HANDBOOK
of
EARLY CHILDHOOD LITERACY

Editorial Advisory Board

HANDBOOK
of
EARLY CHILDHOOD LITERACY

Edited by

NIGEL HALL, JOANNE LARSON AND JACKIE MARSH

SAGE Publications
London • Thousand Oaks • New Delhi

First published 2003

SAGE Publications Ltd
6 Bonhill Street
London EC2A 4PU

SAGE Publications Inc.
2455 Teller Road
Thousand Oaks, California 91320

SAGE Publications India Pvt Ltd
B-42, Panchsheel Enclave
Post Box 4109
New Delhi 100 017

British Library Cataloguing in Publication data

A catalogue record for this book is available from
the British Library

ISBN 0 7619 7437 7

Library of Congress Control Number 2002108284

Typeset by C&M Digitals (Pvt) Ltd, Chennai, India
Printed in Great Britain by The Cromwell Press Ltd, Trowbridge, Wiltshire

Contents

Acknowledgements

The development of an international handbook is, inevitably, a collaborative effort and the editors would like to acknowledge the contributions made by a number of people. First and most importantly, all of the authors, who are some of the most eminent and respected in the field, produced outstanding chapters and the editors would like to thank them for their expert scholarship, diligence and responsiveness. Secondly, we would like to express our gratitude to the original commissioning editor of the handbook, Marianne Lagrange, and her assistant editor Saleha Nessa, for their support and informed guidance throughout the project, in addition to the excellent team at Sage who steered the handbook safely through to completion. Thirdly, we were entirely reliant on the expert skills of the handbook editorial assistants, Lorraine Roe and Rachel Watson of the University of Sheffield, both of whom we would like to thank warmly for their effective administrative management of the project. Finally, all of the chapters were reviewed by an Editorial Advisory Board of esteemed international scholars who completed this task with the utmost rigour and professionalism. We would like to acknowledge the excellent work and collective wisdom of this board and extend our sincerest thanks for their invaluable contribution to the handbook.

Contributors

Patricia Baquedano-López is Assistant Professor in Language and Literacy, Society and Culture at UC Berkeley's Graduate School of Education. She is Co-director of the Center for Urban Education, which is dedicated to supporting school-based research and reform efforts that focus on the problems and issues confronting urban schools. Her ethnographic studies of Latino students in and out of school in California have focused on the relationship of Spanish language maintenance and use to learning and literacy development. Her publications are in *Issues in Applied Linguistics, Language Arts, Theory into Practice, Mind, Culture, and Activity, Narrative Inquiry, The Journal of Linguistic Anthropology* and the *Annual Review of Anthropology*.

Roger Beard taught in primary schools and in a college of higher education before taking up his current post at the University of Leeds, where he is now Reader in Literacy Education. He has published widely in the field and his most recent work includes the *Review of Research and Other Related Evidence* for the National Literacy Strategy (DfEE, 1999) and *Developing Writing 3–13* (Hodder and Stoughton, 2000).

David Bloome is Professor of Education in Language, Literacy and Culture in the School of Teaching and Learning at The Ohio State University. He was President of the National Council of Teachers of English and President of the National Conference on Research in Language and Literacy. His research has focused on the uses of written language in classroom, community, and family settings, the social construction of intertextuality, and the social and cultural nature of literacy practices. His methodological interests have focused on the discourse analysis of classroom literacy events and the ethnographic study of literacy in classroom and community contexts.

Trevor H. Cairney is Master of New College and Adjunct Professor of Education at the University of New South Wales, Australia. He is a past President of the Australian Literacy Educators Association and has over 30 years experience as an educator and literacy researcher. His 180 publications on literacy include books and articles on reading comprehension, children's literature, and the social contexts of literacy. His key publications include *Pathways to Literacy* (Cassell) and *Beyond Tokenism: Parents as Partners in Literacy* (Heinemann). For the past 13 years he has been exploring the relationship between the language and literacy of home, school and community with a number of colleagues and students.

Brian Cambourne is currently Associate Professor in the Faculty of Education, University of Wollongong, Australia. He spent 15 years teaching in New South Wales Department. In his sixteenth year of service for this department he entered the groves of academe as a teacher-educator at Wagga Wagga Teachers' College. He completed his PhD at James Cook University in North Queensland, and was subsequently a Fulbright Scholar and a Postdoctoral Fellow at Harvard. He has also been a Visiting Fellow at the Universities of Illinois and Arizona. Since 1980 Brian Cambourne has been researching how learning, especially literacy learning, occurs. He is best known for his 'conditions of learning' research from which he constructed a grounded theory of classroom learning and teaching, especially as it relates to literacy acquisition.

Victoria Carrington is a Lecturer in Education with the School of Education at The University of Queensland where she teaches a range of undergraduate and postgraduate courses. She is the author of numerous journal articles and book chapters related to early literacy across home and school contexts and has recently published *New Times: New Families* (Kluwer, 2002). Her current research interests include the impact of new communications technologies and consumer culture on early literacy development and the emergence of new literacies.

Frances Christie is Emeritus Professor of Language and Literacy Education at the University of Melbourne and Honorary Professor of Education at the University of Sydney. She was formerly (1990–3) Foundation Professor of Education and Director of the Centre for Studies of Language in Education at the Northern Territory University, Darwin. She holds master's degrees in education and applied linguistics, as well as a PhD in linguistics from the University of Sydney. Her major research and teaching interests are in English language and literacy education. She is particularly interested in writing development, the relationship of talk and writing, teaching about language including pedagogic grammar, and the development of an educational linguistics. Her most recent book is *Classroom Discourse Analysis: A Functional Perspective* (Continuum, 2002).

Gerald Coles is a full-time researcher, writer, and lecturer on literacy, learning and psychology. He is the author of *The Learning Mystique: a Critical Look at 'Learning Disabilities'*, *Reading Lessons: the Debate over Literacy*, *Misreading Reading: the Bad Science that Hurts Children*, and *Reading the Naked Truth: Literacy, Legislation, and Lies*, as well as numerous articles in education, psychology, and psychiatry journals. Before devoting himself to full-time research and writing, he was on the faculties of the Department of Psychiatry at Robert Wood Johnson Medical School, University of Medicine and Dentistry of New Jersey, and the Warner Graduate School of Education and Human Development at the University of Rochester. In 2001 he received a Distinguished Alumnus Award from the University at Buffalo.

Barbara Comber is Director of the Centre for Studies in Literacy, Policy and Learning Cultures at the University of South Australia. Her research interests include literacy, teachers' work, social justice, critical literacies, public education and school-based collaborative research. She has recently co-edited two books: *Negotiating Critical Literacies in Classrooms* (Comber and Simpson, 2001) and *Critiquing Whole Language and Classroom Inquiry* (Boran and Comber, 2001).

Caitlin Dooley taught in urban elementary schools in the United States and is currently pursuing a doctorate degree at the University of Texas at Austin. Her research interests include upper elementary language arts instruction and cultural aspects of literacy education. She conducts research primarily in urban schools and enjoys teaching courses for pre-service teachers in the areas of reading and language arts methods.

Carol Fox is currently Reader in English in Education at the University of Brighton. Her research interests include oral storytelling and literacy, cross-curricular collaboration in teacher education, multicultural English teaching and children's literature about war. She is the author of many journal articles and *At The Very Edge of the Forest* (Cassell, 1993), which is an account of her research on young children's oral storytelling. She is co-editor of *Challenging Ways of Knowing in English, Mathematics and Science* (Falmer, 1997) and of *Ways of Knowing*, a new cross-curricular journal dedicated to alternative ways of thinking about curricula and teaching and learning, published by the University of Brighton. Her most recent book is *In Times of War* (Pavilion, 2000), an anthology of children's literature about war published in collaboration with partners in Belgium and Portugal.

Julia Gillen is Lecturer in Applied Language Studies at the Open University, UK. She is author of the textbook *The Language of Children* (Routledge, 2003). Her main research field is the language of child users of information and communication technologies, in particular the telephone. Since gaining her PhD in 1998, her work has been published in journals such as *Language and Education*, the *Journal of Early Childhood Literacy* and the *British Journal of Educational Studies*. She also enjoys working on flexible education and training resources and was multimedia co-ordinator and co-author of *Shaping the Future: Working with the Under Threes. A Multimedia Training Pack* (Open University Press, 2000). At present she is involved with two international research projects on aspects of young children's communications funded by the Social Sciences and Humanities Research Council of Canada.

Eve Gregory is Professor of Language and Culture in Education at Goldsmiths' College, University of London. She has directed a number of projects funded by the ESRC, Leverhulme and Hamlyn on the out-of-school literacy and learning practices of young children in London's East End and is interested in family literacy in multilingual contexts. Her books include *Making Sense of a New World: Learning to Read in a Second Language* (Sage, 1996), *One Child, Many Worlds: Early Learning in Multicultural Communities* (Fulton and Teachers College Press, 1997) and *City Literacies: Learning to Read Across Generations and Cultures* (Routledge, 2000).

Kris Gutiérrez is Professor in the Graduate School of Education and Information Studies at the University of California, Los Angeles. Professor Gutiérrez also serves as the Director of the Education Studies Minor and the Center for the Study of Urban Literacies. Professor Gutiérrez' research focuses on studying the literacy practices of urban schools. In particular, her research concerns itself with the social and cognitive consequences of literacy practices in formal and non-formal learning contexts. Professor Gutiérrez is currently the Chair of the Standing Committee on Research for the National Council of Teachers of English. Her research has been published in *Human Development, Mind, Culture and Activity, Reading Research Quarterly, Educational*

Researcher, the *Harvard Educational Review, Linguistics and Education, Discourse Processes,* the *Bilingual Review Journal, Urban Education,* the *International Journal of Educational Reform, Education and Urban Society, Theory into Practice, Language Arts*, and the *Review of Education, Pedagogy and Cultural Studies.*

Kathy Hall is Professor of Childhood Education and Head of the Centre for Educational Research at Leeds Metropolitan University, UK. She has directed several research projects including studies funded by the Economic and Social Research Council, the British Council, the Qualifications and Curriculum Authority and Esmé Fairbain. She is currently leading a government-commissioned systematic review of evidence on primary and secondary English teaching. She has published widely on literacy and on assessment and her most recent book is *Listening to Stephen Read: Multiple Perspectives on Literacy* (Open University Press, 2003). She is completing a book entitled *Making Formative Assessment Work* (co-author Winifred Burke) also to be published by the Open University Press.

Nigel Hall is Professor of Literacy Education in the Institute of Education at Manchester Metropolitan University. He is co-editor of the *Journal of Early Childhood Literacy.* He has directed a number of literacy-based projects, including the Punctuation Project, which has been supported by three Economic and Social Research Council awards. He has been on the editorial boards and editorial advisory boards of seven international literacy journals and has authored, co-authored or edited 20 books on literacy and literacy education and has authored over 30 chapters in other people's edited books. Recent books include: *Letter Writing as a Social Practice* (Benjamins), *Looking at Literacy: Using Images of Literacy to Explore the World of Reading and Writing* (Fulton and Heinemann), *Exploring Play and Literacy in the Early Years* (Fulton) and *Learning about Punctuation* (Multilingual Matters and Heinemann).

Peter Hannon is a Professor in the School of Education and member of the Literacy Research Centre at the University of Sheffield, England. His main research and teaching activity is in the areas of literacy and early childhood education. He has directed projects in parental involvement in the teaching of literacy in the early school years, family literacy, preschool literacy development and community-focused programmes for children and adults. He is the author of *Literacy, Home and School* (1995) and *Reflecting on Literacy in Education* (2000).

Cushla Kapitzke is a Lecturer in the School of Education at the University of Queensland, Australia. Her research interests include the literacies and pedagogies of new media and the political economy of information and communication. She is currently undertaking an Australian Research Council project that is investigating the blends of literacies in school libraries in Australia and the US. Key publications include *Literacy and Religion* (Benjamins, 1995) and articles in international journals such as *Educational Theory, Teachers College Record* and *Journal of Adolescent and Adult Literacy.*

Laurie Katz is an Associate Professor in Early Childhood Education in the School of Teaching and Learning at The Ohio State University. Her research and teaching pertains to children with and without special needs from birth through eight years of age and their families. Her research has focused on family and professional relationships, teacher education models and narrative developmental styles of preschoolers.

Charmian Kenner conducted doctoral research at Southampton University into multi-lingualism and early writing, resulting in the book *Home Pages* (Trentham, 2000). From 2000 to 2002 she directed an ESRC-funded project *Signs of Difference* based at the Institute of Education, University of London, on how young children learn to write in more than one script system. She is a Research Fellow in the Department of Educational Studies, Goldsmiths' College, University of London, and also works as a freelance lecturer and consultant in the areas of bilingualism and literacy.

Michele Knobel is an Associate Professor at Montclair State University, New Jersey. Her research interests include school students' in-school and out-of-school literacy practices, new literacies and digital technologies. Her recent books include: *Everyday Literacies, El Estudio Crítico-Social del Lenguaje* and *New Literacies* (both with Colin Lankshear), *Cyber Spaces/Social Spaces: Culture Clash in Computerized Classrooms* (with Ivor Goodson, Colin Lankshear and Marshall Mangan), and the forthcoming *Handbook of Teacher Research* (with Colin Lankshear).

Gunther Kress is Professor of Education/English at the Institute of Education, University of London. His question concerning the English curriculum in schools is: 'What is it that English should be, and offer, in order to prepare young people for productive lives in their world?' He has a specific interest in the interrelations in contemporary texts of different modes of communication – writing, image, speech, music – and their effects on forms of learning and shapes of knowledge. Some of his recent books are: *Reading Images: the Grammar of Graphic Design* (Routledge, 1996), *Multimodal Discourse: the Modes and Media of Contemporary Communication* (Arnold, 2001) (both with Theo van Leeuwen), *Before Writing: Rethinking the Paths to Literacy* (Routledge, 1997), *Early Spelling: between Convention and Creativity* (Routledge, 2000), *Literacy in the New Media Age* (Routledge, 2003), *Multimodal Teaching and Learning: the Rhetorics of the Science Classroom* (Continuum, 2002) and *Multimodal Literacy* (Lang, 2003).

Linda D. Labbo is Professor in the Department of Reading Education at the University of Georgia where she conducts research on early literacy development with a focus on computer-related literacy instruction and pre-service teacher preparation. Dr Labbo's scholarly writing has been published in journals such as *Reading Research Quarterly*, *Language Arts*, *Journal of Literacy Research*, and *The Reading Teacher*. Her co-edited book, *Handbook of Literacy and Technology: Transformations in a Post-Typographic World*, won an American Library Association Award as an Outstanding Academic Book of the year in 1998 and the Edward B. Fry Book Award from the National Reading Conference in 1999. She currently serves as a co-primary investigator (University of Georgia, Teacher's College, Columbia, University of Connecticut, University of Illinois–Chicago) on a research grant Case Technologies in Literacy Education (CTELL) funded by the National Science Foundation and Interagency Education Research Initiative to develop and examine the effectiveness of interactive, multimedia anchor cases on pre-service teachers' professional development and children's reading achievement.

Lesley Lancaster is Senior Lecturer in Education at Manchester Metropolitan University. She has been involved in a number of projects with young children, teachers and parents looking at the development of language and literacy, including projects on narrative and argument. She currently teaches literacy and applied linguistics at undergraduate and post-graduate levels, and directs a project which helps trainee teachers with knowledge and understanding of grammar. Her current research interests are in how very young children understand symbolic forms and systems, in multimodality, and in the development of multimodal systems of description and analysis. She has contributed journal articles in these areas and most recently a chapter in *Multimodal Literacy* (Kress and Jewitt, 2003).

Colin Lankshear is currently a part-time Professorial Research Fellow at the University of Ballarat. He is also an educational researcher and writer based in Mexico, where he has lived since 1999. Formerly a Professor of Education and Research Director, his current academic interests lie mostly in exploring emerging literacies and cultural practices associated with new information and communications technologies, and research methods in qualitative inquiry. His recent books include *Ways of Knowing*, *Maneras de Ver*, and *New Literacies* (all with Michele Knobel), *Teachers and Technoliteracy* (with Ilana Snyder), and *Boys, Literacy and Schooling* (with Leonie Rowan, Michele Knobel and Chris Bigum).

Joanne Larson is Associate Professor and Chair of Teaching and Curriculum at the University of Rochester's Warner Graduate School of Education and Human Development. Her research focuses on literacy as a social practice and examines the ways in which language and literacy practices mediate access to participation in literacy events. Her publications include research articles in *Research in the Teaching of English, Written Communication, Linguistics and Education* and *Discourse and Society*, and co-authored articles in the *Harvard Educational Review, Language Arts, Urban Education* and the *International Journal of Educational Reform*. She is the editor of *Literacy as Snake Oil: Beyond the Quick Fix* (Lang).

Allan Luke is Dean of Research, Centre for Research on Pedagogy and Practice, National Institute of Education, Singapore. He has published numerous books and articles in the field, including *Literacy, Society and Schooling* (Cambridge University Press), *Literacy, Textbooks and Ideology* (Falmer), *Towards a Critical Sociology of Reading Pedagogy* (Benjamins) and *Constructing Critical Literacies* (Hampton), and was a co-author of the New London Group's 'Pedagogy of multiliteracies' work in *Harvard Educational Review* (1997).

Margaret Mackey teaches at the School of Library and Information Studies at the University of Alberta in Canada. She is the author of *Literacies across Media: Playing the Text* (Routledge/Falmer, 2002) and *The Case of Peter Rabbit: Changing Conditions of Literature for Children* (Garland, 1998), as well as numerous articles about young people, their reading, and their media use. She has edited a volume of essays, *Beatrix*

Potter's Peter Rabbit: A Children's Classic at 100 (Scarecrow, 2002), and is the North American Editor of *Children's Literature in Education: an International Quarterly*.

Laurie Makin is Associate Professor, Early Childhood, at the University of Newcastle, Ourimbah Campus, New South Wales, Australia, where she is Director of the Children and Education Research Centre. Laurie has a particular interest in early language and literacy in both monolingual and bilingual children, and has published extensively in this area. She is one of the authors of *Literacies, Communities and Under 5s* (NSW Department of Education and Training, 2001), a professional development resource for early childhood practitioners; is co-editor of *Literacies in Early Childhood: Changing Views, Challenging Practice* (MacLennan and Petty, 2002); and is a Project Leader of the Support at Home for Early Language and Literacies (SHELLS) Project, designed for families with children from birth to three years.

Jackie Marsh is a Senior Lecturer in the School of Education at Sheffield University, where she directs the Literacy, Language and Culture Research Group. Her research interests focus on the role, nature and use of popular culture and media in the early childhood literacy curriculum and out-of-school literacy practices of young children. She has published a number of books in the field of early literacy and is the co-author, with Elaine Millard, of *Literacy and Popular Culture: Using Children's Culture in the Classroom* (Paul Chapman/Sage, 2002). She has written articles published in a range of journals including *British Educational Research Journal*, *Contemporary Issues in Early Childhood*, and *Gender and Education* and is a co-editor of the *Journal of Early Childhood Literacy*.

Miriam Martinez is a Professor of Literacy at the University of Texas at San Antonio and is currently serving as Chair of the Department of Interdisciplinary Studies and Curriculum and Instruction. Her research interests focus on children's and adolescents' responses to literature and their construction of meaning in literary texts. She is co-editor of *Book Talk and Beyond* with Nancy Roser, and is co-author of *Children's Books in Children's Hands* with Charles Temple and Junko Yokota.

Elaine Millard is a Senior Lecturer in the School of Education at the University of Sheffield, Co-director of its distance learning MEd in Literacy and a founder member of the Sheffield Literacy, Language and Culture Research Group. Her main research interests concern the changing patterns of children's literacy practices and preferences and in particular in their relation to gender, social difference and cultural change. She is the author of *Differently Literate: Boys, Girls and the Schooling of Literacy* (Falmer, 1997) and co-author with Jackie Marsh of *Popular Culture: Using Children's Culture in the Classroom* (Chapman/Sage, 2000).

Sharon Murphy is Professor of Education and Associate Dean of the Faculty of Graduate Studies at York University, Toronto, Canada. She has written on the areas of assessment and reading materials. Among her recent publications is *Telling Pieces: Art as Literacy in Middle School Classes*, co-authored with Peggy Albers, which extends theories of emergent literacy for print into the area of art education. Her latest book, co-edited with Curt Dudley-Marling, is *Literacy through 'Language Arts': Teaching and Learning in Context*, a collection of essays from the journal *Language Arts* that provides an introduction to the field of language arts education for pre-service teachers.

Maria Nikolajeva is a Professor of Comparative Literature at Stockholm University. She is the author and editor of several books on children's literature, among them *Children's Literature Comes of Age: Toward the New Aesthetic* (1996), *From Mythic to Linear: Time in Children's Literature* (2000), and *The Rhetoric of Character in Children's Literature* (2002). She has also published a large number of articles in professional journals and essay collections. Her academic honours include a Fulbright Grant at the University of Massachusetts, Amherst, a research fellowship at the International Youth Library, Munich, and Donner Visiting Chair at Åbo Akademi University, Finland. She was the President of the International Research Society for Children's Literature in 1993–7.

Shira May Peterson is a doctoral student in the Warner Graduate School of Education and Human Development at the University of Rochester and a Spencer dissertation fellow for 2003–4. Her dissertation focuses on classroom discourse in preschool, with an emphasis on how young children construct causal explanations through discussion with teachers and peers.

Aria Razfar received his PhD from UCLA's Graduate School of Education and is an Assistant Professor in the Department of Education and Early Child Development at Whittier College. His research is grounded in sociocultural perspectives of literacy development. His current research focuses on how language ideologies mediate classroom discourse practices in urban contexts with a predominantly English language learner population.

David Reinking is a Professor of Education and Head of the Department of Reading Education at the University of Georgia. He is the editor of the *Reading Research Quarterly*, published by the International Reading Association, and he was lead editor for the *Handbook of Literacy and Technology* (Erlbaum, 1998). His main research interest is in the relation between digital technologies and literacy.

Jeanette Rhedding-Jones is Professor of Early Childhood Education at Oslo University College. Before migrating to Norway she taught language and literacy learning in Australian teacher education for almost two decades. From her early twenties to her early thirties she worked as a teacher-carer with children aged five to eight in school and aged three to five in preschools, and mothered four young children. Her publications are in *Contemporary Issues in Early Childhood*, Heinemann's *The Literacy Agenda*, *The British Journal of Sociology of Education*, *Qualitative Studies in Education*, *Gender and Education*, *Journal of Curriculum Studies*. She has taught research methodology in both Australia and Norway. She currently has a large research grant from the Norwegian Research Council to research gender, complexity and diversity in early childhood education.

Muriel Robinson is Principal of Bishop Grosseteste College in Lincoln. She began her career as a primary teacher in Inner London and during this time developed a particular interest in language and literacy in the primary school. This led to a post working on teacher education programmes in the Faculty of Education and Sport at the University of Brighton, and to a PhD on children reading print and television, published as *Children Reading Print and Television* (1997). Other published articles and chapters are in areas extending this topic and in learning and teaching in higher education. In her current role she retains a research interest in the general area of media literacy and is a member of an ESRC-funded seminar group working in this area.

Nancy L. Roser is Professor of Language and Literacy Studies, the Flawn Professor of Early Childhood, and Distinguished Teaching Professor at the University of Texas at Austin. A former elementary teacher, she now teaches undergraduate elementary reading and language arts, as well as graduate courses in teaching the English language arts and children's literature. Her research interests include close inspection of children's book conversations in classrooms. She is co-editor of *Book Talk and Beyond* with Miriam Martinez and *Adventuring with Books* with Julie Jensen, as well as over 100 chapters and articles related to teaching reading and the language arts.

Deborah Wells Rowe is Associate Professor of Early Childhood Education at Peabody College, Vanderbilt University where she teaches courses in literacy education and qualitative research methods. Her ethnographic research focuses on sociocognitive and sociocultural analyses of young children's literacy learning in home and classroom settings. Most recently she has explored issues of identity and access to learning opportunities in classroom activities that link drama, reading, and writing. She is author of *Preschoolers as Authors: Literacy Learning in the Social World of the Classroom* (Hampton).

Patricia L. Scharer is a Professor of Education at Ohio State University and a trainer with OSU's Literacy Collaborative. Her research interests include early literacy development, phonics and word study, and the role of children's literature to foster both literary development and literacy achievement. She has served as co-editor of the *Journal of Children's Literature* and the 'Children's Books' column of the *Reading Teacher.* She is currently co-editor of *Bookbird: a Journal of International Children's Literature.* Professor Scharer is also co-editor of *Extending Our Reach: Teaching for Comprehension in Reading, Grades K–2* and co-author of *Rethinking Phonics: Making the Best Teaching Decisions.*

Rhona Stainthorp is a Senior Lecturer in the School of Psychology and Human Development at the Institute of Education, University of London. Her research interests centre on the development of literacy including reading, text composition, spelling and handwriting. Her work is informed by a background in cognitive psychology and linguistics. She is particularly interested in individual differences in development. She is co-author with Diana Hughes of *Learning from Children Who Read at an Early Age* (Routledge, 1999) which provides an account of her longitudinal research with precocious readers. She is director of the Language and Literacy Research Centre at the Institute of Education. For many years she has been involved with the education of teachers both at initial training level and in continuing professional development.

Radhika Viruru is a Clinical Assistant Professor in the Department of Teaching, Learning and Culture at Texas A&M University. Her research interests include post-colonial theory and its relevance to the field of early childhood education and qualitative research methods in education. She is the author of *Early Childhood Education: Postcolonial Perspectives from India* (Sage). She also co-edits the Childhood and Cultural Studies section of the *Journal of Curriculum Theorizing*.

Jerry Zutell is a Professor of Education at the Ohio State University and Director of the OSU Reading Clinic. His research and scholarship is focused on the study of children's acquisition of word knowledge in reading and writing, with special interests in spelling development, spelling–reading connections, and oral reading fluency. His writings on these topics have appeared in *Research in the Teaching of English, Language Arts, Reading Teacher,* and *Theory into Practice* as well as in other journals, yearbooks and edited volumes. He is a former co-editor of the *National Reading Conference Yearbook* and the developer of the Directed Spelling Thinking Activity (DSTA), an innovative cycle of word study instruction.

Preface

NIGEL HALL, JOANNE LARSON, AND JACKIE MARSH

The last two decades have been powerful ones for the study of early childhood literacy. In many countries, much more attention is being paid to the early years than previously, as politicians recognise just how vital is this period of life. Alongside increased political interest, although largely quite independent of it, has been a resurgence of research as new definitions of early childhood literacy have developed, influenced by a wide range of disciplines (see Chapter 1). There are a number of approaches, therefore, which could have been undertaken in relation to the development of this handbook, given the current complexity and scope of the field. The handbook has 33 chapters, written by 45 authors who come from seven countries across four continents. On the whole, the chapters reflect a particular and distinctive view of early childhood literacy. There are some exceptions, partly because there are still areas of literacy untouched by the approach taken and partly because it is the case that a range of disciplines and approaches will always have an important contribution to make to understanding the relationship between young children and written language. However, the perspectives of many chapters in this book are based on a view that early childhood literacy is a global, social, historical, cultural, and political construct. Many of the chapters suggest that literacy is a social practice that is linked to cultural and linguistic practices and power relationships in specific contexts. As a social practice, literacy learning is mediated by language and accomplished in a context in which social actors position, and are positioned by, each other in verbal, non-verbal, and textual interaction.

This approach was identified for a number of reasons. The first is that the concept of early childhood literacy as a socially-situated practice is a relatively recent development. Its origins lie mostly in the work of anthropologists, social linguists, ethnographers and semioticians who developed their ideas with adult communities. As a recent and still emerging perspective, it has received much less attention than have many others. The second reason is that it is important to focus upon a broad interpretation of early childhood literacy, even though that can sometimes be at odds with contemporary political views of the concept. Researchers must, of course, be interested in the powerful political realities that drive education and schooling, but the extent to which so much research in literacy is driven by the agendas of schooling obscures the other realities of literacy – especially that literacy has a life outside of and beyond schooling. Furthermore, we believe that researchers have both a right and an obligation to think about literacy as a widespread social practice for children as well as for adults. Early childhood literacy can no longer remain the exclusive domain of educationalists and developmental psychologists. The third reason for the approach taken to the shaping of the handbook relates to a recognition of the ways in which literacy is changing in contemporary society. During the late twentieth century, technological developments precipitated a paradigm shift in relation to communicative practices and there was a greater focus on the ways in which people analysed and produced a range of multimodal texts. These changes have impacted greatly on children's lives and today all children, including the very young, are actively participating in their development and use. Many of the chapters in this handbook acknowledge this strong emergent field of research in early childhood literacy and thus broaden traditional conceptions of literacy in the early years.

Given the breadth of areas addressed by the chapters, some readers may feel uncomfortable with one particular absence. Nowhere in this book does any chapter deal with children who, for whatever reason, are finding literacy problematic. This absence is not because we feel this area is unimportant; on the contrary, we do appreciate how significant it is and recognise the many valuable contributions made by scholars conducting research in this field. Nonetheless, the focus of this handbook is on what children can do, rather than what they cannot do. There is already a range of rich literature on children who experience difficulties with literacy. There is a much smaller set of available literature centred around new visions of early childhood literacy.

It is also possible that some readers will feel we have paid too little attention to schooling. However, whilst we acknowledge its importance, we cannot unreflectively accept its dominance. There is no lack of existing research into schooling and literacy; indeed until relatively recently it would be hard to find any other kind. What has been less widely recognised is the integrity of early childhood literacy as a subject of study in its own right, and in this handbook we seek to modestly redress this imbalance by foregrounding a wider range of research than that conventionally associated with formal systems of education.

For the purposes of this handbook, we are defining early childhood as that period from birth to eight-years-old. This is a wider span than many others would accept. However, we recognise that whilst there are some variations in notions of early childhood in the Western world, there are even greater differences across the whole world. By taking a broader stance we increase inclusion, and if we extend beyond some people's preferences for what counts as 'early childhood literacy', then we also offer the opportunity to consider continuity of development across a greater period of time.

The chapters in this handbook, therefore, offer a range of critical perspectives on research and key issues in particular aspects of the field. We do not claim a comprehensive overview of early literacy research in its totality, but suggest that the chapters here represent major themes in which leading authorities in the field provide rigorous social, cultural and historical analyses of aspects of early childhood literacy. The handbook is organised around five main themes.

PART 1: PERSPECTIVES ON EARLY CHILDHOOD LITERACY

The chapters in this section examine the notion of early childhood literacy, its history as a concept, and the way research has historically and contemporaneously positioned it.

They consider the social, cultural, political and economic factors that impact upon the nature, function and use of literacy in early childhood.

PART 2: EARLY CHILDHOOD LITERACY IN FAMILIES, COMMUNITIES AND CULTURES

Early childhood literacy is rooted in family, community and cultural beliefs, attitudes, values and practices. In this section, the chapters centre around literacy as a social practice, exploring different ways in which families, communities and cultures construct, value and use literacy. In particular, these chapters explore how young children respond to these influences and develop ideas about the meanings and functions of literacy for themselves and with their families and communities.

PART 3: EARLY MOVES IN LITERACY

This cluster of chapters focuses on the processes which underpin the acquisition and development of literacy during early childhood. The emphasis in this section is on how children come to understand what literacy is, what are its purposes, and how it functions.

PART 4: LITERACY IN PRESCHOOL SETTINGS AND SCHOOLS

In most countries, but not all, schooling is the institution for controlling children's formal access to the world of written language. Schooling is often controversial, with political agendas rather than research determining the curriculum and teaching practice. In this section, the chapters explore research which has illustrated how teachers and other practitioners create settings for young children's literacy learning, and how children respond to these professional practices and values.

PART 5: RESEARCHING EARLY CHILDHOOD LITERACY

The chapters in this section explore in detail approaches to researching early childhood literacy from a largely qualitative perspective. They are designed to provide a theoretical background rather than offer practical approaches to empirical work, but in doing so provide a foundation for anyone setting out to conduct research in this field.

We hope this book will prove useful to researchers, academics working in the field, students with an academic interest in childhood literacy, and policy makers. While the main audience is likely to be those located within the discipline of education, researchers working in linguistics, cultural studies and sociology will find issues of interest. We are at an early stage in contemporary studies of early childhood literacy. It is our intention that this handbook will provide an informative, critical and helpful introduction to these new and important ideas.

Part I

PERSPECTIVES ON EARLY CHILDHOOD LITERACY

1

The Emergence of Early Childhood Literacy

JULIA GILLEN AND NIGEL HALL

In this chapter we explore, rather briefly, how the approaches researchers bring to studying young children and written language have changed across time, and how in the process critical concepts have been redefined leading to the emergence of early childhood literacy as a major research focus at the beginning of the twenty-first century. We are making the claim that research into early childhood literacy is a very recent phenomenon. This may surprise many people; after all, formal research into the ways in which children have learned about written language has been going on for well over a century, and if an informal definition is adopted then it would be over many centuries, maybe even millennia. However, we want to claim that there are specific attributes of the term *early childhood literacy research* that distinguish it from the many earlier meanings that have underpinned the ways in which previous researchers have examined young children's relationships with written language.

The story of how early childhood literacy emerged as a distinctive and dynamic research area is a fairly complicated one and to do it full justice would require more space than is available to us. To keep control of our account and to contain it within the space allowed us, we have decided to focus on a small number of themes, each of which we see as significant in the emergence of early childhood literacy as now understood. There is, to start with, a crude historical direction in the order of our themes; however, this becomes more difficult to sustain as we move towards the end of the twentieth century and at this point considerable overlap is unavoidable. We are conscious that in this short chapter we have to be selective about the choices made for

discussion. We select mostly book-length studies for particular emphasis; for although ideas tend to find their first output in journals or theses they are then consolidated more comprehensively in books. Our choices are necessarily personal ones and we do not claim that we always use the most significant texts of their kind (although they may be), or that they are themselves the most influential texts, and neither do we claim that together they represent a completely coherent story. We reflect our perceptions at the changing nature of attitudes, values and influences at the particular shifting intersection among disciplines that constitutes research into learning and using written language in early childhood.

THE MOVE TOWARDS 'LITERACY' AND 'CHILDHOOD'

Psychology, written language and young children

We have chosen to start at the end of the nineteenth century. It was a time in which researchers from one discipline had begun to take a specific interest in young children's relationship with written language, although we are certainly not suggesting that it had been completely ignored before this. At this point it would be very unusual to find anyone researching literacy as, according to the *Oxford English Dictionary*, the term 'literacy' was first used in print in 1883. In the nineteenth century researchers, and anyone else, talked about reading and writing rather than literacy.

Even as the modern discipline of psychology emerged in Wundt's laboratories, it took a research interest in reading. The major theme of this early work was that reading is primarily a perceptual activity centred on sound/symbol relationships. The linking of sound and vision made reading susceptible to the interests of perceptual psychologists partly because they focused upon individual behaviour and partly because aspects of perceptual behaviour could be measured (Catell, 1886). A second theme was acceptance of the notion that learning was unlikely to take place unless children were 'ready' (mentally and physically). The notion of *readiness* in association with reading appears to have been used first by Patrick (1899), was supported by Huey (1908) and remained a dominant concept in young children's reading for the next 60 years. Huey's seminal work typifies these characteristics. A lot of it is devoted to visual perception and reading, while in the pedagogy section Huey seeks to reconcile psychological evidence relating to readiness with the current practice of starting children early on reading. His answer seems in some respects to be quite contemporary: root early written language experiences in play.

It was, however, readiness that won. In 1928, two US psychologists began to formally explore reading readiness (Morphett and Washburne, 1931). They claimed reading readiness was closely linked to mental age and, more specifically that, 'It pays to postpone beginning reading until a child has attained a mental age of six years and six months.' This position was supported by a later study which claimed, 'A mental age of seven seems to be the lowest at which a child can be expected to use phonics' (Dolch and Bloomster, 1937). That these studies were based on ludicrous and arbitrary notions of what counted as reading (and for a stunning critical review of these studies see Coltheart, 1979) and 'satisfactory progress in reading' did not stop the educational world from falling in love with their propositions. For the next 50 years books about teaching reading repeated the readiness mantras of these four researchers. A number of consequences followed these research studies. First, an industry emerged concerned with promoting and selling reading readiness, usually with non-print-related activities and materials. Secondly, the limited definition of reading perpetuated a notion of learning to read as an associative activity, centred on perceptual identification and matching. Thirdly, it supported an absolute distinction between being a reader and not being a reader.

The emphasis on measurable behaviour was abetted by the dominance at this time of behaviourism which, in its various guises, claimed to be able to control reading development through systematic reinforcement systems. By breaking down reading into narrow skills and by linking the learning of these skills to reinforcement systems, so children were supposed to acquire mastery of them (Skinner, 1957). Like much research into children's reading, it was based on a number of assumptions: that children's agency was insignificant, that children could learn nothing for themselves, that they were objects to be manipulated by teachers, and that reading and writing were individual acts involving sets of discrete perceptual skills. Behaviourist theories of language learning were dealt a severe theoretical blow by Chomsky (1959) in a major review of Skinner's book *Verbal Behavior*. On the whole, behaviourist approaches to literacy learning only survive in some areas of special education or in more experimental situations using mastery learning.

The major consequence of behaviourism and reading readiness theories was that for much of the twentieth century researchers seemed to have believed that there was simply no point in investigating or even considering very young children's thinking about, understanding of and use of reading and writing; the possibility of this had been defined out of existence until they arrived in school and faced a teacher.

New disciplines and literacy

To a large extent the Second World War provided a new impetus for research into literacy, although the driving notion was 'illiteracy' and it was mostly associated with adults. It was this war with its increased requirements for more advanced skills that really emphasized the significance of low literacy levels. The concept of functional literacy emerged during the war and was widely adopted in development education within mass literacy campaigns (Gray, 1956; and see Akinnaso, 1991, for a personal perspective on this area) and later in adult and employment education. The notion of functional literacy for the first time forced researchers to be interested in what literacy was for and what people did with it in their everyday lives. Almost for the first time research began to consider reading as something more than simply a decoding process and that it had a social element. It also led to the realization that it was not only reading that needed to be considered, but also writing, although it remained true that reading received much greater attention than writing.

Another way in which the Second World War influenced research into literacy was through the emergence and consolidation of newer disciplines: cognitive psychology, the general area of information and communication studies, and psycholinguistics.

These disciplines consistently revealed that communication, especially written communication, was a complex, multilayered, and highly skilled process involving a reflective and strategic meaning-oriented approach to behaviour. While much of this work was related to adults, one book began to powerfully pull threads together and apply it to children learning to read. This book was Frank Smith's *Understanding Reading* (1971). It was not a research study itself, but it used a mass of evidence and theoretical work deriving from these newer disciplines. This evidence came from new studies into cognitive perception (Neisser, 1967; Gibson, 1969), skilled behaviour (Miller et al., 1960), communication and information theory (Pierce, 1961; Cherry, 1966; Miller, 1967), linguistics (Chomsky, 1957; 1965), developmental psycholinguistics (McNeill, 1966) and developmental cognition (Bruner et al., 1956; 1966) and from those educationalists who were beginning to make use of these new disciplines (Goodman, 1968).

Smith's book immediately attracted both huge support and massive opposition and severely divided educationalists. It would not be unfair to describe this division as 'war', with such vitriol were these differences manifested. Despite this substantial opposition, Smith's book regenerated and broadened reading-related research, which swiftly flourished and began to move in directions that even Smith had not anticipated.

Smith's analysis and synthesis had a number of consequences for the emergence of early childhood literacy:

- Reading could no longer be seen simply as an associative process. It had to be recognized as a much more complex activity involving cognitive and strategic behaviour, and the approach of young children to print reflected this complexity and use of strategy.
- The narrowness of research into reading was breached and the area was opened up as a topic for scrutiny and influence from a much wider set of disciplines than psychology (although this was only a beginning).
- Meaning could no longer be seen as simply sitting there in a text. It was readers who assigned meaning to print and children did this in similar ways to adults, although drawing on different experiences.

What Smith had not done in 1971 was (1) move beyond a reading-oriented understanding of print usage, and (2) follow through his own logic and consider whether children who had all these complex abilities were applying them to comprehending and making print long before they moved into formal schooling. However, these newer disciplines had begun to reposition the understanding of written language as a much more dynamic and interactive process. It was these meanings that were carried forward and developed by other researchers.

The emergence of 'emergence'

At the end of the 1970s and the beginning of the 1980s, views on the relationship between childhood and written language were changing dramatically. There had long been interest (mostly from psychologists) in how some children arrived in school able to read (Durkin, 1966; Clarke, 1976; Forester, 1977) but such early engagement with literacy (and again it was always reading) was studied because it was believed to be unusual. Asking explicitly how young children made sense of literacy had begun with psychologists such as Reid (1966) and Downing (1979) but had extended to a crop of studies appearing in the late 1970s and even continuing to the early 1980s. These tended to focus on children in early schooling (Johns, 1976–7; Tovey, 1976). At the same time other researchers were exploring this issue in what was ultimately a more powerful way. Clay (1969), Read (1970) and Goodman (1976) became interested in the strategic behaviour of children engaging in literacy and it was their approach that led to some major shifts in the conceptualization of early childhood and literacy. Rather than ask explicit questions of children, something that is always going to be problematic, they looked at children's actual behaviours while engaged in literacy. They saw that while many of the children's literacy behaviours were technically incorrect, they nevertheless revealed how children were strategic in approaching literacy and were working hard to develop hypotheses about how the system worked. If children aged five and six were bringing sense-making strategies to literacy, and if research from developmental psychology was demonstrating that school-aged young children were actively making sense of their worlds, then how were even younger children responding to literacy? As Ferriero and Teberosky put it in their seminal study:

> It is absurd to imagine that four- or five-year-old children growing up in an urban environment that displays print everywhere (on toys, on billboards and road signs, on their clothes, on TV) do not develop any ideas about this cultural object until they find themselves sitting before a teacher. (1982: 12)

A number of individual case studies, by researchers studying their own children, began to explicitly focus on the period before schooling. Lass (1982) started with her child from birth, Baghban (1984) from birth to three, Crago and Crago (1993) from three to four, Payton (1984), the first British case study, across the fourth year, while Bissex (1980) followed her son during his fifth year. All showed clearly how their children were paying a lot of attention to print. Literacy was certainly beginning before schooling. At the same time researchers began reporting on broader studies involving a wider range of children (Clay, 1975; Mason, 1980; Hiebert, 1981; Harste et al., 1982a; Sulzby, 1985). A revolution was taking place that demanded a revaluation of literacy as something that moved beyond any conventional ability to read and write. Rather than literacy development being something that began at the start of schooling after a bout of reading readiness exercises, it was becoming a much broader continuum that had its origins in very early childhood and drew its meaning from making sense rather than formal teaching.

This rich range of studies during the 1970s and early 1980s, reflected two major moves by researchers:

- There was increasing recognition of the role that young children played in making sense of literacy; that even the very youngest were strategic literacy learners who paid attention to the print world, participated in it in their own ways, and developed theories about how it worked. A new field of study appeared – emergent literacy.
- This change involved a redefinition of literacy, such that literacy began to be viewed as a much broader set of print-related behaviours than those conventionally experienced in education.

If a criticism could be made of much of the research in this period, it would be that research tended to be more pragmatic than deeply theoretically based. Subsequent developments would change this. Nevertheless, early childhood literacy had begun to emerge and this shift was to be greatly facilitated by research that was focusing more closely on the nature of literacy outside of schooling.

THE IMPACT OF SOCIAL AND CULTURAL PERSPECTIVES

It is at this point that any notion of maintaining a chronological sequence, however crude, breaks down, for during the last 20 years of the twentieth century a rich range of research and theoretical perspectives began to impact upon the study of young children and written language, and did so in ways that often overlapped or were inextricably intertwined. As a consequence, the following sections should be viewed in no way as discrete areas, but as aspects of a complex mixture of ideas that would, once again,

redefine how young children's relationship with reading and writing could be understood.

The entry of cultural psychology

We will start with a re-entry of psychology into this story. Chronologically the work of the Russian psychologist Vygotsky belongs to the first part of the twentieth century (he died in 1934). However, after the 1962 translation of *Thought and Language* his work began to have an important influence on research into child development, language and thinking. It was however only more recently (after later translations: Vygotsky, 1978) that his work began to influence research on literacy. The feature of Vygotsky's work that captured the interest of researchers was his recognition of the role of culture in learning, especially that individuals are inseparably connected to cultural history. This made a timely connection with the powerful emergence of sociology and anthropology into literacy research (see next sections).

Vygotsky had a particular interest in the ways in which children use many mediational tools to construct meaning (Lee and Smagorinsky, 2000), an interest shared with more semiotic theorists (see later). In particular, pretence play was seen by him as a very powerful opportunity for children to appropriate the symbols and tools of their culture (Vygotsky, 1967). Vygotsky argued that language, for example, is first experienced around the child and comes to be used by the child; it is within the flow of experience of that participation in society that language is internalized and understanding develops. Vygotsky was also very interested in how the learning relationship between children and their culture developed. In modern research this has primarily revolved around the dyadic exchanges that occur within what is usually termed the zone of proximal development, although Vygotsky himself never studied such exchanges as mother–child problem-solving dialogues (Van der Veer and Valsiner, 1994). Despite this, many scholars have explored naturally efficient pedagogic strategies, especially in dyads, examining how adults can structure children's routes into learning from participation and partial understanding to internalization and expertise. Concepts such as 'scaffolding' (Wood et al., 1976), 'structuring situations', 'apprenticeship' (Rogoff, 1986; 1990) and 'assisted performance' (Tharp and Gallimore, 1988) have been particularly influential.

Ethnography and literacy outside of schooling

That home circumstances made a difference to children's relationship with written language had been known to researchers for a very long time. However, the role of the home was essentially positioned as a handmaiden to schooling. It was sociology and anthropology with their interests in cultural socialization, the development of sociolinguistics with its interest in language as a social practice (Hymes, 1974) and the growing interest in emergent literacy that led researchers in the 1970s and 1980s to look at literacy and homes in different way.

Instead of trying to correlate literacy performance with crude socio-economic indicators, for the first time researchers began to ask in detail how literacy practice operated in homes and how these experiences might influence children's attitudes to and knowledge about literacy. Shirley Brice Heath (1983) brought ethnography to studying literacy in families but, significantly, looked beyond the family to the community. Across a 10-year period she examined how different community language and literacy discourses encultured children. She followed these children into schooling and explored how their early experiences interrelated with the discourses of schooling, demonstrating powerfully different effects on the children's lives in school. In the same year as Heath's book was published another anthropologist, Taylor (1983), introduced the phrase 'family literacy' after spending three years working with six families in exploring how the children developed ideas and knowledge about literacy in their homes and how this related to their literacy experiences in schools. Neither Heath nor Taylor focused specifically upon younger children. They did not have to, as the ethnographic study of family and community literacy life included all participants in relation to each other; young children and their literacy-related behaviours appeared now in context.

Heath and Taylor were part of a significant shift in literacy studies, a shift that began to emphasize the social nature of literacy. Street (1984) after examining different theories of literacy and analysing community literacy practices in Iran concluded that Western academic models of literacy, while widespread, failed to represent the different ways in which literacy was embedded in cultural practices. Describing the Western model as treating literacy like an autonomous object, he developed the ideas of ideological 'literacies' in which different cultural and community discourses led to significantly different ways of valuing and using literacy (something also explored in Africa by Scribner and Cole, 1981, and in Alaska by Scollon and Scollon, 1981). Thus from different cultural contexts children would be bringing very different conceptions of literacy to the autonomous practices of school literacy.

The introduction of ethnography to studying literacy as a social practice was very important.

Uncovering the nature and significance of literacy within family and community life required different approaches, and ethnography – with its focus on detailed description, the evolving of themes, the valuing of participants' perspectives, and the development of different relationships between researchers and subjects – allowed extremely detailed research to flourish.

Considering literacy as a social practice became and remains a dominant theme in literacy studies and most frequently draws heavily, although not always directly, on ethnography. Much subsequent research concentrated on developing more theoretical accounts of literacy (for instance, Gee, 1996; Baynham, 1995; Lankshear, 1997), or on exploring specific community literacy practices (for example, Besnier, 1995; Barton and Hamilton, 1998). Others paid more attention to children (for example, Fishman, 1988; Lofty, 1992) and some have concentrated on older children and adolescents (for example, Voss, 1996; Finders, 1997; Knobel, 1999).

But how was all this work impacting on the emergence of early childhood literacy?

- It demonstrated clearly that literacy cannot be divorced from language as a whole, nor from its wider cultural context. Literacy is given meaning by the cultural discourses and practices in which it is embedded and young children are from birth witnesses to and participants in practices.
- In uncovering young children's literacy lives in families and communities it drew attention to how young children are learning to mean with a much wider notion of literacy than previously considered, thus opening the way for later investigation of broader notions of authorship, young children's relationship to popular culture, and their involvement in the new technologies of communication.
- It has raised and invited powerful questions about the relationship between literacy as a social practice and literacy in schooling at a time when in many parts of the world the autonomous model of literacy was being increasingly privileged by governments.

The literacy classroom as a dynamic social space

The research shifts identified so far had been increasingly opening up literacy as a complex practice, but there still seemed to be both an implicit and often an explicit assumption that in classrooms the activity of teaching literacy was much less problematic. While earlier studies had begun to reveal that young children were strategic, active learners when faced with classroom reading demands, classrooms were still typically viewed as less dynamic situations in which children were positioned as passive consumers of literacy knowledge. Drawing on theoretical stances derived from ethnomethodology and social interactional perspectives (Garfinkel, 1967; Hymes, 1974; Goffman, 1981; Bloome and Green, 1984) a number of researchers began to problematize this instructional space. As they explored in considerable detail the activities and behaviours that made up everyday classroom life, these environments, far from being places where teachers simply taught and children simply learned, were gradually uncovered as complex communicative spaces. Children were not simply learning the academic content of lessons, but were learning (or contesting) the ways of being in classrooms. Classrooms began to be perceived as dynamic spaces that had social structures, academic structures and activity structures, all of which were interlocked and interdependent (Erickson and Mohatt, 1982).

McDermott (1979) explored the discursive construction of identity and how this impacted upon performances of literacy in second-grade classrooms. With the aid of painstaking investigation of frame-by-frame video playback, McDermott demonstrated that children in the apparently chaotic bottom group were actually responding in ways that were as equally strategic as the responses of children in the manifestly achieving top group. McDermott set his analysis not in the context of prior investigations into educational achievement, nor indeed in mainstream psychology, but rather in the micro-sociological questioning of how people in their moment-by-moment behaviour negotiate and construct their roles and identities. This detailed, almost second-by-second examination of classroom activities became a common procedural technique in an effort to locate precisely how literacy sessions were constructed and negotiated during interactions between teachers and students, and between student and student (Green, 1987; Bloome, 1989; Heap, 1989; Floriana, 1993).

One consequence of this research was a growing focus on what it was that children brought to literacy sessions, both academically and socially: for instance, that child participation depended not only on the teacher's rules for participation but the child's standing and relationships with its peers. These more finely focused observations gradually changed from simple comparisons between the language and literacy of home and school in which the child's language in school was seen as somewhat impoverished. Increasingly researchers discovered that whatever the formal agendas of schooling might demand, within them children were nevertheless making rich use of their out-of-school language and literacy lives both in adolescence (Gilmore, 1986) and in early childhood (Dyson, 1989; 1993; 2002).

While the socially oriented work of the researchers in the previous two sections has been highly significant, it has also been criticized for not connecting with wider concerns of a social theory of pedagogy: 'the cross-generational production and reproduction of knowledge and power' and 'the complex fabric of texts and discourses through which social representation and reproduction is effected' (Luke, 1992: 108). These wider perspectives on literacy emerged from the work of theorists associated with discourse studies (Lankshear and Lawler, 1987; Luke, 1988; Baker and Freebody, 1989; Edelsky, 1996; Gee, 1996), although these have their origins in a long history of social, political and philosophical theory (Bourdieu, 1977; 1990; Foucault, 1979; 1988). Discursive approaches broaden the scope of studies in family and classroom life by examining how these social institutions are located in discourse structures and wider ideologies (Gee, 1996). Discourses are deeply embedded and largely invisible to participants within them (although not to those outside them). Some discourses have historically gained immense power and status, something that becomes unproblematic to those subscribing to their ideas and practices. The impact of this area is likely to become increasingly powerful as there is wider appreciation of how discourses and ideologies position participants, materials and practices within early childhood (Cannella, 2002).

Literacy as a semiotic practice

If there is one thing that most of the research written about so far has in common, it is that it focuses on literacy as an activity involving the use of print. To most people this would seem to be an *a priori* condition of researching literacy, but one of the more recent shifts in early childhood literacy has been as a result of social semiotic theory. This theory is concerned with ways in which meaning is made in social contexts (Eco, 1979; Halliday, 1974). Conventionally literacy is an act of meaning making, whether it be in interpreting a text or generating a text, and it has always been acknowledged that there are many other forms of meaning making, e.g. through art, music and dance. Historically these have always been linked generally as 'creative' areas, but specifically separated as cultural practices. Thus, for instance, there is a long history of studies of children's literacy, and a strong history of studies of children's drawings (for example, Kellog,

1969; Goodnow, 1977; Gardner, 1980), giving the impression that these activities are quite distinct. Social semiotic theory points out that as forms of meaning making they, and all other forms of meaning, have as many similarities as differences, and that it is only history and ideology that assign particular values to these differences.

Children from very early on utilize a rich range of ways to make meaning and, while they might be able to distinguish between them as forms, they utilize whatever they feel is appropriate in whichever ways they want to intend a meaning. One of the earliest team of researchers to explore this area, albeit embryonically, was Harste et al. (1984b). They believed that young children's meaning making used exactly the same overall strategies as that of adults, but that their results reflected differences in experience and interest. Although focusing mostly on print-related meaning making by young children, they nevertheless viewed authoring as something that could move across communication systems and which was truly multimodal. This was taken further by Rowe (1994) in her study of preschoolers as authors. She points out that young children do not feel excessively constrained by society's distinctions between communication systems, and the belief of many that young children use a variety of graphic media because they cannot write reflects a major failure to understand how powerfully children were switching between modalities as their intents shifted.

The seminal text in this area is *Before Writing* (Kress, 1997). While acknowledging that children increasingly become aware of the ways in which conventions operate, Kress points out that learning is not simply a unidirectional movement in which children take on board a socially determined world. Children as well as adults transform the world while operating within its conventions. He argues powerfully that children's use of signs, symbols and modalities is not arbitrary but is structured and reflects strategic choices by them to represent things that are important to them. Like Harste et al., earlier, he argues that it is experience and interest that distinguish their meaning making from that of adults, not their strategies. Young children choose what they want to represent and then select the best possible means for doing it (1987: 93). What is best (and often very complex) may come from different modes, means and materials, regardless of whether adult culture uses or sanctions such selections.

In recent years a number of scholars associated with Kress have begun to publish in this area (Pahl, 1999; 2002; Lancaster, 2001; Kenner, 2000). Pahl has examined meaning making in nursery school as well as the home and demonstrates how the texts young children create, while often ephemeral and 'messy', nevertheless represent a crossroads where adults' preoccupations, children's popular culture and interests, and the school and family narratives are played out. Lancaster focuses on how successfully an 18-month child explored in complex ways different forms of graphic representation, while Kenner has more recently explored how five-year-old bilingual children understood different graphic systems of writing, what she termed 'signs of difference'. This stress on the continuity of literacy with other semiotic systems can be linked to an emphasis on the multimodality of all communicative behaviour (Finnegan, 2002) and even the argument that in all modes symbolic representations should logically be defined as 'literacies' (Lemke, 1998).

Finally it should be noted that while very young children have little social or economic power and their transformations may not impact significantly upon the wider world, as children get older this changes when as adolescents their linguistic and multimodal transformations become powerful enough to generate considerable (but ultimately futile) resistance by adults.

CONCLUSION

We are conscious that our survey has necessarily been short, is very selective and partial, and inevitably reflects the histories of the authors. We are keenly aware that nowhere have we been able to do justice to the complexity of the perspectives included (and certainly not to those that have not been included) but know that many of the following chapters offer the opportunity to explore recent perspectives more deeply.

We began this survey at a point where the relationship between early childhood and literacy appeared relatively straightforward and unproblematic, and have explored how this relationship became more complex and problematic during the twentieth century. It is clear that these changes have been dramatic and now reflect a hugely different construct of the relationship between children and written language, a perspective that can now justifiably be termed *early childhood literacy*. We hope we have also shown how these changes are not discrete but are situated in much wider and deeper changes in the way research, culture, and society have been conceived. So what is now implied by the use of the phrase 'early childhood literacy'?

We would want to claim that:

- It is an all-embracing concept for a rich range of authorial and responsive practices using a variety of media and modalities, carried out by people during their early childhood.

- It is a concept that allows early childhood to be seen as a state in which people use literacy as it is appropriate, meaningful and useful to them, rather than a stage on a path to some future literate state. It is not about emergence or becoming literate, it is about being literate; and it allows the literacy practices and products of early childhood to be acknowledged as valid in their own right, rather than perceived as inadequate manifestations of adult literacy.
- It is a concept that allows early literacy to move way beyond the limitations and restrictions of schooling and extend into all domains of the lives of people in early childhood.
- It is a concept that has evolved out of contestation, innovation and reconceptualization and one that has become and continues to be susceptible to the scrutiny of a wide range of theoretical and methodological positions. It is not a concept that has finished evolving, nor will it ever do so. As a position it recognizes that it is a social construct and as such will never achieve fixity.

We would also want to claim that the study of early childhood literacy is in a healthy state. It is a dynamic, fresh and continuously invigorating area, as is shown by the chapters that follow. It is also, unfortunately, an area where much of the contemporary research has had very limited impact upon political views about pedagogic practice. We would, however, want to point out that the study of early childhood literacy is no longer constrained by pedagogic demands; it is now an area of investigation that has integrity in its own right.

REFERENCES

Akinasso, F. Nyi (1991) 'Literacy and individual consciousness', in E. Jennings and A. Purves (eds), *Literate Systems and Individual Lives*. Albany: SUNY Press.

Baghban, M. (1984) *Our Daughter Learns to Read and Write: a Case Study from Birth to Three*. Newark, DE: International Reading Association.

Baker, C. and Freebody, P. (1989) *Children's First School Books*. Oxford: Blackwell.

Barton, D. and Hamilton, M. (1998) *Local Literacies: Reading and Writing in One Community*. London: Routledge.

Baynham, M. (1995) *Literacy Practices: Investigating Literacy in Social Contexts*. London: Longman.

Besnier, N. (1995) *Literacy, Emotion, and Authority: Reading and Writing on a Polynesian Atoll*. Cambridge: Cambridge University Press.

Bissex, G. (1980) *Gnys at Wrk: a Child Learns to Read and Write*. Cambridge, MA: Harvard University Press.

Bloome, D. (1989) 'Beyond access: an ethnographic study of reading and writing in a seventh grade classroom', in D. Bloome (ed.), *Classrooms and Literacy*. Norwood, NJ: Ablex. pp. 53–104.

Bloome, D. and Green, J. (1984) 'Directions in the sociolinguistic study of reading', in D. Pearson, R. Barr, M. Kamil and P. Mosenthal (eds), *Handbook of Research in Reading*. New York: Longman.

Bourdieu, P. (1977) 'The economics of linguistic exchanges', *Social Sciences Information*, 16: pp. 645–68.

Bourdieu, P. (1990) *In Other Words: Essays towards a Reflexive Sociology*. Stanford, CA: Stanford University Press.

Bruner, J., Goodenough, J. and Austin, G. (1956) *A Study of Thinking*. New York: Wiley.

Bruner, J., Olver, R. and Greenfield, P. (1966) *Studies in Cognitive Growth*. New York: Wiley.

Cannella, G. (2002) *Deconstructing Early Childhood Education: Social Justice and Revolution*. New York: Lang.

Catell, J.M. (1886) 'The time it takes to see and name', *Mind*, 11: 63–5.

Cherry, C. (1966) *On Human Communication*. Cambridge, MA: MIT Press.

Chomsky, N. (1957) *Syntactic Structures*. The Hague: Mouton.

Chomsky, N. (1959) 'Review of *Verbal Behavior* by B.F. Skinner', *Language*, 35: 26–58.

Chomsky, N. (1965) *Aspects of a Theory of Syntax*. Cambridge, MA: MIT Press.

Clarke, M. (1976) *Young Fluent Readers*. London: Heinemann.

Clay, M. (1969) 'Reading errors and self-correction behaviour', *British Journal of Educational Psychology*, 39: 47–56.

Clay, M. (1975) *What Did I Write?* London: Heinemann.

Coltheart, M. (1979) 'When can children learn to read – and when should they be taught?', in T. Waller and G. Mackinnon (eds), *Reading Research: Advances in Theory and Practice*, vol. 1. New York: Academic. pp. 1–30.

Crago, M. and Crago, H. (1983) *Prelude to Literacy: a Pre-School Child's Encounter with Picture and Story*. Carbondale, IL: Southern Illinois University Press.

Dolch, E. and Bloomster, M. (1937) 'Phonic readiness', *Elementary School Journal*, 38: 201–5.

Downing, J. (1979) *Reading and Reasoning*. Edinburgh: Black.

Durkin, D. (1966) *Children Who Read Early*. New York: Teachers College Press.

Dyson, A.H. (1989) *Multiple Worlds of Child Writers: Friends Learning to Write*. New York: Teachers College Press.

Dyson, A.H. (1993) *Social Worlds of Children Learning to Write in an Urban Primary School*. New York: Teachers College Press.

Dyson, A.H. (2002) *The Brothers and Sisters Learn to Write: Popular Literacies in Childhood and School Cultures.* New York: Teachers College Press.

Eco, U. (1979) *The Role of the Reader.* Bloomington, IN: Indiana University Press.

Edelsky, C. (1996) *With Literacy and Justice for All: Rethinking the Social in Language and Education.* London: Taylor and Francis.

Erickson, F. and Mohatt, G. (1982) 'Cultural organisation of participation structures in two classrooms of Indian students', in G. Spindler (ed.), *Doing the Ethnography of Schooling: Educational Anthropology in Action.* New York: Holt, Rinehart and Winston. pp. 132–75.

Ferriero, E. and Teberosky, A. (1982) *Literacy before Schooling.* Portsmouth, NH: Heinemann.

Finders, M. (1997) *Just Girls: Hidden Literacies and Life in Junior High.* New York: Teachers College Press/NCTE.

Finnegan, R. (2002) *Communicating: the Multiple Modes of Human Interconnection.* London: Routledge.

Fishman, A. (1988) *Amish Literacy: What and How it Means.* Portsmouth, NH: Heinemann.

Floriana, A. (1993) 'Negotiating what counts: roles and relationships, texts and contexts, content and meaning', *Linguistics and Education,* 5(3 and 4): 241–75.

Forester, A. (1977) 'What teachers can learn from natural readers', *The Reading Teacher,* 31: 160–6.

Foucault, M. (1979) *Discipline and Punish.* New York: Harper.

Foucault, M. (1988) *Technologies of the Self.* London: Tavistock.

Gardner, H. (1980) *Artful Scribbles: the Significance of Children's Drawings.* New York: Basic.

Garfinkel, H. (1967) *Studies in Ethnomethodology.* Englewood Cliffs, NJ: Prentice Hall.

Gee, J. (1996) *Social Linguistics and Literacies: Ideology in Discourses,* 2nd edn. London: Falmer.

Gibson, E. (1969) *Principles of Perceptual Learning and Development.* New York: Appleton-Century-Crofts.

Gilmore, Perry (1986) 'Sub-rosa literacy: peers, play, and ownership in literacy acquisition', in B. Schiefflin and P. Gilmore (eds), *The Acquisition of Literacy: Ethnographic Perspectives.* New York: Ablex. pp. 155–68.

Goffman, E. (1981) *Forms of Talk.* Oxford: Blackwell.

Goodman, K. (1968*) The Psycholinguistic Nature of the Reading Process.* Detroit: Wayne State University Press.

Goodman, K. (1976) 'Miscue analysis: theory and reality in reading', in J. Merritt (ed.), *New Horizons in Reading.* Newark, DE: International Reading Association.

Goodnow, J. (1977) *Children Drawing.* Cambridge, MA: Harvard University Press.

Gray, W.S. (1956) *The Teaching of Reading and Writing.* Chicago: Scott Foresman.

Green, J. (1987) 'In search of meaning: a sociolinguistic perspective on lesson construction and reading', in

D. Bloome (ed.), *Literacy and Schooling.* Norwood, NJ: Ablex. pp. 3–34.

Halliday, M. (1974) *Language and Social Man.* London: Longman.

Harste, J., Burke, C. and Woodward, V. (1984a) 'Children's language and world: initial encounters with print', in J. Langer and M. Smith-Burke (eds), *Reader Meets Author: Bridging the Gap.* Newark, DE: International Reading Association.

Harste, J., Woodward, V. and Burke, C. (1984b) *Language Stories and Literacy Lessons.* Portsmouth, NH: Heinemann.

Heap, J. (1989) 'Sociality and cognition in collaborative computer learning', in D. Bloome (ed.), *Classrooms and Literacy.* Norwood, NJ: Ablex. pp. 135–57.

Heath, S.B. (1983) *Ways with Words: Language, Life, and Work in Communities and Classrooms.* Cambridge: Cambridge University Press.

Hiebert, E. (1981) 'Developmental patterns and interrelationships of pre-school children's print awareness', *Reading Research Quarterly,* 16 (2): 236–59.

Huey, E.B. (1908) *The Psychology and Pedagogy of Reading.* New York: Macmillan.

Hymes, D. (1974) *Foundation in Sociolinguistics.* Philadelphia: University of Pennsylvania Press.

Johns, J. (1976–7) 'Reading is stand-up, sit-down', *Journal of the New England Reading Association,* 12 (1): 10–14.

Kellog, R. (1969) *Analyzing Children's Art.* Palo Alto, CA: National Press Books.

Kenner, C. (2000) 'Symbols make text: a social semiotic analysis of writing in a multilingual nursery', *Written Language and Literacy,* 3(2): 285–66.

Kress, G. (1997) *Before Writing: Rethinking the Paths to Literacy.* London: Routledge.

Lancaster, L. (2001) 'Staring at the page: the functions of gaze in a young child's interpretation of symbolic forms', *Journal of Early Childhood Literacy,* 1: 131–52.

Lankshear, C. (1997) *Changing Literacies.* Buckingham: Open University Press.

Lankshear, C. and Lawler, M. (1987) *Literacy, Schooling and Revolution.* London: Falmer.

Lass, B. (1982) 'Portrait of my son as an early reader', *The Reading Teacher,* 36 (1): 20–8.

Lee, C. and Smagorinsky, P. (2000) 'Introduction: constructing meaning through collaborative enquiry', in C. Lee and P. Smagorinsky (eds), *Vygotskian Perspectives on Literacy Research: Constructing Meaning through Collaborative Enquiry.* Cambridge: Cambridge University Press.

Lemke, J.L. (1998) 'Multimedia literacy demands of the scientific curriculum', *Linguistics and Education* 10 (3): 247–71.

Lofty, J. (1992) *Time to Write: the Influence of Time and Culture on Learning to Write.* New York: State University of New York Press.

Luke, A. (1988) *Literacy, Textbooks and Ideology*. London: Falmer.

Luke, A. (1992) 'The body literate: discourse and inscription in early literacy training', *Linguistics and Education*, 4: 107–29.

McDermott, R.P. (1979) 'Kids make sense: an ethnographic account of the interactional management of success and failure in one first-grade classroom'. PhD dissertation, Stanford University.

McNeill, D. (1966) 'Developmental psycholinguistics', in F. Smith and G. Miller (eds), *The Genesis of Language*. Cambridge, MA: MIT Press.

Mason, J. (1980) 'When do children begin to read? An exploration of four-year-old children's word reading competencies', *Reading Research Quarterly*, 15 (2): 203–27.

Miller, G. (1967) *The Psychology of Communication*. New York: Basic.

Miller, G., Galanter, E. and Pribram, K. (1960) *Plans and the Structure of Behaviour*. New York: Holt, Rinehart and Winston.

Morphett, M.V. and Washburne, C. (1931) 'When should children begin to read?', *Elementary School Journal*, 31: 496–503.

Neisser, U. (1967) *Cognitive Psychology*. New York: Appleton-Century-Crofts.

Pahl, K. (1999) *Transformations: Meaning Making in the Nursery*. Stoke-on-Trent: Trentham.

Pahl, K. (2002) 'Ephemera, mess and miscellaneous piles: texts and practices in families', *Journal of Early Childhood Literacy* 2 (2): 145–66.

Patrick, G. (1899) 'Should children under 10 learn to read and write?', *Popular Science Monthly*, 54: 382–92.

Payton, S. (1984) *Developing Awareness of Print: a Young Child's First Steps towards Literacy*. Birmingham: Educational Review.

Pierce' (1961) *Symbols, Signals and Noise: the Nature and Process of Communication*. New York: Harper and Row.

Read, C. (1970) 'Pre-school children's knowledge of English phonology', *Harvard Educational Review*, 41 (1): 1–34.

Reid, J. (1966) 'Learning to think about reading', *Educational Research*, 9: 56–62.

Rogoff, B. (1986) 'Adult assistance of children's learning', in T.E. Raphael (ed.), *The Contexts of School-Based Literacy*. New York: Random House. pp. 27–40.

Rogoff, B. (1990) *Apprenticeship in Thinking: Cognitive Development in Social Context*. New York: Oxford University Press.

Rowe, D. (1994) *Preschoolers as Authors: Literacy Learning in the Social World of the Classroom*. Cresskill, NJ: Hampton.

Scollon, R. and Scollon, S. (1981) *Narrative, Literacy and Face in Interethnic Communication*. Norwood, NJ: Ablex.

Scribner, S. and Cole, M. (1981) *The Psychology of Literacy*. Cambridge, MA: Harvard University Press.

Skinner, B.F. (1957) *Verbal Behavior*. New York: Appleton-Century-Crofts.

Smith, F. (1971) *Understanding Reading*. London: Holt, Rinehart.

Street, B. (1984) *Literacy in Theory and Practice*. Cambridge: Cambridge University Press.

Sulzby, E. (1985) 'Kindergartners as readers and writers', in M. Farr (ed.), *Children's Early Writing Development*. Norwood, NJ: Ablex.

Taylor, D. (1983) *Family Literacy: Young Children Learning to Read and Write*. Portsmouth, NH: Heinemann.

Tharp, R. and Gallimore, R. (eds) (1988) *Rousing Minds to Life: Teaching, Learning and Schooling in Social Context*. New York: Cambridge University Press.

Tovey, D. (1976) 'Children's perceptions of reading', *The Reading Teacher*, 29: 536–40.

Van der Veer, R. and Valsiner, J. (1994) 'Introduction', in R. Van der Veer and J. Valsiner (eds), *The Vygotsky Reader*. Oxford: Blackwell.

Voss, M. (1996) *Hidden Literacies: Children Learning at Home and at School*. Portsmouth, NH: Heinemann.

Vygotsky, L.S. (1962) *Thought and Language*. Cambridge, MA: MIT Press.

Vygotsky, L.S. (1967) 'Play and its role in the mental development of the child', *Soviet Psychology*, 56–18.

Vygotsky, L.S. (1978) *Mind in Society: the Development of Higher Psychological Processes*. Cambridge, MA: Harvard University Press.

Wood, D.J., Bruner, J.S. and Ross, G. (1976) 'The role of tutoring in problem solving', *Journal of Child Psychology and Psychiatry*, 17: 89–100.

2

Postcolonial Perspectives on Childhood and Literacy

RADHIKA VIRURU

Some of the most fascinating conversations I have ever had have been with a woman whom most people would define as 'illiterate'. When she first came to work for my mother several years ago, she also wanted to open her first bank account. My mother and a neighbour taught her, with great difficulty, to learn to sign her name; until then she had relied on what might be called another official form of literacy, the thumbprint, in situations that demanded identification. That, however, is the beginning and end of her schooled literacy. I know of few people who can read the world around them like she can. Our conversations have included discussions about abortion, marriage, children, schooling, human dignity and globalization, and most of the time I have found myself listening and wondering: about the kind of knowledge that is possible from outside the world of print that so many of us are surrounded by, and about how many other things she could have accomplished if she had indeed been what the world defines as 'literate', as well as what would have been lost if she had. This complex intersection, between the possibilities that literacy affords as well as the loss that accompanies that gain, is one of the central points that this chapter will focus on.

Much of the literature on language and young children portrays literacy as a process of becoming, acquiring, improving and maturing. Rarely, however, is attention directed towards what is lost and shut out in this process of acquisition. In this chapter, the attempt will be to both lay out a theoretical framework that supports such a view and to review the literature that takes a more complex view of the process of young children's interactions

with literacy. The focus in this chapter is deliberately directed towards diverse cultural contexts, where the process of what it means to become literate is in itself being complicated by factors such as global capitalism and its continuing economic colonization of the world. An attempt will be made to look at how young children interact with this complex combination of forces, and how they both use them to empower themselves and are used by them.

DEFINING TERMS

A logical starting place would be to define what one means by such terms as 'literacy', 'postcolonialism' and 'childhood'. However, as postcolonial scholars point out, it is important to recognize the power of ideas such as definitions themselves. As Rassool (1999) has put it, a definition of literacy is a statement of what it means to be literate: thus definitions provide a set of criteria against which a person's abilities are measured. Definitions reflect the power of those who do the defining: the meanings of literacy thus derive from the institutional sites from which they originate. Thus, definitions themselves are not innocent statements of fact, but are powerful tools that emphasize certain meanings and marginalize others: the act of definition in itself is an act of power. It is from within this context that common definitions are explored.

As Guerra (1998) has suggested, defining literacy is far from an easy task. Guerra suggests that the commonly used meanings of literacy can be broadly classified into four different categories:

literacy as entity, literacy as self, literacy as institution and literacy as practice. The umbrella term, literacy as entity, includes the view that literacy is an object that exists 'outside social and individual constraints' (1998: 51). From this range of viewpoints, written texts have an inviolable authority about them: they are not written for individuals to construct diverse meanings with and around them. The second category, literacy as self, consists of metaphors that essentially view literacy as something that an individual possesses, and as such, as something that is very personally constructed. As Guerra points out, such a view also consequently holds individuals personally responsible for the kinds of literacies they do (or do not) possess. The third group, literacy as institution, consists of views that essentially define literacy as something similar to an artifact or currency: the more one possesses of it, the more successful one can be. The final group, literacy as practice, recognizes that there are multiple forms of literacy, and that people blend these multiple literacies as they both create and engage with the world around them.

On a more specific level, according to Powell (1999), common ways of defining literacy include: (1) the ability to decode print into speech, (2) the ability to derive meaning from written texts and (3) the ability to read and write at a specified proficiency level. Rassool suggests that such perspectives reinforce the idea that literacy is a 'quantifiable educational resource' that fits economic criteria: levels of literacy skills can be matched with market needs, and thus literacy can be translated into 'time, work and money, part of the economy' (Gee, 1996, quoted in Rassool, 1999: 6).

Literacy is often defined too by its other: the illiterate. According to Powell (1999), the possession or non-possession of the commodity of literacy is what determine one's access or lack of access to privileges and status. However, as Powell reiterates, the definition of what it is to be literate is not called into question, as this definition is imposed from above. Illiteracy is associated with ignorance, indolence, poverty and the creation of economic havoc that the literate must fix. As Stuckey (1991) has commented, illiteracy is strongly associated with antisocial behavior: even authors such as Jonathan Kozol remark upon the high rates of illiteracy in the prison populations in the United States. Rockhill has also commented upon the discourses which create 'illiterates' as threats to society: illiteracy is seen as 'dangerous, a threat to liberty, to economic and technological development and to the moral well being' of civilized societies (1993: 157). In contrast, as Gee puts it, students who have acquired schooled literacy are seen as having the potential to be adult citizens who are 'innovative,

achievement-oriented, productive, cosmopolitical, media and politically aware, more globally (nationally and internationally) and less locally-oriented, with more liberal and human social attitudes, less likely to commit a crime, and more likely to take education and the rights and duties of citizenship seriously' (Gee, 1990, quoted in Gallego and Hollingsworth, 2000: 6).

In contrast to such views on literacy is the concept of critical literacy, which is in many ways a literacy about literacies. As Luke and Freebody put it, although the idea of critical literacy is by no means unitary, it refers to a broad coalition of viewpoints that 'literacy involves malleable social practices, relations and events that can be harnessed in the service of particular pedagogical projects and agendas for cultural action' (1997: 1). Critical literacy scholars (Lankshear and Lawler, 1989; Walkerdine, 1997) have thus focused in multiple ways on the 'networks of power' that decide how language is used in powerful social institutions and how these practices perpetuate injustice and inequity (Gilbert, 1997). In the 1970s and 1980s, the term 'critical literacy' was often used to describe the work of Freire and his colleagues, who put forth the view that 'language and literacy and control over how issues, problems and aspects of the world are "named" are directly tied to issues of political power' and that (critical) literacy education could empower people to recognize and negotiate these disparities (Luke and Freebody, 1979: 17). More recent work on critical literacy has expanded in multiple directions including gender studies, studies of childhood and studies of the relationship between colonialism and literacy, which is what this chapter will focus on.

POSTCOLONIAL PERSPECTIVES ON LITERACY

Issues of language and literacy have been of great concern to postcolonial theorists as they are seen as deeply implicated in the continuing colonization of the world by Euro-Western ways of being and thinking (Gandhi, 1998; Loomba, 1998). As Seed (1991: 8) has pointed out, language has even been used as a tool to distinguish between 'civilization and barbarism': those civilizations that use written languages are considered superior to those who do not. Scholars of childhood have noted (Walkerdine, 1989; Burman, 1994; Cannella, 1997) that young children too are often referred to as beings who need to be civilized and a vital part of this civilizing process is the acquisition of (proper) language. As Gandhi suggests, language or text, more than any other social or political product, is one of the most 'significant instigators and purveyors of colonial power' (1998: 141). The pertinence of this argument to the lives of young children has been argued elsewhere (Viruru and Cannella, 1999): like many colonized groups, young children have rarely been allowed to define what it means to be a child; the modern construction of childhood as a pure and magical part of one's life is seen as resembling the exotic Western fantasies that came to be called the 'Orient' (which had little to do with the realities of the people these fantasies defined as Orientals). Other common points between the definitions of colonized groups and young children is that children too are often seen as unruly creatures whose bodies need to be strictly controlled and their freedoms restricted; children (like other colonized groups) are often viewed as deficient but 'educable', interested more in what they might become than what they are. Furthermore, one of the key ways in which very young children are seen as 'lacking' is that they do not use language.

However, postcolonial scholars have also pointed out how concepts such as 'print capitalism' have been resisted and used for different purposes by those supposedly lacking in agency (Loomba, 1998: 191). As Chatterjee puts it, for those who saw a foreign language as an imposition, 'language therefore became a zone over which the nation first had to declare its sovereignty and then had to transform in order to make it adequate for the modern world' (1993: 7). As Loomba reminds us, both the 'powerful' and the 'powerless' are not unitary categories, for 'individual and collective subjects can be thought of in multiple ways at any given time, and we must keep open the very meanings of domination' (1998: 240). Furthermore, as Papastergiadis (2000) has commented, the use of a dominant language can both 'ironize and unmask' authority. Papastergiadis' discussion of Bakhtin's theory of hybridity suggests that the hybrid text 'always undoes the priorities and disrupts the singular code by which the dominant code categorizes the other' (2000: 182). Lotman (1991) has suggested that the very existence of a dominant language often leads to hybridity, for the expansion of that language often leads to its 'rigidification', and its becoming more and more distant from the everyday contexts in which it is expected to be used. Thus, he suggests, it becomes more and more prone to disintegration, for the periphery is unlikely to accept conversion passively: the resulting tension produces what Papastergiadis has called a 'dissenting language', which might use the structures of the dominant language, but nevertheless conveys the meanings of the periphery (2000: 185). Lotman has also outlined the mechanisms by which dialogue might occur in the context of difference: originally

'foreign' languages are not seen as a threat, as they are presumed to be superior and can offer a positive contribution. As familiarity builds, however, both ends begin to change and restructure one another, as the 'receiver' sees the potential for its use and begins to transform it to his or her own purposes. The 'foreign' language may then be used to create original texts that represent both assimilation and resistance to the language.

LITERACY AND HYBRIDITY

As the above perspectives illustrate, the process of becoming what the world defines as literate is also, in some ways, a way of losing other ways of knowing, of becoming a 'hybrid'. Young (1995) has pointed out that a hybrid is technically a cross between different species and that the use of such a term invokes botanical images of interspecies grafting. A hybrid was often seen as a monstrous or debased offspring, both weaker and less fertile than either parent (Papastergiadis, 2000). Hybridity, by its very existence, seemed to threaten evocations of social order and disrupt dominant ideas of purity and domination. However, within postcolonial analyses, hybridity has been used to invoke all the ways in which this vocabulary was 'challenged and undermined' (Loomba, 1998: 172). Papastergiadis has suggested that the term 'hybridity' seems to draw some of its strength from its colonial past, from a pleasure in 'taking a negative term and transforming it into a positive sign, to wear with pride the name they were given in scorn' (2000: 169). Bhabha (1990) has differentiated the term 'hybrid' from its earlier connotations: either of 'diabolical stain' or as 'harmonic transcendence between races' (Papastergiadis, 2000: 193). Nandy (1983) has focused on how hybridity emerged as the unseen but inevitable corollary out of the clash of cultures that colonialism invariably created. As one moves away from dualistic thinking, Nandy points out that rather than creating the colonizers as victors and the colonized as victims, colonialism produced new losses and gains, with both sides gaining and losing agency.

Postcolonial scholars have also pointed out the dangers of 'postcolonial desire', a phenomenon through which everything dominant is seen as 'bad' and everything the other is 'good' (Bulbeck, 1998). Thus, it has been suggested that both the 'dominant' and the 'other' are constructed not only in opposition to each other, but through intermingling, which creates hybridity (Loomba, 1998). It underlines the importance of avoiding the temptation to label all practices associated with dominant perspectives on literacy as 'bad' and its opposites as desirable, and furthermore to avoid the use of such dualistic labels altogether (Visweswaran, 1994). Although some postcolonial scholars have cautioned that a focus on concepts such as hybridity distracts from the violence that necessarily accompanies any colonial encounter (Shohat, 1993), others point out it is only through an understanding of diverse hybridities that one can come to understand and appreciate how different communities have, even in colonial conditions, engaged in struggles for emancipation, autonomy and citizenship (Gilroy, 1993).

Thus, it is the contention of this chapter that the above framework is particularly useful in viewing the ways in which young children interact with literacy: as both possibility and limitation. As Millard (in this volume) has pointed out, the processes through which children become literate limit not only the children's identities but also the very definition of literacy itself. As the diverse examples that follow will show, to become literate in one way is to become illiterate in another; to acquire the dominant view of literacy is in some ways gaining access to power, but it is also relinquishing other ways of knowing.

HYBRID LITERACIES

Literacy in a Papua New Guinean village

An interesting perspective on literacy comes from Kulick and Stroud's (1993) description of the complex position of literacy in a Papua New Guinean village. Their ethnographic study of the literary practices of the small (population about 100) village of Gapun are particularly suggestive of complexity. According to Kulick and Stroud, a grammar school was established in the late 1960s in a nearby village and ever since most children from the village have attended it for three to six years. In this school, the language of instruction is English. The children of Gapun thus 'acquire' literacy in a language that they almost never use. What they do acquire however seems to be a literacy about literacy, since most of them 'transfer those skills to Tok Pisin (the language commonly used in the village), thus becoming functionally literate in that language' (1993: 32).

In the social contexts that the children mostly function in, however, this form of literacy is perfectly adequate. Reading and writing in Gapun are not done for purposes of gaining information, nor are people who can do so considered more competent. The most common type of writing in Gapun is

to write notes for practical purposes such as asking for the loan of a chicken. The other most common use of literacy is related to Christianity: most reading is geared towards religious material. Written language itself came to Gapun through the Catholic Church in the 1950s: thus when the villagers learned to read, it was to read Christian literature. Kulick and Stroud suggest that the villagers' relationship with Christianity and literacy reveals both domination and empowerment: on the one hand, Christianity is seen as a link to a more potent Being that can bestow such rewards as 'aeroplanes, money and white skin'; on the other hand, it would appear that by limiting their schooled literacy to religious activities, they maintain their own independence from the world of money, aeroplanes and white skin.

Another remarkable feature of social life in Gapun is the emphasis that people place on personal autonomy: Kulick and Stroud assert that in this village, 'no relationship, not even that between adult and child, is understood by the villagers to legitimately involve the power to order another person to do something against his or her will' (1993: 43).

Viewed from within this context, the ways in which the villagers do and do not use literacy are in sharp contrast to commonly held perceptions of what literacy is. From birth, 'babies in the village are treated as stubborn, big headed individualists' (1993: 43). The babbling of older babies is often interpreted as an expression of anger or dissatisfaction, to which adults might respond by asking what the baby was mad about. Children's first words are often cited as being something that would be translated as 'I'm getting out of here.' What the villagers do seem to consider an important kind of literacy is a quality known as 'save' or the knowledge that one must sometimes compromise one's autonomy for the sake of society: this is a quality that is seen as separating adults and children, though it is not something that can be taught but something that 'breaks open' within a child as they grow older.

Although this is a very brief and necessarily subjective summary of the uses of literacy in one social context, it does seem remarkable that in a social context where human beings are seen as having very little right to control one another, there is a very low emphasis on schooled literacy. As Kulick and Stroud point out also, literacy has been both resisted and accommodated by the villagers in ways that reflect agency and power as well as colonization.

Literacy instruction in Samoa

Duranti and Ochs' (1986) ethnographic study of literacy in a rural Western Samoan village brings out several interesting points that are suggestive of the hybrid nature of literacy acquisition in this context. The authors found that the process of what they called transmitting literacy in school settings was made far more complex as the children were exposed not only to the complexities of written language but to a completely new set of cultural values and expectations, many of which clashed with the ways of the village in which they had been raised. Duranti and Ochs conclude that 'a global effect of literacy instruction is a change in the social identity of the child in Samoan society' (1986: 214).

One interesting aspect of literacy instruction in the village was the kind of alphabet chart that was used. Duranti and Ochs found that children between the ages of three and four were sent to a local pastor's school to learn the alphabet, Arabic and Roman numbers and some passages from the Bible. The alphabet was taught mostly through the use of an alphabet chart, which the authors describe in great detail. The most striking feature of the chart was that the illustrations used on the alphabet chart represent a very clear 'Western' orientation. Although some sounds in the Samoan language were introduced by Europeans, and as such there are no 'indigenous' words that use those sounds, even the other more traditional sounds were associated with Europeanized objects. Thus the authors conclude that in this context the children are being taught not just the alphabet but also to pay attention to a world of 'objects and values' that reflect Western biases.

Duranti and Ochs also contrast the contexts and conventions of literacy use in the village, and compare them to the ones the children encounter in their schooling. Very young children in the village are socialized into what the authors call a 'disposition of attention and accommodation': they are expected to observe the activities going on around them and report on them to others. They are also expected to speak in an intelligible manner: adults do not expect simplified speech from children, nor do they try to 'unravel' unintelligible speech that the children might use. Children between the ages of three and four are also expected to deliver long oral messages to other persons, using appropriate vocabulary. Children are generally not praised for such tasks. Furthermore, in the village, any kind of accomplishment, be it someone driving well on a bumpy road or making a trip to another city, is seen as a collective achievement: 'an individual's competence is defined by his audience appreciation and his merit is framed within the merit of his group' (1986: 222). Thus even if someone is praised for doing something, the general response is for the praise to be returned and for the accomplishment to be generalized into something that was not done by the person alone.

In contrast, the schooling patterns of the children reflected some very different ways of functioning as the school is organized through the Christian Church and the pastors are trained in Western pedagogical methods for four years. Duranti and Ochs found that the kind of 'teacher talk' characteristic of Western middle class environments was common in the school: thus simplification and clarification of terms was common, unlike in the village environment where adults rarely accommodated to what might be called the 'child-like' qualities of children's speech. Thus three- and four-year-old children encounter some very different definitions of what it means to be a child and what it means to use language when they enter the classroom.

In further contrast, children were also frequently praised for having accomplished literacy tasks and the praise is not reciprocated (as would be common in everyday contexts in the village).Thus when a child names an object or identifies an alphabet correctly, the teacher might respond by saying 'good' or 'very good'. The child generally does not respond to such praise, unlike they would in other contexts.

However, as Duranti and Ochs suggest, the reasons that rural Samoans enrol their children in these schools are twofold: they want their children to be able to read the Bible and to be employable. The urban economy that surrounds the village relies heavily not only on literacy related skills but also on the idea of individual accomplishment. Thus to earn a good income, it is essential that one learn not only the skills that are taught in the schools but also the values that undergird those skills.

This brief description of literacy acquisition in this context suggests that acquiring literacy for the children in the Samoan village is very much a process of both loss and gain, of contradiction and accommodation, of colonization and agency.

Literacy acquisition in Inuit contexts

Crago and Allen's (1998) ethnographic study of how Inuit children from the Canadian Arctic acquire their native language, Inuktitut, is also suggestive of the two themes of loss and gain that this chapter is focusing on. There are approximately 28,000 Inuit people in the Canadian Arctic, and nearly 40% of them are below the age of 15. The economy of the Inuit people used to be mostly based on hunting and gathering activities but has now changed to include more 'modern' occupations. Although most families now live in homes and apartments and most children go to school, the schooling and healthcare systems are under local Inuit control and the whole territory has an autonomous government. Crago and Allen's study provides rich detail about the language experiences of four young children (under the age of two) and their families in one Inuit community. The study also included interview data from 20 mothers from the community.

Children in Inuit communities learn language in contexts that Crago and Allen call 'both traditional and evolving' (1998: 249). One interesting feature of many of these communities is the ways in which language is or is not used. It is common for young mothers or couples with their first child to live with their families. Caregiving is also shared among family members; thus young children learn to talk in environments that include many different speakers of different age ranges. Crago and Allen found a striking difference, however, between the language socialization practices of the mothers aged over 45 and the younger, more 'modern' mothers. The older mothers used what the authors called a 'specific baby lexicon, a special register of affectionate talk' and they also tended not to involve children in adult conversations. What, however, was most striking was all the situations in which the mothers did not talk to their children: many activities that from a Western lens have been seen as 'natural' situations for conversations, were in fact conducted in silence. These included such activities as 'bedding, bathing, dressing, eating' as well as more complex ones such as 'companionship and discipline' (1999: 250). The older mothers talked to their children only about one-third as much as the younger mothers within the Inuit community and only one-sixth as much as a comparison group of American white middle class mothers. Most of the children of the older mothers talked more to their siblings and peers, who explicitly modelled accepted ways of behaviour for them. In contrast however many of the younger mothers in Crago and Allen's study used language socialization practices that resemble more generic North American white middle class ways. These changes appear to reflect the influence of many of the white middle class school teachers who came into the community. Many younger parents model their parenting methods on the kind of classroom discourse that is seen in the schools.

Crago and Allen followed the children from their sample into their school. They found that although the practices in their first three years of education, with Inuit teachers, very much reflected the cultural values of their community (for example, children were expected to attend to their peers and were allowed to model their work on that of other children), their later education reflected many discontinuities, as children were looked at much more in terms of individuals rather than as connected to their peer groups.

As Crago and Allen suggest, the Inuit situation is particularly unique in that, even though it has the status of a minority language, there are strong educational and institutional policies that support its continued existence. Almost 100% of the Inuit children in the studied region learn it as their first language. This, however, has both advantages and drawbacks, as many Inuit parents tend to take the continued existence of their language for granted and do not use it as much at home. Furthermore, as many Inuit communities blend more with the larger community around them, complex processes of language shift occur. Inuit communities too are greatly impacted by electronic media, which have contributed to the restructuring of their community as well as their language. As Crago and Allen point out, all of these processes seem to reflect not only 'creative change' but loss as well and it is important to see them as such.

Conflicting perspectives on literacy in India

Studies of literacy acquisition in multiple contexts in India seem to document the hybrid nature of this process particularly well, perhaps due to India's long history of colonization as well as one of its most enduring aftermaths: the widespread use of English. However English occupies rather a unique position in many Indian contexts as both a foreign and an indigenous language (Viruru, 2001). The ways in which children acquire official school literacy in India have been well documented (Kumar, 1993; Sahni, 2001; Alexander, 2001; Viruru, 2001). However two recent studies of literacy and education in India (Urvashi Sahni's 2001 study of literacy acquisition in a North Indian village and Robin Alexander's 2001 comparative study of primary education in five countries) report similar findings but proceed in very different directions.

Alexander's study focuses primarily on descriptions and summaries of the experiences he found in primary schools in the UK, India, Russia, the United States and France. His study provides exhaustive details about classroom practices and educational policy in these five countries, relating both these strands to the cultural contexts particular to those settings. The study was based on the framework that education in the global era had to be 'more generous in its apprehension of time, space, social structure, human relations and the connections between them' than in the past. In India, Alexander's work was based in three North Indian locations (both rural and urban). As Alexander points out, looking at primary education in India is particularly important, since the life experiences of children in India are perhaps more globally representative than those of children in what are commonly referred to as industrialized countries. Furthermore, in 1993 India had the world's largest number of out-of-school children (22% of the global total) and about one-third of the world's 'illiterates'.

Alexander found that the Indian classrooms he studied were characterized by a reliance on ritual and regimentation. As he points out, this was at least partially the result of having larger class sizes (50–60 children in one class). These rituals were largely focused on turn taking in teaching and learning, with the teacher saying something and the children repeating it in unison. One lesson in particular that Alexander observed (focused on the letter/sound A in Hindi) has the teacher asking questions like, 'What word begins with A?', 'What is her name?' (with reference to a particular pupil), 'What have you learned?' and 'What sound can you hear?' To all of these questions the six-year-old children replied in unison. Similar methods were observed by Alexander in other schools, in the teaching of numbers and science. Questioning is thus used by the teachers, initially to engage the students' attention (when they ask more open-ended questions) but more often to elicit specific responses, often from the whole group. Such a structure does not allow for too many individual answers or for much interaction outside of the structure of the lesson. However other accounts of schooling in India have revealed that even though this might appear from the outside to be a very limiting and dehumanized way of educating young children, it in fact represents cultural traditions that are centuries old. Furthermore, there are levels of complex interaction built into this structure that are apparent when the process is studied in more detail (Viruru, 2001).

Sahni's (2001) 'micro-ethnographic' study of a second-grade classroom in rural North India takes an entirely different track, as it looks at what happened when what might be called 'Western' methods of dialogue, representation and conversation were introduced into a research setting. Sahni describes this process as appropriating literacy, which she interprets as adding it (literacy) to 'one's symbolic repertoire, aiding one in interpretive, constructive, creative interaction with the world and others in it' (2001: 19). According to Sahni, this kind of appropriation also involves claiming for oneself a 'power commodity' that has traditionally been outside one's reach. Sahni's study is set in a government run primary school in a village in the northern province of Uttar Pradesh, which served 236 children. Sahni's research was divided into two phases: an observation phase and a participant interaction phase. In the observation phase, Sahni found that the setting was 'alienating, nonresponsive' and uncaring, with phrases like 'no one cares' being used by all the participants a great deal. According to Sahni, the principal, teachers, parents and children all felt disrespected and unsupported, as none of them felt they had any control or investment in the curriculum. Literacy in particular was 'conceived mechanistically, practiced minimally and passively'; the school structures enforced passivity, non-participation and hierarchy. All classroom activity was seen by Sahni as being controlled by the teacher, without the participation of the children. Literacy consisted mostly of copying lines, from textbooks and from the board. There was a great deal of recitation in the classroom. To quote Sahni:

> Literacy was officially defined in terms of decontextualized technical skills of reading and writing, reduced to the bare elements of the alphabet. Reading was defined as decoding of print, and writing was understood as the mechanical transcription of letters. (2001: 21)

Thus far, Sahni's account is quite similar to those related above. Where they differ is in the account of what Sahni calls the participant interaction phase of her research, where she explored the interests of the children in order to construct a curriculum with them, based on their interests and needs. In the redefined classroom, children were given the right to 'make choices, offer consent, play with language, offer suggestions, display their knowledge for peers, express their needs and wishes and have their needs attended to' (2001: 22). The children were given what Sahni calls a more central role in classroom events, as they recited and wrote poetry and songs, read stories (both self and other created), co-wrote stories, wrote picture compositions and enacted dramas in their classrooms. Sahni also provides a detailed description of the experiences of two children in this classroom, both of whom seemed to initially view literacy as the ability to copy print.

This last account of literacy in a rural classroom in India raises many interesting possibilities. The children in the classroom did in fact seem to be able to 'appropriate' literacy for their own purposes. However, as Sahni herself admits, it is not entirely clear where this appropriation may lead them. Although their experiences with literacy may have changed, the social structure around them did not: thus in acquiring this kind of literacy, and in associating it with change and empowerment, in the manner that Sahni describes, one wonders if in some ways they have also not acquired a certain kind of illiteracy about empowerment (in terms of knowing about other ways in which one might empower oneself). Implicit too in Sahni's account is a narrative of deficiency: that the kind of literacy with which these children engaged in their classroom was somehow inadequate, as judged both from a dominant perspective on literacy which views it as something that can be used to empower oneself, and also from the view of the participants themselves. It would be interesting, however, to know more about how the literacy curriculum introduced by Sahni was perceived by the people in the village. One would also like to know more about why Sahni chose to use the methods she did: in particular whether it was because these methods were seen as the 'correct' way in which to engage with literacy or whether these were things that the villagers (including the children) saw as meaningful. It would also be interesting to know how the people in that village perceived literacy and whether they saw what was happening in that school as having anything to do with it.

CONCLUDING THOUGHTS

As all of the above examples illustrate, the process of becoming 'literate' is far more complex than it might appear. Furthermore, what it means to become literate, and how one goes about achieving that, whether it be oral or schooled literacy, is an area that has been greatly impacted by such forces as global capitalism and the kind of languages that fit it, as well as the kinds of skills that empower one to become a part of it. As each one of the studies reviewed has shown, in multiple ways, language reflects as well as creates the cultural context in which it is used: thus power over language is a particularly 'powerful' kind of power. It is, therefore, critically important that scholars and professionals who are interested in how children acquire language should be aware of the complex nature of this process. To look at what children acquire as they become 'literate', is, as many postcolonial scholars would point out, only part of the story. Many would also add that it is not an innocent coincidence that it is the part of the story that we attend to.

REFERENCES

Alexander, R. (2001) *Culture and Pedagogy: International Comparisons in Primary Education*. Malden, MA: Blackwell.

Bhabha, H. (1990) *Nation and Narration*. London: Routledge.

Bulbeck, C. (1998) *Re-orienting Western Feminisms: Women's Diversity in a Postcolonial World*. Cambridge: Cambridge University Press.

Burman, E. (1994) *Deconstructing Developmental Psychology*. London and New York: Routledge.

Cannella, G.S. (1997) *Deconstructing Early Childhood Education: Social Justice and Revolution*. New York: Lang.

Chatterjee, P. (1993) *The Nation and its Fragments: Colonial and Postcolonial Histories*. Princeton, NJ: Princeton University Press.

Crago, M. and Allen, S. (1998) 'Acquiring Inuktitut', in O. Tayor and L. Leonard (eds), *Language Acquisition in North America: Cross-cultural and Cross-linguistic Perspectives*. San Diego, CA: Singular Publishing.

Duranti, A. and Ochs, E. (1986) 'Literacy instruction in a Samoan Village', in Bambi B. Schieffelin and Perry Gilmore (eds), *The Acquisition of Literacy: Ethnographic Perspectives*. Norwood, NJ: Ablex. pp. 213–32.

Gallego, M. and Hollingsworth, S. (2000) 'Introduction: the idea of multiple literacies', in M. Gallego and S. Hollingsworth (eds), *What Counts as Literacy: Challenging the School Standard*. New York: Teachers College Press. pp. 1–23.

Gandhi, L. (1998) *Postcolonial Theory: a Critical Introduction*. New York: Columbia University Press.

Gee, J.P. (1990) *Social Linguistics and Literacies: Ideology in Discourses*. New York: Falmer.

Gee, J.P. (1996) *Social Linguistics and Literacies: Ideology in Discourses*, 2nd edn. London: Taylor and Francis.

Gilbert, P. (1997) 'Discourses on gender and literacy: Changing the Stories', in S. Muspratt, A. Luke and P. Freebody (eds), *Constructing Critical Literacies*. Creskill, NJ: Hampton. pp. 69–76.

Gilroy, P. (1993) *The Black Atlantic: Modernity and Double Consciousness*. London: Verso.

Guerra, J.C. (1998) *Close to Home: Oral and Literate Practices in a Transnational Mexicano Community*. New York: Teachers College Press.

Kulick, D and Stroud, C. (1993) 'Conceptions and use of literacy in a Papua New Guinean village', in Brian V. Street (ed.), *Cross-Cultural Approaches to Literacy*. Cambridge: Cambridge University Press. pp. 25–61.

Kumar, K. (1993) 'Literacy and primary education in India', in P. Freebody and A. Welch (eds), *Knowledge, Culture and Power: International Perspectives on Literacy as Policy and Practice*. London: Falmer Press.

Lankshear, C. and Lawler, M. (1989) *Literacy, Schooling and Revolution*. New York: Falmer.

Loomba, A. (1998) *Colonialism/Postcolonialism*. London: Routledge.

Lotman, Y.M. (1991) *Universe of the Mind*, trans. A. Shukman. London: Tauris.

Luke, A. and Freebody, P. (1997) 'Critical literacy and the question of normativity', in S. Muspratt, A. Luke and P. Freebody (eds), *Constructing Critical Literacies*. Creskill, NJ: Hampton. pp. 1–18.

Nandy, A. (1983) *The Intimate Enemy*. New Delhi: Oxford University Press.

Papastergiadis, N. (2000) *The Turbulence of Migration*. Malden, MA: Polity.

Powell, R. (1999) *Literacy as Moral Imperative: Facing the Challenges of a Pluralistic Society*. Lanham, MD: Rowman and Littlefield.

Rassool, N. (1999) *Literacy for Sustainable Development in the Age of Information*. Clevedon: Multilingual Matters.

Rockhill, K. (1993) 'Gender, language and the politics of literacy', in Brian V. Street (ed.), *Cross-Cultural Approaches to Literacy*. Cambridge: Cambridge University Press. pp. 156–175.

Sahni, U. (2001) 'Children appropriating literacy: empowerment pedagogy from young children's perspective', in B. Comber and A. Simpson (eds), *Negotiating Critical Literacies in Classrooms*. Mahwah, NJ: Erlbaum. pp. 19–35.

Seed, P. (1991) 'Failing to marvel: Atahualpa's encounter with the word', *Latin American Research Review*, 26: 7–32.

Shohat, E. (1993) 'Notes on the postcolonial', *Social Text*, 31/32: 91–113.

Stuckey, J.E. (1991) *The Violence of Literacy*. Portsmouth, NH: Heinemann.

Viruru, R. (2001) *Early Childhood Education: Postcolonial Perspectives from India*. New Delhi: Sage.

Viruru, R. and Cannella, G.S. (1999) 'A postcolonial scrutiny of early childhood education'. Paper presented at the JCT Conference, Dayton, Ohio, October.

Visweswaran, K. (1994) *Fictions of Feminist Ethnography*. Minneapolis: University of Minnesota Press.

Walkerdine, V. (1997) *Daddy's Girl: Young Girls and Popular Culture*. Cambridge, MA: Harvard University Press.

Young, R.J.C. (1995) *Colonial Desire: Hybridity in Culture, Theory and Race*. London: Routledge.

3

Gender and Early Childhood Literacy

ELAINE MILLARD

This chapter considers the multiplicity of ways in which children's gendered identity is implicated in their taking up of literacy practices both at home and in school. The print and media environment which surrounds children from birth, early literacy events in the home and the formalization of literacy encounters within school, all carry messages of what it is to be an effective reader and writer. The education of the young is often overdetermined by parents', teachers' and educators' wish to transmit their own understanding of what is acceptable behaviour in social situations through the medium of story. As a result, the sharing of stories at home and in school becomes overloaded with a multiplicity of value judgements. Learning to read and write, therefore, can be shown to involve children's initiation into social and cultural practices, and of significance amongst these are the multiplicity of narrative and other textual messages that convey aspects of what it might mean to be female, or to be male. Moreover, their gender identification has been shown to play an important role in children's reading and writing choices as well as their growing sense of themselves as learners (Millard, 1994b; 1997; Davies, 1989; 1993; Gilbert, 1989; Walkerdine, 1990). This chapter will examine how research has probed the mechanisms by means of which literacy development and the construction of gendered identity are interwoven and create expectations, not only of what it means to be literate, but also of what it might mean to be a literate boy, or a literate girl. In describing what has been learnt about the process of socialization into gendered literate identities, I shall begin by adopting a definition of

gender which has been widely promoted by earlier researchers into gender and education.

GENDER AS SOCIALLY CONSTRUCTED

The identification of disabling myths about genetic capacities and incapacities influenced a whole generation of feminist theorists to challenge the notion of gender as biologically determined. In order to do this, they first distinguished a definition of male and female arrived at through biological sex from that of gender, which is constructed and reproduced socially, pointing to patriarchy (or the dominance of male thought, culture and power) as the main determinant of gender role (Arnot and Weiner, 1989). Second-wave feminist writers drew widely on the precept of the earlier feminist, Simone de Beauvoir (1972), that one is not born but becomes a woman, in order to draw attention to women's continuing disadvantage in most social and cultural arenas. This was achieved primarily by the identification of women's subjection and derogation through the oppressive dominant discourses of difference and disability. Many feminists, who at this period were themselves involved in education as students, researchers or teachers, began to document, within a discourse of equal rights, the considerable divergence of the routes patterned out by contemporary educational systems for boys and girls. Their project was to expose those embedded habits of gender differentiation which worked against the interests of girls and women (Stacey et al., 1974; Spender and Sarah, 1980; Stanworth, 1981). These researchers argued powerfully that girls' talents, abilities and educational opportunities were severely limited by aspects of both the official and hidden curricula in schools; and moreover, that education was a site where gender difference, imported from experiences outside the school gates, was not only confirmed by the practices of educational institutions, but also more firmly established and even amplified (Delamont, 1980; Marland, 1983; Measor and Sykes, 1992; Acker, 1994).

A new understanding of the place of literacy in education was becoming influential at the same time as the changes to teachers' perceptions of the role of gender in differentiating educational opportunity. Theorists began to redescribe literacy activities (defined previously as a set of cognitive competencies or skills to be acquired developmentally) as socially constructed practices, saturated with power relations and the hierarchical organization of knowledge (Freire, 1972; Street, 1984; Lankshear and McLaren, 1993; Barton and Hamilton, 1998). Literacy, rather than being taken uncritically as a set of universal, abstract, cognitive processes, became recognized as constituted by those socially derived conventions which inform any given culture. Literacy practices could then be shown, as a direct consequence of their constructed nature, to be infused with the dominant ideologies of the culture within which they were transmitted and reproduced (Heath, 1983; Taylor and Dorsey-Gaines, 1988; Street and Street, 1991). As feminists had already shown that gender was constructed through *social practices*, the realization that literacy itself is a set of social practices, rather than cognitive processes, became important in explanations of the interrelationship of (gendered) identity and literacy development (Orellana, 1995; 1999). As an example of this, children can be seen to be forming ideas about for whom a specific activity is most appropriate, whilst being initiated into such seemingly neutral practices as sharing a book with an adult or being supported in writing a message on a birthday card. For in their interactions with adults as carers, or teachers, children begin to establish a sense of their own identities and potentialities as literate beings in a process which Kress has described as forming 'deep-seated dispositions in the person who is literate' (1997: 150). The next section of this chapter will therefore consider the expectations and identifications set up for children by their earliest literacy experiences. In doing this, it is important to emphasize that, although the literacy events in which children participate take place in many different settings (shops, doctors' surgeries and churches, for example), those that have been described most often by researchers occur in homes and classrooms. Not only this, but also most studies

that focus on gendered literacy practices do so in white, middle-class, Western-nation homes. It is important to keep this in mind when considering the reported outcomes of home-based research, for as Orellana has observed, 'researchers often call for attention to intersections of gender, class, race and ethnicity, but rarely explore them in practice' (1999: 65).

LITERACY IN THE HOME

It is in the home that children first encounter the range of literacy practices and resources that enable meanings to be created, transmitted and interpreted and that they are initiated as junior members into what Frank Smith (1988) memorably termed the 'literacy club'. Gunther Kress' (1997) work on multimodality is helpful in explaining how children come to select from the wide range of semiotic resources present in the home. Kress demonstrates that in their early literacy exchanges, children develop an awareness that 'content has a shape' and that this is part of the important things to be learned about the process of communication in a social context. By this, he suggests that children constantly draw on aspects of the materials which they find around them in designing new meanings for themselves. He further suggests (although he does not develop the idea in any detail) that the choice of materials (the stuff) creates possibilities for the differentiation of gender (1997: 31, 145). From this perspective, it can therefore be seen that the materials, as well as the processes encountered in reading, are saturated with inflections of gender appropriateness. In white, middle-class, Western-nation homes, it is mothers who most frequently engage children in the daily practices of text sharing and message making (Millard, 1994). Moreover, in many extended multilingual families, where it is siblings who often engage younger members of the family in such activities, older sisters frequently play the most significant role (Gregory, 1998; 2001).

Because of this, acts of literacy may become feminized in the eyes of the young observers, with the added complication that, in Western cultures, boys appear to resist any activity that might be deemed girl-appropriate and constantly seek to define themselves as both 'not girls' and 'not feminine' (Clark, 1999; Jordan, 1995; Millard, 1997). Moreover, the parents themselves bring expectations of the kind of literacy activities which should be expected from their sons and daughters. In her recent Australian study of parents' construction of their children as gendered, literate subjects, Sue

Nichols (2002) concludes that a notion prevails amongst parents that girls are developmentally more advanced in key literacy-related areas such as speech and that parents also construct girls' literacy learning as natural and unproblematic. In contrast, parent often believe that their sons' masculinity and literacy are in opposition. This creates an expectation of developmental delay in their sons, which is further complicated by parents' attribution of agency to the boys in deciding (or not deciding) when they are ready to learn. Both elements interact to constitute boys' literacy learning as problematic.

Moreover, literacy development has been shown to be heavily dependent on access to available social and cultural capital (Heath, 1983; Taylor and Dorsey-Gaines, 1988; Wells, 1987) and the home is a domain in which gender difference is shown to matter. Judith Solsken (1992), who followed a group of young children from their socialization in the home to the early stages of education, used her observations to identify the dynamics of individual children's literacy. By analysing closely the literacy experiences of four key children, with additional evidence from the activities of their classmates, she demonstrates how children construct concepts about literacy and its practices alongside their evolving identities as readers and writers. She argues that in many social groupings, it is to a large extent women who are assigned the work of supporting young children's literacy and this fact inflects their perceptions of its relevance to children's own identity. Although Solsken provides some examples of boys who experience literacy practices as a positive element of their identity formation, she also demonstrates clearly how children's perception of literacy as adult-sponsored work may bring with it tensions around gender identification. She demonstrates how particular boys who are resisting female models of literacy may be cast at cross-purposes with their teachers, finding written work set for them in schools as 'inactive, difficult and 'boring' (1992: 105). Girls, on the other hand, may experience more links between personal experience and their imaginative worlds, finding literacy activities another source of rich and rewarding forms of play confirmed in the stories they meet both at home and in school. Solsken's findings have clear implications for the understanding of individual gendered positioning, rather than the grand narrative of patriarchal oppression that is assumed to place a limit only on girls' performance. Her work is supported by research findings that many boys report female members of their families as being the key players in reading and writing activities in the home (Millard, 1994; 1997), a position which leads some of them to reject reading as female-appropriate,

passive activity in school (Jordan, 1995; Maynard, 2002). Jordan further suggests that it is because children come to school with already well-defined gendered identities, one of them being the identification of masculinity with 'warriors and fighting fantasy', that it is important during the early school years to explore 'through discussion of television programmes and the children's own writing, that a wider range of behaviour than fighting and resistance to teachers is compatible with the broad parameters of the "warrior" definition' (1995: 81). It is the construction of such gendered identities as princesses and warriors, good guys and bad girls, in play that I will turn to next, before focusing more closely on the engendering of reading and writing activities in school.

LITERACY DEVELOPED IN GENDERED PLAY

Play provides one of the earliest domains both at home and in school where narratives are shaped and take on personal meanings for identity formation. Illuminating perspectives on the interconnectedness of gender and literacy in play have been provided, by teacher/researchers who have closely observed, and then recorded, differences in choice of activity and behaviour in nursery and primary school settings. They show clearly how these feed into children's language and storying behaviour (Clarricoates, 1978; Paley, 1984; Pidgeon, 1993; Francis, 1998; Pahl, 1999). Tales told from the nursery consistently find that children are sensitive to the hidden messages embedded in adult literacy practices taking place all around them. An early account of difference can be found in *Alice in Genderland*, where Julia Hodgeon (1983) describes how four- and five-year-old children, in a nursery located in the north-east of England, appeared to be already established and confirmed in sex-differentiated, gendered roles. She noted, for example, that it was usual for boys to be actively moving around and dominating the space available, jumping, shouting and engaging in boisterous play, whilst girls confined themselves to the edge of play areas, often quietly sharing a book with an adult or participating with peers in domestic roles in a play corner. Children were reinforced in the different orientations of their play by adult expressions of approval or disapproval. This finding is echoed in Nichols' (2002) later study of the role of parents in constructing their children as holding different dispositions towards literacy.

Contemporaneously, Vivian Gussin Paley (1984) was describing similar differences in the children she was closely observing and recording in her classes in a Chicago nursery. Paley gives thick descriptions of her children's retellings of exploits in the creative play area, showing how young children's stories reflect differentiated active and passive engagement with the imagined worlds they create in play. Boys' stories abound in dynamic superheroes and bad guys, girls tell of good little families and passive contentment. She comments that the children make use of story-plays to inform one another of preferred images for boys and girls. She found that when boys were allowed the space to act out their more energetic fantasies, they were more willing to engage later in constructive play. She uses her observations to argue for a greater acceptance of what children bring to their story construction, despite her own wish to counteract their drift towards gender stereotyping. Her work, however, shows clearly how peer group acceptance works to intensify and police the differences of gendered exchanges in the nursery – themes that have been developed by other researchers. These cannot be explored in depth in a chapter whose focus is research on literacy, but nevertheless they are relevant to its contextualization.

EVIDENCE FROM CHILDREN'S WRITING

Those gendered narrative preferences that have been shown to dominate play in the early years are also at work as children move more securely into the scene of writing and the development of their writing preferences. Orellana (1999) has argued that American classroom free-writing workshops are one of the few legitimate arenas in which school-aged children can *play* with (gendered) identities. These 'workshops', which have developed largely influenced by the work of Graves (1983) and Calkins (1986), are mirrored in the independent or elective writing encouraged in both British and Australian schools.

Several researchers have described how learned gender ideologies begin to take concrete form in children's own narrative texts. Minns (1991) provides written pieces from children which bear striking resemblances to Paley's pupils' oral recounts of their narrative play. Minns includes a seven-year-old boy's narrative, based on his drawing of a scene from *Jaws 3* in which a shark bites off a boy's arm and swims through an underground tunnel to attack a whole group of people doing writing. Minns comments on the boy's use of the shark's power and domination to act out a preferred masculine role. In direct contrast, she describes a girl's composition as a 'comfortable story of friendship and support'.

There are strong echoes of the thematic dispositions of the young Chicago storytellers in both tone and content. Moreover, researchers continue to find such differences repeated in the content and style of early compositions. For example, in their article 'Princesses who commit suicide', MacGillivray and Martinez (1998) describe how across age, ethnicity and gender, young children's stories frame boys and men as heroes, girls and women as victims of violence. Maynard, researching children's writing in one UK primary school, also found that, 'boys often positioned themselves as powerful and independent: girls positioned themselves as vulnerable and dependent' (2002: 89). Orellana (2000), analysing stories of Latina and Latino children, comments on the radical difference between the construction of 'good girl' identities in girls' stories and the more heroically conceived 'good guys' of the boys.

Millard and Marsh (2001b) have described similar patterns of active and passive constructions in the drawings which many children create to motivate or illustrate their written narratives. Boys and girls were shown to bring different cultural interests to their work, which were often imported directly from the popular cultural texts targeted separately at them. Clear gender differences were found in the way they related their drawings to their written narratives. Girls tended to draw stylized images of children, houses and flowers, providing decoration rather than illuminating key aspects of the story. Boys embedded scenarios containing cartoon figures and violent action within their narratives (Millard and Marsh, 2001b). Moreover, they argue that that boys' active engagement with visual meaning making often goes unremarked in research, whereas differences in the boys' and girls' choice of appropriate subject matter for writing has been well noted (Poynton, 1985; Tuck et al., 1985; White, 1986; Millard, 1994; 1997).

At first then, the advantage in writing appeared to researchers to be all on the side of girls. Janet White, for example, opines that, by the end of their primary years, most girls possess not only 'a soundly based competence in writing' but also a 'sense of themselves as writers which is similarly robust' (1986: 565). In confirmation of White's earlier findings, Carolyn Millard's (1995) research has shown that in the early years, girls generally write longer, more complex texts, using a wider range of both verbs and adjectives, and develop their texts with more focus on description and elaboration. Kanaris (1999: 261–2) echoes the findings that girls use adjectives more often and use a wider range of verbs. However, as White (1986: 562) went on to remark, this superior performance does not bear fruit outside of school in terms of improved employment. This is because, as Kanaris (1999) found, from an early age girls are rewarded for producing gendered writing in terms of both content and form, and are offered limited opportunities to write in different modes for different audiences. Girls are more likely to remove themselves from the action and tell their stories as the observer, whereas she found that boys placed themselves at the centre of the action. Boys are 'doers in a world of action', girls are 'recipients or observers' (1999: 265).

In contrast with their obedient sisters, much of young boys' elective writing – filled, as often it is, with violent action – may seem to their teachers both disrespectful and trangressive of acceptable norms. See, for example, the Australian nine-year-old boys' story 'Bloodbath EFA Bunnies', which aroused strong feelings of antipathy in both the teacher and the researcher involved in its production (Gilbert and Taylor, 1991: 110–13). Paley (1984), describing her encounters with a plethora of action stories constructed in dramatic play, many of them containing an element of violence, suggests that the first teacherly instinct is to try to counteract aggressive themes by setting limits as to what would be permitted in acting out. However, she came to see that role plays were important to the children's working out of their preoccupations with areas of identity work and that her boys progressed to more table work (that is, work more closely fitted to school literacy activities) when they were allowed more, not less, free play. In a later account of her four-year-old grandson's preoccupations with superhero play, Sue Pidgeon (1998: 33) records her adult, personal distaste for boys' narrative choices, particularly for the incorporation of so many ways to express physical force and dominance of others. In contrast to Pidgeon's lament for the promotion of more responsible role models, Pahl in her insightful book *Transformations* (1999) argues for an acceptance of nursery children's interests in the (gendered) narratives of popular culture. She has provided clear examples of how 'much successful practice in the nursery consists of following and developing ideas from modelling and play, building on the children's trains of thought and allowing their narratives to flower' (1999: 94).

MAKING GOOD USE OF CHILDREN'S CULTURAL PREFERENCES

Children's familiarity with popular cultural discourses which frequently come to teachers' attention through their children's drawing and writing are often suspect in their eyes because of the sexist and racist elements that are embedded in their characterizations and narrative resolutions.[1] Anne Haas

Dyson's work (1995; 1996; 1997; 1999; 2001) and in particular *Writing Superheroes* (1997) examines the role that a discourse which spotlights the children's underlying assumptions and prejudices might play in developing greater insight into sensitive issues. The example she gives, arising from 'author theatre workshops' in which children have incorporated elements of popular culture associated with superheroes, includes a discussion of whether 'a superhero's foxy babe' had to be white (1997: 55, 146), a question raised by the severely limited female roles contained in boys' authored Ninja plays. Dyson writes of the teacher's mediation in the process so that, with guidance, ideological gaps and differences 'could become moments for collective consideration of text fairness and goodness and, also, for individual play with newly salient features' (1997: 162).

It is a course of action that has been shown to be assisted by thoughtful planning, as when Jackie Marsh (1999; 2000) observed a sociodramatic role-play area set up as a Batcave in which literacy elements, particularly opportunities for independent writing, were incorporated. Marsh acknowledges that children's engagement with powerfully desired discourses creates possibilities for both acquiescent and resistant take-up of gendered positionings. She reports that 'many girls demonstrated both assertive, independent characterisation in role-play as Batwoman, as well as acquiescence to hegemonic masculine discourse' (2000: 217). It is worth noting that Marsh used Batwoman, not the comic's preferred Batgirl – a role which, by virtue of its juvenile status, is subordinated to Batman. The whole context of play writing was thought through to encourage equal participation and the exchanging of roles. Marsh's study provides a good example of Dyson's 'pedagogy of responsibility that acknowledges students' pleasures whilst assisting them in the exploration of these pleasures' (1997: 179). There is a balance to be struck between motivating interest and creating an awareness of how particular genres of writing position both reader and writer.

It is positive adult engagements with children's own desires and interpretations which offer the best response to dominant messages of gendered difference and disadvantage. This is an area to which I will return in the closing section on gender and postmodern responses, when I will discuss researchers' advocacy for the use of critical literacy for unsettling simplistic, binary gender categorization.

CHILDREN'S READING CHOICES

The differences that have been described in the main themes and language of children's own storying find an echo in the content and style of the books and magazines that children choose for themselves. The most popular publications found currently on the lowest shelves of a British newsagents, for example, ostentatiously announce their gendered readership, not only in their titles, with *Bob the Builder* and *Thunderbirds* in the one camp and *Princess World* ('for girls who love princesses') and *Pretty Pony Club* in the other, but also in the colours selected for their illustrated covers: racing green, black, red and silver for one set, purple pink and turquoise for the other. Moreover, researchers have shown that in Western cultures, reading is increasingly perceived by the children themselves as an activity more appropriate for girls (Kelly, 1986; Shapiro, 1990; Davies and Brember, 1993; Millard, 1997).

Where the uses and gratifications that pupils take from their reading have been researched, boys have been found to be more interested in searching out factual material and information, girls in their own intrinsic pleasures in story and relationships (Clark, 1976; Greaney and Neumann, 1983; Wheeler, 1984). In Margaret Clark's classic study of British young fluent readers, for example, boys' reading records included daily papers, comics and annuals as well as stories, whereas girls' records featured mainly narratives such as fairytales, Enid Blyton's books and ballet stories. Moreover, it has been shown that girls more readily identify with the male heroes found in their books and take positive pleasure in identification with such constructed heroic selves through a process of double identification than boys do, even with the most 'heroic' women to be found in stories (Golden, 1994).

COUNTERACTING TEXTUAL GENDER STEREOTYPES

In the first wave of analysis of gendered textual difference in the 1970s and 1980s, however, it was girls' disadvantage in the reading curriculum that was most frequently the object of the researcher's attention. One major focus for discussion was the narrative content of the texts used for promoting and practising reading in school, particularly the prevalence of sexist and racist stereotypes in reading books. Representations of girls and women in early (basal) readers and storybooks were seen as prime examples of the passivity and lack of self-assertion which characterized girls' socialization. This passivity, it was argued at the time, worked to disenfranchise girls and young women from the higher levels of attainment in academic performance and future job prospects. It was only when the 'fact' of boys' relative lack of success in the literacy curriculum was brought into prominence

almost simultaneously in Australia and the United Kingdom that the significance of girls' orientation to schooled literacy might be seen as offering some advantage, and that their perceived 'passivity' and lack of risk-taking behaviour be identified as also enabling them to focus more clearly on the reading and writing demands of school. In contrast, boys' written work, although sometimes abundant in energy, creativity and self-expression, was often seen in Australia to be antagonistic to gender equity programmes (MacNaughton, 2000) and in the United Kingdom to be out of keeping with the major genres and attainment targets of the English National Curriculum (Millard, 1994; 1997; Millard and Marsh, 2001a; 2001b).

Having acknowledged the extent of gendered preferences, researchers argued further that it is the children themselves who 'police' what are considered male- and female-appropriate activities, so that while dressing in boys' clothes, playing with boys' toys and taking on masculine roles is part of most girls' early experience, boys engaging in feminine activities is not usually tolerated (Lloyd and Duveen, 1992; Millard, 1994; Paley, 1984). Reading too can easily become a marker of feminization, as noted in what Philip Yearwood (1998) describes as a favourite 'diss' of the older schoolboys he teaches, 'I bet Sir gets books for Christmas'. The next section, then, will consider the role played by books in more detail.

READING BETWEEN THE LINES

A clear objective of early gender and literacy offensives saw feminist researchers fixing their sights firmly on the texts that were used to both teach and develop reading. Their targets were first to describe and then counter the 'sexist' uses of language and stereotypical representations in schoolbooks and basal readers which often worked to emphasize the differences rather than the similarities in girls' and boys' home circumstances, lived experiences and interests (Millard, 1994). Feminists in America (Czaplinski, 1976; Nilsen, 1971; Weitzeman, 1972), in the United Kingdom (Lobban, 1974; Burgess, 1981; Stones, 1983) and in Australia (Bradley and Mortimer, 1972; Gilbert, 1989) used literary critical skills to analyse early books, asking critical questions of both the themes and the language of the children's literature they surveyed which revealed the predominance of male heroes, activities and definitions (see, for example, Stones, 1983).

Reading schemes such as Ladybird (Peter and Jane) and Wide Range Readers (Janet and John) were heavily criticized for their persistent portrayal of patriarchal divisions of activity. For example,

Lobban (1974) found that in all the reading schemes she analysed, the feminine behaviours portrayed were domestic, passive and largely located indoors (note the expression 'her indoors' which is used to denote a wife in British white, male, working-class parlance). The male characters were ascribed a much greater range of activities, as well as more toys and pets. For example, in one early British Ladybird reader, the boy Peter confidently leads his sister Jane safely over the water with all the panache of a full-blown patriarch in the making:

> 'We have to jump this,' says Peter. 'Come after me. I know how to do it. Come after me, but come out of the water.'
> Jane says, 'Mummy said we must keep out of the water.'
> 'I know she said so,' says Peter, 'but we are not going in the water. I know how to do this.'
> Peter jumps again. 'You can do it, Jane,' he says.
> Then Jane jumps.

Of this text, Carol Baker and Bronwyn Davies commented:

> These Peter and Jane sequences, in effect, present married-couple talk in the guise of 'children's play'. The gender dualism here deftly crosses generational boundaries. It is unlikely, however, that any of the millions of children who have been taught to read with such materials have had this pointed out to them … Such reading against the grain is essential to the deconstruction of the male–female dualism and inevitably disruptive to reading lessons and texts as they are currently structured. (1993: 61)

FINDING POSITIVE ROLE MODELS IN CHILDREN'S STORIES

In response to this imbalance, one early strategy of feminist teachers was energetically to weed out the 'sexist', derogatory, limiting and oppressive representations to be found in such children's texts. They labelled such books as sexist and replaced them with narratives with more positive female role models. It is a strategy which relies on the choice of 'quality' texts to convey a set of values, chosen to educate the reader in subtle discriminations of character and ethics. The pro-feminist texts in gender equity programmes were carefully selected for their counter-messages: of female agency and self-sufficiency on the one hand, of male gentleness and/or dependency on the other. Such texts, particularly those which sought to overturn female passivity, however, could come into conflict with children's own desires and were often interpreted idiosyncratically by children if left to their own devices. In her

influential study *Frogs and Snails and Feminist Tales: Preschool Children and Gender* (1989), Davies showed how four- and five-year-olds read alternative fairytales within a normalizing framework of gender role conformity that reintroduced concepts of male supremacy and of female dependency. The children interpreted the stories read to them not as narratives of liberation which offer alternative lifestyles, but as traditional stories in which the counter-traditional heroine/princess had simply got things wrong. This mindset was very persistent and remained intact four years later when the children were interviewed again at age eight and gave similar interpretations of mistaken female behaviour or male supremacy in the face of overwhelming evidence to the contrary. Davies (1993) argues that children are already interpellated as subjects of discourses that create the male/female dualism, which many children have a personal investment in maintaining. Simple exposure to a different point of view has little effect in unsettling their already well-established patterns of thought. Davies and her colleagues, therefore, recommended that young children should be introduced to a more critical analysis of the texts they encounter so that they may be made aware of how they are positioned within them. It is a strategy which is well illustrated by Wing's (1997) use of Anne Fine's story *Bill's New Frock* with older children to explore the construction of male and femaleness within school settings. The point of both Davies' and Wing's work is not to promote an alternative theory of gender through the simple role reversals as portrayed in the counter-narratives, but to introduce the idea of difference within gendered experience through learning to 'read differently'. Part of any such programme would also involve the selection of texts which offer a wide range of experience of cultural and social difference. However, the main emphasis would be on changing how children read, rather than what they read. This is part of a postmodern emphasis on difference and complexity which has replaced older certainties about sex role and textual representation. It forms part of the strategy for developing critical literacy, to which I shall return at the end of this chapter. Before I do so, however, it is important to re-examine in more detail the issue of boys' literacy, which has come to dominate much of the recent discourse on gendered achievement.

TURNING THE FOCUS ON BOYS' 'UNDER ACHIEVEMENT'

In the 1990s, much of the focus of gender research switched from an attention to the analysis of girls' educational disadvantage within a masculinist biased school system, to anxieties about the performance of boys, particularly in literacy oriented subject areas. One reason for this switch can be attributed to the growing attention paid to the role of literacy in the developed capitalist economies, which had begun to rely far less on muscle power and far more on the literacy skills of their respective workforces. The earlier interest in girls' perceived underperformance had come at a time of technological change from an analysis of female underrepresentation and lack of confidence in maths, science and technological subjects, then seen as the key drivers for economic success. The emphasis placed on the development of literacy skills in the economy arrived at a time when traditional heavy industries were in decline and the new employment could be seen to demand more language skills. The focus fell on reading, and the evidence from both classroom-based research and large scale national surveys showed boys to be at a disadvantage to girls. This was attributed to their relative lack of interest in this area of the curriculum and preferences for different genres for personal reading (Davies and Bember, 1993; Barrs and Pidgeon, 1993; White, 1986; Hall and Coles, 1999). In earlier writing about older children's reading choices, I have commented that, when left to their own devices, boys and girls will travel very different roads to literacy (Millard, 1997: 106–7).

Current researchers who have shown that boys perform less well in the literacy curriculum as presented in schools have also commented that this is not a particularly new phenomenon (Millard, 1997; Cohen, 1998). What is new is a globalized pressure for workforces with increasingly advanced literacy skills as the gate to economic opportunity, which have made it each government's driven imperative for boys to 'catch up'. Some commentators have indeed stressed the way that the curriculum or, indeed, teachers' curriculum choices may limit boys' participation or interest in reading and writing (Alloway and Gilbert, 1997; Pahl, 1999; Millard and Marsh, 2001b). However, the intention in such an analysis should be not to separate out the experience of boys from girls, but to stress the importance of a broader interpretation of the literacy curriculum that might encompass a wider range of difference in personal preference and the cultural capital brought to the classroom (Orellana, 1999; Pahl, 1999; Millard and Marsh, 2001b; Dyson, 2001; Marsh, in press).

Yet, much populist work on gender and education in Australia and the United Kingdom has put the emphasis on working with boys alone as a priority for school improvements in literacy (Biddulph, 1997). Recommendations have included the use of male role models as readers and mentors, the production of boy-friendly materials, and even the use of girls as peer role models and guides. This is a core idea of Geoff Hannon (1998), whose work has been widely disseminated amongst teachers in the United Kingdom through in-service courses rather than through research and has had a particular effect on the separation of classes by sex.

The difficulty for many feminist commentators with strategies that direct attention to boys' needs in this way is that boys' education is once more framed as the dominant consideration and girls' real achievements are ignored (Francis, 1998: 166). The result can be an outbreak of what has been described as 'competing victims syndrome' (1995, cited in Alloway and Gilbert, 1997: 57) where different groups compete for attention and, more importantly, funding. Programmes directed solely at boys' underachievement have therefore been interpreted by some as a backlash against feminism (Epstein et al., 1998). It is important, therefore, to turn now to work that moves beyond the reification of binary differences in gender, reinforcing either 'girl-friendly' or 'boy-friendly' approaches, to research which builds towards understandings of both identity formation and the conditions under which social justice and equity programmes can be implemented. For such approaches, we need to make the postmodern turn away from an emphasis on gender role or textual sex role stereotyping towards the more subtle and nuanced approaches arising from poststructuralist analysis and the development of critical literacy.

POSTMODERN ANALYSIS AND CRITICAL LITERACY

In earlier research, the identification of gender difference was central to raising awareness of discrimination and exclusion in order to confront coercive and limiting metanarratives about male and femaleness, success and failure, agency and passivity. The limitation of this view stems from what now seems an oversimplistic understanding of gender as a series of categories that map onto simple binaries (Walkerdine, 1985; 1988; Walkerdine and Lucey, 1989; Luke and Luke, 1992) coupled to an 'othering' of one sex in opposition to another, so that all the virtue (or for that matter, all the disadvantage) is perceived to be located on one side (Paechter, 1998). I have already shown, in discussing developments in the teaching of writing, how more recently, in relation to the narratives of popular culture, researchers such as Anne Haas Dyson in the USA and Jackie Marsh in the UK have been able to shift children's discourse away from a one-dimensional divide into gender positive and gender negative stereotyping of experience. Researchers acknowledge that the popular discourses that are introduced into the classroom to build on children's interests and private pleasures may carry messages that disturb adults through their perpetuation of oppressive norms (Marsh and Millard, 2000). Marsh (1999; 2000) and Dyson (1995; 1996; 1997; 1999) both show how children can be enabled to transform their understanding through sensitive interaction with each other within the guidance of a responsive teacher. Their positioning of the teacher's function as one of helping children to deconstruct gender role in context ties in with current postmodern understanding of the way in which the deconstruction of gender discourse can promote the development of wider possibilities for both boys and girls. Most important to this work is the understanding that an overemphasis on confronting gendered practices in school through anti-sexist programmes which emphasize the differences in boys' and girls' culture may actually work to reify rather than unsettle prevailing norms.

This was the conclusion of Thorne who, in analysing the socializing aspects of play, emphasized the importance of escaping from binary polarities to an understanding that 'gender takes shape in a complex interaction with other social divisions, such as age, class, race, ethnicity and religion' (1993: 109). When gender difference is emphasized by teachers, she suggests that children begin to engage in complex border work which exaggerates rather than ameliorates conflict and difference. It is a process which Francis (1998: 164) has described as gender category maintenance, something that works against an understanding of 'innate equality'.

In contrast to enumerating simple polarities, postmodern theorists, while recognizing the interconnectedness of hegemonic masculinity and emphasized femininity, point to an increasing fluidity and multiplicity in gender identification, which provide increasing possibilities for more diverse understanding of both identity construction and its maintenance. In order to encourage children's understanding, Bronwyn Davies (1989), for example, recommended that children should be shown how to deconstruct the binary oppositions which serve to position them within particular contexts and discourses and be helped to imagine alternatives to the pervasive sense of a simple division in gender. She suggests that educationalists:

> need to work hard to have access to imaginary worlds in which new metaphors, new social relations, new patterns of power and desire are explored. They need the freedom to position themselves in multiple ways, some of which will be recognisably 'feminine', some as we currently understand these terms 'masculine'. (1989: 141)

The literacy teacher needs to make language itself the object of enquiry in order to deconstruct the storylines through which cultural difference is structured and maintained. In a similar vein, both Davies (1993; 1997) and Alloway and Gilbert (1997) focus on the importance of deconstructing masculinities, suggesting that a key task for schools is to help boys to understand the social construction of masculinity, literacy and schooling, and the practices that inscribe them as 'masculine, literate and institutionalised' subjects (1997: 57). Davies further points out how difficult it is for those in the ascendant half of a binary pair to see a need for change because they take their category membership to be 'normal' (1997: 13). Nevertheless, she argues for a more critical, social literacy whereby 'oneself becomes a shifting, multiple text to be read'. This means that the 'construction of that self through discourse, through positioning within particular contexts and moments and through relations of power, is both recognised and made revisable' (1997: 29).

It is also important for teachers and researchers to understand the way in which other binary positionings of class and race intercalate with gender in creating power relations. Glenda MacNaughton (2000) discusses the need to confront both the binary oppositions and the dualistic thinking which privilege race or gender or class. She writes:

> We could see gender identity and racial/ethnic identity as dynamic and mutually constitutive. Each identity is constantly in the process of forming: each identity informs and forms the other. In other words a girl is always in the process of learning what it means to be a girl, because each of us is always in the process of forming and re-forming our gender identity. (2000: 225)

Further, she suggests that children 'could be encouraged to think critically about their own and others' culture and how each forms and informs identity. They could be encouraged to learn about the complexities of who we are rather than about superficial emblems of culture, such as particular foods and dances' (2000: 226). Her emphasis is on helping children develop the emotional skills to help them to confront racism and sexism in their everyday lives. Orellana adds further to this in her proposition that 'no-one is locked into a single position on either end of a system of binary opposites. We can all be both good and bad, both strong and weak, both students and lovers' (1999: 80).

There is as yet, however, little research to show how, in the early years, such a focus might inform teaching and learning; and indeed, for our youngest learners perhaps, such deconstruction will be an area to treat with a sensitive awareness of children's emergent interests and pleasures. It is all too easy for adults to colonize young children's pleasures in order to remedy perceived 'oppressions' and in the process to steal away their delight or force the activity to go underground. As Misson (1998) advises, it is essential that teachers respect children's pleasures and their own cultural choices. However, it is always possible in a complex teaching situation, such as that set up in the shared reading or enactment of a story or in the creation of improvised dramatic play, to enquire with a class about the multiplicity of narrative possibilities available and to consider together, for example, whether alternatives to zapping the aliens, monsters and warriors that dominate many boys' written and dramatic compositions may exist, or whether there can be options other than rejection and suicide for those princesses who face social rejection. Teachers can help their classes, little by little, to unpick the multiplicity of ways in which the texts pupils prefer provide them with different ways of understanding the world by thinking through issues of discourse, knowledge and power. In reading texts together, classes can also be encouraged to understand the changing nature of gender differences and how these are constructed across cultures and time. Teachers may then begin to create further possibilities for learning which encompass new ways of imagining the world and encourage new meanings to be made and new stories to be told, no matter whether the teller of the tale in question is a boy or girl.

NOTE

1 For a more extensive account of the role of children's popular culture in developing literacy, see Jackie Marsh's chapter in this volume.

REFERENCES

Acker, S. (1994) *Gendered Education: Sociological Reflections on Women, Teaching and Feminism.* Buckingham: Open University Press.

Alloway, N. and Gilbert, P. (1997) 'Boys and literacy: lessons from Australia', *Gender and Education,* 9 (1): 49–58.

Arnot, M. and Weiner, G. (eds) (1989) *Gender and the Politics of Schooling*, 2nd edn. London: Unwin Hyman with the Open University.

Baker, C. and Davies, B. (1993) 'Literacy and gender in early childhood', in A. Luke and P. Gilbert (eds), *Literacy in Contexts: Australian Perspectives and Issues.* St Leonards, NSW: Allen and Unwin.

Barrs, M. (1988) 'Drawing a story: transitions between drawing and writing', in M. Lightfoot and N. Martin

(eds), *The Word for Teaching is Learning.* London: Heinemann. Educational Books.

Barrs, M. and Pidgeon, S. (eds) (1993) *Reading the Difference: Gender and Reading in the Primary School.* London: CLPE.

Barton, D. and Hamilton, M. (1998) *Local Literacies: Reading and Writing in One Community.* London: Routledge.

Beauvoir, S. de (1972) *The Second Sex*, trans. and ed. H.M. Parshley. Harmondsworth: Penguin.

Biddulph, S. (1997) *Raising Boys: Why Boys are Different, and How to Help Them Become Happy and Well-Balanced Men.* Melbourne: Celestial Arts.

Bradley, D. and Mortimer, M. (1972) 'Sex-role stereotyping in children's picture books', *Refractory Girl,* 1 (1): 12–16.

Burgess, C. (1981) 'Breakthrough to sexism', *Teaching London Kids,* 17: 79–81.

Calkins, L. (1986) *The Art of Teaching Writing.* Portsmouth, NH: Heinemann.

Clark, M. (1999) *Young Fluent Readers.* Oxford: Heinemann.

Clarricoates, K. (1978) 'Dinosaurs in the classroom: a re-examination of some aspects of the "hidden curriculum"', *Women's Studies International Quarterly,* 1: 353–64.

Cohen, M. (1998) 'A habit of healthy idleness: boys' underachievement in historical perspective', in D. Epstein, J. Elwood, V. Hey and J. Maw (eds), *Failing Boys: Issues in Gender and Achievement.* Buckingham: Open University Press.

Czaplinski, S. (1976) 'Sexism in award winning picture books', in *Children's Rights Workshop. Sexism in Children's Books: Facts, Figures and Guidelines.* London: Writers and Readers. pp. 31–7.

Davies, B. (1989) *Frogs and Snails and Feminist Tales: Preschool Children and Gender.* London: Allen and Unwin.

Davies, B. (1993) *Shards of Glass: Children Reading and Writing Beyond Gendered Identities.* Cresskill, NJ: Hampton.

Davies, B. (1997) 'Constructing and deconstructing masculinities through critical literacy', *Gender and Education,* 9 (1): 9–30.

Davies, J. and Brember, I. (1993) 'Comics or stories? Differences in the reading attitudes and habits of girls and boys in years 2,4 and 6', *Gender and Education,* 5 (3): 305–20.

Delamont, S. (1980) *Sex Roles and the School.* London: Methuen.

Dyson, A.H. (1995) 'Writing children: reinventing the development of childhood literacy', *Written Communication,* 12 (1): 4–46.

Dyson, A.H. (1996) 'Cultural constellations and childhood identities: on Greek gods, cartoon heroes, and the social lives of schoolchildren', *Harvard Educational Review,* 66 (3): 471–95.

Dyson, A.H. (1997) *Writing Superheroes: Contemporary Childhood, Popular Culture, and Classroom Literacy.* New York: Teachers College Press.

Dyson, A.H. (1999) 'Coach Bombay's kids learn to write: children's appropriation of media material for school literacy', *Research in the Teaching of English*, 33: 367–402.

Dyson, A.H. (2001) 'Where are the childhoods in childhood literacy? An exploration in outer (school) space', *Journal of Early Childhood Literacy*, 1 (1): 9–40.

Epstein, D., Elwood, J., Hey, V. and Maw, J. (1998) *Failing Boys: Issues in Gender and Achievement.* Buckingham: Open University Press.

Fisher, E. (1974) 'Children's books: the second sex, junior division', in J. Stacey, S. Beraud and J. Daniels (eds), *And Jill Came Tumbling After.* New York: Dell.

Francis, B. (1998) *Power Play: Primary School Children's Construction of Gender, Power and Adult Work.* Stoke-on-Trent: Trentham.

Freire, P. (1972) *Pedagogy of the Oppressed,* trans. M. Bergman Harmondsworth: Penguin.

Gilbert, P. (with Kate Rowe) (1989) *Gender, Literacy and the Classroom.* Melbourne: Australian Reading Association.

Golden, J. (1994) 'Heroes and gender: children reading and writing', *English in Australia*, 110.

Graves, D. (1983) *Writing: Teachers and Children at Work.* Exeter, NH: Heinemann.

Greaney, V. and Neumann, S. (1983) 'Young people's views of the functions of reading: a cross cultural perspective', *Reading Teacher*, 37 (2): 158–63.

Gregory, E. (1998) 'Siblings as mediators of literacy in linguistic minority communities', *Language and Education*, 1 (12): 33–55.

Gregory, E. (2001) 'Sisters and brothers as language and literacy teachers: synergy between siblings playing and working together', *Journal of Early Childhood Literacy*, 3 (1): 301–22.

Hall, C. and Coles, M. (1999) *Children's Reading Choices.* London: Routledge.

Heath, S.B. (1983) *Ways with Words: Language, Life and Work in Communities and Classrooms.* Cambridge: Cambridge University Press.

Hodgeon, J. (1983) 'A woman's world', in NATE Language and Working Party, *Alice in Genderland.* Sheffield: National Association for the Teaching of English.

Jordan, E. (1995) 'Fighting boys and fantasy play: the construction of masculinity in the early years of school', *Gender and Education*, 7 (1): 68–95.

Kanaris, A. (1999) 'Gendered journeys: children's writing and the construction of gender', *Language and Education*, 13 (4): 254–68.

Kelly, P. (1986) 'The influence of reading content on students' perceptions of the masculinity or femininity of reading', *The Journal of Reading Behaviour*, XVIII (3): 243–56.

Kress, G. (1997) *Before Writing: Rethinking the Paths to Literacy.* London: Routledge.

Lankshear, C. and McLaren, P. (1993) *Critical Literacy: Politics, Praxis, and the Postmodern.* Albany, NY: State University of New York Press.

Lloyd, B. and Duveen, G. (1992) *Gender Identities and Education: the Impact of Starting School.* Hertfordshire: Harvester Wheatsheaf.

Lobban, G. (1974) 'Sex roles in reading schemes', *Forum*, 16 (2): 6–9.

Luke, C. and Luke, A. (1992) 'Just naming? Educational discourses and the politics of identity', in W. Pink and G. Noblitt (eds), *Futures of the Sociology of Education.* Norwood, NJ: Ablex.

MacGillivray, L. and Martinez, A. (1998) 'Princesses who commit suicide: primary children writing within and against stereotypes', *Journal of Literacy Research*, 30 (10): 53–84.

MacNaughton, G. (2000) *Rethinking Gender in Early Childhood Education.* London: Chapman.

Marland, M. (1983) *Sex Differentiation and Schooling.* London: Heinemann.

Marsh, J. (1999) 'Batman and Batwoman go to school: popular culture in the literacy curriculum', *International Journal of Early Years Education*, 7 (2): 117–31.

Marsh, J. (2000) '"But I want to fly too!" Girls and superhero play in the infant classroom', *Gender and Education*, 12 (2): 209–20.

Marsh, J. (in press) 'Superhero stories: literacy, gender and popular culture', in C. Skelton and B. Francis (eds), *Boys and Girls in the Primary Classroom.* Buckingham: Open University Press.

Marsh, J. and Millard, E. (2000) *Literacy and Popular Culture: Using Children's Culture in the Classroom.* London: Chapman.

Maynard, T. (2002) *Boys and Literacy: Exploring the Issues.* London: Routledge Farmer.

Measor, L. and Sykes, P. (1992) *Gender and Schools.* London: Cassell.

Millard, C. (1995) 'Free choice writing in the early years', *Australian Journal of Early Childhood*, 20 (1): 33–7.

Millard, E. (1994) *Developing Readers in the Middle Years.* Buckingham: Open University Press.

Millard, E. (1997) *Differently Literate: the Schooling of Boys and Girls.* London: Falmer.

Millard, E. and Marsh, J. (2001a) 'Sending Minnie the Minx home: comics and reading choices', *Cambridge Journal of Education*, 31 (1): 25–39.

Millard, E. and Marsh, J. (2001b) 'Words with pictures: the role of visual literacy in writing and Its implication for schooling', *Reading*, 35 (1) 54–61.

Minns, H. (1991) *Language, Literacy and Gender.* London: Hodder and Stoughton.

Misson, R. (1998) 'Theory and spice and things not nice: popular culture in the primary classroom', in M. Knobel and A. Healy (eds), *Critical Literacies in the Primary*

Classroom. Newtown: Primary English Teaching Association.

Nichols, S. (2002) 'Parents' construction of their children as gendered, literate subjects: a critical discourse analysis', *Journal of Early Childhood Literacy*, 2 (2): 123–44.

Nilsen, A. (1971) 'Women in children's literature', *College English*, 32 (9) 18–26.

Orellana, M.J. (1995) 'Literacy as a gendered social practice: texts, talk, tasks and take-up in two bilingual classrooms', *Reading Research Quarterly*, 30 (4): 335–65.

Orellana, M.J. (1999) 'Good guys and bad girls', in M. Bucholtz, A.C. Liang and L.A. Sutton, (eds), *Reinventing Identities: the Gendered Self in Discourse.* New York: Oxford University Press.

Paechter, C. (1998) *Educating the Other: Gender, Power and Schooling.* London: Falmer.

Pahl, K. (1999) *Transformations: Meaning Making in Nursery Education.* Stoke-on-Trent: Trentham.

Paley, G. (1984) *Boys and Girls: Superheroes in the Doll's Corner.* Chicago: University of Chicago Press.

Pidgeon, S. (1993) 'Learning reading and learning gender', in M. Barrs and S. Pidgeon (eds), *Reading the Difference: Gender and Reading in the Primary School.* London: CLPE.

Pidgeon, S. (1998) 'Superhero or Prince', in M. Barrs and S. Pidgeon (eds), *Boys and Reading.* London: CLPE.

Poynton, C. (1985) *Language and Gender: Making the Difference.* Deakin University Press.

Shapiro, J. (1990) 'Sex role appropriateness of reading and reading instruction', *Reading Psychology*, 11 (3): 241–69.

Smith, F. (1988) *Joining the Literacy Club: Further Essays into Education.* London: Heinemann.

Solsken, J. (1992) *Literacy, Gender and Work in Families and in School.* Norwood, NJ: Ablex.

Spender, D. and Sarah, E. (1980) *Learning to Lose: Sexism and Education.* London: Writers and Readers.

Stacey, J., Beraud, S. and Daniels, J. (eds) (1974) *And Jill Came Tumbling After: Sexism in American Education.* New York: Dell.

Stanworth, M. (1981) *Gender and Schooling: a Study of Sexual Divisions in the Schoolroom.* London: Hutchinson.

Stones, R. (1983) *'Pour Out the Cocoa, Janet': Sexism in Children's Books.* Schools Council Curriculum Development Committee. London: Longman.

Street, B. (1984). *Literacy in Theory and Practice.* Cambridge: Cambridge University Press.

Street, J. and Street, B. (1991) 'The schooling of literacy', in D. Barton and R. Ivanic (eds) *Writing in the Community.* Newbury Park, CA: Sage.

Taylor, D. and Dorsey-Gaines, C. (1988) *Growing Up Literate: Learning from Inner-City Families.* Portsmouth, NH: Heinemann.

Thorne, B. (1993) *Gender Play: Girls and Boys in School.* Buckingham: Open University Press.

Tuck, D., Bayliss, V. and Bell, M. (1985) 'Analysis of sex stereotyping in characters created by young authors', *Journal of Educational Research*, 78 (4): 248–52.

Walkerdine, V. (1985) 'On the regulation of speaking and silence: subjectivity, class and gender in contemporary schooling', in V. Walkerdine, C. Urwin and J. Steedman (eds) *Language, Gender and Childhood.* London: Routledge and Kegan Paul.

Walkerdine, V. (1988) *The Mastery of Reason.* London: Routledge.

Walkerdine, V. (1990) *Schoolgirl Fictions.* New York: Verso.

Walkerdine, V. and Lucey, H. (1989) *Democracy in the Kitchen.* London: Virago.

Weitzeman, R. (1972) 'Sex-role socialization in picture books for pre-school children', *American Journal of Sociology*, 77 (6): 1125–50.

Wells, G. (1987) *The Meaning Makers: Children Learning Language and Using Language to Learn.* London: Hodder and Stoughton.

Wheeler, M. A. (1984) 'Fourth grade boys' literacy from a mother's point of view', *Language Arts*, 61 (6): 607–14.

White, J. (1986) 'The writing on the wall: beginning or end of a girl's career', *Women's Studies International Forum*, 9 (5): 561–74.

Wing, A. (1997) 'How can children be taught to read differently? *Bill's New Frock* and the hidden curriculum', *Gender and Education*, 9 (4): 491–504.

Yearwood, P. (1998) 'Bringing tenderness to males', in M. Barrs and S. Pidgeon (eds), *Boys and Reading.* London: CLPE.

4

Reconceptualizing Early Childhood Literacy: The Sociocultural Influence

ARIA RAZFAR AND KRIS GUTIÉRREZ

In April 2000, the National Reading Panel presented their analysis of more than 100,000 studies on early literacy and concluded that the five most essential components to a child's ability to read are the following: phonics, phonemic awareness, fluency, vocabulary, and comprehension. What is notably absent from this report are the significant contributions that sociocultural views of literacy and human development have had on understandings of early literacy development and instruction. Over the last 25 years, there has been a growing interest in sociocultural views of language and literacy. In particular, sociocultural perspectives on literacy and learning highlight the important relationships between language, culture, and development. The study of literacy as a socioculturally situated practice in which culture and context take on principal roles presents a fundamentally different conceptualization of early literacy.

In this chapter, we will discuss early literacy studies that are premised upon several key principles of a sociocultural or cultural-historical[1] view of literacy and language which we believe distinguish this view from other prominent views of literacy. The emergent sociocultural theories of human development draw from multiple disciplines, particularly anthropology and psychology. In this way, a cultural-historical theory brings together the history of the development of the individual in relation to the history of both proximal and distal contexts.

We will explore briefly several general theoretical principles that help define a cultural approach to the study of early literacy development. Within this perspective, human beings interact with their worlds primarily through mediational means such as cultural artifacts or tools, and symbols, including language (Vygotsky, 1978). Language from a cultural-historical or sociocultural perspective is considered the pre-eminent tool for learning and human development and is said to mediate individuals' activity in the valued practices of their communities across a lifespan (Cole, 1996; Cole and Engestrom, 1993). Of significance to the focus of this chapter, a sociocultural view of learning centres attention on cultural practices, or valued activities with particular features and routines, as fundamental to understanding the nature of literacy. By focusing on the cultural activity of various communities, the influence of the organization of the valued practices of a community on the nature of learning and participation therein is made visible. Here the role of other participants and the available cultural tools in the social ecology of individuals' lives become key features of learning environments.

Following this perspective, literacy learning is a socially mediated process that cannot be understood apart from its context of development, the forms of mediation available, and the nature of participation across various cultural practices. Thus, in contrast to conceptions of literacy as the acquisition of a series of discrete skills, a sociocultural view of literacy argues that literacy learning cannot be abstracted from the cultural practices in which it is nested. Instead, there is an emphasis on the available tools or artifacts and forms of assistance present in activity (Gutiérrez, 2002).

Culture is central to this view of learning and human development and is said to mediate human activity. Here culture is not treated as an external variable – as something apart from cognition – and thus it cannot be studied directly, or in an isolated, discrete, or causal manner (Cole, 1996). Instead, a more productive approach focuses on studying how people live culturally; that is, how people participate in the quotidian activity of their communities (Moll, 2000). Of significance, a sociocultural view espouses a non-normative, non-integrated dynamic view of culture in which culture is instantiated in the practices and material conditions of everyday life. This focus on activity helps us understand that there is variation in the ways a community's members instantiate and make sense of the valued practices of their community, as well as variation in which practices individual members take up (Gutiérrez, 2002). Thus, both regularities and variation are expected in communities, as culture is not uniformly understood or practised across the members of cultural groups (Gutiérrez and Rogoff, 2003).

This instrumental view of culture is at the core of sociocultural views of literacy and has implications for how we make sense of children's literacy practices and how we study them. Since culture is interwoven in all aspects of human development, sociocultural research necessarily foregrounds the role of culture and context in human development. Accordingly, the development of early literacy practices (and their study) is understood in relation to the contexts in which those practices are culturally, historically, and ideologically situated. From a cultural-historical view, consideration of contextual and cultural influences on language and literacy processes, of language as a lens to understand microprocesses (e.g. shifts in roles and participation over time), or of larger sociological practices and processes, allows us to understand that literacy events have a social history that links the individual to larger sociohistorical practices and processes. Thus, people's literacy practices are necessarily situated in broader social relations and historical contexts.

The concept of literacy as a social activity is illustrated by the literacy practices that people draw on when participating in literacy events (Barton, 1994). This notion of literacy as a sociocultural practice has been developed across an interdisciplinary body of work. Most notably, the work of cultural psychologists contributed new conceptions of literacy as a highly social rather than an individual accomplishment; and they promoted new methods, such as combining ethnographic and experimental studies in order to understand the relationships in indigenous forms of literacy, their practical activity, and the cognitive consequences (Scribner, 1984a; 1984b; Scribner and Cole, 1978; 1981). Within this body of work, cultural psychologists focused on social practice as a unit of analysis to conduct cross-cultural analysis (Scribner et al., 1977). These cross-cultural studies linked the literacy of a cultural group to the larger societal values of the community and illustrated the complexity of the literacy practices in which children engaged outside of formal instructional contexts.

Important to the discussion in this chapter, we highlight how sociocultural theories of literacy have significantly informed our understandings of early literacy development (Bruner, 1977; Snow, 1977). Within this work, we emphasize sociocultural theories of language socialization (Ochs, 1988; Ochs and Schieffelin, 1984), as well as sociocultural studies of early literacy that have advanced our understanding of power relations *vis-à-vis* literacy practices. For example, the new literacy studies (Gee, 2001; Luke, 1994; Luke and Carrington, in press) have illustrated that as children are socialized to particular literacy practices, they are simultaneously socialized into discourses that position them ideologically within the larger social milieu. In addition, sociocultural theories have challenged the role of formal schooling in literacy development (Nicolopoulou and Cole, 1997) and have documented how the social organization of learning of out-of-school settings can promote language and literacy development (Gutiérrez et al., 2001; Hull and Schultz, 2002; Vasquez, 2003).

More recently, especially in the last decade, sociocultural theory's dynamic view of culture has become central to a growing body of literacy studies concerned with the education of poor children, including English language learners (Gutiérrez et al., 1999; Michaels, 1982; Moll et al., 2001; Orellana, 2001; Rueda and McIntyre, 2002; Trueba, 1999). Rather than only raising questions about whether children can read and write, such studies ask what children know about literacy, seeking to learn about the relationship between children's literacy and the nature of literacy practices in which they routinely engage. Of significance to this approach to studying literacy, a cultural-historical theory of learning and development challenges views that equate culture with race and ethnicity and attribute individual traits (including language use) to being a member of a particular group (Gutiérrez, 2002; Lee, 2002; Rogoff and Angelillo, 2002).

We will elaborate on these theoretical principles in our discussion of the following: (1) the historical context in which sociocultural views of early literacy development are situated; (2) emergent literacy constructivist and sociocultural perspectives; (3) sociocultural perspectives on early literacy; (4) mediation and forms of assistance in early literacy development; (5) language socialization and the studies of home and community early literacy practices; and (6) power relations and ideologies as mediators in early literacy practices.

HISTORICAL CONTEXT: FROM THE INDIVIDUAL TO THE SOCIAL

For most of the twentieth century, research on literacy as well as early literacy was dominated first by behaviourist psychology (Skinner, 1957) which conceptualized literacy development as a scripted habit formation, and then by cognitive psychology (Piaget, 1951; 1962) in which development was conceptualized as an individual and linear process. Instruction within these frameworks followed individual development; as a result, literacy practices associated with formal schooling were based on these assumptions of learning and development.

From the late 1800s to the 1920s, the research literature on reading and writing focused primarily (or almost exclusively) on the elementary school years (Teale and Sulzby, 1986). For more than 50 years, it had been widely assumed that children's literacy development began with formal schooling. From this perspective, it was believed that the mental processes necessary for reading were fundamentally intrapersonal cognitive processes that would unfold in concert with biological development (Teale and Sulzby, 1986). Thus, the process of learning to read was highly correlated with biological maturation. The idea that development precedes learning naturally lends itself to the notion of readiness. In 1925, the National Committee on Reading published the first explicit reference to the concept of reading readiness – the dominant theory of reading from the 1920s to the 1950s. In reading readiness programmes children were considered ready to read when they had met certain social, physical, and cognitive competencies (Morphett and Washburne, 1931; Morrow, 1997). Thus, literacy activities occurring in the home and community before formal schooling were not central to the process of acquiring literacy. Instead, the reading readiness paradigm argued for literacy practices that would not interfere with the process of development. In addition, it did not adequately recognize the social dimensions of learning and development. As a result, traditional instructional practices such as whole class instruction and emphasis on formal features of literacy, including phonics-based instruction, dominated instructional practices. In addition, the reading readiness perspective inspired many of the standardized testing batteries used to determine if a child was developmentally ready for reading. For instance, the use of word primers as a stimulus to elicit a conditioning response is an example of reading readiness research and pedagogical practices that were rooted in behaviourist psychological perspectives of human development (Gates et al., 1939; Thorndike, 1921).

EMERGENT LITERACY: FROM SOCIAL CONSTRUCTIVISM TO SOCIOCULTURAL THEORY

The social turn in literacy that occurred in the past few decades was motivated by a series of events and sociocultural phenomena. When the Soviet Union launched the first satellite, Sputnik, in the 1950s, there was growing anxiety that American education was not adequately preparing the next generation. With the state of American education coming under scrutiny, researchers began to question the fundamental assumptions of prevailing educational practice, including the reading readiness paradigm. During this period, Chomsky's classic book *Syntactic Structures* (1957) demonstrated that structural assumptions of language and cognition are incapable of accounting for the fundamental characteristics of language. Chomsky's notion of the language acquisition device (LAD) also was a major breakthrough; it illustrated that children *acquire* the rules to generate complex syntactic structures long before formal schooling. Although Chomsky's work fostered a paradigm shift in cognitive psychology and in the study of literacy and early literacy, applied linguists and linguistic anthropologists argued that Chomsky's notions did not adequately address the communicative and social dimensions of language and language learning (Hymes, 1972; Labov, 1972).

In the last half of the twentieth century, Johnson's 'War on Poverty' in the US coincided with researchers' attempts to understand 'cultural deprivation' and later to challenge deficit-model explanations for the social and educational practices of poor children, many of whom were children of colour. The growing emphasis placed on the social introduced social constructivist views of learning in the field of early literacy. According to Hiebert and Rafael (1996), one of the first and most well-known early literacy movements born out of social constructivist views of learning was the *emergent literacy* perspective (e.g. Clay, 1966; 1975; Mason and Allen, 1986; Sulzby and Teale, 1991).

The emergent literacy framework, with its roots in cognitive psychology and psycholinguistics, was one of the first theories of early literacy to challenge the commonly held assumption that reading and literacy activities in general are intrapersonal and linear mental processes. The term *emergent literacy* was first used in the late 1960s to describe the behaviours of young children when they used books and writing materials in non-conventional ways (Clay, 1966). The term was used to describe the behaviours used by young children with books and when reading and writing, even though the children could not actually read and write in the conventional sense. Whereas the concept of reading readiness suggested that there was a point in time when children were ready to learn to read and write, emergent literacy suggested that there were continuities in children's literacy development between early literacy behaviours and those displayed once children could read independently. This perspective also emphasized the importance of the relationship between reading and writing in early literacy development (Clay, 1975). Until then, it was believed that children must learn to read before they could learn to write.

This body of literature served to broaden the view of children's literacy outside of formal instruction (Mason and Allen, 1986; Sulzby and Teale, 1991). It stressed the importance of parents, caregivers, teachers, and literacy-rich environments in children's literacy development and challenged the view of reading and writing as an individual mental process that begins with formal schooling (Burns et al., 1999; Teale and Sulzby, 1986). As a result, contextual factors that lead to literacy development became a crucial dimension in the study of early literacy. The emergent literacy studies emphasized that in the period prior to formal schooling, children's literacy develops in multiple formal and informal contexts (Ferreiro and Teborosky, 1982; Stahl and Miller, 1989; Sulzby and Teale, 1991; Teale and Sulzby, 1987). Furthermore, children's contributions and participation in adult-directed activities are essential to their development.

The recognition that early literacy development is multifaceted and complex had methodological implications for how early literacy studies would be conducted. The unit of analysis in these studies focused on activity settings and situated literacy practices rather than the performance of literacy skills under controlled experimental conditions. As a result, a number of the emergent literacy studies focused on children's participation in everyday practice and utilized sustained participant observation to gain a deeper understanding of early literacy development (Mason and Allen, 1986). Ethnographic methods allowed researchers to document literacy practices and the process of literacy development as it unfolded in its natural context (both in the home and in other contexts outside of school).

These studies represent a fundamental theoretical and methodological shift from traditional experimental designs that presumed early literacy development to be an individual, discrete process (see Hiebert, 1988, for an overview of emergent literacy studies). This shift also marked a growing realization that culture is fundamental to the development of literacy, and that meaning making and cognition are interactive (with others, including artifacts) and situated in nature.

With the growing importance of culture and context in the study of early literacy came the recognition that the literacy practices of the home were essential to children's literacy development. Some of these studies examined adult–child interactions at home and made them the basis for creating similar contexts in school and other literacy projects.[2] One of the clearest indications that emergent literacy research was having widespread influence was the 1965 inauguration of Project Headstart in the US, a federally funded programme designed to provide children thought to be disadvantaged by poverty with the skills they would need for formal schooling. Longitudinal studies of students enrolled in Headstart programmes showed that Headstart graduates were more likely to be in college and have more educational achievement (Schweinhart and Weikart, 1993). Although Project Headstart illustrated the importance of home literacy practices prior to formal schooling, it was limited in that it did not address the unique factors affecting linguistic and racial minority students. In addition, emergent literacy perspectives tended to apply a deficit view of the home–school disparity, and the problem of low achievement for linguistic and racial minorities was constructed as deficit with the home, that 'families do not read enough or lack book knowledge, that they do not value literacy or model it effectively' (Carrington and Luke, 2003: 9; Mason and Allen, 1986; also see Marvin and Mirenda, 1993; Marvin and Wright, 1997; White, 1982).

These deficit views about the literacy practices of linguistic and racial minority homes can promote narrow conceptions of literacy and culture in which literacy is considered a neutral practice. By privileging the literacy activities of formal schooling – practices that often index the values of white, middle class communities – this work implicitly valued particular forms of literacy (Heath, 1982). Thus, the literacy activities and practices of language minority homes were devalued in relation to the dominant literacy practices. The undervaluing of the literacy practices of non-dominant groups led to beliefs that matching home literacy practices to those valued by schools would solve the chronic underachievement of poor and non-white students. Studies drawing on sociocultural theories of human development have addressed these issues and have argued that literacy cannot be considered independent of a community's culture, history, and values (Cazden, 1979; Heath, 1982; Scribner and Cole, 1981). While emergent literacy perspectives identified the importance of literacy activity prior to school and the role of adults/caregivers in this process, early literacy researchers drawing on sociocultural theories were also able to illustrate the informal contexts in which literacy develops prior to formal schooling (Cazden, 1979; Heath, 1982; Scribner and Cole, 1978; Wells, 1985). Sociocultural theorists also recognized the importance of the adult's role in early literacy development (Bruner, 1983; Cazden, 1983; Vygotsky, 1978; Wertsch, 1978). However, one of the major differences between the emergent literacy perspective and sociocultural views of early literacy development is how adults interact with children *vis-á-vis* literacy practices (Cazden, 1991). Although adults are generally the more expert members of literacy practices, the roles of experts and novices are more fluid as we expect change in the nature of participation over time in literacy activity (Rogoff, 1990); through active participation, children's development is mediated via available material, ideational and cultural tools. Thus, early literacy development is a multidirectional and mutually engaging process between adults and children.

STUDIES OF EARLY LITERACY: A SOCIOCULTURAL PERSPECTIVE

Although much of the work in early literacy has focused on language or reading development, it is important to acknowledge studies of the writing practices of preschool and early primary school children, particularly those studies that illustrate the link between reading, writing, and oral language development. Of significance, sociocultural views of literacy development challenged emergent theories of writing that described stages of writing development along Piagetian lines (Ferreiro and Teberosky, 1982) and instead argued that children's writing emerges coherently but idiosyncratically (Barton, 1994; Hall, 1987; John-Steiner et al., 1994). Read (1971), for example, focused on the invented spellings children use when they begin to create texts. Read argued that these spontaneous spellings serve as a window into how children begin to make sense of the conventions of written text without the help of more expert others. In general, these sociocultural studies have illustrated how writing is embedded in children's everyday practices. Carol Chomsky (1972), for example, examined children's writing as they learned to speak. Hudson (1994) provided a teacher's perspective to capture developmental change in a young child's emergent writing. Similarly, Bissex (1980) and Bissex and Bullock (1987) highlighted the logic revealed in children's early writing as children made hypotheses about language and text. These ethnographic accounts illustrate how reading, writing,

and oral language develop simultaneously in formal and informal contexts and highlight the importance of studying literacy *in situ*.

Unquestionably, there has been significant interest over the last 50 years in the child as a language user and meaning maker. In the early part of the twentieth century, Lev Vygotsky (1978) was among the first to argue the social nature of learning.[3] Sociocultural perspectives across a number of disciplines have influenced the ways educational theorists think about language and literacy. Following Vygotsky, John-Steiner et al. (1994) have argued that the use of a social and functional approach to the study of literacy is common across this work. Specifically, John-Steiner et al. delineate several tenets we believe both help define this approach, and distinguish the model from other models:

1. Sociocultural studies of language and literacy employ functional vs. structural models. Of significance, there is particular focus on communicative intent and on the representational functions of language (Austin, 1962; Grice, 1975; Searle, 1969).

2. Social interaction serves as the generative context for language/literacy mastery. Here the reciprocal nature of language and context is emphasized, for example (Bruner, 1983; Wells, 1981).

3. The study of language is expanded to include meaning, use, as well as structure. Thus, the situated nature of knowledge and its relationship to specific sociohistorical contexts and practices are emphasized (Hickmann, 1987). The situatedness of language suggests that its forms must be understood in terms of context and function (Bruner, 1983; Gee, 1990).

4. Interdisciplinary methodologies, particularly ethnographic and sociological methods, generated a new field, the ethnography of communication. The focus on speech events (Searle, 1969) and the influence of culture (Scribner and Cole, 1981) contributed to a multidisciplinary foundation for the study of literacy. This line of work in particular was instrumental in new research on the literacy in school contexts (Cook-Gumperz, 1985; Gilmore and Glatthorn, 1982; Schieffelin and Gilmore, 1986).

5. There is a shift in emphasis from the individual to understanding literacy practices as socially and historically situated (Goodman and Goodman, 1990; Scribner and Cole, 1981).

6. Research methodologies help explain processes and socially constructed situations. The result is an interest in activity in context (Laboratory of Comparative Human Cognition, 1983) and micro-genetic approaches (Siegler and Crowley, 1991; Tudge, 1990; Wertsch and Hickmann, 1987). (1994: 5–6).

These principles are elaborated in a number of edited volumes on the social origins of literacy, and their visibility signals the growing influence of this perspective. Situating their work across various contemporary contexts and communities, literacy scholars in the neo-Vygotskian tradition elaborate on many of the theoretical and methodological issues relevant to the study of early literacy development (Bloome, 1987; Candlin and Mercer, 2001; Hamilton et al., 1994; Lee and Smagorinsky, 2000; Moll, 1990; Reyes and Halcon, 2001; Wells and Claxton, 2002).

LITERACY AS A SOCIALLY MEDIATED PROCESS: MEDIATION AND FORMS OF ASSISTANCE IN EARLY LITERACY

For researchers drawing on sociocultural theories of cognition, the individual/social dichotomy is a problematic construct in that there is a reciprocal and bilateral relationship between the social and the mental. Human beings participate in activities through the use of *tools* as a means to change themselves, their surroundings, as well as the tools themselves. It is important to emphasize that for Vygotsky, the preeminent tool that mediated human development was the use of signs, which included oral language, writing systems, and number systems. Thus, development constitutes the ability of a child to use these signs in a culturally appropriate way that is mediated by the cultural and historical context in which it is embedded. It is the more expert members of a particular practice that determine what is or is not 'appropriate' participation.

Specifically, a sociocultural understanding of learning and development focuses on the cultural resources that mediate an individual's participation and engagement in social practice. The notion of mediation becomes important to the development of a sociocultural view of literacy and, in particular, how language mediates learning and our experience. Here the notion of language as a medium has several interpretations:

> Firstly, from a constructivist view of the world, all our experience is mediated, nothing is direct. Secondly, by the way they structure reality for us in social interactions, people mediate our experience; and thirdly, texts, whether they are books, films or advertisements, mediate our experience. (Barton, 1994: 68)

In other words, the notion of *mediation* suggests that all human actions, both external and internal, exist in relation to other material and/or symbolic objects that are culturally and historically constructed to make meaning of the world. Thus, the construction of meaning, the basis of literate practices, is always situated and embedded within

human activity systems that are goal directed and rule governed (Wertsch, 1981). For example, the word 'ball' is reconstituted to mean 'not strike' within an activity system such as baseball (Levinson, 1992). Indeed, language is considered the tool of tools mediating human activity (Cole and Engestrom, 1993).

In other words, social relations mediate individual mental processes – relations that are primarily mediated by speech, including inner speech. Although cognitive psychologists also have recognized the importance of inner speech or 'private speech' in early literacy development, cognitive psychological views of inner speech suggest that it is a self-contained, discrete activity (Piaget, 1962). In contrast, Vygotsky (1978; 1987) claimed that internal thought is mediated by meanings and externally by signs. From a sociocultural perspective, individual mental processes are contextually situated and are fundamentally social. The use of private speech as a mediator of thought demonstrates the importance of cultural tools such as language in the development of 'individual' cognition. Studies drawing on sociocultural views of early literacy development have examined the self-regulatory speech of preschool children (Berk and Spuhl, 1995; Elias and Berk, 2002; Patrick, 2000). For example, Patrick (2000) found that preschool children (ages four to six) increasingly used self-regulatory speech to mediate problem solving in more difficult tasks. Another study (Elias and Berk, 2002) found that children's use of self-regulatory speech is situated and mediates the development of literacy practices through participation in problem solving and sociodramatic play. Another type of inner speech, a child's *metalinguistic awareness*, or the ability to think about language and its purposes, is linked to conventional forms of literacy (Olson, 1994). Specifically, the ability to reflect upon an imagined audience and speak to the generalized other is critical to literacy (Applebee, 1978). More importantly, imagined audiences are always situated in a particular cultural context.

Vygotsky's *zone of proximal development* (henceforth ZPD or Zoped), one of the most important constructs growing out of the sociocultural tradition, has special significance to the notion of mediation and early literacy development. The ZPD emphasizes the fact that the development of a child's individual mental processes is socially mediated. Broadly defined, the Zoped is the contrast between what a child can do independently (zone of actual development or ZAD) and the child's potential development or what a child can do with the assistance of a more expert other(s) (Vygotsky, 1978). For example, two children might have the same level of actual development, but given the appropriate form of assistance, one might be able to solve many more problems than the other. Thus, while there is recognition of children's individual capabilities, their individual development is supported by their co-participation with more expert members in a particular literacy or discourse practice. In addition, how adults assist children to navigate the zone is a focal point of a number of sociocultural studies of early literacy.

However, Griffin and Cole (1984) have pointed out that most English-language interpretations have perceived the notion of the zone more narrowly than Vygotsky intended. More traditional conceptions of adult–child assistance strategies construct the child as a passive learner, where the more expert adult usually provides next-step assistance, for example, when an adult asks a question for which the answer is already known. In short, the ZPD places emphasis on what children can do *alone* in relation to what they can do with assistance.

More dynamic notions of the zone of proximal development reshape traditional conceptions where the nature of the adult–child relationship is for the most part top-down and unidirectional (Cole, 1996; Engestrom, 1987; Griffin and Cole, 1984; Stone and Gutiérrez, 2002). Rogoff's (1990) notion of *apprenticeship*, for example, helps to reframe the child as an active participant in his/her literacy development. Moreover, the nature of both adult and child participation and how adults assist children in literacy activities is critical toward understanding how children effectively move through the ZPD (Bruner, 1983; Rogoff, 1990). Activity theoretical views of learning and development expand the notion of the Zoped and illustrate its complexity by documenting the role of conflict and tension inherent in learning activity and, in particular, the potentially productive role of conflict in robust learning activity (Cole, 1996; Cole and Engestrom, 1993; Engestrom, 1987; Gutiérrez et al., 1999).

The focus within this view is on socially supported activities, their organization, the mediational tools, the task, and the participants, and their social relationships. For example, a study of children's writing by Diaz and Flores (2001) is illustrative of this more complex understanding of the Zoped. In this work, the authors describe the importance of the teacher as sociocultural mediator in promoting the emergence of positive or productive Zopeds.

Language socialization research into caregiver–child interactions also supports the view that children are actively engaged in the literacy learning process (Bruner, 1977; Ochs and Schieffelin, 1984; Snow, 1977). The role of caregivers in mediating early literacy development has been well documented by early literacy research based on sociocultural views (Bruner, 1977; Bullowa, 1979; Ochs and Schieffelin, 1984; Snow, 1977). As the more expert participant of various literacy practices, adults mediate children's early literacy development through the various assistance strategies they employ.

Of relevance to this chapter, early literacy activity is often embedded in children's play. According to Vygotsky (1978), play affords children opportunities to move beyond their daily routines and behaviours and 'contains all the developmental tendencies in a condensed form'. In particular, through imagination or imaginary play – where the boundaries are more fluid and dynamic – children can assume roles and engage in activity not afforded them in real life. Play is by nature rule governed and goal directed; however, the rules and goals are subject to manipulation by the participants, which leads to the use of higher cognitive functions. In this way, the roles and forms of participation in play serve as preparation for participation in literacy events and in development (Hall, 1991; Nicolopolou, 1993; Vygotsky, 1978). Thus, play serves as an important leading activity; that is, it becomes a context for reorganizing performance (Griffin and Cole, 1984). Play also affords children opportunities to use cultural symbols and practices to negotiate and navigate social relations, in particular with their peers, to drive the overall meaning making process (Dyson, 1997). Dyson (1997) shows how enabling and less restrictive activities such as 'author's theatre' (compared with the more constraining 'author's chair') provide contexts for the development of more complex literacy tools such as negotiation of conflict, analysis of gender equity, and understanding authoritative voices as they are textually positioned (also see Dyson, 1989; 1993). The wide range of tools that are invoked and utilized through play make it an optimal activity for promoting zones of proximal development.

Another central feature of play is that it creates opportunities to interact with more expert and novice peers. Children's interaction with peers creates contexts for conflict and negotiation, which mediates the use of higher-order literacy practices (Mugny and Doise, 1978; Pellegrini et al., 1998; Pelligrini and Galda, 1990). Moreover, points of conflict are intrinsically emotional and have a strong affective component. This in turn leads to more profound reflection and higher-order cognitive functioning in children (Pelligrini et al., 1998).

LANGUAGE SOCIALIZATION: STUDIES OF HOME AND COMMUNITY EARLY LITERACY PRACTICES

Human beings undergo a lifelong process of socialization whereby they continuously transform into the values of an expected social order. Sociocultural views of early literacy development emphasize that human beings are socialized to particular language practices through language itself. Language socialization is the process whereby novices gain knowledge and skills relevant to membership in a social group (Lave and Wagner, 1991; Ochs, 1991). Cross-cultural studies of language socialization have argued that adults and children actively engage each other in the meaning making process (Geertz, 1959; Ochs and Schieffelin, 1984; Scribner and Cole, 1981; Weisner and Gallimore, 1977; Whiting and Whiting, 1975). From this perspective, language plays a fundamental, dynamic role in the construction of social languages (discourses) and identities. These identities and discourses are subject to constant fluctuation as meaning is constantly negotiated and renegotiated between various segments of society, including adults, caregivers, and children (Gee, 2001; Ochs and Schieffelin, 1986). Studies of caregiver–child interactions have helped us understand the process by which children are socialized to and through language use (Cazden, 1983; Ochs and Schieffelin, 1984). They also helped us reconceptualize the novice child as an agent who assumes roles as author and speaker in the meaning making process (Larson, 1995; Ochs and Schieffelin, 1995; Rogoff, 1990; Schieffelin, 1990). They have helped us understand how children are socialized to various problem-solving practices through various language activities (Goodwin, 1990; Nelson, 1989; Rogoff, 1990). Language socialization studies have demonstrated the powerful ways in which children are socialized to various social identities such as gender, religion, learning disability, and authority (Cook, 1990; Goodwin, 1990; Gutiérrez and Stone, 1997; Mehan, 1996; Schieffelin, 1990). Further, novice members are socialized to these multiple identities through affective features of language practices (Miller et al., 1990; Ochs and Schieffelin, 1989).

The continued underachievement of poor children from cultural and linguistic groups served as the impetus for language socialization studies that compared home literacy practices with those of formal schooling. Prior to the understanding that literacy is fundamentally a cultural practice, these children were labelled as having some type of developmental deficit. Language socialization studies that examined the match between formal schooling practices and the literacy practices of middle class homes served to counter the deficit view. Cook-Gumperz (1973) argued that children who have similar literacy practices in the home and in school tend to be more successful (also see Cook-Gumperz, 1986; Scollon and Scollon, 1981). Teachers were found to rely heavily on question

and language games primarily found in white, middle class homes (Cazden, 1979). Heath's (1982) 10-year study of two communities suggested how different social and linguistic environments and literacy practices of families differentially affected how children learned questioning, storytelling, concepts of print, reading, and writing.

Recent studies have shown the impact of this cultural differential on achievement and school literacy (Vernon-Feagans et al., 2001). For example, Vernon-Feagans et al. (2001) demonstrated that superior narrative skills in poor African-American children are negatively related to literacy, while the narrative skills in Caucasian children in the same classrooms were positively related to achievement and school literacy. In other words, the literacy practices that African-American children come with are not valued in relation to the types of literacy practices that are valued in formal schooling. Other studies have compared the patterns of interaction and language socialization of non-white homes with the socialization patterns prevalent in school (Au, 1980; Erickson and Mohatt, 1982; Philips, 1972; 1982) to illustrate the context specific use of speech. Philips (1972; 1982) compared the patterns of classroom interaction among Native American reservation children and among Anglo children in the same community. She found that the patterns of communication of Native American children varied systematically from one type of situation to another.

This type of emphasis on the context of interaction helped to dispel the notion that Native Americans have a developmental or linguistic deficit. In another cross-cultural study, Duranti and Ochs (1986) examined the difference in adult–child relationships and discourse in Samoan households and school settings. The different socialization practices restricted the ability of Samoan children to be full participants in formal educational contexts.

Understanding and valuing the discursive practices of the home is particularly important for the success of language minority students. Reese and Gallimore (2000) present a case study of the cultural literacy practices that mediate early literacy development of children in some Mexican and Central American immigrant families. They found that parents began to read aloud to their children as a result of the expectations placed on them by school. Nevertheless, the parents' own formal schooling and literacy experiences mediated these read-alouds. Moll et al. (1995) elaborated the concept of *funds of knowledge* to demonstrate the value of working class Latino households in transforming the teachers', parents', students', and even the researchers' views of literacy (also see Moll et al., 1992). The application of this construct has been used to illustrate how the utilization of a child's complete repertoire of cultural knowledge could mediate the development of proficient, biliterate practices in both English and Spanish (Moll et al., 2001).

SOCIOCULTURAL THEORY, POWER RELATIONS AND EARLY LITERACY

The importance of cultural and ideological factors in children's early literacy development led to a body of work in the late 1970s and 1980s that examined the socialization practices of children in their homes. Over the last 25 years, a number of literacy researchers and practitioners who have gravitated toward sociocultural theories of learning and cognition have done so in a particular political context. For years, the cognitive psychologists and behaviourists who presented the dominant view on literacy, learning, and human development suggested that literacy was the cause of rational and abstract thinking which in turn led to modernization and the ability to properly participate in the global markets (Scollon, 2001). Thus, illiteracy, in the narrow sense, was seen as the cause of all social problems, and the relationship between literacy, power, ideologies, and the social distribution of goods became the subject of interest for early literacy research.

Scollon (2001) argued that the 'benefits' of literacy as well as the social problems of illiteracy are derived, not from knowledge of scripts or the lack of this knowledge, but from the ideological power struggles of those who control this knowledge and those who are excluded from participation in 'literate' communities of practice.

The following studies illustrate the significance of examining early literacy development as it is embedded within social contexts of power and privilege. Although some of the studies may not be strictly considered cultural-historical (Bernstein, 1982; Hasan, 1986), they demonstrate the importance for current and future researchers drawing on cultural-historical perspectives of early literacy to consider issues of power and privilege in their analysis of early literacy issues. Bernstein (1982) found that different socialization practices (based on class differences) have direct implications for children's language use. The work of Bernstein and others (Bernstein, 1982; Cook-Gumperz, 1973; Hasan, 1986) shows that mother–child interactions and early language socialization practices are mediated by class and class stratification which have an effect on later literacy development. Scribner and Cole's (1981) study of the Vai community who use multiple scripts (English, Arabic, Vai) in multiple

contexts of power demonstrated that social situation (usually marked by power relations) determines the use of each script. Issues of power and control are even exhibited in early childhood writing practices (Hall and Robinson, 1994).

Similarly, the new literacy studies (NLS) argue that literacy or illiteracy is highly value laden and interest driven (Gee, 2001; Luke and Carrington, in press; Street, 1993; 1995; 2001). These studies aim to understand the learning and language development of children in terms of 'discourses' rather than the more limited notion of 'language'. According to Gee, 'Discourses' are more integrated and comprehensive:

> A Discourse integrates ways of talking, listening, writing, reading, acting, interacting, believing, valuing, and feeling … in the service of enacting meaningful socially situated identities and activities. (2001: 35)

Of importance here are the 'believing, valuing, and feeling' dimensions of discourse because it moves beyond traditional understandings of language as a set of equally valued, abstract mental representations of the world. In addition, becoming a competent member of a particular discourse community always involves how marginally or centrally one participates in specific social situations. NLS challenged what Street (1993) and others (Nicolopoulou and Cole, 1997) have called 'autonomous models of literacy' which presume literacy practices to be discrete and neutral. Sociocultural notions like *event*, *activity*, and *practice* moved literacy studies from 'the individual' as a unit of analysis where autonomous cognitive processes are examined under controlled experimental conditions (Goody, 1968; Ong, 1982) to a broader unit of analysis, 'the social practice' (Heath, 1982; Scribner and Cole, 1981). According to Street, 'Researchers dissatisfied with the autonomous models of literacy … have come to view literacy practices as inextricably linked to cultural and power structures in society' (1993: 7). Thus, 'ideological' models of literacy where literacy is necessarily linked to other dimensions of social life including power structures (authority and power/resistance and creativity) became the focal point of NLS. Thus, literacy practices become a site where these larger social asymmetries converge (Gee, 2001; Luke, 1996; Street, 1987).

SUMMARY

In this chapter, we have aimed to provide the reader with an overview of the orienting principles that guide sociocultural studies of early literacy. Social constructivist views of learning and early literacy, such as the emergent literacy view, challenged the assumption that literacy learning begins with formal schooling. Sociocultural views of early literacy have also helped us understand the nature of learning as a socially mediated process, where even individual cognition is necessarily embedded within a particular social context. The understandings that language is the pre-eminent tool for development, that children are socialized to discursive practices through language, and that learning precedes development have caused a paradigm shift in the field of early literacy research. One of the major consequences, over the last 25 years, has been to move researchers and practitioners beyond the deficit views of linguistic and racial minority homes and communities. These studies have documented the complex ways in which adults and children mediate early literacy development, where the child is an active participant in his/her literacy learning. These social relations are negotiated and renegotiated to construct multiple identities in a constantly changing social reality. Sociocultural views of early literacy have now expanded our understanding of the context of development to include larger ideological and power issues as evidenced by the new literacy studies. Sociocultural theory helps us better understand what it is to be human and how to improve the human situation *vis-à-vis* literacy practices.

NOTES

1 We use the terms 'sociocultural' and 'cultural-historical' interchangeably, although we recognize their distinctions. We prefer cultural-historical as it highlights the importance of historicity.

2 See Dyson (1987) and Martinez et al. (1989) for further references to emergent studies. Dyson (1987) examines the potential for traditionally 'off-task' and informal language practices to be valuable opportunities for the development of school literacy.

3 For a more detailed review of Vygotsky's work see Wertsch (1985) and Van der Veer and Valsiner (1991).

REFERENCES

Applebee, A. (1978) *The Child's Concept of Story.* Chicago: University of Chicago Press.

Au, K.H. (1980) 'Participation structures in a reading lesson with Hawaiian children: analysis of a culturally appropriate instructional event', *Anthropology and Education Quarterly*, 11 (2): 91–115.

Austin, J.L. (1962) *How To Do Things with Words.* Oxford: Clarendon.

Barton, D. (1994) *Literacy: an Introduction to the Ecology of Written Language.* Oxford: Blackwell.

Berk, L. and Spuhl, S. (1995) 'Maternal interaction, private speech, and task performance in preschool children', *Early Childhood Research Quarterly*, 2: 145–69.

Bernstein, B. (1982) 'Codes, modalities and the process of cultural reproduction: a model', in M. Apple (ed.), *Cultural and Production in Education.* Boston: Routledge.

Bissex, G. (1980) *Gnys at Wrk: a Child Learns to Write and Read.* Cambridge, MA: Harvard University Press.

Bissex, G. and Bullock, R. (1987) *Seeing for Ourselves: Case-Study Research by Teachers of Writing.* Portsmouth, NH: Heinemann.

Bloome, D. (1987) *Literacy and Schooling.* Norwood, NJ: Ablex.

Bruner, J. (1977) 'Early social interaction and language acquisition', in H.R. Schaffer (ed.), *Studies in Mother–Infant Interaction.* London: Academic. pp. 271–89.

Bruner, J. (1983) *Child's Talk: Learning to Use Language.* New York: Norton.

Bullowa, M. (1979) 'Introduction: prelinguistic communication: a field of scientific research', in M. Bullowa (ed.), *Before Speech: the Beginnings of Interpersonal Communication.* Cambridge: Cambridge University Press. pp. 5–50.

Burns, M.S., Griffin, P. and Snow, C.E. (eds) (1999) *Starting Out Right: a Guide to Promoting Children's Reading Success.* Washington, DC: National Academy Press.

Candlin, C. and Mercer, N. (2001). *English Language Teaching in its Social Context.* London: Routledge.

Carrington, V. and Luke, A. (2003) 'Reading, homes and families: from postmodern to modern?', in A. Van Kleeck, S.A. Stahl and E.B. Bauer (eds), *On Reading Books to Children: Parents and Teachers.* Mahwah, NJ: Erlbaum. pp. 231–52.

Cazden, C. (1979) 'Language in education: variation in the teacher-talk register', in *Thirtieth Annual Georgetown University Round Table on Languages and Linguistics.* Washington, DC: Center for Applied Linguistics.

Cazden, C. (1983) 'Peekaboo as an instructional model: discourse development at school and at home', in B. Bain (ed.), *The Sociogenesis of Language and Human Conduct: a Multidisciplinary Book of Readings.* New York: Plenum. pp. 33–58.

Cazden, C. (1991) 'Contemporary issues and future directions: active learners and active teachers', in J. Flood, J.M. Jensen, D. Lapp and J.R. Squire (eds), *Handbook of Research on Teaching the English Language Arts.* New York: Macmillan. pp. 418–22.

Chomsky, C. (1972) 'Write first, read later', *Childhood Education*, 47: 296–9.

Chomsky, N. (1957) *Syntactic Structures.* The Hague: Mouton.

Clay, Marie (1966) 'Emergent reading behavior'. Unpublished doctoral dissertation, University of Auckland, New Zealand.

Clay, Marie. (1975) *What Did I Write?* Auckland: Heinemann.

Cole, M. (1996) *Cultural Psychology*. Cambridge, MA: Harvard University Press.

Cole, M. and Engestrom, Y. (1993) 'A cultural historical approach to distributed cognition', in G. Salomon (ed.), *Distributed Cognitions: Psychological and Educational Considerations*. New York: Cambridge University Press. pp. 1–46.

Cook, H.M. (1990) 'The role of Japanese sentence-final particle in the socialization of children', *Multilingua*, 9 (4): 377–95.

Cook-Gumperz, J. (1973) 'Situated instructions: language socialization of school aged children', in S. Ervin-Tripp and C. Mitchell-Kernan (eds), *Child Discourse*. New York: Academic. pp. 103–24.

Cook-Gumperz, J. (ed.) (1985) *The Social Construction of Literacy*. Cambridge: Cambridge University Press.

Cook-Gumperz, J. (ed.) (1986) *The Social Construction of Literacy: Studies in International Sociolinguistics*. Cambridge: Cambridge University Press.

Diaz, E. and Flores, B. (2001) 'Teachers as sociocultural, sociohistorical mediator', in M. Reyes and J. Halcon (eds), *The Best for our Children: Latina/Latino Voices on Literacy*. New York: Teachers College Press. pp. 29–47.

Duranti, A. and Ochs, E. (1986) 'Literacy instruction in a Samoan village', in B. Schieffelin and P. Gilmore (eds), *The Acquisition of Literacy: Ethnographic Perspectives*. Norwood, NJ: Ablex.

Dyson, A.H. (1987) 'The value of "time off task": young children's spontaneous talk and deliberate text', *Harvard Educational Review*, 57: 396–420.

Dyson, A.H. (1989) *Multiple Worlds of Child Writers: Friends Learning to Write*. New York: Teachers College Press.

Dyson, A.H. (1993) *The Social Worlds of Children Learning to Write in an Urban Primary School*. New York: Teachers College Press.

Dyson, A.H. (1997) *Writing Superheroes: Contemporary Childhood, Popular Culture, and Classroom Literacy*. New York: Teachers College Press.

Elias, C. and Berk, L.E. (2002) 'Self-regulation in young children: is there a role for sociodramatic play?', *Early Childhood Research Quarterly*, 17 (2): 216–38.

Engestrom, E. (1987) *Learning by Expanding: an Activity–Theoretical Approach to Developmental Research*. Helsinki: Orienta-Konsultit.

Erickson, F. and Mohatt, G. (1982) 'Cultural organization of participant structures in two classrooms of Indian students', in G.D. Spindler (ed.), *Doing the Ethnography of Schooling*. New York: Holt, Rinehart and Winston.

Ferreiro, E. and Teberosky, A. (1982) *Literacy before Schooling*. Portsmouth, NH: Heinemann.

Gates, A., Bond, G. and Russell, H. (1939) *Methods of Determining Reading Readiness*. New York: Teachers College Press.

Gee, J. (1990) *Social Linguistics and Literacies: Ideology in Discourses*. London: Falmer.

Gee, J. (2001) 'A sociocultural perspective on early literacy development', in S. Neuman and D. Dickinson (eds), *Handbook of Early Literacy Research*. New York: Guilford. pp. 30–42.

Geertz, H. (1959) 'The vocabulary of emotion: a study of Javanese socialization processes', *Psychiatry*, 22: 225–37.

Gilmore, P. and Glatthorn, A. (1982) *Children In and Out of School*. Washington, DC: Center for Applied Linguistics.

Goodman, Y.M. and Goodman, K.S. (1990) 'Vygotsky in a Whole-Language Perspective', in L.C. Moll (ed.), *Vygotsky and Education: Instructional Implications and Applications of Sociohistorical Psychology*. New York: Cambridge University Press. pp. 223–50.

Goodwin, M. (1990) *He-Said-She-Said: Talk as Social Organization among Black Children*. Bloomington, IN: Indiana University Press.

Goody, J. (1968) *Literacy in Traditional Societies*. Cambridge: Cambridge University Press.

Grice, H.P. (1975) 'Logic and conversation', in P. Cole and J.L. Morgan (eds), *Syntax and Semantics: Speech Acts*. New York: Academic. pp. 41–58.

Griffin, P. and Cole, M. (1984) 'Current activity for the future: the Zo-Ped', in B. Rogoff and J. Wertsch (eds), *Children's Learning in the Zone of Proximal Development*. San Francisco: Jossey Bass. pp. 45–63.

Gutiérrez, K. (2002) 'Studying cultural practices in urban learning communities', *Human Development*, 45 (4): 312–21.

Gutiérrez, K. and Rogoff, B. (in press) 'Cultural ways of learning: individual styles or repertoires of practice', *Educational Researcher*.

Gutiérrez, K. and Stone, L. (1997) 'A cultural-historical view of learning and learning disabilities: participating in a community of learners', *Learning Disabilities Research and Practice*, 12 (2): 123–31.

Gutiérrez, K., Baquedano-López, P. and Tejeda, C. (1999) 'Rethinking diversity: hybridity and hybrid language practices in the third space', *Mind, Culture and Activity*, 6 (4): 286–303.

Gutiérrez, K., Baquedano-López, P. and Alvarez, H. (2001) 'Literacy as hybridity: moving beyond bilingualism in urban classrooms', in M. de la Luz Reyes and J. Halcón (eds), *The Best for Our Children: Critical Perspectives on Literacy for Latino Students*. New York: Teachers College Press. pp. 122–41.

Hall, N. (1987) *The Emergence of Literacy*. London: Arnold.

Hall, N. (1991) 'Play and the emergence of literacy', in J. Christie (ed.), *Play and Early Literacy Development*. Albany: State University of New York Press. pp. 3–25.

Hall, N. and Robinson, A. (1994) 'Power and control in young children's scribbling', in M. Hamilton, D. Barton and R. Ivanic (eds), *Worlds of Literacy*. Clevedon: Multilingual Matters. pp. 121–33.

Hamilton, M., Barton, D. and Ivanic, R. (eds) (1994) *Worlds of Literacy*. Clevedon: Multilingual Matters.

Hasan, R. (1986) 'The ontogenesis of ideology: an interpretation of mother–child talk', in Threadgold, T., Grosz, E. and Kress, G. (eds), *Semiotics, Ideology, Language*. SASSC. Sydney: University of Sydney.

Heath, S. (1982) 'What no bedtime story means: narrative skills at home and school', *Language in Society*, 11 (2): 49–76.

Hickmann, M. (ed) (1987) *Social and Functional Approaches to Language and Thought*. Orlando, FL: Academic.

Hiebert, E.H. (1988) 'The role of literacy experiences in early childhood programs', *The Elementary School Journal*, 89 (2): 161–71.

Hiebert, E.H. and Raphael, T.E. (1996) 'Psychological perspectives on literacy and extensions to educational practice', in D.C. Berliner and R.C. Calfee (eds), *Handbook of Educational Psychology*. New York: Macmillan. pp. 550–602.

Hudson, J. (1994) 'Catherine's story: a young child learns to write', in M. Hamilton, D. Barton and R. Ivanic (eds), *Worlds of Literacy*. Clevedon: Multilingual Matters. pp. 188–94.

Hull, G. and Schultz, K. (2002) *School's Out: Bridging Out-of-School Literacies with Classroom Practice*. New York: Teachers College Press.

Hymes, D. (1972) 'On communicative competence', in J.B. Pride and J. Holmes (eds), *Sociolinguistics*. Harmondsworth: Penguin. pp. 269–93.

John-Steiner, V., Panofsky, C. and Smith, L. (1994) *Social Cultural Approaches to Language and Literacy: An Interactionist Perspective*. New York: Cambridge University Press.

Laboratory of Comparative Human Cognition (1983) 'Culture and cognitive development', in W. Kessen (ed.), *Handbook of Child Psychology*, vol. 1. New York: Wiley.

Labov, W. (1972) *The Transformation of Experience in Narrative Syntax. Language in the Inner City: Studies in the Black English Vernacular*. Philadelphia: University of Pennsylvania Press.

Larson, J. (1995) 'Talk matters: knowledge distribution among novice writers in kindergarten', Unpublished PhD dissertation, UCLA.

Lave, J. and Wagner, E. (1991) *Situated Learning: Legitimate Peripheral Participation*. New York: Cambridge University Press.

Lee, C.D. (2002) 'Interrogating race and ethnicity as constructs in the examination of cultural processes in developmental research', *Human Development*, 45: 282–90.

Lee, C. and Smagorinsky, P. (2000) *Vygotskian Perspectives on Literacy Research: Constructing Meaning through Collaborative Inquiry*. New York: Cambridge University Press.

Levinson, S. (1992) 'Activity types and language', in P. Drew and J. Heritage (eds), *Talk at Work: Interaction in Institutional Settings*. Cambridge: Cambridge University Press. pp. 3–66.

Luke, A. (1994) *The Social Construction of Literacy in the Primary School*. Melbourne: Macmillan.

Luke, A. (1996) 'Text and discourse in education: an introduction to critical discourse analysis', *Review of Research in Education*, 21: 3–48.

Martinez, M., Cheyney, M., McBroom, C., Hemmeter, A. and Teale, W. (1989) 'No-risk kindergarten literacy environments for at-risk children', in J. Allen and J. Mason (eds), *Risk Makers, Risk Takers, Risk Breakers: Reducing the Risks for Young Literacy Learners*. Portsmouth, NH: Heinemann. pp. 93–124.

Marvin, C. and Mirenda, P. (1993) 'Home literacy experiences of preschoolers enrolled in Head-Start and special education programs', *Journal of Early Intervention*, 17 (4): 351–67.

Marvin, C. and Wright, D. (1997) 'Literacy socialization in the homes of preschool children', *Language Speech and Hearing Services in Schools*, 28 (2): 154–63.

Mason, J. and Allen, J.B. (1986) 'A review of emergent literacy with implications for research practice in reading', *Review of Research in Education*, 13: 3–47.

Mehan, H. (1996) 'The construction of an LD student: a case study in the politics of representation', in M. Silverstein and G. Urban (eds), *Natural Histories of Discourse*. Chicago: University of Chicago Press. pp. 253–76.

Michaels, S. (1982) '"Sharing time": children's narrative styles and differential access to literacy', *Language in Society*, 10: 423–42.

Miller, P., Potts, R., Fung, H., Hoogstra, L. and Mintz, J. (1990) 'Narrative practices and the social construction of self in childhood', *American Ethnologist*, 17 (2): 292–311.

Moll, L. (1990) *Vygotsky and Education*. New York: Cambridge University Press.

Moll, L. (2000) 'Inspired by Vygotsky: ethnographic experiments in education', in C. Lee and P. Smagorinsky (eds), *Vygotskian Perspectives on Literacy Research: Constructing Meaning through Collaborative Inquiry*. New York: Cambridge University Press. pp. 256–68.

Moll, L., Amanti, C., Neff, D. and Gonzalez, N. (1992) 'Funds of knowledge for teaching: using a qualitative approach to connect homes and classrooms', *Theory into Practice*, 31: 132–41.

Moll, L., Gonzalez, N., Tenery, M., Rivera, A., Rendon, P., Gonzalez, R. and Amanti, C. (1995) 'Funds of knowledge for teaching in Latino households', *Urban Education*, 29 (4): 443–70.

Moll, L., Saez, R. and Dworin, J. (2001) 'Exploring biliteracy: two student case examples of writing as a social practice', *Elementary School Journal*, 101 (4): 435–49.

Morphett, M.V. and Washburne, C. (1931) 'When should children begin to read?', *Elementary School Journal*, 31: 496–508.

Morrow, L. (1997) *Literacy Development in the Early Years: Helping Children Read and Write*. Boston: Allyn and Bacon.

Mugny, G. and Doise, W. (1978) 'Socio-cognitive conflict and structure of individual and collective performances', *European Journal of Social Psychology*, 8: 181–92.

National Reading Panel (2000) US Department of Health and Human Services National Institute of Child Health and Human Development, NIH pub. no. 00–4754.

Nelson, K. (ed.) (1989) *Narratives from the Crib*. Cambridge, MA: Harvard University Press.

Nicolopoulou, A. (1993) 'Play, cognitive development, and the social world: Piaget, Vygotsky, and beyond', *Human Development*, 36: 1–23.

Nicolopoulou, A. and Cole, M. (1997) 'Literacy and cognition', in D.A. Wagner, L. Venezky and B.V. Street (eds), *Literacy: an International Handbook*. New York: Garland. pp. 81–6.

Ochs, E. (1988) *Culture and Language Development: Language Acquisition and Language Socialization in a Samoan Village*. Cambridge: Cambridge University Press.

Ochs, E. (1991) 'Socialization through language and interaction: a theoretical introduction', *Issues in Applied Linguistics*, 2 (2): 143–7.

Ochs, E. and Shieffelin, B. (1984) 'Language acquisition and socialization: three developmental stories and their implications', in R. Shweder and R. Le Vine (eds), *Culture Theory: Essays on Mind, Self, and Emotion*. New York: Cambridge University Press. pp. 276–320.

Ochs, E. and Schieffelin, B. (1986) 'From feelings to grammar', in B. Schieffelin and E. Ochs (eds), *Language Socialization across Cultures*. Cambridge: Cambridge University Press. pp. 251–72.

Ochs, E. and Schieffelin, B. (1989) 'Language has a heart: the pragmatics of affect', *Text*, 9 (1): 7–25.

Ochs, E. and Schieffelin, B. (1995) 'The impact of language socialization on grammatical development', in P. Fletcher and B. MacWhinney (eds), *The Handbook of Child Language*. Oxford: Blackwell. pp. 73–94.

Olson, D.R. (1994) *The World on Paper: the Conceptual and Cognitive Implications of Writing and Reading*. New York: Cambridge University Press.

Ong, W. (1982) *Orality and Literacy*. London: Methuen.

Orellana, M.F. (2001) 'The work kids do: Mexican and Central American children's contributions to households and schools in California', *Harvard Educational Review*, 7 (3): 366–89.

Patrick, E. (2000) 'The self-regulatory nature of preschool children's private speech in a naturalistic setting', *Applied Psycholinguistics*, 21 (1): 45–61.

Pellegrini, A. and Galda, L. (1990) 'Children's play, language, and early literacy', *Topics in Language Disorders*, 10 (3): 76–88.

Pellegrini, A.D., Galda, L., Bartini, M. and Charak, D. (1998) 'Oral language and literacy learning in context: the role of social relationships', *Merrill–Palmer Quarterly*, 44: 38–54.

Philips, S. (1972) 'Participation structures and communicative competence: Warm Springs children in community and classroom', in C. Cazden, P. John and D. Hymes (eds), *Functions of Language in the Classroom*. New York: Teachers College Press.

Philips, S. (1982). *The Invisible Culture: Communication in Classroom and Community on the Warm Springs Indian Reservation*. New York: Longman.

Piaget, J. (1951) *The Child's Conception of the World*. London: Routledge and Kegan Paul.

Piaget, J. (1962) *The Language and Thought of the Child*, trans. M. Gabain. Cleveland, OH: Meridian.

Read, C. (1971) 'Pre-school children's knowledge of English phonology', in *Harvard Educational Review*. Cambridge, MA: Educational Board, Harvard University.

Reese, L. and Gallimore, R. (2000) 'Immigrant Latinos' cultural model of literacy development: an evolving perspective on home–school discontinuities', *American Journal of Education*, 108 (2): 103–34.

Reyes, M. and Halcon, J. (eds) (2001) *The Best for Our Children: Latina/Latino Voices on Literacy*. New York: Teachers College Press.

Rogoff, B. (1990) *Apprenticeship in Thinking: Cognitive Development in Social Context*. New York: Oxford University Press.

Rogoff, B. (2003) *The Cultural Nature of Human Development*. New York: Oxford University Press.

Rogoff, B. and Angelillo, C. (2002) 'Investigating the coordinated functioning of multifaceted cultural practices in human development', *Human Development*, 45: 211–25.

Rueda, R. and McIntyre, E. (2002) 'Toward universal literacy', in S. Stringfield and D. Land (eds), *Educating At Risk Students: One Hundred First Yearbook of the National Society for the Study of Education*. Chicago, IL: University of Chicago Press. pp. 189–209.

Schieffelin, B. (1990) *The Give and Take of Everyday Life: Language Socialization of Kaluli Children*. New York: Cambridge University Press. pp. 75–111.

Schieffelin, B. and Gilmore, P. (1986) *The Acquisition of Literacy: Ethnographic Perspectives*. Norwood, NJ: Ablex.

Schweinhart, L. and Weikart, D. (eds) (1993) *Significant Benefits: High/Scope Perry Preschool Study through Age 27*. Ypsilanti, MI: High/Scope Press.

Scollon, R. (2001) 'Action and text: toward an integrated understanding of the place of text in social (inter)action', in R. Wodak and M. Meyer (eds), *Methods in Critical Discourse Analysis*. London: Sage. pp. 139–83.

Scollon, R. and Scollon, S. (1981) *Narrative and Face in Inter-Ethnic Communicationn*. Norwood, NJ: Ablex.

Scribner, S. (1984a) 'Literacy in three metaphors', *American Journal of Education*, 95 (1): 6–21.

Scribner, S. (1984b) 'The practice of literacy: where mind and society meet', in S.J. White and V. Teller (eds),

Annals of the New York Academy of Sciences: Discourses in Reading and Linguistics, 433: 5–19.

Scribner, S. and Cole, M. (1978) 'Literacy without schooling: testing for intellectual effects', *Harvard Educational Review*, 48 (4): 448–61.

Scribner, S. and Cole, M. (1981). *The Psychology of Literacy*. Cambridge, MA: Harvard University Press.

Scribner, S., Goody, J. and Cole, M. (1977) 'Writing and formal operations: a case study among the Vai', *Africa*, 47: 289–304.

Searle, J. (1969) *Speech Acts*. Cambridge: Cambridge University Press.

Siegler, R. and Crowley, K. (1991) 'The microgenetic method: a direct means for studying cognitive development', *American Psychologist*, 46 (6): 606–20.

Skinner, B.F. (1957) *Verbal Behavior*. New York: Appleton-Century-Crofts.

Snow, C. (1977) 'The development of conversation between mothers and babies', *Journal of Child Language*, 4: 1–22.

Stahl, S.A. and Miller, P.D. (1989) 'Whole language and language experience approaches for beginning reading: a quantitative research synthesis', *Review of Educational Research*, 59 (1): 87–116.

Street, B. (1993) 'Introduction: the new literacy studies', in B. Street (ed.), *Cross-Cultural Approaches to Literacy*. Cambridge: Cambridge University Press. pp. 1–21.

Street, B. (1987) 'Literacy and orality as ideological constructions: some problems in cross cultural studies', in *Culture and History 2*. Copenhagen: Museum Tusculanum Press.

Street, B. (1995) *Social Literacies: Critical Approaches to Literacy in Development, Ethnography and Education*. London: Longman.

Street, B. (ed.) (2001) *Literacy and Development: Ethnographic Perspectives*. New York: Routledge.

Stone, L. and Gutiérrez, K. (2002) 'Microdevelopment and assistance strategies: organizing learning processes in an after-school setting'. Unpublished Manuscript.

Sulzby, E. and Teale, W. (1991) 'Emergent literacy', in R. Barr, M.L. Kamil, P.B. Mosenthal and P.D. Pearson (eds), *Handbook of Reading Research*, vol. 2. New York: Longman. pp. 727–57.

Teale, W. and Sulzby, E. (1986) *Emergent Literacy: Writing and Reading*. Norwood, NJ: Ablex.

Teale, W. and Sulzby, E. (1987) 'Literacy acquisition in early childhood: the roles of access and mediation in storybook reading', in D.A. Wagner (ed.), *The Future of Literacy in a Changing World*. New York: Pergamon. pp. 111–30.

Thorndike, E. (1921) *The Teacher's Word Book*. New York: Teachers College Press.

Trueba, H.T. (1999) 'Critical ethnography and a Vygotskian pedagogy of hope: the empowerment of Mexican immigrant children', *International Journal for Qualitative Studies in Education*, 12 (6): 591–614.

Tudge, J. (1990) 'Vygotsky, the zone of proximal development, and peer collaboration: implications for classroom practice', in L.C. Moll (ed.), *Vygotsky and Education*. Cambridge: Cambridge University Press. pp. 154–74.

Van der Veer, R. and Valsiner, J. (1991) *Understanding Vygotsky*. London: Blackwell.

Vásquez, O.A. (2003) *La Clase Mágica: Imagining Optimal Possibilities in a Bilingual Community of Learners*. Mahwah, NJ: Erlbaum.

Vernon-Feagans, L., Hammer, C.S., Miccio, A. and Manlove, E. (2001) 'Early language and literacy skills in low-income African American and Hispanic children', in S. Neuman and D.K. Dickinson (eds), *Handbook for Research on Early Literacy* New York: Guilford. pp. 192–210.

Vygotsky, L.S. (1978) *Mind in Society: the Development of Higher Psychological Processes*. Cambridge, MA: Harvard University Press.

Vygotsky, L.S. (1987) *The Collected Works of L.S. Vygotsky. Vol. 1: Problems of General Psychology*, (eds), R. Rieber and A. Carton, trans. N. Minick. New York: Plenum.

Weisner, T.S. and Gallimore, R. (1977) 'My brother's keeper: child and sibling caretaking', *Current Anthropology*, 18 (2): 169–90.

Wells, G. (ed.) (1981) *Learning through Interaction: the Study of Language Development*, Vol. 1 Cambridge: Cambridge University Press.

Wells, G. (1985) 'Pre-school literacy related activities and success in school', in D. Olson, N. Torrance and A. Hilyard (eds), *Literacy, Language and Learning*. Cambridge: Cambridge University Press.

Wells, G. and Claxton, G. (2002) *Learning for Life in the 21st Century*. Oxford: Blackwell.

Wertsch, J. (1978) 'Adult–child interaction and the roots of metacognition', *Quarterly Newsletter of the Institute for Comparative Human Development*, 2: 15–18.

Wertsch, J. (1981) *The Concept of Activity in Soviet Psychology*, ed. J.V. Wertsch. Armonk, NY: Sharpe.

Wertsch, J. (1985) *Vygotsky and the Social Formation of Mind*. Cambridge, MA: Harvard University Press.

Wertsch, J. and Hickmann, M. (1987) 'Problem-solving in social interaction: a microgenetic analysis', in M. Hickmann (ed.), *Social and Functional Approaches to Language and Thought*. Orlando, FL: Academic.

White, K. (1982) 'The relation between socioeconomic status and academic achievement', *Psychological Bulletin*, 91: 461–81.

Whiting, B. and Whiting, J. (1975) *Children of Six Cultures*. Cambridge, MA: Harvard University Press.

Part II

EARLY CHILDHOOD LITERACY IN FAMILIES, COMMUNITIES AND CULTURES

5

Researching Young Children's Out-of-School Literacy Practices

MICHELE KNOBEL AND COLIN LANKSHEAR

'Out-of-school literacies' means different things to different people, and has been enlisted in diverse types of research during the past 20 years to serve a range of educational purposes. In this chapter we outline some of the positions that have been adopted and provide examples of the research done under each particular description. Most of the chapter, however, will be devoted to our preferred conception of 'out-of-school literacies'.

Two broad distinctions delineate the main positions available on out-of-school literacy research. One distinction is between views that include as out-of-school literacies *any* literacy practice – including school-like or school-centric literacies – occurring in contexts outside formal school settings, and views that omit school literacies from consideration. Those taking the former position will be prepared to include, for example, caregiver or intergenerational story reading to young children, name writing, print awareness, decoding food product and other brand-related labels, completing school homework, drawing and colouring and oral book-like storytelling, among others (cf. Britto, 2000; Cairney, 2002; Carrington, 2001; Janes and Kermani, 2001; Martens, 1999). Those who take the second position, however, adopt the view that one defining feature of an out-of-school literacy is that it is *not* generally recognized as a characteristic school literacy (cf. Cook-Gumperz and Keller-Cohen, 1993; Hicks, 2002; Hull and Schultz, 2002; Prinsloo and Breier, 1996a). Indeed, from this perspective, out-of-school literacies will typically be literacies that are *not* permitted or tolerated – and are certainly not encouraged – in school. To some extent, however, efforts to legitimate aspects of

literacies based on popular culture or social class within the life of the school may be seen as attempts to 'smuggle' out-of-school literacies into – or endorse them within – classroom curriculum and pedagogy.

The second broad distinction also relates to age. Some researchers recognize out-of-school literacies as practices engaged in by people of any age. Others, however, confine their interest in out-of-school literacies to practices engaged in by persons during their formal preschool to end of high school years. This raises some interesting questions. In some ways, it seems odd to think of someone who does not attend school having 'out-of-school' literacies: at least, in the case of adults beyond compulsory education. It may not be so odd, however, to think of the concept applying to very young children who are becoming initiated into pre-literate and emergent literacy behaviours and other forms of primary socialization that will impact one way or another on their school literacy achievement. The issue is clouded by the emergence of concepts such as 'lifelong learning', which entails people of all ages 'going back to school' in some sense (whether school, a higher education institution, work-based training programmes, ongoing professional development, and so on). The issue is clouded still further by the existence of a set of concepts that nest around the border between school and the wider world. These concepts include community literacies, literacies of popular culture, intergenerational literacy, family literacy, and so on (see related chapters in this volume). There is usually an implication here that school literacy (or literacies) is the *real* one on which other literacies depend for their recognition, in relation to which they are regarded

Table 5.1   *Four available research positions within out-of-school literacy studies*

	Any literacy	Not 'school' literacies
School age range	*Quadrant 1* Any literacy practice engaged in by a (pre)school-age individual in a setting outside the school	*Quadrant 3* Any literacy practice engaged in by preschool and school-age individuals in settings outside the school that is *not* a formally recognized literacy practice within school pedagogy and curriculum
Any age	*Quadrant 2* Any literacy practice engaged in by persons of any age within non-school (i.e. non-formal education) settings	*Quadrant 4* Any literacy practice engaged in by persons of any age within non-school (formal education) settings that is *not* a recognized literacy belonging to a formal education curriculum or pedagogy

as 'unofficial' and less important or valid (if not actually *antagonistic*), or to which they relate in a *service* capacity in order to help enhance school literacy performance.

These two distinctions provide four broad positions so far as defining and distinguishing 'out-of-school literacy practice' are concerned (see Table 5.1).

Our main interest in this chapter lies with research falling within the third quadrant – the study of students and their 'not school' literacies. As we argue later, this approach to investigating children's out-of-school literacies holds rich promise for directly informing effective pedagogical practice, for challenging commonly held but detrimental assumptions and stereotypes regarding traditionally marginalized students and their out-of-school lives, and for helping to shape more equitable literacy education policies. Before discussing this particular body of research, however, it is useful to consider briefly the other three quadrants in our matrix.

Accordingly, there follows a summary explication of quadrants 1, 2 and 4. We present examples from English-language research literature, drawing particularly on published literature – especially from refereed journals – rather than unpublished literature (e.g. dissertations, conference papers), on the grounds of ready availability to readers.

Quadrant 1: any literacy, school age range

Quadrant 1 describes research studies focusing on what children do outside school that contributes directly to them developing (or not developing) sound and efficacious understandings of how written, spoken and visual texts 'operate' (much of what is referred to as 'family literacy studies' falls into this category: see Cairney, in this volume). Within early childhood, this research orientation generally assumes that language and literacy skills 'are

predictive of school literacy success' (Neuman and Celano, 2001: 12), and focuses on documenting young children's literacy development or their 'emergent literacy', that is, acquiring 'literacy concepts and knowledge through ample exposure to and interacting with print' (Xu, 1999: 47). Thus, these studies generally tend to be investigatory or evaluative in nature, rather than interventionist.

The criteria used to judge sound and efficacious literacy understandings are drawn mostly from school-centred definitions of literacy (e.g. correct letter name and sound identification, awareness of print, reading readiness measures), and this group of studies is most often framed theoretically by psycholinguistics, developmental psychology and cultural psychology (especially, by appropriations from Vygotsky). Key concepts include: 'emergent literacy', 'at-home literacy', 'literacy environments', 'disadvantage', 'connection'and 'disconnection', 'collaboration' – and, increasingly, 'meaning making', 'diversity'and 'literacy practices'. Studies falling into quadrant 1 often do not involve the researcher in conducting detailed observations in homes. Instead, these studies rely on parent reporting of home-based literacy practices via interviews or surveys, audiorecordings or videorecordings of literacy events made by children and/or their caregivers, parent-completed inventories, diaries and/or checklists, and so on (cf. Bloome et al., 2000; Gregory, 2001; McCarthey, 1997; Parke et al., 2002; Reese and Gallimore, 2000).

At least three types of purposes characterize this body of research: (1) to document (and sometimes to evaluate, but rarely to intervene in) parent–child interactions with texts in order to identify children's emerging understandings of the functions and purposes of print (e.g. Kenner, 2000; Martens, 1999; Smith, 2001); (2) to compare young children's prior-to-school literacy development with their in-school literacy performance in order to better understand transitions from informal literacy learning at home to formal literacy learning at school (Arthur et al., 2001; Breen et al., 1994; Freebody et al., 1995; Hill et al., 1998); and (3) to respond to what are seen as the limitations of emergent literacy studies that 'do not fully take account of social and cultural variations that exist in young children's literacy learning trajectories' at home and school (Jones Diaz et al., 2000: 231). This last-mentioned group of studies documents a range of in-school and out-of-school literacies and literacy activities – such as popular-culture-related practices, play events, young children's text production, telephone discourse, intergenerational socialization, etc. – and argues for their pertinence to early childhood literacy education (e.g. Arthur, 2001; Cairney and Ruge, 1998; Carrington, 2001; Drury, 2000; Dyson, 2001; Gillen, 2002; Gregory, 2001; Kenner, 2000; McClain, 2000; Moss, 2001; Mulhern, 1997; Parke et al., 2002; Purcell-Gates, 1996; Rodriguez, 1999; Wan, 2000; Williams and Gregory, 2001; see also Marsh, in this volume).

Quadrant 2: any literacy, any age

Quadrant 2 describes studies investigating literacy learning or competent performance regardless of age or non-school location. Studies falling within this quadrant mainly have some family-based intervention programme development in mind – and are often concerned with evaluating the efficacy of an existing family literacy intervention programme (Barton, 1997; Cairney, 2002; Hannon, 1995; Purcell-Gates, 2000; Serpell, 1997; see Hannon, in this volume). Most family literacy programme studies aim at helping parents deliver effective literacy instruction at home (Barton, 1997; Janes and Kermani, 2001; Nason, 1997; Saracho, 1999; Wollman-Bonilla, 2001).

The studies may be:

- *exploratory*, e.g. documenting pregnant teenagers' literacy levels, documenting lower-income families' story-reading practices
- *comparative*, e.g. comparing parents' and grandparents' reading to young children, comparing the home reading practices of diverse families along lines of class and/or ethnicity
- *evaluative*, e.g. evaluating the effectiveness of a storybook reading programme that targeted single mothers.

Interventions developed or evaluated in the course of these wide-ranging studies generally target families with parents who are judged to be struggling with standard literacy themselves. For example, some interventions train parents to engage in talk about texts with their children that is 'lexically rich, includes extended discourses, and is somewhat

distanced from the here and now' (Jordan et al., 2000: 526). Others equip mothers of young babies with free books and instructional materials (e.g. Hardman and Jones, 1999). Others challenge the 'non-neutrality'of literacy instruction and remediation at school by examining a range of discourses operating in the homes and schools of ethnically marginalized children (e.g. Rogers et al., 2000).

Theories used to frame these evaluative studies include, among others: psycholinguistics, cultural psychology (Vygotsky), and emergent literacy theory. Key concepts characterizing this research include: 'transformation', 'disadvantage', 'communities of learners', 'instruction', 'authentic assessment', and, increasingly, 'social context', 'power', and 'discourse'. Data are collected mainly by means of families videorecording literacy events at home, teacher and parent interviews, observing programme participant demonstrations of a new skill or process, and so on. Again, despite claims regarding home literacy practices, it appears that studying actual home literacy events is not a necessary requisite for this body of studies. And, as with studies in quadrant 1, the criteria used to analyse or evaluate home literacies and literacy interventions tend to be drawn from school-focused definitions of literacy.

Quadrant 4: non-school literacies, any age

Studies falling within quadrant 4 focus largely on everyday literacy practices of adults and include work- and community-based activity and learning (cf. Gee et al., 1996; Hull, 1997). This body of research 'explores the functions of literacy' (Hull and Schultz, 2001: 597) in a wide range of practical contexts in order to better understand the literacy requirements and literacy-related social practices of workplaces and adult literacy programmes, and draws attention to ways in which literacy education in schools – including universities – does not always equip adults with the kinds of literacy knowhow required by the world of work (2001: 597).

The rise of the ethnography of communication during the late 1960s and early 1970s as a distinct approach to studying different 'ways of speaking' and doing within a community (e.g. Gumperz, 1982; Hymes, 1972) has generated keen ongoing interest in researching language use within different cultural groups and social contexts. Many such studies in the late 1980s and the 1990s responded to claims alleging a 'literacy' crisis in developed countries. They aimed to show how in their everyday lives so-called 'illiterate' adults engaged in a wide array of literate activities that usually went unrecognized by policy writers, employers and adult educators. Such studies typically address literacies that are not officially recognized in formal school-like or workplace settings yet nonetheless require relatively high degrees of literate competence in order to operate in everyday work, community and home contexts. These 'alternative' literacies include profession-related literacies, like those practised by taxi drivers (Breier et al., 1996), nurses (e.g. Cook-Gumperz and Hanna, 1997), or farm hands (Gibson, 1996); religion-based literacies such as those practised by individuals (cf. Guerra and Farr, 2002), the Amish in the US (e.g. Fishman, 1988), or a community of Seventh Day Adventists in Australia (e.g. Kapitzke, 1995); literacies within economically depressed urban areas (e.g. Cushman, 1998; Barton and Hamilton, 1998); or literacies within prisons (Wilson, 2000); literacies practised by Cape Town gangsters (China and Robins, 1996); the literacy mediation role played by freelance scribes working in a Mexican plaza (Kalman, 1999), by an 'illiterate', middle-aged woman who is a fluent speaker of six languages and responsible for overseeing a range of text-based bureaucratic functions within her community (Kell, 1996), by one man within the day-to-day farming activities in, and bureaucratic systems operating on, a community of Welsh farming folk (Jones, 2001); and so on.

Theories and methodologies drawn on by these studies include: cultural psychology (e.g. Cole, 1996), feminist theory (cf. Gowen, 1992; Heller, 1997), the New Literacy Studies (e.g. Gee, 1996; Prinsloo and Breier, 1996b; Street, 1997) and sociolinguistics (e.g. conversation analysis, language variation studies, critical discourse analysis). Increasingly, this body of research also draws on social semiotics (such as the work of Kress and van Leeuwen, 1996) and poststructuralist feminist theories (such as the work of Walkerdine, 1990). Key concepts include: 'discourse' – including different orders of discourse such as 'dominant discourse' and 'marginal discourse' – 'identity', 'social context', 'social practice', 'language/literacy practice', and 'literacies'. Data are generated by means of detailed interviews and ethnographic-type observations of participants' identity presentation, literacy uses and literacy-related activities.

The remainder of this chapter, however, focuses on research that emphasizes the contextualized study of school children's out-of-school literacies. We believe such research holds most potential for enhancing understanding of the rich literate lives of young people and their sometimes smooth but often fraught literacy learning experiences within school. We pay particular attention to a small but growing body of research that focuses on children in the 'early school years' age range. This orientation toward studying 'out-of-school' literacy resonates

(theoretically, methodologically and conceptually) with studies of adult non-formal literacy practices. It differs, however, from the studies in quadrants 1 and 2 by emphasizing contextualized documentation and analysis of everyday literacy practices that are not constrained by 'school-centric' views of what constitutes 'effective' literacy.

RESEARCHING STUDENTS' OUT-OF-SCHOOL LITERACIES

Studies of out-of-school literacy falling within quadrant 3 in Table 5.1 focus on literacies that are defined *against* the grain of schooled literacies. These are variously referred to as 'everyday' (Prinsloo and Breier, 1996b), 'alternative' (Cook-Gumperz and Keller-Cohen, 1993), 'hidden' (Finders, 1997), 'in-between' (Sarroub, 2002) or 'vernacular' (Camitta, 1993) literacies. These studies begin with the assumption that regardless of what test scores might suggest, most school students are well able to practise and engage competently in literacies outside school. Much of the driving force behind them has been to advocate for a range of children and their rich literate social practices in reaction to narrow, school-based and 'schooled' literacies that privilege particular and normative language and literacy uses – and to teacher-made claims that there is a 'lack of literacy' in poor/working-class/non-white homes. Such views and the privileged literacies associated with them work to further disadvantage already-disadvantaged and marginalized children and social groups within a society (cf. Gee, 1991; Gilmore, 1991; Gilmore and Glatthorn, 1982; Heath, 1983; Lankshear, 1987; Taylor and Dorsey-Gaines, 1988). Research falling within our third quadrant is generally concerned with comparing the in-school and out-of-school literacy competencies and experiences of diverse school children. These studies aim at revealing congruencies and breaches between what children and young people are *already* able to do with literacy outside formal school contexts and what they are *expected* to do and be as 'literate' subjects within school settings.

Out-of-school studies of students' literacies are not, however, interested in *privileging* non-school literacies over school literacies. This research approach recognizes the very real impact and importance of students being able to navigate and produce polished and successful school literacies. Hence, it neither relies on home literacy practices as barometers of school success nor takes school literacy as a benchmark for evaluating students' out-of-school practices. Moreover, a focus on out-of-school literacies does not limit these literacies to home or community settings alone. Out-of-school literacies – particularly those associated with popular youth culture – can be and are brought into classrooms (cf. Alvermann, et al., 1998; Mahiri, 2003), just as school literacies can be and are brought into homes and communities (Street, 1997; Volk and de Acosta, 2001).

The concept of 'practice', in the sense of 'a recurrent, goal-directed sequence of activities using a particular technology and particular systems of knowledge' (Scribner and Cole, 1981: 236, cited in Hull and Schultz, 2002: 20), is integral to studying out-of-school (and in-school) literacies. A concern with literacy *practice* always takes into account knowing *and* doing, and calls into play the notion of *literacies* as a way of describing how people negotiate and construct patterned and socially recognizable ways of knowing, doing and using language to achieve different social and cultural purposes within different social and cultural contexts (Gee, 2001; Lankshear, 1997; Lankshear and Knobel, 2003). The account of Jacques (Knobel, 1999) provides a case in point. Jacques was a young adolescent with a long history of school literacy failure. He could nonetheless participate very successfully in diverse out-of-school practices – including the world of work – and manage the texts these practices entailed (e.g. estimating square metres of gravel needed for surfacing a road, writing a flyer advertising his lawn mowing business). He also participated 'fluently' as an active Jehovah's Witness. This required quite different literate practices and understandings from those employed within the family's earthmoving business (e.g. witnessing every Saturday morning, attending theocratic school, presenting Bible exegesis to large audiences) (see Knobel, 1999; 2001).

Studies of students' out-of-school literacies pursue a diverse range of purposes. These include:

- exploring negotiated gendered identities and practices (e.g. Finders, 1997; Schultz, 1996; 2002)
- mapping multilingual negotiations of identity and cultural, religious and school discourses (Sarroub, 2002; Skilton-Sylvester, 2002)
- documenting the literacy practices of students belonging to marginal youth groups (e.g. gangsters) or youth deemed 'at risk' of failing school (e.g. Moje, 2000; Schultz, 2002)
- investigating differential literacy education outcomes for a range of often-silenced or overlooked children – such as those from white, working-class homes, from marginal ethnic groups, or excluded from school (e.g. Heath, 1983; Hicks, 2002; Pahl, 2002)

- alerting teachers to the literacies in which students are already proficient but which may not have been accommodated in class (Heath, 1983; Pahl, 2002; Volk and de Acosta, 2001)
- undertaking exploratory studies that simply want to know what students do and be with literacy outside school settings (e.g. Knobel, 1999; Moje, 2000; Schultz, 2002).

Such studies often pursue multiple purposes.

Some researchers might argue that studies of children's literacy in after-school programmes should be included within this set of studies (e.g. Hull and Schultz, 2001). We do not engage with such studies here because the programmes concerned with literacy that have been reported tend to be adjuncts to school literacy and, thus, fall outside the scope of our interest here. (Useful introductions to such studies can, for example, be found in Alvermann, 2001; Cole, 1996; Heath and McLaughlin, 1994; Hull and Schultz, 2002.)

RESEARCHING VERY YOUNG STUDENTS' OUT-OF-SCHOOL LITERACIES

Having discussed out-of-school literacy studies involving school-aged children in general, we focus in the remainder of this chapter on out-of-school literacy studies involving young school children. Hull and Schultz report that to their knowledge, no review other than their own of out-of-school literacy research has been conducted (2001; 2002; see also Schultz, 2002). Our search for out-of-school literacy research in the early years bears witness to their claim. Hull and Schultz located close to 50 out-of-school studies across the US, England, Wales, Australia, Mexico, and South Africa. Only one of the studies listed by Hull and Schultz dealt with children eight years old or younger. This was Shirley Brice Heath's classic ethnography of three communities and their literacy practices (Heath, 1982; 1983). Our own review of the literature indicates that out-of-school literacy practices involving children aged eight or younger is a strikingly under-researched area. We found just four exemplary out-of-school literacy studies that focus on documenting in detail young children's everyday lives and their literacy practices (Heath, 1982; 1983; Hicks, 2002; Volk and de Acosta, 2001; Pahl, 2002). These are summarized in Table 5.2 and are described in turn below.

Ways with words

Since Heath's study is summarized elsewhere in this volume (e.g. by Cairney), we will note only

Table 5.2 *Summary overview of four out-of-school studies of young children's literacy practices*

Study	Research design	Participants and location	Duration	Framing theories	Principal concepts
Heath (1982; 1983)	Ethnography	Three communities (working-class African-American, working-class white, middle class); Piedmont Carolinas, USA	10 years +	Ethnography of communication, sociocultural theory, language development theory	Literacy events, ways with words, language habits, patterns, communicative interactions
Volk and de Acosta (2001)	Multiple ethnographic case studies	Three Puerto Rican children (two aged six years, one aged five years). All were Spanish dominant and had older siblings, all belonged to Protestant churches, two were girls and one was a boy, one was a proficient reader, one was making average progress, and the third struggled. They attended the same bilingual preschool and lived in a large city in a Midwestern US state	1 year	Cultural psychology, sociocultural theory, interactional sociolinguistics	Literacy events, developing literacy, syncretic literacy, literacies, resources and resource systems, collaborative learning
Pahl (2002)	Multiple ethnographic case studies	Three boys (aged five to eight years), two of whom have been excluded from school, and one attending a school labelled 'failing'. All boys are from single-parent (mother) families, with a history of domestic violence in two of the three families. Two boys are Indian or Anglo-Indian, and one is Turkish. The study is located in England	18 months	Social semiotics, sociology, sociolinguistics	(Culturally specific) meaning making, representational resources, home pedagogies, strong and weak classification, habitus
Hicks (2002)	Multiple ethnographic case studies	Two white, working-class children living in a large US city. One boy (aged five to seven years) and his family (mother, father, two siblings). One girl (aged five to seven years) and her family (mother, grandmother and two siblings)	3 years +	Cultural psychology, New Literacy Studies, feminist poststructuralism, critical literacy,	Discourse, identity, power, emergent literacy, apprenticeship, relationship, 'doing school'

some key aspects here. Heath conducted a 10-year ethnography of three distinctly different communities in the Piedmont area of the United States. Roadville was a white, working-class community; Trackton was a relatively new African-American community of mill workers and their families; while Maintown was a middle-class community (Heath, 1982: 49). This study was largely a consequence of school desegregation in the late 1960s, when many teachers were unsure of how to teach culturally and linguistically diverse students (Heath, 1983: i). It was also motivated by research reporting patterns of low school achievement for children from working-class homes.

Heath found that the ways of speaking, reading, writing and listening in each of these communities differed markedly. Only the middle-class community in Maintown participated in language practices that were overtly valued and taken up in school (e.g. knowing fairytales and being able to write fantasy stories, asking a question whose answer was known to both the asker and the respondent) and which clearly prepared these middle-class children for operating relatively seamlessly at school.

In contrast, children growing up in Roadville were apprenticed to reading, writing and speaking practices that valued factual information over fiction. Invented stories were regarded generally as lies, and although parents did read bedtime stories to their children prior to school, their engagement with the text emphasized factual or literal engagement, rather than imaginative predictions or innovations on the text. Children were inducted into storytelling by means of factual recounts prescripted for them by their parents. Roadville students did well in the beginning of their first year of schooling, until the teacher began to expect more independent, abstract and creative work which they were unable to carry out successfully.

Children growing up in Trackton were taught from a very young age to be independent and to hold their own in oral engagements with children and adults alike. Thus, young Trackton children were heard playing with words, inventing rhymes, crafting elaborate oral narratives featuring family members and friends, linking seemingly unrelated events in skilfully metaphorical ways, and engaging in witty repartee and teasing word plays with adults and peers. Heath, however, aptly demonstrates how few of these literacies were made space for in the grade 1 curriculum and shows how Trackton children were confused by school practices such as labelling exercises, by 'once upon a time' stories, by item identification worksheets, and by unfamiliar question forms used at school (such as 'what-explanations') (1982: 69). Heath's study confronted taken-for-granted assumptions that children from working-class

families did not engage in rich literacy experiences at home or in their communities. It also called for educators to rethink the ways of speaking, reading, writing and listening they valued most in class, and to make greater efforts to accommodate different ways of being literate, such as those demonstrated by the Roadville and Trackton children.

Collaborative literacy practices and siblings' home–school mediation

Dinah Volk and Martha de Acosta (2001) conducted ethnographic case studies of three Puerto Rican children (two aged six years, one aged five years) and their everyday lives in a working-class area of a large city in a Midwestern US state. All three were 'Spanish dominant', had older siblings, and belonged to Protestant churches. Two were girls. One of the three was a proficient reader, one was making average progress, and the third was struggling with reading. All attended the same bilingual preschool. The study purpose was to address the question: 'What counts as literacy in the bilingual classroom, homes and churches of three Spanish dominant, mainland Puerto Rican children?' (2001: 194). The researchers also hoped to identify what could be learned from the data to usefully inform classroom teaching.

Volk and de Acosta used their study findings to critique research that focuses *solely* on parent–child interactions, thereby missing 'the complexity and richness' of wider support networks and literacy practices occurring within the everyday lives of these children (2001: 216). Older siblings particularly were found to play an important mediating role between home and school for the three focus children. Volk and de Acosta also found that adult members of each child's support network drew directly on their own personal school experiences to help the child with his or her homework. Given traditional approaches to Spanish teaching in Puerto Rico, this literacy support often focused on letter names and sounds rather than on meaning making (Spanish being a highly phonetic language) (2001: 217). Volk and de Acosta also found a direct contrast between the literacies promoted at church – which entailed memorization, repetition, group oral recitation and reading the Bible (and were *not* open to negotiated interpretations) – and the literacy practices promoted in the children's kindergarten class. The latter emphasized 'questioning, individual pleasure, and constructing meaning' from texts (2001: 217). Nevertheless, Volk and de Acosta suggest that far from encouraging rote learning and passivity, church literacy practices and adult help with homework served to induct all three children into literacy learning by enrolling them as '[a]ctive participants with more competent others' in learning 'the language and behaviors valued in many class-rooms' (2001: 218). They argue that the literacy practices of home blended literacy practices valued in schools with practices valued in their churches and in so doing created 'collaborative literacy prac-tices rooted in their culture' (2001: 220).

Interestingly, Volk and de Acosta found that what counted as literacy at home and at church was 'pri-marily social interactions with familiar texts contain-ing significant and useful knowledge' (2001: 219). In contrast, what counted as literacy in school 'was a progression from social to individual interactions with print' (2001: 219–20). Thus, literacy events at home and at church tended to be much more collab-orative than at school, despite the kindergarten teacher's overt interest in group learning and mean-ing making. Volk and de Acosta call on teachers to make explicit to themselves and to families the ways in which they define literacy in their classrooms, and to recognize the out-of-school literacies in which their students engage as significant resources to draw on in classroom-based teaching.

The production of non-schooled texts

Kate Pahl (2002) focuses explicitly on three young boys' text production practices at home, to help inform the development of home-based pedagogies that take account of a wide range of text making processes and conditions. She was especially inter-ested in documenting texts that were so 'localized and so specific' – ephemeral, even – that they would not be recognized as texts by teachers, yet nonetheless demonstrated literate understandings and resourceful improvisation in relation to text production and meaning making (2002: 150). The study participants were aged five to eight years. Two had been excluded from school. One was attending a school labelled 'failing'. All boys were from single-parent (mother) families. Two of the families had histories of domestic violence. Two boys were Indian or Anglo-Indian, and one was Turkish. The study was conducted in England.

Sol (six years old) devoted his time to drawing Pokémon characters and scenes and creating his own Pokémon trading cards, inventing new Poké-mon characters in the process (Pokémon creatures are evolving hybrids that hail from insect, dinosaur and animal worlds). He also made tiny Pokémon-related figures from modelling clay (Fimo). His mother liked to display these neatly but Sol pre-ferred to play with them all over the house.

Fatih (five years old) was a keen drawer and story writer, and drew on a range of influences, like Pokémon, Nintendo's Super Mario video games,

his mother's prayer practices, and 'his own internal landscape of birds and chickens' (2002: 152). Pahl referred to Fatih's literacy practices as syncretic because 'they combined practices from Turkey such as ways of speaking, being, acting, with practices learned in English playgrounds' (2002: 152; see also Kenner and Gregory, and Gregory and Kenner, in this volume).

Edward (eight years old) produced a range of texts, including detailed images of trains and his grandmother's farm in Wales. His great-grandfather had helped build the Indian railways and the family maintained a deep interest in trains – which included numerous models in glass-fronted cabinets in their home. Pahl identified family-oriented resources, like family narratives about farm life, trains and other family experiences, as key iterative resources in Edward's meaning making – rather than, say, popular culture resources.

Besides written and drawn texts, Pahl also docu-ments a range of what she calls 'ephemeral' texts. She argues that these tell as much, if not more, about these three boys' literate understandings as more conventionally recognized texts. These ephemeral texts 'had a necessarily short life as they were hastily constituted, often out of bits of food, old tissues, or anything to hand' (2002: 159). For example, Fatih and his mother regularly used her prayer beads to create – and discuss – outline 'maps' of countries (such as Turkey and England). Pahl argues that researchers do not pay sufficient attention to 'momentary texts' and the literate understandings they reveal. She also discusses dif-ferent ways in which these three families classified text productions (e.g. as things to display, as 'mess', as play). On this basis she calls for researchers to pay closer attention to 'children's meaning making in the home as [being] intimately connected with the space in which it is produced' (2002: 164), to better understand the complexities of young children's meaning making practices. This under-standing can then be brought to bear on articulating a 'home pedagogy' that is tied to the 'aesthetic and moral dimensions' of the home (2002: 165).

Working-class children and their rocky navigation of home and school discourses

Deborah Hicks' ethnographic case study of two white, working-class children living in a large US city focuses on Laurie (female) and Jake (male). Both were five years old at the start of Hicks' three-year study and in the same preschool and primary school classes. Laurie lived with her mother, grandmother and younger brother and sister. Her family had regular financial and childcare worries and was marked by Laurie's loving, but troubled, relationship with her mother and younger sister. Jake lived with his mother and father and two siblings (one older, one younger). He had a particularly strong relationship with his father, and they shared a passion for car racing. Both children demonstrated effective emergent literacy understandings in preschool, but struggled increasingly with literacy as they moved into higher grades.

Hicks' study was partly a reaction to literacy research in the US that has tended to focus on ethnicity and to downplay issues associated with class. She also wanted to advocate on behalf of these two children, their families and teachers (and others like them), and to contribute to educational change for the better, if only on a small scale. With Laurie, advocacy involved Hicks providing specialized tutoring in reading and writing at home. In Jake's case, Hicks made her research findings available to Jake's mother to be used in parent–teacher conferences, and to argue for self-paced, individualized instruction for Jake instead of the rigid, lockstepped instruction that characterized the middle primary grades at his school.

Hicks' study introduces Laurie as a vibrant young girl whose out-of-school life at five years old was filled with imaginary travel to exotic places, mythical beasts, and the desire for a prince (in the form of a loving father) to come and rescue her and her family. Laurie appeared to be a confident emergent reader and writer at home and in kindergarten, and often voiced her plans to be a writer and an artist as an adult. Indeed, Laurie's exuberant understanding of story structure and book language, letter identification and other demonstrated text capabilities suggested she would encounter no academic difficulties in moving from kindergarten to grade 1. By the middle of grade 1, however, Laurie had fallen seriously behind her classmates in reading and writing and required remedial intervention at school. Her escalating academic difficulties were compounded by several factors. The school's reading programme did not match her reading progression. She had difficulty understanding and participating in school/academic practices (for example, when using a letter identification worksheet she painstakingly copied the word stem rather than providing the letter that preceded the stem to make a word). She experienced stresses at home and within the process of negotiating conflicts between what it meant to be a girl at home and a girl at school. Laurie had also been 'acquired by' (2002: 68) an attention deficit disorder in kindergarten, largely on account of her uncontrollable angry outbursts that were often associated with difficulties she was experiencing at home. Pathologizing Laurie's emotions had a profound impact on her personality and school experiences. She was medicated daily, and became depressed and withdrawn at home and school. She also suffered from physical side effects from the medication that plagued her at school: 'I don't feel so good ... 'cause them dumb pills make my stomach hurt' (2002: 64). She increasingly resisted participating in literacy lessons (e.g. tuning out, shrugging sulkily in response to a teacher's question), but at the same time wanted to be a well-behaved student. (Hicks associated Laurie's wish to be well behaved with attempts to compensate for not being a 'good' reader, and as a bid for some degree of power and agency in a setting in which Laurie found herself increasingly powerless and helpless.) Despite Hicks' best efforts, Laurie quickly became a 'disabled reader' at school where reading was defined according to 'grade level expectations' (2002: 75).

Jake's at-home practices showed him as keenly involved in a wide range of literacy practices, and his family regarded him as a 'gifted learner'. Hicks' study of Jake's school literacy practices, however, reveal deep 'dissonances between institutional practices of schooling and working-class values' (2002: 99). At home, Jake moved freely and confidently between a range of literacy-related activities that involved learning by doing ('rather than by talking about parts of a task'; 2002: 99), linking texts to three-dimensional objects (e.g. car racing magazines with his model cars), working collaboratively with his father in building or fixing things needed by the family, being read to by his grandmother, reading or recalling facts from information texts (e.g. on US presidents), and the like. His home was filled with books and magazines. Jake's grandmother and mother were avid readers of novels, and his father was a self-described voracious reader of information texts. Jake had a large collection of children's books (some with supplementary sight word flashcards), along with racing car magazines, and a range of action-oriented video games which he used regularly.

Jake – like his father – was constantly in motion at home and his literacy practices generally involved loud sound effects and whole-body engagement (especially when playing video games). He was also capable of sustained attention to stories, or to engaging in an activity that interested him. Jake's father was particularly influential in his life: a self-taught man who had dropped out of school in grade 9, but who had subsequently – through reading and apprenticeships – become a successful mechanical contractor and a gifted carpenter. Jake was used to working alongside his father (he even had his own powersaw and workspace in his father's home workshop). His father had a huge collection of miniature replicas of racing cars. Jake also had a growing collection. As 'early as his kindergarten year Jake could identify each NASCAR vehicle and its driver by "reading" such details as racing colors and insignia, the shape of different cars and print' (2002: 103). Halfway through the study, Jake was named vice-president of the family's new business and role-played for Hicks how he spoke with clients over the phone.

Jake, however, increasingly experienced troubles with school literacies in grades 1 and 2. He was required to remain seated for long periods of time to complete segmented tasks (e.g. putting spelling words into sentences), to discuss or explain tasks already completed, to engage in abstract, two-dimensional pencil and paper exercises, and so on. These differed greatly from how he accomplished things at home. Hicks watched as Jake increasingly tuned out of lessons – especially reading lessons – and became more and more angrily frustrated with the lockstepped nature of the school's reading programme and the tasks required of him. As one example among many, Hicks recounts Jake's response to a story mapping exercise where he was required to plot information from a story onto a worksheet:

> Jake seemed perplexed. 'I'm not sure what it is,' he commented in frustration. 'What *what* is?' I asked, trying to figure out how he was responding to the story map activity. 'This *paper*,' he said. (Hicks, 2002: 118, original emphases)

For Jake, tasks needed to be meaningful. However, he found many school tasks to be, in his words, just plain 'stupid' and 'dumb' (2002: 104).

Jake – like Laurie – fared somewhat better in the increased reading and writing freedom available in grade 2 and began to write more and longer narratives across the year. These texts invariably dealt with a range of boyhood identities – from playing baseball with his baby brother 'just like the big boys' (2002: 127), to car racing, through to family events such as trips away and outings in a boat. Jake seemed to find space in this classroom to connect his out-of-school 'life worlds' and the discourses of masculinity he was apprenticed to in his everyday life at home with school-valued writing practices (2002: 131). In grade 3, however, he was not allowed to work at his own pace in reading and writing, and – like Laurie – fell further and further behind his classmates. As Jake moved through primary school, he became increasingly resistant to what he perceived as 'dumb' school literacies practised in his classroom.

A key theme running through Hicks' study is 'the ways in which material relations and attachments with others shape early practices of reading' (2002: 41). The cases of Laurie and Jake clearly show the importance and influence of home-based relationships and experiences in these young children's lives. For example, Laurie's need for stable and unconditional relationships in her life translated into utopian stories about family and friends (especially fictional stories that cast her as a flowergirl at her mother's wedding). Jake's out-of-school experiences translated into a preference for reading information texts like his father did at home, and for writing factual recounts about his family. For Hicks, understanding children's literacy practices and abilities at home and school cannot discount the importance of family and class values, parent–child relationships, and the ways in which these are taken up, made room for, or excluded in classrooms.

DISCUSSION

Our summaries have not done justice to the detailed descriptions and analyses of the young children and their literacy practices presented in the four studies. They do, however, indicate the significant contributions such studies can make to understanding the rich and complex literacy practices in which children engage within their everyday lives: notably, children regarded officially as 'literacy failures', or as *not having* 'literacy' at home. These studies demonstrate ways in which literacy practices are always deeply *social:* embedded in and constituting an array of familial, community and school relationships.

Our personal interest in and commitment to the kinds of studies falling within quadrant 3 of our matrix in Table 5.1 stem from their potential to challenge narrow *scholastic* conceptions of literacies that become a basis for allocating and withholding school success in inequitable ways. We also find hope in these studies for informing classroom practice by alerting teachers to young children's existing understandings of and facility with roles and effects of literacy in social contexts, and for suggesting how best to build on these understandings and capabilities in classrooms. This is especially important with regard to studies documenting everyday literacy practices of marginalized children – whether this marginalization is in terms of class, academic performance, gender, behaviour, religion, home language, ethnicity, and so on. Out-of-school studies of young children's literacy practices can also alert researchers and educators to the *complexities* associated with becoming 'school literate' and fluent in school discourses – as exemplified by Laurie's diagnosed 'attention deficit' in Hicks' study, and by the siblings and their mediation-initiation roles studied by Volk and de Acosta.

We are particularly interested in the ways such studies can make young children's 'invisible literacies' visible. Pahl's study of ephemeral texts is a case in point. So is Hicks' account of Jake's information text reading at home. Church-related literacies clearly impact on children's conceptions of texts and meaning making, as Heath's and Volk and de Acosta's respective studies show. Heath's (1983) accounts of Lem's poetic ways with words remain a research exemplar in the way they document what would otherwise be hidden to Lem's white, middle-class teachers when he began school. Lem was a young African-American boy living in Trackton who had been successfully apprenticed to clever word plays and oral language uses of his community. At two and one-half years of age, Lem drew on his church-going experiences in response to hearing a distant bell ring while playing on the front verandah of his house:

Way Far
Now
It a church bell
Ringin'
Dey singin'
  ringin'
You hear it?
I hear it
Far
Now
(1983: 170)

At three years of age he responded to his mother's playful threat to tie him to the railway tracks if he did not keep his shoes on by saying:

Railroad track
Train all big 'n black
On dat track, on dat track, on dat track
Ain't no way I can't get back
Back from dat track
Back from dat train
Big 'n black, I be back
(1983: 110)

Making such language and practices visible may encourage teachers to reconsider the ways 'literacy' is defined in their classrooms, and their own roles in sustaining these definitions. Teachers may also thereby be encouraged to rethink deficit theories that readily associate poor or ethnically marginal children with school literacy failure.

Given the value of these studies, we are left wondering why there is a relative absence of ethnographic-type out-of-school investigations of young children's everyday literacy practices (cf. Hull and Schultz, 2001). Perhaps the answer lies in difficulties regularly encountered in researching young children's practices. Hicks, for example, recounts problems associated with interviewing kindergarten children: 'A few children expressed their response to our request that they reflect on their kindergarten learning experiences by breaking out into song and dance. Others sat stiffly, responding as though they were on a television talk show' (2002: 107). Another difficulty lies in the need for conducting relatively long-term studies in order to better capture the complexities of young children's literacies (Hicks, 2002; Pahl, 2002).

Nonetheless, we detect an increase over the past few years in published out-of-school studies of young children's literacy practices. We hope this indicates an informed and critical response by researchers to the increasingly constricted and test-based conceptions of literacy evident in schools in the US, England, Australia and elsewhere: that researchers are turning to detailed and contextualized accounts of young children's literacies in order to challenge what counts as literacy 'success' and 'failure' at school.

CONCLUSION

Out-of-school literacy studies relying on ethnographic investigation of young children's everyday practices cannot be generalized to wider populations. This, however, is not to deny their theoretical and pedagogical value beyond the scope set by each study. Quite the reverse. Out-of-school studies have enormous value through their *resonances* with other researchers' findings, with teachers' in-class experiences with particular students, and with families' experiences of school–home relationships.

For example, the resonances between Jake in Deborah Hicks' (2002) study and the case of Jacques mentioned previously (see Knobel, 1999; 2001) are uncanny, notwithstanding differences in *age* (Jake was aged five to seven years during the span of Hicks' study, while Jacques was 13 at the start of Knobel's study), *location and citizenship* (Jake was North American, Jacques Australian), and *schooling* (Jake was at the start of his formal primary school, Jacques at the end of his). Both boys shared painful histories of literacy failure and resistance at school (interestingly enough, both feigned sleep during lessons that made no sense to them). Both were extremely independent, active and capable outside school – sharing particularly close 'working' and family relationships with their fathers who each owned his own trades-based business. And both demonstrated they were highly competent in diverse literacy practices out of school.

Other patterns of resonance can be found in the 'synergistic' and ephemeral texts produced by Fatih and his mother – and which were tied to the identities of both – in Pahl's (2002) study and in Loukia Sarroub's (2002) study of the 'in-between literacies' that devout Muslim, Yemeni-American teenage girls used in negotiating home and school worlds. The identity work carried out by Laurie in her textual practices and resistances (Hicks, 2002) resonates with the identity work that young, female, middle-school students call into play via their language use at home and school in Margaret Finder's (1997) study of gender, literacy and adolescence.

Such patterns and similarities across out-of-school studies sound a call to action for researchers and educators alike to pay close attention to students' out-of-school lives. This will help educators build on students' literacy strengths in meaningful and ultimately successful ways, to minimize school experiences such as those endured by children like Laurie and Jake, and to recognize that complex, synergistic relationships exist among home and school discourses – such that one cannot be considered without the other when access to equitable literacy education is at stake.

REFERENCES

Alvermann, D. (2001) 'Reading adolescents' reading identities: looking back to see ahead', *Journal of Adolescent and Adult Literacy*, 44 (8): 676–95.

Alvermann, D., Hinchman, K., Moore, D., Phelps, S. and Waff, D. (eds) (1998) *Reconceptualizing the Literacies in Adolescents' Lives*. Cambridge, MA: MIT Press.

Arthur, L. (2001) 'Popular culture and early literacy learning', *Contemporary Issues in Early Childhood*, 2 (3): 295–308.

Arthur, L., Beecher, B. and Jones Diaz, C. (2001) 'Early literacy: congruence and incongruence between home and early childhood settings', in M. Kalantzis (ed.), *Languages of Learning: Changing Communication and Changing Literacy Teaching*. Melbourne: Common Ground. pp. 65–73.

Barton, D. (1997) 'Family literacy programs and home literacy practices', in D. Taylor (ed.), *Many Families, Many Literacies*. Portsmouth, NH: Heinemann. pp. 101–9.

Barton, D. and Hamilton, M. (1998) *Local Literacies*. London: Routledge.

Bloome, D., Katz, L., Solsken, J., Willett, J. and Wilson-Keenan, J. (2000) 'Interpellations of family/community and classroom literacy practices', *The Journal of Educational Research*, 93 (3): 155–64.

Breen, M., Louden, W., Barratt-Pugh, C., Rivalland, J., Ruhl, M., Rhydwen, M., Lloyd, S. and Carr, T. (1994) *Literacy in its Place: an Investigation of Literacy Practices in Urban and Rural Communities*, vols 1 and 2. Canberra: Department of Employment, Education and Training.

Breier, M., Taetsane, M. and Sait, L. (1996) 'Taking literacy for a ride: – reading and writing in the taxi industry', in M. Prinsloo and M. Breier (eds), *The Social Uses of Literacy: Theory and Practice in Contemporary South Africa*. Bertsham, South Africa: Sached and Benjamins. pp. 213–34.

Britto, P. (2000) 'Family literacy environments and young children's emerging literacy skills'. Unpublished doctoral dissertation, Columbia University, New York.

Cairney, T. (2002) 'Bridging home and school literacy: in search of transformative approaches to curriculum', *Early Childhood Development and Care*, 172 (2): 153–72.

Cairney, T. and Ruge, J. (1998) *Community Literacy Practices and Schooling: Towards Effective Support for Students*. Canberra: Language Australia.

Camitta, M. (1993) 'Vernacular writing: varieties of literacy among Philadelphia high school students', in B. Street (ed.), *Cross-Cultural Approaches to Literacy*. Cambridge: Cambridge University Press. pp. 228–46.

Carrington, V. (2001) 'Emergent home literacies: a challenge for educators', *Australian Journal of Language and Literacy*, 24 (2): 88–100.

China, A. and Robins, S. (1996) '"We can all sing, but we can't all talk": literacy brokers and *tsotsi* gangsters in a Cape Town shantytown', in M. Prinsloo and M. Breier (eds), *The Social Uses of Literacy: Theory and Practice in Contemporary South Africa*. Bertsham, South Africa: Sached and Benjamins. pp. 157–72.

Cole, M. (1996) *Cultural Psychology: a Once and Future Discipline*. Cambridge, MA: Harvard University Press.

Cook-Gumperz, J. and Hanna, K. (1997) 'Nurses' work, women's work: some recent issues of professional literacy and practice', in G. Hull (ed.), *Changing Work, Changing Workers: Critical Perspectives on Language, Literacy, and Skills*. Albany, NY: State University of New York Press. pp. 316–34.

Cook-Gumperz, J. and Keller-Cohen, D. (1993) 'Alternative literacies in school and beyond: multiple literacies of speaking and writing', *Anthropology and Education Quarterly*, 24 (4): 283–7.

Cushman, E. (1998) *The Struggle and the Tools: Oral and Literate Strategies in an Inner City Community*. Albany, NY: State University of New York Press.

Drury, R. (2000) 'Bilingual children in the pre-school years: different experiences of early learning', in R. Drury, L. Miller and R. Campbell (eds), *Looking at Early Years Education and Care*. London: Fulton. pp. 81–91.

Dyson, A. (2001) 'Where are the childhoods in childhood literacy? An exploration in outer (school) space', *Journal of Early Childhood Literacy*, 1 (1): 9–39.

Finders, M. (1997) *Just Girls: Hidden Literacies and Life in Junior High*. New York: Teachers College Press.

Fishman, A. (1988) *Amish Literacy: What and How it Means*. Portsmouth, NH: Heinemann.

Freebody, P., Ludwig, C. and Gunn, S. (1995) *Everyday Literacies In and Out of School in Low Socioeconomic Status Urban Communities*, vols. 1 and 2. Canberra: Department of Employment, Education and Training.

Gee, J. (1991) 'Discourse systems and aspirin bottles: on literacy', in C. Mitchell and K. Weiler (eds), *Rewriting Literacy: Culture and the Discourse of the Other*. New York: Bergin and Garvey. pp. 121–35.

Gee, J. (1996) *Social Linguistics and Literacies: Ideology in Discourses*, 2nd edn. London: Falmer.

Gee, J. (2001) 'Reading as situated language: a sociocognitive perspective', *Journal of Adolescent and Adult Literacy*, 44 (8): 714–25.

Gee, J., Hull, G. and Lankshear, C. (1996) *The New Work Order: Behind the Language of the New Capitalism*. Sydney: Allen and Unwin.

Gibson, D. (1996) 'Literacy, knowledge, gender and power in the workplace on three farms in the Western Cape', in M. Prinsloo and M. Breier (eds), *The Social Uses of Literacy: Theory and Practice in Contemporary South Africa*. Bertsham, South Africa: Sached and Benjamins. pp. 49–64.

Gillen, J. (2002) 'Moves in the territory of literacy? The telephone discourse of three- and four-year-olds', *Journal of Early Childhood Literacy*, 2 (1): 21–44.

Gilmore, P. (1991) '"Gimme room": school resistance, attitude, and access to literacy', in C. Mitchell and K. Weiler (eds), *Rewriting Literacy: Culture and the Discourse of the Other*. New York: Bergin and Garvey. pp. 57–76.

Gilmore, P. and Glatthorn, A. (eds) (1982) *Children In and Out of School*. Washington, DC: Center for Applied Linguistics.

Gowen, S. (1992) *The Politics of Workplace Literacy: a Case Study*. New York: Teachers College Press.

Gregory, E. (2001) 'Sisters and brothers as language and literacy teachers: synergy between siblings playing and working together', *Journal of Early Childhood Literacy*, 1 (3): 301–22.

Guerra, J. and Farr, M. (2002) 'Writing on the margins: the spiritual and autobiographical discourse of two *Mexicanas* in Chicago', in G. Hull and K. Schultz (eds), *School's Out! Bridging Out-of-School Literacies with Classroom Practice*. New York: Teachers College Press. pp. 96–123.

Gumperz, J. (1982) *Language and Social Identity*. Cambridge, MA: Cambridge University Press.

Hannon, P. (1995) *Literacy, Home, and School: Research and Practice in Teaching Literacy with Parents*. London: Falmer.

Hardman, M. and Jones, L. (1999) 'Sharing books with babies: evaluation of an early literacy intervention', *Educational Review*, 51 (3): 221–9.

Heath, S. (1982) 'What no bedtime story means: narrative skills at home and school', *Language and Society*, 11: 49–76.

Heath, S. (1983) *Ways with Words: Language, Life and Work in Community and Classrooms*. Cambridge, MA: Cambridge University Press.

Heath, S. and McLaughlin, M. (1994) 'Learning for anything everyday', *Journal of Curriculum Studies*, 26 (5): 471–89.

Heller, C. (1997) *Until We Are Strong Together: Women Writers in the Tenderloin*. New York: Teachers College Press.

Hicks, D. (2002) *Reading Lives: Working-Class Children and Literacy Learning*. New York: Teachers College Press.

Hill, S., Comber, B., Louden, W., Rivalland, J. and Reid, J. (1998) *100 Children Go to School: Connections and Disconnections in the Year Prior to School and the First Year of School*, vols 1–3. Canberra: Department of Employment, Education, Training and Youth Affairs.

Hull, G. (ed.) (1997) *Changing Work, Changing Workers: Critical Perspectives on Language, Literacy, and Skills*. Albany, NY: State University of New York Press.

Hull, G. and Schultz, K. (2001) 'Literacy and learning out of school: a review of theory and research', *Review of Educational Research*, 71 (4): 575–611.

Hull, G. and Schultz, K. (2002) 'Negotiating the boundaries between school and non-school literacies', in G. Hull and K. Schultz (eds), *School's Out! Bridging Out-of-School Literacies with Classroom Practice*. New York: Teachers College Press. pp. 1–10.

Hymes, D. (1972) 'Toward ethnographies of communication', in P. Giglioli (ed.), *Language and Social Context*. Harmondsworth: Penguin. pp. 21–44.

Janes, H. and Kermani, H. (2001) 'Caregivers' story reading to young children in family literacy programs: pleasure or punishment?', *Journal of Adolescent and Adult Literacy*, 44 (5): 458–67.

Jones, K. (2001) 'Becoming just another alphanumeric code: farmers' encounters with the literacy and discourse practices of agricultural bureaucracy at the livestock auction', in D. Barton, M. Hamilton and R. Ivanic (eds), *Situated Literacies: Reading and Writing in Context*. London: Routledge. pp. 70–90.

Jones Diaz, C., Arthur, L., Beecher, B. and McNaught, M. (2000) 'Multiple literacies in early childhood: what do families and communities think about their children's early literacy learning?', *Australian Journal of Language and Literacy*, 23 (3): 230–44.

Jordan, G., Snow, C. and Porche, M. (2000) 'Project EASE: the effect of a family literacy project on kindergarten students' early literacy skills', *Reading Research Quarterly*, 35 (4): 524–48.

Kalman, J. (1999) *Writing on the Plaza: Mediated Literacy Practices among Scribes and Clients in Mexico City*. Cresskill, NH: Hampton.

Kapitzke, C. (1995) *Literacy and Religion: the Textual Politics and Practice of Seventh-Day Adventism*. Amsterdam: Benjamins.

Kell, C. (1996) 'Literacy practices in an informal settlement in the Cape Peninsula', in M. Prinsloo and M. Breier (eds), *The Social Uses of Literacy: Theory and Practice in Contemporary South Africa*. Bertsham, South Africa: Sached and Benjamins. pp. 235–56.

Kenner, C. (2000) 'Biliteracy in a monolingual school system? English and Gujarati in South London', *Language, Culture and Curriculum*, 13 (1): 13–30.

Knobel, M. (1999) *Everyday Literacies: Students, Discourse and Social Practices*. New York: Lang.

Knobel, M. (2001) '"I'm not a pencil man": how one student challenges our notions of literacy "failure" in school', *Journal of Adolescent and Adult Literacy*, 44 (5): 404–19.

Kress, G. and van Leeuwen, T. (1996) *Reading Images: the Grammar of Visual Design*. London: Routledge.

Lankshear, C. (1987) *Literacy, Schooling and Revolution*. London: Falmer.

Lankshear, C. (1997) *Changing Literacies*. Buckingham: Open University Press.

Lankshear, C. and Knobel, M. (2003) *New Literacies: Changing Knowledge and Classroom Learning*. Buckingham: Open University Press.

McCarthey, S. (1997) 'Connecting home and school literacy practices in classrooms with diverse populations', *Journal of Literacy Research*, 29 (2): 145–82.

McClain, V. (2000) 'Lisa and her mom: finding success in reading the world', *Language Arts*, 78 (1): 21–9.

Mahiri, J. (ed.) (2003) *What They Don't Learn in School: Literacy in the Lives of Urban Youth*. New York: Lang.

Martens, P. (1999) '"Mommy, how do you write 'Sarah'?": the role of name writing in one child's literacy', *Journal of Research in Childhood Education*, 14 (1): 5–15.

Moje, E. (2000) '"To be part of the story": The literacy practices of gangsta adolescents', *Teachers College Record*, 102 (3): 651–90.

Moss, G. (2001) 'Seeing with the camera: analysing children's photographs of literacy in the home', *Journal of Research in Reading*, 24 (3): 279–92.

Mulhern, M. (1997) 'Doing his own thing: a Mexican-American kindergartner becomes literate at home and school', *Language Arts*, 74 (6): 468–76.

Nason, P. (1997) 'Telling tales out of school: the construction of parental literacy in school culture', *School Leadership and Management*, 17 (1): 117–24.

Neuman, S. and Celano, D. (2001) 'Access to print in low-income and middle-income communities', *Reading Research Quarterly*, 36 (1): 8–27.

Pahl, K. (2002) 'Ephemera, mess and miscellaneous piles: texts and practices in families', *Journal of Early Childhood Literacy*, 2 (2): 145–66.

Parke, T., Drury, R., Kenner, C. and Robertson, L. (2002) 'Revealing invisible worlds: connecting the mainstream with bilingual children's home and community learning', *Journal of Early Childhood Literacy*, 2 (2): 195–220.

Prinsloo, M. and Breier, M. (eds), (1996a) *The Social Uses of Literacy: Theory and Practice in Contemporary South Africa*. Bertsham, South Africa: Sached and Benjamins.

Prinsloo, M. and Breier, M. (1996b) 'Introduction', in M. Prinsloo and M. Breier (eds), *The Social Uses of Literacy: Theory and Practice in Contemporary South Africa*. Bertsham, South Africa: Sached and Benjamins. pp. 11–30.

Purcell-Gates, V. (1996) 'Stories, coupons and the TV guide: relationships between home literacy experiences and emergent literacy experiences', *Reading Research Quarterly*, 31 (4): 406–28.

Purcell-Gates, V. (2000) 'Family literacy', in M. Kamil, P. Mosenthall, P. Pearson and R. Carr (eds), *Handbook of Reading Research*, vol. 3. Mahwah, NJ: Erlbaum. pp. 853–70.

Reese, L. and Gallimore, R. (2000) 'Immigrant Latinos' cultural model of literacy development: an evolving perspective on home-school discontinuities', *American Journal of Education*, 108 (2): 103–34.

Rodriguez, V. (1999) 'Home literacy experiences of three young Dominican children in New York City: implications for teaching in urban settings', *Educators for Urban Minorities*, 1 (1): 19–30.

Rogers, T., Tyson, C. and Marshall, E. (2000) 'Living dialogues in one neighbourhood: moving towards understanding across discourses and practices of literacy and schooling', *Journal of Literacy Research*, 32 (1): 1–24.

Saracho, O. (1999) 'Helping families develop emergent literacy strategies', *International Journal of Early Childhood*, 31 (2): 25–36.

Sarroub, L. (2002) 'In-betweenness: religion and conflicting visions of literacy', *Reading Research Quarterly*, 37 (2): 130–49.

Scribner, S. and Cole, M. (1981) *The Psychology of Literacy*. Cambridge, MA: Harvard University Press.

Schultz, K. (1996) 'Between school and work: the literacies of urban adolescent females', *Anthropology and Education Quarterly*, 27: 517–44.

Schultz, K. (2002) 'Looking across space and time: reconceptualizing literacy learning in and out of school', *Research in the Teaching of English*, 36 (3): 356–90.

Serpell, R. (1997) 'Literacy connections between school and home: how should we evaluate them?', *Journal of Literacy Research*, 29 (4): 587–686.

Skilton-Sylvester, E. (2002) 'Literate at home but not at school: a Cambodian girl's journey from playwright to struggling writer', in G. Hull and K. Schultz (eds), *School's Out! Bridging Out-of-School Literacies with Classroom Practice*. New York: Teachers College Press. pp. 61–95.

Smith, C. (2001) 'Click and turn the page: an exploration of multiple storybook literacy', *Reading Research Quarterly*, 36 (2): 152–83.

Street, B. (1997) 'New literacies in theory and practice: what are the implications for language in education?', *Linguistics and Education*, 10 (1): 1–24.

Taylor, D. and Dorsey-Gaines, C. (1988) *Growing Up Literate: Learning from Inner-City Families*. Portsmouth, NH: Heinemann.

Volk, D. and de Acosta, M. (2001). '"Many differing ladders, many ways to climb ...": literacy events in the bilingual classroom, homes, and community of three Puerto Rican kindergartners', *Journal of Early Childhood Literacy*, 1 (2): 193–223.

Walkerdine, V. (1990) *Schoolgirl Fictions*. New York: Verso.

Wan, G. (2000) 'A Chinese girl's storybook experience at home', *Language Arts*, 77 (5): 398–405.

Williams, A. and Gregory, E. (2001) 'Siblings bridging literacies in multilingual contexts', *Journal of Research in Reading*, 24 (3): 248–65.

Wilson, A. (2000) 'There is no escape from third-space theory: borderland discourse and the "in-between" literacies of prisons', in D. Barton, M. Hamilton and R. Ivanic (eds), *Situated Literacies: Reading and Writing in Context*. London: Routledge. pp. 54–69.

Wollman-Bonilla, J. (2001) 'Family involvement in early writing instruction', *Journal of Early Childhood Literacy*, 1 (2): 167–92.

Xu, H. (1999) 'Young Chinese ESL children's home literacy experiences', *Reading Horizons*, 40 (1): 47–55.

6

Language, Literacy and Community

PATRICIA BAQUEDANO-LÓPEZ

Every group in society shares a system of norms, preferences and expectations that organize the linguistic structure of the group's language. Children learn language (from sounds to words, to utterances, to larger discursive constructions) to express, convey, mediate, and manage action, emotions, and knowledge. Acquiring language is thus a process inextricably tied to local social, emotional, and cognitive experience. It entails learning the symbolic systems shared by members of one's cultural group that are used to classify reality in the world. This semiotic property of language is foundational for understanding form–form and form–meaning relations that are constrained by the generative[1] phonological, morphological, and syntactic principles of language. The task for children in their early childhood years is to learn the language spoken around them and learn the comportment that renders that language relevant and adequate across cultural activities. This is also part of the process of literacy development. Children must learn to develop interpretive skills mediated through language, that is, they learn to use existing knowledge in order to generate new knowledge. In this chapter I provide an overview of the work that has contributed to our understanding of the role of language in literacy development. I begin with a discussion of the social nature of language, addressing the implications for children's acquisition and use of language in context. Next, I examine the relationship between language and literacy and the task of the child in using language to develop knowledge and expertise. I conclude with a discussion of the notion of 'community', which has had a significant influence on recent research on language and early childhood literacy, especially in multicultural settings.

LANGUAGE IN ITS SOCIAL CONTEXT

For much of the latter part of the twentieth century, social theorists directed their attention to linguistic phenomena while seeking explanations of linguistic behaviour in social theory. The attention to the role of language in people's engagement with the social world has led to our current appraisal of this period of inquiry as 'the linguistic turn in social theory' (see Fairclough, 1989: 3). This turn has also been interpreted as a response to a set of 'oppositions', some of which were posited by Saussure (1966) in his *Course in General Linguistics*. Saussure had proposed two approaches to the study of language. One was the study of *langue* as the self-sufficient system of signs of a language, potentially available to all speakers of a language. The other was to study *parole*, or speech, which corresponds to the situated realization of that system of signs by a particular speaker. In this model, the expression of individual speech is only possible because there is a larger, more collective system that accounts for it. The relationship between *langue* and *parole* has shaped much of linguistic theory today, including such notions as how language works, and most relevant to this discussion, how language is acquired and used. While a focus on the structure of language is certainly necessary, we cannot disregard the relationship of this system to its speakers who are agential, culturally competent members who acquire language and use it for a number of socially relevant activities.

The distinction between these two aspects of language acquisition and use (*langue* and *parole*) has also been conceptualized as linguistic competence and performance (Chomsky, 1965). Competence refers to the knowledge of a language that speakers and hearers possess, and performance to the actual use of language in concrete situations. From this perspective, the tension between competence and performance lies in the speakers' potentiality in generating an unlimited sequence of grammatically well-formed sentences. There are many advantages to these analytical dichotomies. For one, there is an immediate applicability of the model to the detailed description of the logic and structure of grammar. Indeed, a great number of grammars have been documented and the efforts in language preservation have been most important (cf. Doggett, 1986; Celce-Murcia, 1991).[2] Another area where these structural frameworks have had an impact is in the study of early language development. In Chomsky's language model, children learning language in their communities demonstrate that the process of language acquisition is the result of the innate, and universal, knowledge of language.[3] As children develop, they actively generate hypotheses about language rules that they test against whatever linguistic input is available to them (arguably, this input is limited given the great capacity for language). Children are the best examples of competence. They learn to produce language that is a representation, or rather an instantiation, of the larger system that their linguistic and cultural communities use. Children eventually become adults who use language in creative, generative ways, continuing to display competence. In a critique of this model, Bourdieu (1977) argued that the concept of 'competence' as the capacity to generate grammatically appropriate sentences misses a much larger point. Instead of just being competent at producing sentences, speakers are competent at producing sentences *in socially appropriate ways*. The point of departure in poststructuralist approaches to the study of language lies in its construction as an inherently social phenomenon (Habermas, 1984/1987; 1987), even when constructing language, and oneself as a member of a community, might be purely acts of identity affiliation (Anderson, 1991). The developing child is an intrinsic part of the social world, of a sociocultural milieu, and learns to reproduce language and culture. This growth and development is what Ochs (2002) has recently described as the interactive process of 'becoming speakers of culture'. Novice members of a community learn relevant interactional stances and roles while

engaged in activity. Children learn to become competent members of their communities by attending to cultural expectations, making sense of the ways in which people around them think and act. Sometimes these stances are not necessarily explicitly taught to them, and children must, instead, learn to understand these stances from their own participation in activities with others.

Bourdieu's notion of 'habitus' has been a useful concept to explain the ways in which children come to learn the practices and behaviours that are expected of them. 'Habitus' refers to the set of dispositions that are inculcated and socially structured. These dispositions are also generative, transposable, and durable (Bourdieu, 1977: 82). They are the result of early socialization practices (see also Bernstein, 1970) and reflect the social conditions within which they were acquired. Everyday linguistic exchanges are also situated encounters, so that each linguistic interaction bears the traces of the social structure that constitutes it (Bourdieu, 1977; Derrida, 1974/1976). Speakers use language, and in effect exchange language, in the 'linguistic marketplace' where utterances – not just what is said but how it is said – accrue value. Such linguistic exchanges are not only the result of power; they also reflect relations of power (also Foucault, 1977). This point is the subject of current critical approaches to literacy and pedagogy that have contributed to understanding the unequal acquisition of literacy and knowledge in children, starting with their first contact with formal education (Luke, 1994; Muspratt et al., 1997). Language, as a form of capital, leverages or accentuates differing relations of power, and knowledge can become more a matter of reproduction of existing relations of power than actual competence. Often, to be learned is to be a member and participant of a community of powerful experts and scientists (Lyotard, 1984). These ideas on the power of language and knowledge are extremely relevant to the study of young children acquiring language and literacy. The child learning language engages the social relations and the sociohistorical endowment that comes with using language, that is, its discourses. The acquisition of a range of discourses, speech registers, and genres is thus central to child language development in society (see Gee, 1999, for distinctions of different levels of of 'discourse').

Young children develop language and literacy practices that extend their current capabilities to recreate roles and relationships, even to display appropriate registers, often with the use of available tools and technologies (Andersen, 1986; 1990; Clancy, 1986; Guillen, 2002; Lankshear and Knobel, 1997). An illustrative example is the study of three- and four-year-olds during spontaneous play with a telephone (Guillen, 2002). Children's use of the appropriate speech genres and discourses is activated as they are also developing technological literacies. This is at the core of children's learning: to accord registers to activities, stances to actions, and discourses to social reality. For literary critic Bakhtin (1981), language and discourse (as the sets of norms and preferences that relate language to context) are dialogic in that they invoke histories and social relations. Language is situated in social life; that is, words, phrases, sentences (or the more encompassing term 'utterances') include a past, present, and future orientation that is at once preconditioned and dynamic. Bakhtin speaks of the inherent diversity and heteroglossia in discourse, of the recognition of multiple experiences, speech genres, which are also bound to context. He argues that readers (and we can extrapolate to audiences and even interlocutors) have an active role in co-constructing meaning. Such co-constructions, however, need not be unproblematic or conflict free. Language is a highly contested ground. Across space and time, master narratives give rise to counter-narratives and to alternative discourses that try to break free from normalizing discourses of what constitutes experience, knowledge, and social reality (Anderson, 1991; Bhabha, 1990; Spivak, 1995; Fairclough, 1988; Luke, 1994; Lyotard, 1984). This last point helps explain why there has been concretization and commodification of knowledge and of its accompanying discourses that directly influence children's language and literacy development and reproduce the status quo. A critique of this reproductive process is most evident in the fast growing number of analyses of policy, reform, pedagogical practice, curricula, and institutional accountability aimed towards a more equitable education (Apple, 1996; 2000; Macedo, 1994; Baker and Luke, 1991; McLaren, 1995; 1986/1999; Lankshear and McLaren, 1993; Giroux, 1983; 1992). The efforts to study language in its social context are useful to understand the contexts for development of young children's language and might lead us to the improvement of both language and literacy learning experiences of children, especially of minority children, in multicultural settings.

LANGUAGE AND CULTURE

Discussion thus far has focused on language and the social world and the necessary understanding that children acquire language in social interaction; that is, they acquire knowledge that encodes a sociohistorical trajectory. Culture, like language, is an important conceptual tool for locating the study of the individual in the social world. Largely as a result of feminist critiques to canonical notions of culture and its method of analysis (Behar, 1995; Behar and Gordon, 1995; Pratt, 1986; Visweswaran, 1994) and the lens of the 'native' scientist turned back to the research community (Behar, 1995; Limón, 1991; Narayan, 1993; Rosaldo, 1989), the study of culture has shifted from something to be described, interpreted and explained, to a source of explanation in itself.[4]

One of the earlier definitions of culture, more an effort to reconcile the conflicting views on culture in both sociology and anthropology at the time, underscores the interactional nature of cultural phenomena, the individual and the collectivity. Kroeber and Parsons write:

> We suggest that it is useful to define the concept of *culture* for most usages more narrowly than has been generally the case in the American anthropological tradition, restricting its reference to transmitted and created content and patterns of values, ideas, and other symbolic-meaningful systems as factors in the shaping of human behavior and the artifacts produced through behavior. On the other hand, we suggest that the term *society* – or more generally, *social system* – be used to designate the specifically relational system of interaction among individuals and collectivities. (1958: 583, original emphasis)

As a contractual agreement across disciplinary fields, this definition tied together several important operating concepts of symbols and systems in a relational configuration. The matrix is still useful today. The interest in describing people's behaviours and actions as members constituting society has ranged from an interpretivist (rather than objectivist) perspective in the study of culture (Geertz, 1973), to a more descriptive science highlighting the provisional and contingent nature of the social in the cultural (Rosaldo, 1989), to fiction and description (Visweswaran, 1994), to performance (Bauman and Briggs, 1990), and more recently to the description of the ways in which people live 'culturally' as they engage in everyday practice (Moll, 2000). Ethnography has become the method *par excellence* in the development of interpretive science, particularly through the method of 'thick description'. Linguists, anthropologists, and more recently educators, have since taken on the task of providing accounts of people's (largely differing and conflicting) understandings of their linguistic participation in culturally defined activities, constituting the first efforts to tie language and communicative acts to the study of culture (Wentworth, 1980; also Gumperz, 1982).

The poststructuralist approaches to language and social theory discussed so far have had a significant influence on studies of language and literacy. In fact, several consequences for the study of children's early language and literacy development stem from this conceptual shift. No longer perceived as cultural repositories and producers of language data, children's development and use of language (a field known as developmental pragmatics: cf. Ochs and Schieffelin, 1979) began to be taken as the focus of cross-cultural and cross-linguistic studies. A wealth of research on children's language development has continued to give prominence to the linguistic and the cultural in cognitive development (Cole, 1996; Göncü, 1999; Gopnik et al., 1999; Keenan, 1974; Miller, 1994; Miller et al., 1990; Nelson, 1989; 1996; Ochs, 1988; Ochs and Schieffelin, 1984; Rogoff, 1990; 1993; Saxe, 1994; Schieffelin, 1990). For the young child learning a language, as Ochs (2002) notes, becoming a speaker of culture means to learn to ascertain that there are multiple dimensions of meaning making that take place as children interact with their cultural environment and as they engage people and objects in their world. Scollon (2002), arguing along a similar line, underscores the significance of the interplay between the individual's own development and use of language and her or his community's developmental, ontological trajectories. From this we can conclude that children move within and across these trajectories. And in so doing, they actively construct their own history.

The centrality of language as a tool for socializing young members or novice members to the cultural and linguistic practices (and indeed the history) of a community has launched a new field of child language acquisition studies, language socialization, which involves as much socialization through language as socialization to use language (Schieffelin and Ochs, 1986). Drawing from post-structuralist approaches to the study of the individual in social activity, socialization refers to the lifespan process of becoming a competent member of society. This process presupposes interaction or joint activity between expert and novice members while engaged in culturally meaningful activity (Lave and Wenger, 1991). In such interactions, despite asymmetries in knowledge and power, socialization is always bidirectional in the sense that novices may also socialize experts just as experts socialize novices. Language, thus, mediates the socializing interactions between expert and novice members of a community. Socialization takes place through co-construction during moment-to-moment interaction and it is conditioned by responses, which involve uptake or ratification, challenge, or even reframing (similar to rekeying: see Goffman, 1974).

A number of studies of early childhood literacy development have illustrated the process of socialization (Fader, 2001; Heath, 1986; Phillips, 1983; Ochs, 1988; Ochs and Schieffelin, 1984; Duranti et al., 1995; Schieffelin, 1990; 2000; Pease-Alvarez and Vásquez, 1994). During socializing encounters between experts and novices, cultural norms, preferences, and expectations are socialized vis-à-vis the development of cognition; for example, in the ways one focuses and handles attention, engages in problem solving, or formulates hypothetical thinking, as well as the displays of emotional responses and the appropriate physical demeanour to such states. This perspective on socialization stands in stark contrast to earlier notions of learning where the novice is passive and the expert assumes an active role. This view resembles a process of transmission and not the dynamic process that language socialization tries to capture. Indeed, language socialization is a more integrative, systemic approach to language development and its study has proven to be far more comprehensive than the early oppositions of the past (langue–parole, competence–performance, teaching–learning, and individual–society). Instead, much of the thinking on how people learn and the role that language plays in it has moved to dialectic models that point to synthesis; one of these is activity theory or cultural-historical activity theory. This synthetic approach focuses in studying people's tool-mediated collaborations in shared activity, taking as a starting point that language is a key mediational tool (Cole, 1996; Engestrröm et al., 1999; Lee and Smagorinsky, 2000; Gutiérrez et al., 2000; Vygotsky, 1978).

LANGUAGE, CULTURE, AND KNOWLEDGE: THE TIES TO LITERACY

The notion of language as a tool for meaning making has implications for understanding literacy development and for children's development of interpretive skills in interaction with others. Street (1984) has argued that to properly study literacy processes one must locate them in the interactions of individuals with other members of society and through the context of cultural practices. This link between context, language, and literacy development is further explained by Ochs: 'Meaning is embedded in cultural conceptions of context, and in this respect the process of acquiring language is embedded in the process of socialization of knowledge' (1988: 3). In earlier conceptualizations of knowledge, the role of language was constructed as 'the universal medium' for developing knowledge and understanding (Gadamer, 1975/2000: 389). A less known precursor of language and literacy studies, Gadamer points us to interpretation and knowledge in which language plays a central role. There are many examples from both experimental and longitudinal studies that illustrate the role of language in literacy development, from babies developing knowledge about the world to the development of emergent reading and writing skills (Ferreiro and Teberosky, 1983/1985; Ferreiro, 1986; Goodman 1984; 1986; Gopnik et al., 1999; Nelson, 1996; Scollon and Scollon, 1981/1989; Rogoff et al., 1993; Schieffelin and Cochran-Smith, 1984; Wells, 1985; Williams, 1991). In her case study of Santiago, a Spanish-speaking three-year-old child learning to read and write in Spanish, Ferreiro (1986) documents her extended interactions with Santiago in eliciting his perceptions of sound–letter correspondences while he was learning to write the names of people in his immediate social world. Santiago is seen as moving between many dimensions of knowledge construction: from more static sound–letter correspondences to more abstract symbolism. In another study of four- and five-year-olds' awareness of print and book-handling knowledge and reading procedure, Goodman (1986) concludes that at an earlier age, children know that the printed page carries meaning (pictures, for younger children), but perhaps more telling in the findings she reports is the fact that children verbalize an awareness of the difficulty of the reading task and request help–regardless of actual competence. This suggests an interactional dimension that children learn to engage in the process of learning how to read and write. In a study of African-American middle-class children, Williams (1991) investigates the recounting of literacy experiences that mothers organize for their children, whom, she argues, serve as a way to socialize literacy values. During interactions at home, children are encouraged to talk about successful experiences in school and the church – two important literacy institutions for the children in this study (indeed, churches have been historically important sites for children's literacy socialization[5]). Through these activities, Williams argues, children are being socialized to value school and to see themselves as literate. Of significance, personal storytelling is used to promote literacy development in other contexts (or at least to develop an awareness of literacy). The affiliative, sense making nature of narrative activity was thus employed to begin to generate new knowledge from existing knowledge – a key process in literacy development.

LANGUAGE AND COMMUNITY

The notion of 'community', while widely used in linguistic and developmental research, needs to be seriously problematized. As Pratt (1987) notes of anthropological research, 'community' as a construct has dangerous homogenizing undertones. This assessment is equally applicable to much research in education. In an increasingly global society, where community can no longer be defined in terms of geographical boundaries, or of ethnic affiliation, or even of the languages or dialects of a language spoken in a particular locale (Hymes, 1974; Labov, 1973), community has to take on a more dynamic meaning. Indeed, the literacy development of children in multilingual societies and learning contexts often traverse the traditional fixed geopolitical, ethnic, cultural and linguistic boundaries (Fader, 2001; Garrett and Baquedano-López, 2002; González, 2001; Gutiérrez et al., 1999; Vásquez et al., 1994). The dynamicity of community can best be captured by attending to the practices of members and activity as units of analysis. This focus on practice has led to increasing attention to the study of 'communities of practice' (Lave and Wenger, 1991). At its core, the model presupposes that all individuals of society participate in a myriad of communities of practice (Eckert and McConnell-Ginet, 1992; Garrett and Baquedano-López, 2002; Lave and Wenger, 1991; Wenger, 1998).

To define community in terms of collaborative and relational practices is to recognize the link between the individual and the group and the necessary relationship between tools and participants. It also entails recognizing that there is tension between individual and collaborative goals. Membership in a community of practice is characterized by the socialization of competencies by expert others, and is typified by mutual engagement and by a more dynamic and collaborative deployment of competence and performance in activity (Cole, 1996; Engeström et al., 1999). The community of practice can be a productive, heterogeneous locale for understanding the changes of people's participation over time, i.e. learning (Rogoff, 1993), and the different participation structures that indicate movement from peripheral participation to more central participation (Lave and Wenger, 1991; Larson, 1995; de León, 1998). While the communities of practice model might be most useful in studying people engaged in small-scale, more or less established historical practice, it might prove to be too narrow to account for complex institutional settings, such as classrooms and schools, where unequal relations of power and the sociohistorical endowment of race, gender, and class are at play. It is important to also underscore that even participation in a community of practice is contingent on the ideologies that people and institutions hold about languages and their speakers (Woolard, 1998).

Research on language, literacy, and community must account for different levels of interaction, as well as the ideologies underlying those interactions.

As literacy theorists, we are engaging rich and productive conceptual junctures. The field is healthy in its interdisciplinariness. The lessons learned from the development of social theory, as we address such notions as language, literacy, culture and community, can help improve our practice in the pursuit of answers to the question of how well children can grow to be competent and successful members of the different communities in which they participate and of the many worlds that they are yet to know.

NOTES

1 Generativity refers to the potential for building words, phrases and utterances.

2 It is worth noting here that Fries (1945) in earlier work pioneered much of the call for documenting and teaching of the grammars of the world.

3 The reader is directed to Hanks (1996) for a comprehensive analysis of these programmes.

4 See Kuper (1999) for an important discussion of the engagement of culture in anthropological work.

5 See also Baquedano-López (1997; 2000) Cohen and Lukinsky (1985), Duranti et al. (1995), Fader (2001), Farr (1994), Haight (2002), Heath (1983), Moss (1994), and Zinsser (1986) who have articulated the important role of religious practices in literacy socialization.

REFERENCES

Andersen, E. (1986) 'The acquisition of register variation by Anglo-American children', in B. Schieffelin and E. Ochs (eds), *Language Socialization Across Cultures*. Cambridge: Cambridge University Press. pp. 153–61.

Andersen, E. (1990) 'Acquiring communicative competence: knowledge of register variation', in R. Scarcella, E. Andersen and S. Krashen (eds), *Developing Communicative Competence in a Second Language*. New York: Newbury House. pp. 5–25.

Anderson, B. (1991) *Imagined Communities*. London: Verso.

Apple, M. (1996) *Cultural Politics and Education*. New York: Teachers College Press

Apple, M. (2000) *Official Knowledge: Democratic Education in a Conservative Age*. New York Routledge.

Baker, C. and Luke, A. (1991) *Towards a Critical Sociology of Reading Pedagogy*. Philadelphia: Benjamins.

Bakhtin, M. (1981) *The Dialogic Imagination*. Austin, TX: University of Texas Press.

Baquedano-López, P. (1997) 'Creating social identities through doctrina narratives', *Issues in Applied Linguistics*, 8 (1): 27–45.

Baquedano-López, P. (2000) 'Narrating community in doctrina classes', *Narrative Inquiry*, 10 (2): 1–24.

Bauman, R. and Briggs, C. (1990) 'Poetics and performance as critical perspectives on social life', *Annual Review of Anthropology*, 19: 59–88. Palo Alto, CA: Annual Reviews.

Behar, R. (1995) *The vulnerable observer: Anthropology that breaks your heart*. Boston: Beacon.

Behar, R. and Gordon, D. (1995) *Women writing culture*. Berkeley CA: University of California Press.

Bernstein, B. (1970) *Class, Codes, and Control. Vol. 3: Toward a Theory of Educational Transmission*, 2nd edn. London: Routledge and Kegan.

Bhabha, H. (1990) *Nation and Narration*. London: Routledge.

Bourdieu, P. (1977) *Outline of a Theory of Practice*. New York: Cambridge.

Celce-Murcia, M. (1991) *Teaching English as a Second or Foreign Language*. 2nd edn. New York: Newbury House.

Chomsky, N. (1965) *Aspects of a Theory of Syntax*. Cambridge, MA: MIT Press.

Clancy, P. (1986) 'The acquisition of communicative style in Japanese', in B. Schieffelin and E. Ochs (eds), *Language Socialization Across Cultures* . Cambridge: Cambridge University Press. pp. 213–50.

Cohen, B. and Lukinsky, J. (1985) 'Religious institutions as educators', in M.D. Fantini and R.L. Sinclair (eds), *Education in School and Nonschool Settings*. Chicago: National Society for the Study of Education. pp. 140–58.

Cole, M. (1996) *Cultural Psychology: a Once and Future Discipline*. Cambridge, MA: Belknap.

de León, L. (1998) 'The emergent participant: interactive patterns in the socialization of Tzotzil (Mayan) infants', *Journal of Linguistic Anthropology*, 8 (2): 131–61.

Derrida, J. (1974/1976) *Of Grammatology*. Baltimore: Johns Hopkins University Press.

Doggett, G. (1986) *Eight Approaches to Language Teaching*. Washington, DC: Center for Applied Linguistics/ERIC Clearinghouse on Languages and Linguistics.

Duranti, A., Ochs, E. and Ta`ase, E. (1995) 'Change and tradition in literacy instruction in a Samoan American community', in *Educational Foundations*. pp. 57–74.

Eckert, P. and McConnell-Ginet, S. (1992) 'Think practically and look locally: language and gender as community-based practice', *Annual Review of Anthropology*, 21: 461–90.

Engeström, Y., Miettinen, R. and Punamäki, R. (eds) (1999) *Perspectives on Activity Theory*. Cambridge: Cambridge University Press.

Fader, A. (2001) 'Literacy, bilingualism and gender in a Hasidic community', *Linguistics and Education*, 12 (3): 261–83.

Fairclough, N. (1989) *Language and Power.* London: Longman.

Farr, M. (1994) 'En los dos idiomas: literacy practices among Chicago Mexicanos', in B. Moss (ed.), *Literacy Practices Across Communities*, Cresskill, NJ: Hampton. pp. 9–47.

Ferreiro, E. (1986) 'The interplay between information and assimilation in beginning literacy', in W. Teale and E. Sulzby (eds), *Emergent Literacy: Writing and Reading.* Norwood, NJ: Ablex. pp. 15–49.

Ferreiro, E. and Teberosky, A. (1983/1985) *Literacy before Schooling.* London: Heinemann.

Foucault, M. (1977) *Language, Counter-Memory, Practice: Selected Essays and Interviews.* Ithaca, NY: Cornell University Press.

Fries, C. (1945) *Teaching and Learning English as a Foreign Language.* Ann Arbor, MI: University of Michigan Press.

Gadamer, H. (1975/2000) *Truth and Method.* 2nd. rev. edn, trans. J. Weinsheimer and D. Marshall. New York: Continuum.

Garrett, P. and Baquedano-López, P. (2002) 'Language socialization: reproduction and continuity, transformation and change', *Annual Review of Anthropology*, 31: 339–61. Palo Alto, CA: Annual Reviews.

Gee, J.P. (1999) *An Introduction to Discourse Analysis: Theory and method.* London: Routledge.

Geertz, C. (1973) *The Interpretation of Cultures.* New York: Basic.

Giroux, H. (1983) *Theory and Resistance in Education: a Pedagogy for the Opposition.* South Hadley, MA: Bergin and Garvey.

Giroux, H. (1992) *Border Crossings.* New York: Routledge.

Goffman, E. (1974) *Frame Analysis: an Essay on the Organization of Experience.* Boston: Northeastern University Press.

Göncü, A. (1999) *Children's Engagement in the World: Sociocultural Perspectives.* Cambridge: Cambridge University Press.

González, N. (2001) *I Am My Language: Discourses of Women and Children in the Borderlands.* Tucson, AZ: University of Arizona Press.

Goodman, Y. (1984) 'The development of initial literacy', in H. Goodman, A. Olberg and I. Smith (eds), *Awakening to Literacy.* Exeter, NH: Heinemann.

Goodman, Y. (1986) 'Children Coming to Know Literacy', in W. Teale and E. Sulzby (eds), *Emergent Literacy: Writing and Reading.* Norwood, NJ: Ablex. pp. 1–14.

Gopnik, A., Metzoff, A. and Kuhl, P. (1999) *The Scientist in the Crib: Minds, Brains, and How Children Learn.* New York: Morrow.

Guillen, J. (2002) 'Moves in the territory of literacy? The telephone discourse of three- and four-year-olds', *Journal of Early Childhood Literacy*, 2 (1): 21–43.

Gumperz, J. (1982) *Discourse Strategies.* Cambridge: Cambridge University Press.

Gutiérrez, K., Baquedano-López, P., Alvarez, H. and Chiu, M. (1999) 'Building a culture of collaboration through hybrid language practices', *Theory into Practice*, 38 (2): 87–93.

Gutiérrez, K., Baquedano-López, P. and Tejeda, C. (2000) 'Rethinking diversity: hybridity and hybrid language practices in the Third Space', *Mind, Culture, and Activity*, 6 (4): 286–303.

Habermas, J. (1984/1987) *Theory of Communicative Action*, 2 vols, trans. T. McCarthy. Boston: Beacon.

Habermas, J. (1987) *The Philosophical Discourse of Modernity*, trans. F. Lawrence. Cambridge, MA: MIT Press.

Haight, W. (2002) *African–American Children at Church: a Sociocultural Perspective.* Cambridge: Cambridge University Press.

Hanks, W.F. (1996) *Language and Communicative Practices.* Boulder, CO: Westview.

Heath, S. (1983) *Ways with Words: Language, Life, and Work in Communities and classrooms.* Cambridge: Cambridge University Press.

Heath, S. (1986) 'What no bedtime story means: narrative skills at home and school', in B. Schieffelin and E. Ochs (eds), *Language Socialization Across Cultures.* Cambridge: Cambridge University Press. pp. 97–124.

Hymes, D. (1974) *Foundations in Sociolinguistics: an Ethnographic Approach.* Philadelphia: University of Pennsylvania Press.

Keenan, E.O. (1974) 'Conversational competence in children', *Journal of Child Language*, 1 (2): 163–83.

Kroeber, A. and Parsons, T. (1958) 'The concept of culture and of social system', *American Sociological Review*, 23: 583.

Kuper, A. (1999) *Culture: the Anthropologists' Account.* Cambridge, MA: Harvard University Press.

Labov, W. (1973) *Language in the Inner City.* Philadelphia: University of Pennsylvania Press.

Lankshear, C. and Knobel, M. (1997) 'Literacies, texts, and difference in the electronic age', in C. Lankshear, J.P. Gee, M. Knobel and C. Searle (eds), *Changing Literacies.* Buckingham: Open University Press. pp. 133–63.

Lankshear, C and McLaren, P. (1993) *Critical Literacy: Politics, Praxis, and the Postmodern.* Albany, NY: State University of New York Press.

Larson, J. (1995) 'Talk matters: the role of pivot in the distribution of literacy knowledge among novice writers', *Linguistics and Education*, 7 (4): 277–302.

Lave, J. and Wenger, E. (1991) *Situated learning: Legitimate Peripheral Participation.* Cambridge: Cambridge University Press.

Lee, C. and Smagorinsky, P. (eds) (2000). *Vygotskian Perspectives on Literacy Research: Constructing Meaning through Collaborative Inquiry.* New York: Cambridge University Press.

Limón, J. (1991) 'Representation, ethnicity, and the precursory ethnography: notes of a native anthropologist', in R. Fox (ed.), *Recapturing Anthropology:*

Working in the Present. Santa Fe, NM: School of American Research Press.

Luke, A. (1994) *The Social Construction of Literacy in the Primary School.* Melbourne: Macmillan.

Lyotard, J. (1984) *The Postmodern Condition: a Report on Knowledge.* Minneapolis, MN: University of Minnesota Press.

Macedo, D. (1994) *Literacies of Power: What Americans Are Not Allowed to Know.* Boulder, CO: Westview.

McLaren, P. (1986/1999) *Schooling as a Ritual Performance: Toward a Political Economy of Educational Symbols and Gestures,* 3rd edn. Lanham, MD: Rowman and Littlefield.

McLaren, P. (1995) *Critical Pedagogy and Predatory Culture: Oppositional Politics in a Postmodern Era.* London: Routledge.

Miller, P. (1994) 'Narrative practices: their role in socialization and self-construction', in U. Neisser and R. Fivush (eds), *The Remembering Self: Construction and Accuracy in the Self-Narrative.* Cambridge: Cambridge University Press. pp. 158–179.

Miller, P., Potts, R, Fung, H., Hoogstra, L. and Mintz, J. (1990) 'Narrative practices and the social construction of self in childhood', *American Ethnologist,* 17 (2): 292–311.

Moll, L.C. (2000) 'Inspired by Vygotsky: ethnographic experiments in education', in C. Lee and P. Smagorinsky (eds.), *Vygotskian Perspectives on Literacy Research: Constructing Meaning Through Collaborative Inquiry.* New York: Cambridge University Press. pp. 256–68.

Moss, B. (1994) 'Creating a community: literacy events in African-American churches', in B. Moss (ed.), *Literacy Across Communities.* Cresskill, NJ: Hampton. pp. 147–78.

Muspratt, S., Luke, A. and Peabody, P. (eds) (1997) *Constructing Critical Literacies: Teaching and Learning Textual Practice.* Cresskill, NJ: Hampton.

Nayaran, P. (1993) 'How native is a "native" anthropology?', *American Anthropologist,* 95: 671–85.

Nelson, K. (1989) *Narratives from the Crib.* Cambridge, MA: Harvard University Press.

Nelson, K. (1996) *Language in Cognitive Development: Emergence of the Mediated Mind.* Cambridge: Cambridge University Press.

Ochs, E. (1988) *Culture and Language Development: Language Acquisition and Language Socialization in a Samoan Village.* New York: Cambridge University Press.

Ochs, E. (2002) 'Becoming a speaker of culture', in C. Kramsch (ed.), *Language Acquisition and Socialization.* London: Continuum. pp. 99–120.

Ochs, E. and Schieffelin, B. (eds) (1979) *Developmental Pragmatics.* New York: Academic.

Ochs, E. and Schieffelin, B. (1984) 'Language acquisition and socialization: three developmental stories and their implications', in R.A. Shweder and R.A. LeVine (eds), *Culture Theory: Essays on Mind, Self, and Emotion.* Cambridge: Cambridge University Press. pp. 276–320.

Pease-Alvarez, L. and Vásquez, O. (1994) 'Language socialization in ethnic minority communities', in F. Genesee (ed.), *Educating Second Language Children: the Whole Child, the Whole Curriculum, the Whole Community.* Cambridge: Cambridge University Press. pp. 82–102.

Phillips, S. (1983) *The Invisible Culture: Communication in Classroom and Community on the Warm Springs Indian Reservation.* Prospect Heights, IL: Waveland.

Pratt, M.L. (1986) 'Fieldwork in common places', in J. Clifford and G. Marcus (eds), *Writing culture: the Poetics and Politics of Ethnography* Berkeley, CA: University of California Press. pp. 27–50.

Pratt, M.L. (1987) 'Linguistic utopias', in N. Fabb, D. Atridge, A. Durant and C. MacCabe (eds), *The Linguistics of Writing: Arguments between Language and Literature* Manchester: Manchester University Press. pp. 48–66.

Rogoff, B. (1990) *Apprenticeship in Thinking: Cognitive Development in Social Context.* New York: Oxford University Press.

Rogoff, B. (1993) 'Children's guided participation and participatory appropriation in sociocultural activity', in R. Wozniak and K. Fisher (eds), *Development in Context: Acting and Thinking in Specific Environments* Hillsdale, NJ: Erlbaum. pp. 121–53.

Rogoff, B., Mistry, J., Göncü, A. and Mosier, C. (1993) 'Guided participation in cultural activity by toddlers and caregivers', *Monographs of the Society for Research in Child Development,* 38 (8).

Rosaldo, R. (1989) *Culture and Truth: the Remaking of Social Analysis.* Boston: Beacon.

Saussure, F. de (1966) '*Course in General Linguistics,* trans. W. Baskin. New York: McGraw-Hill.

Saxe, G. (1994) 'Studying cognitive development in sociocultural contexts: the development of practice-based approaches', *Mind, Culture, and Activity,* 1: 135–57.

Schieffelin, B. (1990) *The Give and Take of Everyday Life: Language Socialization of Kaluli Children.* New York: Cambridge University Press.

Schieffelin, B. (2000) 'Introducing Kaluli literacy: a chronology of influences', in P.V. Kroskrity (ed.), *Regimes of Language: Ideologies, Polities, and Identities.* Santa Fe, NM: School of American Research Press. pp. 293–327.

Schieffelin, B. and Cochran-Smith, M. (1984) 'Learning to read culturally: literacy before schooling', in H. Goelman, A. Oberg and F. Smith (eds), *Awakening to Literacy.* Exeter, NH: Heinemann. pp. 3–23.

Schieffelin, B. and Ochs, E. (1986) *Language Socialization across Cultures.* Cambridge: Cambridge University Press.

Scollon, R. (2002) 'Cross-cultural learning and other catastrophes', in C. Kramsch (ed.), *Language Acquisition and Socialization.* London: Continuum. pp. 121–39.

Scollon, R. and Scollon, S. (1981/1989) *Narrative, Literacy and Face in Interethnic Communication.* Norwood, NJ: Ablex.

Spivak, G. (1995) 'Three women's texts and a critique', in B. Ashcroft, G. Griffith and H. Tiffin (eds), *The Post-Colonial Studies Reader.* London: Routledge. pp. 269–72.

Street, B. (1984) *Literacy in Theory and Practice.* Cambridge: Cambridge University Press.

Vásquez, O., Pease-Alvarez, L., Shannon, S. and Moll, L. (1994) *Pushing Boundaries: Language and Culture in a Mexicano Community.* Cambridge: Cambridge University Press.

Visweswaran, K. (1994) *Fictions of Feminist Ethnography.* Minneapolis: University of Minnesota Press.

Vygotsky, L. (1978) *Mind in Society: the Development of Higher Psychological Processes.* Cambridge, MA: Harvard University Press.

Wells, G. (1985) 'Pre-school literacy related activities and success in school', in D. Olson, N. Torrance and A. Hidyard (eds), *Literacy, Language and Learning: the Nature and Consequences of Reading and Writing.* Cambridge: Cambridge University Press. pp. 229–55.

Wenger, E. (1998) *Communities of Practice: Learning, Meaning, and Identity.* Cambridge: Cambridge University Press.

Wentworth, W. (1980) *Context and Understanding.* New York: Elsevier.

Williams, K. (1991) 'Storytelling as a bridge to literacy: an examination of personal storytelling among black middle-class mothers and children', *Journal of Negro Education,* 60 (3): 399–410.

Woolard, K. (1998) 'Introduction/language ideology as a field of inquiry', in B. Schieffelin, K. Woolard and P. Kroskrity (eds), *Language Ideologies: Practice and theory.* New York: Oxford University Press. pp. 3–47.

Zinsser, C. (1986) 'For the Bible tells me so: teaching children in a fundamentalist church', in B. Schieffelin and P. Gillmore (eds), *The Acquisition of Literacy: Ethnographic Perspectives.* Norwood, NJ: Ablex. pp. 55–71.

7

The Out-of-School Schooling of Literacy

EVE GREGORY AND CHARMIAN KENNER

Across generations, families have always ensured that young children have access to important cultural practices through formal classes. Such classes have been particularly crucial to the lives of new immigrant families who are anxious both to preserve the language, literacy and religion of their heritage and to give young children extra tuition in the language and literacy of the new country. Out-of-school schooling thus encompasses a range of different 'community' classes: religious or liturgical, mother tongue language and literacy classes, and Saturday classes in the host language, often covering a range of subjects across the curriculum. This chapter assesses the value of such classes, in terms of cognitive, linguistic and social benefits accruing to young children in their early years in school. It then goes on to review studies describing a range of community classes in different countries, contrasting them with the learning taking place in mainstream schools.

THE OUT-OF-SCHOOL SCHOOLING OF LITERACY

Six-year-old Maruf talks avidly about his Qur'anic class:

Maruf:	There are eighty-three children.
AW (researcher):	Eighty-three children in your Arabic class! And when do you go to that?
Maruf:	Seven o'clock to nine o'clock.
AW:	On?
Maruf:	A night.
AW:	Every night?
Maruf:	Monday to Friday.

AW:	Monday to Friday! You go for two hours every night! Aren't you tired?
Maruf:	I don't feel tired.
AW:	And are you the youngest then?
Maruf:	Yes and I'm on the Qur'an.
AW:	You're on the Qur'an now?
Maruf:	I'm on the last one.

Maruf explains that he is reading the last primer before starting the Qur'an. He goes on to explain more about the structure of his classes:

AW:	How many teachers are there for eighty-three children?
Maruf:	There's two.
AW:	Only two? Who are they?
Maruf:	One is the Qur'an ... you know, all the Qur'an ... he can say it without looking.
AW:	He can? What's his name?
Maruf:	I don't know. And one is ... he can ... he knows all the meanings.
AW:	Does he? Does he tell you the meanings?
Maruf:	Yes he does.
AW:	So do you just read the Qur'an for two hours? Is that what you do?
Maruf:	Yes, but I don't sometimes, I talk sometimes.
AW:	You don't!
Maruf:	I do.

(Gregory and Williams, 2000: 168–9)

The breadth of Maruf's learning reflects that of many young children working in classes established by their local communities throughout the world. This chapter examines existing research studies that describe this 'out-of-school schooling' in which young children engage. It deals only with formal classes taking place outside mainstream school hours, not the more informal ways in which families and communities might foster literacy at home. The classes described are often known as 'community classes', which acts as a blanket term to cover mother-tongue (or national standard heritage language) classes, religious or liturgical classes, or supplementary classes or Saturday schools that may be in either the mother tongue or the host language (or a combination of both) and cover a range of curriculum areas. In different sections, the chapter addresses the following questions: what benefits might accrue to children spending many hours, like Maruf in the excerpt above, participating in this learning? How and why were these classes set up by different communities? What is their scope and what particular classes exist, taking the UK as an example? What is the nature of learning taking place? How different is it from mainstream school learning? Finally, how should mainstream teachers conceptualize this learning?

BILINGUALISM AND BILITERACY:
A THEORETICAL FRAMEWORK

He who knows no other language does not truly know his own. (Goethe quoted by Vygotsky, in John-Steiner, 1985: 368)

Any discussion on mother-tongue classes needs to be situated in the literature relating to the advantages and/or disadvantages of bilingualism and biliteracy as well as that recognizing the inextricable link between language and culture (Vygotsky, 1962; Sapir, 1970). A considerable body of evidence has recently been collected pointing to the advanced development of specific types of linguistic and cognitive skills of bilinguals given certain conditions (summarized in Gregory and Kelly, 1992; Gregory, 1994a). Linguistic skills are expressed in a greater metalinguistic and analytic competence where attention can be focused on isolated components (Feldman and Shen, 1971; Ianco-Worrall, 1972; Ben-Zeev, 1977; Swain and Cummins, 1979; Bain and Yu, 1980; Hakuta, 1986; Arnberg, 1987). Cognitive advantages are most obvious in areas such as conservation of measurement, classification according to shape, colour or size, or manipulating and recognizing visual patterns (Peal and Lambert, 1962; Liedtke and Nelson, 1968; Ben-Zeev, 1977). The crucial question relating to the topic of this chapter is: what are the conditions whereby these advantages accrue?

As early as the 1930s, when Western European research was pointing unambiguously to the negative effects of bilingualism (Jesperson, 1923; Saer, 1924; Goodenough, 1926), a very different direction was taken by Vygotsky (1935, trans. 1962).

Vygotsky's thesis was that bilingualism enabled a child 'to see his language as one particular system among many, to view its phenomena under more general categories… [which] leads to awareness of his linguistic operations' (1962: 110). It is through gaining control over two languages involving different lexical, syntactic and semantic systems, as well as possibly two different scripts, or, put simply, through learning that there are two ways of saying the same thing, that the individual gains an added analytical awareness, which, argued Vygotsky, contributes to a more conscious understanding of linguistic patterns in general. Later research studies in the West support Vygotsky's thesis that this awareness is particularly enhanced through literacy learning in two languages (Verhoeven, 1987; Wagner, 1993; Gregory, 1996; Kenner, 1999; 2000 a&b; Rosowsky, 2001). The skills of young children who are becoming biliterate are examined elsewhere (see Kenner and Gregory, in this volume).

The key to gaining access to this consciousness is the effective mastery of two or more languages, whereby learning a second language is 'added' to the development of the first (Cummins, 1979; 1992). In contrast, for children learning in 'subtractive' contexts, where their first language is 'submerged' (Skutnabb-Kangas, 1984) and seen merely as an obstacle to be overcome, no cognitive or linguistic advantages are likely to accrue. Additionally, it is now widely argued that second-language learning runs parallel with first-language competence and that acquisition of a second language is, indeed, dependent upon the level of development in the first language (John-Steiner, 1985). This thesis has been termed the 'linguistic interdependence principle' which simply states that first- and second-language skills are interdependent.

A number of research studies also support the view of a common underlying cognitive proficiency across languages (Vygotsky, 1962; Cummins, 1981; Hamers and Blanc, 1989) which states that young children are capable of transferring cognitive functioning in their first language at home and in their community classes to their second language in school (Sneddon, 2000; Gregory, 1998; Kenner, 2000 a&b) as well as vice versa. Problems are likely to arise when no transfer is possible because a child has not acquired a certain cognitive functioning in the first language when beginning a second in school (Skutnabb-Kangas, 1984). A recognition of the principle of additive enrichment and common underlying proficiency would provide strong support for the benefits of community language and literacy classes in young children's lives. Not only will young children become proficiently bilingual and biliterate, but strong evidence suggests that mother-tongue proficiency will enhance second-language learning and cognitive skills more generally in their mainstream schools.

COMMUNITY CLASSES: A HISTORICAL PERSPECTIVE

Aumie (aged 78) tells his childhood memories of Hebrew classes in London's East End:

> We would go five times a week. So you'd come home from school ... and then by five o'clock, we would be in Hebrew classes until 7, and, as far as I was concerned, by 8 o'clock I was back in the Synagogue choir for rehearsals twice a week ... You would learn phonetically, the twenty-four letters of the Hebrew alphabet ... we would learn letter by letter and then build up the words ... Learning Hebrew phonetically like this we were soon able to read quite quickly. We would read mechanically without understanding the words. (Gregory and Williams, 2000: 89)

There is a long history of community class teaching and learning in Britain; some studies are auto-biographical (Rosen, 1999) or recount the memories of older citizens such as Aumie above. By the end of the nineteenth century, we know that 30 to 40 'chevras' or religious associations had been established in the East End of London, which took over pastoral care of the poor as well as religious teaching (Fishman, 1979: 78). An important function of the chevras was to teach Hebrew and to prepare children (mostly boys) for their bar mitzvah. By 1891, there were some 200 of these classes in the East End with 2000 boys on their roll (Gregory and Williams, 2000: 55). The children attended in the morning before school, during their lunch break or after school. Their accommodation was sparse – usually one or two rooms of a small house – and materials consisted largely of religious and sacred texts to be learned. These classes were entirely separate from the mainstream school, although evidence is available that some state schools recognized the religious and cultural practices of their communities through holidays and the school kitchen etc. (Gregory and Williams, 2000).

During the first half of the twentieth century, community classes remained largely invisible to the wider host society. However, in 1976 came the publication of a highly controversial draft Directive from Europe. The draft Directive on the education of migrant children proposed the right of all migrant children in European Union states to tuition in their mother tongue. Although the Directive was almost totally rejected by most LEAs in Britain, it led to the setting up of the National Council for Mother Tongue Teaching (NCMTT), an active body campaigning for the recognition of mother-tongue

teaching in mainstream schools. For a short period during the 1980s, following the MOTET (Mother Tongue to English Teaching Project) set up by the DES (Department of Education and Science, 1985), mother tongue teaching even entered mainstream primary classrooms in Bradford (Fitzpatrick, 1987) and Bedford (Tosi, 1984). Although these innovative bilingual education projects provided evidence that young children could operate as well in English in addition to performing better in maths and in their mother tongue than the control group, they were short-lived. Their death knell struck in 1985 with the publication of a major government report, the Swann Report, which stated clearly that the place for mother-tongue teaching lay firmly outside school and within the communities themselves. Any mother-tongue teaching in school should comprise only 'emergency support' until competence in English had been achieved. From that time on, community classes have largely retreated underground to become invisible.

Nevertheless, throughout Britain and particularly in London's East End, community classes have continued to thrive until the present day. The East End Community School set up in 1977 by Mohammed Nurul Hoque and Anwara Begum is one such class in Tower Hamlets. Aiming to teach both English and Bengali language and literature (especially poetry), maths, Arabic, general science, history, geography, singing, needlework, knitting and other crafts and art, it expanded from 13 to 63 students in just 18 months. The school has long hours – from 4.30 to 6.30 p.m. every evening, from 10 a.m. to 5 p.m. on Saturdays, and special activities on Sundays – which bear witness to its popularity. Ros, a 21-year-old graduate from Oxford, tells fondly of her memories of this school:

> We were very lucky – although we didn't think so at the time. We had the East End Community School organised by Nurul Hoque and Anwara Hussein. They are very well known in the community and I think they've done wonders for people of my generation. I have fluent Bengali with GCSE grade A and I owe it to them ... it was incredibly tiring because it was straight after school and we had to go and then we'd miss things like 'Neighbours' ... it was Monday to Friday like 4 till half past 6. We'd have Arabic on Friday and Saturday. It was more Bengali-based, which is why our Bengali is so much better than our Arabic. (Gregory and Williams, 2000: 132)

THE SCOPE OF COMMUNITY CLASS ATTENDANCE IN THE UK

Maruf's description of his community class opening this chapter came as a surprise to his mainstream class teacher. She was unaware of the importance of Qur'anic class learning in his life, since he does not talk about it in school and, like many community classes, it remains invisible to both the mainstream school and the wider host community. In this section, we trace briefly literature detailing the scope of community classes on three levels: that documenting the number of classes overall in Britain; a closer analysis of provision made by three local education authorities during the 1980s; and studies revealing the scope of community class learning in individual children's lives.

Recent work provides details of over 2000 community classes or schools in the UK (Kempadoo and Abdelrazak, 1999). As the compilers of this directory themselves admit, even this huge number represents only a fraction of existing provision made by communities for their children's learning. As well as the more commonly recognized South Asian languages (Bengali, Gujarati, Panjabi, Urdu and Tamil), classes listed include numerous African languages (Tigrini, Yoruba, Swahili, Igbo, Twi, Somali) in addition to Cantonese, Kurdish, Irish, Swedish, Greek, Bosnian, Japanese etc. The London Borough of Tower Hamlets, where Maruf lives, has 59 classes listed, mostly for Bengali and Arabic, but also covering Somali, Panjabi, Cantonese, Vietnamese and Luganda as well as numerous classes offering a combination of a heritage language alongside English, maths and science. Classes in the London Borough of Brent serve as a fine illustration to the wealth of linguistic and cultural diversity in London, with classes in Albanian, Arabic, Gujarati, Bengali, Bosnian, Croatian, Greek, Hindi, Tamil, Irish, Welsh, Mandarin and Somali.

Although the directory provides an excellent bank of information on the scope of community classes in Britain, it leaves many questions unanswered as to the nature of the provision itself. Precisely this finer detail is given in a study by the Linguistic Minorities Project (LMP) (1985). This team of researchers investigated minority languages in three local education authorities (Bradford, Coventry and Haringey). Working together with the National Council for Mother Tongue Teaching, they not only documented the scope of individual community classes in each area, but provided information on the length of time each class had been in existence, the nature of funding, the take-up of provision as well as the age of pupils and their regularity of attendance. Although the researchers stressed the difficulties in collecting trustworthy evidence, the data collected was impressive, showing many classes to be long-established with a large group of regular attenders in spite of lack of local education authority funding. Their questionnaire also attempted to measure the scope of attendance at different classes. It began to highlight the long hours (between 5 and 14) spent per week by children in Qur'anic classes.

However, the survey conducted by the Linguistic Minorities Project team could not show what these apparently long hours might look like in the lives of individual children. This level of detail has been left to ethnographic studies of the literacy lives of small groups of families and their young children. Although some studies document the home literacies of young bilingual children (Minns, 1990) and others show the extent of attendance of older children at community classes (Sneddon, 2000; Saxena, 2000; Rosowsky, 2001), few studies focus on the formal out-of-school learning of *young* children in Britain. However, there is convincing evidence from longitudinal studies that children as young as six also spend up to 11 hours per week in mother tongue and religious classes (Gregory, 1994b; 1996; Gregory and Williams, 2000; Rashid and Gregory, 1997; Robertson, 1997). These studies not only reveal the scope of community class learning in young children's lives, but go on to outline the significant impact such learning might have on their work in mainstream classes. We discuss more closely the nature of this learning in the section following.

OTHER WORLDS OF LEARNING

The class takes place in a neighbour's front room. About 30 children of all ages … line the walls like a human square, seated with their raiel (a beautifully carved wooden stand upon which to place the Qur'an or the initial primers) in front of them. There is a loud hum as they all chant their individual practice piece. Their elderly teacher whom the children affectionately call 'nanna' (grandfather) holds a bamboo cane which he uses only lightly as if symbolically. 'These children need discipline, or they will climb the sky!' … Like many of the children, he (Louthfur) rocks to and fro to the sound of the voices. Children do this because they are encouraged to develop a harmonious voice; they are told Allah listens to his servants and is pleased if time is taken to make the verse sound meaningful. The old man's wife takes children who have already started the Qur'an into a separate room so she can hear the recitations clearly. She comments, 'English is important for this life. But Arabic is required for the life hereafter which is eternal! Therefore, it must be given the greatest importance … Or else, how can our children know?' (Rashid, in Gregory, 1996: 41)

During the last two decades of the twentieth century, ethnographic studies began to provide teachers and researchers with entry into the worlds of community classes. Few such studies existed in the UK before 1990, although longitudinal work conducted in Liberia (Scribner and Cole, 1981), Iran (Street, 1984) and Morocco (Wagner et al., 1986) was beginning to indicate the existence of multiple language and literacy practices taking place in both adults' and young children's lives. This section examines briefly ethnographic studies inviting outsiders into the community classes of young children in three contexts: African-American children in a north-eastern US state; Samoan American children; and Bangladeshi British children in Spitalfields, East London. We extract patterns of similarity and difference in these studies as well as with mainstream classrooms.

Both Heath (1983) and Anderson and Stokes (1984) stressed the importance of Bible reading in the lives of African-American communities but did not follow the children into their religious classes. Taking up these findings, Zinsser (1986) provides a finely tuned analysis of the classes of four- and five-year-old pre-primary children attending two fundamentalist (evangelical) Sunday schools (termed Bible classes). Teachers in these classes were non-professionals, largely mothers of children attending the Sunday school. Important to members of this church was the belief that the Bible was the actual word of God to be taken literally, word for word, rather than more freely, as in other Protestant churches. Through their Bible classes, argues Zinsser, young children learned and were taught a great deal about literacy. The teaching of Biblical texts itself was highly structured and followed tight routines and rituals. Children learned through listening carefully:

Teacher: Does everybody have their listening ears on today?
(Children place their hands on their ears and turn them as though turning knobs.)
(Zinsser, 1986: 60)

By memorization:

Teacher: Every time you have a problem, the Lord can help remind you of memory verses – of verses in the Bible. And that is how you can make the devil run away from you. (1986: 61)

By singing:

The B-I-B-L-E
Yes, that's the book for me!
I stand alone on the word of God
The Bible! (holding Bible aloft) (1986: 62)

And by answering questions directly from the Bible:

Teacher: What have we been learning about?
Children: (chorus) God!
Teacher: God and his son Jesus. (1986: 63)

Crucially, however, children were being taught more than reciting from the Bible and Bible stories. They were becoming familiar with books as a source of important textual material; they were learning about the role of turn taking in learning to read as well as forms of questions and answers and contextualization cues. In a wider sense, they were being taught the importance of the Bible as a source of divine inspiration and knowledge:

Mother: (to daughter) Does David have his Bible?
Daughter: (who is carrying her Bible) He'd better!
Mother: Rachel, go back and look. It was right on top of Mommy's Bible. (1986: 57)

These Bible classes form a very special type of 'community class' in which young children are being 'schooled', not just in literacy particularly and learning more generally, but in becoming worthy and valuable citizens of their community. Mother tongue teaching is not, however, an issue here. This is taken up in different ways in the two ethnographic studies described below.

For the Bangladeshi British community in East London, mother tongue learning is seen as crucial to cultural and identity maintenance. The War of Independence with West Pakistan in 1971 heralded a new beginning for Bangladesh, since victory elevated the language to national status. Pride in Bengali poetry and literature is reflected in the numerous bookshops in Brick Lane (centre of the community in East London). On a more practical level, literacy in Bengali is the means of maintaining contact between children in Britain and their relatives back home. Literacy is also crucial to have access to any form of literature from the heritage country, since the Bangladeshi British community speak Sylheti, a dialect[1] of Bengali without a written form.

Unlike the Bible classes in the congregationalist church, Bengali lessons are focused primarily on the learning of language and literacy; sometimes, indeed, they cover other curriculum areas such as maths and history. They are also held in a variety of different premises, ranging from purpose-built schools to families' living rooms. The particular class referred to below is long established and well organized:

Situated behind Petticoat Lane Market, this Bengali school is funded through the voluntary sector. It comprises two mobile rooms, the walls bare except for a few information posters made by the children. The room I enter has several rows of desks at which children sit quietly – some writing, others practising words under their breath. At the beginning, the teacher sits in front of the room, then starts to walk around. The children who are mumbling are practising the previous day's work and as the teacher passes around, the voice of the child he is listening to is momentarily amplified so that the teacher can correct if necessary before moving on to the next. Later the children read, some at a fast pace whilst others read with careful deliberation. When the teacher reaches the child I have come to observe, she reads confidently and eloquently and the few mistakes she makes are firmly corrected. Parts that are not understood are explained briefly in Sylheti ... and the lesson continues in this way to the end. (Rashid, in Gregory, 1997)

The younger children learn by individual tuition whereby teachers follow the pattern of 'demonstration/practice/test':

Teacher: K, KO, GO
Nazma: (repeats)
Teacher: Go on, read it.
Nazma: (mutters quietly)
Teacher: Read it loudly.
Nazma: (quietly says the alphabet)
Teacher: Say it again.
Nazma: (repeats the letters)
Teacher: Not like that, like this. (stresses the different inflections of the letters)
Nazma: (quietly repeats)
Teacher: Good. What next?
Nazma: (continues)
Teacher: Which one is 'Dho'?
Nazma: This one.
Teacher: Then carry on. No, say it like this 'Pho'.

(Gregory, 1996: 35–6)

Interestingly, the primers used in Bengali classes are mostly imported from Bangladesh, assume a linguistic and cultural familiarity with the text and illustrations by the children, and make no allowances for those who may never have left Britain. The children's parents are generally comfortable with these, since they may well have used the books for their own literacy learning. Nevertheless, Figure 7.1 shows how strange both illustration and text might be for young Bangladeshi British children.

The text rhymes in Bengali and reads: 'The day has gone; put the ducks and chickens in the house; give grandmother her medicine. In auntie's hand there is some rice-pudding; which is very sweet to eat; inside there are different sweet-cakes' (the Bengali text goes on to name a few). Both illustration and text assume a knowledge not just of the language, but of cultural practices (food etc.), simple village life and the extended family living together and caring for each other. All of these might be unknown in the host country but provide a link with the family's heritage.

Community classes may well combine religious practices with formal tuition of the heritage language. Where children are already second- or even third-generation immigrants, it is important to realize that this may no longer be the mother tongue. This is the situation described by Duranti et al. (1995) in their detailed analysis of 'Change and tradition in literacy instruction in a Samoan American community'. Currently more than 90,000 ethnic Samoans live in California, most born and raised there. Local communities view the setting up of a Samoan church as a priority, an important component of which is the religious school, where, like in a Samoan village, very young children are introduced to the Samoan alphabet and numbers. The study presented draws its data from the Samoan Congregational Church in Los Angeles, a church which, like others in the community, provides daily contact to all generations for the preservation of what Samoan parents and grandparents refer to as the 'Samoan way of life'. Crucially, the learning of literacy is set within cultural events such as weddings, funerals and other rites of passage for which special clothes are worn and traditional oratory can be heard. Children sing Christian songs in both languages with traditional Samoan body movements. In this manner, English code interfaces with Samoan expressive gesture, although the church service is almost entirely in Samoan.

In their classes, children aged five and younger are expected to recite and master the very same Pi Tautau (letter, sound, number and word chart) used in pastors' schools throughout the Samoan islands. At first glance, this is what the children seem to achieve, through the method of word-by-word repetition after the teacher. However, the researchers go on to point out ways in which the learning reveals important discontinuities with its village counterpart. Crucially, unlike mother tongue Samoan speakers, American Samoan children have only rudimentary knowledge of Samoan when they begin learning to read the language. Additionally, some of their teachers might not be fluent in the language themselves. A consequence of this is that some children are able to correct the teacher – a practice that would be unthinkable in Samoa. As a result of this linguistic insecurity by both children and teachers, only the actual Pi Tautau recitation takes place in Samoan. Both the introduction and any explanations are given in English. Thus, whereas in Samoa the Pi Tautau is used only to teach *reading,* in California it is used to teach the *language* as well.

Paradoxically, then, reading the Pi Tautau serves a dual function both as an initiator into the traditional

কে কোথায় আছে বল। আব্বার হাতে কি? তিনি কোথা থেকে এলেন?
কাক তাড়াবে কে? কেন? ছেলেমেয়েদের নাম কি?

আম্মা আর আব্বা।
আনু আর আবু।
আমার নাম আনু।
আমার নাম আবু।

উঠানে ধান।
কাক এল।

Figure 7.1 Illustration and text from Bengali primer

religious and linguistic heritage of the Samoan people and as an object of Westernization. In California, the practice is seen as a powerful symbol of Samoan culture; in village Samoa, it would be viewed as predominantly an Anglophile practice. In California, reading the Pi Tautau is seen as part of a wider effort to bolster Samoan identity. Yet its Westernization is revealed through both the objects depicted in the chart (Coca-Cola bottles and ocean liners) and the methods of teaching. Also, the didactic methods customary in Samoa are complemented by an individualized child-centred approach whereby peers help each other. This study, therefore, reveals the syncretism of practices taking place in community classes where children and their families have two 'homes'. By the mid twenty-first century, this situation will be common for many children throughout the world. Pi Tautau may, therefore, be indicative of many community classes throughout the world as immigrants blend different worlds, syncretizing new and old identities in their children's learning.

Although the community classes outlined above take place in different parts of the world and are quite different in the language and culture they are promoting, they share certain key features. First, all implicitly teach not just a language, literacy or religion, but a whole way of life. Importantly, in the last two examples, this way of life cannot directly replicate that of the country of origin, but will *syncretize* the new and the old. Bangladeshi British teachers need to give children individual attention, whereas they would traditionally engage in whole-class teaching, since classes usually have pupils from a variety of ages and stages. Learning, then, takes place through observation of older classmates. Samoan American teachers use English to explain the text and are also adopting more child-centred approaches. Secondly, all the above studies refer to the classroom as a safe 'haven' – a meeting-place where 'members' share common practices and expectations. Thirdly, teachers in all these classes have high expectations for their pupils, never doubting their ability to succeed. Finally, in all these classes, learning takes place within a very definite and familiar structure, using languages, routines and rituals that have been passed down across generations. Parents will not feel lost and excluded when they enter these classrooms but will immediately feel a part of the learning taking place.

CONCLUSION

Millions of new urban settlers around the world are determined to preserve their original languages in addition to acquiring the languages of their new countries.

In the contemporary world, with greater intensity of people movement and with rapid changes in communication, it has become much easier for people to maintain and develop cultural and family ties across diasporas. That, in turn, is playing an important part in the formation of new global cultures. (Gurnah, 2000: 234)

The argument is gaining ground that people with access to different languages, cultural and religious practices have not just funds of knowledge but a range of choices that are inaccessible to monolinguals. During the last two decades of the twentieth century, recognition was finally given to the importance of indigenous languages in countries colonized or conquered by those more powerful. Initial literacy programmes in indigenous languages have been integrated into mainstream classrooms in Mexico, Bolivia, Guatemala, Peru and New Zealand. In Mexico, initial literacy textbooks have been translated into 36 languages – each reflecting families in traditional dress and engaged in appropriate work practices (SEP, 1993). In New Zealand (Aotearoa in Maori), there has been a resurgence of *te reo* and *nga tikanga* (Maori language and culture) (Ministry of Education, 1996). In his work on transnational media and Turkish migrants in Europe, Robbins (2001) argues for the use of satellite TV as providing people with different 'cultural spaces' within which they can both think and have experiences. In similar ways, community classes may provide young children with different cultural and linguistic spaces where they can develop cognitive, cultural and linguistic flexibility with which to tackle the world. It is this capacity to operate across cultures, to think across and through different rituals, routines and languages, that should give children confidence to deal with their future worlds.

NOTE

1 Sometimes referred to as a local language rather than a dialect.

REFERENCES

Anderson, A.B. and Stokes, S.J. (1984) 'Social and institutional influences on the development and practice of literacy', in H. Goelman, A. Oberg and F. Smith (eds), *Awakening to Literacy.* Portsmouth, NH: Heinemann.

Arnberg, L. (1987) *Raising Children Bilingually: the Pre-school Years.* Clevedon: Multilingual Matters.

Bain, B. and Yu, A. (1980) 'Cognitive consequences of raising children bilingually: one parent, one language', *Canadian Journal of Psychology*, 34: 304–13.

Ben-Zeev, S. (1977) 'The influence of bilingualism on cognitive strategy and cognitive development', *Child Development*, 48: 1009–18.

Cummins, J. (1979) 'Linguistic interdependence and the educational development of bilingual children', *Review of Educational Research*, 49: 222–51.

Cummins, J. (1981) *Bilingualism and Minority Language Teaching*. Ontario: Ontario Institute for Studies in Education.

Cummins, J. (1992) 'Heritage language teaching in Canadian schools', *Journal of Curriculum Studies*, 24 (3): 281–6.

Department of Education and Science (1985) *An Education For All: the Report of the Committee of Inquiry into Education for Children of Ethnic Minority Groups (the Swann Report)*. London: HMSO.

Duranti, A., Ochs, E. and Ta'ase, E.K. (1995) 'Change and tradition in literacy instruction in a Samoan American community', *Educational Foundations*, fall: 57–75.

Feldman, C. and Shen, M. (1971) 'Some language-related cognitive advantages of bilingual five year olds', *Journal of Genetic Psychology*, 118: 235–44.

Fishman, J. (1979) *The Streets of East London*. London: Duckworth.

Fitzpatrick, F. (1987) *The Open Door*. Clevedon: Multilingual Matters.

Goodenough, F. (1926) 'Racial differences in the intelligence of schoolchildren', *Journal of Experimental Psychology*, 9: 388–97.

Gregory, E. (1994a) 'Non-native speakers and the National Curriculum', in G. Blenkin and V. Kelly (eds), *The National Curriculum and Early Learning*. London: Chapman.

Gregory, E. (1994b) 'Cultural assumptions and early years pedagogy: the effect of the home culture on minority children's interpretation of reading in school', *Language, Culture and Curriculum*, 7 (2): 111–24.

Gregory, E. (1996) *Making Sense of a New World: Learning to Read in a Second Language*. London: Chapman.

Gregory, E. (ed.) (1997) *One Child, Many Worlds: Early Learning in Multicultural Communities*, London: Fulton.

Gregory, E. (1998) 'Siblings as mediators of literacy in linguistic minority communities', *Language and Education*, 12 (1): 33–54.

Gregory, E. and Kelly, C. (1992) 'Bilingualism and assessment', in G. Blenkin and V. Kelly (eds), *Assessment in Early Childhood Education*. London: Chapman.

Gregory, E. and Williams, A. (2000) *City Literacies: Learning to Read across Generations and Cultures*. London: Routledge.

Gurnah, A. (2000) 'Languages and literacies for autonomy', in M. Martin-Jones and K. Jones (eds), *Multilingual Literacies*. Amsterdam: Benjamins.

Hakuta, K. (1986) *Mirror of Language: the Debate on Bilingualism*. New York: Basic.

Hamers, J.F. and Blanc, M.H. (1989) *Bilinguality and Bilingualism*. Cambridge: Cambridge University Press.

Heath, S.B. (1983) *Ways with Words: Language and Life in Communities and Classrooms*. Cambridge: Cambridge University Press.

Ianco-Worrall, A. (1972) 'Bilingualism and cognitive development', *Child Development*, 43: 1390–400.

Jesperson, O. (1923) *Language*. London: Allen and Unwin.

John-Steiner, V. (1985) 'The road to competence in an alien land: a Vygotskian perspective on bilingualism', in J.V. Wertsch (ed.), *Culture, Communication and Cognition: Vygotskian Perspectives*. Cambridge: Cambridge University Press.

Kempadoo, M. and Abdelrazak, M. (1999) *Directory of Supplementary and Mother-Tongue Classes*. London: Resource Unit for Supplementary and Mother-Tongue Schools.

Kenner, C. (1999) 'Children's understandings of text in a multilingual nursery', *Language and Education*. 13 (1): 1–16.

Kenner, C. (2000a) 'Children writing in a multilingual nursery', in M. Martin-Jones and K. Jones (eds), *Multilingual Literacies*. Amsterdam: Benjamins.

Kenner, C. (2000b) *Home Pages*. London: Trentham.

Liedtke, W.W. and Nelson, L.D. (1968) 'Concept formation and bilingualism', *Alberta Journal of Education Research*, 14: 225–32.

Linguistic Minorities Project (1985) *The Other Languages of England*. London: Routledge and Kegan Paul.

Ministry of Education (1996) 'Statement of desirable objectives and practices for chartered early childhood services', *New Zealand Education Gazette*, 3 October.

Minns, H. (1990) *Read It To Me Now!* London: Virago.

Peal, E. and Lambert, W.E. (1962) 'The relation of bilingualism and intelligence', *Psychological Monographs: General and Applied*, 76 (546): 1–23.

Rashid, N. and Gregory, E. (1997) 'Learning to read, reading to learn: the importance of siblings in the language development of young bilingual children', in E. Gregory (ed.), *One Child, Many Worlds: Early Learning in Multilingual Communities*. London: Fulton.

Robbins, K. (2001) 'Beyond imagined community? Transnational media and Turkish migrants in Europe'. Inaugural lecture, Goldsmiths' College, London.

Robertson, L. (1997) 'From Karelia to Kashmir: a journey into bilingual children's story-reading experiences within school and community literacy practice', in E. Gregory (ed.), *One Child, Many Worlds*. London: Fulton.

Rosen, H. (1999) *Are You Still Circumcised?* London: Five Leaves.

Rosowsky, A. (2001) 'Decoding as a cultural practice and its effects on the reading process of bilingual pupils', *Language and Education*, 15 (1): 56–70.

Saer, D.J. (1924) 'An inquiry into the effect of bilingualism upon the intelligence of young children', *Journal of Experimental Psychology*, 6: 232–40, 266–74.

Sapir, E. (1970) *Culture, Language and Personality*. Berkeley, CA: University of California Press.

Saxena, M. (2000) 'Taking account of history and culture in community-based research on multilingual literacy', in M. Martin-Jones and K. Jones (eds), *Multilingual Literacies*. Amsterdam: Benjamins.

Scribner, S. and Cole, M. (1981) *The Psychology of Literacy*. Cambridge, MA: Harvard University Press.

SEP (1993) Maaya T'aan, 1st edn. Secretaria de Educacion Publica. Mexico: Comision National de los libros de texto gratuitos.

Skutnabb-Kangas, T. (1984) *Bilingualism or Not? The Education of Minorities*. Clevedon: Multilingual Matters.

Sneddon, R. (2000) 'Language and literacy practices in Gujarati Muslim families', in M. Martin-Jones and K. Jones (eds), *Multilingual Literacies*. Amsterdam: Benjamins.

Street, B. (1984) *Literacy in Theory and Practice*. Cambridge: Cambridge University Press.

Swain, M. and Cummins, J. (1979) 'Bilingualism, cognitive functioning and education', *Language Teaching and Linguistics Abstracts*, 12 (1): 4–18.

Tosi, A. (1984) *Immigration and Bilingual Education*. Oxford: Pergamon.

Verhoeven, L. (1987) *Ethnic Minority Children Acquiring Literacy*. Dordrecht: Foris.

Vygotsky, L. (1962) *Thought and Language*. Cambridge, MA: MIT Press.

Wagner, D.A. (1993) *Literacy, Culture and Development: Becoming Literate in Morocco*. Cambridge: Cambridge University Press.

Wagner, D.A., Messick, B. and Spratt, J. (1986) 'Studying literacy in Morocco', in B. Schieffelin and D. Gilmore (eds), *The Acquisition of Literacy: Ethnographic Perspectives*. Norwood, NJ: Ablex.

Zinsser, C. (1986) 'For the Bible tells me so: teaching children in a fundamentalist church', in B. Schieffelin and D. Gilmore (eds), *The Acquisition of Literacy: Ethnographic Perspectives*. Norwood, NJ: Ablex.

8

Literacy within Family Life

TREVOR H. CAIRNEY

Many educators have viewed the home as an important foundation for later learning, and as the site for the emergence of practices such as literacy. But most have failed to appreciate its significance for learning in other institutional settings, particularly school. The 1990s was a period in which the work of sociolinguists, social psychologists, anthropologists, critical and cultural theorists and literacy researchers led to the questioning of previous assumptions concerning the nature of family and community literacy and its relationship to the literacy of schooling.

Increasingly, researchers have come to realize that the influence of family members and caregivers does not cease at age five. Indeed, while the role of the teacher has been shown to be vital in children's school learning, differences in family backgrounds also appear to account for a large share of variance in student school achievement. This is reflected in findings of high positive correlations between parent knowledge, beliefs and interactive styles, and children's school achievement (see Schaefer, 1991, for a detailed review). Some even suggest that the cumulative effect of a range of home-related factors may account for the greatest proportion of variability in student literacy performance (Rutter et al., 1970; Thompson, 1985).[1] As a result, family involvement in children's education has become widely recognized as an important element in effective schooling (Epstein, 1983; Delgado-Gaitan, 1991). This involvement is diverse and consists of contributions from varied household members, including parents, caregivers and extended family members such as grandparents and siblings (Taylor and Dorsey-Gaines, 1988; Gregory, 1997).

Just as we have learned a great deal about the importance of families and the home in recent times, we have also learned much about the nature of literacy. Our work in a variety of settings suggests that literacy is not a single unitary skill; rather, it is a social practice, which takes many forms, each with specific purposes and specific contexts in which they are used (Cairney, 1995a; Luke, 1993; Welch and Freebody, 1993; Gee, 1990). Children negotiate a world in which there are multiliteracies and within this complex world there are different life chances (Cope and Kalantzis, 2000).

In this chapter, 'family literacy' is defined as social and cultural practices associated with written text. The research reviewed is that which relates to how literacy is constructed, developed, valued and defined in families.[2] It has attempted to focus primarily on studies that have examined these practices in the families of preschool children. However, several studies have been included that focus on family literacy practices for young school-aged children because of the relevance of much of this work to the preschool years.

What has not been included in this chapter are studies that focus on initiatives to support family literacy practices, educate parents about school literacy, build partnerships between home and school and so on. Peter Hannon's chapter on family literacy programmes (in this volume) provides a review of this research. Other reviews of this topic have been provided by Purcell-Gates (2000) and Cairney (2002).

Before exploring what we now know about literacy learning in the family, it is essential first to provide a brief overview of foundational research in the language and literacy field.

HOW EMERGING THEORIES ON EARLY LANGUAGE AND LITERACY DEVELOPMENT SHAPED VIEWS ON THE ROLE THAT FAMILIES PLAY IN EARLY LITERACY LEARNING

It is fair to say that research on literacy in families was rather limited prior to the 1980s. While there was a great deal of research about children's early language development within the home, little specific attention was given to family literacy. Until the 1980s the prevailing view of literacy researchers and teachers was that children arrived at school in varying stages of readiness for literacy learning.[3] New school entrants were seen largely as 'blank slates' in relation to literacy. The exception to this was that some attention was given to the impact of environmental print in the 1960s and 1970s (e.g. Clark, 1976; Clay, 1979; Mason, 1965) but even this research was viewed as of interest because it helped us to understand children's early literacy learning at school.

As well as being driven by the school agenda, interest in early language learning (and hence literacy) prior to the 1960s was shaped by behavioural theories. Such theoretical foundations led to views of literacy that assumed that children were not ready to read and write until age five or six, and that this required instruction in schools if it was to be achieved (Hall, 1987). Studies of language acquisition were shaped by attention to the number, variety and frequency with which words were used, and the grammatical structures within which they were embedded.

There were two dominant perspectives during this period: maturational readiness and developmental readiness (Crawford, 1995). Maturational readiness, with its roots in the work of researchers such as Gesell (1925), argued that children pass through a number of stages that reflect biological maturation. Developmental readiness was an extension of this work and reflected strongly the work of developmental psychologists such as Piaget and Thorndike. Advocates of developmental readiness (e.g. Chall, 1967; Durkin, 1966) argued that children needed to be 'ready to read' if they were to have success. Hence, they placed greater importance on the alphabetic code. Families were seen, at best, as having a minor role in literacy development, and even then, only as they contributed to support of school literacy learning.

However, the 1960s and 1970s also saw the emergence of important changes in our understanding of oral language development that were eventually to alter the way we viewed the role of the family in development. Harste et al. have argued that developmental psycholinguistics 'altered the

profession's view of language learning. Instead of passively awaiting external reinforcement, children came to be seen as actively attempting to understand the nature of the language spoken around them, making predictions and testing hypotheses about how language worked' (1984: 56).

But it was not until the 1980s that the first significant changes in the positioning of families occurred as two new perspectives emerged. The first has become known as emergent literacy and had its roots in the work of Clay (1966), Holdaway (1979), Wells (1982; 1986), Harste et al. (1984), Mason and Allen (1986), Teale and Sulzby (1986) and others. Hall (1987) provided one of the earliest syntheses of the emergent literacy research and did much to translate this work into a form that could inform early childhood practice. The emergent literacy work was influenced strongly by disciplines other than developmental psychology, particularly psycholinguistics (e.g. K. Goodman, 1965; 1967; Y. Goodman, 1978) and linguistics (Halliday, 1973; 1975; Wells, 1986) as well as research on early writing development (e.g. Teale and Sulzby, 1986). These different influences each contributed to new perspectives on the social dimensions of literacy, the way in which meaning is constructed as part of the reading and writing processes, and the role that adults in and outside the school play in children's literacy development.

What these perspectives contributed to an emerging knowledge of families and family literacy was an increased understanding of the critical role that early literacy experiences play in children's school literacy learning. This included a new appreciation that:

- Family support of literacy experiences was foundational to later literacy learning.
- Guided interaction between parents/caregivers and children in relation to story reading or early print experiences was important.
- The development of the alphabetic code had its foundations in children's early experiences of environmental print.

Almost in parallel to the development of emergent literacy was the rise of constructivist and sociolinguistic perspectives that were based strongly on the work of Vygotsky (1978). Researchers such as Harste et al. (1984) and Cook-Gumperz (1986) rejected developmental psychologists' staged notions of children's early learning. Drawing instead on the work of social psychology, anthropology and sociolinguistics, these researchers saw spoken language and literacy as cultural tools that shape individuals as they grow and transform behaviour as it is internalized. Rich literacy experiences, scaffolded support (Bruner, 1983; 1986; Rogoff, 1990) and encouragement of meaning making and risk taking were more fully appreciated as a vital part of child language learning.

Sociolinguistic theories of language derived from writers like Bahktin (1935/1981), Gumperz (1986), Halliday (1975) and Hymes (1974) also played a major role in this shift. These theories built upon the basic understanding that language is made as people act and react to one another. From this was derived a number of key related constructs. First, people learn to be literate primarily in groups as they relate to others to accomplish social and communicative functions. Secondly, literacy is purpose driven and context bound. Thirdly, people react to the actions of others as well as to set patterns of group interaction. Fourthly, people may act with and react to each other through sequences of actions, not just single acts.

One final influence on how family literacy has been viewed was the emergence of 'critical literacy' (Crawford, 1995). This perspective draws heavily on the work of critical theorists, sociolinguistics and cultural studies. Its major contribution to our understanding of family literacy is that:

- Differences between the discourses of home and school can make a difference to the success of some children (Gee, 1990).
- An acceptance of cultural differences between home and school can lead to more responsive curricula that offer all children greater chances of success in learning.
- Some families are disadvantaged by power relationships that fail to value the funds of knowledge that some children and their families bring to school, while others are advantaged (see Moll, 1992; Moll et al., 1992).

As Solsken points out, the major contribution of this work has been to help us to identify 'the social practices by which schools, families and individuals reproduce, resist and transform hierarchies of social relations and their positions within them' (1993: 7). Furthermore, it has enabled research and educational initiatives concerned with family literacy to be critiqued in new ways.

The combined and overlapping impact of these quite disparate scholarly traditions was to bring about a significant shift in the way literacy was defined and studied and an increased understanding of the relationship between the literacy of home and school.

RECENT FINDINGS FROM FAMILY LITERACY RESEARCH

Building on the foundations of the above literacy research and the work across a variety of other related disciplines, much more is now known about literacy in families. I want to discuss what the literature tells us under four key headings, each of which reflects a broad insight into the nature and importance of family literacy:

- Children acquire literacy as part of complex processes of enculturation.
- There are differences between the literacy practices of home and school that impact on literacy learning at home and school.
- Shared reading plays a key role in family literacy practices.
- The literacy practices of home are complex and varied.

Children acquire literacy as part of complex processes of enculturation

There have been a number of studies that are based on the foundational premise that children learn and develop as they try to make sense of their world. They are seen as socialized from birth into the cultural practices of families and community members with whom they share their lives. As McNaughton (1995) points out, literacy, like other cultural practices, functions to socialize children into specific ways of acting and thinking which are seen as appropriate by the group or community within which the actions are embedded.

It appears from practical experience and extensive research that from the beginning of life, parents introduce children to the complexities of language. Parents communicate with their children and jointly make sense of a shared world. The parent's role is complex and includes adopting the role of listener, prompter, information giver, asker of questions, and fellow meaning maker interested in the communication process (Cairney, 1989; 1990; Lindfors, 1985; McNaughton, 1995; Snow, 1983; Wells, 1985; 1986).

As Clay points out: 'Remarkable learning has already occurred before children pass through the school doors. Even those who are most reluctant to speak have learned a great deal about the language of community' (1998: 1–2). From birth, parents and their children construct meaning together and the child is socialized into the cultural practices of community through language. Families do this by selecting, arranging and using specific experiences, which serve to show what is valued and seen as useful by family members (Cairney, 2002).

What the above work demonstrates is how literacy is developed within families as part of the social practices of life. Literacy is not developed in a culturally neutral way; rather it is interwoven with the enculturation of each child, as written text is implicated in human relationships. As such, differences exist in the way literacy is viewed, defined, supported and used as part of family cultural practices.

There are differences between the literacy practices of home and school that impact on literacy learning at home and school

There has been a long interest in the social differences[4] that exist between families and individuals, and in particular the linguistic differences that might impact on later learning and achievement. As Wells (1986) suggests, because language is a social activity it is not unreasonable to expect differences between children that may be related to their membership of social groups such as families. As a result, there has been strong interest in understanding variations in early language and literacy development across various social and cultural groups.

This body of work has also helped us to understand the cultural variation that occurs across communities and families in the way that literacy is defined and supported. One of the most significant early studies to document cultural variations in literacy acquisition was the work of Scribner and Cole (1981). They found that the Vai people of Liberia used three different writing systems for different purposes. Arabic literacy was learned by rote as part of religious practices, English was learned as part of formal schooling, and finally, the Vai language was learned informally at home and in the community and for personal communication such as letters. What Scribner and Cole concluded was that each of these 'literacies' was acquired and used for different social and cultural purposes.

Heath (1983) found in her well-known ethnography in the Piedmont Carolinas that there was significant variation in the use of literacy practices across three communities. There was variation in the acquisition of oral language, and the manner in which parents introduced children to literacy and its purposes. By focusing on story reading she was able to document significant differences in community styles of literacy socialization.

In a white middle class community (Maintown), children were socialized into a life in which books and information gained from them was seen as having a significant role in learning. Parents and other adults interacted with children from six months using book reading events. They asked information questions about these books, and related the content to everyday situations, encouraging them to share their own stories. Children in a second white working class community (Roadville) took part in book reading where the texts were more likely to be alphabet or number books, real life stories, nursery rhymes or Bible stories, rather than written narratives. The parents asked factual questions about the books, but did not encourage the children to relate the books to events in their lives. Within a third working class African-American community (Trackton), parents rarely provided book reading events. Instead, they used oral stories that focused primarily on fictional stories or the positioning of familiar events into new contexts. These literacy forms were equally sophisticated, but they were not privileged in schools, nor did they prepare children for school literacy practices.

Duranti and Ochs (1986) found that the children of families in a Samoan village needed to cope with different forms of interaction across home and school settings. In the family, for example, complimenting and praising was a much more reciprocal process than in schools and the achievement of task at home was seen as a social product dependent on the participation of different group members.

Snow (1977) also found that there were variations across class groups, with working class mothers using more directives than middle class and upper class mothers. She also identified a key difference across social class groups and observed that middle class families prepared their preschool children to understand decontextualized language. This involved active scaffolding of children's interaction with text as they expanded, extended or clarified their children's utterances

The demonstration of diversity across different social contexts has also led to an interest in how such diversity compares to the seeming uniformity of schooling (see, for example, Cairney et al., 1995a; Freebody et al., 1995) and has an impact on school learning. Much of the research in the last decade on matches and mismatches between the literacies of home and school can be traced to early work on social differences in spoken language in the preschool years. One of the earliest studies to impact on this field of inquiry was the influential (but often misused and misunderstood) work of Bernstein. Bernstein (1964; 1971; 1972) argued that educational disadvantage (that had long been identified as in some way related to social class) was related not to linguistic abilities but rather to the ways in which these abilities had been used as part of daily life. He argued that working class as opposed to middle class families were more likely to emphasize specific relationships in their families and through these relationships to use language resources in different ways. Hence, rather than lacking linguistic resources, working class families simply use different resources in different ways. Bernstein suggested that as a result, these families used what he referred to as a 'restricted' linguistic code in which a great deal of the speaker's meaning was implicit because it was already assumed to be known. Middle class families on the other hand showed in their interactions with children more personal relationships and were more explicit in their use of language, making their views much clearer. This he termed an 'elaborated' linguistic code.

Bernstein's research spawned a number of other studies (see, for example, Hawkins, 1969; Tough, 1977) of early language development that collectively gave credence to what has been an enduring (if somewhat simplistic) belief that children of middle class families generally have linguistically more complex language than those from the working class. The interpretation of Bernstein's earliest work also gave rise to a number of less than helpful deficit theories[5] of children's early language and literacy development. However, Bernstein's later work has gone some way towards redressing this misinterpretation (see, for example, Bernstein, 1996).

The Bristol Study (see Wells, 1986; C.G. Wells, 1982) provided evidence that undermined simplistic attempts to make causal links between social class and early language development. In this project information was compiled on home background (primarily education and occupation) for each of 128 children to create four social class subgroups. When these groups were compared on a variety of language measures there were no statistically significant differences. On the basis of these findings Wells (1986) concludes that there is little evidence to suggest class stereotypes have validity in relation to spoken language development of children at the point when they enter schooling.

But just as many have asked questions about the relationship between family background and early language development, so too researchers have considered the impact of differences in families on early literacy achievement. As argued elsewhere (e.g. Cairney, 1994; 1995b; Cairney and Munsie, 1995a; 1995b) the match and mismatch in language and literacy between home/community and school, are of vital importance in addressing the specific needs of all students, particularly those who experience difficulties with literacy and schooling. Differences in school literacy achievement are not due to differences in the volume of preschool or home literacy experiences. Indeed, many researchers have shown that virtually all children in highly literate countries such as the USA have extensive experiences with written language (Heath, 1983; Harste et al., 1984; Teale, 1986). Rather than reflecting deficits in skills and experiences, these differences in school literacy achievement seem to have more to do with some students'

lack of familiarity with the literacy practices of schooling, and schools' failure to recognize and build on the literacy practices children bring with them from home.

The work of Luis Moll and his colleagues (Moll, 1992; Moll et al., 1992; Gonzales and Moll, 1994) has provided an important alternative perspective that suggests that variations across families are in fact a resource rather than a set of determinants of literacy success. Moll and his colleagues argue that all children live in families that have resources and that part of these resources is the knowledge that family members possess, which they argue represents 'funds' that can be used by the children as part of later learning in school and the world. The role of teachers and schools is seen by Moll as to acknowledge and work with community funds of knowledge to design more effective literacy curricula.

Similarly, Weinstein-Shr and Quintero (1995) and Taylor (1983) argue that diversity in family means of support is a rich resource rather than a deficit for children. They argue that schools need to spend less time trying to conform families to school practices and more time understanding how schools can extend literacy opportunities outside the narrow definitions of classroom practices. Furthermore, we need to understand learners' different identities and the ways in which they learn best.

What this area of research highlights is that differences do exist in the literacy practices of home and school, and that understanding these variations is important.

Shared reading plays a key role in family literacy practices

A number of detailed accounts of children's early storybook reading (Butler, 1979; Crago and Crago, 1983; White, 1954) have increased understanding of how shared reading experiences in the home are intertwined with the daily fabric of life and how they are an extension of human relationships in the children's world. Each of these accounts demonstrates how the process of learning to read is socially complex, and involves parents and children sharing in an imaginative process that integrates factors of language, thought and feeling (Meek, 1991).

However, while research suggests that reading to children is important, it is less certain how prevalent this is as a family literacy practice and what form it takes.[6] Meek (1991) suggests that traditionally we have assumed that it is the amount of reading that is critical, that picturebooks are the beginning text type for all children, and that the parent reads and the child listens. The limited evidence that we do have suggests that the picture is more complex than this. These views are borne out by some of the early research on parent language interactions with children where texts were evident (e.g. Wells, 1986).

A number of detailed accounts of reading inter-actions within researchers' families have been help-ful in providing some insights into the complexity of this partnership. For example, the work of Crago and Crago (1983) showed how one child in a literature-rich home moved in the first four years of life from being a listener to stories to a reteller and finally a narrator of her own stories. Similarly Ninio and Bruner (1978), in their research on two different families from two different social classes, identified that a joint book reading cycle could be identified that involved joint construction based around pointing to pictures, page turning and con-stant conversation, positive parent feedback and naming behaviour. Miller et al. (1986) also studied the early reading behaviour of three families with a child at age two. Reading with a partner was com-mon and consisted of an initial agreement on the nature of the activity (e.g. 'Let's look at books'), followed by the act of reading which consisted in turning pages, pointing to pictures and much verbal activity. Parents used naming to gain the child's attention and engagement (e.g. 'Let's look', 'See the rabbit' etc). Children also used language to gain the parent's engagement but this was typically what the researchers called a 'notice verb' (e.g. look, see). This was followed (as Ninio and Bruner found) by cycles of 'query' (e.g. 'What's this? Say "bird"') and 'label' (e.g. squirrel). Positive feed-back was also given, and finally 'storytelling' occurred, with narratives being told that were asso-ciated with the text.

Phillips and McNaughton (1990) explored the nature of storybook interactions based on observa-tions of 10 families who had identified themselves as interested in books and book reading. The families had incomes that placed them in the top two socio-economic groups. Analysis of the multiple readings within families showed that parents concentrated on the narrative in first readings but over time they reduced this emphasis and increased efforts to make links between the text and experiences. Nevertheless exchanges about the narrative accounted for 86% of all interactions. Children also initiated more questions over subsequent readings of the same text. While this work provides useful insights into the story reading practices of more wealthy white families, there are still many unanswered questions concerning families from dif-ferent cultural backgrounds and those who are from lower socio-economic classes.

Snow (1993) attempted to compare low-income families that evidently supported their children's learning well to those who did not. She found that the parents' most significant contributions were non-print-related activities, particularly language interaction and talk. She found that effective home talk provided children with definitions that assisted learning. They also exchanged information with their children, showed affection and support, enforced discipline and kept them on task, and expressed feelings. Snow concluded that these interactions supported children's early literacy learning. These findings have been supported by a study in Australia by Hill et al. (1998).

Williams (1990) compared the shared reading practices of two groups of mothers. One group sent their children to a disadvantaged preschool in a poor neighbourhood; the other group sent their children to a privately run preschool. He noted four main differ-ences in home reading practices from transcripts of reading sessions. First, mothers from the disadvan-taged preschool (DPS) tended to read lengthy sections of the text with little linguistic interaction when compared to mothers from the private preschool (PPS). Secondly, there was more demand from the children at the PPS to display shared knowl-edge in the form of ritual displays than the DPS children. Thirdly, the conversation of the children at the DPS was closely tied to the fictional world of the book, whereas the children from the PPS linked their own world more regularly to the text. Finally, children from the PPS were given more opportunities to choose the texts than the children from the DPS.

The actual nature of the adult interactions with the child has also received attention by researchers. For example, Resnick et al. (1987) found that parental behaviour during reading had an impact on children's emergent literacy. Parental behaviours that fostered shared reading were evaluated and it was concluded that the amount of exposure to read-ing materials and the degree of facilitative verbal-izations by parents (e.g. describing pictures, whispering, 'cooing' etc.) were important.

The above research confirms that shared reading is an important family literacy practice and that the interaction with family members can vary in form across social and cultural contexts. However, there is still limited research on the exact impact of this practice on a wide range of families across different social and cultural groups. Further work is needed to document the relative importance of shared read-ing. While it is a common literacy practice and has been widely researched, its prevalence should not lead us to overlook the importance of the many other varied forms of literacy present in the daily lives of families.

The literacy practices of home are complex and varied

What the above discussion has shown is that while a great deal is known about early literacy development, there have been relatively few studies that have provided a detailed description of literacy practices within a wide range of families. This section summarizes several major research studies that have spent time in families attempting to understand the complexity of literacy practices.

Any discussion of literacy within families would be deficient without a treatment of the significant work of Denny Taylor. It was Taylor's (1983) work that spawned the term 'family literacy' and it has provided some of the most detailed insights into the nature of literacy practices within homes. Her series of ethnographic investigations began in 1977 with the study of a single family and by 1979 had grown to six white middle class families living in suburban areas within 100 km of New York City. Her study spanned a period of three years and involved her becoming part of the lives of her informants.

Taylor's work has contributed a number of critical insights. First, literacy is implicated in the lives of family members and discussions of literacy included reference to its place in the memories of the past, particularly in relation to schooling and the sharing of key literacy experiences. Secondly, the way parents mediated literacy experiences varied across and within families (e.g. in relation to the latter, even different siblings had different experiences). Thirdly, there were 'shifts' in parents' approaches to the 'transmission of literacy styles and values' which coincided with children beginning to learn to read and write in school (1983: 20). Fourthly, older siblings had an influence on shaping their younger siblings' experiences of literacy. Fifthly, literacy experiences within families are rich and varied and include reading and writing necessary for the running of the household (e.g. keeping financial records, reading junk mail), reading for information and pleasure, communicating with others (e.g. letters, notes) and establishing social connections with other people. Sixthly, literacy surrounds family members and is part of the fabric of life. Finally, children's growing awareness of literacy involves experiences that are woven into daily activities and could go 'almost unnoticed as the children's momentary engagement merges with the procession of other interests' (1983: 56).

The findings of Taylor's early work informed a number of later studies that similarly provided 'thick descriptions' and offered additional insights. In particular, her work with Dorsey-Gaines in conducting an ethnography of black families living in urban poverty (Taylor and Dorsey-Gaines, 1988) added much to her earlier descriptions of white middle class families. What this work also did was offer a theoretical frame for the literacy practices observed that was lacking in Taylor's previous study. This framework built on the work of Heath (1983) and Taylor (1983) and described literacy practices in 22 categories. These examples included instrumental reading (i.e. to gain information, accomplish tasks or meet practical needs); social-interactional reading (to gain information linked to relationships, to build relationships etc.); news-related reading; recreational reading; writing as a substitute for oral messages (notes and messages); writing as an aid to memory (grocery lists, telephone numbers etc.); financial reading (reading stock reports, reading forms etc.); recreational writing (puzzles, crosswords etc.); work-related writing (job applications, forms etc.); and so on.

Based on their observations, Taylor and Dorsey-Gaines drew a number of conclusions that are important. In particular, their work showed that within these poor black families there was a richness of literacy experience that previous studies had not been able to recognize, and that institutional factors rather than a lack of parental support had a far greater impact on lack of school success for these families. This supports Auerbach's (1995) view that the extent to which families use literacy in socially significant ways as an integral part of family life is a key factor in shaping literacy acquisition. These findings are important because they suggest that race, economic status and social setting should not be used as significant correlates of literacy. They support the conclusion that there is a rich diversity of literacy practices within families that should be acknowledged and tapped.

The difficulty of making sense of the varied literacy practices that are observed in families is common to many studies. A major problem has been that few studies use comparable categories or even broad definitions of literacy practices. Some of these studies tend to define and list separate literacy events[7] (see, for example, Leichter, 1984; Teale, 1986) and others use a mix of reader and writer purpose and function (e.g. Heath, 1983; Taylor and Dorsey-Gaines, 1988); some use a combination of audience and purpose (e.g. Cairney et al., 1995b; Barton and Padmore, 1991) and others use linguistic categories such as written genres.

Another study that attempted to consider literacy practices across different social and cultural groups was conducted by McNaughton (1995) in New Zealand. He concluded from detailed case studies of 17 families in New Zealand that what happens in the families is the most critical determinant of children's early literacy development. His description of the literacy practices of Maori, Samoan and Pakeha families whose income earners were from non-professional occupations provided a picture of resourceful families able to support their children's early literacy learning. What is useful about McNaughton's analysis is that he was able to describe the variable way in which families use time, space and varied resources to help preschool children to learn literacy. He noted three different ways in which families supported literacy learning:

- joint activities – where another person (parent, relative, sibling) provided guidance in a specific literacy event such as story reading
- personal activities – involving the child practising a specific form of literacy on their own (e.g. scribbling)
- ambient activities – involving literacy practices in which the child is immersed as part of daily life, those practices that occur 'around' the child while they go about life.

Like Taylor's work, McNaughton's research demonstrates the 'everydayness' of literacy in the family and provides detailed analysis of common literacy practices in the home.

As part of an Australian government project that sought to examine the relationship between home, school and community literacy, Cairney and Ruge (1998) described the literacy practices evident within 27 families. From these 27 families, a total of 37 children were observed. While these children were of primary school age, the families also had approximately 20 preschool children. Each participating family was asked to collect a range of data including audiotape literacy events, an audit of home literacy resources, a log of all reading and writing activities, and photographs of significant literacy events in the home (using disposable cameras supplied by the researchers). One member of each family was also asked to act as co-researcher. The child and family member co-researchers involved in this phase of data collection recorded a range of home literacy events. A total of 130 home literacy events were recorded.

Cairney and Ruge (1998) identified four distinct purposes for literacy in the homes and classrooms in their study: literacy for establishing and maintaining relationships; literacy for accessing or displaying information; literacy for pleasure and/or self-expression; and literacy for skills development. Table 8.1 below lists the identified literacy practices, as well as sample home literacy events in each category.

One important finding from this study was that the data showed that specific literacy practices may contribute to, and constitute part of, different literacy events in different contexts depending on the understandings and purposes of the participants. For example, the intended purpose of a newsletter from school may be to give parents access to information about school policies or activities. Alternatively, the intended purpose may be to maintain communication between home and school and thereby develop the relationship between families and the school. However, in reading the newsletter at home, families may have very different purposes and 'use' the newsletter in different ways (e.g. one family used it for oral reading practice).

Cairney and Ruge (1998) also found that the families in their study differed greatly in the extent to which literacy was *visible* in everyday life, ranging from the ever pervasive nature of literacy in one family home to the seemingly rare occurrence of literacy events in another household. There was considerable variation in the amount and types of literacy resources available in each home.

One of the striking features of literacy practices in the homes of many of the families in this study was the extent to which 'school literacy' dominated home contexts. That is, the particular types and uses of literacy usually associated with schooling were prominent in many families. This prominence was manifest primarily in the amount of time spent on homework activities and, to a lesser extent, siblings 'playing schools'. While this might seem irrelevant for a review of early childhood family literacy practices, it is important to remember that once the first child in any family is five years old then that family is effectively under the strong influence of school literacy practices (see Cairney and Ruge, 1998; Freebody et al., 1995). As well, there is evidence to suggest that the literacy practices privileged right from the birth of a first child are strongly shaped by the parents' experience of school literacy as well as the desire to prepare the preschool child for later schooling (Cairney and Ruge, 1998).

CONCLUSION

As suggested at the commencement of this chapter, the last 20 years have seen a deepened interest in understanding literacy within the home. As a result, a great deal has been learned about the importance of families and the home as sites for early literacy development. Research suggests that children experience multiliteracies at home, and that literacy is defined, used and supported in accordance with social and cultural differences.

As well, literacy in the home is diverse. Young children encounter print on food products, on television, in books, magazines and computer games,

Table 8.1 *Classification of Cairney and Ruge's (1998) literacy practices and examples of home literacy events in each category*

Literacy practices	Sample literacy events
• Literacy for establishing or maintaining relationships	Reading/writing letters to/from relatives or friends Making/writing birthday cards Reading 'bedtime' stories Writing/reading notes to/from school Playing 'schools'
• Literacy for accessing or displaying information	Completing homework activities Doing school projects Reading/discussing newspaper articles Reading store catalogues, 'junk' mail Reading/discussing non-fiction texts Study related (e.g. TAFE coursework) Use of computer/Internet/fax Reading TV guide Reading maps, timetables, calendars, menus Writing/reading notes to/from family members Reading/writing recipes Writing/reading shopping list Reading/writing labels or instructions Reading street signs Reading TV subtitles Writing/reading appointment diary Filling in forms Writing/reading list of jobs/chores Writing/reading for financial, accounting or banking purposes
• Literacy for pleasure and/or self-expression	Practising writing own name Drawing/labelling pictures Reading books, magazines or comics Playing card or board games Doing crossword puzzles, find-a-word puzzles Writing/reading stories or poems Writing/drawing cartoons or comics Keeping a personal diary Writing own life history Writing songs Playing computer/ Sega/ Nintendo games
• Literacy for skills development	Completing homework activities 'Read aloud' practice Phonics drills Writing the alphabet

flashing at them on the freeway, and even on clothing. The typical preschool child experiences more diverse forms of literacy than at any time in human history. Print is everywhere. Children also 'read' a myriad of pictures, images, words and sounds as they observe others using automatic teller machines, writing letters, collecting faxes, reading messages on mobile phones, and playing video games. Increasingly, they watch members of their families purchasing products via computer, answering e-mail, interacting with their televisions, and downloading images, recipes, and other documents from the Internet (Cairney, 1995a). In the increasingly digital age there also appears to be greater opportunity for the interactive experience of multiple media than ever before.

However, it is evident from the studies reviewed here that much work still needs to be done in understanding family literacy practices. We still know little about the diversity of reading experiences and early writing. We know even less about the way in which the multiliteracies of life interact and shape each other and the people who use them. There are three main reasons for this. First, much of the early writing research still uses definitions of literacy that are limited and hence researchers restrict observation to a more limited range of literacy practices that appear far too often to simply mirror school literacy.[8] Secondly, a concern with how family literacy impacts on school learning has led almost inevitably to efforts to examine family literacy as subordinated to the primary concerns of researchers to improve school learning. Thirdly, the methods that have been used to examine family literacy have been very limited. Except for a small number of significant ethnographies, few get 'close enough' to, or spend enough time with, families to gain insights into the depth and diversity of literacy practices at home. The major challenge for researchers is to address these issues as we attempt to gain further insights into literacy within families.

As well as the above general issues, there are a number of specific areas of great need in relation to ongoing research. First, we need more studies that consider factors such as gender, social class and culture while examining literacy across diverse contexts. For example, Razey (2002) has recently examined gender differences in the literacy practices of home and school for children aged five years. In her study gender construction was examined by observing and analysing the literacy interactions of six kindergarten children at school and home. Her analysis showed that there were differences in the ways that teachers interacted with boys and girls. Boys were asked more questions and in turn asked more questions themselves than girls. Within homes, Razey found that each child's pattern of interactions with parents was unique. As well, what counted as literacy was seen differently in many homes. This was in contrast to school lessons where far less diversity was observed, consistent with the work of Cairney and Ruge (1998) and Freebody et al. (1995). In considering both home and school contexts, Razey was able to conclude that for the families studied, school was a 'linguistic leveller' that failed to acknowledge and build on the linguistic diversity of families.

There is also a need to examine in more detail the synergistic relationship between the literacies of home and school. While this chapter has examined some of the research on mismatches between the literacies of home and school, we need further research that examines the impact of school literacy on the shaping of family literacy practices as well as an increased understanding of how family literacy intersects with community literacy. Rather than studying home literacy in order to shed light on

learning at school, we need to give more attention to understanding how school literacy practices shape home literacy – and why. As well, there is a need to understand the cultural diversity of literacy in families to inform the development of more responsive curricula (Cairney, 1997).

Another area of urgent need is the examination of how multimedia and digital literacy demands are impacting on literacy practices within the family and how this intersects with the forgotten part of the literacy context triad, the community. While we know that literacy practices in our world are changing (see, for example, Cairney, 1995a; Cope and Kalantzis, 2000; Lankshear, 1997; Makin and Jones Diaz, 2002), far less is known about the impact this has had on the literacy practices of the average family. Accounts like those of Lankshear (1997) are helpful in enabling us to understand the increasing complexity and multimodal nature of literacy, but there is still more to learn about what it means for literacy acquisition. While there is much (almost polemical) writing about how literacy is changing and how the literacy practices of the digital age are different, little definitive work has been done within families to assess the impact of such changes on the way children experience literacy in the first years of life.

Finally, we need to remember that literacy is not culturally and ideologically neutral (Street, 1995). Hence we need to examine what this means for literacy acquisition and the relationship of family literacy to life and, in particular, public institutions such as schools. It is important to understand how family literacy practices and their relationship to school literacy are implicated in power relationships that affect life chances.

The research reviewed in this chapter is rich in its findings concerning the importance of the family as the first and perhaps most critical site for literacy acquisition. The evidence also shows that interactions between adults and children as they encounter literacy are significant in shaping literacy practices and the human relationships that surround and are embedded in literacy. There is also a richness in literacy experience that transcends social class and culture. However, there is also evidence to suggest that there are significant variations in the way that literacy is culturally defined and used and that understanding this complexity may well be important for understanding the role that later institutions play in literacy and learning. Children experience a richness of literacy practices at home that is not replicated in school. This richness appears to have been affected by the increase in multimodal literacy experiences as we enter an increasingly digital age. Understanding variations across the contexts of home, school and community, and how these relate to other factors such as social disadvantage, gender and language diversity, is perhaps the greatest challenge for literacy researchers in the future.

NOTES

1 There has been great debate over the last 10 years concerning the reason for such a relationship. However, this is outside the scope of this chapter. Broadly, there appear to be two extreme positions. At one end of the continuum we have what can be called deficit driven explanations. These are based on the faulty assumption that there are families who lack the specific skills to enable them to create an environment of support that will enable children to succeed at school. At the other end of the continuum is what could be called an educational inadequacy explanation, which suggests such problems simply represent a failure of educational institutions to develop student strengths and abilities. Neither of these explanations is very helpful because each assumes that social practices such as literacy are skills to be mastered that are dependent on the possession of the right mix of abilities and access to 'appropriate' teaching practices. Much of the variability of student achievement in school reflects discrepancies that exist between school resources and instructional methods, and the cultural practices of the home (Au and Kawakami, 1984; Auerbach, 1989; 1995; Cairney, 1995a; Cazden, 1988; Heath, 1983; Moll, 1992), not deficiencies.

2 Family is defined here as any group of people that includes at least one parent/caregiver and one child. Such units may include combinations of biological parents, step-parents, *de facto* partners, other adult family members and children of other members of the same family unit.

3 It is important to note that while I use the term 'literacy' throughout this chapter to encompass the multiliteracies within the domains of reading and writing, this was not the case prior to the late 1970s. To this point in time the terms 'reading' and 'writing' were used separately. When using the term 'literacy' in relation to the 1970s and earlier, I am referring to the combined fields of reading and writing research.

4 This is a term that Gordon Wells (1986) uses to avoid problems caused by the use of the terms 'social class' or 'socio-economic status'.

5 There have been a number of useful descriptions of the various explanations of the relationship between social difference and variable school achievement (e.g. Au, 1995; Ogbu, 1993). Wells (1986) discusses three explanations: deficit views (i.e. children and families are deficient linguistically); mismatches between the school and the students' dialect and language capabilities (i.e. schools need to be responsive); and in between a societal limitations view (i.e. society at large had problems in terms of

distributions of power and control). These three positions are variously reworked in other work by Au (1995), Cairney (1994; 1995a), Cairney and Ruge (1998), Comber (1999), Comber et al. (2001) and Luke (1993).

6 It is worth mentioning that similarly little is known about how parents listen to their children read, something that largely replaces parents reading to their children in the school years. For an interesting discussion of this issue and details of his own research see Hannon (1995).

7 It is important to differentiate between literacy events and practices. The term 'literacy event' has its roots in the sociolinguistic idea of speech events dating back to the work of Dell Hymes in 1962, but the concept was developed further by Heath (1982; 1983) to describe a distinct communicative situation where literacy has a key role. For Heath, a literacy event is 'any occasion in which a piece of writing is integral to the nature of the participants' interactions and their interpretive processes' (1982: 23). According to Barton, 'literacy *events* are the particular activities in which literacy has a role: they may be regular repeated activities. Literacy *practices* are the general cultural ways of utilizing literacy that people draw upon in a literacy event' (1991: 5).

8 There are many interesting discussions concerning how one's definition of literacy shapes one's research, writing or practice. Street (1995), for example, would suggest that such limited approaches reflect 'autonomous' models of literacy that see it as a culturally and politically neutral technical skill.

REFERENCES

Au, K. (1995) *Literacy Instruction in Multicultural Settings*. Fort Worth: Harcourt Brace Janovich College Publishers.

Au, K. and Kawakami, A. (1984) 'Vygotskian perspectives on discussion processes in small-group reading lessons', in P. Peterson and L.C. Wilkinson (eds), *The Social Context of Instruction*. Portsmouth, NH: Heinemann.

Auerbach, E. (1989) 'Toward a social-contextual approach to family literacy', *Harvard Educational Review*, 59: 165–81.

Auerbach, E. (1995) 'Which way for family literacy: intervention or empowerment?', in L.M. Morrow (ed.), *Family Literacy: Connections in Schools and Communities*. Newark, DE: International Reading Association.

Bakhtin, M. (1935/1981) 'Discourse in the novel', in M. Holquist (ed.), *The Dialogic Imagination*. Austin, TX: University of Texas Press.

Barton, D. (1991) 'Literacy: an Introduction to The Ecology of Written Language', Oxford: Blackwell.

Barton, D. and Padmore, S. (1991) 'Roles, networks and values in everyday writing', in D. Barton and R. Ivanic (eds), *Writing in the Community*. London: Sage. pp. 58–77.

Bernstein, B. (1964) 'Aspects of language and learning in the genesis of the social process', in D. Hymes (ed.), *Language in Culture and Society*. New York: Harper and Row.

Bernstein, B. (1971) *Class, Codes and Control*, vol. 1. London: Routledge and Kegan Paul.

Bernstein, B. (1972) 'A sociolinguistic approach to education with some references to educability', in J.J. Gumperz and D. Hymes (eds), *Directions in Sociolinguistics*. New York: Holt, Rinehart and Winston.

Bernstein, B. (1996) *Pedagogy, Symbolic Control and Identity: Theory, Research, Critique*. London: Taylor and Francis.

Bruner, J. (1983) *Child's Talk: Learning to Use Language*. Oxford: Oxford University Press.

Bruner, J. (1986) *Actual Minds, Possible Worlds*. Cambridge, MA: Harvard University Press.

Butler, D. (1979) *Cushla and Her Books*. London: Hodder and Stoughton.

Cairney, T.H. (1989) 'Text talk: helping students to learn about language', *English in Australia*, 90: 60–8.

Cairney, T.H. (1990) *Teaching Reading Comprehension: Meaning Makers at Work*. Milton Keynes: Open University Press.

Cairney, T.H. (1994) 'Family literacy: moving towards new partnerships in education', *Australian Journal of Language and Literacy*, 17 (4): 262–75.

Cairney, T.H. (1995a) *Pathways to Literacy*. London: Cassell.

Cairney, T.H. (1995b) 'Developing parent partnerships in secondary literacy learning', *Journal of Adolescent and Adult Literacy*, 38 (7): 520–6.

Cairney, T.H. (1997) 'Acknowledging diversity in home literacy practices: moving towards partnerships with parents', *Early Child Development and Care*, 127–8: 61–73.

Cairney, T.H. (2002) 'Bridging home and school literacy: in search of transformative approaches to curriculum', *Early Child Development and Care*, 172 (2): 153–72.

Cairney, T.H. and Munsie, L. (1995a) *Beyond Tokenism: Parents as Partners in Literacy*. Portsmouth, NH: Heinemann.

Cairney, T.H. and Munsie, L. (1995b) 'Parent participation in literacy learning', *The Reading Teacher*, 48 (5): 392–403.

Cairney, T.H. and Ruge, J. (1998) *Community Literacy Practices and Schooling: Towards Effective Support for Students*. Canberra: DEET.

Cairney, T.H., Lowe, K. and Sproats, E. (1995a) *Literacy in Transition: an investigation of the Literacy Practices of Upper Primary and Junior Secondary Schools*, vols 1–3. Canberra: DEET.

Cairney, T.H., Ruge, J., Buchanan, J., Lowe, K. and Munsie, L. (1995b) *Developing Partnerships: The Home, School and Community Interface*, vols 1–3. Canberra: DEET.

Cazden, C. (1988) *Classroom Discourse*. Portsmouth, NH: Heinemann.

Chall, J.S. (1967) *Learning to Read: the Great Debate*. New York: McGraw-Hill.

Clark, M.M. (1976) *Young Fluent Readers*. London: Heinemann.

Clay, M. (1966) 'Emergent reading behaviour', Unpublished PhD thesis, University of Auckland.

Clay, M.M. (1979) *Reading: the Patterning of Complex Behaviour*. Exeter, NH: Heinemann.

Clay, M.M. (1998) *By Different Paths to Common Outcomes*. New York: Stenhouse.

Comber, B. (1999) 'IT's got power in it: critical literacies and information technologies in primary schools', *Reading Forum New Zealand*, 3: 12–26.

Comber, B., Badger, L., Barnett, J., Nixon, H. and Pitt, J. (2001) *Socio-economically Disadvantaged Students and the Development of Literacies in School*, vol. 1. Adelaide: Department of Education, Training and Employment.

Cook-Gumperz, J. (1986) *The Social Construction of Literacy*. Cambridge: Cambridge University Press.

Cope, B. and Kalantzis, M. (2000) *Multiliteracies: Literacy, Learning and the Design of Social Futures*. Melbourne: Macmillan.

Crago, H. and Crago, M. (1983) *Prelude to Literacy: a Preschool Child's Encounter with Fiction and Story*. Champaign, IL: Southern Illinois University Press.

Crawford, P. (1995) 'Early literacy: emerging perspectives', *Journal of Research in Childhood Education*, 10 (1): 71–86.

Delgado-Gaitan, C. (1991) 'Involving parents in schools: a process of empowerment', *American Journal of Education*, 100: 20–45.

Duranti, A. and Ochs, E. (1986) 'Literacy instruction in a Samoan village', in B. Schieffelin and P. Gilmore (eds), *The Acquisition of Literacy: Ethnographic Perspectives*, vol. 21. Norwood, NJ: Ablex. pp. 213–32.

Durkin, D. (1966) *Children Who Read Early*. New York: Teachers College Press.

Epstein, D. (1983) *Effects on Parents of Teacher Practices of Parent Involvement*. Baltimore: John Hopkins University report no. 346, pp. 277–94.

Freebody, P., Ludwig, C. and Gunn, S. (1995) *Everyday Literacy Practices In and Out of Schools in Low Socio-economic Status Urban Communities: a Descriptive and Interpretive Research Program*. Canberra: DEETYA.

Gee, J. (1990) *Social Linguistics and Literacies: Ideology in Discourses*. London: Falmer.

Gesell, A. (1925) *The Mental Growth of the Preschool child*. New York: Macmillan.

Gonzalez, N. and Moll, L. (1994) 'Lessons from research with language-minority children', *Journal of Reading Behaviour*, 26 (4): 439–56.

Goodman, K.S. (1965) 'A linguistic study of cues and miscues in reading', *Elementary English*, 42: 639–43.

Goodman, K.S. (1967) 'Reading: a psycholinguistic guessing game', *Journal of the Reading Specialist*, 4: 639–43.

Goodman, Y. (1978) 'Kidwatching: observing children in the classroom', *Journal of National Elementary Principals*, 57 (4): 41–5.

Gregory, E. (1997) *One Child, Many Worlds: Early Learning in Multi-Cultural Communities*. New York: Teachers College Press.

Gumperz, J. (1986) *Discourse Strategies*. New York: Cambridge University Press.

Hall, N. (1987) *The Emergence of Literacy*. London: Hodder and Stoughton.

Halliday, M.A.K. (1973) *Explorations in the Functions of Language*. London: Arnold.

Halliday, M.A.K. (1975) *Learning How to Mean: Explorations in the Development of Language*. London: Arnold.

Hannon, P. (1995) *Literacy, Home and School*. London: Falmer.

Harste, J., Woodward, V. and Burke, C. (1984) *Language Stories and Literacy Lessons*. Portsmouth, NH: Heinemann.

Hawkins, P. (1969) 'Social class, the nominal group of reference', *Language and Speech*, 12: 125–35.

Heath, S.B. (1982) 'What no bedtime story means: narrative skills at home and at school', *Language in Society*, 11: 49–76.

Heath, S.B. (1983) *Ways With Words: Language, Life and Work in Communities and Classrooms*. New York: Cambridge University Press.

Hill, S., Comber, B., Louden, W., Rivalland, J. and Reid, J. (1998) *100 Children Go to School*, vol. 2, Canberra: Department of Employment, Education, Training and Youth Affairs.

Holdaway, D. (1979) *The Foundations of Literacy*. Sydney: Ashton Scholastic.

Hymes, D. (1974) *The Foundations of Sociolinguistics: Sociolinguistic Ethnography*. Philadelphia: University of Philadelphia Press.

Lankshear, C. (1997) *Changing Literacies*. Buckingham, Open University Press.

Leichter, H.J. (1984) 'Families as environments for literacy', in H. Goelman, A. Oberg and F. Smith (eds), *Awakening to Literacy*, London: Heinemann.

Lindfors, J.W. (1985) 'Oral language learning: understanding the development of language structure', in A. Jagger and M.T. Smith-Burke (eds), *Observing the Language Learner*. Urbana, IL: IRA.

Luke, A. (1993) 'Stories of social regulation: the micropolitics of classroom narrative', in B. Green (ed.) *The Insistence of the Letter: Literacy Studies and Curriculum Theorising*. London: Falmer.

McNaughton, S. (1995) *The Patterns of Emergent Literacy*. Oxford: Oxford University Press.

Makin, L. and Jones-Diaz, C. (2002) *Literacies in Early Childhood: Challenging Views, Challenging Practice*. Sydney: Maclennan and Petty.

Mason, G. (1965) 'Children learn words from commercial TV', *Elementary School Journal*, 65: 318–20.

Mason, J.M. and Allen, J. (1986) 'A review of emergent literacy with implications for research and practice in reading', Technical Report no. 379, Center for the Study of Reading, Champaign, IL.

Meek, M. (1991) *On Being Literate*. London: Bodley Head.

Miller, P., Nemoianu, A. and DeJong, J. (1986) 'Early reading at home: its practice and meanings in a working-class community', in B.B. Schieffelin and P. Gilmore (eds), *The Acquisition of Literacy: Ethnographic Perspectives*, Norwood, NJ: Ablex.

Moll, L. (1992) 'Literacy research in community and classrooms: a sociocultural approach', in R. Beach, J. Green, M. Kamil and T. Shanahan (eds), *Multidisciplinary Perspectives on Literacy Research*. Urbana, IL: National Council of Teachers of English.

Moll, L., Amanti, C., Neff, D. and Gonzalez, N. (1992) 'Funds of knowledge for teaching: using a qualitative approach to connect homes and classrooms', *Theory Into Practice*, 31 (2): 132–41.

Ninio, A. and Bruner, J. (1978) 'The achievements and antecedents of labelling', *Journal of Child Development*, 5: 1–15.

Ogbu, J. (1993) 'Frameworks – variability in minority school performance: a problem in search of an explanation', in E. Jacob and C. Jordan, (eds), *Minority Education: Anthropological Perspectives*. Norwood, NJ: Ablex.

Phillips, G. and McNaughton, S. (1990) 'The practice of storybook reading to preschool children in mainstream New Zealand families', *Reading Research Quarterly*, 25 (3): 196–212.

Purcell-Gates, V. (2000) 'Family literacy', in M.L. Kamil, P.B. Mosenthall, P.D. Pearson and R. Carr (eds), *Handbook of Reading Research*, vol. 3. Mahwah, NJ: Erlbaum. pp. 853–70.

Razey, M. (2002) 'Gender differentiation in kindergarten: literacy at home and school', Unpublished doctoral thesis, University of Western Sydney.

Resnick, M.B., Roth, J., Aaron, P.M., Scott, J., Wolking, W.D., Laren, J.J. and Packer, A.B. (1987) 'Mothers reading to infants: a new observational tool', *The Reading Teacher*, 40: 888–95.

Rogoff, B. (1990) *Apprenticeship in Thinking: Cognitive Development in Social Context*. Oxford: Oxford University Press.

Rutter, M., Tizard, J. and Whitmore, K. (1970) *Education Health and Behaviour*. London: Longmans.

Schaefer, E. (1991) 'Goals for parent and future parent education: research on parental beliefs and behaviour', *Elementary School Journal*, 91: 239–47.

Scribner, S. and Cole, M. (1981) *The Psychology of Literacy*. Cambridge, MA: Cambridge University Press.

Snow, C. (1977) 'The development of conversation between mothers and babies', *Journal of Child Language*, 4: 1–22.

Snow, C. (1983) 'Literacy and language: Relationships during the preschool years', *Harvard Educational Review*, 53 (2): 165–89.

Snow, C. (1993) 'Families as social contexts for literacy development', in C. Daiute (ed.), *The Development of Literacy Through Interaction*. San Francisco: Jossey Bass. pp. 11–24.

Solsken, J.W. (1993) *Literacy, Gender and Work: in Families and in Schools*. Norwood, NJ: Ablex.

Street, B. (1995) *Social Literacies: Critical Approaches to Literacy Development, Ethnography and Education*. London: Longman.

Taylor, D. (1983) *Family Literacy: Young Children Learning to Read and Write*. Portsmouth, NH: Heinemann.

Taylor, D. and Dorsey-Gaines, C. (1988) *Growing Up Literate: Learning From Inner City Families*. Portsmouth, NH: Heinemann.

Teale, W. (1986) 'Home background and young children's literacy development', in W. Teale and E. Sulzby (eds), *Emergent Literacy: Writing and Reading*. Norwood, NJ: Ablex.

Teale, W. and Sulzby, E. (1986) *Emergent Literacy: Writing and Reading*. Norwood, NJ: Ablex.

Thompson, W.W. (1985) 'Environmental effects on educational performance', *The Alberta Journal of Educational Psychology*, 31: 11–25.

Tough, J. (1977) '*The Development of Meaning*. London: Allen and Unwin.

Vygotsky, L.S. (1978) *Mind in Society: the Development of Higher Psychological Sociocultural Processes*, trans. M. Cole, V. John-Steiner, S. Scribner and E. Souberman. Boston: Harvard University Press.

Weinstein-Shr, G. and Quintero, E. (eds) (1995) *Immigrant Learners and Their Families: Literacy to Connect the Generations*. Washington: ERIC Clearinghouse on Languages and Linguistics.

Welch, A.R. and Freebody, P. (1993) 'Introduction: explanations of the current international "literacy crises"', in P. Freebody and A. Welch (eds), *Knowledge, Culture and Power: International Perspectives on Literacy as Policy and Practice*. London: Falmer.

Wells, C.G. (1982) 'Some antecedents of early educational attainment', *British Journal of Sociology of Education*, 2: 181–200.

Wells, C. G. (1985) *Language Development in the Preschool Years*. Cambridge: Cambridge University Press.

Wells, G. (1986) *The Meaning Makers: Children Learning Language and Using Language to Learn*. Portsmouth, NH: Heinemann.

White, D. (1954) *Books Before Five*. Portsmouth, NH: Heinemann.

Williams G. (1990) 'Variations in home reading practices', paper presented to the Fifteenth Australian Reading Association Conference, Canberra.

9

Family Literacy Programmes

PETER HANNON

Family literacy research has become indispensable for a full understanding of how young children learn literacy and how they may be taught or helped to acquire it. This chapter focuses on family literacy *programmes*. These are ways of teaching literacy that recognize the family dimension in individuals' learning. The aim of the chapter is, first, to offer a way of conceptualizing family literacy programmes and the research base that provides their rationale. The development of such programmes – so far in English-speaking countries – over the past two decades or so will then be summarized. Family literacy programmes belong to the field of adult education as well as to early childhood education but, for the purposes of this volume which is concerned with early childhood literacy, programmes are viewed mainly from the perspective of early childhood education. There are several research issues in the field. Seven key ones will be reviewed: deficit approaches, targeting of programmes, evidence of effectiveness, gender, bilingualism, training for practitioners, and policy research. Some of these have attracted considerable research interest and activity; others remain under-researched or under-conceptualized. The chapter makes suggestions about what we know about family literacy programmes and what we still need to know.

CONCEPTUALIZING FAMILY LITERACY PROGRAMMES

The term 'family literacy' has had two basic meanings. In the first it refers to interrelated *literacy practices within families*. Taylor (1983) appears to have coined the term with this meaning. Her

original research, which involved qualitative case studies of middle-class white families in the United States, showed how young children's initiation into literacy practices was shaped by parents' and other family members' interests, attitudes, abilities and uses for written language. Many other studies have shared this focus even if they have not all used the term 'family literacy': Heath (1983), Teale (1986), Taylor and Dorsey-Gaines (1988), Hannon and James, 1990; Baker et al. (1994), Moss (1994), Purcell-Gates (1995), McNaughton (1995), Voss (1996), Weinberger (1996), Gregory (1996), Cairney and Ruge (1998), Barton and Hamilton (1998), Hirst (1998). These studies can generally be classed as descriptive-analytic in that they have sought to understand existing family literacy practices rather than to evaluate any attempt to change them (although Cairney and Ruge, 1998, combined this approach with a study of innovative literacy programmes). All studies have involved qualitative methods but some have also made use of quantitative survey or longitudinal data (e.g. Hannon and James, 1990; Baker et al., 1994; Weinberger, 1996; Hirst, 1998). This body of research – now covering different societies, and different social classes and ethnic groups within those societies – constitutes a rich archive which opens our minds to the variety of language and literacy practices that can be found in families and therefore the many ways in which children can be drawn into literacy without the direct agency of schools. Not much more will be said about 'family literacy' in this sense as it is addressed more fully in other chapters in this volume, notably that by Trevor Cairney.

It is the second meaning of 'family literacy' that is the focus of this chapter. Here the term refers to certain kinds of *literacy programmes involving families*. The origin of this meaning is not so clear but it appears to have emerged (again in the United States) in the late 1980s, one of the earliest documented instances being the University of Massachusetts English Family Literacy Project (Nash, 1987). This meaning is now so common as almost to obliterate the first – a matter of some regret for, as Hannon (2000b) has argued, it was very useful to have a term which referred to literacy practices which occur independently of any programme. Without such a term, programme designers and practitioners can easily overlook valuable language and literacy activities in which family members engage, separately and interactively, independently of any programme.

Family literacy programmes can be defined as *programmes to teach literacy that acknowledge and make use of learners' family relationships and engagement in family literacy practices*. An obvious example of a programme fitting this definition would be a school involving parents in the teaching of reading to their children. This acknowledges that many parents do, to some degree, assist their children's reading development, and makes use of their motivation to do more, their opportunities at home to do so and the likelihood that, because of their relationship to their parents, children will enjoy and benefit from the experience. Another example would be an adult literacy programme for parents that made use of their desire to help their children learn to write and which created shared writing activities to enable both parent and child to learn together.

It may be helpful to contrast family literacy programmes with non-instances of the concept, i.e. programmes in which members of families may participate but in which no account is taken of their being family members. Most traditional schooling and adult education of the past century or two has been of this character. This is not necessarily a bad thing where it is desirable or appropriate to treat learners as individual children or adults. For example, if some parents value adult literacy classes because they offer a respite from childcare rather than an extension of it, it is sensible to take account of their wishes. It should also be noted that not all learners – especially in the case of adults – are members of families and in these cases the question of providing family literacy programmes does not arise.

At this point it is necessary to acknowledge that the terms 'family', 'literacy' and 'teaching' can have many different meanings. The concept of *family* employed in this chapter is intended to be inclusive of the full range of groups within which children are cared for and grow up. Carers of young children can be biological parents, step-parents, foster parents, grandparents, siblings, or others in the home. In general one would expect children to learn from carers but the reverse is also possible: carers can learn some things from children and there can be joint learning. However, family literacy programmes may sometimes be based on narrow concepts of family and of who learns from whom. There can be unexamined assumptions about family structure, e.g. that children in programmes have fathers at home. Regarding *literacy*, current research and theory tends to conceptualize it either as a set of social practices involving written language or as a skill. These are not necessarily mutually exclusive conceptions since social practices do involve skills (often transferable from one practice to another) but it does still matter whether one gives primacy to the social practices or to the skills. Although some family literacy programmes give primacy to skills, the approach underlying this chapter is that it is the social practices that matter. Reference will be made later to *literacy inequalities*. By this is meant unequal access to those literacy practices associated with power in society or those literacy practices valued in formal education. Teaching literacy cannot by itself reduce literacy inequality but it can contribute to that goal. Finally, the concept of *teaching* itself needs unpacking. It includes many ways in which those engaged in literacy practices can help others – whether children or adults – to become proficient in those practices. Hannon (2000a) has suggested that there is a teaching spectrum with 'instruction' at one end and 'facilitation' at the other. *Instruction* involves deliberate, planned teaching to meet curricular objectives, often carried out with one instructor teaching many students in settings distanced from real-life contexts. *Facilitation* is support of on-task learning, embedded in real-life contexts – well captured by the Vygotskian notion of learners doing in cooperation with others today what tomorrow they will be able to do on their own. Broadly speaking instruction can be said to be characteristic of schools and other formal learning situations; facilitation is characteristic of learning in out-of-school settings, particularly families. Family literacy programmes vary in the balance struck between instruction and facilitation, those giving primacy to teaching literacy skills being more likely also to emphasize instruction.

A consequence of there being different concepts of family, literacy and teaching is that, depending upon which ones are applied, there can be many different kinds of family literacy programmes. A further source of variation amongst programmes concerns their aims. These can be limited to teaching children and adults how to participate in specific literacy practices or they can be broader in enhancing families' awareness of their own literacy and that of others in society and how literacy may play a part in maintaining or changing their position in society. This issue will be considered in a later section on 'deficit approaches'.

A wide variety of family literacy programmes over the last two decades have been documented (McIvor, 1990; Nickse, 1990; ALBSU, 1993b; Dickinson, 1994; Meek Spencer and Dombey, 1994; Cairney and Munsie, 1995; Hannon, 1995; Morrow, 1995; Morrow et al., 1995; Wolfendale and Topping, 1996; Taylor, 1997; Tett, 2000; Auerbach, 2002; Cairney, 2002). A fundamental way in which programmes vary is in whose literacy they aim to change. Some focus on children, some on adults, some on both. Programmes vary in aiming for outcomes in individuals' literacy in homes, schools, other educational institutions, communities or workplaces. Then there are variations in whether programme input is to children, adults or both. If both, there may be separate inputs to each or they may be combined in shared activities. Inputs may be to one family member with outcomes sought in another (e.g. work with parents to affect children's literacy). The location of work with families can vary. In some programmes it is carried out in families' homes; in others it is in centres/schools, libraries, workplaces, football clubs or elsewhere in the community. The workers can be early childhood educators, adult educators, paraprofessionals, or volunteers. Teaching can involve different mixes of instruction and facilitation. There are variations in the target populations for programmes, e.g. bilingual or ethnic groups, fathers, adolescent mothers, prison inmates. The underlying concept of literacy could vary from an emphasis on conventional activities within written language to broader conceptions involving media texts, oral language and additional language learning. Some programmes extend literacy to health awareness, parenting and life skills. Some make critical awareness of literacy itself the object of learning.

How to conceptualize this complexity, and the potential for countless permutations of focus, input, location, workers, target populations and conceptions of literacy? It is hardly surprising that such categorizations of programmes as have been proposed tend to be illuminative rather than comprehensive. Nickse suggested that 'Family and intergenerational literacy programs are organized efforts to improve the literacy of educationally disadvantaged parents and children through specially designed programs' with the basic idea that 'parents and children can be viewed as a learning unit and may benefit from shared literacy experiences' (1990: 2). She proposed a fourfold typology according to whether programmes target the adult directly and the child indirectly, vice versa, both directly, or both indirectly. This is helpful as far as it goes but clearly leaves out many features that

could be important to researchers, practitioners and policy makers. Morrow and Paratore (1993) distinguished two categories of programmes: home–school partnerships and intergenerational interventions. Cairney (2002) suggested similar categories (home/school programme initiatives, intergenerational literacy programmes) but added a third, termed 'partnership programmes', in which the focus is on links at the level of schools, families and communities. Some agencies – notably in the United States the National Center for Family Literacy (Darling, 1993) and in England the Adult Literacy and Basic Skills Unit (ALBSU, 1993b) – have insisted on a specific definition of family literacy that refers to programmes which combine basic skills and parenting input for parents with early literacy education for their children and joint parent–child activities. This definition, whilst having the virtue of clarity, has been so restricted as to exclude most programmes other than those the agencies themselves promoted (Hannon, 2000b). It excluded 'home–school partnerships' or 'parental involvement', leaving only what Morrow and Paratore (1993) and Morrow et al. (1995) term 'intergenerational' programmes. The confused and contested status of the term led Morrow et al. to conclude rather weakly that 'family literacy refers to a complex concept associated with many different beliefs about the relationships between families and the development of literacy' (1995: 2). Wolfendale and Topping (1996) characterized family literacy as a broadening of parental involvement in early literacy to include a wider range of activities often also concerned with the needs of parents and carers. Auerbach (1997a) proposed that programmes be grouped according to three paradigms whose assumptions, goals and practices are informed by different ideological and theoretical perspectives: the 'intervention prevention' approach, the 'multiple literacies' approach and the 'social change' approach. Categorization according to these three paradigms is not straightforward but the categories rightly draw attention to the fundamental aims and purposes of programmes, and the extent to which they enable families to challenge social forces that marginalize them. Taylor argued for a redefinition of family literacy programmes as ways to 'organize the advantaged and disadvantaged to read, write, and do other kinds of work together to increase the opportunities available to all' (1997: 4). Recent reviewers (Purcell-Gates, 2000; Wasik et al., 2001; Padak et al., 2002) have accepted that it is extremely difficult to impose any overall conceptualization on the field. Given the heterogeneity of current family literacy programmes, and the continuing inventiveness of practitioners in developing new ones, it is probably best to work with the general definition offered earlier, that we are dealing with a class of *programmes to teach literacy that acknowledge and make use of learners' family relationships and engagement in family literacy practices.* The programmes thus encompassed vary considerably; some of their variations are significant for research, practice or policy.

From the viewpoint of early childhood educators, family literacy programmes could be conceptualized simply as another method for achieving historic aims regarding teaching literacy to young children. This, however, would be a rather narrow view: for the concept, fully appreciated, means educators shifting their focus from the individual child to the family, acknowledging that their role may be secondary to that of parents, recognizing pre-existing family literacy practices, and seeing that teaching aims might be better achieved by also taking an interest in the learning of other family members. It means rethinking some pedagogical assumptions in early childhood education and a two-way professional exchange with adult education. This has research implications to be discussed later.

RATIONALE FOR FAMILY LITERACY PROGRAMMES

What is the justification for taking seriously the concept of a family literacy programme? We can look to studies in literacy, language, child development and education for a rationale. The research of most relevance concerns children's, rather than adults', literacy and was carried out in the period leading up to the emergence of family literacy programmes in the late twentieth century. That emergence no doubt owed much to political and ideological factors but the ground for it had been well prepared by research.

The most influential research is that showing the importance of home (for which one can generally read 'family') factors in school literacy achievement – throughout all the years of schooling. Achievement in school literacy and in reading tests reflects proficiency in only one kind of literacy practice but it is one valued by many families. Compelling evidence comes from large-scale surveys. In the USA, for example, studies within the National Assessment of Educational Progress have shown the very strong association between the extent of literacy materials (newspapers, magazines, books, dictionaries) in homes and children's reading test scores at ages nine, 13 and 17 (Applebee et al., 1988). By the end of schooling, children in families having 'many' as opposed to 'few' such materials enjoyed approximately four years' superiority in reading achievement. In the UK one could cite the National Child Development Study which showed that the likelihood of children being 'poor' readers or 'non-readers' at age seven was very strongly related to social class (Davie et al., 1972). It can be argued from such evidence that efforts to reduce literacy inequalities are unlikely to be successful if they are confined to school learning; literacy education needs also to address learning at home – in families.

Research concerning parental involvement in children's early literacy development also underpins family literacy programmes. In the UK, for example, studies have shown that such involvement – not necessarily encouraged by specific programmes – is very common (Newson and Newson, 1977; Hannon and James, 1990) across all social groups and that within disadvantaged groups it is strongly associated with literacy achievement (Hewison and Tizard, 1980; Hannon, 1987; Bus et al., 1995). It should not be surprising that parents involve themselves in this way. For most parents, it is intrinsically motivating to be involved in their children's development – it being one reason for becoming a parent in the first place – and literacy is a part of that development. That alone might be considered sufficient justification for family literacy programmes.

Parental motivation matters particularly in the case of parents who feel they have literacy difficulties. Adult literacy tutors are familiar with the situation where an adult decides to do something about their literacy at the point when their young children are beginning to learn to read and write. The fact that parents' motivation to help their children and to help themselves can peak at the same time, and reinforce each other, suggests that family literacy programmes that provide opportunities for both could be very effective.

Another line of research serving to justify family literacy programmes is that from the 1980s which showed the (previously overlooked) extent of young children's knowledge of literacy before formal schooling. Some of this work has been in the emergent literacy tradition (Goodman, 1980; Goelman et al., 1984; Teale and Sulzby, 1986; Hall, 1987). Knowing about literacy practices and skills valued by schools confers advantages on some children starting formal education, just as lack of it disadvantages others (Heath, 1983; Harste et al., 1984). The relevant knowledge can include awareness of the purposes of literacy (Heath, 1983), awareness of story (Heath, 1982; Wells, 1987), knowledge of letters (Tizard et al., 1988) and phonological awareness (Bryant and Bradley, 1985; Maclean et al., 1987). If children have this knowledge at school entry it seems reasonable to infer that they have acquired it in their families. If they do not have it (and if it is desirable that they should) there is a case for family literacy programmes to help them acquire it.

More generally, research into preschool language and literacy learning has forced a re-evaluation of the power of home learning. On the basis of studies such as that by Tizard and Hughes (1984) comparing children's early language experiences at home and in preschool classes, Hannon (1995) identified many ways in which home learning can be more powerful than school learning (e.g. in being shaped by immediate interest and need, in often seeming to be effortless, in spontaneity, in being a response to real rather than contrived problems, in being of flexible duration, in having a high adult–child ratio, in being influenced by adult models, and in allowing a 'teaching' role for younger family members). Hannon further suggested that families can provide children with four requirements for early literacy learning: (1) *opportunities* to read texts and attempt writing, (2) *recognition* of early literacy achievements, (3) *interaction* with more proficient literacy users, usually through facilitation rather than instruction, and (4) *models* of what it is to use literacy. Nutbrown and Hannon (1997) and Hannon and Nutbrown (1997) have shown that this framework (generally abbreviated to ORIM) can be used to construct family literacy programmes.

Finally a strong research justification for family literacy programmes comes from those studies, cited at the beginning of this chapter, which have revealed the nature and extent of families' uses for literacy and family members' interrelated literacy practices. Once these practices are recognized, children's literacy learning is deindividualized. It is seen as part of a larger system – a system moreover that from a social learning perspective has the capacity to scaffold and otherwise facilitate young children's literacy development.

THE DEVELOPMENT OF FAMILY LITERACY PROGRAMMES

Early childhood educators tend to see family literacy programmes as the latest form of parental involvement in early literacy education. That is true up to a point but fails to do justice to the contribution of adult educators who, not unreasonably, tend to see such programmes as a new form of *their* practice. It is better to see the development of family literacy programmes as stemming from both of these strands of education.

Taking first the early childhood education strand, it is worth noting at risk of some oversimplification that parental involvement in the teaching of literacy is a fairly recent development. In industrialized countries, mass compulsory schooling, since its beginnings in the late nineteenth century and throughout most of the twentieth, was characterized more by parental exclusion than by involvement (Hannon, 1995). This was probably not planned or even conscious and can be attributed, at least in the early years of the system, to a lack of space and physical resources in schools, to a lack of cultural resources (an educated teaching force, literature for children), and to an ideology that took it for granted that children should be educated outside their homes, in large groups, in specially dedicated educational institutions (i.e. schools) where it was assumed that school teaching methods, often characterized by rote learning, were superior to home learning. Even when more sophisticated methods were developed later (e.g. systematic reading schemes), the effect was often to privilege professional knowledge and distance parents further from their children's literacy development.

It was not generally until the last quarter of the twentieth century that, in industrialized societies, early literacy educators began to see parents differently. The change reflected interest in parental involvement as a tool for reducing persistent educational inequalities, increased adult literacy in society, rethinking of professional knowledge concerning literacy development, more print in the environment (including children's books), and a recognition of families as active users, rather than passive beneficiaries, of educational services.

Parental involvement in the teaching of literacy developed gradually. Parents were enjoined to support their children's school literacy learning through encouragement and showing an interest. To this end they were informed about schools' policies and practices. Parental involvement was often seen as a matter of coming into school, it being assumed that school, not home, was the key site for literacy learning. Reading was prioritized over writing (with the term 'literacy' at first rarely used). Later, involvement became more direct, for example in the UK, when schools began encouraging and supporting parents of young children to 'hear' children read aloud books that they brought home from school. A pioneering programme with six- to seven-year-olds in Haringey, London, was found to have measurable outcomes in terms of children's reading test performance (Tizard et al., 1982) and had a national impact on practice. Parents in the Haringey programme were not given any particular method for assisting their children's oral reading but other, more prescriptive programmes, most importantly 'paired reading', were developed and also spread rapidly (Bushell et al., 1982; Topping and Lindsay, 1991; 1992). In New Zealand, another prescriptive programme, 'pause, prompt and praise', was developed and evaluated (McNaughton et al., 1981). In the US, prescriptive programmes have included giving quite explicit directions to parents (Edwards, 1994) and 'dialogic reading' (Whitehurst et al., 1994). The 'hearing reading' programmes (whether 'open' or 'prescriptive') have been the most clearly documented and evaluated but they emerged at the same time as a multitude of less easily catalogued approaches to involving parents and families (Dickinson, 1994; Hannon, 1995; Wolfendale and Topping, 1996). Some programmes have reached into the preschool years (Hannon, 1996) and a few have gone beyond books to focus also on writing and oral language (Wade, 1984; Green, 1987; Hannon, 1998). A recent national initiative in England has involved several thousand parents in courses to familiarize them with changes in the school literacy curriculum and to help them support their children's learning (Brooks et al., 2002).

In summary, within the early childhood education strand, parental involvement in the teaching of literacy began, after a long period of routine parental exclusion, with a focus on parents helping children's oral reading. It has gradually evolved to take on a broader concept of literacy, preschool as well as school-aged children, and support for a wider range of at-home as well as in-school activities. These actions by schools can be counted as family literacy programmes in that they clearly 'acknowledge and make use of learners' family relationships', but it must be admitted that the learners with which they are concerned are mainly young children and that on the whole programmes have been concerned not so much with 'engagement in family literacy practices' as with families' engagement in school literacy practices.

Within the adult education strand there has been, as one would expect, more concern for parents as learners. In the United States, McIvor (1990) documented eight family literacy programmes, all of which were devised and delivered by agencies whose mission was primarily to do with adults (libraries, colleges, adult education services, prison organizations, services to users of day care or Head Start). In England, it was the Adult Literacy and Basic Skills Unit that did more than any other organization to promote 'family literacy' by securing and distributing government funding for a particular model of family literacy – taken from the US – that clearly aimed to aid parents' literacy development as well as children's (ALBSU, 1993a; 1993b). The introduction of adult literacy educators into family literacy reinforced concern for families' own literacy values and practices. For example, in the US, Nickse, in a foreword to McIvor (1990), pointed out

that family literacy programmes required extra sensitivity from providers who had to become aware of different cultural and literacy practices in families. She suggested, 'When families are involved together for literacy, more of their lives are shared with us, and adults become more vulnerable. This is a trust not to be taken lightly' (1990: 5). These considerations are not always uppermost in the minds of early years educators whose focus is the child in a school setting.

Family literacy programmes in the twenty-first century can thus be seen as a merging of literacy teaching in early childhood education and in adult education. Future development will depend upon success in combining the strengths and avoiding the weaknesses of each strand. Future research in the field also needs to draw upon traditions associated with each strand.

RESEARCH ISSUES IN THE FIELD

Family literacy programmes now constitute a large field of educational activity in which can be found, in some form or other, most issues of interest to early childhood literacy researchers. The following are singled out because, to this reviewer, they seem currently to have high theoretical or practical interest.

Deficit approaches

It has already been noted that family literacy programmes developed by early childhood educators tend to emphasize the engagement of families in school literacy rather than the engagement of schools in the families' literacy. Some adult educators do the same but many take a more sceptical view of the value of school literacy (which has often been problematic in their students' lives) and a more positive view of the strengths of parents and families in relation to everyday life and literacy. There have been critiques (by Auerbach, 1989; 1995; 1997b; Grant, 1997; Taylor, 1997) of what is termed a 'deficit approach' in family literacy programmes. Families may be heavily engaged in literacy practices and have many literacy skills but these may not be the practices and skills valued by schools. Cairney (2002) points out that many family literacy programmes are about taking school literacy into families. Further, it is probable that there are family literacy programmes that proceed on ignorant, and even offensive, assumptions concerning what certain families do *not* do or what they are supposed to be *incapable* of doing. That is, some programmes ignore the family literacy research cited earlier in the section 'Rationale for family literacy programmes'. They are also ignoring research that has shown more generally the extent to which families' knowledge is undervalued by schools (Moll et al., 1992). Such assumptions, as well as being educationally unsound, have political consequences in 'explaining' the situation of poor families in terms of their literacy being less than, rather than simply different from, that of the powerful in society whose hegemonic definition of what counts as literacy goes unchallenged.

This issue may not, however, be quite as straight-forward as stated and it is one that could benefit from further research – both conceptual and empiri-cal. The term 'deficit approach' is not entirely help-ful, for there is a sense in which there is nothing wrong with deficits – with learners acknowledging they have them or with teachers seeking to address them. None of us would ever engage in any con-scious learning if we did not feel we had some deficit we wanted to make up. Problems arise if dif-ferences (e.g. in literacy practices) are uncritically viewed as deficits, if deficits are imputed to learn-ers without their assent, if deficits are exaggerated or if deficits are seen as *all* that learners have (i.e. their cultural strengths are devalued). These prob-lems can arise in any form of literacy education – indeed in any form of education – but they are more exposed in the case of family literacy programmes within which the cultural values and practices of homes and schools are brought together. The chal-lenge for family literacy educators is to value what families bring to programmes but not to the extent of simply reflecting back families' existing literacy practices (for it is patronizing to suppose families need help with their existing literacy practices). Somehow they must offer families access to some different or additional literacy practices but through collaboration and negotiation rather than imposi-tion. If educators fail either to facilitate families' entry into powerful literacy practices or to empower them to challenge those practices, they will simply perpetuate families' continued exclusion from whatever benefits participation in those practices confers. Some family literacy programmes do take up this challenge (e.g. several in Taylor, 1997) but their efforts are documented rather than rigorously evaluated. Using and valuing what families already know in order to teach them what they do not know is a subtle process that can easily go wrong. Research can help by elucidating teaching possibil-ities and pitfalls. Studies of particular programmes by Delgado-Gaitan (1990), Moll et al., (1992) and Tett (2000) – as well as others discussed by Auerbach (1997a) – have begun to provide insights into this, but more research in a wider range of cultural settings is needed.

Targeting of programmes

A recurrent idea in family literacy discourse is that there are families in which parents have literacy dif-ficulties and in which it is supposed the children are consequently destined to have low literacy achieve-ment, at least by school measures. The policy and professional literature in family literacy, if not the research literature, abounds with claims that there is a 'cycle of underachievement' which be can be broken, but only by targeting parents' and children's literacy at the same time and in the same programmes. Conspicuous advocates of this view in the US have included Nickse (1990) and Darling (1993a), and in the UK the Adult Literacy and Basic Skills Unit (1993a). It leads directly to the idea that targeting intergenerational family literacy programmes on families where parents have liter-acy difficulties will have a major impact on literacy levels in society.

Despite a certain common-sense appeal, this idea is poorly supported by research evidence. It is actu-ally two propositions wrapped together: (1) that parents with literacy difficulties will have low achieving children; and (2) that low achieving children have parents with literacy difficulties. Both have to be true for the 'cycle of underachieve-ment' claim to be accepted as an explanation for literacy inequalities in society (and for targeted family literacy programmes to be seen as the remedy). It is not easy to conduct research into the literacy of parents and children in a representative sample large enough to permit statistical analyses, but one such study has been carried out in the UK and reported by the Adult Literacy and Basic Skills Unit (1993c). 'Low literacy achievement' for children was operationalized in terms of perfor-mance in the lowest quartile of a nationally stan-dardized reading test and for adults in terms of whether or not they reported having reading diffi-culties. The research claimed to have found 'the first objective evidence of the link between a par-ent's competence in basic skills and the competence of their children' (1993c: 3), but a reinterpretation of the data by Hannon (2000b) showed that, even if one were to accept the validity of the measures used, the link is far weaker than first appears. According to ALBSU (1993c) those few children who had parents reporting reading difficulties were three times more likely than other children to have reading test scores in the lowest quartile. This might appear to support proposition (1) were it not for the fact that around half the children in these families did *not* have low scores. There was practically no evidence for proposition (2) since the overwhelm-ing majority (92%) of children in the lowest quar-tile did *not* have parents reporting reading difficulties. Literacy inequalities amongst children in a society such as the UK therefore cannot, on the available evidence, plausibly be attributed to parental literacy difficulties. It follows that targeting family literacy programmes only on those families where parents acknowledge that they have literacy difficulties can make no more than a modest contribution to reducing literacy inequalities amongst young children.

Evidence of effectiveness

There have been many studies of the effectiveness of parental involvement in the teaching of early literacy, i.e. the early childhood strand of family literacy programmes. A review of over 30 studies by Hannon (1995), which also built upon several earlier reviews by previous researchers, concluded that there was substantial evidence of benefits, and no reports of negative consequences, of involving parents. Most evaluations concerned open or prescriptive approaches to parents hearing children read. A more recent review of 35 studies since 1990 of US family literacy programmes reached broadly similar conclusions (Padak et al., 2002). It should be noted, however, that there have been very few randomized control trial (RCT) evaluations. One does not have to believe RCTs are the only way of conducting evaluations, or that they are the gold standard, to wish that now and again they could be used in comparing family literacy programmes to alternatives, especially in view of the bold claims made for effectiveness (Hannon, 2000b). Emerging findings from an RCT evaluation of a preschool parental involvement literacy programme conducted at 11 sites in Sheffield, England, indicate immediate post-programme effectiveness with an effect size of 0.40 (Hannon and Nutbrown, 2001). Many other evaluations have relied upon quasi-experimental controls or pre-test/post-test comparisons using standardized tests (in effect using a test standardization sample as a quasi-experimental control group). Nevertheless the sheer weight of positive findings is probably sufficient to conclude that parental involvement generally 'works'. What is harder to judge, given the weakness of research designs, is how well it works. There is no evidence that any programme so far developed is guaranteed to have profound effects for all families involved. Some programmes in some circumstances appear to have considerable impact on some families but in other cases the effects may be rather modest. The problem of take-up has often been overlooked in evaluations even though, from a policy perspective, programmes with low take-up cannot make much impact at community level. Apart from Hewison (1988) there is a lack of follow-up studies of

parental involvement programmes. Neither is there sufficient evidence to compare the effectiveness of different kinds of programmes. In practice the conditions for direct comparison do not often arise. Research has, however, helped identify factors to be kept in mind in choosing between programmes. For example, Hannon (1995) concluded that some programmes are costly in professionalsals' time but may be helpful for older children having continued difficulties with reading; others might be suitable for all children at a younger age but may not be sustainable over a long period. Little is known about the effects of combining different forms of involvement. Another gap concerns involvement in writing, the predominant focus having been book reading. In summary, a great deal still needs to be researched but enough has been done to conclude that the parental involvement form of family literacy programme is effective.

What about family literacy programmes that aim to change parents' literacy too? Here there are numerous small-scale, largely qualitative studies but few well-designed quantitative studies. The former are interesting in revealing issues in programme design, the nature of effects and factors limiting effectiveness (e.g. Finlay, 1999; Tett, 2000; Padak et al., 2002). The latter have found positive effects for both children and parents (St Pierre et al., 1995; Brooks et al., 1996). Brooks et al. (1997) in a follow-up study also found that effects persisted. However, there is as yet no evidence that intergenerational programmes combining provision for adults with provision for children (including parent–child sessions) have greater effects, or are more cost-effective, than separate child-focused or adult-focused programmes (Hannon, 2000b). One seriously under-researched issue in those family literacy programmes that require parents' participation as literacy learners is take-up. If take-up is low (and Hannon, 2000b, suggests there are signs this is often the case) the value of such programmes is greatly diminished. Finally, it is unfortunate, and perhaps a little surprising, that no study has yet set out directly to test the strong claims made for the synergistic benefits of intergenerational programmes as compared to stand-alone programmes. It is easy to agree with Padak et al. that 'for the most part, evaluation of family literacy programs is still in its infancy' (2002: 22).

Gender

This chapter has consistently referred to 'parents' in programmes when generally it would be more accurate to talk of 'mothers'. This is not to say that fathers or male carers are never involved in programmes, only that the numbers are generally low (typically well under 10% in centre-based programmes). Using the word 'parent' is inclusive and helps maximize the number of fathers who are involved (if programmes referred only to mothers the gendered nature of parental involvement would be reinforced and it is likely that there would be even fewer fathers). Sticking to 'parent', however, must not blind us to the highly gendered nature of parental involvement. Many programmes are sensitive to this issue and have made serious efforts to include men, in some cases adopting this as a primary goal (Haggart, 2000; Lloyd, 2001; Millard, 2001; Karther, 2002). There are at least three research challenges here. First, it would be helpful to understand more about the gendered nature of family literacy practices and how they vary in different economic and family circumstances (e.g. as men in industrialized countries respond to increased literacy demands in the workplace). Quantitative, as well as qualitative, studies could make a contribution. It would be interesting to know whether men's lower involvement is an artefact of school-based programmes where employment and cultural expectations reduce fatherss' attendance; they may be more involved, if less visibly so, in home-based programmes. Secondly, research could usefully distinguish different kinds of family structure referred to earlier in this chapter and the different roles that men and women now perform as parents, step-parents, grandparents, foster parents and carers within them, whether or not they are in daily contact with children. Thirdly, it would be helpful to have detailed evaluations of those programmes that have made special efforts to involve men. To be really helpful such studies need to go beyond documentation of interesting cases to a quantitative evaluation of key issues such as take-up and outcomes.

Bilingualism

More research is needed into programmes for bilingual or multilingual families. There have been valuable reports either of research or concerning programme design by Auerbach (1989; 2002), Delgado-Gaitan (1990), Hirst (1998), Brooks et al. (1999), Blackledge (2000), Kenner (2000) and Cairney (2002). These point out how such families can be different (e.g. in relation to the gendering of parenting, expectations of children) but also how they can often be similar (e.g. in parents' aspirations for their children). What also emerges is how families are perceived by educators (who may grossly underestimate the cultural resources of homes). However, much of the literature on family literacy programmes concerns monolingual, English-speaking families. As we enter the twenty-first century and take an international perspective it

becomes ever clearer that bilingualism and multilingualism, rather than monolingualism, will be the norm. Some of the issues to be investigated are very complex. For example, the first language of some families may not have a written form or, if it does, it may not be much used by family members. Parents' literacy can appear limited in comparison with what is familiar in industrialized countries. Parents' aspirations for their own and their children's literacy may or may not accord with the assumptions of programme designers and national policy makers. Different cultures, different concepts of childhood and different pedagogies may require their own programmes and desired outcomes. Research still needs to catch up with global realities.

Training and professional development

If early childhood educators are to play a full part in family literacy programmes they need appropriate training and professional development opportunities. Working with adults demands a different awareness and set of skills than does working with groups of children. Nutbrown et al. (1991) proposed a framework for pre-service and in-service provision within which early childhood educators could become better equipped to meet the demands of family literacy programmes and they urged research into key issues. Since then there has been very little progress either in the provision of training and professional development or in associated research. Hannon and Nutbrown (1997) investigated teachers' use of the ORIM framework referred to earlier but that is only one variety of family literacy work. Potentially, there are as many issues worth researching in training and professional development in relation to family literacy work as there are in relation to wider aspects of early childhood and adult education. There is the issue, for example, of whether family literacy teachers/tutors should be reflective practitioners or technicians implementing – and obediently following – prescriptions of programme designers (Hannon et al., 1997). Another issue is the role of organizations providing or accrediting training who may use the opportunity to impose their particular models of family literacy. Research can enable a more open and critical approach to programme development and to related professional development.

Policy relevance and policy research

It is by no means clear what role family literacy programmes should play in relation to mainstream, compulsory early childhood education. It could be argued that all education should take a family approach; alternatively that family literacy programmes can never be more than an adjunct to mainstream provision, perhaps only in areas of disadvantage. Research has a role to play here, not only in providing evidence – particularly about take-up and effectiveness – to inform family literacy policies but also in examining and critiquing those policies. One area where there is scope to do this concerns the claims made for family literacy programmes. Some of these seem rather extravagant. In the US, the National Center for Family Literacy has claimed that family literacy programmes enable 'at risk families with little hope to reverse the cycle of undereducation and poverty', bringing about changes that 'pave the way for school success, and thereafter life success' (1994: 1). Brizius and Foster have claimed family literacy 'provides disadvantaged children with educational opportunities that can enable them to lift themselves out of poverty and dependency' (1993: 11). Although it is to be hoped that family literacy programmes can make a useful contribution to these goals, promising more than the research evidence warrants may store up trouble for the future.

CONCLUSIONS

This review has shown that family literacy programmes have, over the past two decades, come to occupy an important role in early childhood literacy education. There is some fuzziness in the conceptualization of family literacy programmes but this reflects the variety that has been, and continues to be, developed. The effectiveness of programmes is reasonably well established in a general sense but there remain significant unanswered questions about the extent and duration of effects, the benefits of combining the different components of programmes, and the limiting effect of low take-up. There are also other areas to be developed, relating for example to implied deficits, gender, bilingualism, training and policy. These are to be expected in any field of education but may be more exposed in family literacy programmes. All of them can be illuminated by future research.

NOTE

I am grateful to Elsa Auerbach, Greg Brooks, Kath Hirst, Jackie Marsh and Jo Weinberger for their comments on an earlier draft of this chapter.

REFERENCES

ALBSU (1993a) *Family Literacy News, no. 1*. London: Adult Literacy and Basic Skills Unit.

ALBSU (1993b) *Framework for Family Literacy Demonstration Programmes*. London: Adult Literacy and Basic Skills Unit.

ALBSU (1993c) *Parents and Their Children: the Intergenerational Effect of Poor Basic Skills*. London: Adult Literacy and Basic Skills Unit.

Applebee, A.N., Langer, J.A. and Mullis, I.V.S. (1988) *Who Reads Best? Factors Related to Reading Achievement in Grades 3, 7 and 11*. Princeton, NJ: Educational Testing Service.

Auerbach, E.R. (1989) 'Toward a social-contextual approach to family literacy', *Harvard Educational Review*, 59 (2): 165–81.

Auerbach, E.R. (1995) 'Which way for family literacy: intervention or empowerment?', in L.M. Morrow (ed.), *Family Literacy: Connections in Schools and Communities*. Newark, DE: International Reading Association. pp. 11–27.

Auerbach, E.R. (1997a) 'Family literacy', in V. Edwards and D. Corson (eds), *Encyclopaedia of Language and Education. Vol. 2: Literacy*. Dordrecht: Kluwer. pp. 153–61.

Auerbach, E.R. (1997b) 'Reading between the lines', in D. Taylor (ed.), *Many Families, Many Literacies: an International Declaration of Principles*. Portsmouth, NH: Heinemann. pp. 71–82.

Auerbach, E.R. (ed.) (2002) *Community Partnerships*. Alexandria, VA: TESOL.

Baker, L., Sonnenschein, S., Serpell, R., Fernandez-Fein, S. and Scher, D. (1994) *Contexts of Emergent Literacy: Everyday Home Experiences of Urban Pre-kindergarten Children*. Reading Research Report no. 24. Athens, GA: National Reading Research Center.

Barton, D. and Hamilton, M. (1998) *Local Literacies: Reading and Writing in One Community*. London: Routledge.

Blackledge, A. (2000) *Literacy, Power and Social Justice*. Stoke-on-Trent: Trentham.

Brizius, J.A. and Foster, S.A. (1993) *Generation to Generation: Realizing the Promise of Family Literacy*. Ypsilanti, MI: High/Scope Press.

Brooks, G., Gorman, T., Harman, D. and Wilkin, A. (1996) *Family Literacy Works: the NFER Evaluation of the Basic Skills Agency's Family Literacy Demonstration Programmes*. London: Basic Skills Agency.

Brooks, G., Gorman, T., Harman, J., Hutchison, D., Kinder, K., Moor, H. and Wilkin, A. (1997) *Family Literacy Lasts: the NFER Follow-up Study of the Basic Skills Agency's Demonstration Programmes*. London: Basic Skills Agency.

Brooks, G., Harman, J., Hutchison, D., Kendall, S. and Wilkin, A. (1999) *Family Literacy for New Groups: the*

NFER Evaluation of Family Literacy with Linguistic Minorities, Year 4 and Year 7. London: Basic Skills Agency.

Brooks, G., Cole, P., Davies, P., Davis, B., Frater, G., Harman, J. and Hutchison, D. (2002) Keeping Up with the Children: Evaluation for the Basic Skills Agency by the University of Sheffield and the National Foundation for Educational Research. London: Basic Skills Agency.

Bryant, P. and Bradley, L. (1985) Children's Reading Problems. Oxford: Blackwell.

Bus, A.G., Van Ijzendoorn, M.H. and Pellegrini, A.D. (1995) 'Joint book reading makes for success in learning: a meta-analysis on intergenerational transmission of literacy', Review of Educational Research, 65 (1): 1–21.

Bushell, R., Miller, A. and Robson, D. (1982) 'Parents as remedial teachers: an account of a paired reading project with junior school failing readers and their parents', Journal of the Association of Educational Psychologists, 5 (9): 7–13.

Cairney, T.H. (2002) 'Bridging home and school literacy: in search of transformative approaches to curriculum', Early Child Development and Care, 172 (2): 153–72.

Cairney, T.H. and Munsie, L. (1995) Beyond Tokenism: Parents as Partners in Literacy. Portsmouth, NH: Heinemann.

Cairney, T.H. and Ruge, J. (1998) Community Literacy Practices and Schooling: Towards Effective Support for Students. Canberra: Department of Employment, Education, Training and Youth Affairs.

Darling, S. (1993) 'Focus on family literacy: the national perspective', NCFL Newsletter, 5 (1): 3.

Davie, R., Butler, N. and Goldstein, H. (1972) From Birth to Seven: a Report of the National Child Development Study. London: Longman/National Children's Bureau.

Delgado-Gaitan, C. (1990) Literacy for Empowerment: the Role of Parents in Children's Education. London: Falmer.

Dickinson, D. (ed.) (1994) Bridges to Literacy: Children, Families and Schools. Oxford: Blackwell.

Edwards, P.A. (1994) 'Responses of teachers and African-American mothers to a book-reading intervention program', in D. Dickinson, (ed.), Bridges to Literacy: Children, Families and Schools. Oxford: Blackwell.

Finlay, A. (1999) 'Exploring an alternative literacy curriculum for socially and economically disadvantaged parents in the UK', Journal of Adolescent and Adult Literacy, 43 (1): 18–26.

Goelman, H., Oberg, A.A. and Smith, F. (eds) (1984) Awakening to Literacy. Portsmouth, NH: Heinemann.

Goodman, Y.M. (1980) 'The roots of literacy', in M.P. Douglas (ed.), Claremont Reading Conference Forty-Fourth Yearbook. Claremont, CA: Claremont Reading Conference.

Grant, A. (1997) 'Debating intergenerational family literacy: myths, critiques, and counterperspectives', in D. Taylor (ed.), Many Families, many Literacies: an International Declaration of Principles. Portsmouth, NH: Heinemann. pp. 216–25.

Green, C. (1987) 'Parental facilitation of young children's writing', Early Child Development and Care, 28: 31–7.

Gregory, E. (1996) Making Sense of a New World: Learning to Read in a Second Language. London: Chapman.

Haggart, J. (2000) Learning Legacies: a Guide to Family Learning. Leicester: National Institute of Adult and Continuing Education.

Hall, N. (1987) The Emergence of Literacy. London: Hodder and Stoughton.

Hannon, P. (1987) 'A study of the effects of parental involvement in the teaching of reading on children's reading test performance', British Journal of Educational Psychology, 57: 56–72.

Hannon, P. (1995) Literacy, Home and School: Research and Practice in Teaching Literacy with Parents. London: Falmer.

Hannon, P. (1996) 'School is too late', in S. Wolfendale and K. Topping (eds), Family Involvement in Literacy: Effective Partnerships in Education. London: Cassell.

Hannon, P. (1998) 'How can we foster children's early literacy development through parent involvement?', in S.B. Neuman and K.A. Roskos (eds), Children Achieving: Best Practices in Early Literacy. Newark, DE: International Reading Association.

Hannon, P. (2000a) Reflecting on Literacy in Education. London: Routledge Falmer.

Hannon, P. (2000b) 'Rhetoric and research in family literacy', British Educational Research Journal, 26 (1): 121–38.

Hannon, P. and James, S. (1990) 'Parents' and teachers' perspectives on preschool literacy development', British Educational Research Journal, 16 (3): 259–72.

Hannon, P. and Nutbrown, C. (1997) 'Teachers' use of a conceptual framework for early literacy education with parents', Teacher Development, 1 (3): 405–20.

Hannon, P. and Nutbrown, C. (2001) 'Outcomes for children and parents of an early literacy education parental involvement programme'. Paper presented at the Annual Conference of the British Educational Research Association, Leeds.

Hannon, P., Nutbrown, C. and Fawcett, E. (1997) 'Taking parent learning seriously', Adults Learning, 9 (3): 19–21.

Harste, J.C., Woodward, V.A. and Burke, C.L. (1984) Language Stories and Literacy Lessons. Portsmouth, NH: Heinemann.

Heath, S.B. (1982) 'What no bedtime story means: narrative skills at home and school', Language in Society, 2: 49–76.

Heath, S.B. (1983) Ways with Words: Language, Life and Work in Communities and Classrooms. Cambridge: Cambridge University Press.

Hewison, J. (1988) 'The long term effectiveness of parental involvement in reading: a follow-up to the

Haringey Reading Project', *British Journal of Educational Psychology*, 58: 184–90.

Hewison, J. and Tizard, J. (1980) 'Parental involvement and reading attainment', *British Journal of Educational Psychology*, 50: 209–15.

Hirst, K. (1998) 'Pre-school literacy experiences of children in Punjabi, Urdu and Gujerati speaking families in England', *British Educational Research Journal*, 24 (4): 415–29.

Karther, D. (2002) 'Fathers with low literacy and their children', *The Reading Teacher*, 56 (2): 184–93.

Kenner, C. (2000) *Home Pages: Literacy Links for Bilingual Children*. Stoke-on-Trent: Trentham.

Lloyd, T. (2001) *What Works with Fathers*? London: Working With Men.

Maclean, M., Bryant, P. and Bradley, L. (1987) 'Rhymes, nursery rhymes, and reading in early childhood', *Merrill–Palmer Quarterly*, 33 (3): 255–81.

McIvor, M.C. (1990) *Family Literacy in Action: a Survey of Successful Programs*. Syracuse, NY: New Readers Press.

McNaughton, S. (1995) *The Patterns of Emergent Literacy*. Oxford: Oxford University Press.

McNaughton, S., Glynn, T. and Robinson, V. (1981) *Parents as Remedial Tutors: Issues for Home and School*. Wellington: New Zealand Council for Educational Research.

Meek Spencer, M. and Dombey, H. (eds) (1994) *First Steps Together: Home–School Early Literacy Collaboration in European Contexts*. Stoke-on-Trent: Trentham.

Millard, E. (2001) *It's a Man Thing! Evaluation Report of CEDC's Fathers and Reading Project*. Coventry: CEDC.

Moll, L., Amanti, C., Neff, D. and Gonzalez, N. (1992) 'Funds of knowledge for teaching: using a qualitative approach to connect homes and classrooms', *Theory into Practice*, 31 (2): 132–41.

Morrow, L.M. (ed.) (1995) *Family Literacy: Connections in Schools and Communities*. Newark, DE: International Reading Association.

Morrow, L.M. and Paratore, J. (1993) 'Family literacy: perspectives and practices', *Reading Teacher*, 47: 194–200.

Morrow, L.M., Tracey, D.H. and Maxwell, C.M. (eds) (1995) *A Survey of Family Literacy in the United States*. Newark, DE: International Reading Association.

Moss, B.J. (ed.) (1994) *Literacy across Communities*. Cresskill, NJ: Hampton.

Nash, A. (1987) *English Family Literacy: an Annotated Bibliography*. Boston: English Family Literacy Project, University of Massachusetts.

National Center for Family Literacy (NCFL) (1994) 'Communicating the power of family literacy', *NCFL Newsletter*, 6 (1): 1.

Newson, J. and Newson, E. (1977) *Perspectives on School at Seven Years Old*. London: Allen and Unwin.

Nickse, R.S. (1990) *Family and Intergenerational Literacy Programs: an update of 'Noises of Literacy'*. Columbus, OH: ERIC Clearinghouse on Adult, Career and Vocational Education, Ohio State University.

Nutbrown, C. and Hannon, P. (eds) (1997) *Early Literacy Education with Parents: a Professional Development Manual*. Nottingham: NES–Arnold.

Nutbrown, C., Hannon, P. and Weinberger, J. (1991) 'Training teachers to work with parents to promote early literacy development', *International Journal of Early Childhood*, 23 (2): 1–10.

Padak, N., Sapin, C. and Baycich, D. (2002) *A Decade of Family Literacy: Programs, Outcomes, and Future Prospects*. Information Series no. 389. Columbus, OH: ERIC Clearinghouse on Adult, Career, and Vocational Education, Ohio State University.

Purcell-Gates, V. (1995) *Other People's Words: the Cycle of Low Literacy*. Cambridge, MA: Harvard University Press.

Purcell-Gates, V. (2000) 'Family literacy', in M.L. Kamil, P.B. Mosenthal, P.D. Pearson and R. Barr (eds), *Handbook of Reading Research*, vol. III. Mahwah, NJ: Erlbaum. pp. 853–70.

St Pierre, R., Swartz, J., Gamse, B., Murray, S., Deck, D. and Nickel, P. (1995) *National Evaluation of the Even Start Family Literacy Program*. Washington, DC: US Department of Education, Office of Policy and Planning.

Taylor, D. (1983) *Family Literacy: Young Children Learning to Read and Write*. Exeter, NH: Heinemann.

Taylor, D. (ed.) (1997) *Many Families, Many Literacies: an International Declaration of Principles*. Portsmouth, NH: Heinemann.

Taylor, D. and Dorsey-Gaines, C. (1988) *Growing Up Literacy: Learning from Inner-City Families*. Portsmouth, NH: Heinemann.

Teale, W.H. (1986) 'Home background and young children's literacy development', in W.H. Teale and E. Sulzby (eds), *Emergent Literacy: Writing and Reading*. Norwood, NJ: Ablex.

Teale, W.H. and Sulzby, E. (eds) (1986) *Emergent Literacy: Writing and Reading*. Norwood, NJ: Ablex.

Tett, L. (2000) 'Excluded voices: class, culture, and family literacy in Scotland', *Journal of Adolescent and Adult Literacy*, 44 (2): 122–8.

Tizard, B. and Hughes, M. (1984) *Young Children Learning: Talking and Thinking at Home and in School*. London: Fontana.

Tizard, J., Schofield, W.N. and Hewison, J. (1982) 'Collaboration between teachers and parents in assisting children's reading', *British Journal of Educational Psychology*, 52: 1–15.

Tizard, B., Blatchford, P., Burke, J., Farquhar, C. and Plewis, I. (1988) *Young Children at School in the Inner City*. London: Erlbaum.

Topping, K. and Lindsay, G.A. (1991) 'The structure and development of the paired reading technique', *Journal of Research in Reading*, 15 (2): 120–36.

Topping, K. and Lindsay, G.A. (1992) 'Paired reading: a review of the literature', *Research Papers in Education*, 7 (3): 199–246.

Voss, M. (1996) *Hidden Literacies: Children Learning at Home and at School*. Portsmouth, NH: Heinemann.

Wade, B. (1984) 'Story at home and school'. Educational Review Publication no. 10, University of Birmingham, Faculty of Education.

Wasik, B.H., Dobbins, D.R. and Hermann, S. (2001) 'Intergenerational family literacy: concepts, research, and practice', in S.B. Neuman and D.K. Dickinson (eds), *Handbook of Early Literacy Research*. New York: Guilford. pp. 444–58.

Weinberger, J. (1996) *Literacy Goes to School: the Parents' Role in Young Children's Literacy Learning*. London: Chapman.

Wells, G. (1987) *The Meaning Makers: Children Learning Language and Using Language to Learn*. London: Hodder and Stoughton.

Whitehurst, G.J., Epstein, J.N., Angell, A.L., Payne, D.A., Crone, D.A. and Fischel, J.E. (1994) 'Outcomes of an emergent literacy intervention in Head Start', *Journal of Educational Psychology*, 86 (4): 542–55.

Wolfendale, S. and Topping, K. (eds) (1996) *Family Involvement in Literacy: Effective Partnerships in Education*. London: Cassell.

10

Early Childhood Literacy
and Popular Culture

JACKIE MARSH

By the end of the nineteenth century, the school saw itself as a place where working-class children might be compensated for belonging to working-class families. (Steedman, 1985: 156)

One could argue that, as a means of developing this compensatory role, schooling across centuries and continents has celebrated particular versions of 'high' culture in the hope of leading the populace to 'the best that has been thought and known in the world' (Matthew Arnold, *Culture and Anarchy*, 1869). This is no less true of schooling for young children as it is for the education of their older counterparts. This chapter focuses on research that has challenged this hegemonic construction of the literacy curriculum, research which has thrust issues relating to the study of the popular firmly onto the educational agenda. Indeed, the inclusion of a chapter focusing on the role of popular culture in early literacy in this handbook is an indication of the growing impact of the field. Despite its relatively recent history, there has been a range of work which has served to illustrate the complex relationship between popular culture and literacy in the early years. In this chapter, key themes and issues that have emerged from this body of research are reviewed and future research agendas identified.

The chapter begins with an exploration of the concept of popular culture itself and discusses the relationship between literacy and popular culture. The role of popular culture in the literacy practices undertaken in the home is then identified, before the chapter moves on to discuss research which has focused on the use of popular culture in nurseries and schools. In the final part of the chapter, ways in which future research agendas might be shaped by contemporary issues and concerns are discussed. What is not addressed in these pages is the question of the need for such a focus on popular culture in the first place. For this discussion, see Williams (1965) and Willis (1990) who remind us that schools should not exist to compensate children for their cultural experiences, but should, in fact, recognize and build on them. As many children's cultural experiences are located firmly within the realm of the popular, it is necessary to turn first to a critical examination of this concept.

POPULAR CULTURE AND LITERACY

Definitions of popular culture are as varied and contradictory as those of culture itself (Jenks, 1993). The strict dichotomy between high and low culture which has been posited for many years can no longer be sustained. There is much evidence that texts which have long been assumed to represent 'high' culture actually began their days within the popular realm, as is the case with the work of Shakespeare, for example (Levine, 1991). However, it is clear that there are inherent divisions and cultural hierarchies and, therefore, it is possible to identify those texts and artefacts which may be seen as popular:

Popular culture refers to the beliefs and practices, and the objects through which they are organized, that are widely shared among a population. This includes folk beliefs, practices and the objects rooted in local traditions, and mass beliefs, practices and objects generated in political and commercial centers. It includes elite cultural forms that have been popularized as well as popular forms that have been elevated to the museum tradition. (Mukerji and Schudson, 1991: 3)

Such a postmodern construction of the term allows us to recognize that popular cultural forms are constantly changing and are bound by sociocultural contexts. Children's popular cultural pursuits are obviously inflected by local concerns and contexts and thus there can be no comprehensive account of the texts that might be involved in children's popular cultural practices. For some children in majority world cultures, or in economically disadvantaged communities in minority world countries, artefacts of popular culture may be few in number, might be adaptations of cultural products aimed at adults, or may be locally produced and fashioned from the materials to hand – paper, stone, wood, metal and so on, having little to do with manufactured, globalized narratives derived from television or film. This is not the case, of course, in all majority world or economically disadvantaged communities, and Ritzer's (1996) critique of the 'McDonaldization' of global cultures is an incisive account of how multinational industries have ruthlessly expanded global operations, discounting localized practices and cultural knowledge and values. However, children's agency in the ways in which global narratives are taken up is rarely acknowledged and there needs to be a much more careful study of how these texts are appropriated and adapted in specific cultural contexts. In addition, children engage in popular cultural practices which are not always a part of these Westernized narratives. For example, many children, in Asia and across the world, watch Indian movies, many of which are made in Bombay and which are an integral part of their families' leisure pursuits (see Kenner, 2000, whose research is located in the UK). These movies are often referred to as 'Bollywood' films, but this appears to make it a marked binary term, with 'Hollywood' as the privileged concept. Dyson also notes that in one Mexican-American community in the USA, children consumed popular car magazines such as *Lowrider* and, in a Chinese-American neighbourhood, children enjoyed Asian animation (Dyson, 1996: 473). There is a growing body of work which attests to the culturally specific popular cultural interests of teenagers and young people (Mahiri, 1998; Moje, 2000). However, there is little research as yet into similar practices in early childhood and therefore, whilst this chapter draws primarily from research conducted in minority world locations, it is important to recognize that popular culture can be both hegemonic and non-hegemonic in nature and

is differently indexed in localized communities of practice.

Children's popular culture includes a wide range of cultural objects. Figure 10.1 outlines some of the texts and artefacts which may be included in any exploration of the term. This is not, of course, an exhaustive list. As suggested earlier, access to and use of the texts and artefacts which are contained within this web are obviously dependent on culture, economic capital and social context.

Manufacturers and media industries have been swift to exploit the possibilities afforded by the interrelationships between these texts. Narratives are developed across computer games, television programmes, toys, cards, stickers, fast food and gifts and many children are able to play with, watch, listen to, eat, wear and sleep on texts and artefacts which are linked to their favourite characters and media texts. This 'transmedia intertextuality' (Kinder, 1991: 3) contributes to the development of peer culture and means that children can engage in specific narratives even if they own only a relatively minor part of the system, for example stickers and cards (Marsh and Millard, 2000). More recently, Gunter Kress has indicated the importance of these 'communicational webs' (2000: 143) as children's multimodal meaning making crosses sites and media (see also Nixon, 2001).

Once the extent and richness of the range of texts and artefacts that constitute children's popular culture have been recognized, it is a short step to understanding the way in which popular culture can impact upon literacy experiences and development. Many of the texts included in Figure 10.1 contain printed text (books, comics, magazines), other texts are embedded into children's new literacy practices (television, film, computer games, mobile phones) and others (toys, games) have books and literacy materials linked to them. There is evidence that children read material which is related to their popular cultural interests (Millard, 1997). Computer gamers, for example, often are avid readers of computer magazines as they glean information about 'cheats' and games (Roe and Muijs, 1998). This chapter will examine research that has indicated ways in which children engage in reading and writing texts which are located within their popular cultural worlds in out-of-school contexts, but it will also review work which has explored how far popular culture can be used within the early years curriculum as a resource and stimulus for literacy activities.

POPULAR CULTURE IN THE HOME

Most of the studies which have explored children's literacy practices within the home have focused

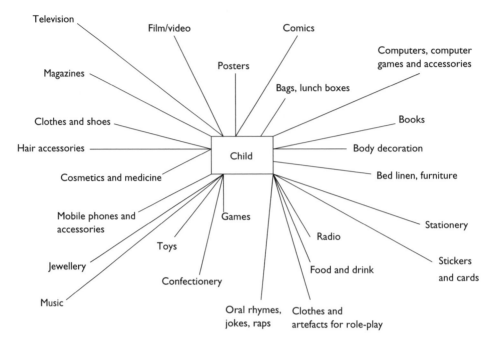

Figure 10.1   Texts and artefacts in children's popular culture

upon print-based text, although many throw light on the way in which texts that are located within children's popular culture are an integral part of this literacy network. There are four key themes which emerge from a review of this work. The first is the extent to which popular cultural texts are deeply embedded within the literacy lives of families. The second is the way in which such texts become an integral part of children's literacy practices in households. The third theme to emerge is that, generally, in the research reported here, parents appear to view children's engagement with popular cultural texts in a positive light. Finally, the dissonance between home and nursery/school practices in relation to popular culture is a thread which runs through a number of studies. These themes will be addressed in turn.

The range of popular cultural texts in the home

There is evidence to suggest that popular cultural texts are an integral part of the literacy environment in many homes. Although not a specific focus of most studies located within domestic sites, research which has documented the literacy texts and practices situated in young children's homes has

demonstrated that, within this sphere, children and parents encounter a range of cultural and media texts. Purcell-Gates (1996) examined the home literacy practices of 20 families from 'low socio-economic status' groups in the USA, located within a range of ethnic communities. Families were observed by researchers over a period of one week and all literacy practices taking place within the home were recorded. Members of the project families engaged with a range of texts which included TV guides, junk mail and food labels.

This trend was identified by Weinberger in her 1996 study of 42 families in the UK. Weinberger traced the literacy practices of children aged three to six over three years. Weinberger found that much of the print in homes was related to everyday life and included junk mail, newspapers and magazines. Many of the children's books in the home were related to popular television characters (1996: 48). Again in the UK, Moss (2001) constructed a study in which children aged seven to nine took photographs which tracked how reading resources were made available to them in the home. Children photographed themselves and siblings reading popular storybooks (e.g. Disney), comics and magazines, took pictures of posters, catalogues, sticker albums and a range of environmental print including shopping bags and food packaging. For these children, the literacy environment consisted of a wide range of texts and the boundaries between popular and canonical texts were blurred. Corresponding patterns which indicate the significant place of popular cultural texts in young children's households have also been found in Australia by Cairney et al. (1996). In addition, it is clear that the pervasiveness of media and popular cultural texts in many homes crosses cultural and linguistic boundaries and there is evidence of bilingual children accessing a range of popular and media texts in more than one language (Kenner, 2000; Rodriguez, 1999; Xu, 1999).

Children's popular cultural literacy practices in the home

The second theme to emerge from a consideration of the literature relating to popular culture in the home is that children draw readily from these texts and artefacts in their home-based literacy practices. In Marsh and Thompson's (2001) study in the UK, 18 families in a white, working-class community in the north of England were asked to keep literacy diaries for a period of four weeks. These literacy diaries documented the number and titles of texts which three- and four-year-old children read over that four-week period, including televisual texts. Key findings were that, as is the case with older children (Livingstone and Bovill, 1999), televisual texts were a primary source of narrative satisfaction (Hilton, 1996), with children watching television and films far more than they engaged in any other type of literacy activity. However, embedded within children's literacy practices in the home were a range of popular cultural texts such as computer (mainly console) games, comics, books based on television characters and environmental print linked to media texts (stickers, labels, video labels and computer game boxes). The role of television in preschool children's meaning making in the home was also a pattern noted by Rodriguez (1999) in her study of three Dominican preschool children aged two and a half to five years, living in New York City. The children were observed in the home over a period of nine months. Rodriguez reported that children engaged with a wide range of texts within the home, but were particularly drawn to television and were highly attentive to the print which appeared on the screen. In addition, they were not passive viewers, but were constantly asking questions and talking about what they were watching, demonstrating meaning making practices that have been noted in relation to older children (Buckingham, 1993; Palmer, 1986; Robinson, 1997).

Children draw from their popular culture not only when reading televisual texts, but also when engaging in multimodal productive practices within the home. Popular culture provides part of the cultural store of semiotic texts from which children draw when meaning making in whatever context (Dyson, 1997a). Kenner (2000) outlines the literacy practices of three bilingual children in their London homes. Three-year-old Billy's favourite literacy item, his mother noted, was a Thai karaoke video that displayed the words of the songs in Thai script across the screen, which Billy enjoyed watching and singing along with. Meera, also aged three, copied Gujerati script from magazines, encouraged by her father. Four-year-old Mohammed used a song tape to learn Arabic letters and loved to identify the names of different makes of cars when out in the community. In Pahl's (2001; 2002) ethnographic studies of children's multimodal meaning making in homes, children can be seen moving seamlessly between multilingual sites as they mine whatever they can to produce texts that reflect a range of media and cultural interests. This rich seam of popular texts from which children draw has also been identified in a number of other studies that have analysed children's semiotic practices in the home (see Anning and Ring, 1999; Barrs, 1988; Carrington and Luke, 2003; Hicks, 2001).

In many countries, popular cultural and media texts often form the majority of young children's first encounters with spoken and written English. In a number of studies, children's engagement with popular culture in the home has been linked to the development of English as an additional language. Xu (1999) documented the home literacy practices of six Chinese-American children aged between five and six. She found that children often read, alongside their parents, the TV guides in order to find out about their favourite programmes. All of the children watched television for at least one hour per day. For the children in Xu's study, popular culture was an important means of developing an understanding and use of English as an additional language. Orellana (1994) also found, in an analysis of three Spanish-speaking children's superhero play, that watching popular television programmes helped to develop the children's American English. There are complex issues relating to cultural imperialism and hegemonic constructions of cultural identities within media texts which need to be traced in this process. This work does suggest that popular culture has a role to play in young children's acquisition of language and, for bilingual children, it can provide a means of creating cultural and linguistic shared spaces between home, school and community (Kenner, 2000).

Parental attitudes

Despite the unease of a number of early years educators concerning the influence of popular culture on young children (see Levin and Rosenquest, 2001), it would appear that many parents view things rather differently. Makin et al. (1999) interviewed 60 parents across 79 early years settings in Australia. The researchers noted that, in discussions with Aboriginal parents and other groups of parents who spoke languages other than English, the use of technology such as TV, video and computer games was highly valued by them as a means of acquiring English as an additional language (Makin et al., 1999: 130). In a number of studies in which parents have been interviewed on this topic, there is evidence that many parents not only provide popular cultural and media resources for their children and recognize their role in promoting early literacy development, but are positive about the place of such texts in their children's lives (Arthur, 2001; Marsh and Thompson, 2001; Weinberger, 1996; Xu, 1999). This is, as the next sections illustrate, in direct contrast to the way in which popular culture is viewed in early years settings and schools.

Home–school differences

Congruency between home and educational sites is an important concept if institutions are to build upon the richness of children's media literacy backgrounds (Arthur et al., 2001; Jones Diaz et al., 2000; Makin et al., 1999; Marsh and Thompson, 2001). In a study of 79 early childhood education sites in Australia, in which the research team interviewed two staff members at each site and conducted focus group interviews with 60 parents, Makin et al. (1999) found that literacy practices embedded within technology and popular culture were pervasive in homes, yet few early years settings incorporated such resources into the curriculum. Although 71% of parents identified technology and popular culture as important to their child's literacy development, only 13% of staff acknowledged such practices occurred within the home, with many staff expressing concerns about these literacy events, in particular the viewing of television.

This dissonance between home and school practices with regard to popular culture has also been identified in a number of other studies (Comber et al., 2001; Hill et al., 1998; Marsh, 2003a). Hicks (2001) provides a detailed case study of one working-class white child growing up in the USA. She observed and documented the home and school learning experiences of the boy Jake over a three-year period, between the ages of four and seven. Hicks reports that, in the home, 'Jake's fictional world seemed largely constructed around physically

enacted texts, texts that involved a high degree of movement and that often involved media forms' (2001: 220). Jake, for example, liked to play Sega computer games, which involved him in corporeal modes of meaning making. However, when Jake started school, the curriculum did not reflect his interests or areas of expertise; he became disengaged from activities and was soon identified as a 'struggling' reader. Carrington and Luke (2003) also use children's experience of the disjuncture between home and school literacy practices to argue that so-called 'at-risk' students are placed in risky situations because of the lack of attention paid by educational settings to literacy practices embedded within popular culture and new technologies. The lack of continuity between homes and schools with regard to popular culture and new technologies has been extensively noted (Carrington, 2001; Kress, 1997; Luke, 1999; Luke and Luke, 2001; Makin and Jones Diaz, 2002; Marsh and Millard, 2000; Marsh and Thompson, 2001), yet the situation still persists in many societies. In the following section of this chapter, work is examined which has, despite the apparent lack of interest from policy makers, addressed the way in which such texts are used and can be utilized within the literacy curriculum of nurseries and schools.

POPULAR CULTURE, LITERACY AND SCHOOLING

Any study of the relationship between popular culture, literacy and schooling in early childhood must acknowledge the way in which the official curriculum in most institutions serves to exclude popular cultural and non-canonical texts. The work of cultural reproductionists offers insight into how the official literacy curricula of early years settings and schools reflect the interests of the powerful and governing classes (Bourdieu and Passeron, 1977; Bernstein, 1996), although this work has been criticized for being overly deterministic (Sharp, 1980). In addition, the work of Freire (1972), Apple (1993) and Giroux (1988; 1994) has been central to the exploration of this relationship between pedagogical practices and culture, although the extent to which they share the reproductionist models or draw from Marxist discourses differs. In relation to literacy, the work of Luke (1994) in particular has demonstrated how 'dominant literacies' (Lankshear et al., 1997: 74) become enshrined in the curriculum and draw from the 'cultural capital' (Bourdieu, 1977) of particular socio-economic groups at the same time as they marginalize the cultural capital of other groups. An examination of the way in which the curriculum frames knowledge and excludes popular culture in this process must also address the issue of the 'null curriculum' (Eisner, 1979: 83). Eisner suggests that any study of the curriculum should contain an analysis of what educational institutions do not teach, as that impacts on what is taught. Britzman goes further to say that:

> The null curriculum signifies all that is not selected as well as all that occurs but which remains unnamed and acknowledged. Housed within official school discourse but situated behind the backs of teachers, the null curriculum can be thought of as 'renegade' knowledge. Such knowledge exists outside the boundaries of institutional sanctions and defies institutional order. The null curriculum is represented by silences, deliberate omissions, and what the institution of school designates as cultural taboos, controversy, or matters deemed extraneous to the values of efficiency and standardization. Its exclusion is most evident when 'covering the material' mandates the silencing of student voice and, concurrently, the diminishment of student experience. (1989: 143)

The phrase 'behind the backs of teachers', however, may suggest that teachers are not complicit in the exclusion of students' interests. This is not always the case (see Marsh, 2003b; Seiter, 1999). Despite the lack of attention paid to media and popular texts by many early childhood educators, however, children's resourcefulness means that they find a myriad ways to circumvent such exclusionary tactics and draw from their popular cultural worlds in classroom literacy events.

Unofficial worlds and appropriated texts

In 1985, Carolyn Steedman outlined how Amarjit, a Punjabi girl living in a northern UK town, created a song using the materials she had to hand which were, in this case, a reading primer and her own voice. Steedman notes that:

> An act of transformation like this can be seen as an act of play, in the same way as reading and writing are play, a way of manipulating the symbols of a social and emotional world, and of abstracting meaning from a particular reality. (1985: 138)

Nowhere has children's playful transformation and reconceptualization of media texts been traced more powerfully than in Anne Haas Dyson's work. Dyson's corpus of work (see 1994; 1995; 1996; 1997a; 1997b; 1998; 1999a; 1999b; 2000; 2001a; 2001b; 2002) has been central to the development of our understanding of the ways in which children transgress the restrictions of the 'null curriculum' in early childhood classrooms. Her writing demonstrates how children take up media and popular cultural texts in their creation of an 'unofficial curriculum' (Dyson, 1997a) in which they negotiate teacher-mandated tasks but reconstruct them in order that their own interests and desires are woven into the daily fabric of classroom life. Dyson's extensive work on popular culture has focused specifically on the writing curriculum, but much of what she has to say about the potential of media texts can be applied more widely across the literacy curriculum.

In an early study, Dyson (1994) observed a second-grade classroom class in San Francisco for a period of three months. The data reported on in her paper focus on observations relating to the use of 'author's theatre', in which children wrote stories which were then performed by peers of their choosing. In the study, Dyson illustrates how the children's media stories generated power struggles in which class, race and gender were used as markers of identity and agency and informed how the children's stories were developed and performed. In a book which provides more extensive details of the research undertaken in this school (Dyson, 1997a), she describes how further data were collected by means of extensive observations of children in their second- and third-grade classrooms and through the collection of their written texts, audiotapes of the author's theatre and the recording of conversations with the children and their teacher. These rich data provided further information about the way in which children constructed their unofficial social worlds and how popular culture informed that construction. In choosing which of their classmates were to act out their stories, children played with notions of exclusivity and inclusivity and were negotiating their social worlds as much as they were creating written ones. In this study, Dyson outlines the attraction of superhero stories for young children and indicates how they are both liberating (in providing a forum in which children's knowledge can be drawn upon) and limiting (in providing a forum in which stereotyped roles are rife). The worlds created by children were unofficial in the sense that the popular material was not introduced by Kristin, the teacher involved in the study, although she obviously sanctioned its use. Despite the lack of official recognition of popular texts in mandated curricula, children throughout Dyson's studies have imaginatively exploited this rich source of semiotic material as they create media-saturated 'figured worlds' (Holland et al., 1998) within the realm of the classroom.

Children use this cultural agency to refashion media discourses in a playful and inventive manner. Dyson (1999a) outlines five ways in which media were appropriated by children for use in schooled texts in one of her studies. Table 10.1 provides an

Table 10.1 *Children's appropriation of media texts*

Kinds of appropriation	Example
Content	Names of baseball/ football teams; sports events; knowledge of sports
Communicative forms	Textual forms such as games results; discourse features of those forms, e.g. use of location adjectives (Dallas Cowboys)
Graphic conventions	Symbols of teams
Voiced utterances	Particular lines spoken by narrators or characters
Ideologies	Children appropriated ideologies of gender and power embedded in sports narratives

Source: Dyson, 1999a: 379–80

overview of these categories, illustrated by the examples Dyson provides in relation to children's use of sports media. These five categories can be traced in the ways in which children appropriate media texts in a range of other studies outlined in this chapter and indicate the extent to which media discourses permeate children's meaning making. This process of requisition serves to validate children's own cultural resources and, in addition, it enables them to negotiate and navigate peer relationships. Seiter (1993) has suggested that popular culture is the lingua franca of playgrounds and, as such, it can offer a means for children from disparate linguistic, cultural and economic backgrounds to forge common links and develop dialogic communities of practice (Dyson, 1997a; Marsh, 2000b; Suss et al., 2001). One discourse which is regularly subject to such border crossing is that of the superhero.

Superheroes

Superheroes offer an iconic embodiment of the concept of 'good' which is engaged in the fight against its binary opposite, 'evil', and this elemental, mythic narrative can be attractive to young children (Dyson, 1997a). In addition, daring costumes and technological wizardry offer children performative narratives of autonomy and adventure (Marsh, 2000a). In Dyson's (1997a) work, the superhero cult has been shown to hold a particular attraction for young children. This is also the case in other work undertaken in North America and Australia (Clark, 1995; Paley, 1984). A number of studies have examined the way in which superhero play can inform children's language and literacy development (Barrs, 1988; Marsh, 1999) and have suggested that it can provide a means of encouraging language acquisition. Orellana (1994) focused on superhero play as a means of developing oral language in her study of three bilingual preschool children's language use in such play. She suggested that American popular culture, and in particular the superhero narrative, was a useful tool in developing English as an additional language.

There has been work which suggests that superhero play is particularly attractive to young boys. Vivian Gus Paley (1984) observed young children in a kindergarten in the United States of America. She found that boys in particular were attracted to the superhero genre and acted out narratives based on this genre in their play. Clark (1995) conducted a study over three years in Canada, which focused on 46 children aged six to seven. The researcher studied the narratives of the children and analysed the differently gendered elements in boys' and girls' stories. Clark (1995: 10) suggested that boys in particular focused on superheroes as the key characters in their stories and that the girls in her study responded in similar ways to those in Paley's (1984) work in that they were not attracted to the superhero genre. However, in the work of Dyson (1997a) and Marsh (1999; 2000a), girls were clearly attracted to the superhero genre but encountered resistance from boys who engaged in furious 'borderwork' (Thorne, 1993) to keep them at bay. For a more extensive discussion of issues relating to gender and popular culture, see Millard's chapter in this volume.

Hybrid texts

In Dyson's (1997a) study, popular culture provided the material for the children's writing and social relationships in the classroom and bridged the domains of schooled literacy and the literacy practices of the children's unofficial worlds of home and community. As the children refashioned superhero stories for classroom use, the teacher introduced Greek myths to the class and the children subsequently interwove the narratives of these archetypal myths into their writing and superhero play. Thus, Dyson notes, 'Venus had entered the classroom image store, along with the Power Rangers, the X-men, and Rosa Parks' (1997a: 143).

In later studies, Dyson has examined in closer detail the way in which media discourses are recontextualized by children in their production of classroom texts (Dyson, 1999a; 2001a; 2001b; 2002) and outlines how these hybrid texts present an opportunity to examine both conjuncture and disjuncture between official and unofficial worlds. In a classroom ethnography undertaken over a year in an elementary classroom, Dyson observed children for four to six hours per week over an eight-month period, in addition to collecting the work of all 20 children in the class. In a close analysis of the way in which two children used media texts to inform their social and cultural landscape, Dyson (2001a; 2002) outlines how the children appropriated narratives from cartoons, songs and classroom texts to inform their writing. She argues that the children were:

> recontextualizing material from diverse sources. That recontextualizing necessitated some negotiating among the conventions of different symbolic media, and it led as well to a highlighting of the social expectations of different words. (2001a: 28)

The children deftly negotiated the different textual, social and ideological practices embedded within these various media as they produced hybrid texts which included snippets from pop songs and cartoon videos alongside more canonical classroom texts such as non-fiction books on space and picture books.

Hicks suggests that schools need to develop 'hybrid pedagogical spaces' (2001: 226) in which children's out-of-school interests are given due recognition within the curriculum. There are a number of compelling accounts of how such hybrid pedagogical spaces have been developed successfully across a range of social and cultural contexts (see Au and Kawakami, 1991; Kenner, 2000; Millard, 2003; Moll et al., 1992). Such a move with regard to children's experiences could provide opportunities to address some of the difficulties identified by Hicks (2001) and Carrington and Luke (2003) regarding children's lack of motivation to engage in literacy practices as framed by schools. Throughout much of the literature on the use of popular culture in educational settings, a key tenet has been that it can provide a useful means of motivating children to take part in schooled literacy events. The following section reviews this body of work.

Motivation

Motivation is key to literacy learning (Guthrie et al., 1996; Turner, 1995; Turner and Paris, 1995). There is growing evidence of the way in which popular culture can orientate children towards taking part in schooled literacy practices. Helen Bromley (1996) analysed the way in which children she taught in a reception class drew from video films in their oral and written narratives and outlined how

films provided an exciting stimulus for literacy work for these children as they retold favourite stories and read video covers. The stories recreated in many of the videos watched by children, the majority produced by Disney, drew on fairytales, myths and legends, all of which encapsulate and replay deep narratives of desire (Hilton, 1996: 41). It is inevitable, therefore, that these are the texts which magnetically draw children to literacy events in classrooms.

In Marsh (1999), a Batman and Batwoman HQ was set up in a base shared by two vertically grouped classes containing 58 children aged between six and seven. Data were collected through observation, videorecording of the role-play area and analysis of children's written texts. The study indicated that the superhero theme was extremely appealing for the majority of the children in the class, but proved to be particularly attractive to a group of boys who had been identified by the teachers as underachieving in literacy. These boys were observed engaging in a wide range of literacy practices in the HQ and took more interest in literacy activities outside of the 'Batcave' (Marsh, 1999; 2000a). This also proved to be the case in relation to younger children who attended two nurseries in the north of England (Marsh, 2000b). Sixty-three three- and four-year-old children took part in a range of literacy activities based on 'The Teletubbies' television programme, which included making 'Tubby custard' and then writing their own 'Teletubby' recipes. Data were collected using observation, analysis of written texts and interviews with nursery staff. Again, analysis of the data indicated that the discourse was very attractive to the children and the nursery staff expressed astonishment at the response of children previously identified as not being orientated towards schooled literacy practices (Marsh, 2000b). In addition, the activities promoted discussion by the children of their knowledge of the shared texts and thus enhanced the opportunities to build dialogic communities in the multilingual environments of the nurseries.

A number of other case studies also indicate that the use of popular cultural texts in early childhood classrooms can enhance motivation, whether that is through the use of popular computer games such as Super Mario (Hill and Broadhurst, 2002) and Pokémon (Arthur, 2001), television characters such as the Smurfs (O'Brien, 1998), or comics featuring a range of popular characters (Millard and Marsh, 2001). In addition, such work can provide a means of recognizing the 'funds of knowledge' (Moll et al., 1992) from which children draw and which arises from their saturation in popular culture at home and the community. (This is an issue explored further in Carrington, 2001; Comber,

1998; Comber and Simpson, 2001; Dyson, 1999a; Hicks, 2001; Marsh and Millard, 2000.)

It is important to point out that the work outlined above does not subscribe to a romantic vision in which children's popular culture is idealistically celebrated and used uncritically as a means of orientating children towards schooled literacy practices. Although the role of the consumer industry in a post-Fordist, globalized economy is recognized, and the way in which children are inscribed within that discourse acknowledged (see Kenway and Bullen, 2001), children are not bereft of agency as they engage with media texts. In addition, their critical literacy skills can be utilized and extended in work on media texts in the classroom. Nor does an emphasis on the use of popular culture in the curriculum suggest simplistically that such work will provide a platform for democratic pedagogical practices, an issue which has been addressed more extensively in relation to critical literacy.

Critical media stories

'Critical literacy' is a term which has been applied to practices which involve the examination of the sources, uses and effects of power within a text (Comber and Simpson, 2001; Knobel and Healy, 1998). Popular cultural texts lend themselves to this kind of critical analysis because of the vast amount of knowledge that children bring to an examination of the production and consumption of these texts, and there has been an emphasis on developing critical literacy skills in order to deconstruct the discourses of power embedded within popular texts. Although some of the research in this area has been concerned with older children (see Alvermann et al., 1999), there are a growing number of researchers working in the early childhood field (Comber, 1998; 2000; Comber and Simpson, 2001; Jones Diaz et al., 2002; Knobel and Healy, 1998; O'Brien, 1998; Vasquez, 2001).

As Comber's chapter in this volume suggests, work in this area demonstrates how children's lived experiences develop their capacity to explore critically the texts they encounter in a range of contexts, skills which can be drawn upon in enlightened and imaginative ways in classrooms (Comber, 1992; 1994; 1998; 2000; Comber and Kamler, 1997; Comber and Simpson, 2001; Comber et al., 2001). Comber's work demonstrates that, although we can enhance children's critical literacy skills, they do not begin this process as empty ciphers; they enter classrooms with a wealth of understanding about the popular cultural world around them. Misson (1998) also reminds us that we must approach this work with an understanding of the pleasures such texts bring to children and seek to respect this pleasure, not destroy it.

If the rich practices identified within this corpus of work are to be embedded fully in policies, curricula and early years practice, then educators need to be convinced of the ways in which such work can develop 'powerful literacies' (Crowther et al., 2001). Initial research in this area would suggest, however, that this recognition of the potential role of popular culture is, as yet, not widespread amongst early years professionals.

Teacher attitudes

Research on teacher attitudes to the use of popular culture and media in the curriculum is very limited but, nonetheless, provides some illuminating glimpses into the way in which such work is viewed by professional educators. Dyson (1997a) reports on the discussions of 10 primary school teachers from San Francisco, in which they reflected on their experiences of and attitudes towards the use of popular culture in their classrooms. Some of the teachers reported on how they had used some forms of popular culture in their classroom, e.g. videos, magazines, and reproductions of popular fast-food outlets in sociodramatic play areas. Dyson suggests that 'The genres associated with commercial media (e.g. videos, advertisements, and television shows) did not, in and of themselves, cause any ideological uneasiness. But the *content* of media forms could' (1997a: 174). Thus, some teachers expressed concern over representations of women in magazines or the violence which permeated some of the media stories. The teachers reported a number of strategies to deal with this such as censoring materials, discussing their objections with children and replacing the texts with more acceptable alternatives. One teacher, Kristin, took an approach which involved children in reflecting on the ideological tensions in the media material they reworked in their stories, developing their critical literacy skills. In this way, the responsibility for challenging racist, sexist and exclusive discourses was not just the teachers', but also the children's.

Green et al. (1998) interviewed 28 teacher graduate students in Australia. They asked the teachers to compare the amount of time the children they taught engaged with electronic media with their use of print media. In their feedback, the teachers complained about the individualistic nature of the games, the gender imbalance in the use of the games and the way in which reading was a less favoured pursuit of the children. Green et al. suggest that a number of this new generation of teachers:

seem to be thinking and talking about Nintendo in ways that are more like their parents than their little brothers and sisters. They are concerned to make a link between computer game play and antisocial, aggressive, 'non-literate' behaviour. On this basis, it would seem that teacher education has a long way to go. (1998: 35)

Makin et al. interviewed 158 early years teachers in Australia and, from their negative attitudes and lack of knowledge about the discourse, concluded that:

There is wide divergence between parents and early childhood staff in terms of their beliefs about the role technology and popular culture can play in young children's early literacy. Because staff do not seek or understand parents' knowledge about children's early literacy at home and in the community, most staff seem unaware of the literacy learning potential of technology as well as other aspects of early literacy at home and in the community. (1999: 115)

This negative attitude towards popular computer games is not confined to Australian teachers. A study by Sanger et al. in the UK demonstrated that most of the teachers who took part in their survey disapproved of the kinds of games likely to be used by many children and banned computer magazines from their classrooms, despite being ignorant of the content of these publications (Sanger et al., 1997: 39).

Disapproval of computer games is usually founded on misgivings about the level of violence, racism and sexism involved in many of the texts and on fears of addiction. Whilst these fears are not to be dismissed, there are ways in which children can challenge these discourses effectively within the classroom (see Comber's chapter in this volume; and Marsh and Millard, 2000). The studies outlined above have been conducted with primary teachers. Research which has documented the views of nursery and kindergarten teachers indicates that such disapproval of media texts is widespread also in this sector.

In a study of children's media use in Finland, Spain and Switzerland, the researchers report that, 'The gap between children's own media culture and media use at home and the media preferred by teachers is especially clear in Switzerland where electronic media and media-related toys are in some ways taboo in many kindergartens' (Suss et al., 2001: 34). There are, however, notable exceptions within the literature. In the USA, Seiter (1999) reports on a project in which 24 preschool teachers and childcare workers were interviewed about their attitudes towards the use of media in preschool settings. Seiter found that the teachers displayed a diverse range of opinions on the subject and illustrates some of the themes which emerged from her work in a case study of two very different settings. In one setting, a Montessori school, the teacher, Sarah, banned videos and Disney films from the classroom. She held very negative attitudes towards media texts, felt that they encouraged children to be passive and worried that they introduced them to inappropriate material. In the classroom, children were discouraged from media play and even prevented from talking about the programmes they had watched and enjoyed. In contrast, Seiter (1999) provides a description of the practice of Gloria, who taught in a private nursery. Gloria was enthusiastic about television for children and encouraged its use in the nursery. Children were allowed to watch videos and engage in fantasy play related to the programmes. Seiter suggests that these two contrasting views are located in two very different paradigms in which children are viewed either as active constructors of meaning in their world, in the case of Gloria, or as passive victims who need to be protected from the ravages of media, as Sarah imagined to be the case.

Given the intransigence displayed by many teachers, it is not surprising, therefore, to find some resistance in the use of popular cultural and media texts by pre-service teachers (Marsh, 2003b; Xu, 2001b). Xu's work (2000a; 2000b; 2001a; 2001b) demonstrates how initial teacher education programmes can effectively challenge such negative attitudes and support student teachers in ensuring that they plan a literacy curriculum which reflects the lives and cultural interests of children. Such work is essential if the cycle which perpetuates the trivialization of children's pursuits and the marginalization of media texts in early years settings and schools is to be broken.

CONCLUSION

From the research reviewed within this chapter, it can be seen that much is now known about the way in which popular culture penetrates children's home literacy practices and the means by which it can inform the early childhood literacy curriculum. Nevertheless, there is clearly still much work to be done in the field. In particular, there needs to be much more detailed research undertaken that helps to identify what children's popular cultural interests are across a range of cultural and social contexts. Much of the large survey work which examines children's use of media texts and identifies their leisure pursuits does not include children under five (Livingstone and Bovill, 1999). We also need to look closely at how children appropriate or resist hegemonic popular cultural discourses in their localized contexts. In addition, ways in which young children take up or contest discourses in relation to ethnicity, class, gender, sexuality, disability and other forms of identity should be analysed, for popular culture and media texts provide prime sites for marginalization, stereotyping and oppression (Dyson, 1997a; Giroux, 1994).

In identifying areas in which research might usefully shape our understanding of this field in the future, it is clear that the role of families is central. Parents' and siblings' roles in recognizing, fostering and celebrating children's popular cultural interests could be usefully studied. Families and communities are central to young children's development as literate agents, as other chapters in this volume demonstrate (see, for example, chapters by Cairney, Kenner and Gregory, Knobel and Lankshear, and Hannon in this volume). Popular culture infuses the literacy lives of communities and families (Barton and Hamilton, 1998) and there needs to be a clearer focus on the ways in which this informs young children's literacy development.

Although we have a rich array of work, as evidenced in this chapter, on the role of popular culture in children's literacy practices, we are only just beginning to appreciate ways in which popular culture can inform the literacy curriculum of early years settings and schools. Research agendas which extend this arena so that we develop further understanding about the ways in which work on popular culture in educational settings can motivate, extend and challenge children's critical literacy skills will be useful in providing further evidence to educators and policy makers that the lack of attention to such material is an 'urgent question' (Luke and Luke, 2001: 118) which needs immediate attention. Finally, research which analyses how pre-service and in-service teachers' professional development in early childhood education can ensure that the educators who populate early years settings and schools are fully conversant with theoretical and pedagogical discourses in this field needs to be extended. If this issue is not embedded into teacher education courses across the globe, then literacy in early childhood education will continue to reflect the concerns of a twentieth, not a twenty-first, century.

Above all, we need to pay close attention to patterns emerging from studies in the forefront of this sphere of scholarly study as it evolves over the next decades and attempt to draw together the common themes and issues. In this way, we can avoid the fate that Stahl assigns to the field of phonics research when he asserts in a recent review that, 'We seem to be asking the same questions as we did 40 years ago, with the same results' (2001: 343). Parker, in a book aimed at elementary teachers, written in 1919, discussed the influence of movies on his son:

Recently, seeing Griffiths' moving picture 'Intolerance' gave a vivid notion of the life of Babylon, of Belshazzer's feats, of the battles of the Persians and the Babylonians ... Thus as a result of a peculiar combination of adventure reading, fourth-grade history, the movies, and current events he has developed an active

desire, an active 'reaching out' for more Biblical reading. Perhaps it may result in a permanent abiding interest in biblical matters. (1919: 49–50)

Over 80 years later, we are still asking the same question about the potential of popular culture and the media to create 'a permanent abiding interest' in literacy learning because we have hardly, as yet, begun to answer it.

REFERENCES

Alvermann, D., Moon, J.S. and Hagood, M.C. (1999) *Popular Culture in the Classroom: Teaching and Researching Critical Media Literacy*. Newark, DE: IRA/NRC.

Anning, A. and Ring, K. (1999) 'The influence of sociocultural context on young children's meaning-making'. Paper presented at the British Educational Research Association Annual Conference, Brighton, September.

Apple, M.W. (1993) *Official Knowledge: Democratic Education in a Conservative Age*. New York: Routledge.

Arthur, L. (2001a) 'Popular culture and early literacy learning', *Contemporary Issues in Early Childhood*, 2 (3): 295–308.

Arthur, L., Beecher, B. and Jones Diaz, C. (2001) 'Early literacy: congruence and incongruence between home and early childhood settings', in M. Kalantzis (ed), *Languages of Learning: Changing Communication and Changing Literacy Teaching*. Melbourne: Common Ground. pp. 65–73.

Au, K. and Kawakami, A.J. (1991) 'Culture and ownership: schooling of minority students', *Childhood Education*, 67 (5): 280–4.

Barrs, M. (1988) 'Maps of play', in M. Meek and C. Mills (eds), *Language and Literacy in the Primary School*. London: Falmer.

Barton, D. and Hamilton, M. (1998) *Local Literacies: Reading and Writing in One Community*. London: Routledge.

Bernstein, B. (1996) *Pedagogy, Symbolic Control and Identity: Theory, Research, Critique*. London: Taylor and Francis.

Bourdieu, P. (1977) *Outline of a Theory of Practice*. Cambridge: Cambridge University Press.

Bourdieu, P. and Passeron, J.C. (1977) *Reproduction in Education, Society and Culture*. London: Sage.

Britzman, D.P. (1989) 'Who has the floor? Curriculum, teaching and the English student teachers' struggle for voice', *Curriculum Inquiry*, 19 (2): 143–62.

Bromley, H. (1996) '"Did you know that there's no such thing as Never Land?" Working with video narratives in the early years', in M. Hilton (ed.), *Potent Fictions: Children's Literacy and the Challenge of Popular Culture*. London: Routledge. pp. 71–91.

Buckingham, D. (1993) *Children Talking Television: the Making of Television Literacy*. London: Falmer.

Cairney, T.H., Lowe, K., Munsie, L., Ruge, J. and Buchanan, J. (1996) *Developing Partnerships: the Home, School and Community Interface*, vols 1–3. Canberra: DEET.

Carrington, V. (2001) 'Emergent home literacies: a challenge for educators', *Australian Journal of Language and Literacy*, 24 (2): 88–100.

Carrington, V. and Luke, A. (2003) 'Reading, home and families: from postmodern to modern?', in A. van Kleeck, S.A. Stahl and E.B. Bauer (eds), *On Reading Books to Children: Parents and Teachers*. Mahwah, NJ: Erlbaum. pp. 231–52.

Clark, E. (1995) 'Popular culture: images of gender as reflected through young children's story'. Paper presented at Annual Joint Meeting of the Popular Culture Association/American Culture Association, Philadelphia.

Comber, B. (1992) 'Critical literacy: a selective review and discussion of recent literature', *South Australian Educational Leader*, 3 (1): 1–10.

Comber, B. (1994) 'Critical literacy: an introduction to Australian debates and perspectives', *Journal of Curriculum Studies*, 26 (6): 655–68.

Comber, B. (1998) 'Coming ready or not! Changing what counts as early literacy?'. Keynote address to the 7th Australia and New Zealand Conference on the First Years of School, accessed at http://www.schools.ash.org.au/litweb/barb2.html.

Comber, B. (2000) 'What really counts in early literacy lessons?', *Language Arts*, 78 (1): 39–49.

Comber, B. and Kamler, B. (1997) 'Critical literacies: politicising the classroom', *Interpretations*, 30 (1): 30–53.

Comber, B. and Simpson, A. (eds) (2001) *Negotiating Critical Literacies in Classrooms*. Mahwah, NJ: Erlbaum.

Comber, B., Thompson, P. and Wells, M. (2001) 'Critical literacy finds a "place": writing and social action in a neighbourhood school', *Elementary School Journal*, 101 (4): 451–64.

Crowther, J., Hamilton, M. and Tett, L. (eds) (2001) *Powerful Literacies*. Leicester: NIACE.

Dyson, A.H. (1994) 'The Ninjas, the X-Men, and the Ladies: playing with power and identity in an urban primary school', *Teachers College Record*, 96 (2): 219–39.

Dyson, A.H. (1995) 'Writing children: reinventing the development of childhood literacy', *Written Communication*, 12 (1): 4–46.

Dyson, A.H. (1996) 'Cultural constellations and childhood identities: on Greek gods, cartoon heroes, and the social lives of schoolchildren', *Harvard Educational Review*, 66 (3): 471–95.

Dyson, A.H. (1997a) *Writing Superheroes: Contemporary Childhood, Popular Culture, and Classroom Literacy*. New York: Teachers College Press.

Dyson, A.H. (1997b) 'Rewriting for, and by, the children: the sociological and ideological fate of a media miss in an urban classroom', *Written Communication*, 14 (3): 275–312.

Dyson, A.H. (1998) 'Folk processes and media creatures: reflections on popular culture for literacy educators', *The Reading Teacher*, 51 (5): 392–402.

Dyson, A.H. (1999a) 'Coach Bombay's kids learn to write: children's appropriation of media material for school literacy?, *Research in the Teaching of English*, 33: 367–402.

Dyson, A.H. (1999b) 'Transforming transfer: unruly children, contrary texts and the persistence of the pedagogical order', in A. Iran-Nejad and P.D. Pearson (eds), *Review of Research in Education*, vol. 24. Washington, DC: American Educational Research Association.

Dyson, A.H. (2000) 'On reframing children's words: the perils, promises and pleasures of writing children', *Research in the Teaching of English*, 34: 352–67.

Dyson, A.H. (2001a) 'Where are the childhoods in childhood literacy? An exploration in outer (school) space', *Journal of Early Childhood Literacy*, 1 (1): 9–39.

Dyson, A.H. (2001b) 'Donkey Kong in Little Bear country: a first-grader's composing development in the media spotlight', *The Elementary School Journal*, 101 (4): 417–33.

Dyson, A.H. (2002) *The Brothers and Sisters Learn to Write: Popular Literacies in Childhood and School Cultures*. New York: Teachers College Press.

Eisner, E. (1979) *The Educational Imagination*. New York: Macmillan.

Freire, P. (1972) *Pedagogy of the Oppressed*. Harmondsworth: Penguin.

Giroux, H.A. (1988) *Schooling for Democracy: Critical Pedagogy in the Modern Age*. London: Routledge.

Giroux, H.A. (1994) *Disturbing Pleasures: Learning Popular Culture*. New York: Routledge.

Green, B., Reid, J. and Bigum, C. (1998) 'Teaching the Nintendo generation? Children, computer culture and popular technologies', in S. Howard (ed.), *Wired-Up: Young People and the Electronic Media*. London: UCL Press. pp. 19–41.

Guthrie, J.T., Van Meter, P., Dacey Mcanu, A., Wigfield, A., Bennett, L., Poundston, C.C., Rice, M.E., Faibisch, F.M., Hunt, B. and Mitchell, A.M. (1996) 'Growth of literacy engagement: changes in motivation and strategies during concept-orientated reading instruction', *Reading Research Quarterly*, 31: 306–25.

Hicks, D. (2001) 'Literacies and masculinities in the life of a young working-class boy', *Language Arts*, 78 (3): 217–26.

Hill, S. and Broadhurst, D. (2002) 'Technoliteracy and the early years', in L. Makin. and C. Jones Diaz (eds), *Literacies in Early Childhood: Changing Views and Challenging Practice*. Sydney: Maclennan and Petty. pp. 269–88.

Hill, S., Comber, B., Louden, W., Rivalland, J. and Reid, J. (1998) *100 Children Go to School: Connections and Disconnections in Literacy Development in the Year Prior to School and the First Year of School*. Canberra: DEETYA.

Hilton, M. (ed.) (1996) *Potent Fictions: Children's Literacy and the Challenge of Popular Culture.* London: Routledge.

Holland, D., Lachicotte, W., Skinner, D. and Cain, C. (1998) *Identity and Agency in Cultural Worlds.* Cambridge, MA: Harvard University Press.

Jenks, C. (1993) *Culture.* London: Routledge.

Jones Diaz, C., Arthur, L., Beecher, B. and McNaught, M. (2000) 'Multiple literacies in early childhood: what do families and communities think about their children's literacy learning?', *Australian Journal of Language and Literacy,* 23 (3): 230–44.

Jones Diaz, C., Beecher, B. and Arthur, L. (2002) 'Children's worlds and critical literacy', in L. Makin and C. Jones Diaz (eds), *Literacies in Early Childhood: Changing Views and Challenging Practice.* Sydney: Maclennan and Petty.

Kenner, C. (2000) *Home Pages: Literacy Links for Bilingual Children.* Stoke-on-Trent: Trentham.

Kenway, J. and Bullen, E. (2001) *Consuming Children: Education – Entertainment – Advertising.* Buckingham: Open University Press.

Kinder, M. (1991) *Playing with Power in Movies: Television and Video Games from Muppet Babies to Teenage Mutant Ninja Turtles.* Berkeley, CA: University of California Press.

Knobel, M. and Healy, A. (eds) (1998) *Critical Literacies in the Primary Classroom.* Newtown: Primary English Teaching Association.

Kress, G. (1997) *Before Writing: Rethinking the Paths to Literacy.* London: Routledge.

Kress, G. (2000) 'A curriculum for the future', *Cambridge Journal of Education,* 30 (1): 133–45.

Lankshear, C. with Gee, J.P., Knobel, M. and Searle, C. (1997) *Changing Literacies.* Buckingham: Open University Press.

Levin, D.E. and Rosenquest, B. (2001) 'The increasing role of electronic toys in the lives of infants and toddlers: should we be concerned?', *Contemporary Issues in Early Childhood,* 2 (2): 242–7.

Levine, S. (1991) 'William Shakespeare and the American people: a study in cultural transformation', in C. Mukerji and M. Schudson (eds), *Rethinking Popular Culture: Contemporary Perspectives in Cultural Studies.* Berkeley, CA: University of California Press. pp. 157–97.

Livingstone, S. and Bovill, M. (1999) *Young People, New Media.* London: London School of Economics.

Luke, A. (1994) '*The Social Construction of Literacy in the Primary School'*, Melbourne: Macmillan.

Luke, C. (1999) 'What next? Toddler netizens, playstation thumb, techno-literacies', *Contemporary Issues in Early Childhood,* 1 (1): 95–100.

Luke, A. and Luke, C. (2001) 'Adolescence lost/childhood regained: on early intervention and the emergence of the techno-subject', *Journal of Early Childhood Literacy,* 1 (1): 91–120.

Mahiri, J. (1998) *Shooting for Excellence: African American Youth Culture in New Century Schools,* Urbana, IL: National Council of Teachers of English.

Makin, L. and Jones Diaz, C. (2002) *Literacies in Early Childhood: Changing Views and Challenging Practice.* Sydney: Maclennan and Petty.

Makin, L., Hayden, J., Holland, A., Arthur, L., Beecher, B., Jones Diaz, C. and McNaught, M. (1999) *Mapping Literacy Practices in Early Childhood Services.* Sydney: NSW Department of Education and Training and NSW Department of Community Services.

Marsh, J. (1999) 'Batman and Batwoman go to school: popular culture in the literacy curriculum', *International Journal of Early Years Education,* 7 (2): 117–31.

Marsh, J. (2000a) '"But I want to fly too!" Girls and superhero play in the infant classroom', *Gender and Education,* 12 (2): 209–20.

Marsh, J. (2000b) 'Teletubby tales: popular culture in the early years language and literacy curriculum', *Contemporary Issues in Early Childhood,* 1 (2): 119–36.

Marsh, J. (2003a) 'One-way traffic? Connections between literacy practices at home and in the nursery', *British Educational Research Journal,* 29 (3): 369–82.

Marsh, J. (2003b) 'Taboos, tightropes and trivial pursuits: pre-service and newly-qualified teachers' beliefs and practices in relation to popular culture and literacy'. Paper presented at the Annual Meeting of the American Educational Research Association, Chicago, April 2003.

Marsh, J. and Millard, E. (2000) *Literacy and Popular Culture: Using Children's Culture in the Classroom.* London: Chapman.

Marsh, J. and Thompson, P. (2001) 'Parental involvement in literacy development: using media texts', *Journal of Research in Reading,* 24 (3): 266–78.

Millard, E. (1997) *Differently Literate: Boys, Girls and the Schooling of Literacy.* London: Falmer.

Millard, E. (2003) Transformative pedagogy: towards a literacy of fusion', *Reading, Language and Literacy,* 37 (1): 3–9.

Millard, E. and Marsh, J. (2001) 'Sending Minnie the Minx home: comics and reading choices', *Cambridge Journal of Education,* 31 (1): 25–38.

Misson, R. (1998) 'Theory and spice, and things not nice: popular culture in the primary classroom', in M. Knobel and A. Healy (eds), *Critical Literacies in the Primary Classroom.* Newtown, NSW: PETA. pp. 53–62.

Moje, E. (2000) 'To be part of the story: the literacy practices of gangsta adolescents', *Teachers College Record,* 102 (3): 651–90.

Moll, L., Amanti, C., Neff, D. and Gonzalez, N. (1992) 'Funds of knowledge for teaching: using a qualitative approach to connect homes and classrooms', *Theory into Practice,* 31 (1): 132–41.

Moss, G. (2001) 'Seeing with the camera: analysing children's photographs of literacy in the home', *Journal of Research in Reading*, 24 (3): 279–92.

Mukerji, C. and Schudson, M. (1991) *Rethinking Popular Culture: Contemporary Perspectives in Cultural Studies*. Berkeley, CA: University of California Press.

Nixon, H. (2001) 'The book, the TV series, the web site: teaching and learning within the communicational web of popular media culture'. Paper presented at the Australian Association of the Teaching of English Annual Meeting, 2001, accessed at http://www. cdesign.com.

O'Brien, J. (1998) 'Experts in Smurfland', in M. Knobel and A. Healy (eds), *Critical Literacies in the Primary Classroom*. Newtown, NSW: PETA. pp. 13–25.

Orellana, M.F. (1994) 'Appropriating the voice of the superheroes: three preschoolers' bilingual language uses in play', *Early Childhood Research Quarterly*, 9: 171–93.

Pahl, K. (2001) 'Texts as artefacts crossing sites: map making at home and school', *Reading, Literacy and Language*, 120–5.

Pahl, K. (2002) 'Ephemera, mess and miscellaneous piles: texts and practices in families', *Journal of Early Childhood Literacy*, 2 (2): 145–66.

Paley, V.G. (1984) *Boys and Girls: Superheroes in the Doll Corner*. Chicago: University of Chicago Press.

Palmer, P. (1986) *The Lively Audience: a Study of Children around the TV Set*. Sydney: Allen and Unwin.

Parker, S.C. (1919) *General Methods of Teaching in Elementary Schools, Including the Kindergarten*. Boston: Ginn.

Purcell-Gates, V. (1996) 'Stories, coupons and the TV guide: relationships between home literacy experiences and emergent literacy experiences', *Reading Research Quarterly*, 31 (4): 406–28.

Ritzer, G. (1996) *The McDonaldization of Society*, rev. edn. Thousand Oaks, CA: Pine Forge/Sage.

Robinson, M. (1997) *Children Reading Print and Television*. London: Falmer.

Rodriguez, M.V. (1999) 'Home literacy experiences of three young Dominican children in New York City', *Educators for Urban Minorities*, 1 (1): 19–31.

Roe, K. and Muijs, D. (1998) Children and computer games: a profile of the heavy user', *European Journal of Communication*, 13 (2): 181–200.

Sanger, J. with Wilson, J., Davies, B. and Whittaker, R. (1997) *Young Children, Videos and Computer Games*. London: Falmer.

Seiter, E. (1993) *Sold Separately: Children and Parents in Consumer Culture*. New York: Rutgers University Press.

Seiter, E. (1999) 'Power Rangers at preschool: negotiating media in child care settings', in M. Kinder, (ed.), *Kids' Media Culture*. Durham, NC: Duke University Press.

Sharp, R. (1980) *Knowledge, Ideology and the Politics of Schooling: Towards a Marxist Analysis of Education*. London: Routledge and Kegan Paul.

Stahl, S.A. (2001) 'Teaching phonics and phonological awareness', in S. Neuman and D. Dickinson (eds), *Handbook of Early Literacy Research*. New York: Guilford.

Steedman, C. (1985) '"Listen, how the caged bird sings": Amarjit's song', in C. Steedman, C. Urwin and V. Walkerdine (eds), *Language, Gender and Childhood*. London: Routledge and Kegan Paul.

Suss, D., Suoninen, A., Garitaonandia, C., Juaristi, P., Koikkalainen, R. and Oleaga, J.A. (2001) 'Media childhood in three European countries', in I. Hutchby and J. Moran-Ellis (eds), *Children, Technology and Culture: the Impacts of Technologies in Children's Everyday Lives*. London: Routledge/Falmer.

Thorne, B. (1993) *Gender Play: Girls and Boys in School*. Buckingham: Open University Press.

Turner, J. (1995) 'The influence of classroom contexts on young children's motivation for literacy', *Reading Research Quarterly*, 30: 410–40.

Turner, J. and Paris, S.G. (1995) 'How literacy tasks influence children's motivation for literacy', *The Reading Teacher*, 48: 662–73.

Vasquez, V. (2001) 'Constructing a critical curriculum with young children', in B. Comber and A. Simpson (eds), *Negotiating Critical Literacies in Classrooms*. Mahwah, NJ: Erlbaum. pp. 55–66.

Weinberger, J. (1996) *Literacy Goes to School: the Parents' Role in Young Children's Literacy Learning*. London: Chapman.

Williams, R. (1965) *The Long Revolution*. Harmondsworth: Penguin.

Willis, P. (1990) *Common Culture*. Buckingham: Open University Press.

Xu, S.H. (1999) 'Young Chinese ESL children's home literacy experiences', *Reading Horizons*, 40 (1): 47–64.

Xu, S.H. (2000a) 'Preservice teachers integrate understanding of diversity into literacy instruction: an adaptation of the ABC's model', *Journal of Teacher Education*, 51: 135–42.

Xu, S.H. (2000b) 'Preservice teachers in a literacy methods course consider issues of diversity', *Journal of Literacy Research*, 32 (4): 505–31.

Xu, S.H. (2001a) 'Exploring diversity issues in teacher education', *Reading Online*, 5 (1), accessed at http://www.readingonline/org.

Xu, S.H. (2001b) 'Preparing teachers to use students' popular culture in connecting students' home and school literacy experiences'. Paper presented at the Annual Meeting of the American Educational Research Association, Seattle.

11

Film and Television

MURIEL ROBINSON AND
MARGARET MACKEY

Today's children become literate in a context that includes many forms of televisual text as part of their daily environment. In this chapter we will explore current evidence which illuminates our understandings of the relationship between televisual texts and children's literacy development, and of the complexities of the exchanges between print and televisual forms. The *Oxford English Dictionary* defines 'televisual' as relating exclusively to television, but we will use it slightly more broadly to include television and also the other formats that provide moving image and sound: film, video, and DVD.

Literacy occurs as a set of situated practices (Barton and Hamilton, 1998); that is, we read as part of a social world in real contexts, and our literate behaviours are influenced by and influence the world we are in. One impact of televisual texts, and television in particular, has been to reposition children both in the world and in their relation to texts. Children now approach all their texts as multiliterate interpreters (New London Group, 1996). Their plural understandings of literacy inflect all their dealings with text. Those who wish to explore those literary understandings must take account of *all* the kinds of text that contribute to children's growing relationship with literacy.

The complexities of the relationship between print and televisual texts are insufficiently understood, and too much research is conducted within parameters that simply do not make enough space for complex analysis. Much existing research has set up a simple opposition between print and television in which the televisual environment is posited as some kind of deficit to be battled. Other research

is more neutrally framed but focuses narrowly on laboratory-style testing of singular elements of televisual literacy, often ignoring larger questions of motivation and pleasure. Such an approach misapprehends the intertextual and cross-media understandings that young children develop from their earliest months, as we shall explore below.

DISPLACEMENT AND INTERFERENCE: A DEFICIT MODEL

Much existing research into children and television assumes a deficit model in which television interferes with other activities and displaces more 'valuable' activities. An assumption underlying much past research was anxiety about displacement; it was thought that children could not continue to read as much with so many other activities to displace reading time. Recent research demonstrates that children are as likely to be avid or reluctant readers in the same proportion as ever (Wright, 2001) and that the average time spent reading for leisure – 15 minutes per day – is still the same as that found by studies in the 1940s and 1950s (Livingstone and Bovill, 1999; Neuman, 1995). Sales of books are now closely linked to televised or cinematic versions.

Potter suggests that each new technology, rather than displacing others, causes a realignment:

> As each new medium comes to prominence, the preceding ones tend to take on new functions or become specialised in what they do best. (1994: 162)

The notion of displacement was taken further by work which argued not only that television interfered with literacy development by displacing reading in children's use of time, but also that it damaged them psychologically so that their mental abilities were dulled or distorted by the act of watching television. Such work is perhaps most extremely demonstrated in Marie Winn's book *The Plug-In Drug* (1985), but still occurs today. Minow first famously described American television as a 'vast wasteland' in 1961; in 1995, he was still describing the situation of children as 'abandoned in the wasteland' (Minow et al., 1995).

Neuman (1995) produces a thorough and thoughtful critique of displacement theories. Nevertheless, the opposition between reading and viewing which is a central tenet of effects and deficit studies also influences much research design in this area. Thus we find many research papers which try to create clearly distinguishable behaviours which can then be studied to identify difference (e.g. Terrell and Daniloff, 1996; Calvert and Gersh, 1987). To control variables, such work is often laboratory based or constructed in such a way as to be far removed from the everyday practices of young children as they move between and within media boundaries.

Such work is often influenced by Salomon's (1983) schema theory, as in the case of Tidhar's (1996) investigation into Israeli kindergarten children. This study, which used pre- and post-testing to discover the impact of adult mediation on children's understandings of television material, operated entirely in the cognitive domain, asking the children about their understanding of fantasy effects, logical and temporal gaps and technical elements of camera work. The children's answers to the 20-question tests were judged as correct or incorrect according to the quality of logical reasoning demonstrated. The affective aspects of viewing were not deemed relevant to the experiment. Those studies seeking to establish what children do alone often seem designed to measure what can be measured (such as visual and vocal responses to television by infants, as in Hollenbeck and Slaby, 1979; Richards and Cronise, 2000).

The findings of such research tend to be remarkable only for their demonstration of what might seem obvious, for example that one-year-old children are more likely to sustain their attention to a television screen if it is depicting movement (Takahashi, 1991), and do little to help us understand how young children begin to interact with the wide range of televisual and print texts that surround them today. As Hodge and Tripp suggest:

the problem, we will argue, is that these 'experts' have been trying to answer the wrong questions in the wrong order, with theories and methods that have been overly partial and inadequate. (1986: 2)

Where research is more positive, it is often unhelpful for our purposes since much of it focuses on one medium, usually television or video (with video often being treated as television, in that there are rarely opportunities for the children to pause or rewind or even view repeatedly). Such work can offer interesting insights (see, for example, Lowe and Durkin, 1999, who indicate that even first-graders can remember police dramas with flashbacks as well as when the same drama is presented in canonical or chronological order) but does little to illuminate our understandings of how children operate in a multiliterate world.

For many researchers, TV is not only seen as damaging because it displaces more worthwhile activities or because of its general psychological impact. The deficit view also inflects experiments seeking to demonstrate the pernicious impact of violence on television which have been shown to offer contradictory and inconclusive findings (Buckingham, 2000; Buckingham and Allerton, 1996). No other question leads to such utter disagreement.

Direct causality is accepted by such prestigious organizations as the American Psychological Association and the (American) National Institute of Mental Health (Freedman, 2002: 9). Yet other scholars describe their warnings about the dire impact of violent television as 'junk science; pop psychology of the worst sort based on nothing but some vague extrapolations from research that is not cited and may not exist' (2002: 11). There is not space here to investigate all the complexities of this polarized and highly contentious debate, which is explored thoroughly in such work as that of David Buckingham (1996) and through Barker and Petley's (1997) response to the Newson Report. These more balanced debates demonstrate the problematic nature of the existing research, and the whole 'effects' debate is aptly summed up by Gauntlett in his very helpful examination of a wide range of research projects in this area:

All too often the television effects research evidence is interpreted as 'inconclusive', or as showing nothing. In fact, if nothing else, it *has* answered its own question: television does not have predictable, direct effects. The mass of studies, which individually may be inconclusive or flawed, when taken as a whole must surely demonstrate that. The lack of 'positive' results showing effects in the real world do not constitute an informational void, but have to be taken as a conclusion in themselves. (1995: 115)

It is worth noting that the opposing sides take very differing views on how actively children process the narrative that contains violent scenes. Those who favour a hypothesis of active processing are less likely to assume that children are at the mercy of copycat instincts; they are also more likely to draw clear distinctions between the impact of fictional and of non-fictional scenes. As Gunter points out with regard to adults:

> Analyses of audience response to TV materials, whether at behavioural, emotional or perceptual levels, have indicated many subtle distinctions that viewers make between violent portrayals. (1985: 11)

An intriguing insight from research with eight- and nine-year-old British children was that the children, when asked to suggest what was appropriate for them to watch and what might be too violent, adopted a technique common among adult lay critics of violent television programmes. They saw themselves as discerning and mature viewers, able to handle even adult horror films such as the *Nightmare on Elm Street* series, but were very clear that younger children should not be allowed to watch such films, in a finding confirming that of Buckingham (1993):

> there seems to be something at issue here about the need for these children to see themselves as autonomous and in control whilst displacing anxieties onto younger children in very much the way in which adults who are worried by television violence see themselves as in no danger but worry about the effect on others. (Robinson, 1997: 92)

As this exploration of the violence debate shows, there are researchers actively seeking to explore this very difficult territory who do not start from a deficit model. The work of such people as Dyson, Seiter and Livingstone offers a very different view of the ways in which young children interact with televisual and printed texts as they make sense of the world, as we shall demonstrate below. Before we explore the specific findings of such researchers, we would like to present an alternative to the deficit model which may offer a more fruitful way forward.

SOME REAL-WORLD EXAMPLES: AN ASSET MODEL

Tyner has coined a useful phrase, talking of 'an asset model' of someone's media experience: 'An asset model for media teaching assumes that mass media and popular culture content can work as a benefit to literacy instead of as a social deficit' (1998: 7). She argues that we may increase our understanding by exploring what assets a person

brings to bear on a literacy event. Tyner does not develop this model further, but we find it a useful concept to bring to bear on the idea of the interrelationship between print and televisual literacies. A few examples will help to make it clearer:

- Verónica, from Mexico City, develops a deep interest in dinosaurs when she is just two. The first sign is a request to own two very small remaindered books. Watching videos of the BBC's 'Walking with Dinosaurs' leads to the moment six months later when the family drive past a huge billboard for the Disney film *Dinosaur*. Verónica's assets are sufficient for her to ask if this is a poster for a film about dinosaurs, and if so, whether she can go and see it. She negotiates with her parents that they will take her but that if she doesn't like it she can leave. She watches the whole film and this viewing is the spur for a continued interest in all things to do with Aladar in particular and dinosaurs in general, still alive two years after the first interest, and registered through the use of many different media.

- Philip, a Canadian six-year-old, is a passionate ice hockey fan. His first successful reading experience comes when he shows his grandmother his hockey sticker book and recognizes players of the Toronto Maple Leafs by reading the distinctive shapes of their names on their jerseys. He has cheered for them on television, and played them on his PlayStation game; his mediated experience supplies a strong emotional core to his reading repertoire.

- Batanai, aged five, lives in a mixed suburb of Harare. He is an ardent viewer of 'Thomas the Tank Engine' which appears weekly on Zimbabwean television. He owns only one 'Thomas' book, and certainly does not have any access to accoutrements such as pyjamas or nightlights, but he is able to hold his own with vigour and enthusiasm in discussions about Thomas with British and Canadian visitors. Reinforced as an expert on the topic, he continues his engagement with these popular stories.

Rather than worrying about this broad range of media experience as a kind of interference with the virtues of print literacy, it makes much more sense to explore the values of the enriched repertoires which these children are all enabled to bring to bear on their encounters with print. Their media experiences are undeniably assets in their literate lives.

It is difficult to express the complexities of the situation in which contemporary literacies are rooted without oversimplifying things. However, in Figure 11.1 we schematically indicate the major elements in the literacy engagement of a contemporary

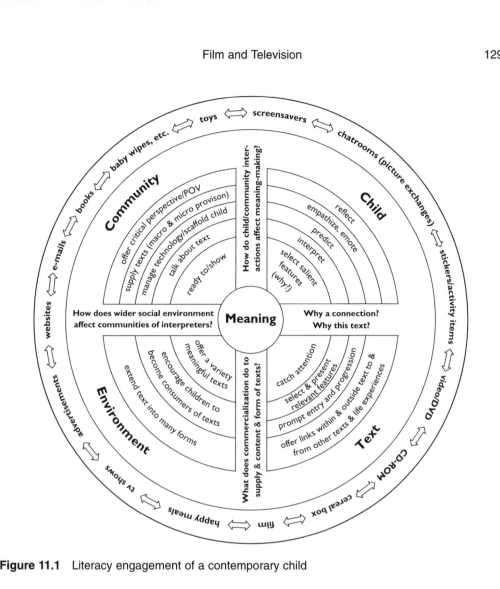

Figure 11.1 Literacy engagement of a contemporary child

child: the child, the text, the community, and the broader environment. The ingredients in each quadrant should be read from the centre outwards and summarize the behaviours involved for each element. The questions on the spokes represent some important issues that arise in the overlap between the main players in this engagement. Around the outer perimeter we have indicated the wide range of texts we believe to be part of a child's experience of literacy in the modern world, many of which are dealt with more extensively in other chapters in this book but which need to be seen as a totality even where the discussion, as here, emphasizes televisual and printed texts.

In addition to learning how to interpret specific conventions of particular televisual texts, children also learn what programmes or films speak to their needs in a particular context. Meaning, as

Livingstone (1990) reminds us, is negotiated between text and interpreter. Both are important and we ignore either at the risk of an impoverished understanding.

In the course of developing this chapter, we explored many reports on research into televisual comprehension and more conventionally understood literacy. Research that explores such complexity in the lives of the very young is difficult to organize, but some practitioners accomplish it successfully and their work illuminates our understanding. It is noticeable that their studies are often located in the wider framework of popular culture rather than confined to more narrow issues of print and televisual literacy (see, for example, Berry and Asamen, 1993; Hilton, 1996; Kenway and Bullen, 2001; Kline, 1993; Luke, 1988; Marsh, 2000; Marsh and Millard, 2000; Messenger Davies, 2001; Seiter, 1999a).

THE CIVICS OF EARLY LITERACY:
THE CHILD AND THE WIDER
SOCIAL ENVIRONMENT

Social theories of literacy explore the situated practices that comprise literate engagements in particular contexts. Such approaches open up many complexities in how we observe and understand literacy, increasing our attention to the political, economic, social and cultural aspects of our interactions with texts. In Figure 11.1 we refer to the role of the environment in providing meaningful texts in many forms and in encouraging children to engage with these. In this section we look at how this happens and what impact it may have on children's developing understanding of literacies. This leads us to ask about the impact of commercialization on supply, content and form, questions which are only partly satisfactorily answered by the existing research and which deserve fuller investigation.

Few, if any, contemporary children live in circumstances that actively exclude numerous media, yet some research is reluctant to acknowledge this reality. Livingstone points out how, for much modern sociology, the child is represented as living a *non-mediated* childhood: this is 'a carefree child playing hopscotch with friends in a nearby park, not a child with music on the headphones watching television in her bedroom' (1998: 438). Yet the emergent literacies of small children often do not feature very significantly within the framework of social theories of literacy. Kalantzis and Cope describe literacy teaching as 'always ... a civic act' (2000: 140), but it is unusual to consider early literates as young citizens. Small children are often not regarded as political, economic, social or cultural agents in their own right. Very often we consider their main literate activity as *being read to*, a phrase that emphasizes passivity. Children's learning about literacy is still more often perceived as developmental or cognitive; they will achieve agency one day but for the present they are simply learning how to 'belong to the club' (Smith, 1983), in specific, observable, and non-political ways. Such a perspective denies the complexity of children's agency as they learn to place themselves within the world of multiple literacy demands.

Television plays a constituent role in the development of literacies in a variety of ways. Its address incorporates small children into the economic world from which we often assume they are naturally shielded. National variations in the quantity and address of advertising permitted on children's television also help to establish civic differences. Kenway and Bullen remind us of the complex relationship between Western consumer children and those children who produce the goods: 'Without doubt, the consuming child of the West is the beneficiary of labouring children of such countries as Indonesia, China and Pakistan' (2001: 37).

But the picture is not completely one-sided with TV as a purely Western phenomenon. Children all over the world watch television. Ownership figures vary hugely: according to Hart (2002: 16), there is at least one colour television set in 98.3 out of 100 households in the United Kingdom, compared to 0.6 per 100 households in Bangladesh (2002: 16). Euromonitor's *International Marketing Data and Statistics* for the year 2000 lists figures for the possession of black-and-white and colour televisions for 40 countries around the world. Their figures for television ownership in 1998 are shown in Table 11.1. The ubiquity of television is a significant social factor around the world, as these figures demonstrate. With such widespread domestic ownership, it is clear that small children everywhere are learning to make sense of televisual text.

Small children are, in fact, busy making sense of the whole world and responding to the different ways in which they are addressed. Even though adults may not explicitly notice the role of the toddler consumer, children use the information they are given and respond to the different ways they are spoken to.

Implicitly, scholars of early literacy do take note of the way that little children are integrated into society as consumers. We read descriptions of how children develop scripts that outline an expected sequence of events, and what to expect on a trip to McDonald's is sometimes presented as a neutral specimen of such scripts (for example, see Neuman, 1995: 21). Similarly, McDonald's golden arches are presented as an early specimen of the interpretable symbol (Harste et al., 1984: 27). But televisual texts play a more complex role in children's lives than simply developing their economic roles. Television locates children in an economic world, it provides information about the social world, it locates them as fully fledged participants in popular culture, and it also provides some forms of explicit instruction on literate behaviours – perhaps the most researched aspect of television experience for children. Programmes such as 'Sesame Street', 'The Teletubbies', 'Blue's Clues', and 'Reading Rainbow' are intensively researched both by those making the programmes and by outsiders (see, for example, Fisch et al., 1999, and Sell et al., 1995, on 'Sesame Street'; Anderson et al., 2000, on 'Blue's Clues'; Wood and Duke, 1997, on 'Reading Rainbow'; and Marsh, 2000, and Howard and Roberts, 2003, on 'The Teletubbies'). 'Sesame Street' in particular takes account of small children as international citizens with its production of many different national inserts for the programme.

Table 11.1 *Television ownership, 1998 (% of households)*

	Black and white	Colour
Algeria	38.0	65.0
Argentina	7.1	89.6
Australia	1.5	97.5
Azerbaijan	28.0	89.0
Bolivia	16.8	51.9
Brazil	10.0	87.2
Canada	1.0	99.4
Chile	7.5	83.3
China	44.3	95.6
Colombia	7.2	83.0
Ecuador	12.1	62.0
Egypt	26.0	16.0
Hong Kong	3.2	99.3
India	18.5	26.0
Indonesia	12.3	36.1
Israel	7.0	87.5
Japan	0.2	99.6
Jordan	9.2	90.7
Kazakhstan	39.0	46.0
Kuwait	7.1	86.0
Malaysia	1.2	89.2
Mexico	8.5	89.8
Morocco	14.0	67.0
New Zealand	3.2	98.2
Nigeria	24.7	44.0
Pakistan	19.0	30.6
Peru	11.0	63.2
Philippines	33.2	37.5
Saudi Arabia	2.5	97.0
Singapore	0.2	99.1
South Africa	4.5	37.0
South Korea	9.5	98.2
Taiwan	9.3	99.5
Thailand	17.3	78.2
Tunisia	7.3	66.0
Turkmenistan	29.0	34.0
United Arab Emirates	5.7	95.4
USA	0.8	98.1
Venezuela	8.1	87.5
Vietnam	42.2	28.3

Source: Euromonitor, *International Marketing Data and Statistics*, 2000, p. 746, Table 1607 'Possession of durables'

On a daily basis, television also supplies constant and ongoing examples of storytelling that children must learn to interpret. Video is often viewed as 'safer' by parents and offers new forms of control, especially providing a potential for interpretive autonomy for toddlers who know what buttons to push. And DVD, with its large memory, frequently offers interpretive lessons for particular films and has the potential to be a major tool for the specific development of more sophisticated forms of televisual literacy. Disney DVDs, for example, offer very young viewers a great deal of information about how animations are made. According to *The New York Times*, video has also played a role in improving telecasters' understanding of children's capacity to be absorbed by lengthy texts:

> Parents who read to their children have always known that they could sit still for long stretches if a story interested them. But the realization didn't sink in with television programmers until the advent of the VCR, which showed that preschoolers could watch movies they liked over (and over) again. (Salamon, 2002)

To understand fully the ways in which children become literate and take on the civics of literacy, in connection with televisual texts and particularly as they pertain to the youngest children, more research of the kind undertaken by Seiter (1999b) (discussed further by Marsh, in this volume) is needed. However, it is also important to consider the ways in which such social encounters are part of the ways in which children make meanings.

COMMUNITIES OF INTERPRETERS: CHILD–COMMUNITY INTERACTIONS AND MEANING MAKING

As well as being situated in a broadly defined social world, children are active members of a range of particular communities, all of which are themselves influenced by and forces for change in the wider environment discussed above. A significant factor for any user of media is the network of communities of interpreters we draw on when making meaning. Fish (1980) first set out the principle of interpretive communities as a way of describing the interactions by which we make meanings and assign intentions to texts as a collaborative act. We have extended the idea to describe the ways in which each of us belongs to a series of communities with whom we have a dialectic relationship and from which emerges our understanding of any text (Robinson, 1997). For young children, the communities of interpreters are particularly significant since one of the roles of the more experienced reader is to mediate the text to the child. As shown in Figure 11.1, the child relies on the community to read and show texts in the first instance, but also for talk about text, for help with the technology, for supply of texts and for a critical perspective and point of view. As we explore the ways in which this interaction happens, it is important also to ask, as we do in Figure 11.1, about the impact of such interactions on the meaning-making process.

We do not yet know enough about the ways in which mediation acts to support the child in becoming a full member of the interpretive communities to which he or she belongs, but we do know that parents and other significant adults or older siblings can make a difference (see, for example, Rodriguez, 2000; St Peters et al., 1991; Dombey, 1983). For the young child, any encounter with texts can be a social one, regardless of medium: books are read to and with children, and watching will rarely happen entirely alone, even where television is being used as a babysitter and the main company is other children. Access to televisual texts may well be controlled by adults until children have mastered the technology and even beyond. Thus many of the child's meaning-making acts will be in a social setting; they will be able to see the responses of their siblings, peers and adult carers and will in many cases be encouraged to respond themselves with scaffolded questions. Parent–child conversations are particularly important, as Lemish and Rice demonstrate in their participant-observer study:

> Unlike book-reading, it is not necessary to set aside time for television viewing, or to formally break ongoing activities to establish a separate communicative framework. Instead, the children's talk about television was embedded in a stream of conversational interactions with other members of their families. (1986: 267)

Research into media usage at home (see, for example, Lull, 1988, for a global perspective on this topic; and Anderson, et al., 1986, for a study of the home viewing habits of 99 American families, each containing a five-year-old child) has shown that, along with the specific lessons about how to read and react to texts, children learn many social lessons from the ways in which those around them use technology. Power relationships may be inextricably intertwined with the choice of channel, with use of the family television set or computer, and with book purchase. Zhao-Bin (1996) shows the complexity of parent–child power relationships in modern China, linking the interpretive processes children use to the broader sociocultural context to explore parental control strategies with the generation of pampered only children known as the little emperors. Thus young children also learn from these communities of interpreters that literacy and meaning making are social and political acts which have broader implications than might at first appear to be the case.

Sanger et al.'s (1997) study of the use of video in the homes of approximately 100 children aged four to nine also explores some of the social roles revolving around the domestic small screen. Their study reveals interesting local gender issues in terms of who actually understands how to programme the video recorder. Their work also draws attention to some of the distinctions between television and video; the parents they interviewed were much more uneasy about television than about video, which children tended to be left to watch on their own since parents could be more comfortable about content. Sanger et al. also testify to the importance of conversation, though from a more negative perspective, talking about:

> a role that seems to be largely missing in most children's lives – that of the mediating adult, helping children to make sense of their experience. With parents reneging, generally, on this role and teachers rejecting popular culture, children were very often adrift, with no support from a significant adult. (1997: 122)

These social dimensions are nowhere more apparent than in the playground talk and play of young children. We know that with older children (Buckingham, 1993) knowledge about televisual texts is crucial to maintain social standing; the child needs at least sufficient knowledge to engage in discussion and role play, even if they have not seen the text in question. However, there seems to be a lack of systematic research into these social pressures with regard to the early years, though Marsh (2000) indicates that adults can actually exclude potential communities of interpreters by banning or ignoring popular culture in the nursery classroom. Much of the most interesting work in the area of the social currency of literacies focuses much more heavily on televisual texts than on print or on the intersections and overlaps between media. There is a need for more research with young children to address the concerns identified in Figure 11.1 more systematically.

THE CONTINUUM OF TEXTS: BOUNDARIES AND DIRECTIONALITY

We are increasingly aware that a simple opposition between printed books and televisual texts is an inadequate model of the complexities of textual interrelations which exist in the world today. The outer perimeter of our diagram, as explained above, represents this complexity, but can only do so imperfectly: as Livingstone and Bovill point out, research on what are collectively known as new media 'involves studying a moving target' (1999, 1: 6). This chapter was originally intended to focus on television and literacy but to do so would present an artificial picture of the realities of reading today even for very young children. Within the definition of televisual texts, therefore, we include:

- film as shown in a conventional cinema – bearing in mind that what is conventional about any cinema experience is culturally bounded
- television – terrestrial, satellite and cable
- video – displaying either recorded television or recorded film or special made-for-video features
- home video – showing 'local' scenes in either analogue or digital form
- DVD – which at present is likely to display feature films or complete series of television episodes, rather than material directly recorded in this format.

At one level, it may not much matter which of these formats a child is watching, but in terms of the phenomenological detail of the experience there are substantial differences. Conventions designed for the big screen (pan shots, for example) 'read' differently on the small screen; close-ups designed for the intimacy of television viewing may appear differently if shown on a large screen by a video projector (see Willems, 2000). Even a brief analysis of each format reveals substantial differences in the quality of experience.

Film seen in a cinema is an 'event', with attendant rituals (sitting in separate seats in the dark, eating or at least smelling popcorn), and usually involving planning and anticipation. The scale of the screen, the loudness of the surround sound, and the need for a certain level of social decorum all feature in the experience. In contrast, television is familiar and domestic. Rather than being a special, ritualistic event, it occurs on a daily basis alongside many other mundane activities. Viewers may opt in and out of the experience as they choose, but once a moment is past it may not be recovered at will. Children often attend to television in very partial ways, using sound as a cue for visual attention, for example. Bickham, et al. speak of the child as 'making continuous decisions about attention based on partial information' (2001: 105). Another highly salient quality of television is its 'flow' (Williams, 1974: 86), its ongoing continuity. A televiewing experience may vary substantially according to whether it is a specially selected programme or a mere tuning into whatever happens to be onscreen at the moment. The flow includes station breaks, advertisements, previews of upcoming shows, as well as the programmes themselves, and viewers learn early that a discontinuous form of viewing is often appropriate. Video often represents a reformatting of material designed for film or television. Watching a video is also a domestic experience and the large-scale elements of movies are reduced to the smaller screen and more modest speakers of domestic equipment. At the same time, while the experience of watching a video resembles television viewing in many ways, it is not exactly the same.

Crucially, of course, the video is both skippable and repeatable. The viewer is much more in charge of the experience than with either film or television; and a videotape actually shares some qualities with a book in terms of ready accessibility and repeatability. Home video offers a route to a different kind of understanding of televisual experience. Children who live in a home with a camcorder see much more of the production process in action and most likely develop a different understanding of representation (just watch a two-year-old check out that grandma is still sitting behind him even as he looks at her image on the screen).

DVD offers many of the same elements as video with some important differences. Browsability is probably the most significant improvement; as with a book, random access is possible (and it is, of course, no accident that DVDs use the book vocabulary of 'chapters' to describe the divisions). DVDs also offer the potential to watch the same scene with different soundtracks, so even a very young viewer can alternate between the diegetic soundtrack of the story itself and an explanatory commentary. DVDs first introduced the deleted scenes and outtakes that are now a feature of many children's intellectual understanding of the construction of story. Even an animated cartoon such as *Toy Story* or *Monsters, Inc.* will now include simulations of outtakes, and all but the youngest viewers are expected to get the joke.

Some children will possess a broader range of such televisual experiences than others. Many contemporary Western children will be familiar with several of the items on the list; many non-Western children will have experience of at least one or two.

The contents of these different formats may also vary. Children's viewing may include any or all of the following categories:

- story (real world or cartoon)
- information
- a loose blend of the two (a child-oriented programme such as 'Sesame Street' or 'Blue Peter' or an adult genre such as a cookery programme)
- recreational non-narrative such as sports
- persuasive material (mainly in advertisements but also in other forms)
- music with associated visuals.

All of these formats (with the possible exception of home video) and many of these content areas 'leak'. Material that appears on television or film reappears in the child's world in many other ways: in books related to the televisual production, in toys and commodities, in environmental print of many different kinds. If film and television had no other impact on print literacy than to serve as a repertoire of background information, their role would be significant.

Table 11.2   *Three sets of television-related texts*

	Teletubbies[1]	Sesame Street[2]	General Disney texts[2]
DVD	2	11	247
Videos	23	84	893
Books	87	590	3011
Toys and Games	7	26	34
Software/ computer games	4	6	117
Music	2	44	534
Websites[3]	220,000	270,000	4,610,000

[1]www.amazon.co.uk, accessed 27 December 2001.
[2]www.amazon.com, accessed 27 December 2001.
[3]www.google.com, accessed 26 December 2001.

Figure 10.1 (by Marsh, in this volume) provides an overview of the extraordinary range of texts and artefacts available to at least Western children. Table 11.2 takes a close-up look at some textual elements of that larger set, and gives the numbers of related texts listed by amazon.co.uk or amazon.com for 'Teletubbies', 'Sesame Street', and a general search term of 'Disney'. The numbers of different texts available to small children are truly remarkable. But the textual world is even broader than this table represents; for example, the 'Sesame Street' listing also offers a variety of other products including flushable baby wipes, Band-Aids, a soft potty seat, and so forth. The salience and virtues of environmental print suddenly acquire a price tag, and the infant consumer is inculcated into a world where literacy includes the concept of brand recognition.

The kind of information laid out in Table 11.2 represents the heart of another significant contemporary change as well. Today's children grow up within the context of a multimedia bath of symbol systems. While adults readily differentiate print from audio from television from computer text, small children start from scratch and may observe these texts quite differently. It is striking how much of the research about television/film and print literacy works on the assumption that these operations represent discrete categories, when, as we see above, much of children's early textual experience washes across media boundaries. A noteworthy exception is the study by Livingstone and Bovill, which starts from a recognition that:

> In their everyday lives children and young people weave together a huge diversity of activities. This interconnection across activities may be more or less *ad hoc*, but it may also be deliberate, as in the intertextual integration of content themes across diverse media forms. (1999, 1: 13)

Adults often see texts as operating in a single direction: first you have the original and then all the spin-offs. Child consumers of these texts often do not perceive such a singular directionality, and deal happily with a set of coexisting plurals.

Some elements transfer directly across media. In the simplest cases, as shown above, it is a straightforward reworking of familiar content. But access to a variety of media texts enables other kinds of transfers involving cognitive developments, such as the need to sort out the relationship between size and distance (see Abelman, 1989), or the development of story schemata (see Neuman, 1995; Tobin, 2000). Other aspects of literate processing of texts in different media are distinct: pace is determined by the producer in television and film (though video and DVD restore some control to the user) but it is negotiable in print, for example (though it may be a site of contestation between children and the adults reading to them) (see Wright et al., 1984, for a discussion of pace and attention in television).

A BROADER VIEW: WHERE TEXTS AND YOUNG CHILDREN CONNECT

In our view, the most useful research into the interrelationship between televisual and print literacies is that which takes account of the complexities outlined above. This is where, in Figure 11.1, the child and the text interact and we are led to ask about the nature of the connection and the reasons why particular texts resonate for particular children. Unfortunately, many of the studies that explore contemporary multiliteracies do not deal with the youngest children.

Those researchers who do take a holistic approach to the literacies of the youngest children often produce findings that confirm that children are aware of the complexities that surround them. As Sipe expresses it:

> it would seem that the children know that stories do not merely *lean* on other stories; stories are so *porous* to each other that they can be combined, stitched, woven together, and fused into more all-encompassing imbrications and palimpsests. (2000: 85)

This observation is based on his analysis of children aged five, six, and seven, and their responses to the stories read to them at school. His young subjects make use of textual repertoires based in a variety of media, and televisual texts clearly fuel their developing understanding.

Dyson (1994; 1997; 1999; 2000; in press) has worked for years with children aged between six and nine, and her full, rich reports of their literate lives are perhaps the most powerful contemporary testimony to how children make sense of the world through the use of an enormous variety of textual filters. Dyson's explorations of children's own written and drawn creations and their ongoing conversations provide deeper and more complex insights into their textual understandings than any amount of testing of the 'learning' of details could ever do, as the much fuller account of Dyson's work given by Marsh in this volume attests.

Dyson's extensive ethnographic work with small children is in a category of its own with its striking combination of close-up and wide-angle vision, but useful smaller-scale projects also testify to the importance of locating the learning of small children within the context of the culture as a whole. Hilton (1996), Marsh (2000), and Marsh and Millard (2000) all explore developing literacies in terms of children's exposure to many elements of popular culture. Kline (1993) and Cross (1997) look at questions of children's developmental play as rooted in the toy industry and its strong links to television programmes and advertising. Kinder (1991) explores questions of agency in text interpretation across a range of children's programmes and texts.

PROCESSING ISSUES: DEALING WITH THE TEXT

It is often assumed that words are abstract entities made up of the straight and rounded lines of individual letters, and requiring intense training to decode, while moving images can be interpreted by the application of intuitive knowledge about the real world. Such assumptions do not acknowledge the true complexity of the situation, and in Figure 11.1 we have attempted to represent the need to consider the role of the child in processing the text and the need to examine the text to see how it prompts the child to engage with it and to make connections with other texts and with the world. Small children have much to learn before they can make sense of moving images – and on some occasions the context of print makes the translation of its arbitrary shapes into meaning almost transparent.

The elements of print decoding are amply dealt with elsewhere in this book, so here we will concentrate on what is needed to interpret moving images, and the connections to print literacy. Although we found little evidence of detailed research comparing the strategies of young children across media, there is research which suggests that for older children there are processes which are significant for both print and televisual texts. Robinson

(1997) has shown how eight- and nine-year-old children use very similar strategies to make sense of narratives in print and television. In each case they engage emotionally with the story, they draw on their prior knowledge of other texts and of the world to interpret and predict the text in front of them, and they do this as active members of a series of interpretive communities which influence their interpretation. In particular, they use textual and visual cues wherever available 'to predict, to retell, to confirm individual positions and to develop collaborative reconstructions' (Robinson, 1997: 150). However, there are particular strategies which children need to develop in order to make sense of televisual texts which deserve more specific attention here.

A primary requirement is to learn that the images represent three-dimensional 'reality'. Children who have access to home video images develop this understanding in a different way from those children whose viewing is confined to externally provided texts. Children who have access to one or many toys related to televisual texts with which they are familiar will also operate within a different ontological framework from those who only ever see the characters portrayed as moving images in the two dimensions of the screen. Little research explores these complex contingencies of what and how small children learn about comprehending moving images.

The grammar of cut, camera angle, zoom, and edit is not intuitively clear to young children. These elements of the moving image provide spatial and temporal information that young viewers must learn how to process into their final interpretation. Viewers must also learn to coordinate the language of soundtrack (musical underlining or foreshadowing, sound effects, dialogue) with the content of the images that run in parallel – not to mention the more complex processing challenge when the soundtrack for one scene continues to underlie a change of visual images. Much evidence suggests that small children actually make use of the audiotrack to help them decide when to expend visual attention on the screen (see, for example, Rolandelli et al., 1991; Calvert and Scott, 1989; Calvert, 2001). As with print processing, comprehension of these features must reach a level of automaticity before it can be relied on not to interfere with the creation of meaning; the interpretation of moving images, like the interpretation of print, calls for an ability to orchestrate many sources of information within the limits of a finite capacity for attention.

There is rather more research on the subject of modality, of how children develop an understanding of the relationship of a particular set of moving images to reality. Early on, children distinguish between cartoons and images of real people. Their grasp of the fictionality of live-action drama and of the relationship to daily life of the news and documentaries is more subtly developed (Hodge and Tripp, 1986; Flavell et al., 1990; Howard, 1994; 1996; Chandler, 1997). Comparable work with print fiction (Lewis, 2001) shows that the idea of fiction in print is also a complex conceptual development. It is, of course, rather more difficult with print to operate a default position that all images are real until proven otherwise. Television, with its moving images of real people, is often misleadingly close to our own daily experience and children must learn the ontological implications of the framing mechanisms. This task is complicated by the modality variations of the daily television schedule in particular, as news, advertisements, cartoons, game shows, and dramatic representations mingle on the screen. Film, video and DVD, in contrast, are usually framed apart from real life in various formal and pragmatic ways and need rather less sorting out.

In addition to developing generic understandings of conventions, modality, and the framing of different formats, children learn to make local decisions about how to attend to any given programme. Bickham et al., in an attempt to resolve the active and passive models of television viewing into a single and more useful picture, describe a viewer as engaged in moment-to-moment decisions:

> As sampling occurs, the viewer gains information from the features observed. Animation, character voices, and production style can notify the viewer of content type, age of intended audience, and other program-specific information. The viewer, now more knowledgeable about the show's content, can consider specific cognitive and motivational questions: Is this a program I recognize? Is it a program for people like me? Can I understand it? Does it meet my current viewing goals? Will it be fun to watch? Positive answers to these questions lead to further attention. This attention, however, is constantly re-evaluated: Am I understanding this? How much mental energy is required to continue to understand? Is this memorable enough to merit my investment of energy? Transitions in the program elicit a requestioning of the current attentional state based on the cognitive and motivational goals of the child viewer. (2001: 108)

Television is based on a flow of programming but it is a flow designed to take interruptions into account, and thus more resembles magazine reading with a series of relatively short items loosely linked together – spatially in the case of a print magazine, temporally on television. Child viewers learn to manage their own attention in the context of this flow.

CONVENTIONS OF INTERPRETATION

We would argue that one reason why the research we have been citing fails in many cases to illuminate our understandings of the ways in which children in the early years become literate across a range of media is that the questions which would allow such an understanding to be developed have rarely been asked. One starting point for future work would be to consider conventions of interpretation in different media and how these might be learned. Rabinowitz (1987) has produced a useful list of grouped protocols for interpretation which could be used in this way and which informed the development of our diagram. He bases them on conventional nineteenth and twentieth century narrative prose and calls them, somewhat misleadingly, 'rules of reading'. It is instructive to apply his 'rules' to the processes of televisual interpretation, for they have a generic utility that draws out surprising parallels.

Rabinowitz's first rules are the *rules of notice*. How do you decide what to pay attention to? In print, there are numerous conventions for attracting notice: something mentioned in a sentence that opens or closes a paragraph, for example, receives extra attention; a single-sentence paragraph receives even more. Chapter titles, punctuation, repetition, question and answer may all draw attention.

What are the televisual parallels? Obviously camera angles, zooms, and close-ups are features that attract and direct attention, perhaps even more peremptorily than their print counterparts. The grammar of these televisual rules of notice is no more intuitive than the print version; viewers, like readers, have to learn how to interpret these pointers. Clearly the audiotrack also has an important role to play in establishing what to notice.

Rules of signification are applied after rules of notice. When we have decided what to pay attention to, we must then decide how to attend to it. Is a narrator reliable? Is a character trustworthy? Is a particular account of a situation merely a set-up to delude unwary readers? What is going on that the author or director is *not* drawing our attention to?

With televisual texts, one element of signification that we probably need to take account of is the trustworthiness of the camera angle. What is happening outside the range of the viewfinder? Other ingredients are extraneous to the internal world of the story but highly relevant to our interpretive operation: for example, if we recognize a well-known actor we are likely to attend to that character rather differently, at least initially, expecting her to play an important part in the story. A significant character can be 'slid into' a print story rather more unobtrusively in many cases.

Rabinowitz's third category involves the *rules of configuration*. These protocols help us to assemble the elements of the story into a workable whole. An event early in the story will likely have consequences later on. Rabinowitz's account of this convention is that in a story we can expect that *something* will happen but that *not anything* can happen once the parameters of the story are laid down. Genre expectations feed into how we put plot elements together. Whether our expectations are met or shattered, they still play a part in how we construct the story.

Of all the protocols, the rules of configuration are the most straightforward and apply the most universally across media. If a character forgets her keys in the early stages of a story, we are entitled to expect some later outcome of that event and our anticipation of such a development plays a part in how we compose the story. Whether this happens televisually or in print is not a major consideration.

The final set of protocols is the *rules of coherence*, which we generally apply after we have finished the story. These enable us to make the best possible sense of the story as a whole. We tidy loose ends, decide where particular details fit into the story as a whole, reinterpret events and characters – and also gaps and/or excesses – so they make metaphoric or thematic sense.

Partly because they are retrospectively applied, there is likely to be a stronger social element in the assessment of the rules of coherence. It is rather more likely that a televisual text will be experienced socially in the first place, and discussions about coherence often follow quickly: witness the cinema-goers discussing the film as they leave the theatre or the television viewers commenting on the latest episode of a favourite programme on the playground next morning. Occasionally a print story will create its own powerful community that operates on a relatively immediate basis. For example, the drive to acquire and read the newest 'Harry Potter' title is at least partly related to the urge to participate in the first conversations after the story is finished; a strong social imperative is mingled with the private experience of the text.

Rabinowitz does not explore the activities of readers to validate his categories of rules, and there is not space here to extend this discussion to detail how these rules might be understood in print and televisual literacy; but one of us has made substantial use of his interpretive schema and found it to apply usefully both to print and also to texts in other media (see Mackey, 1995; 2002). It would be valuable to extend and develop this work with a wider group of younger children.

As well as similarities in text processing experiences across media, there are also differences. One area in which – at least at first glance – there is a clear discrepancy is that of the rhythm of the experience. To some extent, this difference in rhythm is linked to the difference between a moving and a still picture. The flow of narrative or action is different in print and televisual texts; we create the pace of action from the words in print, with moments in time frozen for us by the illustration. Even the jerkiest animation has more sense of flow than any still image, and one convention which those becoming literate have to learn differently in the different media is the understanding of motion. With still images, we have to build in the motion for ourselves or learn where there is none (as in a reference text); televisual texts supply the opposite challenge of learning to attend to the relevant details in a flow of activity, a point ably demonstrated by Chatman (1978) in his comparison of books and film. As Kress (1998: 69–71) points out, still images are spatial and simultaneous in their organization; language is temporal (though writing certainly includes a spatial component); and moving images combine the two. Children growing up between and among these different semiotic systems must master what usefully transfers and what does not.

Selecting these relevant details is another difference of interpretation which we must learn. In print, some at least of the selection has been done for us; the author has set out a limited number of words and in the case of a picturebook chosen which images should be included. Every drawing has a selected set of content created by the artist. (Even so, the research evidence – see Goodman, 1969 – suggests that experienced readers still sample and make meaning from a selection from the words provided.) With televisual images, we can see and hear much more and thus there is even more necessity to learn what is important and what we need to see. The director uses camera angles and edits to help us in the task of distinguishing figure from ground, but the constant flow of background information is very often much more assertive in moving images than in still ones. The soundtrack conveys further information and helps direct attention. The different codes and conventions of the media assist us in learning these lessons, as do the communities of interpretation which can include the texts themselves. Children may not learn technical terms, such as *mise-en-scène*, but they learn implicitly how to attend to the concepts that these terms describe.

A common metaphor for the reading process is orchestration (Bussis et al., 1985: 67; Chittenden et al., 2001: 73). In terms of reading televisual media, the metaphor holds good. The selection of what is relevant and helpful may be more complex where the text has many potential channels through which to offer information. So a televisual text, with its range of points of view, movement, multiple voices, background music, sound effects and even subtitles, offers a rich experience from which to select. But as Lewis (2001) has shown, the polysemic world of picturebooks offers a challenge of similar kind to the beginning reader: do they choose between competing stories in *Come Away from the Water, Shirley*, (Burningham, 1977) or attempt to synthesize the two? Across all media, to use Margaret Meek's (1988) famous phrase, texts teach what readers learn.

Research into very young children has tended to work at a relatively simplistic level with regard to television. Thus we know that young children are more likely to pay attention to a programme if there is sound and vision than to vision alone (Hollenbeck and Slaby, 1979) but not much about how young children construe meaning from the range of sources which is offered. It seems that some codes are learned very young; Verónica at three and a half chose to tell us that some of the music in *Dinosaur* was *muy feo* (very ugly or nasty) and that this meant something bad was going to happen. More systematic research into such phenomena might add to our understanding of the interactions between the processes of becoming literate in a range of media more helpfully than the more limited research currently available.

MAPPING THE TERRITORY

In this chapter we have attempted to show what we already know from research about the complex interrelationships of print and televisual literacies and how children become expert meaning makers of all kinds of texts. Although there is a huge corpus of research into certain aspects of this territory, there are still too many areas which seem to us to be central but which have been neglected by research. There is a tendency to research what is easily measurable rather than to start, as Dyson does, by observing what children are doing and trying to understand the significance of their behaviour and what it shows about how the key lessons of cross-media literacy are learned. Other very valuable work focuses on either televisual or print texts rather than on the interaction. For example, Livingstone and Bovill's (1999) revisiting of the classic Himmelweit et al. (1958) study of children and television provides a fascinating insight into the ways in which children use media but takes as its central focus the 'electronic screen' and the ways in which children from six to 17 use this. This offers much useful insight along the way but does not address as a central question the ways in which the interactions of very young children with a *range* of media, including print on paper, are connected with the ways in which they learn to read those media.

In Figure 11.1 we set out a series of issues concerning the interaction between the four quadrants of our diagram. Throughout the chapter we have attempted to show what evidence is available to answer such questions with regard to young children. To summarize, we believe that if we are to understand fully how children under seven learn to be literate across a range of printed and televisual texts, we need to ask not simply separate questions about the ways the child learns to process information, the ways in which the texts themselves invite interpretation, and the roles of the community and the wider environment in developing children as literate members of society. We have begun to suggest the questions which allow the *interaction* of child, text, community and environment to be problematized and have argued that much existing research fails to address these crossover questions sufficiently.

We have argued that the corpus of research based on a deficit model is fundamentally flawed, since it sets up oppositions between print and television which cannot be justified. We have suggested that a more helpful way forward might be an asset model, which looks at what children actually do and how their understandings are extended by encounters with a wide range of texts, mediated by the interpretive communities to which they belong and by the broader social contexts in which they live. However, much of the more thoughtful research cited here, which does attempt to explore children's understandings, either focuses on one medium or pays more attention to children over the age of seven. Nor are there enough researchers who are attempting to answer the questions we identified in Figure 11.1. We have suggested that one fruitful way forward would be to build on Rabinowitz's 'rules of reading' reinterpreted as conventions of interpretation. What is clear is that, despite the huge corpus of work which purports to explore the nature of children's literacy development, we still have few real answers as to how the four quadrants of our diagram – child, text, community and environment – work together as young children become literate. As the media world of even the youngest children becomes ever more complex, more multifaceted research is urgently needed.

NOTE

The authors would like to thank Shelagh Genuis of the University of Alberta for her contributions to the literature search that underpins this chapter.

REFERENCES

Abelman, R. (1989) 'From here to eternity: children's acquisition of understanding of projective size on television', *Human Communication Research,* 15 (3); 463–81.

Anderson, D.R., Lorch, E.P., Field, D.E., Collins, P.A. and Nathan, J.G. (1986) 'Television viewing at home: age trends in visual attention and time with TV', *Child Development,* 57: 1024–33.

Anderson, D.R., Bryant, J., Wilder, A., Santomero, A., Williams, M. and Crawley, A.M. (2000) 'Researching *Blue's Clues*: viewing behavior and impact', Research Synthesis Essay, *Media Psychology,* 2: 179–94.

Barker, M. and Petley, J. (eds) (1997) *Ill Effects: the Media/Violence Debate.* London: Routledge.

Barton, D. and Hamilton, M. (1998) *Local Literacies: Reading and Writing in One Community.* London: Routledge.

Berry, G.L. and Asamen, J.K. (eds) (1993) *Children and Television: Images in a Changing Sociocultural World.* Newbury Park, CA: Sage.

Bickham, D.S., Wright, J.C., and Huston, A.C. (2001) 'Attention, comprehension, and the educational influences of television', in D.G. Singer, and J.L. Singer (eds), *Handbook of Children and the Media.* Thousand Oaks, CA: Sage. 101–19.

Buckingham, D. (1993) *Children Talking Television: The Making of Television Literacy.* London: Falmer.

Buckingham, D. (1996) *Moving Images: Understanding Children's Emotional Responses to Television.* Manchester: Manchester University Press.

Buckingham, D. (2000) *After the Death of Childhood: Growing Up in the Age of Electronic Media.* Cambridge: Polity.

Buckingham, D. and Allerton, M. (1996) *Fear, Fright and Distress: a Review of Research on Children's Emotional Responses to Television.* London: Broadcasting Standards Council.

Burningham, J. (1977) *Come Away from the Water, Shirley.* New york: Crowell.

Bussis, A.M. Chittenden, E.A., Amarel, M. and Klausner, E. (1985) *Inquiry into Meaning: an Investigation of Learning to Read.* Mahwah, NJ: Erlbaum.

Calvert, S.L. (2001) 'Impact of televised songs on children's and young adults' memory of educational content', *Media Psychology* 3: 325–42.

Calvert, S.L. and Gersh, T.L. (1987) 'The selective use of sound effects and visual inserts for children's television story comprehension', *Journal of Applied Developmental Psychology,* 8: 363–75.

Calvert, S.L. and Scott, M.C. (1989) 'Sound effects for children's temporal integration of fast-paced television content', *Journal of Broadcasting and Electronic Media,* 33 (3): 233–46.

Chandler, D. (1997) 'Children's understanding of what is "real" on television: a review of the literature', *Journal of Educational Media,* 23 (1): 67–82.

Chatman, S. (1978) *Story and Discourse: Narrative Structure in Fiction and Film.* Ithaca, NY: Cornell University Press.

Chittenden, E. and Salinger, T. with Bussis, A.M. (2001) *Inquiry into Meaning: an Investigation of Learning to Read,* rev. edn. New York: Teachers College Press.

Cross, G. (1997) *Kids' Stuff: Toys and the Changing World of American Childhood.* Cambridge, MA: Harvard University Press.

Dombey, H. (1983) 'Learning the language of books', in M. Meek (ed.), *Opening Moves: Work in Progress in the Study of Children's Language Development.* London: Bedford/Heinemann.

Dyson, A.H. (1994) *The Ninjas, the X-Men, and the Ladies: Playing with Power and Identity in an Urban Primary School.* National Center for the Study of Writing, Technical Report no. 70.

Dyson, A.H. (1997) *Writing Superheroes: Contemporary Childhood, Popular Culture, and Classroom Literacy.* New York: Teachers College Press.

Dyson, A.H. (1999) 'Coach Bombay's kids learn to write: children's appropriation of media material for school literacy', *Research in the Teaching of English,* 33: 367–402.

Dyson, A.H. (2000) 'On reframing children's words: the perils, promises, and pleasures of writing children', *Research in the Teaching of English,* 34: 352–67.

Dyson, A.H. (in press) 'The stolen lipstick of overheard song: composing voices in child song, verse, and written text', in N. Nystrand, and J. Duffy (eds), *Towards a Rhetoric of Everyday Life.* Madison, WI: University of Wisconsin Press.

Fisch, S.M., Truglio, R.T. and Cole, C.F. (1999) 'The impact of *Sesame Street* on preschool children: A review and synthesis of 30 years', research.' Research Synthesis Essay, *Media Psychology,* 1: 165–90.

Fish, S. (1980) *Is There a Text in This Class? The Authority of Interpretive Communities.* Cambridge, MA: Harvard University Press.

Flavell, J.H., Flavell, E.R., Green, F.L. and Korfmacher, J.E. (1990) 'Do young children think of television images as pictures or real objects?', *Journal of Broadcasting and Electronic Media,* 34 (4): 399–419.

Freedman, J.L. (2002) *Media Violence and its Effect on Aggression: Assessing the Scientific Evidence.* Toronto: University of Toronto Press.

Gauntlett, D. (1995) *Moving Experiences: Understanding Television's Influences and Effects.* London: Libbey.

Goodman, K. (1969) 'Psycholinguistic universals in the reading process', in F.V. Gollasch, (ed.) (1982), *Language and Literacy: the Selected Writings of Kenneth S. Goodman.* Boston: Routledge and Kegan Paul.

Gunter, B. (1985) *Dimensions of Television Violence.* Aldershot: Gower.

Harste, J.C., Woodward, V.A. and Burke, C.L. (1984) *Language Stories and Literacy Lessons.* Portsmouth, NH: Heinemann.

Hart, J. (2002) 'This vision thing', *Times Educational Supplement*, 7 June: 15–18.

Hilton, M. (1996) *Potent Fictions: Children's Literacy and the Challenge of Popular Culture*. London: Routledge.

Himmelweit, H.T., Oppenheim, A.N. and Vince, P. (1958) *Television and the Child: an Empirical Study of the Effect of Television on the Young*. London: Oxford University Press.

Hodge, B. and Tripp, D. (1986) *Children and Television*. Cambridge: Polity.

Hollenbeck, A.R. and Slaby, R.G. (1979) 'Infant visual and vocal responses to television', *Child Development*, 50 (1): 41–5.

Howard, S. (1994) '"Real bunnies don't stand on two legs": five-, six- and seven-year-old children's perceptions of television's "Reality"', *Australian Journal of Early Childhood*, 19 (4): 35–43.

Howard, S. (1996) '"Bananas can't talk": young children judging the reality of Big Bird, Bugs and the Bananas', *Australian Journal of Early Childhood*. 21 (4): 25–30.

Howard, S. and Roberts, S. (2003) 'Winning hearts and minds: television and the very young audience', *Contemporary Issues in Early Childhood. International Marketing Data and Statistics 2000*. London: Euromonitor.

Kalantzis, M. and Cope, B. (2000) 'Changing the role of schools', in B. Cope and M. Kalantzis (eds), *Multiliteracies: Literacy Learning and the Design of Social Futures*. New London Group. London: Routledge.

Kenway, J. and Bullen, E. (2001) *Consuming Children: Education–Entertainment–Advertising*. Buckingham: Open University Press.

Kinder, M. (1991) *Playing with Power in Movies, Television, and Video Games: from Muppet Babies to Teenage Mutant Ninja Turtles*. Berkeley, CA: University of California Press.

Kline, S. (1993) *Out of the Garden: Toys and Children's Culture in the Age of TV Marketing*. Toronto: Garamond.

Kress, G. (1998) 'Visual and verbal modes of representation in electronically mediated csommunication: the potentials of new forms of text', in I. Snyder (ed.), *Page to Screen: Taking Literacy into the Electronic Era*. London: Routledge.

Lemish, D. and Rice, M.L. (1986) 'Television as a talking picture book: a prop for language acquisition', *Journal of Child Language*, 13 (2): 251–74.

Lewis, D. (2001) *Reading Contemporary Picturebooks: Picturing Text*. London: Routledge/Falmer.

Livingstone, S. (1990) *Making Sense of Television: the Psychology of Audience Interpretation*, London: Routledge.

Livingstone, S. (1998) 'Mediated childhoods: a comparative approach to young people's changing media environment in Europe', *European Journal of Communication*, 13 (4): 435–56.

Livingstone, S. and Bovill, M. (1999) *Young People, New Media*. London: LSE.

Lowe, P.J. and Durkin, K. (1999) 'The effect of flashback on children's understanding of television crime content', *Journal of Broadcasting and Electronic Media*, 43 (1): 83–97.

Luke, C. (1988) *Television and Your Child: a Guide for Concerned Parents*. Toronto: Kagan and Woo.

Lull, J. (ed.) (1988) *World Families Watch Television*. London: Sage.

Mackey, M. (1995) '*Imagining with words: the temporal processes of reading fiction*'. Unpublished PhD dissertation, University of Alberta.

Mackey, M. (2002) *Literacies across Media: Playing the Text*. London: Routledge/Falmer.

Marsh, J. (2000) 'Teletubby tales: popular culture in the early years language and literacy curriculum', *Contemporary Issues in Early Childhood*, 1 (2): 119–133.

Marsh, J. and Millard, E. (2000) *Literacy and Popular Culture: Using Children's Culture in the Classroom*. London: Chapman.

Meek, M. (1988) *How Texts Teach What Readers Learn*. Stroud: Thimble.

Messenger Davies, M. (2001) *'Dear BBC': Children, Television Storytelling and the Public Sphere*. Cambridge: Cambridge University Press.

Minow, N.N. and Lamay, C.L. (1995) *Abandoned in the Wasteland: Children, Television, and the First Amendment*. New York: Hill and Wang.

Neuman, S.B. (1995) *Literacy in the Television Age: the Myth of the TV Effect*, 2nd edn. Norwood, NJ: Ablex.

New London Group (1996) 'A pedagogy of multiliteracies: designing social futures', *Harvard Educational Review*, 66: 60–91.

Potter, F. (1994) 'Media education, literacy and schooling', in D. Wray, and S. Medwell (eds), *Teaching Primary English: the State of the Art*. London: Routledge.

Rabinowitz, P.J. (1987) *Before Reading: Narrative Conventions and the Politics of Interpretation*. Ithaca, NY: Cornell University Press.

Richards, J.E. and Cronise, K. (2000) 'Extended visual fixation in the early pre-school years: look duration, heart rate changes, and attentional inertia', *Child Development*, 71 (3): 602–20.

Robinson, M. (1997) *Children Reading Print and Television*. London: Falmer.

Rodriguez, M.V. (2000) 'Home literacy in the everyday life of three Dominican families', Paper presented at the American Educational Research Association, New Orleans.

Rolandelli, D.R., Wright, J.C., Huston, A.C. and Eakins, D. (1991) 'Children's auditory and visual processing of narrated and nonnarrated television programming', *Journal of Experimental Child Psychology*, 51: 90–122.

St Peters, Michelle, Oppenheimer, S., Eakins, D.J., Wright, J.C. and Huston, A.C. (1991) 'Media use among preschool children as a function of income and media options'. Paper presented at The Society for Research in Child Development, Seattle, Washington.

Salamon, J. (2002) 'Children's TV catches up with how kids watch', *New York Times*, 9 June, accessed at http://www.nytimes.com.

Salomon, G. (1983) 'Beyond the formats of television: the effects of student preconceptions on the experience of televiewing' in M. Meyer, (ed.), *Children and the Formal Features of Television: Approaches and Findings of Experimental and Formal Research*. Munich: Saur

Sanger, J. with Willson, J., Davies, B. and Whittaker, R. (1997) *Young Children, Videos and Computer Games: Issues for Teachers and Parents*. London: Falmer.

Seiter, E. (1999a) *Television and New Media Audiences*. Oxford: Oxford University Press.

Seiter, E. (1999b) 'Power Rangers at pre-school: negotiating media in child care settings', in M. Kinder (ed.), *Kids' Media Culture*. Durham, NC: Duke University Press.

Sell, M.A., Ray, G.E. and Lovelace, L. (1995) 'Preschool children's comprehension of a *Sesame Street* video tape: the effects of repeated viewing and previewing instructions', *Educational Technology Research and Development*, 43 (3): 49–60.

Sipe, L.R. (2000) '"Those two gingerbread boys could be brothers": how children use intertextual connections during storybook readalouds', *Children's Literature in Education*, 31 (2): 73–90.

Smith, F. (1983) *Essays into Literacy*. Exeter, NH: Heinemann.

Takahashi, N. (1991) 'Developmental changes of interests to animated stories in toddlers measured by eye movement while watching them', *Psychologia: an International Journal of Psychology in the Orient*, 34 (1): 63–8.

Terrell, S.L. and Daniloff, R. (1996) 'Children's word learning using three modes of instruction', *Perceptual and Motor Skills*, 83: 779–87.

Tidhar, C.E. (1996) 'Enhancing television literacy skills among pre-school children through an intervention programme in the kindergarten', *Journal of Educational Media*, 22 (2): 97–110.

Tobin, J. (2000) *'Good Guys Don't Wear Hats'*: *Children's Talk about the Media*. New York: Teachers College Press.

Tyner, K. (1998) *Literacy in a Digital World: Teaching and Learning in the Age of Information*. Mahwah, NJ: Erlbaum.

Willems, M. (2000) 'Video and its paradoxes', in Russell Jackson (ed.), *The Cambridge Companion to Shakespeare on Film*. Cambridge: Cambridge University Press.

Williams, R. (1974) *Television: Technology and Cultural Form*. London: Fontana/Collins.

Winn, M. (1985) *The Plug-In Drug*. Harmondsworth: Viking Penguin.

Wood, J.M. and Duke, N.K. (1997) 'Inside "Reading Rainbow": a spectrum of strategies for promoting literacy', *Language Arts,* 74: 95–106.

Wright, J.C., Huston, A.C., Ross, R.P., Calvert, S.L., Rolandelli, D., Weeks, L.A., Raeissi, P. and Potts, R. (1984) 'Pace and continuity of television programs: effects on children's attention and comprehension', *Developmental Psychology*, 20 (4): 653–66.

Wright, R. (2001) *Hip and Trivial: Youth Culture, Book Publishing, and the Greying of Canadian Nationalism*. Toronto: Canadian Scholars' Press.

Zhao-Bin (1996) 'The little emperors' small screen: parental control and children's television viewing in China', *Media, Culture and Society*, 18: 639–58.

Part III

EARLY MOVES IN LITERACY

12

Moving into Literacy: How it All Begins

LESLEY LANCASTER

There is very little research into the development of literacy much before the age of three. There are a number of studies of its development between the ages of three and five or six (Torrey, 1973; Clark, 1976; Bissex, 1980; Luria, 1983; Ferreiro and Teberosky, 1982; Kress, 1997; 2000), and although there are references to earlier stages of literacy in some of these, there is no substantive study of literacy below this age. This is perhaps unsurprising since very young children are not likely to be literate in the commonly understood sense of the term, and therefore, so the argument might go, there is not a great deal of evidence to consider. However, this does leave a significant gap in the account of children's development of literacy. It would be surprising if, from an apparent position of no serious engagement with print at all, children are suddenly able to explode into the type of rampant, creative, independent and reasoned relationship with the medium which is described in most of the studies cited above. It appears as if much groundwork has been laid before. However, there are both theoretical and practical reasons why this has not invited a great deal of attention in educational circles.

The influence of Jean Piaget on educational thinking about children's cognitive development has been considerable over the years. Critiques of aspects of his work have been accepted for some time now (Donaldson, 1978; Deloache and Brown, 1987; Feldman, 1987; Thelen and Smith, 1994), but the legacy has persisted. Two claims of Piaget can be held to partial account for the lack of attention to early literate activity. First, there is the suggestion that learning happens in fairly discrete stages, with the very earliest involving little more than reflexive responses to the external environment. In other words, children have to reach the right stage before they are able to cope with the physical, cognitive and symbolic demands of reading and writing. Secondly, there is the view that a common process of development pervades all areas of cognition, rather than there being different domains of cognition and learning. So, very young children would not be capable of recognizing features of literacy as a unique symbolic system, distinguishable from other such systems.

A second factor influencing the investigation of early literacy comes from the study of the development of writing itself, and in particular its relationship to speech. A traditional view holds that writing is predominately a transcription of speech (Havelock, 1976; Gelb, 1952); that it developed in order to enable talk to be written down. It would therefore be quite reasonable to suggest that until children have reached a fair level of proficiency with spoken language, they are not going to have the requisite skills to understand or produce written language; they cannot read or write down talk if they are not yet producing it. The marks that children do make prior to being able to make this connection are frequently described as 'scribble', with its rather unhelpful association with marks that are purposeless, illegible or meaningless. Within the literature, it tends to refer specifically to a stage of development prior to there being any real connection being made between letter forms and spoken meaning; Sulzby refers to the way in which children of five or six who are aware of 'conventional spelling' will revert to the use of 'lower-order forms like scribbling' (1986: 70) in certain situations. The suggestion here is that where the connection between spoken and written modes is not made, these features of children's 'written' productions have 'lower-order' communicative intention and representational purpose.

The third reason why this early stage of literacy has not been researched to the same extent as literacy beyond infancy is a practical one. Once children reach the age of three, many attend nursery classes and playgroups. The population of children under two, however, is very widely located, with children mostly being looked after at home or by childminders. Access, in other words, is difficult. It is also problematic to work with children this young without the cooperation and help of someone the child knows and trusts. Whilst this can have many benefits, it does add practical and organizational difficulties to research. The other side of this is that the relative ease of working with children in institutional settings also contributes to what Street (1995) calls the 'pedagogization' of literacy: the reduction of reading and writing to social practices predominantly associated with schooled learning. This contributes to the exclusion of the literacy practices of infants and children who are not yet part of the formal educational system from serious consideration.

In spite of the sparsity of research studies concerned exclusively with children's development of literacy before the age of three, studies from disciplines like art education show that these children are capable of a range of representational behaviour. Far from this being a quiescent period, children of this age avidly explore graphic systems, much as do children later on. In this chapter, I shall look at evidence that they are able to systematically explore graphic systems as a way of representing significant features of their personal, social and cultural experiences, long before any direct connection with language is made. I shall show that they are capable of recognizing the unique features of different domains of representation – writing, drawing and number – and I shall look at how even the very earliest marks made by children reflect intention and meaning. Finally, I shall discuss the view that they are already actively acquiring parallel systems of representation within these domains between the ages of 12 and 24 months. In other words they are already actively producing and interpreting different levels and genres of written language and different means of representing them.

PREAMBLE

In certain very obvious senses, it can be said that literacy begins at the beginning. At the start of the twenty-first century, most children are born into cultures which are in one way or another driven or affected by a complex array of literacy practices. The social and material evidence of their operation is pervasive, although it goes without saying that individual exposure to this is variable, both within and across cultures and communities. And long before they might be expected to understand much about it, babies and toddlers are on the receiving end of a kind of intense semiotic acculturation, which includes writing of many kinds in many forms. Clothes, bed covers, eating and drinking utensils, toys, videos, books: a host of merchandise covered in pictures, logos, numbers and print of all kinds, representing characters and objects from media events of the moment. These are part of a huge industry producing an array of items which are directed at the families of very young children and ultimately, of course, at young children themselves. Marsh in this volume (Figure 10.1) demonstrates the extent of the modes and media involved.

Initially it is the adults who respond to the particular characters, narratives and images signified by these various objects. However, their cultural significance is mediated through talking, showing, shaking, touching, and the countless other ways in which adults communicate with babies about significant things. The baby's first response is likely to be to their material qualities, and its exploration to involve senses like vision, touch and taste. However, the fact that, initially at least, a baby finds putting an object in its mouth an effective mode of exploration, does not preclude it from being responsive to its other signifying features. Nor does it preclude it from directing the focus of its attention to objects and images not in the least designed to be interesting or attractive to an infant. Very young children are notorious for finding unpredictable things salient. I recall my son, as a young baby, screaming when being moved from one part of the room to another so that he could watch the movement of what I considered to be a really interesting mobile. I eventually realized that in his original spot, he was watching the movement of the leaves of a tree, reflected through a sunny window as flickering shadows onto the ceiling. I had interrupted some serious semiotic work.

Even the best intentioned adults have a tendency to disrupt this kind of intense engagement which young children have with seemingly unimportant or irrelevant objects and activities often, of course, for their own protection and safety. My mother remembers an incident which happened when she was probably less than a year old. She was crawling along a beach when she spotted what she considered to be the most brightly coloured and desirable object she had ever seen. She crawled towards it with delight and anticipation, and was just about to grab it when a hand came down and snatched it away from her grasp. What the object had been, she realized much later, was a Swan Vestas matchbox, with its highly coloured images and lettering. Eighty years later, she can still recollect the feeling of devastating loss and disappointment!

These examples illustrate some important things about how very young children engage with visual and graphic representations of meaning. In both cases, the activity is independently constructed; it is purposeful and compelling, involving, potentially at least, a commitment of time and effort to find out more. In the case of the matchbox, the compulsion was also a physical and bodily one: to hold and scrutinize the desired object. Watching shifting patterns of shadowy images, on the other hand, requires prolonged visual concentration. It also requires considerable intellectual engagement with what amounts to a fluctuating sequence of abstract images. This kind of intense desire to find out more, the need to be physically involved, and the extended concentration and interest in things at an abstract level, are also the qualities which very young children require to start engaging with all the cultural paraphernalia and attendant semiotic systems which surround them; including, of course, systems of writing. Whether they are just generally aware and responsive to all of this, or whether they start to sort out how these systems work as soon as they are aware of them, is central to a consideration of how literacy develops.

RECOGNIZING DIFFERENT DOMAINS

Harste et al. (1984) claim that by the time they reach the age of three, children are quite insistent about there being a distinction between drawing and writing. Evidence comes from the marks that children make and what they say about their function and purpose. Although there is not necessarily a consistency between the types of marks which are used to represent these different modes, nevertheless, whatever form is chosen is used consistently and systematically. So, children might use circular shapes for drawing and linear strokes for writing. Whatever and however marks are produced, they are always 'a serious expression of meaning' (Goodman, 1986: 7). A number of factors can be significant in how this choice of marks is made, including the dominant writing script in their communities (Harris and Hatano, 1999). Useful evidence comes from the productions of slightly older children who have access to more than one writing script from an early age. Gregory and Williams (2000) show the skill and proficiency with which such children move between two very different writing systems that use marks in quite different ways, Bengali and English. Kenner (2002; and Kenner and Gregory, in this volume), in her study of young children learning to write in two different writing systems at the same time, demonstrates that at five and six, children are able to clearly articulate

distinctions between the semiotic principles operating for the different systems they are using. This includes being able to point out that there is a distinction between a logographic system like Chinese and a pictorial system. In other words, the decisions which children make at this stage about which system is which and how they are constructed are consistent, rational and well informed. As has already been suggested, it looks as if in order to have the capacity to reach such a sophisticated conceptual level by the time they are five or six, children will have been engaged in serious analyses of the systems of representation around them for some time. In contrast with Piagetian thinking about this, they will have recognized different domains of cognition and learning and made a start on working out their distinctive features long before they reach the age of three.

Deloache et al. (1979) show that already at five months old, children are able to recognize relatively abstract pictures of objects. Karmiloff-Smith (1992) notes that by the time they are 10 to 18 months, children readily differentiate between drawing and writing in their productions. They are 'adamant', she says, about the distinction between a mark that is a drawing and one that is writing. However, the relationship between process and product has to be taken fully into account when considering the intentions of children this young. The mark on its own is likely to be ambiguous without the context of its production, since toddlers go about the *processes* of drawing and writing differently, even though the outcome might be largely undifferentiated. So, for example, they tend to lift the pen from the page much more frequently when pretending to write than when pretending to draw. Lancaster (2001) shows that before they are two, children are also able to use other modes of communication to help ascribe meaning to their notations: language and gesture, for example, can be used to ascribe identity to otherwise undifferentiated marks, along the lines of, 'This mark I am pointing to is writing because I say it is writing, this one is a cat because I say it is a cat.' The interpersonal interactions involved in this kind of symbolic activity are central to the process of production (Halliday, 1975; Trevarthen, 1990). Both communicative processes, in the form of the informal involvement of adults and other children, and processes of physical and material production are an integral part of the outcome. The final production cannot really be understood without taking into account the circumstances which gave rise to it. However, it is interesting to note that whilst this multimodality is central to very young children's ability to communicate distinctions of meaning, it is not a quality that simply disappears as they develop fuller linguistic and graphic repertoires. Mackey (2003), in describing a project set up to explore readers processing texts in a variety of media, shows how children of 14 still manifest an understanding of the story they are reading in a variety of tactile ways. They too use gaze, a range of gestures, and their hands and fingers to process the print. In other words, the use of the body to mediate symbolic meanings (see Johnson, 1987) is not something which children move on from as they develop the ability to talk, draw, and read and write in more adult ways, but a process which has a developmental momentum of its own.

Karmiloff-Smith (1992) has also looked at slightly older children's ability to discriminate between drawing, writing and number, as well as between drawing and writing. Working with children of four years, she found that they apply clearly differentiated constraints to the three modes of notation: drawings are not acceptable as either number or written language; single elements are acceptable as number, but not as writing, as are repeated identical elements; linkage between elements is accepted for writing, but not for number; and a limited number of elements is accepted in a written string, but the same constraints do not apply to numbers. Clearly this involves sophisticated analyses and a considerable degree of understanding of the salient features of the different modes of notation. It is unlikely that the ability to additionally recognize numerical properties is something which happens suddenly at this later stage, particularly in view of evidence which suggests that babies as young as four months old can distinguish between different number arrays (Treiber and Wilcox, 1984), and by six months they can detect numerical correspondence between auditory and visual inputs (Starkey et al., 1985). It also seems unlikely, given a very young child's ability to deploy the most salient resources to deal with the task in hand (Kress, 1997), that such useful insights would be ignored. Whilst children under two might not be able to articulate the differences between writing, drawing and number in the same way that the four-year-old can, this does not mean that they are not aware of them; more likely the problem lies in the difficulty of gaining access to what it is they know and how they come to know it. What it does suggest is that children's learning about domains of symbolic representation is a continuous, developing and expanding process, which starts very early on in their lives.

EXPANDING WAYS OF MEANING IN EACH DOMAIN

If children are able to distinguish between writing, drawing and number before they are two, then it follows that this is based on their experience and perceptions of how each of these domains individually represent meaning. This is far from being a straightforward thing to sort out, however, since the domains also have features in common, at least in certain circumstances, and sometimes they do not behave 'in mode' at all. So writing can be represented graphically, two-dimensionally on a page, using a simple tool like a pencil, as can drawing and numbers; numbers can also be represented by writing; writing and numbers can be incorporated into drawings; but then writing can also be read aloud, numbers can be represented three-dimensionally by an abacus, quantity and spatial organization can be incorporated into written meanings, drawings can be made to move in cartoons, and so on.

If one starts to consider the sheer range of possibilities which each domain of symbolic representation presents to young children at the outset of the twenty-first century, then it is not difficult to reach the conclusion that to view them as principally pedagogical practices is to significantly misrepresent the nature of the task facing children, as well as the complex nature of symbolic systems involved. Indeed Teale (1986) concludes that for preschool children, 90% of their reading and writing experiences occur as part of the daily lives of their families and communities, rather than as being seen and acknowledged as literacy activities *per se*. As Goodman (1986) points out, children know that most things in their lives are organized systematically, and this insight is applied to the complexities of symbolic representation as they present in the course of daily routines and interactions. Pahl (1999) shows how they interpret things according to the information and resources to which they have access at the time, and according to what is currently salient to their thinking. She cites the example of a child in a nursery copying every feature of an adult's rendition of his name, including mistakes and superfluous dots; the same child could also produce his own version quite independently. Pahl's explanation is that to the child, these tasks are quite different: the first he constructed as a design task, whilst the second 'required subjective decisions about what constituted his name' (1999: 63). In other words, to see this task as a process with a single outcome is to entirely misunderstand the complexity of the child's understanding of the ways in which meanings can be represented graphically.

Both writing and drawing suffer from being dominated by pedagogical concerns and by being frequently reduced to a single endpoint: in the case of writing, correctly making links between sounds and letters; and in the case of drawing, the achievement of realistic picturing. Wolf and Perry (1988) suggest that in fact, drawing involves a wide repertoire of visual languages. In investigating how young children develop drawing skills, they identify three broad areas of development: the invention of drawing systems; the construction of distinctions between different graphic genres (between maps, drawings and diagrams, for example); and the evolution of specific renditions of visual images. Here, their definition of 'drawing' also included features of the process of production. Looking at the creations of children between 12 and 15 months, they identified the appearance and use of a series of distinguishable systems.

Significant analogies can be drawn here with features of writing development. Wolf and Perry describe one of the earliest of these systems, evident at between 12 and 14 months, as 'object-based representations', where drawing materials and tools are substituted for the referents which the child has in mind. So the pen might be rolled up in the paper to signify the object 'hot dog', rather than being used to make marks which represent it graphically. Kress (1997) describes a range of creative constructions devised by children moving into literacy, which could be similarly characterized. Rowe (1994) also shows how immediate and transformative children can be at this stage: turning a paper plate into a note by pencilling across it, giving it to someone, and then throwing it into the air to demonstrate how it flies. Labbo (1996) shows how children use the computer screen to similarly explore symbols and objects. These children are slightly older, between three and five, but they are still using the same multimodal strategies as the younger children, though arguably at a more developed level. The system is also broadly the same whether it is being considered as drawing or writing. As Kress points out, the principles deployed in the learning of writing are much the same as for other sign systems, 'employing the strategy of using the best, most apt available form for the expression of a particular meaning' (1997: 17). This is central to all children's early representations of symbolic meaning.

Another system which Wolf and Perry identify as appearing at about the same age is that of 'gestural representations', where gestures are incorporated into the process of signifying meanings. They give the example of a child saying 'bunny' and hopping a marker across the page, making a trail of dotted footprints. Vygotsky (1978) suggests that gesture is also linked to the development of written signs in much the same way, and many of his examples are very similar in structure and concept to those cited by Wolf and Perry. Lancaster (1999) describes a child of 23 months using gesture to 'read' writing. Looking at a line of print on a title page, she moves her pointing hand rhythmically back and forth

along the line, saying in unison with the movement, 'says writing David's, writing David's'. The gesture models the movement of her older brother's hand as he writes. These signs, with their precise integration of language and gestural action, comprise the most useful and appropriate forms available to these children at these times to express these meanings. As to whether a distinction between gestural signs which are characterized as drawing and those characterized as reading and writing can be made, more research would need to be done. However, gestures of different kinds are an important means by which very young children signify meanings, both within and across both these domains.

The third system of drawing activity which Wolf and Perry identify, they describe as 'point–plot representations'. At around 20 months, children start to make 'planful' use of graphic properties. They are able to record the number and location of an object's features by linking the graphic properties of the marks with the spatial features represented on the surface of the paper. So a human body might be represented by a line above another line and two lines at the bottom: top half, bottom half, and feet. This 'planful' linking of marks, properties of marks, and spatial organization is also well documented in the development of children's writing between three and school age, and is discussed in detail in a number of the studies referred to at the start of this chapter. Marks are made and placed systematically to express ideas and concepts. Ferreiro and Teberosky (1982) describe how a child might make a very large mark because it signifies a big animal, or conversely a small one because it signifies a small animal; and a mark might be placed adjacent to another mark because it signifies something which is part of or owned by the object or person represented by that mark. Luria (1983) shows how children also ascribe meaning to otherwise very similar marks by how they are located on the page.

Thelen and Smith (1994) point out that the facility to organize and classify space symbolically is clearly evident by the time children are 18 months old. Lancaster (1999) shows the same kind of systematic organization of marks and space at 23 months. The child in this study is making a card for her mother, with the support and collaboration of her father. The page she is working on is organized so that the same mark can be used to represent different things according to how it is placed on the page: for example, one side of the page has 'cat' marks and the other 'drawing' marks; 'writing' marks are placed at the very bottom of the page, as close to the edge as possible. These constraints reveal that she already understands significant things about symbolic practice and representative domains. A graphic mark can be used to represent different systems (drawing and writing) and objects (cats); these have different relationships to the surrounding space, with drawing and object marks being less constrained and linear in their relationship than writing. Kress (1997), Matthews (1994) and Pahl (1999) have also observed the keen interest which very young children have in organizing space, including the ways in which they physically inhabit it, and the ways in which this experience informs their perception of symbolic space. Space is of itself a significant meaning making resource (see Kress and van Leeuwen, 1996), which young children use to very good effect.

In my example, principles of spatial organization are used to structure a simple narrative based around a cat involving a sequence of possessive 'events' where activity is implied by this ownership: cat's tree; cat's house; cat's treehouse. For very young children, ownership tends to involve a physical relationship with an object or person: holding, touching or being very close to what is desired. Tomasello (1992) reports on how such social encounters and relationships are reflected in the ways in which children construct a linguistic system. He notes that by 17 months, a child is able to express possession by saying the one 'next' to the other, as in 'mummy sock'. So, both physical experience and language provide vital tools in dealing with the difficult problem of how to represent a narrative with a temporal organization involving a sequence of different events, on the fixed and two-dimensional space of the page, in a consistent and repeatable way. The principle of adjacency, of locating a mark representing someone close to the mark representing the thing that they own, is one approach adopted by the child in this study. This suggests the beginnings of an insight into two significant and distinct features of writing: generic structure and grammatical organization. This is derived from thoughtful and reasoned activity, and investigation of consistencies and regularities in these domains, long before it might considered that any explicit connections could be made between different graphic and linguistic forms and modes.

MAKING MARKS

Consistent reference has been made throughout this chapter to the marks that children under two make, and the systematic ways in which they are generated and presented. Reference has also been made to the way in which they are frequently described as 'scribble', with all the negative connotations associated with the term. None of the evidence discussed so far suggests that this characterization is likely to be an accurate one. The fact that children's earliest marks are seen as falling short of intentionally representing alphabets, or images which closely resemble real objects, has often meant that they have been regarded as simply part of a stage to be passed through, on the way to the real thing. However, whilst there is limited research on how young children construe the material structure of written notation, what there is provides evidence of their systematic engagement with its basic elements.

Dissanayake (1992) says that children of this age require the physical trace of a marker in order to remain interested in what they are doing. If the marker fails to leave a mark, they lose interest in the activity. The related actions and movements are not in themselves enough: the visual sign is after all an essential characteristic of writing and of artistic practices, and children are surrounded by evidence of these in every possible medium. A significant distinction between these domains, however, is that in the case of print, its signifying status remains fixed in spite of local variation: letters of the alphabet, logograms and ideograms are identifiable as such whether they are handwritten, printed or typed, and in spite of variations in handwriting, print type, size or location (see Goodman, 1976). It is most unlikely that children's early ability to discriminate between drawing and writing does not include a level of understanding about this defining feature of systems of written notation.

According to Kellogg (1970), there are 20 distinct kinds of markings which have been identified in the graphic productions of children of two years old and under. On the basis of the overall direction of the movement of the hand making them, these can be grouped into six categories: vertical, horizontal, diagonal, circular, alternating, and no line movement; the category 'alternating' includes wavy lines and zigzags; 'no line movement' refers to dots. These categories also include single line markings and multiple line versions: so vertical, horizontal and diagonal lines can be represented singly or multiply. The alternating lines include a 'roving' line which meanders and one which doubles back on itself, creating enclosed areas. One might surmise, though, that this is more likely to be the case when they are 'drawing' than when they are 'writing'. Fein (1993) has identified similar categories of markings, and her evidence also shows interesting individual variation within categories. So, for example, a meander (Kellogg's 'zigzag' within the 'alternating' category) can be made with either a rounded or a sharp turning point. In this case the mark remains fixed in spite of local variation, presaging systems of print: handwriting of a sort. Baghban (1984) shows evidence of this range of marks being used in the productions of her daughter between the ages of 18 and 24 months. Both Kellogg and Fein show how these marks continue to be used and to develop in complexity as children get older, and Kellogg points out that the different categories of mark evolve into the construction of both written forms and forms used for artistic expression and design.

Whilst the marks themselves do not constitute a recognizable system of written notation, nevertheless, qualities intrinsic to them can be incorporated into the structure of the 'point–plot organization' which I have described. In the example discussed previously, (Lancaster, 1999), a single type of mark, a zigzag, is used throughout the making of the card. The use of a constant category of mark means that it is its placement that is the variable factor which signifies distinctions of meaning. Variation to qualities of the mark itself has the potential to introduce a further level of distinction. An extended zigzag, going from the top to the bottom of the page, is assigned the ascription 'tree'; with its length and span, it also resembles a tree. Acknowledging the resemblance, the little girl adds 'branches' at the top; this time the zigzag is curved in an wide arch going from the 'tree' into the middle of the page, maintaining a link between representation and resemblance. The 'writing' at the bottom of the page also has a structural resemblance to that which it represents, being a linear sequence of small zigzags. These intentional and systematic variations to the graphic device itself suggests the operation of a basic morphology.

CONTINUOUS DEVELOPMENT

The evidence already discussed in this chapter suggests that children between the ages of one and two have the capacity to distinguish confidently between writing and drawing, and to recognize and produce certain features, qualities and marks, characteristic of both these modes; even well before this age, they have the capacity to recognize many of these features. One construction which has been put on the relationship between these modes is that writing evolves from drawing, both developmentally and historically. Martlew and Sorsby (1995) suggest that children's ability to draw writing provides evidence of this. However, the boundaries between writing and drawing are far from being fixed and absolute, and children move comfortably around them, using whatever is most salient and useful to interpret and communicate what is needful. In doing this, they are using not only elements which are characteristic of each mode, but also those which they have in common; and at this stage in life, they will commonly experience texts where writing and pictures operate in tandem. To draw writing is as reasonable as to write about a drawing, and would seem to demonstrate a sound understanding of the semiotic functions which are distinct to each mode, as well as those which are common to both.

A parallel can be drawn with interpretations of early writing systems, which suggest that they evolved through a highly pictographic stage to become increasingly abstract systems. However, evidence from the very earliest systems suggest that this is not the case (Schmandt-Besserat, 1978), and that graphic marking has always been used for different purposes, with drawing and writing having different representational functions, then as now. Writing developed to communicate information by graphic means (Harris, 2000; Gaur, 2000; Olson, 1994), whereas drawing developed for the purposes of aesthetic expression, even though the two modes might have drawn on similar types and methods of marking. It is likely that young children's recognition of the distinction between the modes is also based on an understanding of this fundamental difference in function. Kenner's example of a young Chinese boy who dismisses a fellow pupil's idea that an oval shape could represent a mouth in Chinese, on the basis that in Chinese you have to write, 'not draw pictures', demonstrates this point nicely. However, this still leaves open questions about development in each domain: what happens to these very early representational methods and structures which children construct and operate. Wolf and Perry claim that children's early drawing systems are frequently regarded as being simply preparatory. Luria makes a similar point with respect to early writing systems, describing them as 'primitive techniques' that are 'similar to what we call writing' and which 'served as necessary stages along the way' (1983: 237). In other words, the outcomes of all that intense semiotic exploration simply wither away. The conclusions which Wolf and Perry draw about children's early drawing systems, however, suggest a much more likely developmental path. Each of the systems which they develop and use is not so much a stage on the way to realism, as a system which continues to evolve and to remain useful; nothing is wasted. Mackey's (2003) work demonstrates a similar path for the early use of bodily modes like gesture in communicating graphic meaning, with it continuing to have a significant communicative role to play in the interpretative strategies of much older children. At the same time, new systems are acquired, as and when they are needed: what Pariser calls 'a kitbag of graphic strategies' (1999: 104).

Important parallels can again be drawn. The ways in which infants and young children set about the interpretation and production of writing suggest that, like drawing, writing is also a multiply constituted mode. By the time they are two, children have been grappling with different genres, ways of displaying and representing meanings and information, spatial organization, systems of marking, fixed and flexible representations, morphological distinctions, and the movement between the interpretation and expression of writing. Each of these constituents of early writing continues to be used and to evolve. To reduce writing to the making of correct links between letters and sounds is to misrepresent both the nature of writing and children's ways of constructing it. This is not to underestimate the significance of this feature of writing, but to make the point that it is one of many. Children discover a great many things about writing as a system before they reach the point of needing to investigate its relationship to speech. Development, in other words, is continuous. Far from this being a stage of limited semiotic activity, restricted by a lack of cognitive, social and linguistic development, it is a time when children are actively and independently interested and involved in representational matters.

REFERENCES

Baghban, M. (1984) *Our Daughter Learns to Read and Write: a Case Study from Birth to Three*. Newark, DE: International Reading Association.

Bissex, G.L. (1980) *Gnys at Wrk: a Child Learns to Read and Write*. Cambridge, MA: Harvard University Press.

Clark, M.M. (1976) *Young Fluent Readers*. London: Heinemann.

Deloache, J. and Brown, A. (1987) 'The early emergence of planning skills in children', in J. Bruner and H. Haste (eds), *Making Sense: the Child's Construction of the World*. London: Methuen. pp. 108–30.

Deloache, J., Strauss, M. and Maynard, J. (1979) 'Picture perception in infancy', *Infant Behavior and Development*, 2: 77–89.

Dissanayake, E. (1992) *Homo Aestheticus: Where Art Comes From and Why*. New York: Free.

Donaldson, M. (1978) *Children's Minds*. London: Collins.

Fein, S. (1993) *First Drawings: Genesis of Visual Thinking*. Pleasant Hill: Exelrod.

Feldman, C.F. (1987) 'Thought from language: the linguistic construction of cognitive representations', in J. Bruner and H. Haste (eds), *Making Sense: the Child's Construction of the World*. London: Methuen. pp. 131–46.

Ferreiro, E. and Teberosky, A. (1982) *Literacy before Schooling*. Portsmouth, NH: Heinemann.

Gaur, A. (2000) *Literacy and the Politics of Writing*. Bristol: Intellect.

Gelb, I.J. (1952) *The Study of Writing: the Foundations of Grammatology*. London: Routledge and Kegan Paul.

Goodman, N. (1976) *Languages of Art*. Indianapolis: Hacket.

Goodman, Y. (1986) 'Children coming to know literacy', in W. Teale and E. Sulzby (eds), *Emergent Literacy: Writing and Reading*. Norwood, NJ: Ablex. pp. 1–15.

Gregory, E. and Williams, A. (2000) *City Literacies: Learning to Read across Generations and Cultures*. London: Routledge.

Halliday, M.A.K. (1975) *Learning How To Mean: Explorations in the Development of Language*. London: Arnold.

Harris, M. and Hatano, G. (eds) (1999) *Learning to Read and Write: a Cross-Linguistic Perspective*. Cambridge: Cambridge University Press.

Harris, R. (2000) *Rethinking Writing*. London: Athlone.

Harste, J.C., Woodward, V.A. and Burke, C.L. (1984) *Language Stories and Literacy Lessons*. Portsmouth, NH: Heinemann.

Havelock, E.A. (1976) *Origins of Western Literacy*. Toronto: OISE.

Johnson, M. (1987) *The Body in the Mind: the Bodily Basis of Meaning, Imagination, and Reason*. Chicago: University of Chicago Press.

Karmiloff-Smith, A. (1992) *Beyond Modularity: a Developmental Perspective on Cognitive Science*. Cambridge, MA: MIT Press.

Kellogg, R. (1970) *Analyzing Children's Art*. Palo Alto, CA: National Press.

Kenner, C. (2002) 'Signs of difference: how children learn to write in different script systems: an ESRC-funded project'. Paper presented at Manchester Metropolitan University, 13 June.

Kress, G. (1997) *Before Writing: Rethinking the Paths to Literacy*. London: Routledge.

Kress, G. (2000) *Early Spelling: between Convention and Creativity*. London: Routledge.

Kress, G. and van Leeuwen, T. (1996) *Reading Images: the Grammar of Visual Design*. London: Routledge.

Labbo, L. (1996) 'A semiotic analysis of young children's symbol making in a classroom computer center', *Reading Research Quarterly*, 31 (4): 356–85.

Lancaster, L. (1999) 'Exploring the need to mean: a multimodal analysis of a child's use of semiotic resources in the mediation of symbolic meanings'. Unpublished PhD thesis, University of London.

Lancaster, L. (2001) 'Staring at the page: the function of gaze in a young child's interpretation of symbolic forms', *Journal of Childhood Literacy*, 1 (2): 131–52.

Luria, A. (1983) 'The development of writing in the child', in M. Martlew (ed.), *The Psychology of Written Language: Developmental and Educational Perspectives*. Chichester: Wiley.

Mackey, M. (2003) '"The most thinking book": attention, performance and the picturebook', in E. Bearne and M. Styles (eds), *Art, Narrative and Childhood*. Stoke-on-Trent: Trentham. pp. 101–13.

Martlew, M. and Sorsby, A. (1995) 'The precursors of writing: graphic representation in preschool children', *Learning and Instruction*, 5: 1–19.

Matthews, J. (1994) *Helping Children to Draw and Paint in Early Childhood: Children and Visual Representation*. London: Hodder and Stoughton.

Olson, D. (1994) *The World on Paper*. Cambridge: Cambridge University Press.

Pahl, K. (1999) *Transformations: Meaning Making in a Nursery*. London: Trentham.

Pariser, D. (1999) 'Children of Kronos: what two artists and two cultures did with their childhood art', *The Journal of Aesthetic Education*, 33 (1): 62–72.

Rowe, D. (1994) *Preschoolers as Authors: Literacy Learning in the Social World of the Classroom*. Cresskill, NJ: Hampton.

Schmandt-Besserat, D. (1978) 'The earliest precursors of writing', *Scientific American*, 238 (6): 38–47.

Starkey, P., Gelman, R. and Spelke, E.S. (1985) 'Detection of number or numerousness by human infants', *Science* 222: 179–81.

Street, B.V. (1995) *Social Literacies: Critical Approaches to Literacy in Development, Ethnography and Education*. London: Longman.

Sulzby, E. (1986) 'Writing and reading: signs of oral and written language organisation in the young child', in W. Teale and E. Sulzby (eds), *Emergent Literacy: Writing and Reading*. Norwood, NJ: Ablex. pp. 50–89.

Teale, W.H. (1986) 'Home background and young children's literacy development', in W. Teale and E. Sulzby (eds), *Emergent Literacy: Writing and Reading*. Norwood, NJ: Ablex. pp. 173–206.

Thelen, E. and Smith, L.B. (1994) *A Dynamic Systems Approach to the Development of Cognition and Action*. Cambridge, MA: MIT Press.

Tomasello, M. (1992) *First Verbs: a Case Study of Early Grammatical Development*. Cambridge: Cambridge University Press.

Torrey, J.W. (1973) 'Learning to read without a teacher: a case study', in F. Smith (ed.), *Psycholinguistics and Reading*. New York: Holt, Rinehart and Winston. pp. 147–57.

Treiber, F. and Wilcox, S. (1984) 'Discrimination of number by infants', *Infant Behavior and Development*, 7: 93–100.

Trevarthen, C. (1990) 'Growth and education in the hemispheres', in C. Trevarthen (ed.), *Brain Circuits and Functions of the Mind*. Cambridge: Cambridge University Press.

Vygotsky, L.S. (1978) *Mind in Society*. Cambridge: Harvard University Press.

Wolf, D. and Perry, M.D. (1988) 'From endpoints to repertoires: some new conclusions about drawing development', *Journal of Aesthetic Education*, 22 (1): 17–34.

13

Perspectives on Making Meaning: The Differential Principles and Means of Adults and Children

GUNTHER KRESS

Children come into the world with an absolute interest in meaning. To them, knowing what the world means is of more than academic interest. Yet even if they are born into a 'literate society', the technology of the script systems of their parents' cultures is just one part of the vast web of meanings that makes up the world they will need to understand and learn to deal with. Nor is it a particularly focal part for them; it certainly has none of the overwhelming significance that it has for many of the adults around them; it is as important or less than many other aspects of their world. It is there to be dealt with like so much else, and that is that.

This is a fundamental difference in orientation and perspective of child and adult toward the issue of meaning, and to writing and reading specifically, one that it is crucial to recognize if we, the adults, wish to facilitate the entry of the young into full use of that resource. Whether it is in an attempt to understand the paths that children take into the world of writing, or to develop pedagogies – formal or informal – around the learning of writing and reading, an understanding of the child's perspective is a *sine qua non* for the success of any attempts in that direction.

From these two perspectives the issue of (meaning and) meaning making looks different in several respects. Adults, having been 'socialized', are oriented toward convention – the frame of rules which their societies have erected to regulate social action. Children are oriented to 'truth', to that which the evidence of their senses seems to tell them is incontrovertibly the case. Convention hovers close to 'law'; what conforms to convention is 'correct', and

what does not conform is therefore to be avoided. So an orientation to convention leads to a focus on correctness, while an orientation to 'truth' leads to a focus on accuracy. As far as making meaning is concerned, adults focus on what their cultures provide and their societies have taught them to regard as the proper means for making meaning. Language as speech is one such ready-made means, and in 'literate societies', language as writing is the most valued. Children focus on that which best serves the purpose, given what is to hand for making the meaning that they wish to make.

Last but by no means least there is a deep difference in perspective on how meaning is made. The adult's focus is on the correct use of culturally ready-made resources, used in accord with convention. In that approach the means for making meaning exist already, as 'signs' which come with (clear, often strict) instructions for their use. Dictionaries and grammars enshrine the sense both of ready-made signs and of correct rules of use. Children make their means for making meaning, according to two distinct needs. On the one hand, they make signs to express – to make *real as a sign*, to *realize* – that which they wish to represent. On the other hand that which they wish to represent is governed by their *interest* at the moment of making the sign. This 'interest' works in at least two ways: to select that which is to be represented, and to select those aspects of the thing to be represented which are the focus of their interest at the moment of making the sign. Interest focuses on that which is criterial of what is represented in the moment of representation.

The sign making stuff (the signifier) is chosen so as to best represent that which is to be meant (the signified). It is chosen according to its aptness for the purpose. To choose an actual example that I have used on several occasions, if the sign is to be of 'car', and the child's interest in 'car' at that moment sees wheels as criterial, then wheels will be the signifier stuff, to be joined with the signified 'car'. Wheels themselves can be signified aptly by the 'signifier stuff' of 'circles'. Children's early meaning making is governed by the very fact that they do not use ready made signifiers: and so their meaning making is led both by that which is to hand, and by that which is apt for the purpose.

Neither the adults' nor the children's view is accidental. The adults' view is the outcome of ceaseless theoretical work over the history of their society; and the dominant theory itself is always shaped by the highest-level social and political arrangements, and reflects the ideologies which sustain such arrangements. The adults' view derives from and is buttressed by such theory, appearing in the guise of 'common sense'. The children's view is the result of their need to understand that which is everywhere yet to be understood – and what is to be understood includes the adults' views of things. It is no wonder that adults see a path ready-made that children should take 'towards' literacy; and it is no wonder that this path makes no real sense to children, for in most ways it does not match their interest that shapes how they see their world.

Yet here I need to make it clear that I am not talking about the reality of adult meaning making; I am talking about *perspectives*, not *practices*. The process of meaning making is the same for adults as it is for children: both use the means which are available and which seem most apt to make the meanings that their interests lead them to make. Both transform the means for making meaning. The difference lies in the fact that adults have already learned so much more than children have: they have learned what they should regard as the "apt means" as much as the correct ways for making meaning; and they have learned to believe that their actions do not transform the means they use in making meaning. They have learned to accept a perspective that tells them that they must operate within convention. When they do not do so, as is often the case, they nevertheless feel that there were rules that they have transgressed, rules which they should have observed. Some children, in their turn, have picked up adults' concerns with correctness, and may strive for that in their practices of making meaning.

So here, in a schematic form, is the contrast between adults' views and the practices of children:

- convention versus 'truth'
- correctness versus accuracy
- culturally made means used conventionally versus apt use of that which is to hand for the purpose
- language as writing versus whatever is to hand that is apt for the purpose.

These distinct principles exist together with a difference in approach to meaning making which can be characterized as *the use of ready-made signs in line with convention versus signs-to-be-made with interest governing both sign making and sign use.*

From these flow differing dispositions to practices. In this chapter I will focus on each of the principles in turn and draw out some consequences of the distinctive dispositions towards representation and communication of children and adults, and explore some of the implications for views on learning through the use of examples. The recognition of the differences in principle is needed as the basis on which to build new practice. There already exists a strong body of work that looks newly at children's making of meaning and at questions of learning, knowing and the making of meaning through many more means than those of language alone. I will make reference to this work where it becomes relevant, including some work that goes outside the age range envisaged in this handbook, and including some work with a strictly theoretical focus. Inevitably all this work constitutes a challenge to dominant notions of literacy, of learning as much as to theories of (making of) meaning much more widely.

At the same time, such thinking and such work is not new. Many of these insights have been developed by academics working in this field over a considerable period. What is the case is that their effect on mainstream theory has been relatively limited, and their effect on practice and application less than it might or should have been. The early work of Read (1968) stands in that line, as does some of the work of Clay later (1975); of course the insights of her work have had profound effects in practical ways, as in the project of Reading Recovery. There is also the work of Dyson (1986) and Bissex (1980). Barr's article 'Maps of play' (1988) has been highly influential in extending the boundaries of thinking about meaning making and representation in the field of literacy and learning. Of course some of the theoretical work of Vygotsky (1978), on which Barr for instance draws, as of Piaget (1990), points in this direction. However, for these two theorists, language remained in its central 'place' – even though Vygotsky had a strong interest in representations other than language. The 'truth' of convention remained more or less unchallenged.

Nodelman (1988) is laden with insight and inspiration. All this work is diverse in terms of its origin and location in disciplines – from education, psychology, linguistics, literary theory; and that, in part, may account for the fact that its impact has been less than one might have expected, given the plausibility of the accounts provided.

That is one difference with a now growing – and to some extent already considerable – body of research and writing which attempts to provide material for that rethinking, retheorizing, and reorientation, and a considerable amount of this is focused on quite young children. It takes the social semiotic theory of multimodal representation and communication as one starting point (see Hodge and Kress, 1988; Kress and van Leeuwen, 2002), even if at the moment in quite different ways. In that work speech and writing are accorded the place that they have in representational practices, and so are other modes. In what follows here, I wish to provide a theoretical framing for that work. One strand which unifies all this work – even if in different ways, with differing emphases – is its location in a semiotic framework (rather than say, a linguistic or psychological one), and an interest in exploring speech and writing in an environment seen as multimodal, one where there are many culturally shaped resources – modes – for making meaning.

THE MEANS FOR MAKING MEANING: WRITING AND SPEECH IN THE FULL ENVIRONMENT OF COMMUNICATION

The first difference in principle focuses on the means for making meaning: *language as (speech or) writing* versus *whatever is to hand that is apt for the purpose*. For the adult the resource which is, almost inevitably, in focus is language, in nearly all environments and for nearly all purposes; and language as writing is most highly valued. For the child there is, initially, no focal resource. Anything that is to hand which will 'make a mark' that is apt for the purpose will be drawn into the making of a sign: speech, of course, but other kinds and uses of sound as well, whether banging a saucepan, or using the voice in imitating some other sound; making a 'graphic' mark on a surface as in drawing, scratching, smearing food; building, making models, using blankets, boxes, bits of paper or cardboard, coat-hangers, in fact any material thing at all that turns out to be suited for the realization of the meanings to be meant. And whereas for the adult both the means for making meaning and even the meanings themselves seem to pre-exist their use in meaning making – a sense in which everything we do or say is a cliché – for the child the (potentials for) meanings are in principle unbounded.

This immediately leads to a difference in how the resources and their use are seen. Adults simply 'know' that there are rules of use (even if they would not be able to articulate them); while for most of the materials that children press into service to make their meanings there are no rules; and if there were, children either would not know them, or would not necessarily observe them if they did. However, at this point we already have the question of 'orientation'. Children are very attentive to what the potentials of the materials are for making the meanings that they want to make. Lack of knowledge of convention or absence of rules is replaced by and substituted for by acute observation. There are no rules that say what a cardboard box of a certain size might be made to mean. However the acutely observant and evaluating eye and hand of the child can determine that it can become a boat, or a room, or a car: its qualities as container give it a potential for meaning which is open to use in transformations of various kinds. The adult's reliance on convention is replaced by an acutely analytic assessment of the meaning potentials of the material object. The analytic assessment is founded on principles of meaning (making) of a rigorous kind – a seriousness of 'reading' of the object for its sign making potential.

Two things emerge from that: to the adult there appears to be a fixed set of resources, with convention to guide their use in action; for the child there is no limitation – other than what is to hand – and aptness for purpose guides use.

Let me then take as an example the notion of 'car'. I say "notion" because as will become clear in a moment, there is no stable 'concept' or meaning of 'car'. The car that I had described just above was the car as represented by a three-year-old. Its focus and meaning was 'car-as-wheels'. We might notice that this graphically realized car has no lexical equivalent in either speech or writing. If we wanted to represent it in either one, we would be forced into a quite lengthy description: it is not a car-with-wheels, but a car-as-wheels. Speech or writing, as much as drawing, have, in that respect as in others, different 'affordances': you can do certain things with the graphic mode of image that you cannot do (so easily) with the written, and vice versa. But the interest of the sign maker shifts, both from occasion to occasion and through age. Age, in the case of children, is often described by the term *development*, though it might be better to see it as the process whereby they increasingly work themselves into the meanings of their social group – as socialization.

The car in Figure 13.1 was made by the child who made the 'circles car', some three years later. This car is the representation of a very different meaning: the extremely sleek, aerodynamic arrow shape speaks of speed and power; the high level of sheen is achieved by intense pressure in thickly applying the crayon; the red colour has a small black trimming; all these express a specific interest and a specific meaning of 'car', one that is a long way from the 'wheels-car' of three years earlier. The meanings are difficult to reproduce in the mode of writing: it is quite simply the case that they are meanings best expressed in this graphic mode (or graphic modes, if we take colour to be a mode). The car has been cut out with great precision from the sheet of paper on which it had been drawn, so that it is no longer a *representation on a page*, it is now *an object in the world*. As such it can participate in actions *in* the world in ways that words cannot. But the fact that we cannot easily provide a gloss on the meaning in speech or in writing is not to say that the meaning is vague, ambiguous or imprecise; far from it. The problem is no other than that of providing an image representation of a spoken or written text.

It is clear that precise meanings are being made, with apt means, the means that are to hand. The lexical item, the word 'car', is imprecise by comparison; it applies in meaning to both these cars and yet covers the meaning of neither. Words, it turns out, are quite vague, maybe too vague – unless heavily modified – to convey the meanings that are here wanted to be conveyed. A third car is different yet again. Figure 13.2 shows a further example of 'car'. It differs in meaning yet again: power is very much in focus, but this time it is power in the service of violence: the violence of the powerful engine spewing flames, of the wheels kicking up dirt and gravel, producing sparks and flames on the road; as well as the violence of the weaponry attached to the car, and of the rocket just fired. Here the agent in control of all the power is shown, so that we have a more complex sign 'the power that the driver of this car has at his command'. This drawing has also been cut out: but this time it is not so much the car as object in the world, but as the picture of a car which can be transported away from the page. The cutting-out is far less careful, and clearly the aim has not been to produce an object in the world: no effort is expended on the object as such, it is a drawing of a car in motion, not the production of an object. As a drawing it can be moved, it has become transportable, not as object in the world but rather as 'image of the object'.

Again we might reflect on the task of representing this cut-out drawing in words, and realize that

Figure 13.1 Arrow car

Figure 13.2 Rocket car

what would result would be an entirely different representation: it would either be a description of this image; or it would be a re-presentation of this image, where what is here shown as a *display* would become a representation of events and actions related by words in sequence, a simple *narrative*. That is, it would be a representation in which time and sequence would dominate: 'There is a car, travelling at great speed along a road, the driver has just fired a rocket, its engines are belching flames and smoke, etc.'

The translation, whichever one we chose, would not be the original, of course. It would be different: it would not be more accurate, more precise, more clear. It would be different; and it would not do what the original does. This is important to realize: the graphic representation is precise; it is complex in its meanings; it is neither ambiguous nor vague. It is meaning made with apt and available means. It is ontologically different to the written or spoken representation that might have stood in its place.

I will discuss another car, also made by this child at this time. It is three-dimensional, made from lego blocks. This looks like a car which – more even than the last – has been influenced by a number of models: above all both super-fast speedboats and space vehicles. But in this it shows us the flexibility and the openness of the potentials for making meaning which exist outside of the conventionally given means. Three-dimensionality makes new demands and also opens up new possibilities for meaning. It demands symmetry, for instance, in a way that was not the case with the graphic representations. An unbalanced three-dimensional 'car' would not function; it would lean over or topple, apart from its aesthetically displeasing shape.

In all these examples we are touching on the issue of meaning to be made and on the meaning potentials of the means for making meaning. What is clear is that 'word' is quite limited compared to the means employed here. What is also clear is that these representations are complex: they belong to and draw on the cultural world of their makers; they display very clear principles of meaning; and they function very differently to words, whether in speech or in writing. Above all, in each instance the representations realize the varying interests of their makers, and do so by using means aptly, so that the signifier stuff in its arrangement realizes the meanings that were meant to be meant. The signs are not, at any point and in any way, arbitrary conjunctions of form and meaning.

WHAT THE CULTURE PROVIDES, AND WHAT IS TO HAND

In the examples just discussed, the ready-made means that culture provides are words in speech or in writing – the word 'car' as well as words to modify it, 'a *sleek red* car', 'a *fast heavily armoured* car', and so on. The child maker of the meaning 'car' made his own means of making meaning, graphic means, and in the case of the three-dimensional model, Lego blocks. The use of the Lego blocks is the use of culturally made means, though whether they are used conventionally in this case is in question. In the case of the drawn cars there is no doubt that these are means made by the child. The issue of *culturally made means used conventionally* versus *apt use of that which is to hand for the purpose* is a difficult one in the case of children. On the one hand, culture makes many ready-made means for them – 'toys', by and large, of various kinds. The set of objects that provides the child with the means to assemble a farmyard with animals, machinery, buildings, fences, is a resource for making meanings. And quite clearly the resource comes as a set of signs with rules for their use attached. I am talking here not of any 'instructions' that might come with the box, but rather of the inbuilt structure that says that the roof goes on the house; that the fences surround the garden and the fields; that the machinery is stored in the barn; and so on.

On the other hand, however, children are notoriously eager to go beyond and against the set of signs and the rules coded with them, and they extend both the inventory of object signs, and with equal facility the rules that regulate the larger structures that are made. In so far as they do so, they transform the ready-made signs into quite new signs, and create quite new rules which may have little affinity with the rules as they were. So nearly any toy at all can be brought into the farmyard structure, for instance. As with all other signs that they make, the relevant point for them is 'aptness' for purpose, and their interest which determines what is to be criterial. If a female doll is, by adult judgement, far too large to fit into the arrangement, the fact that there might have been a need for a farmer's wife easily overrules the now irrelevant matter of size. The doll is what is to hand; it is female and a female figure is what is needed, so this criterial feature becomes the basis for the making of the new sign. The principles of sign making persist, and are not threatened.

What emerges from examples such as these is that in all cases, the notion of the *culturally made means used conventionally* is not or is barely tenable. Even the signs that seem to be there ready-made are treated as material from which to make new signs. Children's semiotic actions, that is, their work in making meaning, are always transformative of the materials used.

Nevertheless, the use of ready-made materials brings some constraints – perhaps less for children than for adults or older children – deriving from the histories of prior use of the material, which both endows the materials with the meanings of past action, and in doing so constrains the extent of transformations for present use. Yet the childish gaze falls on many materials which do not bear such constraining meanings, but where we can nevertheless clearly see the principle of the *apt use of that which is to hand for the purpose* of making meaning.

Take my next example, Figure 13.3. The helmet is made from the very strong shiny cardboard box which had contained barbecue briquets. It has some holes cut into it, to allow the wearer to peer out, and has the bottom knocked out, so that it will fit over the wearer's head. What is important here – as in other meaning making – is that purpose and intent, *interest,* precede the making of the sign. There is an intent to make a helmet, because a helmet is needed for a game involving fighting with swords; the child's interest lights on the solidity and sheen of the material. The material that is to hand becomes the signifier for the signified 'helmet', and so the sign *helmet* is made. It is important to be aware of the steps involved in the making of this sign here, because what might appear as fairly random action is actually the result of a complex process of design. What is produced is not just one sign, but the complex set of signs of a game and all its essential elements. The game itself is designed, as are its individual elements. The material to serve as the signifier stuff for the sign 'helmet' is selected for its aptness in relation both to that one sign, this object sign, and to the function of the larger design made here.

With the notion of design we have moved a considerable distance from randomness in the selection of the apt signifier material: design implies intent in relation to specific imagined features and tasks of the meaning to be made, whether that meaning is expressed as the complex sign of a verbal text, or the complex sign of the objects and relations of a game. The application of meaning making principles is the same, though the materials, the means for making meaning, are not linguistic.

In design, as in all sign making, the process of transformation is crucial. Some existent material is selected as the means for realizing a meaning, and in its fusion with the meaning to be expressed, the material in its potential to mean changes, a new sign is produced; and the semiotic resources have been transformed.

Figure 13.3   Helmet

THE 'TRUTH' OF CONVENTION AND THE 'TRUTH' OF THINGS EXPERIENCED

As adults we know that 'truth' is a semiotic construct; children take a different view. Social truths derive from the exertion of power sustained over time, and individuals meet that truth in the guise of 'convention'. Children do not initially have access to this 'truth', and are instead reliant on the evidence of their senses to tell them the 'truth' about the world. 'Spelling', to move the discussion a bit closer to language and literacy, is a very good case in point. Spelling is 'knowing how to write words correctly'; it is very much the 'truth' of convention. We need not detain ourselves long on arguing this issue. In my examples here I refer to spelling in standard (British) English; other languages have different 'truths'. Instead of the argument, I wish to look briefly at the spellings of a child, where the 'truth' is what the senses perceive, and what his attempt at interpretation tells him as the sense of the world that is spelled (Figure 13.4).

Let me focus on two aspects of this example in turn. Take first 'spelling', this time as transcription of sounds into letters. We notice that James spells *their* as *there*, *little* as *littel*, and *nothing* as *nofing*; he also spells *can't* as *con't*, though in this case instead of *spelling* incorrectly, he might just have been 'miswriting' the letter *a* as an *o*. In the case of *nofing*, however, the *f* is definitely what he will hear in his (north) London dialect. And there is nothing at all that would make plausible for him the *th* letter sequence as a means of transcribing what he hears as an *f*. In the case of *littel*, speakers of his dialect insert the 'weak' vowel 'schwa' between the two consonants in these contexts, rather than treating the *l* as a semi-vowel. The spelling of *there* is an instance where he is unaware of the 'truth' of convention, which separates two lexical items which are identical in the sound of speech by a difference in orthography. Another six-year-old from the same dialect area spells *breathe* as *brev*, following the same 'truth' as James, and she spells *under* as *uda*, because in this dialect the *n* before the voiced dental plosive has just about disappeared by nasalizing the preceding vowel. For both children this is the 'truth' of the evidence of their ears: and both, as do all children who have no hearing difficulties, transcribe the sounds of the speech they hear with razor-sharp accuracy; they are acute analysts of the sounds of speech.

But there are other 'truths' as well: and most strikingly these are the 'truths' of meanings that are made here. The phrase 'frog's spawn' is obviously not known to James, but that does not mean that he does not need to know its 'truth'. In this case he is asked to perform a semantic 'transcription' rather than the phonetic one just exemplified. He takes the route that seems most promising: 'this topic is about the life-cycle of frogs', he seems to say to himself, 'so clearly this phrase is about frogs (being) born'. This too is the 'truth' of evidence – not the evidence of his ears, but the evidence of his rigorous logic. The six-year-old girl (from a different school in north London) who wrote *brev* faced the same problem as James, though she took a different route to the 'truth' of this phrase. She wrote *I have learnt that tadpole come out of frog's sporn*. This is a 'truth' which is in part phonological (and therefore conventional): she knows that in English

word-initial consonant clusters such as *sp* (as in *sporn*) are permitted, but that *sb* is not (a problem that James did not have to deal with, as in his 'spelling' he had separated the *s* and the *b* in frog*s born*. And in part it is a 'truth' which is syntactic: English has many noun phrases such as *X's Y*: – 'my mum's bag', 'the dog's collar', – and this is the 'truth' that leads to her transcription and spelling. It is the 'truth' of the syntax of her language that she knows already: a paradoxical solution from the point of view of the adult, the 'truth' of convention utilized to tell the 'truth' of experience.

In these cases here the 'truth' of experience is modified somewhat: the act of perception is never neutral, it is always an act which transforms that which is perceived, apprehended, transformed in the light of existing knowledge. In the case of these six-year-olds, perception is already shaped by considerable cultural knowing, though the principle of 'truth to experience' remains. But these examples also 'belong' to the same principles of meaning making that I discussed in relation to the 'car' examples: a bit of the world around the child is drawn into the designs of the child, whether in articulation (the signs made outwardly) or in interpretation (the signs made inwardly). There is no difference in the principles of meaning making: a bit of the world around the child is focused on and becomes the material which serves to make a new sign in conjunction with that which is to be meant – here a 'syntactic truth' and a 'semantic truth'.

The principles of meaning making, of the construction of signs, are shared by all these examples, whether in speech, writing, or three-dimensional making. This is the reason I think that we cannot hope to understand children's meaning making if we focus on language alone, the mode in which convention rules most strongly as far as common sense and reality both are concerned. Of course, the same principles of sign making apply to language as apply elsewhere; most of the time, however, they are somewhat harder to trace. In the last example that I wish to discuss here I want to bring together the two principles as yet not directly discussed: *correctness* versus *accuracy*; and *the use of ready-made signs in line with convention* versus *signs-to-be-made with interest governing both sign making and sign use*. In fact both have been implicitly there in all of the previous discussion, but here I want to focus on them explicitly.

Take my last example, Figure 13.5. The written text, in 'translation', is

Flowers
I pick the flowers
From my garden I turn around
And stop to see the

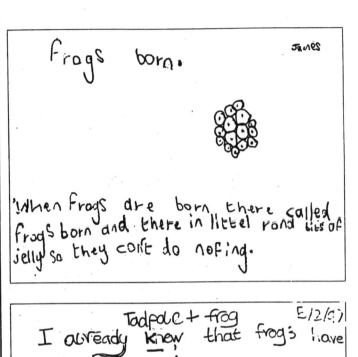

Figure 13.4 Frogs born

Yellow rose I go to pick one
A thorn gets stuck in my finger

Appearances seemingly to the contrary, I want to say that this child poet is oriented toward the "truth" of experience, attempting to transcribe as fully as she can that which she wishes to realize. For a start, being a poem, aesthetic principles – transcribing and realizing beauty – are first: from the beautifully handwritten and displayed graphic aspects of the poem, to the attempt at a 'heightened' diction achieved through the graphic representation of phonic means. The sounds which are suggested here are not simply the sounds of language in the ordinary mode, but the sounds of a heightened diction. The lengthening is suggested in the spelling of *flawase*, to be pronounced slowly; and similarly with *pike*, where the final *e* is meant to produce a

Figure 13.5   Flawase

lengthening of the medial vowel (as she will have been told by her teacher with words like *care, sore, nine,* and so on). The *i* sound in *gadin,* not lengthened here by a word-final *e,* but 'raised' to a clear *i* sound rather than the lower, lax sound of the weak vowel 'schwa', as in the usual pronunciation of 'garden' with the final 'schwa'. In the *areawd* the child strives to ensure that the reader who reads this aloud is forced into great deliberateness and care in the pronunciation of the word. All these – to give just some of the instances here – are attempts to produce and transcribe (or to produce in transcription) all the marks of 'poetic diction'. It is the 'truth' of accuracy to poetic form which is striven for here.

The visual image elements – in the original they are in colour – parallel the verbal signs: from the intense neon-yellow of the rose, to the (only slightly heightened) dense spacing of the thorns on this rose, and the beautifully drawn petals of the rose;

the precision of the drawing of the injured finger, and the flowers in the vase. All these speak of the same register, the aesthetic. Correctness is absolutely not the issue here; accuracy in terms of the (here aesthetic) interest of the sign maker is. And even though ready-made signs are available for use, the child poetess makes the signs that correspond to her interest. Clearly the *signs-to-be-made* are made *with the interest of the sign maker governing both sign making and sign use*.

We might ask at this point, 'What sets this off from adult sign making?' My response would be: on the one hand, the *general* processes of sign making are the same for both; on the other hand the adult would never stray from convention in the way child has done. But above all, and linked to all this, the child focuses in a deeply different way on 'that which is to be transcribed'. For the adult 'that which is to be transcribed' has already become shaped by convention, in this case by syntax and orthography; it would not include the aesthetic concerns of the child *in the way they are represented/transcribed here*. We know of course that poets use alliteration as a meaning making device; but it is a device that stays within the bounds of convention.

For the child and for the adult that which is perceived differ profoundly, so the child's and the adult's senses of what is to be recorded and transcribed differ. As well as that, the forms of transcription used by the child differ entirely from those which convention provides, and which adults would use.

THE CONTEST OF PRINCIPLES AND MEANS: A NEED FOR A THEORETICAL RE-ORIENTATION

In 'moving into' the technologies of representation and recording of their cultures, children are faced with a dual task. As my last example has shown, they must 'reduce' that which they wish to transcribe, and in order to do that they must in effect change their criteria of seeing and valuation. If their society says that the aesthetic dimension is not important, is irrelevant, or is not wanted, or is wanted only in rare moments, or is possible only for selected individuals, and is in any case only ever to be handled in specific ways, then that is what children will have to learn. They must learn to represent through and with the means that their society says to them are the appropriate means for representing. That means forgoing the use of the many means that they have used for making meaning, and it means forgoing the adherence to the principle of aptness for purpose – at least ostensibly.

Of course all sign making, adult as much as child, is founded on the principle of aptness of the material/formal means for realization of the immaterial/conceptual means. But at the moment, that cannot be acknowledged. Children must therefore abjure the theory of meaning which they have held implicitly and acted on explicitly in all their meaning making, and exchange it for the implausible theory that adults subscribe to. They have to learn to give up public confession of one kind of 'truth' and learn the public confession of another, the 'truth' of convention. They have to give up adherence to accuracy, and learn to live with correctness. That of course is a slow and difficult path; it is the path that schooling still lays out for them.

In the meantime the theories held by the adults – whether the adults in the school or those who have power elsewhere – have ceased to be serviceable. The truth of convention – that is, knowledge as the product of social power – was serviceable in the Western nation-states of the nineteenth century and of the early part of the twentieth. It produced allegiance to authority, and reduced both the scope and the desire for individual variation and (to some extent) the reality of that as well. In the information-based and consumption-led societies of the early part of this century, this theory is no longer serviceable. Its lack of fit with the social world now is everywhere visible to those who will take a moment to look. At the moment there is a lack of registration between the two; children bear the brunt of that, and society the cost.

As I have said, the principles of meaning making are the same for adult and students; what differs is the theory which provides the explanatory framework, and all that flows from that difference. There is no or at best a very poor 'registration' between the two. The theoretical and then practical task now is to bring the principles in line with the theory.

RETHINKING REPRESENTATION, MEANING AND LEARNING

As I indicated at the beginning, there is now a growing – and to some extent already considerable – body of research and writing which attempts to provide material for that rethinking, retheorizing, and reorientation, and a considerable amount of this is focused on the quite young. It takes the social semiotic theory of multimodal representation as a starting point, even if at the moment in quite different ways. In that work speech and writing are accorded their place in the multimodal representational environment characteristic of the present period; but so are other modes. Kress (1996; 2000), Kenner (2000; 2003), Pahl (1999), Moss (2001; 2003), Kress and Jewitt (2003), as well as a special edition of the journal *Reading: Literacy and Language* (Bearne and Kress, 2001), all attest to the many and varied modes which appear in children's making of meaning. In Lancaster (2003) a multimodal approach is used to describe both communication/representation and 'attention' in the joint 'reading' of a picturebook by a father and his two-year-old daughter. The work of Mavers (2003) applies multimodal social semiotic theory to the work of children in primary schools. The implications of multimodal ways of thinking and describing have had a particular effect in the work of South African educators (Stein, 2003) for whom the rich variety of cultures present in that new nation, with their differing orientations to and valuations of representation, present a particular theoretical and pedagogical problem.

The implications of the approach sketched here are far-reaching. They affect still largely dominant conceptions of language: as central, whether as writing or as speech; as a full means of representation and communication; and as definitive of human rationality. In the approach sketched here it can be seen that rationality resides in all making of meaning, as do affect and emotion. It becomes apparent that writing or speech are never 'full' means for representation, they are always partial; and so the question arises in what ways *all* modes, speech and writing no less than image, or gesture, or body movement, or three-dimensional objects, are partial, what their potentials are and their limitations. But in asking that question, we are shifting our conception of meaning making decisively in the direction of the real – yet never unconstrained – agency of every maker of signs. Making meaning is now seen, from a social/political perspective, as a question of rhetoric: 'What are the best means to represent that which I wish to communicate here, now, for this audience?'. And from a semiotic point of view it is seen as a question of design: 'What are the means that I have available to me, and how do I deploy them in the most apt fashion to realize the design that I have here, arising out of my interest in this environment?' These are requirements that go beyond 'competence', and they incorporate the aims of 'critique'; for now I need to have full awareness of the potentials of the resources I use in relation to that with which I wish make my representation as a successful message in this social environment.

The aim of 'competence in use' related to an era of stability; its goal was to ensure continued stability. The aim of 'critique' related to an era of the challenge of stable systems, and its goal was to 'bring into crisis' that which was no longer seen as adequate, just, equitable. We are no longer in a period of stability, and stable systems are difficult to spot. We are in an era of radical instability, so that new aims are essential: the fostering of a disposition in which I feel capable of shaping my designs, in environments which I understand, with resources whose potentials, limitations, and relations to my audience now I fully understand. The new goal is to allow me to act meaningfully in an unstable environment. This requires a disposition to the making of meaning which goes entirely beyond 'competence', and incorporates its aims and those of 'critique' in a constantly innovative and transformative response to the communicational demands of my environment.

Such a conception places the maker of meaning at the centre, aware of the cultural and social shape of the resources for representing, aware of the social shape of the environments of communication and of its constraints, and yet meaningfully agentive and always innovative. That might serve as the basis of new theories of learning, as much as of representation and communication.

REFERENCES

Barr, M. (1988) 'Maps of play', in M. Meek and C. Mills (eds), *Language and Literacy in the Primary School*. Lewes: Falmer.

Bearne, E. and Kress, G.R. (eds) (2000) *Reading: Literacy and Language*, 35 (3).

Bissex, G.L. (1980) *Gnys at Work: a Child Learns to Write and Read*. Cambridge, MA: Harvard University Press.

Clay, M. (1975) *What Did I Write? Beginning Writing Behaviour*. London: Heinemann.

Dyson, A.H. (1986) 'The imaginary worlds of childhood: a multimedia presentation', *Language Arts*, 63 (8): 799–808.

Hodge, R.I.V. and Kress, G.R. (1988) *Social Semiotics*. Cambridge: Polity.

Kenner, C. (2000) *Homepages*. Stoke-on-Trent: Trentham.

Kenner, C. (2003) 'Embodied knowledges: young children's engagement with the act of writing', in G.R. Kress and C. Jewitt (eds), *Multimodal Literacy*. New York: Lang.

Kress, G.R. (1996) *Before Writing: Rethinking the Paths to Literacy*. London: Routledge.

Kress, G.R. (2000) *Early Spelling: between Convention and Creativity*. London: Routledge.

Kress, G.R. and Jewitt, C. (eds) (2003) *Multimodal Literacy*. New York: Lang.

Kress, G.R. and van Leeuwen, T. (2001) *Multimodal Discourse: the Modes and Media of Contemporary Communication*. London: Arnold.

Lancaster, L. (2003) 'Beginning at the beginning: how a young child constructs time multimodally', in G.R. Kress and C. Jewitt (eds), *Multimodal Literacy*. New York: Lang.

Mavers, D. (2003) 'Communicating meanings through image: composition, spatial arrangement and links in student mind maps', in G.R. Kress and C. Jewitt (eds), *Multimodal Literacy*. New York: Lang.

Moss, G. (2001) 'To work or play: junior age non-fiction as objects of design', *Reading Literacy and Language,* 35 (3): 106–10.

Moss, G. (2003) 'Putting the text back into practice: junior-age non-fiction as objects of design', in G.R. Kress and C. Jewitt (eds), *Multimodal Literacy*. New York: Lang.

Nodelman, P. (1988) *Words about Pictures: the Narrative Art of Children's Picture Books.* London: University of Georgia Press.

Pahl, K. (1999) *Transformations: Meaning Making in a Nursery* School. Stoke-on-Trent: Trentham.

Piaget, J. (1990) *The Child's Conception of the World*. London. Rowman and Littlefield.

Read, C. (1986) *Children's Creative Spelling*. London: Routledge and Kegan Paul.

Stein, P. (2003) 'The Olifantsvlei fresh stories project: multimodality, creativity and fixing in the semiotic chain', in G.R. Kress and C. Jewitt (eds), *Multimodal Literacy*. New York: Lang.

Vygotsky, L.S. (1978) *Mind in Society: the Development of Higher Psychological Processes*. Cambridge, MA: Harvard University Press.

14

Brain Activity, Genetics and Learning to Read

GERALD COLES

What is the relationship between brain functioning, genetics, and learning to read – and should reading educators care? Do reading educators really need to know about what's going on in the brain and in DNA when devising effective reading instruction and helping students learn to read? Knowledge about these connections might be interesting, but isn't it enough to focus on the children's visible reading activity and outcomes when making decisions about instruction and its implementation? Or, addressing a more immediate question, why is this chapter in a handbook on literacy?

In recent years claims have insisted that if reading teachers are to be effective, they *must* know about the brain and genetics. As the editor of the newsletter of The Center for Education Reform stated, 'Teachers are rarely if ever taught about how reading gets accommodated in the brain. And of course without that knowledge, we'll never be a nation of readers, and the nearly 40 percent of children who are mainly disadvantaged will never reverse that label' (2001: 1).

The need to know about the brain and genetics is also asserted on the website of the International Dyslexia Association (2002). Answering the question, 'How do people get dyslexia?', the Association states, 'The causes for dyslexia are neurobiological and genetic. Research shows that individuals inherit the genetic links for dyslexia. One of your grandparents, parents, aunts or uncles is dyslexic, and chances are that one or more of your children will be dyslexic.'

A press release from the Office of Public Information of the University of Florida summarized for the nation's media the findings of campus researchers: 'Brain structure may play a role in children's ability to learn to read' (Ramey, 1998). And the Child Development Institute (1997) told readers of its 'award winning' website that '10 Years of Brain Imaging Research Shows The Brain Reads Sound By Sound'. More specifically, it stated the instructional implications of the research: 'The new brain research shows why intensive phonics is also the best way for everyone to learn to read.' Buttressing these kinds of claims is a stream of media headlines. *The New York Times* (1999) informed readers that 'Scientists Find the First Gene for Dyslexia'. *The Times* reported, 'Changes in Brain a Clue to Dyslexia'. An implication of these claims was summarized in the *Education Week* headline, 'Demands Grow to Link Neuroscience with Education' (Jacobson, 2000).

These 'demands' have, in fact, already been transformed into reading policy that has mandated particular kinds of classroom instruction and excluded others (Coles, 2000; 2003). Consequently, reading educators, to the extent that they understand this research, would be better able to make informed judgements about the research linked to these demands and policy – which should be supported or opposed. The purpose of this chapter is to contribute to that understanding.

BRAIN ACTIVITY AND BEGINNING READING SKILLS

A discussion of the research on brain activity, genetics, and learning to read must begin with the observation that most of this work has been guided by *a priori* assumptions about how children *should* be taught to read. Foremost among these has been the judgement that beginning readers will learn best if they first master the basic skill of making sound–symbol relationships, then continue in a 'building block' sequence to erect skill upon skill, eventually gaining competence in the skill of comprehending text (National Institute for Literacy, 2001). The opposite has also been assumed: if beginning readers do not first master basic skills, they will be at risk of becoming reading disabled. Phonological awareness (distinguishing and manipulating sounds in words) is considered to be the first building block within the sequence, as well as the core deficit in reading disabilities – an assumption, according to reading researchers such as Sally Shaywitz, consistent 'with what neuroscientists know about brain organization and function' (1996: 99).

Much recent research on brain malfunctioning and reading acquisition aimed at demonstrating this primary belief has been funded by the Child Development and Behavior Branch of the National Institutes of Child Health and Human Development (NICHD), whose viewpoint was expressed in a paper reporting an NICHD-funded study co-authored by Reid Lyon, chief of the branch. The relationship between 'brain activation patterns' and tasks of 'sounding out words', Lyon and his co-authors concluded, 'provided neurobiologic evidence of an underlying disruption in the neural systems for reading in children with dyslexia and indicate that it is evident at a young age' (Shaywitz et al., 2002: 101). Findings like these have, according to Lyon, contributed to his anticipating a time in the foreseeable future when scientists will 'confidently' be able to 'design a classroom curriculum based completely on neuroscience' (Hotz, 1998: 1).

The following section reviews representative studies associated with this interpretation of brain functioning and reading success. Although much of the research reviewed in this chapter used adults rather than children as subjects, the researchers of and commentators on this work have assumed that the findings are directly applicable to classroom reading instruction. In order to give the reader an adequate sense of the quality of the research and because of space limitations, I will offer in-depth discussions of key, representative studies, rather than brief summaries of many studies.

A 'brain glitch'

Studying 29 'dyslexic' readers (14 men and 15 women, ages 16–54 years), in an NICHD-supported investigation, Sally Shaywitz and her colleagues (1998) used functional magnetic resonance imagery (MRI), a technology that provides information about the structure and function of the brain, while the subjects engaged in a sequence of reading and reading-related tasks. Whether or not the adults actually met criteria for being 'dyslexic' cannot be determined because, except for their IQ score range, we are told nothing else about them. For the sake of the primary focus of my appraisal, however, I will accept this categorization.

The study used a sequence of five tasks, beginning with one that required no ability with written language (asking subjects to decide whether or not lines matched: \\V versus \V\).

The second task asked subjects to match patterns of upper- and lower-case letters (bbBb versus bbBb). This required letter, but not phonological, knowledge.

The third task asked the subjects if letters rhymed ('Do T and V rhyme?'). This added 'a phonological processing demand' requiring knowing and comparing the sounds of the letters.

The fourth task asked the subjects if non-words rhymed ('Do leat and bete rhyme?'). This task required 'analysis of more complex structures'.

The fifth and last task required that the subjects know complex sound–symbol relationships and the meaning of words ('Are corn and rice in the same category?'), requiring both phonological and semantic knowledge and processing.

Clearly, this study is not simply about the brain and reading, but is linked to skills-emphasis theory and pedagogy, of which phonological awareness is the centrepiece. That is, using this viewpoint, the researchers contrived a study around their conception of what is causal in beginning reading, namely, phonological awareness. In addition, to assume that this study enables one to draw conclusions about 'reading' begs the question because the attenuated reading-related tasks that were used, while providing activities for potentially useful functional MRI information about language, cannot be thought to represent 'reading'. At best, they pertain to delimited skills. Alternative definitions of 'reading' certainly would have led to the creation of very different 'reading' tasks – perhaps even one in which the subjects actually 'read' sentences! (For other definitions see, for example, Ruddell et al., 1994.) The study was also infused with an assumption that a neuropsychological deficit (or, as Shaywitz has described it, 'a brain glitch') can cause reading problems in otherwise normal children (Kolata, 1998). When we look at the results, we see how the researchers' presumptions influenced interpretation of the data.

Shaywitz and her colleagues found group differences in brain patterns while the subjects were engaged in the various tasks. The good readers showed 'a systematic increase in activation' in the brain areas studied, when going from the second (matching letter patterns) to the fourth task (determining if non-words rhyme). That is, there was an increase in brain activation as the tasks increased demands for applying phonological awareness abilities. In contrast, the dyslexics showed a fairly steady level of brain activation, rather than an increase, in response to these tasks. Generally speaking, the brain activation for these tasks was higher for the good readers than for the dyslexics, although one area of the brain showed the reverse pattern.

Examining the activation in the brain hemispheres, the researchers found that for good readers the activation was greater in the left, and for dyslexics it was greater in the right. This pattern held across all tasks.

Shaywitz and her colleagues concluded that 'for dyslexic readers, these brain activation patterns provide evidence of an imperfectly functioning system for segmenting words into their phonological constituents'. This malfunctioning was 'evident' to the researchers when they asked the dyslexics to respond to increasing demands on phonological analysis. The dyslexic readers demonstrated 'a functional disruption' in the rear area of the brain in which visual and sound identification and associations are made during reading. These findings, according to the researchers, added 'neurological support' to evidence obtained through studies at the behavioural and cognitive levels that pointed 'to the critical role of phonological analysis and its impairment in dyslexia' (1998: 2640).

The problem with these interpretations is that functional MRI data themselves do not carry an imprint of their meaning, that is, they do not point to a cause of the specific brain activation. The specific activation linked to responses generated by the five tasks tells us nothing about the *processes* that *produced* the activation. The specific activation facts would actually make possible various reasonable explanations, and given the limited data in this study, they would all have equal legitimacy.

For example, the study disregarded problem solving approaches, learning experiences, personal meanings, emotions, motivation, and confidence, to name but a few potential influences that could have affected the group outcomes. Studies have shown that during tasks of this kind, altering any one of these background and processing factors could result in altered patterns of brain functioning (Coles, 1987). Furthermore, since there were ability differences between the groups, why would anyone assume that the brain activity for the two groups would be the same when doing these tasks?

Czechlexia?

Another NICHD-funded study, led by Bennett Shaywitz, with Sally Shaywitz and Reid Lyon among the co-authors, also used the functional MRI to identify brain areas that were active when good and poor readers did non-word and real word tasks. Normal readers showed more activation in the back of their brain, while the dyslexic group showed more activation in the front and side regions.

Continuing to be guided by the assumption that 'converging evidence indicates a functional disruption in the neural systems for reading in adults with dyslexia' (Shaywitz et al., 2002: 101), an NIH–NICHD (2002) press release stated, 'Children who are poor readers appear to have a disruption in the part of their brain involved in reading phonetically.'

The study does not provide the means for supporting these conclusions, however, because it is only one more investigation containing methodological confusion of correlation and causation. That is, as was true for the NICHD-supported study just discussed, the fact that there is a difference in the brain activation between good and poor readers does not mean that the brain activation is the *cause* of the respective reading abilities. Rather, we know only that the activation is correlated with reading ability. Consider the following experiment. If two groups of normal people were asked to read a Czechoslovakian text, and if only one group could read Czechoslovakian, who would expect the brain activation of the two groups to be the same? And who would think that differences in brain activity revealed dysfunctions (Czechlexia), not differences? This failure to distinguish between correlation and causation fosters the single-minded interpretation of the data represented by this and similar studies. We do know from the study that the brain activity of good and poor readers differs when they do reading tasks, but that is all we know. Certainly nothing can be concluded about the cause of the reading problems or the best way to teach reading.

Learning and brain changes

A study that sheds light on the question of causation is one Leonide Goldstein and I did on differences in brain hemisphere activation in adult beginning readers as they were learning to read (Coles and Goldstein, 1985). We found that these adults did, indeed, have greater right hemisphere activation initially, when they were poor readers or non-readers, but as their reading improved the activation of their hemispheres also changed toward the greater left activation pattern common to good readers. We interpreted these data as evidence that new knowledge and competencies were linked to concomitant changes in brain structure and functioning. More generally, these brain changes associated with written language acquisition were representative of the kinds of changes that would occur through all kinds of learning. There was nothing in the data to suggest that these beginning readers started learning to read with anything but normal brains that were initially configured as they were because the students had not learned to read; no data suggested that the educational intervention somehow repaired or circumvented dysfunctional brain areas.

Unfortunately, in later studies using educational intervention that produced similar findings, the researchers concluded that the brain changes were evidence that a neurological dysfunction had caused the reading problems. Under the subtitle 'New evidence on neurobiological causes', Reid Lyon and Jack Fletcher (2001) described a study in which 60 hours of intensive educational intervention produced brain changes in the left brain hemisphere. Before intervention, MRI analysis revealed unactivated portions of the left hemisphere – 'the standard activity pattern of children with reading disabilities' noted Lyon and Fletcher. After intervention, they said, 'brain activation patterns shifted to the normative profile seen in nonimpaired readers'. The authors concluded that although environmental factors can influence brain organization and activity, the results were part of 'a sizable body of evidence' that indicates 'poor readers exhibit disruption primarily, but not exclusively, in the neural circuitry of the brain's left hemisphere, the part that serves language'. Why they drew these conclusions is not apparent because they offered no evidence to demonstrate that the minimal activity in the circuitry that serves language was caused by a 'disruption' rather than by merely the absence of knowledge and skills that the educational intervention later provided.

In another educational intervention study with a comparable outcome, a similar interpretation was offered: the brain changes produced through educational intervention demonstrated faulty brain wiring in poor readers and the possibility of rewiring. 'We now know that people with reading problems are using the wrong hardware in their brains, and if we can get them to switch to the right hardware, we might be able to improve their reading' said NICHD-supported principal investigator Andrew Papanicolaou (Suriano, 2002). Again, there was no evidence that these readers began learning with the 'wrong hardware'. Of course it is true that the brain areas were rewired, but there was no evidence that this rewiring was different in any way from the rewiring that goes on throughout our learning lives.

Regrettably, although the functional MRI is a potentially valuable technology for literacy studies, it is rendered worthless when used with flawed theories, methods, and data interpretations. In making this criticism, I do not want to lose sight of the potential value this technology can provide for understanding the complex phenomenon of learning to read and for addressing questions such as, 'Will alternative teaching approaches configure brain activity in alternative ways?' Clearly, the reading field could benefit from objective studies that employ good teaching and use a developmental method that appraises brain activity as reading ability evolves in the reading acquisition process.

GENETICS AND READING

Explanations of genetic causes of reading problems parallel much of the brain research. In a House of Representatives Committee on Education and the Workforce hearing, for example, Reid Lyon (1997) stated, 'our NICHD studies have taught us that the phonological differences we see in good and poor readers have a genetic basis'. In another overview of 'major findings' from NICHD research programmes, Lyon declared, 'There is strong evidence for a genetic basis for reading disabilities, with deficits in phonological awareness reflecting the greatest degree of heritability' (1996: 65).

A 'correction'

One example of this 'strong evidence' was an NICHD-financed study published in the prestigious journal *Science* (Cardon et al., 1994). Lon Cardon and his colleagues reported locating a gene for reading disability on chromosome 6, a finding that appeared especially compelling because the gene was shared to a much greater extent – an extraordinary extent – by subjects with 'extreme deficits in reading performance' than by a group of poor readers with serious but relatively fewer problems. Similarly, the families of the subjects with 'extreme deficits' were found to have the gene more frequently than the families of poor readers with fewer problems. In other words, the worse the reading deficit, the greater the evidence of a relationship to a gene on chromosome 6.

The results were even more striking when the researchers grouped the twins who had 'more extreme deficits' in reading and found that their genetic sharing on a portion of chromosome 6 soared to an astronomical 0.00001! In contrast, the same analysis for siblings with 'more extreme deficits in reading' found a correlation just short of significance (0.066). In short, Cardon and his colleagues presented what they regarded as considerable evidence suggesting a 'broad heritability' of reading disability.

Although these findings certainly seemed to provide exceptionally strong evidence, seven months after the article appeared, the researchers wrote a letter to *Science* offering a 'correction' of the previously reported results (Cardon et al., 1995). 'Reanalyses of the twin data revealed that four identical twin pairs had been inadvertently included in the [fraternal pair] sample.' This, it turned out, accounted for the highly statistically significant correlations. How this mistake occurred was not explained, but one can reasonably wonder how researchers with precision enough for mapping chromosomes and for performing intricate statistical analyses could have missed recognizing the inclusion of four pairs of identical twins.

When the four pairs of identical twins were removed from the fraternal twin group, the researchers' correction letter explained, the extraordinarily high statistical results reported in the original paper essentially disappeared. Overall, the 'correction' letter repudiated the researchers' original conclusions: 'In order to confirm evidence for a possible [linkage] for reading disability on chromosome 6', the researchers conceded, 'analyses of data from additional twin pairs will be required' (1995: 1553). A later study by these researchers, using over 100 pairs of twins categorized by degrees of severity of reading problems, failed to salvage the initial claims (DeFries et al., 1997). Remarkably, current reviews of the genetics of reading disability continue to cite the findings of the original study and completely omit the reanalysis in the 'correction' letter or later failures by the same group of researchers (Olson and Gayan, 2001).

The decline in statistical significance that resulted from the removal of only four of 50 twin pairs in the original study demonstrates how the weight of only a small number of heavily loaded scores can dramatically shift correlations, and cautions against placing strong confidence in a single group of subjects in this kind of genetics research. This is no small matter because the evaporation of the evidence was exactly what happened in the earlier research on chromosome 15. At first there were 'breakthrough' findings linking the gene to 'dyslexia', but added subjects, researchers later found, reduced the level of statistical significance. Furthermore, one investigator, using a different group of subjects, failed to duplicate the original research. Eventually, the researchers of the original 'breakthrough' study on this chromosome repudiated their own initial 'findings' (Coles, 1987; 1998).

Reading disability genes in families

Another study that looked for a reading disability gene on chromosome 6 examined six families of adults who had had serious reading problems as children (Grigorenko et al., 1997). The families were divided according to five measures or phenotypes: (1) phonological awareness, (2) phonological decoding, (3) single-word reading, (4) rapid naming automaticity, and (5) a discrepancy score between IQ and reading score.

The investigators reported that an association with chromosome 6 varied for each phenotype, with phonological awareness having the highest association and single-word reading the least. Presumably, this was a striking piece of evidence for the phonological awareness explanation of reading success and failure.

To assess these findings we need to look closely at the results by themselves and in relationship to previous studies on genetics and reading, particularly the ones just discussed. Key outcomes of such an assessment are these:

- The statistical significance for a portion of chromosome 6 found in the first twin group study reported by Cardon et al. (1994) was not found in this research.
- For another portion of chromosome 6, this study found a strong correlation for the phonological awareness phenotype, but the correlation was largely due to the strong contribution by one family, which made up for the lack of any such correlation for phonological awareness in two families at this or any other portion of chromosome 6. If there is a powerful association between reading and chromosome 6, why did one-third of the six families show no consequential association at all?
- The investigators of this study claimed that their results for 'chromosome 6 are consistent with the results' of the previous research (Cardon et al., 1994) I have discussed. There is, however, little overlap of significant findings for any of the regions explored on chromosome 6. In fact, in contrast to the researchers' assertions, comparing the two results demonstrates that this is not a replication study!

Other questions may be raised about this family study with respect to the now familiar theory of reading disabilities that underpins it and to the actual reading abilities of the subjects. The investigators acknowledged that because 'a number of individuals with a phonological awareness deficit – including all affected cases in the largest family

(26 members) – exhibit normal single-word scores, it follows that this hypothetical gene on chromosome 6 is not itself sufficient for the full syndrome of dyslexia' (Grigorenko et al., 1997: 35). In other words, although the individuals scored poorly on tests of phonological awareness, their scores on word reading tests were those of normal readers. This discrepancy between purported cause and effect can be stated even more strongly: what is the actual impact of the supposedly genetically generated phonological awareness deficit if these adults, who had been classified as 'reading disabled' in childhood, did not in adulthood have single-word reading problems? The word recognition score is, of course, inadequate for a satisfactory picture of the reading abilities of these 'affected cases', but the researchers provided no other reading profile information. Presumably, the word reading results indicated that the subjects could read sufficiently well, therefore making unapparent a clear link between phonological deficits and actual reading.

The question of whether a phonological awareness gene contributes to the creation of reading problems is further complicated by the fact, as the researchers themselves acknowledge, that it is phonological decoding skills, not phonological awareness, that has been identified as a 'central, disproportionate deficit in dyslexia' (1997: 29). What, therefore, do the phenotype results in this research mean, if they do not jibe with the decisive skills the researchers believed were associated with reading achievement?

When the researchers added two families to their subject pool (Grigorenko et al., 2000), they only duplicated the previous results and inconsistencies contained in the report of the six families. The phonological phenotype continued not to play the causal role that the researchers initially expected. No other phenotype stood out as having a determinant connection to poor reading. Furthermore, the outcome of this kind of investigation, the researchers acknowledged, was dependent upon the very analytical method of identifying an area of a gene and, of course, upon how frequently a 'phenotype of interest' appears 'in a given sample' – an explanation apparently meant to explain why the phenotype the researchers expected to find was not found (2000: 721).

Findings in additional studies that, on the surface, appeared to support claims about a dyslexic gene on chromosome 6, were questionable because of inconsistencies over whether the word-identification phenotype was associated with chromosome 6 or 15; inconsistencies over the association between word identification and phonological phenotypes with reading problems; and contradictory conclusions about effect sizes and purported gene actions

(Fisher et al., 1999; Gayan et al., 1999). In addition, the results of these studies were not replicated by researchers who reported finding an 'absence of linkage of phonological coding dyslexia to chromosome 6' (Field and Kaplan, 1998). Finally, all of these studies suffer from a complete lack of exploration of (1) the precise nature of the reading problems that were conveniently clumped together as 'dyslexia' in order to categorize the subjects for the studies, and (2) alternative experiential explanations, such as family and school influences, that could explain the subjects' reading problems.

As is true for the brain function studies, sophisticated genetics techniques cannot compensate for the flawed theories, methods, and data interpretations. Are there genes that determine the effectiveness of portions of the brain that process sound–symbol relationships and are root causes of reading success or failure? To answer this question, or to answer any question about genes and reading, and brain functioning and reading, research must be based on accurate models of brain functioning. In the next sections, I will discuss these models.

HOW THE BRAIN WORKS: MODULES?

An understanding of the relationship between brain functioning, genes and reading acquisition requires examining the extent to which the premises of the research accord with current findings in neuroscience. A chief premise holds that the brain has specific modules for specialized operations that work in sequence and in coordination with other modules in learning written language. As we have seen in the research discussed above, one or more modules that process basic sound–symbol skills are believed to be fundamental in the hierarchy and organization of modular brain activities that underpin learning to read. That is, unless these fundamental modules first process written sounds and symbols, other brain modules involved in learning to read will not be able to function adequately.

Explanations of reading acquisition based on a modular model rely heavily on an assumption that the fundamental modules – those that process written sounds and symbols – must first be activated and stocked because a beginning reader has limited working memory that restricts the amount of attention that can be allocated to various aspects of written language. If, for instance, a beginning reader has to give equal attention to sound–symbol correspondence of words *and* to the meaning of what he or she is reading, working memory would be overloaded. To avoid this, the focus of beginning reading instruction must be consistently narrow, aiming the student's learning on sound–symbol skills (Adams, 2001).

However, the basic assumptions of brain modules and working memory that underpin this view of the mental requirements in beginning reading are rejected by many neuroscience researchers. Merlin Donald, for example, a psychologist who has written extensively on human consciousness, argues that conclusions about limited working memory come primarily from laboratory studies that have used a brief time frame methodology in which 'short-term memory, visual imagery, perceptual illusions and the allocation of attention, must be crammed' (2001: 47). Because of 'this built-in, albeit unintended, bias, such experiments look only at the lower limits of conscious experience' (2001: 47). In real-life activities, Donald stresses, 'the width and depth of working memory in such situations are much larger than those suggested by traditional laboratory techniques' (2001: 50). Consequently, these laboratory models 'have very limited real-world generality' (2001: 52). He argues that the memory system is composed of both short-term and 'intermediate-term awarenesss' that constantly update working memory. Hence, there is much more that working memory can address, incorporate, and apply in these more elaborate mechanisms. If this is so, then even if the modular view of reading acquisition were correct, the beginning reader would have no cognitive need to focus almost exclusively on modules assumed to be foundational in the sequenced organization of modular activity.

With respect to the theory that there are modules that do 'specialized operation', such as deciphering language (2001: 3), Donald argues that the columnar unit within the 'now-mythical Broca's region, once believed to be the language region of the dominant hemisphere' (2001: 101) is only one among several hundred thousand in the brain that are interconnected, 'woven into various brain-wide networks by millions of long communication fibers' (2001: 101). In other words, learning written language – as learning all else – involves an extensive network (a polyphony) of brain areas activated and communicating simultaneously and interactively. It is *not* a predetermined network.

Donald notes that 'many researchers trained in the sixties', including himself, 'sought to discover the neurological "magic module" that might explain human language and symbolic thought', a tradition that extends 'back to the early heroes of the Great Module Hunt' such as Wernicke and Broca. The results of that search, Donald concludes, 'were largely negative' because there is no modular 'table of elements' that make humans more unique than chimpanzees in some 'modular redesign of the nervous system' (2001: 111).

Furthermore, Donald criticizes the 'isolated mind' bias in cognitive science that treats the 'cognitive system' as though it were a 'self-contained entity or monad' – an isolated organ with the modules in place to acquire written language (2001: 150). Instead, although the brain has fundamental mechanisms for beginning to learn written language, it is learning and experience that shape the brain's circuits and how they are used in learning to read. The brain 'has no fixed pattern of connectivity to start'. There are basic mechanisms that are innate, but the brain's 'connectivity pattern is set by experience' with 'countless interconnection points, or synapses, which connect neurons to one another in various patterns' (2001: 103).

The view of a 'connectivity pattern' that emerges and is activated as children learn to read contrasts with the model of step-by-step progression from module to module. If the former is an accurate model of brain organization and functioning, it suggests that the connectivity pattern should be the focus of research because only by looking at the overall pattern can researchers begin to determine the functioning and interrelationships of any part, and the causal, consequential, or interactive function of that part within the entire pattern.

From the perspective of a connectivity pattern model, not only do the brain areas involved in grasping the sound–symbol correspondence not have to be primed first before other areas of the pattern can become effectively operable, but the functioning of these areas depends on connections within the entire pattern. And because the pattern is not innately fixed, if instruction were to stimulate certain areas more than others, a particular connectivity pattern would emerge. That specific pattern, however, might not necessarily be the sole one required for reading success or the one superior over other connectivity patterns. Moreover, if conceptions of limited working memory are incorrect, a more complex connectivity pattern could be created through richer written language learning.

Linguist Philip Lieberman (2000) too has criticized modular explanations, calling them 'neophrenological theories', that is, theories that 'map complex behaviors to localized regions of the brain, on the assumption that a particular part of the brain regulates an aspect of behavior' (2000: 3). In these theories, the functional organization of the brain is run by 'a set of petty bureaucrats each of which controls a behavior' (2000: 2). Like Donald, he proposes that:

> converging behavioral and neurobiological data indicate that human language is regulated by a distributed network that includes subcortical structures, the traditional cortical 'language' areas (Broca's and Wernicke's

areas), and regions of the neocortex associated with 'nonlinguistic' aspects of cognition. (2000: 2)

Complex processes 'are regulated by neural networks formed by circuits linking populations of neurons in neuroanatomical structures that may be distributed throughout the brain', not by a hierarchical system (2000: 4). Lieberman stresses:

> although specific operations may be performed in particular parts of the brain, these operations must be integrated into a *network* that regulates an observable aspect of behavior. And so, a particular aspect of behavior usually involves activity in neuroanatomical structures distributed throughout the brain. (2000: 4, emphasis in original)

Such a view of functioning that is distributed, not localized, undercuts a fundamental premise upon which the research on brain activity and reading acquisition is grounded. Pertinent to explanations of genetic bases of reading and reading disabilities is Lieberman's (1998) judgement that there is no genetic 'blueprint' for learning functional language or aspects of it, such as phonological awareness. The 'details of syntax, speech, and the words of the languages that a person knows' are not learned by specific genes for these details, but 'appear to be learned by means of the associative processes that enable us to learn other complex aspects of behavior' (1998: 132).

Putting this another way, there are neural systems that include language-related portions of the brain, but learning written language is not determined solely by the functioning of these specific parts or by the genes for these specific parts. Learning language, spoken and written, is based on the inferential aspects of our thinking that are part of a larger neural network that includes functions and systems used for other kinds of thinking. No one gene determines phonological awareness or word recognition because there is not that kind of specificity for the details of language. It is a larger thinking system that orchestrates language learning.

'COGNITION' AND READING: THE ABSENCE OF EMOTIONS

The assumption that 'cognition' actually describes the brain processes associated with reading also needs to be examined. Skills-emphasis/' building-block' brain research has assumed that 'cognition' – that is, the process of images, concepts, and mental operations – is an independent reality, not a construct, and in doing so has ignored ever-growing evidence suggesting that thinking is an inseparable interaction of both cognition *and* emotion (feelings, desires, enthusiasms, antipathies etc.), not cognition alone.

Neurologist Antonio Damasio (1994), for example, rejects the traditional distinction between cognition, thought to be neocortical, and emotions, thought to be subcortical. There are no 'higher' and 'lower' brain centres, he argues: the neocortex – the 'high level' part of the brain – does not handle reason, while the subcortex – the 'low level' part of the brain – handles emotions (1994: xiii). Rather, he maintains, the neural substrates for cognitive responses are associated with neural substrates for emotions: both so-called 'high' and 'low' levels are integrated in thinking processes. His work supports conceptualizing cognition and emotions, to use the metaphor of paediatric researcher Michael Lewis, as a 'continuous and interwoven fugue' (Lewis et al., 1984: 264) that is operative in every facet of learning to read.

The work of neural scientist Joseph E. LeDoux (1996), which has identified brain pathways that carry sensory signals to sites of emotion and of cognition, also reveals the error of focusing solely on 'cognition' in studies on brain activity and reading acquisition. LeDoux has found that the thalamus, an area that relays sensory information, conveys sensory stimuli to the amygdala (a site of basic emotional memory) *and* to the cortex, where 'cognition' occurs. From the cortex the stimuli go on to the hippocampus, a site involved in memory and linked to the amygdala. This interconnection of pathways means that an emotional response can, in terms of pathway activity, precede a cognitive perception and response, and that emotions and cognition are integrated and interactive. Consequently, reading researchers who focus only on cognition when studying the brain are ignoring the areas of networks whose emotional activation are part of 'cognition'. Faulty or insufficient activity identified in a portion of the brain of someone doing a reading task might be a consequence of an emotional response, in that emotional memories can exert a powerful influence on 'thought processes'. What these connections are remains for future research to determine, but there is no question that research on brain activity and reading that fails to account for the fugue of cognition and emotion is severely insufficient research.

INSTRUCTION AND THINKING

Although most reading research does not delve into brain activity, some of it can offer insights into how thinking is organized in relation to learning to read, especially if the investigation explores the question,

'Does the particular way in which "reading" is defined and taught shape the kind of readers students become?' If different reading approaches result in different kinds of thinking among students who become competent readers, according to conventional definitions of reading success, this outcome would contradict the modular view of reading acquisition. That is, one could conclude that thinking related to reading acquisition is organized through learning, but does not have to be organized in one way only in order for someone to learn to read. On the other hand, if youngsters successfully learn to read with different approaches, but their thinking is organized the same way, that would suggest that the modular view is correct. A study by reading researcher Penny Freppon (1991) provides some insights into these issues.

Freppon compared reading outcomes for first-grade children taught with either skills-based or literature-based/whole-language instruction and found that the test results were similar for both groups. But her study went beyond these outcomes by looking closely at the way in which the children processed written language while reading and at the conceptions of reading they held. She found that even though the literature-based/whole-language instruction did not explicitly teach skills, the children in both forms of instruction 'were knowledgeable about the importance of decoding' and 'successfully used' it in reading (1991: 159). There was no evidence that whole-language instruction diminished children's sense of the value of this aspect of reading.

Freppon's finding accords with Lieberman's view: as children learn to read they problem solve, and by doing so attain increased ability to understand causal and reciprocal relationships. As part of this problem solving, they grasp that a key problem to be solved in learning to read is the mastery of connections between graphemes and phonemes.

The similar group knowledge of decoding did not mean that each group used the strategy the same way – that there is an invariable mental organization necessary for learning to read. The skills-emphasis group used decoding as a primary strategy, while the whole-language group used it to a lesser degree because that group employed a greater variety of strategies, such as rereading, using context, and skipping words. An unexpected finding was that even though the whole-language children 'attempted to sound out words less often' when they did attempt it, they 'achieved a higher success rate of correctly sounding out words'. Their rate was 53% compared to 32% for the skills-emphasis children (1991: 139).

These findings suggest that a particular reading approach is likely to produce particular kinds of thought processes. Presumably, the neural networks created in learning to read included the necessary activation of a subnetwork facilitating learning of sound–symbol skills, but this subnetwork, as part of the larger one, was not any more foundational than other subnetworks that were used for learning to read. The implicit definition of 'reading' in whole-language instruction made decoding 'a' key, not 'the' key, in orchestrating the thought processes. For the skills group, the grapheme–phoneme task loomed larger both as a strategy and as the meaning of 'reading' and was more 'the' key than 'a' key. In the skills classroom, reading for meaning was included but it was 'incidental' to word skills instruction (1991: 144).

In the literature-based instruction, decoding skills were focused on as needed but more of the students' attention was drawn to meaning, with the teacher encouraging the children to think about what was going on in the story. Interviews with the children found that the literature-based group expressed greater 'understandings of the use of multiple strategies in reading' and 'associated reading with language' (whether something makes sense or sounds like a sentence), whereas the skills-emphasis group 'expressed understanding of sounding out as a primary reading strategy' and 'associated reading with getting words correct' (1991: 152). Almost all of the children in the literature group 'said that understanding the story or both understanding and getting words right is more important in reading'. In contrast, only half the children in the skills group chose these explanations; nearly all of the remaining half chose 'getting words right as most important' (1991: 153).

Asked about the 'characteristics of good readers', the skills group emphasized 'knowing and learning words and sounding out words'. In contrast, the literature-based group discussed characteristics such as 'reading a lot' and 'understanding the story'. The skills group included 'paying attention to the teacher' and 'knowing their place in the book', characteristics that were not mentioned by the literature group (1991: 152).

These findings also put in serious doubt the assumption that children have a limited working memory requiring that they focus on only one kind of beginning reading strategy. It would appear that children can orchestrate successfully several strategies in working memory while not diminishing their ability to identify words and comprehend stories.

The Freppon study suggests an extremely important conclusion: instruction itself contributes to the construction of the thinking process to a considerable degree, and different instruction produces different thinking processes. And it also suggests that the assumptions about mental organization and activity that underpin most of the research on brain activity and learning are erroneous.

CONCLUSION

Philip Lieberman offers a caveat worth emphasizing in appraising contemporary research and conclusions about brain activity, genetics, and reading acquisition: 'We must remember that we stand on the threshold of an understanding of how brains really work. The greatest danger perhaps rests in making claims that are not supported by data or that inherently cannot be subjected to rigorous tests' (1998: 132). Unfortunately, not only have reading researchers who have undertaken this work seldom been guided by such a caveat, but they have tended to misconstrue the data and draw conclusions that serve to justify unwarranted beliefs and instructional policy that have driven the research in the first place.

The review in this chapter also suggests that there are fundamental theoretical problems in the assumptions about modular brain organization and 'cognition' that guide the research. Given these problems, the research does not allow us to conclude that a modular organization of the brain requires one form of instruction, that a dysfunction in a skills module creates reading disability, or that cognition, independently of affect, can explain reading acquisition. Genetics research thus far adds nothing to our understanding of reading outcomes both because of the faulty data of the studies and the highly questionable premise that there are genes that can cause dysfunctional modules.

Deficiencies like these do not mean that brain research cannot contribute to our understanding of reading acquisition. Continued understanding of whether brain functioning is organized as neural networks or as sequential modules can provide a sounder basis for appraising the logic of instructional approaches and for devising sound instruction. More specifically, such knowledge can help evaluate arguments that give special weight to particular aspects of beginning reading instruction. Understanding how emotions are involved in neural networks can help teachers appraise the degree and contributions of affect in classroom literacy instruction. With greater understanding of the brain we can also better determine the interaction between children's personal knowledge and their literacy learning, and thereby better grasp and devise an interplay between the two. Finally, greater understanding of the relationship between brain functioning and reading acquisition can help promote ecological approaches that are grounded in an understanding of the unified interrelationships of brain, active child, and learning

environment, and that eschew instructional views that are 'brain based' or that conceive of the brain as an extraneous 'black box.'

REFERENCES

Adams, M.J. (2001) 'Alphabetic anxiety and explicit, systematic phonics instruction: a cognitive science perspective', in S.B. Neuman and D.K. Dickinson (eds), *Handbook of Early Literacy Research*. New York: Guilford. pp. 66–80.

Cardon, L.R., Smith, S.D., Fulker, D.W., Kimberling, W.J., Pennington, B.F. and DeFries, J.C. (1994) 'Quantitative trait locus for reading disability on chromosome 6', *Science*, 266: 276–9.

Cardon, L.R., Smith, S.D., Fulker, D.W., Kimberling, W.J., Pennington, B.F. and DeFries, J.C. (1995) 'Quantitative trait locus for reading disability: correction', *Science*, 268: 1553.

Center for Education Reform (2001) 'Reading, 'riting and common sense', *Monthly Letter*, no. 72: 1.

Child Development Institute (1997) '10 years of brain imaging research shows the brain reads sound by sound', www.aboutdyslexia.com.

Coles, G. (1987) *The Learning Mystique: a Critical Look at 'learning disabilities'*. New York: Pantheon.

Coles, G. (1998) *Reading Lessons: the Debate Over Literacy*. New York: Hill and Wang.

Coles, G. (2000) *Misreading Reading: the Bad Science that Hurts Children*. Portsmouth, NH: Heinemann.

Coles, G. (2003) *Reading the Naked Truth: Literacy, Legislation and Lies*. Portsmouth, NH: Heinemann.

Coles, G. and Goldstein, L. (1985) 'Hemispheric EEG activation and literacy development', *International Journal of Clinical Neuropsychology*, 7: 3–7.

Damasio, A.R. (1994) *Descartes' Error: Emotion, Reason, and the Human Brain*. New York: Putnam's Sons.

DeFries, J.C., Filipek, P.A., Fulker, D.W., Olson, R.K., Pennington, B.F., Smith, S.D. and Wise, B.W. (1997) 'Colorado Learning Disabilities Research Center', *Learning Disabilities*, 8: 7–19.

Donald, M. (2001) *A Mind So Rare: the Evolution of Human Consciousness*. New York: Norton.

Field, L.L. and Kaplan, B.J. (1998) 'Absence of linkage of phonological coding dyslexia to chromosome 6p23–p21.3 in a large family data set', *American Journal of Human Genetics*, 63: 1448–56.

Fisher, S.E., Marlow, A.J., Lamb, J., Maestrini, E., Williams, D.F., Richardson, A.J., Weeks, D.E., Stein, J.F. and Monaco, A.P. (1999) 'A quantitative-trait locus on chromosome 6p influences different aspects of developmental dyslexia', *American Journal of Human Genetics*, 64: 146–56.

Freppon, P. (1991) 'Children's concepts of the nature and purpose of reading in different instructional settings', *Journal of Reading Behavior*, 23: 139–63.

Gayan, J., Smith, S.D., Cherny, S.S., Cardon, L.R., Fulker, D.W., Brower, A.M., Olson, R.K., Pennington, B.F. and DeFries, J.C. (1999) 'Quantitative-trait locus for specific language and reading deficits on chromosome 6p', *American Journal of Human Genetics*, 64: 157–64.

Grigorenko, E.L., Wood, F.B., Meyer, M.S., Hart, L.A., Speed, W.C. and Shuster, A. (1997) 'Susceptibility loci for chromosomes 6 and 15', *American Journal of Human Genetics*, 60: 27–39.

Grigorenko, E.L., Wood, F.B., Meyer, M.S. and Pauls, D.L. (2000) 'Chromosome 6p influences on different dyslexia-related cognitive processes: further confirmation', *American Journal of Human Genetics*, 66: 715–23.

Hotz, R.L. (1998) 'In art of language, the brain matters', *Los Angeles Times*, 18 October: 1.

International Dyslexia Association (2002) 'About dyslexia', www.interdys.org.

Jacobson, L. (2000) 'Demand grows to link neuroscience with education', *Education Week*, 22 March: 5.

Kolata, G. (1998) 'Scientists track the process of reading through the brain', *New York Times*, 3 March: F3.

LeDoux, J. (1996) *The Emotional Brain: the Mysterious Underpinnings of Emotional life*. New York: Simon and Schuster.

Lewis, M., Sullivan, M.W. and Michalson, L. (1984) 'The cognitive-emotional figure', in Carroll E. Izard, Jerome Kagan and Robert B. Zajonc (eds), *Emotions, Cognition, and Behavior*. New York: Cambridge University Press. pp. 264–88.

Lieberman, P. (1998) *Eve Spoke: Human Language and Human Evolution*. New York: Norton.

Lieberman, P. (2000) *Human Language and Our Reptilian Brain: the Subcortical Bases of Speech, Syntax, and Thought*. Cambridge, MA: Harvard University Press.

Lyon, G.R. (1996) 'Learning disabilities', *The Future of Children*, 6: 54–76.

Lyon, G.R. (1997) 'Testimony of G. Reid Lyon on children's literacy'. Committee on Education and the Workforce, US House of Representatives. Washington, D.C.

Lyon, G.R. and Fletcher, J.M. (2001) *Early Warning System*. Stanford, CA: Hoover Institution. www.education next.org.

National Institute for Literacy (2001) *Put Reading First: the Research Building Blocks for Teaching Children to Read*. Washington, DC: National Institute for Literacy.

NIH–NICHD Press Release (2002) 'Children's reading disability attributed to brain impairment', 2 August, http://www.nih.gov/news/pr.

Olson, R.K. and Gayan, J. (2001) 'Brains, genes and environment in reading development', in S.B. Neuman and D.K. Dickinson (eds), *Handbook of Early Literacy Research* New York: Guilford Press. pp. 81–94.

Ramey, P.E. (1998) 'Brain structure may play role in children's ability to learn to read'. University of Florida Health Science Center, Office of Public Information. 4 November, www.vpha.ufl.edu.

Ruddell, R.B., Ruddell, M.R. and Singer, H. (eds) (1994) *Theoretical Models and Processes of Reading* 4th edn. Newark, DE: International Reading Association.

Shaywitz, B.A., Shaywitz, S.E., Pugh, K.R., Mencl, W.E., Fulbright, R.K., Skudlarski, P., Constable, R.T., Marchione, K.E., Fletcher, J.M., Lyon, G.R. and Gore, J.C. (2002) 'Disruption of posterior brain systems for reading in children with developmental dyslexia', *Biological Psychiatry*, 52: 101–10.

Shaywitz, S.E. (1996) 'Dyslexia', *Scientific American*, November: 98–104.

Shaywitz, S.E., Shaywitz, B.A., Pugh, K.R., Fulbright, R.K., Constable, R.T., Mencl, W.E., Shankweiler, P., Liberman, A.M., Skudlarski, P., Fletcher, J.M., Katz, L., Marchione, K.E., Lacadie, C., Gatenby, C. and Gore, J.C. (1998) 'Functional disruption in the organization of the brain for reading in dyslexia', *Proceedings of the National Academy of Sciences*, 95: 2636–41.

Suriano, R. (2002) 'Brain studies may lead to reading revolution', *Orlando Sentinel*, 15 December, www. orlandosentinel.com/news/education.

The New York Times (1999) 'Scientists find the first gene for dyslexia', 7 September: 2.

The Times (2001) 'Changes in brain a clue to dyslexia', 17 February: 11.

15

Becoming Biliterate

CHARMIAN KENNER AND EVE GREGORY

More children in the world are bilingual than monolingual, and more children are being educated bilingually or in a second language than only in their mother tongue, according to Tucker (1996). This may seem an unusual statistic from the point of view of Anglo-centric countries, where mainstream schooling tends to be monolingual in English and bilingualism is perceived as outside the norm, but children in many other countries are indeed learning to read and write in more than one language and often in more than one script. Datta (2000) describes how in India, for example, children in every region learn three languages in school. These include a regional or local language such as Bengali in Calcutta, and Hindi as the national language, as well as English. Each of these is written in a different script, and Datta herself had become literate in all three languages simultaneously via home tuition from her mother before entering school at age seven (Datta, 2000: 3).

Thus it clearly is possible for very young children to become multiliterate, and in many settings internationally this is seen as a normal part of literacy development. This chapter will focus on minority-language children whose development is taking place in majority-language contexts, since young learners in these situations face particular challenges. In England, North America and Australasia, for example, where English is seen as the dominant world language, there is relatively little support for children to develop a minority-language literacy such as Bengali or Spanish. However, families and communities persist in their efforts to accomplish this goal, and evidence for the cognitive and cultural advantages of bilingualism and biliteracy suggests that mainstream education should broaden in these directions (see Gregory and Kenner, in this volume).

We will begin by looking at the ways in which young children may encounter writing in different languages through literacy practices at home and in their communities. We will then discuss the processes involved in becoming biliterate, looking particularly at how children transfer cultural and linguistic knowledge between their literacies. Finally, the chapter will consider research on promoting biliteracy in mainstream classroom contexts.

EARLY ENCOUNTERS WITH BILITERACY

It is only recently that researchers have begun to investigate young children's participation in literacy events in bilingual homes, and to reflect on the implications for early learning. In this section we outline several aspects arising from this research: children's understanding of the purposes of writing and reading, the varying nature of multiliterate experience, and children's awareness of different scripts.

Purposes for reading and writing

The propensity for young children to take note of family literacy events is recorded by Minns (1990), who researched the literacy lives of four-year-olds growing up in the English Midlands. The parents of Gurdeep, for example, commented that even when he was a baby 'you'd be reading or writing and he'd be out there sitting in that corner and quickly he would pick it up' (1990: 7). He would be the first to want to open birthday cards and wedding invitations, which would be read out to him, and would try to copy his parents when he saw them writing in Panjabi and English.

Children in Kenner's (2000a) study of a multilingual nursery in South London showed a similar desire to participate as readers and writers, as shown in the following example:

> Danny, a four-year-old who had recently arrived with his mother from Ecuador, attended the primary school nursery class where he was beginning to learn to read in English. Meanwhile, Danny was engaged in a variety of Spanish-based literacy activities at home.
>
> When his mother wrote letters to Ecuador in Spanish, Danny would sit beside her and dictate what he wanted her to include. At the same time, he would rapidly cover pages with emergent writing to make his own letter.
>
> Another important source of literacy knowledge for Danny was the Bible. He and his mother read the Bible together in Spanish regularly and Danny would open the book himself to read again, saying for example 'Papá Dios nos da las flores' ('Our Father God gives us the flowers').
>
> Danny's uncle had given him a storybook called *El Rey León* (based on the Disney film *The Lion King*), with an accompanying audiotape. Danny derived considerable enjoyment from simultaneously listening to the tape and looking at the book. He entered into the spirit of the story, enunciating the words with resonance, and knew when to turn the page. He could also perform the song from the tape, strumming along on an imaginary guitar. (discussed in Kenner, 2000a: 13–14)

Thus even before attending the more formal lessons provided at community language schools, children are likely to be involved in writing and reading in their immediate environment. Bilingual family literacy practices tend to be based around key social purposes, as identified by ethnographic researchers Martin-Jones and Bhatt (1998) in their work on the experience of Gujarati-speaking families in the English Midlands. For these families, the main reasons for using Gujarati literacy included:

- keeping in touch with relatives living abroad
- maintaining links with the wider community in Britain
- religious observance
- supporting cultural interests.

From the description of Danny's home activities in Spanish, we can see that he is involved from an early age with writing to family abroad and with religious literacy. Cultural interests are also a significant reason for wanting to read, although with this particular text Danny is being introduced to the global media-associated culture of Disney rather than the more traditional literary heritage of Ecuador.

The varying nature of multiliterate experience

Purposes for writing and reading in bilingual families involve both continuity and change. Some communities, such as the mainland Chinese families described by An (2000), are expecting to return to their home country after a few years' stay abroad, and parents concentrate on maintaining children's literacy in their home language, with fairly intensive home teaching taking place from the age of six or so. In other cases, parents and grandparents will be maintaining religious or other cultural practices as discussed above, but the family's intention to stay in a new country will also give rise to further literacy needs. Most of the thirty Pakistani-origin families with children aged two, three or four interviewed by Hirst (1998) in an English inner-city area wanted their children to become competent in four languages: English for everyday life and education, Urdu to write to relatives, Panjabi (spoken) to use with the family, and Arabic to participate in the Muslim religion. Hirst documented the print-rich environments of the children growing up in these families, who were from a range of socio-economic backgrounds. Twenty-seven of the 30 children were said to be given opportunities to share books and stories at home, and more than half of the children owned between four and 12 books. The children participated in many family literacy events, from writing greetings cards to religious worship. Often books were in English and greetings cards, for example, were written in English as well as Urdu.

Delgado-Gaitan (1990; 1996) found similar concerns amongst Latino-American parents in the United States, who wanted to give their children access to literacy in both Spanish and English. In settings where parents feel unconfident about their knowledge in English, researchers have found that older siblings take on the role of teacher, particularly in helping younger children to learn to read (Rashid and Gregory, 1997; Volk, 1999; Blackledge, 2000). With an awareness of literacy practices from both mainstream and community schools, siblings are well placed to combine these practices in their teaching. Thus a range of interactions around literacy may occur through young bilingual children's participation in home and community events with a variety of family members (Rodriguez, 1999; Xu, 1999; Volk and de Acosta, 2001).

English literacy will figure to a greater or lesser extent in the lives of most bilingual families living in an English-dominant society. In fact, as families settle into their new environment, English may become the main literacy. Luke and Kale (1997) describe how six-year-old Elsey, a Torres Strait Islander child living in Queensland, Australia, would read functional print such as an advertising flyer with her grandmother in English, although the talk around the text was conducted in both English and Torres Strait Creole. Zentella's (1997) study of second-generation Puerto Rican families in New York indicated that most literacy materials (storybooks, magazines, and the Bible) were in English.

Zentella's study also points to the effects of technological change on literacy. Most of the reading done by adults was from the television screen: advertisements, credits, and programme scheduling. This was in English, along with the instruction manuals for operating the technology. However, in the years since Zentella's study a further change has taken place. Many more cable and satellite channels are now available in minority languages and these are being tuned into enthusiastically in homes around the world. Visits to bilingual children's homes in London in 2001 (Kenner, forthcoming) gave a window onto this highly varied world, in which a family might be watching 'Who Wants To Be a Millionaire?' in English one moment and then switch to the news on Arabic satellite TV. Print in the family's other writing system, such as Arabic or Chinese, was thus present on screen as well as in dictionaries on the shelf or posters and calendars on the wall. These multilingual media possibilities, in an otherwise English-dominated world, may help in motivating children to develop their other languages and literacies.

Children's awareness of different scripts

There is evidence that very young children take note of the symbols being used for writing and reading as well as the overall purpose of each literacy event. Saxena (1994: 100) provides us with a case study of a Panjabi Hindu family living in Southall, West London. The four-year-old son encounters a variety of languages and a variety of scripts during a typical day. Although teaching only occurs in English at his primary school, as he enters the building he sees bilingual signs in the Gurmukhi and Devanagari scripts, designed for the multilingual school community. The Gurmukhi script is usually used for Panjabi and the Devanagari script for Hindi, although as Saxena points out, both languages can be written in both scripts. When the child gets home from school in the afternoon, his grandmother sends him to the local shop with a shopping list written in Hindi/Devanagari, and the shopkeeper records the goods sold in the same language and script.

During the day, the four-year-old can also observe his parents and grandparents reading and writing; for example, his mother reads Hindi film magazines and novels, and together with his grandmother writes to relatives in India in Panjabi–Hindi mixed code using Devanagari script. The family also uses English for a number of purposes, such as when the father reads a newspaper in the morning or the grandfather reads his grandson a storybook in English brought home from primary school. The complexity of this multiliteracy environment is not lost on the little boy; Saxena states that he can already distinguish between the Gurmukhi and Devanagari scripts and the Roman script in which English is written.

Similarly, Kenner's (2000a; 2000b) case study of four-year-old Meera, from a Gujarati-speaking family, shows how a young child who had been receiving no formal instruction in her home language literacy still recognized the difference between that script and English. Meera stated clearly that she wished to work with Gujarati – 'I want my Gujarati' – and began to produce her own emergent 'Gujarati' symbols, using her mother's writing as a resource.

THE PROCESSES INVOLVED IN BECOMING BILITERATE

It is clear from the above discussion that children growing up in bilingual or multilingual homes tend to have access to a variety of texts and literacy practices involving different languages. This experience is supplemented by their school learning, whether at community-run classes (as discussed by Gregory and Kenner, in this volume) or in mainstream school. What do children make of these inputs and what factors come into play which can aid or hinder the development of biliteracy? This section looks at research on children's learning about different writing systems and different cultural worlds, and then considers to what extent children can transfer aspects of knowledge between their literacies.

Knowledge about different writing systems

One part of the process of becoming biliterate involves producing the symbols which make up different writing systems and recognizing what they stand for. Research with young children shows that they are capable of differentiating two or more script systems and of beginning to distinguish the principles on which these are based. Datta (2000: 100) gives an example of a five-year-old, Raki, who spontaneously produced three types of script in one text, demonstrating her knowledge of letters from the Bengali, Arabic and English alphabets. Raki was also experimenting with ways of forming words by combining consonants and vowels in Bengali.

Kenner et al. (forthcoming) have followed six-year-olds in London learning to write in Chinese, Arabic or Spanish as well as English, and have found that children understand the form–meaning relationship in their different writing systems. In this project, the participant bilingual children were asked to conduct 'peer teaching sessions' – teaching their mainstream primary school classmates how to write in their home language system. Tala, who was attending Arabic Saturday school, showed that she understood how each Arabic letter has four different forms: as well as the main form in which it appears in the alphabet, there are initial, medial and final forms which must be used when the letter appears joined to others at the beginning, in the middle or at the end of a word respectively. Tala explained to her primary school peers which letters she used from the Arabic alphabet chart to construct her name, and how they looked different 'because I joined them up'. Pointing to the letter which began her name, she said 'There's a T in Arabic like this', and as she demonstrated how to join this letter to the following one, she stated 'and now I change it, because Arabic is magic'. Yazan, who attended the same community language school as Tala, was clear about the directionality of books in Arabic as compared to English. When showing his Arabic textbook to his primary school class, Yazan pointed to the front cover. Recognizing that his audience would have expected this to be the back of the book, he stated 'Not the end'. He then turned to the back cover, emphasizing 'This is the end', and reinforced the concept by returning to the front and stating 'This is the first'.

The principles mentioned so far had been directly taught to Tala and Yazan at Arabic school, but children in the study also showed that they were making their own deductions about how writing systems worked. For example, teachers at the Chinese community school were not observed to discuss the conceptual basis of the Chinese writing system as compared to English. Yet in a peer teaching session, Ming compared the three characters which represented his full Chinese name (Lai Sei Ming) on the front of his Chinese school exercise book to his name as written in English school, 'Ming'. He remarked 'That one's got three words and the English one's got four' (i.e. four letters). Later he said 'Ming is four, seven if it's together', referring to the seven letters needed for his full name in English, 'Ming Lai'. Here Ming was distinguishing between the characters used to represent whole words in Chinese, and the alphabetic letters which form the building blocks of English.

These young children also demonstrated that they were able to produce complex symbols with care and accuracy, often from memory (Kenner and Kress, forthcoming). This ability has surprised teachers from mainstream schools, who would be expecting emergent writing – as yet relatively unsophisticated – from children of this age. An extract from Selina's exercise book (see Figure 15.1) in her first year of Chinese school, when she was aged five, shows how she was learning the particular sequence of strokes with which to build up a character, and then practising the whole character numerous times. Children were required to pay great attention to the detail of each stroke, so that the character could not be confused with another similar one, and to ensure that the character was harmoniously balanced in the centre of each square.

Knowledge about different cultural worlds

Children's engagement with their different writing systems occurs in particular cultural contexts – such as home, community school or place of worship – and is thus part of the meanings they encounter as they represent and experience their complex bilingual worlds. Their engagement with the overall purpose and content of text also opens out a variety of cultural knowledge. The Welsh Language Board (1999) includes the following aspects in its list of advantages arising from bilingual education: 'twice the enjoyment of reading and writing' and 'access to two cultures and worlds of experience'.

An example comes from Gurdeep, the four-year-old mentioned above who was growing up in the English Midlands. Minns (1990) commented on the literary worlds which were opened up for Gurdeep by reading the sacred Sikh text, the *Guru Granth Saheb*, with his mother and by hearing her tell folktales in Panjabi with their clear moral messages. Meanwhile, Gurdeep also experienced children's stories in English written out of a different cultural tradition, both in his primary school class and when his father read him books borrowed from the local library.

Datta (2000) emphasizes how children's knowledge is strongly based in the oral, written and media discourses encountered at home and in their communities, the content and the style of which influence children's learning. She quotes a student teacher who began to investigate the multilingual literacy worlds of eight-year-old English–Gujarati bilinguals in her primary school class and concluded 'it appears that their linguistic and literary experiences are mostly embedded in cultural and religious experiences' (2000: 21). If young children's home-based literacy experience is very different from that offered in

Figure 15.1 From Selina's first-year exercise book: learning the stroke sequence to build up a character (in the right-hand column) and practising the whole character

mainstream school, teachers may need to cater specifically for this difference, as will be discussed below.

Transfer between literacies

Concepts and ideas which bilingual children develop in one language can interact with those developed in another, as explained by Cummins (1991). Some examples of how this could happen with literacies are given by Baker (2000): once children understand that letters stand for sounds, or that words can be guessed from the storyline, these principles can be applied when reading or writing in another language.

Several researchers have found evidence for this kind of transfer. Verhoeven (1994) studied the early biliteracy learning of Turkish children in the Netherlands and found that word decoding skills and reading comprehension skills developed in Turkish predicted corresponding skills when Dutch was acquired later. Transfer can also occur when literacies have different orthographies: Wagner (1993) found a positive interaction between the learning of French and Arabic in Morocco.

The process of creating and interpreting textual meanings can be enriched through multilingual experience. When Sneddon (2000) studied children from a Gujarati- and Urdu-speaking Muslim community in north-east London, she found that children who had opportunities to develop their language through using the cultural and leisure facilities of the local Gujarati community centre had a higher level of linguistic vitality in Gujarati than those who did not have this opportunity. This led to children being more creative storytellers in both Gujarati and English. Meanwhile, the children were becoming literate in Urdu for religious purposes, via community classes in which they answered complex questions on textual comprehension, with discussion taking place in English and Gujarati as well as Urdu. Sneddon suggests that this negotiation of meanings between three languages may provide strategies which can also be used when reading in the English mainstream classroom.

Researchers have also observed that young bilingual children have the propensity to write in more than one language within the same text, combining the resources available from their different literacies. Mor-Sommerfeld (2002) gives examples of children writing stories and messages in both Hebrew and English, switching from one language to the other and finding inventive ways to deal with the different directionalities of each script. She gives this process the apt name of 'language mosaic'. Kenner (forthcoming) noted that six-year-old Brian, growing up in London with Spanish as his home language, combined Spanish and English literacy resources within one phrase in order to write a caption for his drawing of a flying bear (see Figure 15.2). For the Spanish phrase 'un oso que vuele' ('a bear that flies') Brian wrote '1osokwle'. The number '1' represented 'un' ('un' can mean both 'a' and '1' in Spanish) – thus Brian was making use of the number system as a resource here too. The word 'oso' was familiar to Brian and he could write it spontaneously. He then called upon his knowledge of the English alphabet (the letter-name K and the sound of /w/) to give a good representation of the sounds he needed at this point. The final part 'le' is the rather more standard ending to the word 'vuele'.

As well as the possibility of transferring understandings across the variety of writing systems already mentioned in this section, logographic systems such as Chinese can also be combined with alphabetic systems in order to represent meaning. Selina, one of the children in Kenner's study (forthcoming), produced drawings of her mother and sister accompanied by both Chinese and English writing. In an increasingly multilingual world, this kind of linguistic creativity is likely to stand children in good stead later on in life. Pennington (1996) examines the prevalence of mixing and borrowing between Chinese and English in texts in Hong Kong, and the need for readers and writers in a bilingual society to be able to produce and interpret such texts. She argues that users of more than one linguistic code can use the differences in formal properties, semantics, and symbolic associations 'to produce a range of expressive effects which involve the differential contrastive meaning potential of the available languages' (1996: 254).

Cognitive and cultural challenges involved in biliteracy learning

As well as being able to transfer skills, children meet various challenges when they learn a second or third written language, especially if the new literacy is not immediately connected with their home language and culture. These challenges may be phonological, syntactic, semantic and textual, and young learners will have particular advantages and disadvantages when they set out to deal with them.

It is often found that bilingual children are more confident about decoding words than about answering comprehension questions on a whole text, for example. Rosowsky (2001) discovered that bilingual learners may be more accurate than monolingual peers when reading aloud, and he suggests that decoding skills are reinforced by the teaching of this aspect in community classes. However, overall comprehension of a passage involves grammatical and cultural knowledge which is less easily available in a second language, and here the monolingual children in Rosowsky's study tended to do better.

Within the area of phonology, some aspects will also be easier for bilingual learners than others. Gregory (1996) points out that in a first language, children will be familiar with the usual patterns of sounds: for example, sounds which tend to occur in clusters, or tend to start or end words. In a second language, children have less experience from which to build this understanding.

Thus it is possible to analyse the likely strengths and difficulties which second-language learners will have in the areas of phonological, syntactical, lexical, semantic and bibliographic knowledge respectively. The following list shows examples based on a fuller discussion by Gregory (1996: Chapter 3).

Figure 15.2   Brian's drawing and caption of 'un oso que vuele' ('a bear which flies')

Grapho-phonic knowledge

Strengths: Concept of matching symbols to sounds can transfer.

Difficulties: Hard to distinguish/pronounce sounds not used in own language.

Syntactic knowledge

Strengths: Awareness that different grammatical structures exist.

Difficulties: Don't yet have a 'feel' for grammar in the new language.

Lexical knowledge

Strengths: Awareness that words have different forms and properties.

Difficulties: May not know collocation (e.g. 'grind' goes with 'corn').

Semantic knowledge

Strengths: Awareness that different cultural experiences will exist.

Difficulties: Cultural content will be unfamiliar, so hard to predict text.

Bibliographic knowledge

Strengths: Experience of different kinds of texts.

Difficulties: Format and style of English story-book may be unfamiliar.

In the final section of this chapter, we discuss how teachers can help bilingual children to build on their strengths and increase their knowledge base in both or all of their literacies.

THE TASK FOR EDUCATORS

Throughout the chapter, we have highlighted a number of areas which educators of bilingual children need to keep in mind in order to support the development of biliteracy. Now we consider research evidence on tackling the cognitive and cultural challenges just described, and bring together examples of successful classroom practice regarding biliteracy work with minority-language children in mainstream schools, identifying the common factors involved.

Building new knowledge bases

Second-language researchers have emphasized that a clearly organized approach is necessary to ensure children become more deeply acquainted with the structure and content of a new literacy. Gregory (1996) lays out the varied activities that can be undertaken to introduce emergent bilinguals to the unfamiliar aspects of another written language. For example, with regard to building lexical knowledge, teachers can provide experiences which will highlight certain words so that these become meaningful and memorable for children. Words can also be introduced in lexical sets, grouped around a theme, which again makes it easier to store and recall them.

Bates (1995) recommends that when teaching children to write stories in a second language, the different elements of story structure are clearly explained. Young writers can be encouraged to elaborate on their texts, and to use pronouns and definite articles for reference within their writing, through feedback from an audience which requires them to clarify what they have produced. This kind of detailed approach, based on an analysis of children's language needs, is brought together by NALDIC (1998) in a guide to good practice for the teaching of literacy in English as an additional language, showing how direct interactive teaching can give children models of language use for different

purposes and contexts and enable learners to make this language part of their repertoire.

Building on knowledge which children already have

The NALDIC authors emphasize the importance of selecting culturally relevant texts and drawing on children's own experience, and also of encouraging the use of home languages to build concepts and negotiate meaning (1998: 6).

Several authors show how work which connects with home language experience can be a springboard for children's development in a second literacy. McWilliam (1998) suggests asking children to compare the use of vocabulary in their different languages, to highlight awareness of specific meanings and word classes. Datta (2000) gives striking examples of how to connect with children's rich imaginative worlds which arise from texts and events encountered in homes and communities. These experiences can then become a starting point for writing in English. The young writer of a ghost story could draw on knowledge of ghost stories from Bangladesh, whilst the writer of poetry could draw on the rich imagery and use of metaphor in Bollywood film songs, or ideas from the Buddhist tradition about peace and harmony. Meanwhile, through this 'intercultural literate community approach' (2000: 135) children can also be introduced to the metaphors and imaginative devices used in English literature.

Gregory (1996: Chapters 4 and 5) argues that both an 'inside-out' approach (starting from the known) and an 'outside-in' approach (introducing the unknown) are needed when teaching reading. These two approaches complement each other in order to fully develop bilingual children's literacy capabilities in their second language.

Developing literacy in children's home language

In majority-language contexts, the balance of power is heavily in favour of the dominant language and literacy. Few opportunities are offered for children to study their home literacy: as discussed by Gregory and Kenner (in this volume), such opportunities are almost always in voluntary-run, underfunded out-of-school classes. As a result, children tend to focus more strongly on the dominant literacy, and this may limit development of their full potential as biliterates.

A number of researchers have therefore devised and implemented action-research projects to develop children's literacy in the minority language alongside the majority language. Such research has demonstrated that when children have the opportunity to work with their home languages and literacies in supportive mainstream classroom environments, their English development also benefits. The projects described below share certain key factors, including the integration of bilingual work into the curriculum, parental involvement, and an increase in the status of the minority literacy.

In Feuerverger's (1994) research in an elementary school in inner-city Toronto, extending the provision of dual-language and first-language books in the school library built up skills and confidence for bilingual children as readers. These texts could be taken home to read with parents, and became part of classroom work when teachers encouraged children to write book reports and stories based on their reading, or to read the books to the whole class group. Kenner (2000a) found that bringing texts such as newspapers, videos and calendars in different languages from homes into a South London nursery class, supported by parents writing in the classroom, was successful in stimulating literacy work by both bilingual and monolingual children.

The importance of relevant cultural themes for literacy work is emphasized by Masny and Ghahremani-Ghajar (1999), who found that Somali children in a Canadian elementary school who were thought by their teachers to be illiterate began to demonstrate literacy skills when the teacher-researcher brought in books such as the Qur'an. The same teacher drew on Somali themes for language work and invited participation from parents in spoken Somali. With this approach of 'weaving multiple literacies', children began to make progress in their learning.

Multilingual computer-based texts show considerable potential for biliteracy work. They are linguistically flexible and motivating, enabling children to manipulate different scripts and realize ideas on screen. Edwards (1998: 71–2) describes how an 'Urdu club' with computer access in a multilingual English primary school aided literacy development for children. Meanwhile, parents used the resources to produce dual-language books and other teaching materials, gaining the status of expert within the school. Anderson (2001) found that producing web pages helped secondary school pupils in London to extend their writing in both English and Bengali; this approach could be adapted for young children, who are keen to experience web page authorship.

Bilingual education

Whilst identifying the above projects as ways of supporting bilingual children's literacy learning in mainstream English classrooms, we would emphasize that biliteracy development would be greatly enhanced if dual-language education was more widely available. Verhoeven (1999) points out that literacy in two languages can be acquired either successively or simultaneously. Since ethnographic studies have shown that literacy in the mother tongue may help to enhance community and cultural identity, 'both cognitive and anthropological arguments speak in favor of a biliteracy curriculum' (1999: 147). Given the importance of raising the status of minority literacies in order to promote additive bilingualism (see Gregory and Kenner, in this volume), this biliteracy curriculum is most likely to be successful if it is participated in by all children rather than by bilingual pupils only. Collier's (1995) longitudinal assessment of the effects of different types of bilingual education in the United States showed that the most effective were two-way immersion programmes involving children from both Spanish-speaking and non-Spanish-speaking backgrounds.

Biliteracy futures

Children's early learning experiences lay the foundations for later development, and for this reason it is particularly important that educators should pay attention to young children's biliterate development in the mainstream classroom. Otherwise children may feel that the domains in which their home literacy can be used are highly restricted, and even if community classes are on offer, their motivation to attend and learn can be diminished. Hardman (1998) found that in a Cambodian community in the United States, children had pride and confidence in their family's spoken language, but little interest in writing Cambodian. Hardman comments 'Possibly, because there is no room for L1 literacy in the children's school, there is no room for it anywhere in their lives' (1998: 72).

Access to a wide variety of print materials in the home language can also aid children in finding their individual paths to biliteracy. Tse (2001) interviewed 10 adults who had grown up in the United States, to find out how they had developed relatively high levels of literacy in their home languages of Spanish, Cantonese and Japanese respectively. One important common factor was reading for pleasure, which could involve novels, magazines, newspapers and comic books for example. Tse notes the results of a survey which showed the lack of Spanish-speaking materials in elementary school libraries even where schools had populations of over 90% Spanish-speaking children, and she argues that more books in minority languages should be provided by the mainstream.

CONCLUSION

As explained earlier in this chapter, for young children who live bilingually or multilingually, there are many links between their experiences as well as differences. When schools address the child as a whole person and give status to the minority literacy as a valued part of mainstream education, these links are strengthened with all-round benefits for self-esteem and learning.

As an example of the possibilities for biliterate children, we return to Gurdeep, the four-year-old introduced at the beginning of the chapter from the work of Minns (1990). Minns followed Gurdeep's progress, and described his 'enormously wide range of literacies' as a 10-year-old (1993: 65–8). Gurdeep was reading a whole variety of texts, from *The Concise Oxford Dictionary* to Teenage Mutant Turtles comics and his father's books on engineering. His weekly Panjabi classes at the Sikh temple were preparing him to study the sacred book, the *Guru Granth Saheb*. The words of this text were part of his daily act of worship, and related to his music making activities since he was also learning to play the drums at the temple. Gurdeep was drawing on his two languages to extend his literacy learning. He commented: 'In Panjabi, there are new words that I learn when I translate them into English. I've never heard of them before, and I find the meanings and I learn new words as well' (1993: 66).

When Minns (1997) reported on Gurdeep's progress again at age 15, he was heavily involved in academic-related reading and writing in English, but still found time to read teenage horror novels and write business letters for his mother on the computer. Meanwhile, through his classes at the temple he had already passed both GCSE and A-level in Panjabi by age 14: these levels of examination are usually taken at age 16 and age 18 respectively in the English system, but biliterate children are often ready earlier. From this rare longitudinal research study we can see how, as Minns commented in 1997, Gurdeep's early experiences had shaped his literacy life. His deep connection with Panjabi literacy had continued alongside his attainment of a high level of English. This development had been made possible by the strength of family and community support as well as mainstream school input. The cognitive and cultural advantages of biliteracy would accrue to Gurdeep, as we hope that they could accrue to many other potentially biliterate children.

REFERENCES

An, R. (2000) 'Learning to read and write at home: the experience of Chinese families in Britain', in M. Martin-Jones and K. Jones (eds), *Multilingual Literacies*. Amsterdam: Benjamins. pp. 71–90.

Anderson, J. (2001) 'Web publishing in non-Roman scripts: effects on the writing process', *Language and Education*, 15 (4): 229–49.

Baker, C. (2000) *A Parents' and Teachers' Guide to Bilingualism*. Clevedon: Multilingual Matters.

Bates, L. (1995) 'Promoting young ESL children's written language development', in M. Verma, K. Corrigan and S. Firth (eds), *Working with Bilingual Children*. Clevedon: Multilingual Matters. pp. 109–27.

Blackledge, A. (2000) *Literacy, Power and Social Justice*. Stoke-on-Trent: Trentham.

Collier, V. (1995) *Promoting Academic Success for ESL Students*. New Jersey: New Jersey Teachers of English to Speakers of Other Languages – Bilingual Educators.

Cummins, J. (1991) 'Interdependence of first and second language proficiency in bilingual children', in E. Bialystok (ed.), *Language Processing in Bilingual Children*. Cambridge: Cambridge University Press. pp. 70–89.

Datta, M. (2000) *Bilinguality and Literacy: Principles and Practice*. London: Continuum.

Delgado-Gaitan, C. (1990) *Literacy for Empowerment: the Role of Parents in Children's Education*. Lewes: Falmer.

Delgado-Gaitan, C. (1996) *Protean Literacy: Extending the Discourse on Empowerment*. London: Falmer.

Edwards, V. (1998) *The Power of Babel: Teaching and Learning in Multilingual Classrooms*. Stoke-on-Trent: Trentham.

Feuerverger, G. (1994) 'A multicultural literacy intervention for minority language students', *Language and Education*, 8 (3): 123–46.

Gregory, E. (1996) *Making Sense of a New World: Learning to Read in a Second Language*. London: Chapman.

Hardman, J. (1998) 'Literacy and bilingualism in a Cambodian community in the USA', in A. Durgunoglu and L. Verhoeven (eds), *Literacy Development in a Multilingual Context: Cross-Cultural Perspectives*. Mahwah, NJ: Erlbaum. pp. 51–81.

Hirst, K. (1998) 'Pre-school literacy experiences of children in Punjabi, Urdu and Gujerati speaking families in England', *British Educational Research Journal*, 24 (4): 415–29.

Kenner, C. (2000a) *Home Pages: Literacy Links for Bilingual Children*. Stoke-on-Trent: Trentham.

Kenner, C. (2000b) 'Biliteracy in a monolingual school system? English and Gujarati in South London', *Language, Culture and Curriculum*, 13 (1): 13–30.

Kenner, C. (forthcoming) 'Living in simultaneous worlds: difference and integration in bilingual script-learning', *International Journal of Bilingual Education and Bilingualism*.

Kenner, C. and Kress, G. (forthcoming) 'The multisemiotic resources of biliterate children', *Journal of Early Childhood Literacy*.

Kenner, C., Kress, G., Al-Khatbib, H., Kam, R. and Tsai, K-C. (forthcoming) 'Finding the keys to biliteracy: how young children interpret different writing systems', *Language and Education*.

Luke, A. and Kale, J. (1997) 'Learning through difference: cultural practices in early childhood language socialization', in E. Gregory (ed.), *One Child, Many Worlds: Early Learning in Multicultural Communities*. London: Fulton. pp. 11–29.

McWilliam, N. (1998) *What's in a Word? Vocabulary Development in Multilingual Classrooms*. Stoke-on-Trent: Trentham.

Martin-Jones, M. and Bhatt, A. (1998) 'Multilingual literacies in the lives of young Gujaratis in Leicester', in A. Durgunoglu and L. Verhoeven (eds), *Literacy Development in a Multilingual Context: Cross-Cultural Perspectives*. Mahwah, NJ: Erlbaum. pp. 37–50.

Masny, D. and Ghahremani-Ghajar, S. (1999) 'Weaving multiple literacies: Somali children and their teachers in the context of school culture', *Language, Culture and Curriculum*, 12 (1): 72–93.

Minns, H. (1990) *Read It To Me Now!* London: Virago.

Minns, H. (1993) 'Three ten year old boys and their reading', in M. Barrs and S. Pidgeon (eds), *Reading the Difference: Gender and Reading in the Primary School*. London: Centre for Language in Primary Education. pp. 60–71.

Minns, H. (1997) 'Gurdeep and Geeta: the making of two readers and the nature of difference'. Paper given to IEDPE (UK) Conference, Hidden Europeans: Working with Minority Language Groups in Different School Systems, London, 17 October.

Mor-Sommerfeld, A. (2002) 'Language mosaic: developing literacy in a second-new language – a new perspective', *Reading, Literacy and Language*, 36 (3): 99–105.

NALDIC (1998) *Provision in Literacy Hours for Pupils Learning English as an Additional Language*. Watford: National Association for Language Development in the Curriculum.

Pennington, M. (1996) 'Cross-language effects in biliteracy', *Language and Education*, 10 (4): 254–72.

Rashid, N. and Gregory, E. (1997) 'Learning to read, reading to learn: the importance of siblings in the language development of young bilingual children', in E. Gregory (ed.), *One Child, Many Worlds: Early Learning in Multicultural Communities*. London: Fulton. pp. 107–21.

Rodriguez, M.V. (1999) 'Home literacy experiences of three young Dominican children in New York City', *Educators for Urban Minorities*, 1 (1): 19–31.

Rosowsky, A. (2001) 'Decoding as a cultural practice and its effects on the reading process of bilingual pupils', *Language and Education*, 15 (1): 56–70.

Saxena, M. (1994) 'Literacies amongst the Panjabis in Southall (Britain)', in J. Maybin (ed.), *Language and Literacy in Social Practice*. Clevedon: Multilingual Matters. pp. 96–116.

Sneddon, R. (2000) 'Language and literacy: children's experiences in multilingual environments', *International Journal of Bilingual Education and Bilingualism*, 3 (4): 265–82.

Tse, L. (2001) 'Heritage language literacy: a study of US biliterates', *Language, Culture and Curriculum*, 14 (3): 256–68.

Tucker, R. (1996) 'Some thoughts concerning innovative language education programmes', *Journal of Multilingual and Multicultural Development*, 17 (2–4): 315–20.

Verhoeven, L. (1994) 'Transfer in bilingual development', *Language Learning*, 44 (3): 381–415.

Verhoeven, L. (1999) 'Second language reading', in D. Wagner, R. Venezky and B. Street (eds), *Literacy: an International Handbook*. Oxford: Westview. pp. 143–7.

Volk, D. (1999) 'The teaching and the enjoyment and being together: sibling teaching in the family of a Puerto Rican kindergartner', *Early Childhood Research Quarterly*, 14 (1): 5–34.

Volk, D. and de Acosta, M. (2001) 'Many differing ladders, many ways to climb: literacy events in the bilingual classrooms, homes and community of three Puerto Rican kindergartners', *Journal of Early Childhood Literacy*, 1 (2): 193–224.

Wagner, D. (1993) *Literacy, Culture and Development: Becoming Literate in Morocco*. Cambridge: Cambridge University Press.

Welsh Language Board (1999) *Two Languages: Twice the Choice*. Cardiff: Welsh Language Board.

Xu, S.H. (1999) 'Young Chinese ESL children's home literacy experiences', *Reading Horizons*, 40 (1): 47–64.

Zentella, A. (1997) *Growing Up Bilingual: Puerto Rican Children in New York*. Oxford: Blackwell.

16

Playing the Storyteller: Some Principles for Learning Literacy in the Early Years of Schooling

CAROL FOX

THE CENTRALITY OF NARRATIVE

While oral storytelling has received much attention from the research on literacy development, major collections of oral stories are rare in the literature and those narrated by young children even more so. In spite of this rarity, literacy educationalists have long acknowledged that narrative is central to the way our minds order experience, whether real or virtual, and over the years, the literature from domains of study as diverse as psychoanalysis, anthropology, linguistics, literary theory and cognitive psychology has tended to confirm the view that human minds order experience in the mode of story. Half a century ago Suzanne Langer (1953: 261) called narrative a major mental 'organizing device'; more recently Bruner (1986: 1994) proposed that narrative is a fundamental mode of thought through which we construct our world or worlds, while Barbara Hardy (1968) suggested that narrative, 'a primary act of mind', is the medium through which we filter virtually all our experience. Theorists of the way memory works, from Bartlett in the 1930s to the structuralists and cognitive psychologists of the 1960s, 1970s and 1980s, show that our memory reorders our experience as stories, since narrative structure is organized along the dimension of time; it is, according to Scholes (1981), 'a temporal icon'. While the literary theorist Roland Barthes (1977) claims that narrative is 'international, transhistorical,

transcultural', sociologists and ethnographers have demonstrated that narratives are deeply culturally embedded, suggesting that universal structures for stories are subject to local variation in different social groups (Labov, 1972a; Scollon and Scollon, 1981; Heath, 1983). Historians of literacy remind us that both phylogenetically and ontogenetically the first texts are usually oral stories written down or written stories presented in the styles of oral narrations (Ong, 1982). Harold Rosen (1984) once remarked that:

> Stories break the surface of our discourse not as great edifices but as spontaneously constructed coherences – cheap as dirt, common currency, a popular possession. You will not need reminding that in our society common property is suspect. What everyone possesses is scarcely worth possessing.

The theme that I want to develop in this piece is that, given the enormous knowledge we now have of storytelling in all its variety and universality, we are still not making the essential links to literacy learning that are implicit in the research.

In spite of our recognition of the centrality of narrative in our lives and our knowledge that oral stories begin to emerge in young children at the onset of connected language, we are still unsure about how to make direct use of young children's storytelling skills in language and literacy learning. The research on oral storytelling comes from several major fields, each of which illuminates our understanding of what children (and adults) are capable of as narrators, but somehow we have trouble in incorporating these discoveries into our curricula and pedagogies; schooling seems inimical to this 'common coin'. In this piece I shall briefly outline some of the major contributions to children's storytelling research in the last 40 years or so, and then go on to discuss some implications of that research, linking narrative, verbal play and play to show the huge potential that is often neglected in literacy learning.

RESEARCH ON CHILDREN'S ORAL STORYTELLING

We might start by looking at collections of transcribed stories told by children. The data themselves fall into two categories: collections from large numbers of children who told one or two stories each, and collections from small numbers of children or individuals who told several stories each. In 1963 Pitcher and Prelinger collected two narratives each from 137 children aged three to five, and for many years their collection remained a basic resource for other researchers (Ames, 1966; Sachs, 1972; Applebee, 1978). The narratives were invented fantasy stories and the orientation both of Pitcher and Prelinger and of Ames was psychoanalytic, leading to an emphasis on content rather than form or structure. In looking at children's ego development as it was reflected in the stories, an interesting finding was that the use of fantasy (rather than realistic) material increases as the children move towards the age of five and become more confident that the real world is as it is and that they are safe to play with fantasies of different kinds. This finding is borne out by most subsequent studies of young children's stories. Using the same material, Ames' focus was on children's developing sense of causality in their stories, a theme developed by Sachs in his famous analysis of a two-clause story in the data told by a child of 24 months, 'The baby cried, the mommy picked it up'. Sachs argues that this is a narrative because the second clause is understood by the listener to be temporally and causally connected to the first. Sachs' work suggests that storytelling begins as soon as children are able to construct simple sentences and provides a useful basic definition of a narrative.

Applebee (1978) used the Pitcher and Prelinger data for different purposes, those more closely linked to literacy. His aim was to trace the development of language 'in the spectator role' (Harding, 1974; Britton, 1970), that is the language of fiction and of story as an aesthetic art. Applebee's study of narrative structure is unique in its use of Vygotsky's stages of concept development as the analytic tool. He found that two major linking devices were at work in young children's stories: events linked to other events by a chain mechanism, *chaining*; and events related to an overall central theme, *centring*. His focus is primarily on cognitive development as it is revealed through story structure, and although he claims that chaining and centring are the structuring forces at work in major novels and dramas, the link to literature is weakened by the fact that the *language/discourse* of the children's stories is neglected in favour of a focus on the organization of events.

Brian Sutton-Smith made a major story collection in the 1970s taking one or more narratives from 350 children age two to 10, published as *The Folk Stories of Children* (1981). He also collected large numbers of stories from individual children, in nurseries and school settings, in relaxed and informal conditions. The methodological issue about how story data are garnered is an important subtheme of the literature; in societies with strong oral traditions, stories belong to leisure time when the day's work is done. The most interesting and expressive story data usually emerge in naturalistic contexts where the tellers can feel valued and confident, a point that needs to be taken seriously if we are considering storytelling in school settings. Sutton-Smith uses a Piagetian framework for his analysis of story structure, with a focus on conservation and reversibility, a focus that again bypasses the discourse of the stories and instead relates to story events. An interesting suggestion by Sutton-Smith was that children's stories develop analogously to folksong forms in oral traditions. He found that early narratives were stitched together through the use of oral formulae and prosodic features – 'a poetic orientation' (1981: 19), which tended to be replaced by causal and logical relationships as the child became more literate. While the work of Pitcher and Prelinger and of Ames suggested that children's oral stories express deep affective themes, Applebee and Sutton-Smith, in different ways, lead us in the direction of literature and the verbal arts.

Labov's (1972a) sociolinguistic work on the narratives of inner-city black adolescents in the US excludes young children, but it is nevertheless seminal in several major respects. It establishes the methodological point that stories ought to be elicited in relaxed, unthreatening settings, especially if they are to be collected from non-powerful subcultures. It establishes a very satisfying account of narrative structure, one which extends beyond beginnings, middles and ends and instead places 'evaluation', of the narrator's stance to the narrative being told, at the heart of narrative structure. At once the category of evaluation includes the events being narrated, the narrator's affective stance to those events and the discourse which tells the story – all of which had tended to be excluded from earlier oral story analyses. An important sociological point made by Labov's work is that his most successful and skilled narrators tended to be leaders and also the least oriented to literacy and school success in their groups. Labov's work also links verbal play (as ritual insults) to narrative in that the linguistic skills in both forms are highly developed and complex in the groups he studied but not harnessed to literacy learning in the education system. Other researchers were able to use Labov's narrative structure to analyse the stories of younger children (Kernan, 1977; Menig-Peterson and McCabe, 1978; Umiker-Sebeok, 1979; Bennett, 1980; Fox, 1993). In the UK Rosen (1988) published an account of her work on the oral stories of working-class adolescent boys in an inner London comprehensive school. As with Labov's work, the oral stories revealed talents and verbal skills not hitherto recognized in school, and suggested that the reasons for the failure of such groups in the education system, both in the UK and in the US, did not lie in the verbal deficits of the pupils.

The diversity of storytelling traditions has been exemplified by other research. Scollon and Scollon (1981) contrasted the narratives of their two-year-old daughter with those of Athabaskan Alaskan children. Their findings argue that their own child's stories reflected relationships that were intertextual rather than interpersonal and were already turned in a literate direction, where meanings tend to reside in the text. Athabaskan stories by contrast reflected different cultural norms, contrasting story structures and values other than those of the dominant society. Heath's (1983) major study of the contrasting literacy practices of three distinct communities in the Southern US shows an orientation to school literacy in one group, Maintown, but very different practices in the other two, Roadville and Trackton – practices which led to literacy and school failure because they were not understood by educational institutions. As well as demonstrating that young black children in the Trackton community 'come up as talkers' through exposure to the storytelling traditions of the family, Heath also shows that oral and written modes operate along fluid continua:

> written information almost never stood alone in Trackton: it was reshaped and reworded into an oral mode. In so doing adults and children incorporated chunks of the written text into their talk. (1982: 100)

Heath argues that schools need to understand the literacy practices and narrative traditions of the communities they serve and adapt to the students.

Heath's work initiated new ethnographic perspectives on literacy. The diversity of cultural practices exposed by several in-depth studies of narrative and literacy practices in different parts of the world and in different communities has led to the conception of plural notions of literacy, to *literacies*, and the proposition that the white middle-class norms of teachers and schools in the West tend to exclude and be ignorant of the cultural forms brought to school by different groups (Street, 1993; Barton, 1994; Gregory and Williams, 2000). Literacies are now conceived of as sets of ideological practices whose values and norms can be deconstructed and examined. The polarization of literacy/illiteracy is destabilized along with a real weakening of the older notion of an oral–literate discontinuity.

It needs to be said that in the 1970s and 1980s many narratologists attempted to describe story grammars and schemata using experimental work based on children's ability to recall and retell simple stories (Maranda and Maranda, 1971; Mandler and Johnson, 1977; Rumelhart, 1975; 1977; Stein and Glenn, 1978). In these studies the stories used were often devised by the researchers as idealized forms, stripped of the elaborative elements that make stories interesting and, indeed, worth listening to. Stories in these kinds of experiment become 'problem-solving' formats (Rumelhart, 1977: 269), or information for 'retrieval' (Mandler and Johnson, 1977: 112). While such studies have led to interesting findings about the links between narrative structure and memory, their methodological limitations make them poor models for discovering what the full extent of children's storytelling competencies looks like.

During the 1980s I collected 200 oral invented stories from five preschool children who had had an extensive exposure to children's literature read aloud in the early years (Fox, 1993). Using analytic systems based on Labov (1972a), Genette (1972, trans. 1980), and Barthes (1970, trans. 1974), my intention was to show the enormous influence of written language on the children's narrations at every level – vocabulary, syntax, story structure, and complex literary techniques found in fiction for both children and adults. In 1988 Meek published a slim but seminal work *How Texts Teach What Readers Learn,* which set out the complexity of the literary competencies even very young children could learn from the texts of skilled children's authors. Very recently Barrs and Cork (2001) have shown with older schoolchildren that an intense exposure to specific works of children's fiction can lead to considerable advances in writing and composing competencies. I theorized the work by regarding the stories as acts of verbal play in which cognitive and affective factors were equally implicated. I proposed that in this kind of linguistic production – often performance in the case of five-year-old Sundari, an astonishingly precocious narrator – the metaphoric principles which lie at the heart of language as play, come into operation (Fox, 1997; 1998). One of the major implications for education of my storytelling study is that unless we find out what children are capable of in their narrating we are in danger of grossly underestimating their capabilities – cognitive, linguistic and narrative. Betty Rosen (1988) found that the stories told by adolescent boys in a London comprehensive school, boys who were not credited with much literary talent in the school system, were extraordinarily complex, sensitive and skilful. Heath, in an article about the storytelling of US teenagers very like the London boys of Betty Rosen's book, claims that the stories of adolescents have received too little attention in the literature on oral storytelling, and she offers a good summary of some of the implicit skills:

> The stories embody description, persuasion, exposition, with argument implicit; but they must also include humour – achieved through character development, word play and satire … they must also achieve humour through exaggeration and hyperbole in abundance. Tellers include much internal dialogue thought, though not expressed, at the time of the actual event. In addition, during the story's telling, they create on-the-spot dialogues between teller and other participants to increase the liveliness and participatory nature of the story. (1994: 210)

Over the years there have also been studies of individual children's storying: Bissex (1980), Paley (1981), and Dyson (1994) are examples. In these studies we watch the interaction of the oral and the literate as writing develops from talk and talk develops from writing, along the kinds of fluid continua described by Heath. In these studies literacy does not emerge in a simplistic progress from written language read loud, to written language internalized and employed in oral stories, to written stories, but is a more complex mix of both cultural source material and the spoken and written channels:

> children's language repertoires include stories, songs, jokes, and other language genres that reflect the folk traditions of their community, the popular media that pervade their lives, and also the written literature they have experienced at school and at home. (Dyson, 1994: 156)

Although my own study foregrounds the literary qualities of my children's stories and their sources in books, nevertheless the equation is never as simple as that. In a long and highly entertaining story about God, St Peter, Dracula and Frankenstein, a story told by five-year-old Josh about which I have written extensively (see Fox, 1993: Chapter 11), the complexity of the story language and structure is woven from material taken from popular culture (Frankenstein and Dracula), ordinary everyday conversations (most of the story is conducted in dialogue) and written texts (several children's books).

What I want to develop in the second part of this chapter is the notion that there are major sources of literacy and the language of literacy *other than book experience* surrounding children in the early years; that the deep, underlying processes of metaphor making in storying, role-play and verbal play of all kinds may be pretty universal among children; and that there are some strong and widely established linguistic practices in groups often identified with low literacy that are surprisingly consistent across many cultures and seem in many ways to offer satisfactory parallels to what my children were doing when they made up stories. My themes are organized under three headings – 'Play', 'The patterns of language', and 'The interaction of the oral and literate'.

PLAY

To regard children's oral storytelling as play can be problematic. On the face of it the storytellings in my study seem perfect examples of symbolic play activities which conform in almost all respects to what the major psychologists have told us about play. There is no doubt that most of the defining characteristics of play were present. The storytellings were voluntary, pleasurable, inconsequential to the tellers, and highly conventional, employing complex sets of rules and regularities self-imposed by the storytellers – Vygotsky's 'rule that has become a desire' in symbolic play (1978: 99). The stories do indeed provide opportunities to deal with dangerous, threatening or subversive material in a safe way, free from consequences in the real world. Additionally the stories themselves could be regarded as Freudian forms of wish fulfilment (1978: 93), as adaptive behaviour which is primarily assimilative (Piaget, 1951: 159) and as strongly linked to future development (Vygotsky, 1978: 101–3; Piaget, 1951; Bruner, 1976: 49). In these respects the storytellings accord with descriptions of play by the major psychologies of development. The children were not only making words into play material (the content of their stories) but they were playing at being the author, the storyteller, all the characters and even the audience. If you listen to my children's tapes it is not difficult to recognize the play context: there is giggling and laughter, pleasure and delight, silliness and fun. But there are also stories which seem to be much more serious, not only in their content but also in the struggle and effort that goes into the telling. They show fierce concentration over quite long periods of time, a carefulness to get things right and an urgent commitment to the story as a finished piece, even in five-year-old Sundari's case as a sound–voice performance. These stories sound much more like hard work. In the past I have called this 'serious play' though I wish there were a better term for it (Fox, 1998). What I think it represents is a transition that is rooted in play but is on its way to becoming something far more striven for, less inconsequential and more like what older pupils or adults do when they voluntarily read a very demanding book for pleasure, learn their part in amateur theatricals or even practise their tennis shots. Freud (1920) and Vygotsky (1978) propose that the pleasure of play lies in mastery, and there is no doubt that several kinds of mastery are implicated in the children's storying; their power over what they are doing is very obvious in some of the stories, most notably from the two five-year-olds, and is the basis of their pleasure and satisfaction. They are striving very hard to get better at something for the pure pleasure and ambition of doing it.

This kind of transition from the basis of play to something still pleasurable but more demanding and serious must be an almost ideal way of learning, something that teachers would want their pupils to experience, to read and write for pleasure, to want to work at it independently of the teacher for the satisfaction it brings. Piaget observed that it was towards the middle years of childhood that play turns in the direction of adaptation to reality (rather than to the ego formation of the egocentric stage) and notes that it now has the beginnings of serious intellectual and artistic work (1951: 140–2). The developmental trajectory seems to be from play at the beginning to serious work later, and would suggest that learning in school needs to be embedded in a play-like basis for longer than the kindergarten years. Stories, storytelling, reading and writing, and role-play of all kinds particularly lend themselves to the maintenance of playful qualities. They are all forms of symbolic transformation, all involve imaginative activity, all are capable of giving pleasure and satisfaction, and many children undertake these literacy practices independently and voluntarily, and not only those from bookish backgrounds.

How many of us have been stopped from reading under the desk in school, or in bed at home? How many of us have played at writing out our gang rules, sending imaginary letters, keeping secret diaries? Isn't text messaging very often creative, inventing spelling in the way that young children do

when they are allowed to, and isn't it voluntary and pleasurable (and probably subject to banning or adult disapproval in school)? And don't almost all children role-play from infancy as Vygotsky suggests? By maintaining a play basis for the early years of schooling we do not need to abandon practice in useful skills; we simply need to avoid separating them from what children enjoy and find meaningful. Are there not the most delightful and hilarious phonics in Dr Seuss' works, not to mention Lewis Carroll, Edward Lear and Spike Milligan? Hall and his associates have shown us very clearly over the years that emergent writing can be embedded in all kinds of role-play activities created in school settings (Hall, 1989; 1999; Robinson et al., 1990; Hall and Robinson, 1995). *So the first principle I would extrapolate from the story study is that we ought not to put the desire to learn voluntarily for its own sake and for satisfaction and pleasure at risk by abandoning the principles of learning through play in the early years of schooling.*

Most countries start formal schooling at age six or seven. In Britain many children are under five when they begin. If some children have not had the pleasure of hearing stories read aloud in the early years, or of joining in with rhymes, poems and songs, or of role-playing of all kinds with their friends, or of doing play writing (to name but a few literacy practices, never mind all the other creative activities that young children enjoy), then those years in school between the ages of four and seven need to be filled with them. When the two five-year-olds in my study started school at the age of five their story competencies were not in any way given the scope to be part of what they were supposed to be learning. Sundari was never invited to tell a story, while Josh was tested on suspicion of 'language retardedness' during the period when he was recording 29,000 words of narrative at home. The children still learned to read and write quickly, but like many of the young fluent readers in Margaret Clark's (1976) famous study it was at the price of concealing what they already knew about literacy and at the even greater cost of their enjoyment of school learning.

THE PATTERNS OF LANGUAGE

Young children who hear books read aloud are usually hearing stories that are structured and written according to folktale traditions. There are very often rhymes, rhythms, repetitions, refrains and other prosodic features, and openings and endings taken from folk-story formulae. Even many picturebooks written for older readers employ such devices from oral literature, for example *Rose Blanche* (Gallaz, 1985) and *The Tin-Pot Foreign General and the Old Iron Woman* (Briggs, 1984), two serious works for older readers about real and tragic historic events. I would therefore expect that children who frequently heard oral stories that are *not* from books before going to school would also be well set up for future literacy, if that literacy is taught primarily through storybooks, since much of the language of young children's literature is the oral tradition written down. These children would be familiar with all the formulaic patterns of their own traditions of oral stories. The oral traditions of the Trackton community described by Heath in *Ways with Words* (1983) also look like good literacy preparation, although these children were not successful in the school system because their cultures were not understood.

The young black children from Trackton are observed to develop as talkers from the start through the storying which is constantly present in the community around them. Heath tells us that in Trackton culture stories are valued not for their truthfulness or for their conformity to the structures of book stories, but for their prosodic features, alliteration, rhythm and rhyme, together with highly exaggerated language and embellishments of style. She shows that Trackton children's story traditions of repetition, variation and straying from a main storyline are misunderstood by their white teachers and therefore are not utilized in becoming literate: they are rejected as somehow not fitting story 'norms' (beginnings, middle and ends, logical outcomes, sticking to the main point, and so on). Yet the imaginative, creative and deeply social ways that Trackton children develop language and linguistic style through storying would fit all the play criteria outlined earlier and seem ideally suited for an introduction to lively and enjoyable stories in books and to lots of patterns and stylized conventions for writing.

Heath goes on to talk about how Trackton children's talk later develops into ritual insults and stories which are highly sexually suggestive and full of *double entendre* and taboo themes, while remaining stylistically skilful both in prosody and in metaphor (1983: 183). When I began to look at studies of language play around the world in the late 1980s I was surprised at how similar the practices were. I managed to locate studies, all made at a time in the 1970s when anthropologists were recognizing the linguistic qualities of the talk of young people from subcultures in the USA and in former colonized societies, from widely diverse locations, including the Caribbean (Abrahams, 1972a; 1972b), Central Africa (Albert, 1972), Turkey (Dundes et al., 1972), urban ghettos in the USA (Brown, 1972; Kochman,

1972; Labov, 1972b; Mitchell-Kernan, 1972); Mexico (Bricker, 1976; Gossen, 1976) and Hawaii and the Philippines (Conklin, 1964; Frake, 1964; Watson-Gegeo and Boggs, 1977). The type of ritual insult described in these studies is usually played by adolescent boys, and is called 'talking sweet', 'talking broad', 'signifying', 'verbal duelling', 'rapping', 'stylin out', 'playing the dozens', 'frivolous talk' and 'truly frivolous talk', and 'talking through the straw'.

Such linguistic usage, still happening in groups of adolescent boys and increasingly girls, has now become part of commercialized popular culture as rap and it will be familiar to many readers, though there is less awareness of its long history and its ubiquity. Poets who write for children, especially those with Caribbean roots like John Agard and Benjamin Zephaniah, are good at making books for kids using the same poetic devices. Although on the face of it the five children in my study might have little in common with the traders of ritual insults over the world, at a deep level there are some fundamental characteristics that the story language of these pre-literate white young children shares with these older adolescent subgroups (usually described as having limited school literacy). They have in common a huge awareness of language as play material, with prosodic features that are infinitely flexible and mnemonic; an enormous emphasis on style as the prime value; a facility for constructing metaphors, allusions, puns, double meanings and similes; and, most importantly, an awareness that language play frees one from the restrictions of society's taboos, dangers and politenesses. The tendency of stories from young boys to lean towards the disorderly has been noted by Nicolopoulou et al. (1994) in a fascinating study of the gender dimensions in stories invented by four-year-olds, while violent, thrilling and dramatic content has been noted by the collectors of oral stories from Pitcher and Prelinger in the 1960s, Labov, Heath, myself and many others. Within either the storytelling or the rituals of competitive rapping the player is free to subvert the real social world without consequences, although Labov points out that if the opening gambit in a verbal duel is not recognized as symbolic but taken for 'real', then there is a danger of violence, even death in extreme cases (1972b: 343).

The kinds of language described above are recognizable as poetic forms; they are present in nursery rhymes and jokes, in comic books and ballads, and in canonical literature world-wide; their rudeness and subversion are an extension of the kinds of danger and violence found in the more innocent oral productions of much younger speakers like my five children. There are of course big differences, too, and not only cultural ones. Most of the subcultures described above use oral vernaculars or dialects as far removed from the standard languages of writing as it is possible to get. Labov asserts that the failure of literacy by the best players of verbal duels in the USA ghettos is attributable to teachers' ignorance of these language varieties and their undervaluing of students' highly developed verbal skills, which are surely ideal foundations for literacy – a judgement similar to Heath's on the schooling of Trackton children. He describes the dominant values of what is now called rap as 'toughness, smartness, trouble, excitement, autonomy and fate' (1972b: 344), values far removed from school notions of literacy which at their worst can be more concerned with conformity, standardization, politeness, protectiveness (from violence), lack of autonomy and formal assessment. More recently some research has suggested that imaginative writing is the particular strength of African-American students who use BEV (black English vernacular) and urges teachers to use the 'rich reservoir' of these cultural discourses in the teaching of writing (Smitherman, 1994). There is nothing new in the observation that the street talk of black adolescents in cities in the UK is much admired in the white peer group for its style and coolness. In-depth studies of the influence and cross-fertilization between the vernaculars spoken by minority groups in the UK and the dialects of the mainstream groups can be found in Hewitt (1986) and Rampton (1995). But perhaps we are arriving at a new evaluation of verbal play in popular culture. Very recently I saw in a television programme about new languages and literacies a London infant teacher of literacy using in her literacy hour her pupils' ability to rap ('BBC Knowledge', February 2002). My second principle for literacy learning then is that *we should find out about and make full use of children's delight and skill in playing with language patterns of all kinds, especially the prosodic and metaphorical, to advance their literacy, and we should choose stories and poems that reflect these values.*

THE INTERACTION OF THE ORAL AND LITERATE

I do not think that the evidence for linguistic continuity and the constant overlapping and interdependence between speech and writing needs to be repeated at any great length here. The work of anthropologists of literacy has established that literacy is not an autonomous, homogeneous mental entity but is more accurately described as a plural set of cultural and social practices many of which

have yet to be understood in education (Heath, 1983; Street, 1993; Barton, 1994). My story study shows that the interflow back and forth between oral language and the language of storybooks can be strongly established by the time children go to school. But it would be a great mistake to assume that hearing stories read aloud is the only way that young children get to hear written language read aloud. They also hear a great deal of it in scripted broadcasts in a variety of media, radio, TV, films, videos, computer games, pop songs and the like. In my data, pretend newsreadings and weather forecasts were offered as stories from time to time by five-year-old Josh. His grasp of the discourse patterns appropriate to these broadcasts was strong and clear and they are immediately recognizable to the listener. Indeed, the imitations of radio newsreaders produced some of the most complex syntax in the study. He uses a high number of passive constructions in his newsreadings, together with collections of political names and terminology, albeit in a playful, mocking manner. His weather forecasts are characterized by long adverbial phrases and the future tense. These grammatical features are not common in his storytellings but come from another frequently heard aural source – the radio.

We really know too little about the knowledge of specific discourses, some of them written or at least scripted, that children have in the early years of schooling. This is partly because, to children themselves, knowing how to do the voices and tunes of particular discourses is natural and inconsequential and usually comes out in their play. At present there is a perception that what children take from broadcast media is detrimental to their language and literacy rather than potentially useful in a bridge-building sense. Myra Barrs (1990) has made the point that television narrative conventions are known by many children who incorporate them into their writing and who are critical of storytellers who depart too far from the narrative rules. Pop songs and advertising jingles, however banal, use the linguistic devices of poems and nursery rhymes. They have the advantage of being repetitive and are often enjoyable. As children get older they often have considerable knowledge of quite specific discourses in popular culture, ranging from football commentaries (and the songs sung on the terraces) to the current language of *Star Wars*, *Lord of the Rings* (whose literary origins are impeccable) and 'Harry Potter'. There is no great gulf between these discourses and those of the stories and poems that may be first encountered in books. In the case of films and videos the passage from book to film and back again to book has now become a significant cultural process, not just for children's works but for adults too. Many children pick up the rhythms and lexical features quickly and use them in their improvised play. My point is that although these forms seem somewhat removed from storybook reading, they are like the oral stories and verbal duels of Trackton in having the potential to be used for literacy if they are not rejected by schools and teachers. They are often highly patterned and structured according to specific recognizable conventions, usually popular, shared and widely known, often (but not always) part of children's culture and belonging to children, and sometimes subversive and dangerous in the ways that children enjoy. So here I come to my third principle for literacy learning: *we need to develop a better understanding of the knowledge of distinct discourse styles and structures that children bring with them to school from the outside world, to see how spoken and written channels overlap and inter-flow in those discourses, and to recognize how linguistic knowledge of this kind can be used to make literate transformations from speech to reading and writing and back again.* One way to discover this kind of discourse knowledge would be to place oral storytelling and role-play close to the centre of the early years curriculum.

THE WORLD OF THE STORY

To read a story is to write it, to construct it yourself, to be a story maker, in a sense to become the author of the text (Barthes, 1970). The reader's activity makes the story mean, and what the story means will be slightly or even greatly different for each reader and for each reading by the same reader. The reader brings a whole set of identifications, 'selves', social roles and experiences, expectations, preconceptions and histories to the text, as well as understandings from all the other texts read or heard or seen. Reading cannot really be possible without such interactions with texts. The story is a symbolic representation of experience whose materials are words and often pictures too upon which we are required to act to bring its meanings into being. It is a form of metaphor making in which we are obliged not only to recognize and understand the metaphors but to reinvent them for ourselves and, some would claim, reinvent ourselves in the process as teller and as told.

Such notions of the role and importance of stories in becoming literate are not new and I, especially in the light of the story study I began so many years ago, am completely committed to an induction to literacy for every child that will lead not only to reading and writing as practices to be developed over a lifetime but also to literature and the imaginative uses of language as a source of lifelong pleasure and enlightenment. The three principles that I

have focused on here are a plea for us to be more inclusive in the means we employ to recruit children to the literacy club. The potential for becoming literate is not confined to bookish children but is present in all children who act out different kinds of symbolic transformation in their play, and all children who hear and enjoy richly patterned stylistically distinct language, whether it is because they are situated within specific oral traditions or because they are surrounded by familiar media texts and discourses on a daily basis.

REFERENCES

Abrahams, R.D. (197a) 'The training of the man of words in talking sweet', *Language in Society*, 1: 15–30.

Abrahams, R.D. (1972b) 'Joking: the training of the man of words in talking broad', in T. Kochman (ed.), *Rappin' and Stylin' Out*. Chicago: University of Illinois Press.

Albert, E.M. (1972) 'Culture patterning of speech behaviour in Burundi', in D. Hymes and J.J. Gumperz (eds), *Directions in Sociolinguistics*. New York: Holt, Rinehart and Winston.

Ames, L.B. (1966) *Children's Stories*. Chicago: University of Chicago Press.

Applebee, A. (1978) *The Child's Concept of Story*. Chicago: University of Chicago Press.

Barrs, M. (1990) 'Children's theories of narrative', *English in Education*, 24 (1): 32–9.

Barrs, M. and Cork, V. (2001) *The Reader in the Writer*. London: Centre for Language in Primary Education.

Barthes, R. (1970) *S/Z: an Essay (1974)*. New York: Hill and Wang.

Barthes, R. (1977) 'Introduction to the structural analysis of narratives', in A.K. Pugh, V. Lee and J. Swann (eds), *Language and Language Use*. London: Heinemann. pp. 244–73.

Barton, D. (1994) *Literacy: an Introduction to the Ecology of Written Language*. Oxford: Blackwell.

Bennett, R. (1980) 'Proficiency in storytelling', in *Proceedings of the Sixth Annual Meeting of the Berkeley Linguistics Society*. Arcata, CA: Humboldt State University Press. 120–32.

Bissex, G (1980) *Gnys At Wrk: a Child Learns to Write*. Cambridge, MA: Harvard University Press.

Bricker, V.R. (1976) 'Some Zinacanteco joking strategies', in B. Kirschenblatt-Gimblett (ed.), *Speech Play*. Philadelphia: University of Pennsylvania Press.

Briggs, R. (1984) *The Tin-Pot Foreign General and the Old Iron Woman*. London: Hamish Hamilton.

Britton, J. (1970) *Language and Learning*. Harmondsworth: Penguin.

Brown, H. Rap (1972) 'Street talk', in T. Kochman (ed.), *Rappin' and Stylin' Out*. Chicago: University of Illinois Press.

Bruner, J. (1976) 'The nature and uses of immaturity', in J. Bruner, A. Jolly, and K. Sylva (eds), *Play*. Harmondsworth: Penguin.

Bruner, J. (1986) *Actual Minds, Possible Worlds*. Cambridge, MA: Harvard University Press.

Bruner, J. (1994) 'Life as narrative', in A.H. Dyson and C. Genishi (eds), *The Need for Story*. Urbana, IL: NCTE. pp. 28–37.

Clark, M. (1976) *Young Fluent Readers*. London: Heinemann.

Conklin, H.C. (1964) 'Linguistic play in its cultural context', in D. Hymes (ed.), *Language in Culture and Society*. New York: Harper and Row. pp. 295–300.

Dundes, A., Leach, J.W. and Ozkok, B. (1972) 'The strategy of Turkish boys' duelling rhymes', in D. Hymes and J.J. Gumperz (eds), *Directions in Sociolinguistics*. New York: Holt, Rinehart and Winston. pp. 130–60.

Dyson, Anne Haas (1994) '"I'm gonna express myself": the politics of story in the children's worlds', in A.H. Dyson and C. Genishi (eds), *The Need for Story*. Urbana, IL: NCTE. pp. 155–71.

Fox, C. (1993) *At the Very Edge of the Forest*. London: Cassell.

Fox, C. (1997) 'Children's conceptions of imaginative play revealed in their oral stories', in N. Hall and J. Martello (eds), *Listening to Children Think: Exploring Talk in the Early Years*. London: Hodder and Stoughton. pp. 54–63.

Fox, C. (1998) 'Serious play: the relationship between young children's oral invented stories and their learning', *Current Psychology of Cognition*, 17 (2): 211–28.

Frake, C.O. (1964) 'How to ask for a drink in Subanun', *American Anthropologist*, 66 (6) Part 2.

Freud, S. (1920) *Beyond the Pleasure Principle*, Standard edn (1955). Harmondsworth: Pelican.

Gallaz, C. (1985) *Rose Blanche*. London: Cape.

Genette, G. (1972) *Narrative Discourse*, trans. 1980. Oxford: Blackwell.

Gossen, G.H. (1976) 'Verbal duelling in Chamula', in B. Kirschenblatt-Gimblett (ed.), *Speech Play*. Philadelphia: University of Pennsylvania Press.

Gregory, E. and Williams, A. (2000) *City Literacies*. London: Routledge.

Hall, N. (1989) *Writing with Reason: the Emergence of Authorship in Young Children*. London: Hodder and Stoughton.

Hall, N. (1999) *Interactive Writing in the Primary School*. Reading: University of Reading.

Hall, N. and Robinson, A. (1995) *Exploring Writing and Play in the Early Years*. London: Fulton.

Harding, D.W. (1974) 'Psychological processes in the reading of fiction', in M. Meek, G. Barton and A. Warlow (eds), *The Cool Web*. Oxford: Bodley Head. pp. 58–72.

Hardy, B. (1968) 'Towards a poetics of fiction: an approach through narrative', in B. Hardy (ed.), *Novel: a Forum on Fiction*. Providence, RI: Brown University. pp. 12–23.

Heath, S.B. (1982) 'Protean shapes in literacy events: ever-shifting oral and literate traditions', in D. Tannen (ed.), *Spoken and Written Language*. Norwood, NJ: Ablex. pp. 91–117.

Heath, S.B. (1983) *Ways with Words*. Cambridge: Cambridge University Press.

Heath, S.B. (1994) 'Stories as ways of acting together', in A.H. Dyson and C. Genishi (eds), *The Need for Story*. Urbana, IL: NCTE. pp. 206–20.

Hewitt, R. (1986) *White Talk, Black Talk*. Cambridge: Cambridge University Press.

Kernan, K.T. (1977) 'Semantic and expressive elaboration in children's narratives', in J. Ervin-Tripp and C. Mitchell-Kernan (eds), *Child Discourse*. New York: Academic. pp. 91–102.

Kochman, T. (1972) 'Toward an ethnography of black American speech behaviour', in T. Kochman (ed.), *Rappin' and Stylin' Out*. Chicago: University of Illinois Press.

Labov, W. (1972a) 'The transformation of experience in narrative syntax', in W. Labov (ed.), *Language in the Inner City*. Oxford: Blackwell. pp. 354–96.

Labov, W. (1972b) 'Rules for ritual insults', in W. Labov (ed.), *Language in the Inner City*. Oxford: Blackwell. pp. 297–353.

Langer, S. (1953) *Feeling and Form*. London: Routledge and Kegan Paul.

Mandler, J.M. and Johnson, N.S. (1977) 'Remembrance of things parsed: story structure and recall', *Cognitive Psychology*, 9: 111–51.

Maranda, E.K. and Maranda, P. (1971) *Structural Models in Folklore and Transformational Essays*. The Hague: Mouton.

Meek, M. (1988) *How Texts Teach What Readers Learn*. Stroud: Thimble.

Menig-Peterson, C.L. and McCabe, A. (1978) 'Children's Orientation of a Listener to the Context of their Narratives', *Developmental Psychology*, 14 (6): 582–92.

Mitchell-Kernan, C. (1972) 'Signifying, loud talking and marking', in T. Kochman (ed.), *Rappin' and Stylin' Out*. Chicago: University of Illinois Press.

Nicolopoulou, A., Scales, B. and Weintraub, J. (1994) 'Gender differences and symbolic imagination in the stories of four year olds', in A.H. Dyson and C. Genishi (eds), *The Need for Story*. Urbana, IL: NCTE. pp. 102–23.

Ong, W. (1982) *Orality and Literacy*. London: Methuen.

Paley, V. (1981) *Wally's Stories*. Cambridge, MA: Harvard University Press.

Piaget, J. (1951) *Play, Dreams and Imitation in Childhood*. London: Routledge and Kegan Paul.

Pitcher, E.G. and Prelinger, E. (1963) *Children Tell Stories*. New York: International Universities Press.

Rampton, B. (1995) *Crossing: Language and Ethnicity among Adolescents*. London: Longman.

Robinson, A., Hall, N. and Crawford, L. (1990) *'Some Day You Will No All About Me'. Young Children's Explorations in the World of Letters*. London: Glasgow.

Rosen, B. (1988) *And None of It Was Nonsense*. London: Glasgow.

Rosen, H. (1984) *Stories and Meanings*. Sheffield: NATE.

Rumelhart, D.E. (1975) 'Notes on a schema for stories', in D.G. Bobrow and A. Collins (eds), *Representation and Understanding* New York: Academic. pp. 211–36.

Rumelhart, D.E. (1977) 'Understanding and summarizing brief stories', in D. La Berget (ed.), *Basic Processes in Reading*. Hillsdale, NJ: Erlbaum. pp. 265–304.

Sachs, H. (1972) 'On the analyzability of stories by children', in D. Hymes and J.J. Gumperz (eds), *Directions in Sociolinguistics*. New York: Holt, Rinehart and Winston. pp. 325–45.

Scholes, R. (1981) 'Language, narrative and anti-narrative', in W.J.T. Mitchell (ed.), *On Narrative*. Chicago: University of Chicago Press.

Scollon, R. and Scollon, S. (1981) *Narrative, Literacy and Face in Inter-Ethnic Communication*. Norwood, NJ: Ablex. pp. 57–98.

Smitherman, G. (1994) 'The blacker the berry, the sweeter the juice: African American student writers', in A.H. Dyson and C. Genishi (eds), *The Need for Story*. Urbana, IL: National Council of Teachers of English. pp. 80–101.

Stein, N.L. and Glenn, C.G. (1978) 'An analysis of story comprehension in elementary school children', in R.O. Freedle (ed.), *New Directions in Discourse Processing*. Norwood, NJ: Able. pp. 53–119.

Street, B. (1993) *Cross-Cultural Approaches to Literacy*. Cambridge: Cambridge University Press.

Sutton-Smith, B. (1981) *The Folk Stories of Children*. Philadelphia: University of Pennsylvania Press.

Umiker-Sebeok, D.J. (1979) 'Pre-school children's intra-conversational narratives', *Journal of Child Language*, 6: 91–109.

Vygotsky, L. (1978) *Mind in Society*. Cambridge MA: Harvard University Press.

Watson-Gegeo, K.A. and Boggs, S.T. (1977) 'From verbal play to talk story: the role of routines in speech events among Hawaiian children', in S. Ervin-Tripp and C. Mitchell-Kernan (eds), *Child Discourse*, New York: Academic. pp. 67–90.

17

Uncovering the Key Skills
of Reading

ROGER BEARD

This chapter attempts to provide an overview of research that has been undertaken to uncover the key skills of reading. It will outline the debates that have been a feature in this area of literacy studies over many years and examine more recent theoretical stances that have tried to reconcile the earlier debates. The chapter will also briefly consider the implications of the advent of hypertext for our understanding of what key reading skills comprise.

It needs to be stressed that the chapter is focused on the key skills of interpreting and comprehending text in printed or electronic media in written English. Similar discussions that are focused on other languages will raise different issues, particularly if the languages are not alphabetic ones like English. As will be seen, some of the key skills of reading written English are related to the fact that written English comprises a code in which alphabetic letters represent the phonemes of spoken language (Byrne, 1998).

Much of the research on reading skills has been of an experimental kind and the chapter will inevitably reflect this. However, the discussions in the chapter have been written to take account of the fact that the audience for this handbook is likely to be predominantly from an educational background. One of the few substantial naturalistic studies is by Bussis et al. (1985). Their conceptual framework regarding reading skills has much in common with the experimental work in the field, discussing the relative importance of decoding, anticipation of grammatical sequences and so on, although they report the use of observational and interview methodologies and place a relatively greater emphasis on the importance of constructing meaning from text.

There is a huge literature on this topic and the publications that the chapter focuses upon have been selected either because they have been particularly influential or because they are representative of a certain perspective. Where these references are rather dated, other more recent publications have been suggested. It is also important to note that, although the chapter focuses on certain technical skills of literacy, these skills are developed within social processes in homes, classrooms and the wider world. The chapter will conclude by noting that becoming a successful reader involves both key skills and meaningful social practices.

THE LANGUAGE BASE OF LITERACY

It is widely agreed that language has generally preceded literacy, both historically in the evolution of humankind and individually in normal patterns of childhood development (Liberman, 1995). This precedence suggests that the understanding of reading will benefit from a consideration of language, on which literacy is in some ways 'parasitic'. In attempting to uncover the key skills of reading, the structure of language is a useful starting point. Key skills are taken to be the centrally important abilities that can be developed through training and/or practice, in a process described by Bussis et al. (1985: 67) as orchestrating personal resources to achieve a particular result.

Some influential linguists (e.g. Crystal, 1976) have shown how the structure of spoken English can be helpfully represented by three strands:

pronunciation (sounds and spellings), grammar (syntax and morphology) and meaning (words and discourse).

Although different terms may be used, the three-strand distinction is common in linguistic description. Such a model is also likely to contain the elements for the 'encoding' of the language. In English this is centred on the use of the graphology, the system of vowels, consonants etc., to represent the phonology, the system of sounds (phonemes). Written language often involves a more deliberate use of vocabulary and grammar, in order to fulfil the sociocultural contexts which have led to the decision to use written language in the first place. Written language also follows certain conventions of space and direction: in English normally left to right, down the page. Written language uses various kinds of punctuation that compare, in a limited way, with pauses in speech. Written language is also pragmatically different. The reader is typically distant from the creator of the written language in both space and time, whereas the use of speech normally involves a face-to-face interaction. The respective genres and registers used often reflect this.

It is important to add that subdivisions such as the one outlined above are rarely all-embracing and some strands of language may cut across others. For instance, grammatical rules apply within words (morphology) as well as between words (syntax). Meaning is conveyed at word level (vocabulary) as well as at discourse or text level. Punctuation is part of the graphology but also plays an important role in confirming the grammatical rules that are being used.

Analysing the strands of language in this way provides a helpful starting point for attempts to undercover the key skills of reading. Taking the three strands in turn, the letter–sound relationships of unfamiliar words have to be decoded; grammatical sequences have to be followed; words have to be recognized; and the meaning attributed to them has to be understood. Such an analysis seems to imply that successful reading and writing may involve effective use of information from a range of sources. Descriptions of these sources of information have often fallen into one of two groups, often described as 'bottom-up' or 'top-down'. The two groups approach the language base of literacy from different directions. The former gives emphasis to the code that is used in written language to represent the spoken; the latter emphasizes the meaning that is conveyed by the written language. The distinction is clearly made by Jeanne Chall (1983: 28–9). She explains that 'bottom-up' approaches are those that view the reading process as developing from perception of letters, spelling patterns, and words, to sentence and paragraph meaning.

'Top-down' approaches stress the first importance of language and meaning for reading comprehension and also for word recognition. The reader theoretically samples the text in order to confirm and modify initial hypotheses. Each approach will now be briefly discussed in turn before a third approach is considered, one that deals with the interactive nature of reading skills.

ARE THE KEY SKILLS 'BOTTOM-UP' ONES?

One of the best-known bottom-up models of reading has been outlined by Philip Gough (1972) and is focused on 'one second of reading'. The following summary of Gough's model is derived from that provided by David Rumelhart (1985). The visual information (written characters) from the text is seen and registered in an 'icon' that holds the information while it is scanned. The written characters are then processed by a 'pattern recognition' device. This device identifies the letters, which are then read into the 'character register'. While the letters are being held in this way, a 'decoder' converts the character strings into the underlying phonemic representation. The phonemic representation of the original character strings serves as an input to a 'librarian', which matches up these phonemic strings against the vocabulary store (lexicon). The resulting entries are then fed into 'primary memory'. The four or five lexical items held in primary memory at any one time provide input to a 'wondrous mechanism', which applies its knowledge of the syntax and semantics to determine the meaning of the input. This 'deep structure' of meaning is sent on to the final memory register, TPWSGWTAU ('the place where sentences go when they are understood'). When all inputs of the text have found their final resting place in TPWSGWTAU, the reading is complete.

Gough goes on to consider the implications of this model for the young learner. He emphasizes that children of school age bring several important capacities to learning to read. They can produce and understand sentences; they have a vocabulary; they have the ability to understand language; and they have a phonological system. Gough also concedes that identifying letters, 'blank, stark, immovable, without form or comeliness', does not come naturally. He stresses that letter recognition has to be accomplished, 'whether by means of alphabet books, blocks, or soup'. However, the fundamental challenge in learning to read, according to Gough, arises in what is commonly referred to as 'decoding', converting characters into phonemes. After discussing the limitations of teaching approaches that use word recognition ('look-and-say') techniques, Gough argues that children should be helped to map the letter–sound code from the start, while assuring them that the code is solvable. Gough stresses that he does not see phonics as a method of teaching children grapheme–phoneme correspondence rules. The rules that children learn are not the rules they must master, but rather heuristics for locating words through auditory means. The lexical representations of those words then provide data for the induction of the real character–phoneme rules. Skill in phonics provides children with a valuable means of data collection about the writing system. According to Gough, the reader appears to go from print to meaning as if by magic. But this is an illusion. The reader really plods through the sentence, letter by letter, word by word. Good readers need not guess what the text conveys; poor readers should not.

Another well-known bottom-up model is that of David LaBerge and Jay Samuels (1974). This model consists of three memory systems. As the text is processed, the three systems hold different representations. The visual memory system holds visually based representations of the different elements that make up the text (letters, spelling groups, and so on). The phonological and semantic memory systems similarly hold phonological and semantic representations. Visual information is analysed by a set of specialized 'feature detectors', most of which are fed directly into 'letter codes'. The letter codes feed into 'spelling pattern codes', which in turn feed into 'visual word codes'. There are a number of routes whereby words can be mapped into meanings, either directly (necessary to distinguish between homophones like 'pair' and 'pear') or through word group and phonetic codes (necessary for a word group meaning like 'time out').

Some criticisms of bottom-up models

In discussing these two bottom-up models, Rumelhart draws attention to several research findings that are difficult to account for with either model.

First, the perceptions of letters often depend on the surrounding letters. Ambiguous symbols, such as a poorly written *w*, may be interpreted as an *e* and a *v* as in *event*. The reader is saved from this ambiguity if the symbol appears in a sentence like 'Jack and Jill *went* up the hill'.

Secondly, the perception of words depends on the syntactic environment in which we encounter them. Studies of oral reading errors made by children and adults show that over 90% of reading errors are grammatically consistent with the sentence to the point of error (Weber, 1970). Rumelhart argues that such findings are difficult to reconcile with the bottom-up models discussed above. In the Gough model, for example, syntactic processing occurs later in the sequence than the findings imply.

Thirdly, the perception of words depends on the semantic environment in which we encounter them. This environment can be seen at work in our perception of homonyms ('*wind* up the clock' versus 'the *wind* was blowing') and also in resolving ambiguities ('They are eating apples' could mean either 'The children are eating apples' or 'The apples may be eaten'). The importance of semantic context in letter identification was noted as early as 1886 by Catell. He found that that skilful readers can perceive whole words as quickly and easily as single letters, and whole phrases as quickly and easily as strings of three or four unrelated letters (cited by Adams, 1990: 95).

The authors of the most influential bottom-up theories have in time accepted that their original theories have been overtaken by evidence. In subsequent publications, Gough, and LaBerge and Samuels, have conceded the weaknesses in their models of reading. Gough (1985) accepts that predictable texts facilitate word recognition, although he warns that most words are not predictable and so can only be read bottom-up. He accepts that his model did not pay sufficient heed to the problems of understanding text, but believes that it still points in the right direction. Similarly, LaBerge and Samuels' model has been revised to include feedback loops from semantic memory to earlier stages of processing (Samuels, 1985).

ARE THE KEY SKILLS 'TOP-DOWN' ONES?

In contrast with the bottom-up models of reading, one of the best known of the top-down models actually includes the word 'guessing'. According to David Crystal (1976) 'psycholinguistics' is the study of language variation in relation to thinking and to other psychological processes within the individual. Kenneth Goodman (1967), however, has given the term a more radical connotation in literacy research. His 'psycholinguistic guessing game' model of reading assumes a close and direct parallel between the learning of spoken and written language. He asserts that learning to read is as natural as learning to speak. He suggests that the basis of fluent reading is not word recognition but hypothesis forming about 'the meanings that lie ahead'. He argues that reading involves the selection of maximally productive cues to confirm or deny these meanings.

In a later paper, Goodman (1985) stresses the tentative information processing that is involved in reading. He argues that reading is meaning seeking, selective and constructive. Inference and prediction are central. Readers use the least amount of available text information necessary in relation to their existing linguistic and conceptual schemata to get to meaning.

Frank Smith's (1971; 1973) model of reading drew heavily on the seminal work of Noam Chomsky (1957). Chomsky had shown how human language acquisition could not be explained by a linear model. Children did not just learn language by imitation or by connecting together various bits of language (e.g. sounds, words or phrases). Using their inherited capacity for language learning (a kind of 'language acquisition device'), children all over the world seemed to learn to speak by a process of hypothesis testing and discovery, through authentic interaction with others. Smith argued that precisely the same kind of argument may be applied to reading. A child is equipped with every skill that he or she needs in order to read and to learn to read. Given adequate and motivating experience with meaningful text, learning to read should be as natural as learning to talk.

As with Goodman's model, there is a strong emphasis on the 'non-visual' information that the reader brings to the text. Reading comprises a process of 'reducing uncertainty' as hypotheses about the structure and meaning of the text are mediated by sentence, word and letter identification if they are needed. Smith argues that readers normally can and do identify meaning without, or ahead of, the identification of individual words. Smith argues that skilful readers do not attend to individual words of text, that skilful readers do not process individual letters and that spelling – sound translations are irrelevant for readers.

Some criticisms of top-down models

As with the bottom-up theories, there have been recurrent criticisms of the top-down ones. Eleanor Gibson and Harry Levin (1975) point out that Goodman's model of reading does not explain how the reader knows when to confirm guesses and where to look to do so. Philip Gough (1981) has consistently challenged how predictable written language is. His studies suggest that, at most, we can only predict one word in four when all the succeeding text is covered. Furthermore, the words that are easiest to predict are often the words that are most easily recognized. When skilled adult readers read a text with content words missing, prediction rates may fall as low as 10% (Gough, 1983; see also Gough and Wren, 1999).

One of the most searching critiques of Goodman's theories has been provided by Jessie Reid (1993). She notes that Goodman oscillates between using the terms 'predicting', 'anticipating', 'expecting' and 'guessing'. These terms, though closely related, are not synonymous. Reid asks a number of questions: how does the reader know which cues will be most productive? Are the criteria fixed for any given word? If the predicted word is not on the page, what then? Can readers sample for the most productive cues in the word they did not expect? Most fundamentally, is the guessing game model optimally efficient?

One of the most detailed attacks on Smith's theories was made by Marilyn Jager Adams in 1991. Adams acknowledges that Smith's argument was, in some respects, insightful: he was correct in arguing that skilful reading does not proceed on the basis of identifying one letter or word at a time. But extending the ideas about the language acquisition device, the details of which were only speculative, was, according to Adams, an enormous and gratuitous leap.

Adams examines several of Smith's assertions in the light of recent psychological research and shows how misleading they can be, including those mentioned earlier in this chapter. In examining the assertion that skilful readers do not attend to individual words of text, Adams refers to research involving computer-mediated eye movement technology. She cites evidence that fluent readers do skip a few words, mostly short function words, but that most words are processed either in eye fixations or in the peripheral vision of the saccades of eye movements (Just and Carpenter, 1987; see also Carver, 1990; Rayner, 1992). Adams feels that Smith is right in warning against an over-concentration on individual words, but wrong to imply that readers should not process them. Skilful readers have learned to process words and spellings very quickly but such automaticity comes from having read words, not from skipping them.

Adams also considers the assertion that skilful readers don't process individual letters. Adams acknowledges that skilful readers do not look or feel as if they are processing individual letters of text as they read, but research has repeatedly shown that they do (McConkie and Zola, 1981; Rayner and Pollatsek, 1989). Individual letters and spelling patterns are processed interdependently as the text is perceived and comprehended, in a process of 'parallel processing' (McClelland and Rumelhart, 1986; Rumelhart and McClelland, 1986). According to Adams, to deny letter identification in reading is like saying that there is no such thing as a grain of sand. Skilled readers can process letters so quickly because of visual knowledge of words. This knowledge is based on their memories of the sequences of letters, which make up words. The more we read, the more this knowledge is reinforced and enriched.

Unlike Gough, and LaBerge and Samuels, however, there was no retraction from the most influential top-down theorists. In his sardonically titled *Phonics Phacts*, Goodman (1993) reasserts the 'natural' view of learning to read. In responding to the many research studies reviewed in Adams' *Beginning to Read* (1990) which, he acknowledges, sought to undermine his arguments, he replies that his is a 'real-world' (as opposed to an instructional and laboratory studies) view of reading. However, less convincingly, he relies for evidence on experiments with short, decontextualized and disfigured texts (i.e. not from the 'real world') in support of his case. Frank Smith also reflects a lack of willingness to accept any limitations in his theories by producing a fifth edition of his book *Understanding Reading* (1994) without any substantial changes to his original theories.

On both sides of the Atlantic, however, there is a clear consensus that the most influential top-down theories have also been overtaken by evidence. In three recent independent reviews of research commissioned by central government bodies in the UK, Roger Beard (1999), Jane Hurry (2000) and Colin Harrison (2002) all reach a similar conclusion. Hurry concludes as follows: 'It is now very clear that Goodman and Smith were wrong in thinking that skilled readers pay so little attention to the details of print. Research on the reading process in the 1980s produced clear evidence that skilled readers attend closely to letters and words and in fact that it is the less skilled readers who rely more heavily on contextual clues to support their reading' (2000: 9). Colin Harrison also spells out the implications of recent research in some detail:

What we now believe, on the basis of eye-movement research with equipment far more accurate and faster than used to be available, is that fluent readers fixate nearly every word as they read, and that, far from simply sampling letters on the page in a partial and semi-random fashion, and looking closely at the letters in a word when it seems necessary, a good reader processes just about every letter in every word, very rapidly and very accurately. This is almost the opposite of the model of a good reader that some of us read about in the works of Ken Goodman (1970; 1967) or Frank Smith (1971). (2002: 18)

ARE THE KEY SKILLS INTERACTIVE ONES?

One of the most influential publications in support of an 'interactive-compensatory' model of reading was written by Keith Stanovich (1980). Drawing on over 180 sources, Stanovich argues that fluent reading is an interactive process in which information is used from several knowledge sources simultaneously (letter recognition, letter–sound relationships, vocabulary, knowledge of syntax and meaning). Various component subskills of reading can cooperate in a compensatory manner. For example, higher level processes can compensate for deficiencies in lower level processes: the reader with poor word recognition skills may actually be prone to a greater reliance on contextual factors because these provide additional sources of information.

Indeed, in contrast to the top-down theories, Stanovich shows that good readers do not use context cues more than poor readers do. In contrast, it is weaknesses in word recognition that lead to relatively greater use of contextual cues as reading proficiency of continuous text develops. Better readers may appear to use context cues more effectively in cloze procedure activities when words are artificially deleted and the surrounding text is visible. But what is at issue here is not the presence of contextual knowledge in good readers, but their use of and reliance upon it in normal reading of continuous text (good readers may be more sensitive to context, and yet less dependent upon it, because information is more easily available to them from other sources). Stanovich draws on dozens of studies to show that fluent readers are distinguished by rapid word recognition and effective comprehension strategies.

In the UK a similarly extensive research review has been brought together by Jane Oakhill and Alan Garnham (1988; see also Oakhill, 1993). Like Stanovich, they question top-down theories in the light of the relative speeds of the processes involved. They show how, in fluent reading, the use of contextual cues to help identify a word is usually unnecessary because words are recognized from visual information so quickly.

Perfetti (1995: 108) notes that research findings suggest that the role of contextual cues in word recognition and in comprehension is radically different from that assumed by top-down models: 'the hallmark of skilled reading is fast *context-free* word identification combined with a rich *context-dependent* text understanding' [author's original italics].

Some criticisms of the interactive model

Perhaps not surprisingly, the main criticisms of the interactive-compensatory model have come from the bottom-up and top-down theorists. Gough, for example, is concerned that:

> It is easy to create a model which is 'right'; all you need do is make one interactive or transactional enough such that everything in reading influences everything else. The result will be 'right' because it will be impervious to disprove; it will yield no falsifiable predictions. But my view has always been that such models are not really right, they are simply empty, for a model which cannot be just proved is a model without content. (1985: 687)

Smith is similarly unconvinced. In the third edition of *Understanding Reading*, Smith (1988: 193) suggests that no top-down theorist would want to claim that reading is not an interaction with the text. He goes on to warn, though, that many interaction theories tend to be 'bottom-up in disguise; they sound more liberal but they still tend to give the basic power to the print'.

Nevertheless, the interactive-compensatory model does seem to be generally accepted by many in literacy education as one of the most valid ways of representing the key skills of reading. Stanovich (2000: 7) notes that his 1980 paper has received over 350 citations. Harrison (2002) reports that the paper is widely regarded as one of the most important of recent years and that it remains broadly speaking uncontested (for discussion of some of the implications for policy and practice, see Perfetti, 1995; Stanovich and Stanovich, 1995; Pressley, 1998).

Stanovich himself, in reviewing the powerful impact of his work, suggests that 'at the gross level, the results have stood the test of time – as have the general theoretical analyses' (2000: 8). He goes on to identify two studies that have advanced the theory. First, Nation and Snowling (1998) found that individuals with poor comprehension may be at risk for poor development in word recognition because they lack the language prediction skills that are needed to add contextual information to partial phonological information. Stanovich suggests that such individuals may reflect another form of the 'Matthew effect' that he himself has proposed in earlier publications: 'the facilitation of further learning by a previously existing knowledge base that is rich and elaborated' (2000: 185; see also Stanovich, 1986). Secondly, Tunmer and Chapman (1998: 60) report that good decoders do not need to rely on context so often because of their superior ability to recognize words. When such readers do use context they are much more likely to identify unfamiliar words than are less skilled readers (see also Share, 1995). Stanovich (2000: 11) suggests that this work elaborates and builds upon the interactive-compensatory model in an attempt to explain more of the variance in reading ability.

ONE REMAINING ISSUE

This chapter has brought together a range of sources on a complex, and sometimes controversial, topic. There are signs that something of a consensus has now been reached among the majority of researchers in the field. One remaining issue, however, is how an interactive-compensatory model can be effectively summarized, perhaps diagrammatically, for wider dissemination among practitioners. For some years, a kind of overlapping circles diagram has been used, apparently being particularly promoted in the work of Routman (1988) and others. Adams (1998) describes the way in which this diagram has been adopted in teacher education and is concerned that it may sometimes be used to underplay the role of phonics, as 'grapho-phonic cues' are tucked away at the bottom of the model, perhaps suggesting that such cues are a last resort in reading. Instead, in her own publications, Adams prefers a triangular model, based on the work of McClelland and Rumelhart (1986), in which the role of the 'phonological processor' in the decoding of unfamiliar words is shown by a phonological loop. The analytic and iconic aspects of this issue may be worth considering further by readers of this chapter.

CONSOLIDATING THE LEARNING OF KEY SKILLS

In recent years, research has examined in greater depth the particular importance of several of these key skills. Three in particular have received sustained attention: fluency, comprehension and phonics. While all three are in some ways assumed in the models discussed in this chapter, recent studies suggest that each of them can be positively developed by specific teaching approaches. The significance of all three has been recently confirmed by the report of the National Reading Panel (2000) in the United States of America.

As much of the Panel's work was based on research syntheses of research, reference to individual studies may be misleading; the interested reader is referred to the Panel's full report and discussion. Improvements in reading fluency can be effected especially by guided oral reading, combined with feedback and guidance. These improvements have resulted in increases in overall achievement, affecting word recognition and comprehension.

Independent silent reading is also likely to play a positive role, although the research base is less well established (2000: Section 3).

Similarly, reading comprehension can be promoted by a variety of techniques, including those that focus on vocabulary, on text comprehension instruction, and on teacher preparation and comprehension strategies instruction (2000: Section 4).

The National Reading Panel report also concludes that systematic phonics instruction makes a bigger contribution to children's growth in reading than alternative programmes that provide unsystematic or no phonics teaching. Phonics teaching was found to be effective when taught individually, in small groups, and as classes. No one approach differed significantly from the others in this respect. On the basis of its research review, the Panel concludes that systematic phonics teaching produces the biggest impact on growth in reading before children learn to read independently. To be effective, systematic phonics teaching introduced in the kindergarten age range must be appropriately designed for learners and must begin with 'foundational' knowledge involving alphabet letters and phonemic awareness.

The research perspective adopted by the NRP has been criticized by Cunningham (2001), who argues that the Panel adopted an excessively positivist philosophy of science. At the same time, Cunningham generally endorses the Panel's conclusions on all three aspects referred to above. In relation to phonics, for example, he argues that: 'the preponderance of logic and evidence is against those who contend that it is all right to provide young school children with reading instruction containing little or no phonics, with any phonics included being taught unsystematically' (2001: 332). On the role of guided oral reading in developing fluency, Cunningham concludes that the findings of the Panel seem likely to hold up over time in the real world. Furthermore, the section on comprehension he describes as more interesting and potentially valuable than the other parts of the Panel's report because it does not adhere too closely to *a priori* methodological standards.

NEW MEDIA: NEW SKILLS?

With the advent of electronic texts, new questions are raised about the nature of these texts and the skills that they require. According to David Reinking (1998: xxiv), hypertext has become the quintessential example of how printed and electronic texts differ. The former are generally linear and hierarchical; the latter are fluid, a set of different potential texts awaiting realization. Hypertext elements are verbal or graphic units and the links that join them. Hypertexts are multilinear, constructed so that the textual elements can be read in any order (Bolter, 1991).

Such distinctions suggest that the key skills in reading hypertext will need to be underpinned by an understanding of the availability of different routes through the material. These 'navigational' skills (Kamil and Lane, 1998) have been further delineated by Landow (1992) as an ability to deal with 'departures' (understanding where a particular link may take a reader) and 'arrivals' (the evaluation of a new textual location).

As with much electronic text, another key requirement is the ability to evaluate and make effective complementary use of visual images. This realization points up two possible relations between word and image in electronic media: hypermedia or interactive television that may evolve in time. Both have very different cultural implications from the print-based verbal culture to which educational institutions are still adapted (Bolter, 1998). Nevertheless, it is salutary to note that explorations of these issues are still largely located in printed texts, often with little visual supporting material (see Reinking, 1998, for a discussion of this apparent paradox).

There is less agreement about the particular reading skills required by hypertext. Horney and Anderson-Inman (1994) have categorized hypertext reading as involving skimming, checking, reading, responding, studying and reviewing, although these might also be described as reading strategies. However, an underlying issue, according to Kamil et al. (2000), is that when a reader encounters a hypertext link, there is often no way of predicting whether the information to be acquired is useful. This may explain why Gillingham (1993), even when working with adults, found that hypertext may interfere with comprehension when the goal is to answer specific questions.

A recent study has underlined the complex issues that need to be addressed in understanding the key skills of reading electronic texts. Pang and Kamil (2002) report a study of 18 third-grade students. The sample included good and poor readers; all were experienced with computers, and about half were experienced with hypertext. The students each read four passages selected from an Internet-based children's newsletter, with hypertext links. Hard copy versions were also provided. The majority of the students expressed a preference for reading the hard copy versions of the texts. A majority also preferred reading the whole text first before exploring any hyperlinks.

In general, the advent of hypertext seems not to alter the significance of the key reading skills discussed in this chapter, but instead to raise new questions about their strategic use in the new information age contexts created by electronic media.

CONCLUSION

If something of a consensus about the key skills of reading has now been reached, this consensus can be used as a kind of conceptual infrastructure for policy and practice decisions. Although the chapter has inevitably drawn primarily on experimental research, the infrastructure can be accommodated and built upon by others who use different theoretical perspectives (see Oakhill and Beard, 1999). Moreover, other chapters in this handbook are testimony to the fact that becoming a successful reader involves the development of key skills and involvement in many social processes. These processes help learners, for example, to understand what reading is for and what it does; to develop positive attitude towards reading; to link the acts of reading and writing; to have access to a range of rich and interesting texts; and to be essentially concerned with making meaning.

Definitions of literacy are changing as new kinds of communication skill evolve and are better understood. This chapter has shown how the study of reading processes has also evolved, leading to a more informed understanding of what goes on when we interact with written language.

REFERENCES

Adams, M.J. (1990) *Beginning to Read: Thinking and Learning about Print*. Cambridge, MA: MIT Press.

Adams, M.J. (1991) 'Why not phonics *and* whole language?', in W. Ellis (ed.), *All Language and the Creation of Literacy*. Baltimore, MD: Orton Dyslexia Society. pp. 40–53.

Adams, M.J. (1998) 'The three-cueing system', in J. Osborn and F. Lehr (eds), *Literacy for All: Issues in Teaching and Learning*. New York: Guilford. pp. 73–99.

Beard, R. (1999) *The National Literacy Strategy: Review of Research and other Related Evidence*. London: Department for Education and Employment.

Bolter, J.D. (1991) *Writing Space: the Computer, Hypertext and the History of Writing*. Hillsdale, NJ: Erlbaum.

Bolter, J.D. (1998) 'Hypertext and the question of visual literacy', in D. Reinking, M.C. McKenna, L.D. Labbo and R.D. Keiffer (eds), *Handbook of Literacy and Technology*. Mahwah, NJ: Erlbaum. pp. 3–13.

Bussis, A.M., Chittenden, E.A., Amarel, M. and Klausner, E. (1985) *Inquiry into Meaning*. Hillsdale, NJ: Erlbaum.

Byrne, B. (1998) *The Foundations of Literacy: the Child's Acquisition of the Alphabetic Principle*. Hove: Psychology Press.

Carver, R.P. (1990) *Reading Rate: a Review of Research and Theory*. San Diego, CA: Academic.

Chall, J. (1983) *Learning to Read: the Great Debate*, updated edn. New York: McGraw-Hill.

Chomsky, N. (1957) *Syntactic Structures*. The Hague: Mouton.

Crystal, D. (1976) *Child Language, Linguistics and Learning*. London: Arnold.

Cunningham, J.W. (2001) 'The National Reading Panel Report', *Reading Research Quarterly*, 36 (3): 326–35.

Gibson, E.J. and Levin, H. (1975) *The Psychology of Reading*. Cambridge, MA: MIT Press.

Gillingham, M. (1993) 'Effects of question complexity and reader strategies on adults' hypertext comprehension', *Journal of Research and Computing*, 26: 1–15.

Goodman, K.S. (1970/1967) 'Reading: a psycholinguistic guessing game', *Journal of the Reading Specialist*, 4 (1): 11–30.

Goodman, K.S. (1985) 'Unity in reading', in H. Singer and R.B. Ruddell (eds), *Theoretical Models and Processes of Reading* 3rd edn. Newark, DE: International Reading Association. pp. 813–40.

Goodman, K.S. (1993) *Phonics Phacts*. Ontario: Scholastic.

Gough, P.B. (1972) 'One second of reading', in J.F. Kavanagh and I.G. Mattingly (eds), *Language by Ear and Eye*. Cambridge, MA: MIT Press. pp. 331–58.

Gough, P.B. (1981) 'A comment on Kenneth Goodman', in M.L. Kamil (ed), *Directions in Reading: Research and Instruction*. Washington, DC: National Reading Conference. pp. 92–5.

Gough, P.B. (1983) 'Context, form, and interaction', in K. Rayner (ed.), *Eye Movements in Reading*. New York: Academic. pp. 203–11.

Gough, P.B. (1985) 'One second of reading: a postscript', in H. Singer and R.B. Ruddell (eds), *Theoretical Models and Processes of Reading*, 3rd edn. Newark, DE: International Reading Association. pp. 687–8.

Gough, P.B. and Wren, S. (1999) 'Constructing meaning: the role of decoding', in J. Oakhill and R. Beard (eds), *Reading Development and the Teaching of Reading: a Psychological Perspective*. Oxford: Blackwell.

Harrison, C. (2002) *The National Strategy for English at Key Stage 3: Roots and Research*. London: Department for Education and Skills.

Horney, M.A. and Anderson-Inman, L. (1994) 'The electrotext project: hypertext reading patterns of middle school students', *Journal of Educational Multimedia and Hypermedia*, 3: 71–91.

Hurry, J. (2000) *Intervention Strategies to Support Pupils with Difficulties in Literacy during Key Stage 1: Review of Research*. London: Qualifications and Curriculum Authority.

Just, M.A. and Carpenter, P.A. (1987) *The Psychology of Reading and Language Comprehension*. Boston: Allyn and Bacon.

Kamil, M.L. and Lane, D.M. (1998) 'Researching the relation between technology and literacy: an agenda for the 21st century', in D. Reinking, M.C. McKenna, L.D. Labbo and R.D. Keiffer (eds), *Handbook of Literacy and Technology*. Mahwah, NJ: Erlbaum. pp. 323–41.

Kamil, M.L., Intrator, S.M. and Kim, H.S. (2000) 'The effects of other technologies on literacy and literacy learning', in M. Kamil, P.B. Mosenthal, D. Pearson and R. Barr (eds), *Handbook of Reading Research*, vol. III. Mahwah, NJ: Erlbaum. pp. 771–88.

LaBerge, D. and Samuels, S.J. (1974) 'Towards a theory of automatic information processing in reading', *Cognitive Psychology*, 6: 293–323.

Landow, G.P. (1992) *Hypertext: the Convergence of Contemporary Critical Theory and Technology*. Baltimore: Johns Hopkins University Press.

Liberman, A.M. (1995) 'The relation of speech to reading and writing', in B. De Gelder and J. Morais (eds), *Speech and Reading: a Comparative Approach*. Hove: Erlbaum, Taylor and Francis. pp. 17–31.

McClelland, J.L. and Rumelhart, D.E. (eds) (1986) *Parallel Distributed Processing. vol. 2: Psychological and Biological Models*. Cambridge, MA: MIT Press.

McConkie, G.W. and Zola, D. (1981) 'Language constraints and the functional stimulus in reading', in A.M. Lesgold and C.A. Perfetti (eds), *Interactive Processes in Reading*. Hillsdale, NJ: Erlbaum. pp. 155–75.

Nation, K. and Snowling, M.J. (1998) 'Individual differences in contextual facilitation: evidence from dyslexia and poor reading comprehension', *Child Development*, 69: 996–1011.

National Reading Panel (2000) *Teaching Children to Read: an Evidence-Based Assessment of the Scientific Research Literature on Reading and its Implications for Reading Instruction*. Washington, DC: National Institute for Child Health and Human Development.

Oakhill, J. (1993) 'Developing skilled reading', in R. Beard (ed.), *Teaching Literacy: Balancing Perspectives*. London: Hodder and Stoughton.

Oakhill, J. and Beard, R. (eds) (1999) *Reading Development and the Teaching of Reading: a Psychological Perspective*. Oxford: Blackwell.

Oakhill, J. and Garnham, A. (1988) *Becoming a Skilled Reader*. Oxford: Blackwell.

Pang, E.S. and Kamil, M. (2002) 'Reading Hypertext: Comprehension and Strategies of Third Grade Readers', in D. Schallert, C.M. Fairbanks, J. Worthy, B. Maloch and J.V. Hoffman (eds) *51st Yearbook of the National Reading Conference*. Wisconsin: National Reading Conference.

Perfetti, C. (1995) 'Cognitive research can inform reading education', *Journal of Research in Reading*, 18 (2): 106–15.

Pressley, M. (1998) *Reading Instruction that Works: the Case for Balanced Teaching*. New York: Guilford.

Rayner, K. (ed.) (1992) *Eye Movements and Visual Cognition: Scene Perception and Reading*. New York: Springer.

Rayner, K. and Pollatsek, A. (1989) *The Psychology of Reading*. Englewood Cliffs, NJ: Prentice Hall.

Reid, J. (1993) 'Reading and spoken language: the nature of the links', in R. Beard (ed.), *Teaching Literacy: Balancing Perspectives*. London: Hodder and Stoughton.

Reinking, D. (1998) 'Introduction: synthesizing technological transformations in literacy in a post-typographic world', in D. Reinking, M.C. McKenna, L.D. Labbo and R.D. Keiffer (eds), *Handbook of Literacy and Technology*. Mahwah, NJ: Erlbaum. pp. xi–xxx.

Routman, R. (1988) *Transitions: from Literature to Literacy*. Portsmouth, NH: Heinemann.

Rumelhart, D.E. (1985) 'Towards an interactive model of reading', in H. Singer and R.B. Ruddell (eds), *Theoretical Models and Processes of Reading*, 3rd edn. Newark, DE: International Reading Association. pp. 722–50.

Rumelhart, D.E. and McClelland, J.L. (eds) (1986) *Parallel Distributed Processing. vol. 1: Foundations*. Cambridge, MA: MIT Press.

Samuels, S.J. (1985) 'Towards a theory of automatic information processing in reading: updated', in H. Singer and R.B. Ruddell (eds), *Theoretical Models and Processes of Reading*, 3rd edn. Newark, DE: International Reading Association. pp. 719–21.

Share, D.L. (1995) 'Phonological recoding and self-teaching: *sine qua non* of reading acquisition', *Cognition*, 55: 151–218.

Smith, F. (1971) *Understanding Reading*, 3rd edn (1988), 5th edn (1994). New York: Holt, Rinehart and Winston.

Smith, F. (ed.) (1973) *Psycholinguistics and Reading*. New York: Holt, Rinehart and Winston.

Stanovich, K.E. (1980) 'Towards an interactive-compensatory model of individual differences in the development of reading fluency', *Reading Research Quarterly*, 16: 32–71.

Stanovich, K.E. (1986) 'Matthew effects of reading: some consequences of individual differences in the acquisition of literacy', *Reading Research Quarterly*, 21: 360–407.

Stanovich, K.E. and Stanovich, P.J. (1995) 'How research might inform the debate about early reading acquisition', *Journal of Research in Reading*, 18 (2): 87–105.

Stanovich, K.E. (2000) *Progress in Understanding Reading*. New York: Guilford.

Tunmer, W.E. and Chapman, J.W. (1998) 'Language prediction, skill, phonological recoding and beginning reading', in C. Hulme and R.M. Joshi (eds), *Reading and Spelling: Development and Disorder*. Hove: Erlbaum. pp. 36–67.

Weber, R.M. (1970) 'First graders' use of grammatical context in reading', in H. Levin and J.G. Williams (eds), *Basic Studies in Reading*. New York: Basic.

18

Phonology and Learning to Read

RHONA STAINTHORP

The subject of this chapter is phonology, its development and its relationship to the development of reading and writing.

One of the defining characteristics of being human is language. Thus Noam Chomsky in *Language and Mind* wrote, 'When we study human language, we are approaching what some might call the "human essence", the distinctive qualities of mind that are, so far as we know, unique to man' (1972: 100). We can never know for certain when language first emerged as a human skill. Indeed, in 1886 the Linguistics Society of Paris 'outlawed' papers that speculated on this. However, all human societies have developed their own highly complex language, with each language being based on the production of sounds.[1] Anthropologists believe that the human species has existed for at least one million years (Fromkin and Rodman,1998). This means that for the major part of history people have been speaking and listening without being able to read and write, and still today many languages exist only in a spoken form.

About 5000 years ago societies such as those of the Sumerians and Akkadians, existing in Mesopotamia, developed in complexity so much that there became a need to keep permanent records rather than rely on spoken language and memory for evidence. This led to people being faced with the problem of developing symbols to represent the ideas they wished to record. The first attempts were in the form of tokens or counters that represented quantities. These were eventually replaced with symbols and this ultimately led to the development of more formal systems for representing the world (Schmandt-Besserat, 1992). This early cuneiform writing was initially only capable of recording concrete information but as it developed so more abstract ideas began to be represented. Later the Egyptians developed their hieroglyphic system in such a way that it could record abstract concepts from the start and was much more nearly a record of the spoken language. Though we tend to think of hieroglyphs as pictorial representation, they also included phonograms to represent sounds. However, the great leap forward was in the development of systems that use a more abstract system to represent the sound structure of the language in graphic form – what we call an *alphabet*. The adults – and we must assume that they were creative, intellectually insightful adults – who developed alphabets must have had an intuitive understanding of the phonemic structure of their language.

Today, children who are learning to read and write in alphabetic scripts are all required to solve the same problem: how do the shapes of the written language encode and represent the sounds of the spoken language? But young children have to solve this problem without necessarily having spontaneous insights about the sound structure of the language. They need the support of teachers or others to help them. This means that their teachers need explicit knowledge and understanding of the development of phonology in young children and how this relates to written language.

SOME TERMINOLOGY

Because phonology is the subject of this chapter, it seems sensible to begin with some essential information about the sound structure of language and the terminology that is used particularly to describe phonological units. Those readers who have this terminology at their fingertips might want to move now to the next section.

Language is composed of a number of different interrelated systems, namely the pragmatic, semantic, syntactic, morphological, and phonological systems. The phonological system is the sound system of the language. Humans are capable of producing an infinite number of ideas in an infinite number of ways. However, they produce these infinite ideas using words from a finite though extensive lexicon using the combinatory rules of syntax and morphology. Words are the commonest free-standing units in a language. They are, however, composed of smaller units. Where meaning is concerned, the smallest units are morphemes. Phonology is the study of the system of units below the level of the word and the segmental units of phonology are meaningless sounds – *phonemes*. Phonemes are defined as the smallest units in the sound system that can signal a change in meaning. Though humans are capable of producing a wide range of speech sounds, the actual units of sound are relatively few in number. In English, there are 44 phonemes: 20 vowels and 24 consonants.[2] In this chapter, when the words *vowel* and *consonant* are used on their own, I will be referring to the phonemes, the sounds not the letters, and any examples will be presented within slash marks. Thus the public place where animals are kept is a /zu/. (The symbol list for each phoneme is given in the appendix to this chapter.)

Each language has its own set of phonemes but also its own set of phonotactic rules which specify what combinations of phonemes are permitted and where in a word they may occur. English is a language which permits consonant blends without intervening vowels: e.g. /steI t/ and /streI t/. Positional constraints mean that the consonant blend /mp/ can occur in word-final position as in /stæmp/ but not in word-initial position. Not all languages permit consonant clusters. Italian is an example of a European language that permits few consonant clusters and Japanese is a good example of a language that has no consonant clusters. Thus though MITSUBISHI is written in the Roman script with the letters TS this stands for the single consonant sound /ts/.

The words, as the smallest units of meaning, are composed of phonemes, as the smallest units of sound.[3] However, there are also significant sound segments that are larger than phonemes but smaller than words. The largest of these is the *syllable*. All syllables must consist minimally of a vowel but may include any associated consonants to form an articulated unit. The number of syllables in a word is synonymous with the number of vowels. Thus /sɪt/ has one syllable but /seti/ has two. Syllables can be *open* or *closed* depending on whether the final phoneme of the syllable is a vowel (open) or a consonant (closed): e.g. /bi/ and /bit/.

Syllables themselves can be further segmented into subsyllabic units. The segmental units of the syllable are the *onset* and the *rime.* The onset is always any consonants that precede the vowel. In English there can be up to three consonants in an onset: e.g. /reI t/, /treI t/, /streI t/. The rime is the vowel and any succeeding consonants: e.g. /pæn/, /pænt/, /pænts/. Rime units can be further subdivided into the *peak* and the *coda.* The peak is the vowel and the coda any succeeding consonants. Onsets and codas are optional and can be single or multiple phonemes. The peak is obligatory and a single vowel phoneme. Vowel phonemes appear to be the 'strongest' elements in syllables. We have to remember that spoken language appears seamless. When speech is made 'visible' through speech spectroscopy, spaces between or even within words do not map onto the beginnings and ends of words as we see them written on the page. The phonemes in syllables are folded into each other and coarticulated. This means that as one is preparing to produce the first phoneme in a word one is also anticipating the production of the second phoneme and so on. Observe the shape of your mouth in a mirror as you get ready to say /mi/ and /mu/. Even as you are preparing to produce the phoneme /m/ your lips will be stretched ready for the /i/ in /mi/ or more rounded for the /u/ in /mu/. Languages differ in their syllabic structure. Japanese, as mentioned above, is an example of a language that has a different syllabic structure from English. It is mainly composed of open syllables with single consonant onsets. Italian on the other hand has mainly open syllables but permits polyphonemic onsets.

PHONOLOGICAL DEVELOPMENT

When people first become interested in bird watching they are clearly able to discriminate between birds and other animals, but their ability to discriminate between different species of birds may be limited and based on fairly gross features. However, with time, experience and motivation the dedicated ornithologist can make the finest discriminations and so distinguish between one LBJ and the next. An LBJ is a nondescript small brown bird that to the uninitiated looks like any other – hence the name 'little brown job'. This ability to make increasingly finer distinctions going from large to small units is a common feature of perception across all modalities. However, in linguistics the idea that phonological organization may move from large-grained to fine-grained units was not really considered until the 1970s. In 1975, Ferguson and Farwell put forward the idea that the word is the first unit of contrast in the developing phonological system. From this it followed that as language develops there has to be a restructuring of the lexicon with the sublexical units emerging gradually. This means that first words will be represented holistically and then, as sublexical units emerge, these words will be restructured to be represented by these smaller phonological units. Later acquired words will be represented by smaller units in the first place.

This notion seems initially to be counter-intuitive because early phonological production tends to take the form of babbling in small units. There is also evidence that long before language emerges infants show an adult-like ability to differentiate between phonemes. Eimas et al. (1971) showed that one-month-old infants could discriminate between phonemes. In a habituation task they showed that babies could recognize when a generated syllable, e.g. /pʌ/, changed to /bʌ/. The difference between the phonemes /b/ and /p/ is that /b/ is voiced and /p/ is unvoiced. They are both bilabial stop consonants. It is possible to generate sounds that change from /b/ to /p/ along a continuous dimension but people tend to perceive the sounds categorically as either one or the other. This finding was used to support the view that phonemes are innately specified and therefore biologically determined. However, subsequently there was evidence that this ability to show categorical perception of phonemes can also be found in chinchillas (Burdick and Miller, 1975) and macaque monkeys (Kuhl and Padden, 1982), suggesting that this behaviour may be evidence of general auditory ability rather than of *linguistic* behaviours. In addition, infant ability to perceive the differences between the phonemes may result at that stage from holistic perception of the stimuli rather than from specific perception of the segmental differences. In other words, the infants could have been responding to something being different *per se* rather than *what* was different. It is important to recognize that phonological awareness is different from audition.

In 1992 Jusczyk developed a model of word recognition and phonetic structure acquisition (WRAPSA), which proposes that phonemic segments are *emergent* units of speech perception rather than being units that are innately specified. Such a model assumes that children have to learn which differences in the acoustic stream are important and therefore need to be attended to and which can be ignored. Differences between the liquid phonemes /l/ and /r/ are important in English because in similar phonological environments they signal different referents. Thus a /leɪ k/ is different from a /reɪ k/. This contrast between the phonemes /r/ and /l/ is not a significant one in Japanese. Children have to learn, almost certainly implicitly, that the phoneme is a salient unit, and probably the smallest salient unit. Below the level of the phoneme, differences at the phonetic level do not affect meaning. The realizations of the phonemes /æ/, /p/ and /t/ for example in the words /pæ t/, /æ pt/ and /tæ p/ are all different at the phonetic level but they have to be treated as equivalent. The individual phonemes also have to be articulated slightly differently depending on the different sequences.

Ferguson and Farwell (1975) suggest that words may be the first unit of differentiation. Children's early vocabulary is small, and indeed the first 50 words of vocabulary are acquired relatively slowly so there is no need to have a fine-grained system to discriminate between them. However, from roughly 18 months onwards there is a sudden growth spurt in the lexicon. This results in pressure to develop more fine-grained representations so therefore sublexical segments begin to emerge. The necessity for this is because many words begin to be only discriminable on the basis of minimal phonemic differences. For example, in received pronunciation of English /bæ t/, /bæ k/, /bæg/, /bæʃ/, /p æ t/, /f æ t/, /m æ t/ are all high-frequency words that differ by just one phoneme. Thus the necessity for an enlarged vocabulary is a *causal* factor in the movement from whole to part representation. The exemplar words given here differ by a single phoneme and are of course all single syllabic words. However, Jusczyk (1986; 1992) suggests that the syllable is the first sublexical unit to emerge and only after this does the phoneme emerge. This means that phonological development proceeds from large through intermediate to small units.

Metsala and Walley (1999) have developed a further model – the lexical restructuring model (LRM). The use of the term *restructuring* is crucial. They note that after the initial early spurt in lexical growth, though the rate of increase slows down, there is still considerable expansion throughout childhood and even into adolescence. Their model incorporates the idea that young children's word recognition is more holistic than older children's and adults'. It also includes the notion that the growth of the lexicon is causal in providing the pressure for segmental restructuring of the representations of lexical items (Walley, 1993). They suggest, however, that this restructuring may be quite gradual and word specific.

One important dimension along which words differ from one another is in terms of the number of other words that are close to them phonologically. This is known as *neighbourhood density* (Luce, 1986; Logan, 1992) and has nothing to do with the number of semantic neighbours that a word may have. The neighbourhood density of a specified word is defined as the number of words in the lexicon that differ from the target by the substitution, addition or deletion of a single phoneme. The word /mIθ/ has a relatively low neighbourhood density (5) and /hæt/ has a relatively high neighbourhood density (33). However, if you work out all the neighbours for yourself you will realize that the neighbourhood density of a word is not an absolute psychological characteristic because it depends on the size of the individual person's lexicon which, particularly in the early years, will be constantly growing. You may not agree with the neighbourhood sizes given here and this may be because of differences in regional (and national) accents. Sensitivity to regional variations in the phonemic structure of words is very important particularly when working with young children. Over time a word may change from being in a relatively dense neighbourhood to a relatively sparse neighbour and vice versa during lexical expansion. Metsala and Walley argue that there will be a greater push towards more a fine-grained representation for words that are in dense neighbourhoods in the early stages. Because these words are holistically phonologically similar to a relatively large number of other words, they need to become restructured and thereby represented by smaller units in order to ensure accurate differentiation.

This account of phonological restructuring should not be taken to imply that it is happening at a conscious level. Metsala and Walley specifically state that 'the phoneme emerges first at an implicit level for the perceptual representation and processing of spoken words' (1999: 102). It is only after lexical restructuring at the *implicit* level happens that the phoneme emerges as a cognitive unit at the *explicit* level. This is similar to Gombert's (1992) characterization of awareness as being either *epilinguistic* or *metalinguistic*. When the phoneme is available at the explicit level the child is able to reflect upon and manipulate the phonemes in words and therefore demonstrate explicit phoneme awareness. It is this explicit or metalinguistic phoneme awareness that has been the focus of much research into the relationship between phonology and early literacy.

Chaney (1992) found that lexical development in four-year-olds as measured by *spoken* vocabulary was related to their phonological awareness. This is what would be predicted by the lexical restructuring model, since as the lexicon expands so the items need to be represented subsyllabically. However,

Garlock et al. (2001) found that *receptive* vocabulary did not predict phonological awareness. In our work tracking the skills of precocious readers (Stainthorp and Hughes, 1998; 1999) we matched precocious and non-precocious readers on the basis of receptive vocabulary using the British Picture Vocabulary Scales (Dunn et al., 1982), but we found there were highly significant differences in phonological awareness at the age of five years. The precocious readers demonstrated clear evidence of good explicit phonemic awareness whereas the non-precocious readers only showed evidence of implicit awareness through rhyming ability.

A prediction of the lexical restructuring model is that lexical restructuring of words will have begun to take place prior to literacy so that some words will be represented at the phoneme level at this time. There is likely, therefore, to be some phonemic awareness emerging prior to literacy. For example, Metsala and Stanovich (1995) presented four- and five-year-olds with words and pseudowords. Pseudowords are items that conform to phonotactic rules but which have no meaning and therefore no lexical representation: e.g. /kib/. They found differential performance between words and pseudowords on a phoneme identification task and an onset–rime blending task. All the word stimuli used were within the children's vocabularies, so the result suggests that the words were represented in the lexicon at subsyllabic levels whereas the pseudowords obviously had no representations. However, this awareness is generally at the implicit rather than the explicit level – epilinguistic rather than metalinguistic, in Gombert's terms.

WRITING SYSTEMS

The word 'phonology' can be traced back to the Phoenicians who inhabited the land between the mountains of Lebanon and the Mediterranean during the second millennium BCE. It was the Phoenicians who invented an alphabet for their writing system. They created a simple code whereby each consonant phoneme in the language was represented by a unique visual symbol – and so the history of alphabetic reading and writing began. The Greeks later extended the Phoenician system to include letters which stood for vowel phonemes and then, in turn, their system was adapted by the Etruscans (c. 800 BCE). This alphabet is the model of all the Western alphabets in use today. There was a letter for every phoneme in the language. Thus, reading and writing were a matter of translating from visual to phonological structure and from phonological to visual form using a transparent

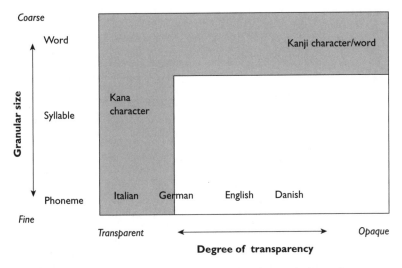

Figure 18.1 Schematic representation of the hypothesis of granularity and transparency (Wydell and Butterworth, 1999)

mapping system. It does not seem to be too much of a flight of fancy to speculate that those unknown early benefactors of humanity must have had insight into the sound structure of their language in order to make the decision to represent phonemes with letters. They invented the alphabetic principle. From the beginning, therefore, the basis of literacy in an alphabetic system was phonological or more specifically the phoneme. However, this view was not reflected in the literature on the development of reading until the 1970s, although teaching programmes based on phonics had moved in and out of fashion for well over a century.

All writing systems solve the problem of systematically representing transient spoken language as permanent visual patterns but they do so in different ways. In their 'hypothesis of granularity and transparency', Wydell and Butterworth (1999) argue that orthographies can be described in two orthogonal dimensions: transparency and granularity (see Figure 18.1). The granularity dimension relates to the size of the phonological unit that is the basis of the mapping system. The transparency dimension relates to the degree to which the mapping is regular, uniform and consistent. English falls in the area of the two- dimensional space with a high degree of opaqueness but a fine grain size.[4] Goswami has also evoked the concept of 'grain size' in the 'psycholinguistic grain size' theory of reading (Goswami, 2002; Goswami et al., 2001). She suggests that the sequence of phonological development may be language universal, beginning with the word as the unit followed by the emergence of

syllabic and subsyllabic units. However, the way the mapping of sounds to visual units is solved is language/orthography specific.

Language is above all a system for conveying meanings, so it is not surprising that some early attempts at writing used visual symbols that stood for meaning units (Gelb, 1963). These systems would be at the extreme large-grained end of the grain-size dimension. The problem with words is that they represent referents in an arbitrary way, and representing meaning units by unique visual patterns presents an extremely taxing task to the learner. Systems today that use meaning units as the basis of representation such as Chinese and Japanese Kanji take a long time to learn and may never be completely mastered.[5] This can be recognized when we think about the size of a child's spoken vocabulary. Estimating the size of children's vocabulary is fraught with difficulties, but various estimates put the size of an average three-year-old's vocabulary at about 1000 words (Dale, 1976) and by the time a student finishes school it has risen to 30,000+ (Mason et al., 1991). A fluent reader needs to be able to recognize with ease as many of the words in the spoken lexicon as possible. Though mastering all the characters in Chinese or Japanese is laborious, it is clearly possible. However, it does limit the independence of the child to read anything he or she chooses. During their primary school years Japanese children are introduced to 996 Kanji characters, which they learn by rote using repeat writing. By the end of compulsory education at the age of 16 years they will have been introduced to about 2000 characters, but it is estimated that to read a newspaper an adult needs to know about 3000 characters (Wydell and Butterworth, 1999). This is clearly very different from the number of words that a child can read when learning in an alphabetic system.[6]

A development from writing with meaningful units as the basis of the system was to represent the meaningless sound-based units – for example the syllable. The Japanese kana systems of hiragana and katakana exemplify such systems and can be characterized as being in the middle of the granularity dimension. In Japanese there are 71 katakana 'letters' representing each of the morae.[7] The kana systems are very transparent, so each of the 71 letters represents the five vowels, the 65 consonant– vowel combinations and the nasal code uniquely. Therefore learning the mappings poses little problem. As long as the child can abstract the morae from the acoustic string and learn the kana–mora combinations it is possible to access the phonological identity of each word written in a kana script. As we have seen, both Jusczyk's WRAPSA and Metsala and Walley's LRM models would predict that the syllable emerges as a unit earlier than the phoneme, so mapping syllable-like units onto letters should be a reasonably easy task. There is also an advantage for the Japanese child in that the grain size of the writing system in kana maps directly onto the grain size of the salient unit of the spoken language – the mora (Goswami, 2002).

The final development in the history of writing systems was the invention of the alphabet, whereby the unit of representation is the phoneme. These systems are at the finest end of the granularity dimension. This type of system is highly efficient. In a perfect alphabetic system there is one letter for each phoneme, and each phoneme is represented by that letter uniquely. Such systems are said to be *transparent* or *shallow* – e.g. Serbian (the transparent end of the transparency dimension). However, most alphabetic systems, though based on letter–phoneme mappings, are not completely transparent. They may, for example, need graphemic parsing whereby more than one letter stands for a single phoneme: e.g. the letters T and H each have their own sound value when written alone, but when written together stand for the phonemes /θ/ or /ð/. Some languages may be consistent for reading but not for spelling. This means that a letter or grapheme may always represent the same phoneme but that phoneme may be realized in a number of different ways. An example from English would be where the letters SH consistently represent the phoneme /ʃ/,[8] but /ʃ/ is spelt in a number of different ways: **SHOP, CHUTE, NATION, MISSION**. This shows phoneme–grapheme correspondence (PGC)

inconsistency with one-to-many mappings. In English, there are also inconsistencies in grapheme–phoneme correspondences (GPC). For example the grapheme EA may represent the phonemes /i/, /e/, / eɪ / or even /i æ / as in BEAD, HEAD, GREAT, REACT. Learning the mappings for phonemes and letters in English is a very complex problem.

This problem of mapping phonemes and letters is one that has to be solved by all beginning readers and spellers in alphabetic systems. In each language the spelling system is fixed so every learner may appear to have to solve the same problem by learning the same mappings. However, because of differences in accents, the mappings may be subtly different. All teachers need to take account of regional and ethnic accents within the wider political communities. As with many languages, English spoken in England varies depending on region, social and ethnic context and these accents are different again from the accents of the English spoken in Scotland, Ireland and Wales or from the accents of the English spoken in Canada, the USA, Australia and South Africa. The word written with the letters CAR has two phonemes (/k/ and /ɑ/) in 'southern English' but three phonemes in Scottish and some US accents (/k/ /ɑ/ /r/). The word written with the letters HILL has two phonemes (/I/ and /l/) in a South London accent but three in received pronunciation (/h/ /I/ /l/). When I first began teaching in an outer London school the pupils found it a great source of amusement that I talked about '/h æ f/ /pæ st /' whereas they said '/hɑf/ /pɑst/'. The important point to note is that all accents have their own systematic phonemic structure, but that none of these map exactly on to English orthography. In ensuring that children achieve explicit, metalinguistic phonemic awareness teachers have to become particularly sensitive to the children's accents so that they work with them and not against them.

The basis of any alphabetic writing system is the *alphabetic principle*. Children have to understand this principle and how it works and in doing so they gain a powerful tool for working out new words independently (Byrne, 1998; 2002). However, in order to come to an understanding of this principle and to use it in grapheme–phoneme correspondence as a tool for identifying words on the page, they have to be able to abstract the phonemes of their own accents and become explicitly phonologically aware.

PHONOLOGY AND READING

We now therefore turn to the importance of phonological awareness for reading. One of the earliest,

Table 18.1   *Results from the phoneme and syllable tapping task study by Liberman et al. (1974)*

		Nursery	Kindergarten	First Grade
Mean % achieving criterion of six trials without demonstration	Phoneme	0	17	70
	Syllable	46	48	90
Means trials to criterion	Phoneme	(no children achieved criterion)	26	25.6
	Syllable	25.7	12.1	9.8
% reaching criterion in the minimum of six trials	Phoneme	0	0	0
	Syllable	7	16	50

most important papers in this field is the seminal work by Liberman et al. (1974). They argued that in order to represent any segment of speech, writers must be able to extract it explicitly. Since alphabetic systems represent language at the level of the phoneme, readers and writers must be able to segment language down to this level. In other words they need to be phonemically aware. The WRAPSA and LRM models of phonological development both incorporate the notion that phonemes are late emerging units and the last to emerge. Liberman et al., had specifically proposed that phonemic awareness is a later development than syllabic awareness. Their study was the first to provide empirical, experimental evidence that pre-reading children have greater difficulty in identifying the phonemes in words explicitly than in identifying syllables.

They developed a 'tapping' task, whereby children had to tap once for each phoneme or syllable that they could identify in words. The children they tested were from age 4 years 7 months to 7 years 4 months and came from nurseries, kindergartens and first-grade classes. Their results are presented in Table 18.1.

In order to do the task successfully the children needed to be *explicitly* aware and these results showed (1) that awareness of phonemes is a later development than awareness of syllables, and (2) that in a task requiring segmentation of words, phonemic segmentation is more difficult than syllabic segmentation. Though in this study they did not investigate the reading ability of the children, they speculated that one of the major differences between reading and listening and between writing and speaking is that the 'literacy partner' in each of these pairs requires specific segmentation. They noted that children often find the task of learning the sound values of the individual letters *per se* not particularly challenging. However, if children are not able to abstract the phoneme from the acoustic stream they only have one half of the mapping code

available to them. Learning the sound values of the individual letters means learning that the 'name' of the shape Bb is /b/. This task is probably not that dissimilar from learning that the name of the shape □ is 'square'. This simply requires stimulus–response learning, and as mentioned above, when Japanese children learn the names of the katakana and hiragana characters they achieve a high level of success. However, because letters represent phonemes, it is necessary that children achieve an understanding of the alphabetic principle in order to utilize their letter–sound knowledge. In addition, English has many examples of words that contain letters which are not sounded.

Liberman et al., ended their paper by pointing out that it would be:

> of primary interest to learn in future research whether first grade children who do not acquire phoneme segmentation are, in fact, deficient in reading and spelling as well … we should think, as Elkonin (1973) does, that it would be possible (and desirable) to develop this ability by appropriate training methods. (1974: 211)

In this final paragraph they mapped out one significant agenda for reading research for the next 25 years. Their prescience about possible phonological deficits of children with reading difficulties has been acutely accurate (Snowling, 1981; 1995; 2000). The term 'phonological awareness' was not in the title of their paper but it has become the shorthand for much subsequent research investigating the relationship between phonology and reading.

Reading in an alphabetic orthographic system is founded on phonological processing. This means that in order to read words children (and adults) have to be able to develop an ability to make an accurate translation from the visual stimulus – the printed word – to its phonological counterpart – its spoken equivalent. Classically, the dual route model of reading (Coltheart et al., 1993; Stuart, 2002) proposes that a word can be read both by a direct, lexical route and by an indirect, sublexical route. When a word is read by the direct route, there is a straight translation from print to meaning and the phonology is only accessed after the word has been recognized. A word read by this route is assumed to have a representation in the orthographic (visual) lexicon. When a word is read by the indirect route, grapheme–phoneme correspondences are used to generate the phonological identity and the meaning is accessed via this. In the very early stages children who have not developed any skills in decoding words may only be able to read words directly. They are unlikely to have built up an extensive orthographic lexicon and so have to rely on others to identify any unknown words. They may also use contextual strategies but this is slow, and the inflexibility of relying too much on context tends to be a backup strategy of poor readers (West and Stanovich, 1978). Frith (1985) proposed that direct 'logographic' reading was the first in a six-step reading acquisition process, but Stuart and Coltheart (1988) suggest that a logographic stage is not a necessary one when learning to read in an alphabetic system.

The beauty of an alphabetic system is that once the learner has cracked the alphabetic code and learned to map the letter sounds there is an opportunity for becoming an independent *word* reader without having to rely on others to supply the sound of an unknown sequence of letters. Being able to read the words successfully is one of the first steps to becoming an independent reader with good understanding of the meaning of the text. However, the 'simple definition' of reading proposed by Gough et al. (1992) states that reading is the result of decoding *and* comprehension. This means that word reading is necessary but not sufficient for independent reading to be achieved as success also depends on knowing what the word means once it has been phonically identified.

When an orthography is transparent this mapping problem poses few difficulties, with the result that accurate word reading is achieved at a very early stage in the learning process (Goswami, 2002). However, with an opaque orthography like English the mapping problem may be considerable. Nevertheless, as Goswami argues, developing high-quality phonological representations at the phoneme level is the key factor in successful reading acquisition in all alphabetic systems.

Share has suggested that the role that phonology plays in early reading acquisition is to provide a self-teaching mechanism to enable children to bootstrap their way into reading (Jorm and Share, 1983; Share, 1995; 1999). By recoding from letters to phonemes the reader is able to identify the written word: 'each successful decoding encounter with an unfamiliar word provides an opportunity to acquire word specific orthographic information that is the foundation of skilled word recognition' (1999: 155). This means that individual word entries in the orthographic lexicon are created as a result of the evidence obtained from successful word reading via the sublexical route initially. This is characterized as a self-teaching mechanism whereby the reader develops a means of identifying the sound of unknown words independently. With increasing facility and exposure to print the reader develops more general orthographic knowledge. This means that the patterns that have previously been encountered in other words will be processed more efficiently and require less processing capacity. This is another important feature of the self-teaching mechanism: 'the process of phonological recoding becomes increasingly "lexicalised" in the course of reading development' (1995: 156). Lexicalization is an interesting 'reversal'. The WRAPSA and LRM models of phonological development both point to the movement from holistic to small unit representations of words; and there is an overwhelming body of research pointing to individual differences in phonemic awareness accounting for differences in later reading performance (Wagner and Torgeson, 1987; Snowling, 1991; Shankweiler et al., 1992; Stainthorp and Hughes, 1998). However, once the self-teaching mechanism is under way, readers can begin to use larger visual sequences that map onto larger phonological units so that their reading may be indistinguishable from whole word reading. The two developmental models of Frith (1985) and Ehri (1995; 2002) suggest that there is a movement from using small units to identify words to using larger units as children develop their word reading proficiency. Nevertheless, ability to read pseudowords accurately is evidence that the sublexical route is still active. Pseudoword reading may be the purest measure of individual differences in phonological recoding. Share suggests that a minimum level of phonemic awareness *and* letter-sound skill may enable a child to acquire a rudimentary self-teaching system that then becomes self-sustaining. This is always assuming that the child has sufficient encounters with print to practise any developing skills.

PHONOLOGY AND THE TEACHING OF READING

Throughout its history the teaching of reading through phonics instruction has had a mixed press, especially during recent decades (Smith, 1971; 1973; Goodman, 1973; 1993). Yet the majority of the empirical evidence from psychological research chosen for review by Adams (1990) indicated that children who are taught about the alphabet and letter–sound correspondences go on to be better readers and spellers. They are given privileged information that helps to kick-start the self-teaching mechanism. To put the kindest gloss on it, it may well have been the case that historically, the teaching of phonics did not involve any notion of teaching about phonology. This meant that children were taught their letter–sound correspondences and were expected to induce the sound structure of words for themselves. The phonological linkage hypothesis articulated by Hatcher et al. (1994) suggests that it is important that children should be taught explicitly about the phonemic structure of words and then given opportunities to apply this knowledge directly to reading. Byrne (1998) has demonstrated that the majority of children are helped if they receive specific instruction in phoneme identity because it cannot be assumed that children will have this knowledge explicitly available to them (cf. Liberman et al., 1974).

The early intervention study by Bradley and Bryant (1983) showed that there were long-lasting positive effects of instruction in sound categorization on later reading performance, particularly when this instruction was coupled with instruction in letter knowledge. The teaching programme they used was one where children had to make judgements about which word was the odd-one-out from sets of three or four words. The target item could be unique on the basis of initial, medial or final phoneme, although subsequently it was realized that many of the judgements were made on the basis of rhyming. This research was carried out with nursery children using playful activities that were not based on rigid phonic drills. More recently Byrne and Fielding-Barnsley (1991a; 1993; 1995) have developed a programme to teach preschool children about phoneme identity. They argue that we need to make sure that children learn explicitly that spoken language is constructed from phonemes and that alphabetic writing represents the phonemes. Their programme is designed for preschool children and so capitalized on gaming activities that are compelling in themselves so that children enjoy the games. They included stories, poems and fantastic pictures about sounds to capture the children's imagination as well as some more formal pencil and paper games. Because children need to gain mastery over this knowledge, it is important to capitalize on their enjoyment of games. Kirtley et al. (1995) have produced a series

of card games for children that have integrity in their own right. The fact that the units being played over happen to be phonemes, rhymes and letters is almost incidental. Achieving good phonemic knowledge requires lots of practice just like any other skill, and games are one of the most absorbing ways of practising.

Within the framework of Metsala and Walley's lexical restructuring model, the aim is not to rely on the phonemes to emerge as a unit automatically but to provide specific teaching to ensure that they do emerge. There is some evidence from adults who have not yet learned to read that explicit phonemic awareness does not arise spontaneously but may be dependent on early literacy teaching (Morais et al., 1986). *Sound Foundations* (Byrne and Fielding-Barnsley, 1991b) begins with a small subset of phonemes and their associated letters and through silly rhymes, stories, games and object identification aims to enable children to be able to identify phonemes as discrete segments of words. The results are impressive, with children who received the training showing a significant advantage when they begin to receive reading instruction. This work has been cited because it is based on a sound methodology with a programme that has a clearly articulated theoretically based rationale.

Teaching programmes that are grounded in the notion of developing phonemic awareness are becoming more the norm in the English-speaking world. In the United States the alphabetic sub-panel of the National Reading Panel (2000) conducted a meta-analysis of all the papers appearing in peer refereed journals that had investigated the unconfounded effect of instruction in phonemic awareness training on subsequent reading performance. This meta-analysis showed that phonemic awareness training was effective in teaching children to become explicitly aware of the phonemic structure of words themselves. This is an important finding in itself and one that is confirmed across many studies (although the study has not been without its critics). The evidence selected by this report shows that it is possible to intervene in the course of development to make children explicitly aware of the sound structure of words at the smallest grain size. However, as Share points out, it is not enough to be phonologically aware if there is no impact of this on the self-teaching mechanism. However, the sub-panel's meta-analysis was designed to answer questions about the effectiveness of phonemic awareness instruction on subsequent learning to read. They found that there was clear evidence that in achieving phonemic awareness children were given a tool, which helped them to bootstrap their way into literacy. Early phonemic awareness training boosts word reading accuracy but also has a significant effect on comprehension.

CONCLUSION

In this chapter, I have presented evidence that the phoneme is an emergent unit of phonology and not an innate one. When language first emerges, words are represented holistically. However, as vocabulary grows there is a push towards more fine-grained representation because holistic representations do not permit sufficient discrimination to be made. It seems that the phoneme, as the smallest unit of phonology, is the last to emerge. At the point when children begin to receive reading instruction, they may not yet be explicitly aware of the phonemes. However, awareness of the phoneme seems to be instrumental in achieving literacy. Awareness of the phoneme enables children to map the letter–sound correspondences when learning to read in an alphabetic language and so establish a self-teaching mechanism to bootstrap their way into skilled word reading. There is strong evidence that children's phonemic awareness can be accelerated through direct instruction. Early high levels of phonemic awareness, coupled with letter knowledge, lead to better word reading and effective word reading leads to higher levels of comprehension.

Of course this is not the whole story: other factors necessarily contribute to early literacy achievement. As many chapters in this book demonstrate, long before schooling children are constructing hypotheses about the nature and purpose of written language. They may have seen significant others using written language, they may have had stories and rhymes read to them, they may have been encouraged to explore ways of representing the world through drawing and writing, and they may have been included in the literacy activities that occur in homes. Such activities may have interested children in reading and writing and helped them appreciate that they are meaningful to those who use them. In addition to having a more general effect on vocabulary development (Castles et al., 1999; Cunningham and Stanovich, 1998; Senechal et al., 1998), such activities may lead to the emergence of explicit phonological awareness. Children who can build on these may even bring some emerging phonemic knowledge to their first experiences of formal instruction (Read, 1970).

When children do not develop explicit phonemic awareness they may not be able to capitalize on their social experiences of literacy. These are the children who may be at risk for developing reading problems because they do not have all the tools for figuring out how the system works. The NRP study suggests that early instruction in phonemic awareness will help children to understand about the alphabetic principle and so enable them to use their understandings about literacy to achieve success as readers and writers.

APPENDIX

The phonemes (sounds) of English

Consonant sounds		Vowel sounds	
p	peg	i	tree
b	bad	I	sit
t	tip	e	wet
d	dog	æ	cat
k	king	ɑ	father
g	goat	ɒ	plot
f	fish	ɔ	saw
v	vase	ʊ	put
θ	thumb	u	shoe
ð	they	ʌ	duck
s	soon	ɜ	girl
z	zoo	ə	banana
ʃ	shop	eɪ	play
ʒ	treasure	əʊ	go
tʃ	chip	ai	sigh
ʤ	jug	aʊ	now
m	milk	ɔɪ	boy
n	nice	ɪə	here
ŋ	sing	ɛə	there
l	leg	ʊə	pure
r	red		
j	yellow		
w	watch		
h	house		

NOTES

1 It is acknowledged that all the different sign languages in use by the deaf community are languages in their own right.

2 This figure of 44 is only approximate. It varies depending on the regional accent, the form of English that is being studied (e.g. British English, Australian English etc.) and the system of classification used.

3 For the purposes of this explanation, *word* is used as if it were synonymous with *morpheme* which is the smallest unit of meaning. It is acknowledged that many words are polymorphemous.

4 Although English orthography is generally considered to be phonemically based, there are aspects of spelling that are morphological. For example, the past tense morpheme is spelled with the letters ED in regular verbs: e.g. KISSED, PLAYED, MELTED. This is a morphological unit and not a phonological unit since the phonological unit is different in each case: /kɪst/, pleɪd/,/meltɪd/.

5 Though Chinese and Kanji are generally cited as being logographic/ideographic systems, characters do include phonetic radicals that give sound relation clues.

6 When talking about our precocious reader research in Hong Kong (Stainthorp and Hughes, 1995) we encountered an interesting cultural clash. The Chinese audience wanted to know how many recognizable words the children knew. All we could say was that they were fluent and appeared to be able to read anything they chose. We, of course, had no idea how many words the children could recognize.

7 A mora is in fact a subsyllabic rhythmic unit, but most Japanese syllables comprise single morae and are represented by a single kana letter.

8 English is always problematic and there are times when the letters SH are not parsed together. In the word MISHAP the letter S is at the end of the initial morpheme and H is at the beginning of the next. A common misreading of this even amongst adults is /m ɪ ʃ æ p/.

REFERENCES

Adams, M.J. (1990) *Beginning to Read: Thinking and Learning about Print.* Cambridge, MA: MIT Press.

Bradley, L. and Bryant, P.E. (1983) 'Categorising sounds and learning to read: a causal connection', *Nature*, 301: 41–421.

Burdick, C.K. and Miller, J.D. (1975) 'Speech perception in the chinchilla: discrimination of sustained /a/ and /i/', *Journal of the Acoustical Society of America*, 58: 415–27.

Byrne, B. (1998) *The Foundation of Literacy: the Child's Acquisition of the Alphabetic Principle.* Hove: Psychology Press.

Byrne, B. (2002) 'The process of learning to read: a framework for integrating research and educational practice', in R. Stainthorp and P. Tomlinson (eds), *Learning and Teaching Reading.* Leicester: British Psychological Society. pp. 29–44.

Byrne, B. and Fielding-Barnsley, R. (1991a) 'Evaluation of a programme to teach phonemic awareness to young children', *Journal of Educational Psychology*, 83: 451–5.

Byrne, B. and Fielding-Barnsley, R. (1991b) *Sound Foundations: an Introduction to Pre-reading Skills.* Sydney: Leyden.

Byrne, B. and Fielding-Barnsley, R. (1993) 'Evaluation of a programme to teach phonemic awareness to young children: a 1-year follow-up', *Journal of Educational Psychology,* 85: 104–11.

Byrne, B. and Fielding-Barnsley, R. (1995) 'Evaluation of a programme to teach phonemic awareness to young children: a 2- and 3-year follow-up and a new pre-school trial', *Journal of Educational Psychology,* 87: 488–503.

Castles, A., Datta, H., Gayan, J. and Olson, R. (1999) 'Varieties of developmental reading disorder: genetic and environmental influences', *Journal of Experimental Child Psychology*, 72: 73–94.

Chaney, C. (1992) 'Language development, metalinguistic skills and print awareness in three-year-old children', *Applied Psycholinguistics,* 13: 485–514.

Chomsky, N. (1972) *Language and Mind.* New York: Harcourt Brace Jovanovich.

Coltheart, M., Curtis, B., Atkins, P. and Haller, M. (1993) 'Models of reading aloud: dual route and parallel-distributed-processing approaches', *Psychological Review*, 100: 589–608.

Cunningham, A.E. and Stanvovich, K.E. (1998) 'The impact of print exposure on word recognition', in J.L Metsala and L.C. Ehri (eds), *Word Recognition in Beginning Literacy.* Hillsdale, NJ: Erlbaum. pp. 235–62.

Dale, P.S. (1976) *Language Development: Structure and Function.* New York: Holt, Rinehart and Winston.

Dunn, L.M., Dunn, L.M., Whetton, C. and Pintilie, D. (1982) *The British Picture Vocabulary Scale.* Windsor: NFER-Nelson.

Ehri, L.C. (1995) 'Phases of development in learning to read words by sight', *Journal of Research in Reading*, 18: 116–25.

Ehri, L.C. (2002) 'Phases of acquisition in learning to read words and implications for teaching', in R. Stainthorp and P. Tomlinson (eds), *Learning and Teaching Reading.* Leicester: British Psychological Society. pp. 7–28.

Eimas, P.D., Siqueland, E.R., Jusczyk, P.W. and Vigorito, J. (1971) 'Speech perception in early infancy', *Science*, 171: 304–6.

Ferguson, C.A. and Farwell, C.B. (1975) 'Words and sounds in early language acquisition', *Language*, 51: 419–39.

Frith, U. (1985) 'Beneath the surface of phonological dyslexia', in K. Patterson, J. Marshall and M. Coltheart (eds), *Surface Dyslexia.* London: Erlbaum.

Fromkin, V. and Rodman, R. (1998) *An Introduction to Language.* New York: Harcourt Brace.

Garlock, V.M., Walley, A.C. and Metsala, J.L. (2001) 'Age-of-acquisition, word frequency, and neighbourhood density effects on spoken word recognition by children and adults', *Journal of Memory and Language*, 54: 468–92.

Gelb, I.J. (1963) *A Study of Writing.* Chicago: University of Chicago Press.

Gombert, J.E. (1992) *Metalinguistic Development*. Hemel Hempstead: Harvester-Wheatsheaf.

Goodman, K.S. (1973) 'The 13th easy way to make learning to read difficult: a reaction to Gleitman and Rozin', *Reading Research Quarterly*, 8: 484–93.

Goodman, K.S. (1993) *Phonics Phacts*. Toronto: Scholastic Canada.

Goswami, U. (2002) 'Orthography, phonology and reading development: a cross-linguistic perspective', in press (paper presented to the NATO Advanced Studies Institute, Tuscany, 2001).

Goswami, U., Zeigler, J.C., Dalton, L. and Schneider, W. (2001) 'Pseudohomophone effects and phonological recoding procedures in reading development in English and German', *Journal of Memory and Language,* 45: 648–64.

Gough, P.B., Juel, C. and Griffith, P. (1992) 'Reading, spelling and the orthographic cipher', in P.B. Gough, L.C. Ehri and R. Treiman (eds), *Reading Acquisition*, Hillsdale. NJ: Erlbaum. pp. 35–48.

Jorm, A.F. and Share, D.L. (1983) 'Phonological recoding and reading acquisition', *Applied Psycholinguistics*, 4: 103–47.

Jusczyk, P.W. (1986) 'Towards a model of the development of speech perception', in J.S. Perkell and D.H. Klatt (eds), *Invariance and Variability in Speech Perception*. Hillsdale, NJ: Erlbaum.

Jusczyk, P.W. (1992) 'Developing phonological categories from the speech signal', in C.A. Ferguson, L. Menn and C. Stoel-Gammon (eds), *Phonological Development: Models, Research, Implications*. Parkton, MD: York.

Kirtley, C., Brychta, A. and Goswami, U. (1995) *Oxford Reading Tree: Rhyme and Analogy Card Games*. Oxford: Oxford University Press.

Kuhl, P.K. and Padden, D. (1982) 'Enhanced discriminability at the phonetic boundaries for the voicing feature in macaques', *Perception and Psychophysics*, 32: 542–50.

Liberman, I.Y., Shankweiler, D., Fischer, F.W. and Carter, B. (1974) 'Explicit syllable and phoneme segmentation in the young child', *Journal of Experimental Child Psychology*, 18: 201–12.

Logan, J.S. (1992) 'A computational analysis of young children's lexicons'. Research on Spoken Language Processing, Technical Report no. 8, Department of Psychology, Speech Research Laboratory, Bloomington, IN.

Luce, P.A. (1986) 'Neighbourhoods of words in the mental lexicon'. Research on Speech Perception, Report no. 6, Department of Psychology, Speech Research Laboratory, Bloomingtom, IN.

Mason, J.M., Herman, P.A. and Au, K.H. (1991) 'Children's developing knowledge of words', in J. Flood, J.M. Jensen, D. Lapp and J.R. Squire (eds), *Handbook of Research on Teaching the English Language Arts*. New York: Macmillan.

Metsala, J.L. and Stanovich, K.E. (1995) 'An examination of young children's phonological processing as a function of lexical development'. Paper presented at the annual meeting of the American Educational Research Association, San Francisco. Cited in K.E. Stanovich (2000), *Progress in Understanding Reading: Scientific Foundations and New Frontiers*. London: Guilford.

Metsala, J.L. and Walley, A.C. (1999) 'Spoken vocabulary growth and the segmental restructuring of lexical representations: precursors to phonemic awareness and early reading ability', in J.L. Metsala and L.C. Ehri (eds), *Word Recognition in Beginning Literacy*. Hillsdale, NJ: Erlbaum.

Morais, J., Bertelson, P., Cary, L. and Alegria, J. (1986) 'Literacy training and speech segmentation', *Cognition*, 24: 45–64.

National Reading Panel (2000) *Report of the National Reading Panel: Report of the Subgroups*. NICHD Clearinghouse. www.nichd.nih.gov.

Read, C. (1970) 'Pre-school children's knowledge of English phonology*', Harvard Educational Review,* 41 (1): 1–34.

Senechal, M., LeFevre, J.-A., Thomas, E.M. and Daley, K.E. (1998) 'Differential effects of home literacy experiences on the development of oral and written language', *Reading Research Quarterly,* 96: 523–68.

Shankweiler, D., Crain, S., Brady, S. and Macaruso, P. (1992) 'Identifying the causes of reading disability', in P. Gough, L.C. Ehri and R. Treiman (eds), *Reading Acquisition*. Hillsdale, NJ: Erlbaum.

Share, D.L. (1995) 'Phonological recoding and self-teaching: *sine qua non* of reading acquisition', *Cognition*, 55: 151–218.

Share, D.L. (1999) 'Phonological recoding and orthographic learning: a direct test of the self-teaching hypothesis', *Journal of Experimental Child Psychology*, 72: 95–129.

Schmandt-Besserat, D. (1992) *How Writing Came About*. Austin, TX: University of Texas Press.

Smith, F. (1971) *Understanding Reading: a Psycholinguistic Approach*. New York: Holt, Rinehart and Winston.

Smith, F. (1973) *Psycholinguistics and Reading*. New York: Holt, Reinhart and Winston.

Snowling, M.J. (1981) 'Phonemic deficits in developmental dyslexia', *Psychological Research,* 43: 219–34.

Snowling, M.J. (1991) 'Developmental reading disorders', *Journal of Child Psychology and Psychiatry*, 32: 49–77.

Snowling, M.J. (1995) 'Phonological processing and developmental dyslexia', *Journal of Reading Research*, 18: 132–8.

Snowling, M. J. (2000) *Dyslexia*, 2nd edn. Oxford: Blackwell.

Stainthorp, R. and Hughes, D. (1995) 'Young early readers: the cognitive characteristics and educational experiences of children who can read before they go to school'. Paper presented to the 11th World Conference on Gifted and Talented Children, Hong Kong.

Stainthorp, R. and Hughes, D. (1998) 'Phonological sensitivity and reading: evidence from precocious readers', *Journal of Research in Reading*, 21: 53–67.

Stainthorp, R. and Hughes, D. (1999) *Learning from Children Who Read at an Early Age*. London: Routledge.

Stuart, M. (2002) 'Using the dual-route cascade model as a framework for considering reading development', in R. Stainthorp and P. Tomlinson (eds), *Learning and Teaching Reading*. Leicester: British Psychological Society. pp. 45–60.

Stuart, M. and Coltheart, M. (1988) 'Does reading develop in a sequence of stages?', *Cognition*, 30: 139–81.

Wagner, R. and Torgeson, J. (1987) 'The nature of phonological processing and its causal role in the acquisition of reading skills', *Psychological Bulletin*, 101: 192–212.

Walley, A.C. (1993) 'The role of vocabulary development in children's spoken word recognition and segmentation ability', *Developmental Review*, 13: 286–350.

West, R.F. and Stanovich, K.E. (1978) 'Automatic contextual facilitation in readers of three ages', *Child Development,* 49: 717–27.

Wydell, T.N. and Butterworth, B. (1999) 'A case study of an English–Japanese bilingual with monolingual dyslexia', *Cognition*, 70: 273–305.

19

Young Children's Literary Meaning Making

MIRIAM MARTINEZ, NANCY ROSER
AND CAITLIN DOOLEY

Much recent attention to young children's literacy has focused on their acquisition and understanding of the alphabetic nature of English – and on the instruction that ensures their ability to segment spoken language into phonemes and attach those phonemes to graphemes *en route* to independent decoding (e.g. National Reading Panel, 2000; Snow et al., 1998). Less attention (at least within recent reviews in the US) has focused on compiling evidence for the complexity of children's willingness and ability to make sense of their reading. Contending that meaning making is the gateway through which young children enter the world of literacy, this chapter reviews research and inquiry that provide insights into young children's *literary* meaning making. In particular, we focus on ways in which children from preschool to approximately age eight construct meaning as they read, listen, and respond to *written* stories. Of course children's literary experiences are not limited to stories in written form, and there is research that focuses on how children respond to other forms of stories (e.g. Robinson, 1997). However, because the most extensive body of research on children's literary responses focuses on written stories, we have chosen to make this the focus of our review.

Margaret Donaldson (1978) argues that early in their lives children are working to make sense of their worlds. Although they have their own purposes and intentions, children are soon capable of escaping from their own point of view. Perhaps it is the ability to figure out others' intentions that signals children's ability to follow storylines and

make literary meaning. Stories invite young people into a complex web of communities and cultures (Robinson, 1997), and figuring out what other people *mean* – understanding other people's stories – presents complex linguistic and experiential demands. We examined the research literature to determine how young children seem to rise to the challenging tasks of constructing the intentions and meanings of written texts.

Stories are the most prevalent form of texts with which children are initiated into literacy, yet young children have literary experiences long before they learn to read (Rosenblatt, 1938/1976: ix). Fox describes the development of literary meaning making as children 'playing themselves into the discourses of literature and literacy' (1993: ix). Through their 'storying', children reveal their grasp of narrative intent, their openness to layered meanings, their efforts toward character building, and their dexterity with 'talking like a book' (Fox, 1993). Likewise, students often encounter narrative texts on television and other media which also influence their storying abilities and interpretations (Robinson, 1997). Narrative, in all its forms, creates an avenue for children to explore the texts, language, and culture of their worlds.

According to Langer (1995) literary meaning making involves (among other things) knowing how to 'move through' story worlds. Moving through story worlds, or following the narrative strands of a story, requires a reader, viewer, or listener who is actively involved not only in determining the intentions of story characters, but also in understanding how characters both shape the storyline and are, in turn, shaped by it. Literary meaning making involves connecting pieces of the story – filling in the many gaps that stories naturally offer. To do this, children must draw on their personal experiences and knowledge about the world, including a host of linguistic and cognitive abilities.

Picturebooks are the most likely text encountered by young children, at least in societies in which tradebooks are published for children. When children listen to or read picturebooks, (see Nikolajeva, in this volume), they must process not only written information but pictorial information as well. According to Sipe (1998a), written language is processed in a sequential fashion while the processing of visual art is predominantly simultaneous in nature. So the child in contact with a picturebook story must process and then integrate two quite different kinds of information, contributing to the complexity of meaning making.

During the past quarter century, diverse strands of research have focused on how young children construct text meanings. Much of the earliest research, rooted in schema theory, gave insights into children's memory representations of stories and how stories become assimilated into what children already know. However, this research was somewhat limited by its reliance on simple, contrived texts. More recently, another body of research has emerged. Conducted from the perspective of literary response theory, this strand has yielded rich insights into how young children construct meanings from authentic works of literature (e.g. Galda et al., 2000; Martinez and Roser, 2002). Much of this latter research has drawn on the theoretical thinking of Louise Rosenblatt, who describes the relationship between reader and text as a 'transaction' in which the reader attends not only to 'what the words point ... to in the external world ... [but also] to the images, feelings, attitudes, associations and ideas that the words and their referents evoke' (1978: 10). Rosenblatt argues that readers attend *both* to the text (including the 'texts' of illustrations) *and* to the 'poem' (or evoked meanings).

Although a number of investigations have focused on *older* children's responses, increasingly researchers have attempted to describe and to interpret the literary responses of *young* children both at home and in school. In this chapter we review the research on response to storybook reading that provides insights into some ways children are initiated into meaning making. We have gathered investigations that examine the literary meaning making of young children from preschool to approximately grade three (about the ages four to eight). We have included studies that describe the nature of young children's literary responses as well as explore what

these responses reveal about the ways young children engage in literary making meaning. We have also included a body of research (stemming from the influence of Vygotsky, 1978, and others) that considers the role social interaction plays in shaping children's literary thinking.

CURRENT UNDERSTANDINGS FROM RESEARCH ON CHILDREN'S LITERARY MEANING MAKING

From our review of studies of children's responses, several characterizations of children's responses to literature seem to emerge: (1) children's responses are rich and varied, centring both on texts and upon the child's transaction with the 'evoked poem' (Rosenblatt, 1978); (2) children exhibit distinct response profiles; (3) responses vary across age groups; (4) responses change when the texts become familiar; and (5) responses often reflect the nature of guidance/modelling by the adult involved.

Children respond in rich and varied ways

Text-centred responses

Early investigators of young children's responses such as Applebee (1978) and Hickman (1981) found that the *story world* was of primary importance to young respondents. Subsequent studies confirmed young children's attention to and interest in the story world (e.g. Martinez and Roser, 1994; McGee, 1992; Sipe, 2000a). However, the earliest descriptions of children's text-based responses yielded a somewhat narrow view of children's responses. For example, Applebee (1978) found that his younger subjects (six- and nine-year-olds) focused on story actions as they retold or summarized stories. In fact, Applebee argued that young children are developmentally unable to analyse and generalize about stories.

However, as researchers broadened their methodology beyond structured interviews to include more naturalistic, observational methods, and as they broadened their views about what constituted response, they found vast evidence that children can respond in rich and diverse ways. Using ethnographic (e.g. Frank et al., 1998), sociolinguistic (e.g. Flint, 2000) and other qualitative lenses, researchers have revealed the complexity of children's responses. Hickman (1981), for example, viewed response as any behaviour that revealed a connection between children and literature. In her investigation, she found that five- and six-year-olds responded to literature through body movements such as dance and applause, by sharing discoveries in books, through actions and drama, and by making representations based on literature. Similarly, Paley (1997) described how a student in her kindergarten classroom, deeply involved in the study of Leo Lionni's picturebooks, began to interpret her own world through the perspectives of Lionni's characters. Seemingly, children reveal their responses in multiple ways, including through group dramatization such as readers' theatre (Trousdale and Harris, 1993), as well as through individual projects such as illustrating or role-playing (Kelly, 1990). Several researchers have also examined how written responses (including those of beginning-stage writers) develop and how children's attempts to write in response to texts both enhance their writing and feed their oral responses (e.g. Kelly, 1990; Martinez et al., 1992; Wollman-Bonilla and Werchadlo, 1995). By viewing children's responses more broadly and dynamically, researchers have gained clearer understandings of the ways in which children reveal literary meanings.

Recent investigators have found children's engagement with the story world to be active and interpretive, in contrast with early researchers who characterized the young child as responding primarily at *literal* levels. This attention to the active, thoughtful role of the reader sensitizes the child to the non-neutral text – 'the substance on which the [reading] process works' (Meek, 1988: 5). In an investigation focusing on the literature discussion of a group of six- and seven-year-olds with their teacher, McGee (1992) found that approximately one-third of the children's responses were inferences and interpretations. Additionally, in his investigation of the responses made by six-, seven-, and eight-year-olds during storybook reading, Sipe (2000a) found that 40% of the children's total talk was interpretive in nature. Typically this talk occurred as the children actively worked out meaning and focused on the unfolding storyline. Sipe described the range of the children's interpretive responses:

> The children described, evaluated, speculated, or made inferences about story characters' actions, made frequent use of prediction ... commented about the structure of the story, made thematic or quasi-thematic statements ... [and] made evaluative comments about the story. (2000a: 265)

Similarly, Sipe (2001) found that a great deal of urban kindergartners' talk (about 75%) was reflective of the children's *analysis* of stories. Children discussed the significance in format, language, illustrations, plot meanings, and character relations. Additional evidence suggests that after children move through more literal responses, they are more likely to offer inferential, interpretive, and thematic responses (Kelly, 1990; Sipe, 1996). Although there is evidence that younger children are more firmly bound to the story world during their literature discussions than are older students (Martinez and Roser, 1994), it is also evident that young children actively construct meaning and use sophisticated interpretive strategies. There is some evidence that preschoolers are sensitive to (and respond differently to) varying literary genres (Shine and Roser, 1999). Seemingly, the more opportunities young children have to respond to literature, the more adept they become (McGill-Franzen and Lanford, 1994).

Just as Sipe found that his young participants offered thematic interpretations of stories, Lehr (1988; 1991), in her in-depth investigation of children's ability to infer thematic meanings, found that even five- and seven-year-olds could successfully generate thematic statements. In particular, she found that when children talked at length about characters and their internal motivations, their talk frequently became the pathway through which they were able to discuss story themes. Lehr concluded that children who understood the inner workings of characters were able to take that information and 'generate an overarching construct for the story' (1991: 52). The thematic statements made by Lehr's five-year-old subjects often differed from those offered by adults; nonetheless, the young children's theme statements were congruent with the texts. Lehr (1988) concluded that although young children process meaning with different perspectives than adults, even young children construct meaning at thematic levels when the texts themselves are within their grasp.

Young children's text-focused responses also include attention to the author's and illustrator's craft. In her model of literary meaning making, Langer (1995) describes a stance in which readers step outside the story world to 'objectify' their experience with text, achieving the distance necessary to consider the author's or illustrator's artistry. Evidence suggests that young children might actually be more attuned to the illustrator's rather than the author's craft. That is, they may be more likely to objectify the illustrations than the text. For example, a child might make an evaluative comment about an illustration ('Wow! That dragon's scary') rather than the text ('Wow! Those words are scary'). Kiefer noted that 'as children communicate with and about picture books, they seem to develop a growing awareness of aesthetic factors and of the artist's role in choosing these factors to express meaning' (1988; 264). Sipe (2000a) found that 23% of the responses of the six-, seven-, and eight-year-olds in his study involved taking an analytical approach to illustrations. His subjects discussed artistic media, the arrangement of illustrations, as well as artists' choices of colour and perspective – talk Sipe interpreted as 'sophisticated'.

Children's skilful reliance on illustration to make literary meaning has been documented by other researchers as well. Wolf and Heath (1992) produced a case description of how a three-year-old child gained insights into stories using information conveyed through illustrations. In their analysis of children's responses to Anthony Browne's *Zoo*, Styles and Arizpe (2001) found that children as young as four used visual cues to infer the unhappiness of the animals in the story. Because the crafting that illustrators and authors achieve is closely linked with the meanings they seek to convey, attention to text as a crafted object provides young readers and listeners with an additional pathway to meaning.

It is possible that attention to the illustrator's craft makes clearer to children the notion that text, too, is artistically constructed. Wolf and Heath observed that 'a child accustomed to illustrative metaphors will quickly recognize the honesty, mischievousness, or inner beauty of a character and use the clues of costume or expression to define character and predict outcomes' (1992: 57). A number of researchers have documented young children's attention to the text as an 'object' crafted by an author (Green, 1982; Kelly, 1990; Wollman-Bonilla, 1989). Although young children's responses to the features and qualities of text appear to occur less frequently than other types of response (Martinez et al., 1992; McGee, 1992; Sipe, 1998a), this type of response is, nonetheless, important in terms of the ways in which children construct meaning.

Children seem especially likely to focus on the artistry of literature in contexts in which their attention is directed toward features of craft. Bloem and Manna (1999) described classroom author/illustrator studies as one way to engage readers in thoughtful literary analysis. These researchers found that the eight-year-olds in their investigation attended to the artistry of the texts and illustrations as well as to the teacher models of response. The children took pleasure in the nuances of texts and in querying how an author/illustrator (Patricia Polacco) crafted her work. Madura described an approach to the teaching of language arts through the 'world of the picturebook', documenting how her students came to understand themselves as readers and writers in a learning environment that valued 'beauty, personal reflection, and the process of creating visual and written compositions' (1995:

116). Keifer (1983; 1988) suggests that through picturebooks, children can learn that illustrations as well as texts carry meaning. After working for over six years with students from kindergarten through fourth grade, Kiefer found that children's appreciation for craft develops over time and with many opportunities for response.

Reader-centred responses

While attention to text is critical as children respond to literature, researchers have also acknowledged the vital importance of reader-centred responses. As children build bridges between their personal experiences and the stories they read, they are involved in a fundamental act of literary meaning making. Hickman's (1981) seminal study described the personal associations young children make with literature. Subsequent studies have confirmed her findings (e.g. Martinez et al., 1992; Short, 1992; Sipe, 1998b; Wollman-Bonilla, 1989; Wollman-Bonilla and Werchadlo, 1995). The six-, seven-, and eight-year-olds in Sipe's (2000a) investigation relied on experiences from their own lives to understand various facets of stories. Studies by McGee (1992) and by Wollman-Bonilla and Werchadlo (1995) identified yet another way in which children use personal experiences to better understand stories: The subjects in these investigations became vicariously involved with character as they stepped into the characters' roles and made judgements about how they would feel if they found themselves in a similar situation. Wollman-Bonilla and Werchadlo also found that the number of reader-centred responses, especially personal reactions to stories, grew as children were encouraged to respond to texts over time.

A number of studies have found that young children not only use personal experiences to understand text better, but also use text to understand some facet of their own lives – a type of response Cochran-Smith (1984) labels as 'text-to-life' connections. Langer (1995) has described a text-to-life connection as a stance in which readers 'step out' of stories (even momentarily) to reflect on how the events, ideas, or characters relate to their own lives or the lives of others. McGinley and Kamberelis (1996) found that, for the eight- and nine-year-olds in their study, literature served both a personal and a social function. Their participants used literature as a means of reflecting on experiences and imagining possibilities, but they also attempted to use stories as vehicles to help them better understand and negotiate social relationships and address significant social problems. In effect, the children in

McGinley and Kamberelis' investigation used literature as a lens through which they could better understand their own personal experiences and their world. Wolman-Bonilla and Werchadlo (1995) found that these connections increased over time and with experience.

Children bring their experiences with other texts to literature study, and various researchers have found that young children make valuable and insightful intertextual connections when responding to literature (Oyler and Barry, 1996; Short, 1992; Sipe, 2000a) – producing what Cochran-Smith (1984) calls a 'text-to-text' connection. Sipe (2000b) maintains that these intertextual connections are important to children's developing literary understanding. In his investigations of five-, six-, and seven-year-olds, Sipe found that children use intertextual connections to interpret or analyse the language, narrative elements, and symbolic aspects of stories. In particular, Sipe's subjects used intertextual connections to 'interpret story characters' appearance, feelings, motivation, and the plot' (2000b: 80). Based on an investigation of young children's responses to five variants of a traditional tale, Sipe (2001) found that opportunities to explore variants enabled the children to build schemata for traditional tales. In particular, the children analysed the story, 'understanding the function of characters, the plot sequence, the setting, and the other narrative elements' (2001: 347).

Individuals have distinct response profiles

While it is possible to address text-centred and reader-centred responses in general, it is also important to acknowledge that individuals respond to stories and make their own meanings from stories in their own ways. Wolf and Heath (1992), for example, found that two sisters had distinctive ways of responding to stories. Lindsey, the older sister, saw books as opportunities for social interaction. She chose drama as her way to represent her meaning making. Ashley, the younger sister, preferred to sit quietly alone, intently studying the illustrations in stories. Ashley preferred reflection to acting out stories; in addition, she showed appreciation for story language. Sipe (1998b; 2000a) also found distinctive response styles among the beginning readers in his study. He analysed the ways in which four of his subjects, Sally, Charles, Krissy, and Jim, responded to stories. The typical way in which Sally responded to literature was through close analysis and logical reasoning. Further, Sally used intertextual references to substantiate the points she made during discussions and was concerned with identifying relationships between fictional stories and reality. Another defining feature of Sally's response style was her sensitivity to the feelings of story characters and to issues of equity and justice. Charles was a 'performative responder' who often used story worlds as springboards for his own flights of fancy. Charles seemed to relish taking on the roles of characters and creating voices for them. Charles' responses were typified by his predictions of upcoming story events. The most distinctive feature of Krissy's response style was her tendency to suggest story-based creative activities in which she and her classmates might engage – art activities, drama activities, and others. Krissy also delighted in inventing alternatives to the plots of stories and sharing her speculations about stories with classmates. She was especially interested in craft and frequently talked about the artistic styles and techniques used by illustrators. The defining feature of Jim's response style was his ability to take a broad perspective on stories; frequently during story discussions, Jim shared thematic and quasi-thematic statements.

Like Sipe, Keenan (1993) evaluated the various ways in which first-graders responded in writing to characters in fairytales and found that while some children made personal connections ('text-to-self') with the characters (e.g. writing to characters for advice or as conversation), others made more 'text-to-text' and 'text-to-life' connections (e.g. writing to a character from one fairytale about a character from another, or introducing a character to one's own home and family). The work of Wolf and Heath, Sipe, and Keenan suggests that even very young children may go about the process of constructing meaning in highly individualistic ways.

Children respond differently across age levels

Even though children develop their own preferred styles of response, they are also developing as responders and meaning makers in ways that can be broadly sketched. Although most researchers seem to agree that development occurs, fine-tuned understandings about that development are still being shaped. In an early investigation focused on the developmental nature of children's literary responses, Applebee (1978) looked at literary thinking across four age groups. He asked his younger subjects (six- and nine-year-olds) to identify, tell about, and evaluate favourite stories. Applebee examined the children's objective responses (i.e. those responses concerned with a story's publicly verifiable characteristics) as well as their subjective or personal responses. In their objective responses, the children focused on story actions rather than story characteristics such as point of view or theme. However, the forms of objective responses differed between the six- and nine-year-olds, with the younger children typically producing detailed retellings while the older children produced synopses or summaries. Further, the six-year-olds typically offered global evaluations (e.g. 'It's good') in their subjective responses, while the nine-year-olds evaluated by placing stories in categories with clearly marked attributes (e.g. 'dreary' or 'interesting').

More recent research demonstrates changes in how children choose to express their responses as they get older. In a longitudinal case study of her daughter's responses to various editions of *Hansel and Gretel*, Wolf (1991) found changes in the style of response with age and exposure to a text. At ages three and four, the child responded more physically (e.g. pantomiming and acting out the story), whereas at ages five and six, her gestures became 'more subdued and her talk opened up into comments, questions, [and] tentative hypotheses' (1991: 389). In the same manner, Hickman (1981) observed differences in children's responses in three multi-age classrooms (five- and six-year-olds; seven- and eight-year-olds; and nine- and ten-year-olds). As noted earlier, Hickman broadened the definition of response to include both verbal and physical responses. Although Hickman found instances of both modes of response in each of the three classrooms in which she collected data, she found that some modes were more characteristic of particular age levels. For example, the younger children were more likely to use their bodies to respond. These five- and six-year-old children frequently dramatized the action of stories read aloud and in teacher-led discussions, and they enacted parts of stories during dramatic play. Hickman observed that the seven- and eight-year-olds appeared to be at a transitional level. At times they responded in much the same way as did the younger children. However, at other times they appeared to be more like the nine- and ten-year-olds whom Hickman characterized as being intensely attentive to books, sometimes becoming 'lost in books'.

In their oral responses, five- and six-year-olds in Hickman's study expressed more interest in stories than in the authors of stories. Although they were very concerned with sorting out plot, they often reduced stories to 'lessons' when invited to interpret meaning. The personal statements these younger children made were only loosely tied to stories. Finally, these children expressed concern with the reality of stories by talking about whether stories were 'true' or 'possible'. Even though the seven- and eight-year-olds sometimes responded in similar ways, at other times they showed less need

to focus on the story world in their verbal responses and instead revealed connections between their own experiences and story meanings. In addition, they were beginning to recognize the role of the author as the creator of a story.

Lehr (1988) found developmental trends in children's (ranging in age from five to 10) ability to identify and articulate story themes. Lehr asked her subjects to identify realistic books with related themes as well as folktales with related themes. Although all the children were more successful in identifying related themes of realistic stories, the older children (ages seven to 10) made the same selections as adults more often than did the younger children (ages five and six). The older children were also more successful in making their own thematic statements for the stories. Lehr also found differences across age levels in children's awareness of character motivation. The older children 'identified with characters and expected characters to change, whereas [younger] children typically did not want to change actions of characters' (1988: 351).

A number of researchers have documented differences in children's literary thinking across grade levels; however, it is not yet clear the extent to which differences may reflect the influence of factors such as instruction and experience rather than developmental constraints. For example, in examining children's responses, Lehr found that her subjects' previous experiences with literature were tied to the sophistication of their responses.

Children talk differently when the text is familiar

In yet another effort to gain understanding about the complexities and shifts in children's meaning making efforts, several investigators have examined children's responses across time when the same story is reread (cf. Crago and Crago, 1976; Hickman, 1979; Kiefer, 1986; Yaden, 1988). In both homes and classrooms, adults repeatedly read the same story to children, and these repetitions appear to affect children's responses. Martinez and Roser (1985) examined changes in preschool children's naturally occurring responses as they listened to stories read aloud repeatedly across intervals of time. Focusing on the storytime interactions of a four-year-old and her father and a group of four-year-olds and their preschool teacher, the researchers identified four changes that signalled the differences in children's responses as they repeatedly listened to stories. First, the child at home and those in a preschool storytime talked more about familiar than unfamiliar stories. Secondly, the form of children's responses changed when listening to unfamiliar and familiar stories, i.e. the child reading with her father asked more questions when a story was read for the first time and shared more comments when listening to familiar stories. In the preschool, the children also made more comments when stories were familiar. Further, the focus of responses (i.e. whether on characters, events, details, title, setting, story language, or theme) changed over repeated readings of stories. The actual pattern of change varied from story to story; however, the shifts in focus suggest that, as children gain control over particular aspects of stories, they are able to attend to other dimensions. Finally, when children chose to talk about a particular aspect of a story across multiple readings, the discussion that occurred suggested that the children were probing the story more deeply than they had initially.

Morrow (1988) examined the number and complexity of four-year-olds' responses to literature. She also investigated children's responses to stories read to them repeatedly. The children, all from low socio-economic backgrounds attending urban childcare centres, were assigned to two experimental groups and one control group. The children in the first experimental group were read a different book each week for 10 weeks on a one-to-one basis. Children in the second experimental group heard repeated readings of only three different books. The children in the control group were involved in traditional reading readiness activities. Morrow found that participation in one-to-one readalouds increased the quantity and complexity of the children's responses. Children in both experimental groups asked more questions and made more comments than those in the control group, and children in the 'different-book' group asked more questions, while those in the 'repeated-book' experimental group made more comments about the stories they heard. From Morrow's intervention, it seems that repeated experiences with stories fostered a wider variety of response and more complex, interpretive comments than did single readings of stories.

The results of these investigations suggest that increased opportunities to listen to a story result in more complex literary meaning making. Seemingly, increased familiarity with a story appears to enrich a child's literary meaning making by giving licence to explore different facets of stories.

THE SOCIAL NATURE OF RESPONSE

For the most part, young children's responses to literature are being observed and learned about within social contexts – during classroom readalouds, literature circles, and family story readings.

Vygotsky (1978) and others have characterized the vital role that social interactions play in shaping and clarifying language and thought. Similarly, teachers and researchers have long recognized the importance of opportunities for learners to work together to share ideas, and make meaning. Through opportunities to interact with peers around a shared experience (such as a story), children shape their thoughts and feelings about the experience. Researchers argue that the deepest levels of understanding are made possible though social interaction. While researchers have examined storybook reading in both home and school as contexts for initiating children into meaning construction, in large part we limit this section of our review to the school context which is arguably, for many children, the primary social setting for literary meaning making (Langer, 1995).

Storybook readalouds

Storybook readalouds in the school may well serve as the best possible impetus to literary meaning making. Langer suggests that:

> through literary experience, teachers can help students become aware of and use their various cultural selves to make connections, explore relationships, examine conflicts, and search for understandings through the literature they read and the interactions they have. (1995: 38)

While reading aloud storybooks, adult readers can initiate children into the intricacies of meaning construction as they step into the roles of model, guide, and fellow discussant; concurrently, children have the opportunity to tell what they understand, to ask questions, to extend their ideas, and to develop social and intellectual allies (Pellegrini and Galda, 1998). Hepler and Hickman have observed that the 'literary transaction, the one-to-one conversation between author and audience, is frequently surrounded by other voices' (1982: 279). The conversations around literature in which different ideas, conjectures, and backgrounds are shared allow for enriched understanding and experience (Bakhtin, 1986; Lindfors, 1999; Pellegrini and Galda, 1998). However, Eeds and Wells (1989) remind us that a rich exchange of ideas is likely to occur only when adults use strategies that foster 'grand conversations' rather than 'gentle inquisitions'.

Cochran-Smith (1984) conducted a comprehensive 18-month study of preschoolers' socialization into literacy. She found that the three- to five-year-olds in her investigation learned to interpret stories during group story reading:

> In the verbal interaction around books, the story reader instructed her listeners in how to make sense of texts by

helping them to use – or using for them – various kinds of world and literary knowledge. She also guided the children in ways to use book knowledge in their lives. (1984: 6)

Through readalouds and the conversation that surrounded them, the adult story reader in Cochran-Smith's study tried to make more transparent for children the internal reading processes of adult readers. Cochran-Smith characterized the interactions that occurred during the storybook readings in the preschool as being dialogic or conversational in nature. The children answered questions, made comments, and offered interpretations, while the adult reader guided the children based on their responses. The adult story reader and children constructed meaning together.

In her analysis of the data, Cochran-Smith identified two major types of interaction sequences – 'life-to-text' interactions and 'text-to-life' interactions. The life-to-text interactions, which accounted for the majority of interaction sequences, 'helped listeners make sense of the events, characters, action, and information in the particular books being shared' (1984: 169). In the life-to-text interactions, children learned to use extratextual information to make sense of the text. In particular, the adult reader modelled how to use four kinds of knowledge to read and interpret stories: (1) knowledge of the world; (2) knowledge of literary conventions; (3) knowledge of story or narrative; and (4) knowledge of how to respond as a member of a reading audience. According to Cochran-Smith, under the tutelage of the adult story reader, the children learned to use both knowledge of the world and personal knowledge to fill in gaps in the story and to integrate story information. When the children lacked necessary world knowledge, the story reader supplied it and then guided the children in using that knowledge. The story reader also guided the children in acquiring knowledge of literary conventions, including genre conventions. For example, she showed them the titles of stories they read, and signalled to the children that titles are likely to hold clues to what the story will be about. She also identified stories by genre and signalled how books in a particular genre should be read (e.g. 'This is a wordless picture book. Be sure to look carefully at each picture to create a story').

The story reader also helped the students understand the basics of narrative, which Cochran-Smith identified as characters and action. Story readers placed a great deal of emphasis on both characters and action through the use of questions such as: 'Who is this character?', 'How does she feel?', 'Why?', 'What do the character's actions tell you about how she feels?' In effect, the storybook reading interactions told the children that (1) it was important to make inferences about characters by integrating the information in pictures and texts; and (2) this information 'played an important role in what happened in a story' (1984: 21). Finally, the adult story reader shared with the children knowledge of how to respond as a member of the story audience. The adult shaped the children's responses by modelling how she felt as a member of the audience and suggesting feelings the children might have. Children learned to talk about what they might do if they found themselves in the same situation as the story characters as well as what the story told them.

The roles of the teacher

While Cochran-Smith has done an extensive analysis of what young children learn about literary meaning construction during readalouds, others have also added to this understanding. Both Sipe (1998a) and Wolf and Heath (1992) found that the adult story reader helps young children learn to integrate textual and pictorial information. Wolf and Heath observed that children can learn a great deal about interpreting character during the read aloud, both through the reader's prosodic oral interpretation and through the talk that occurs around stories *following* the readaloud. These researchers also found that through readalouds children learn about features of particular literary genres.

The roles teachers assume and the strategies they use seem to be critical elements of story sharing experiences. McGee et al. (1994) coded and analysed discussions led by three first-grade teachers and found that the teachers took on five roles: (1) facilitator; (2) helper/nudger; (3) responder; (4) literary curator (i.e. drawing attention to the literary elements in a story); and (5) reader. They suggest that in order to lead 'grand conversations' (Eeds and Wells, 1989), teachers in their study invited students' responses and allowed children to initiate topics of conversation. They found, however, that the teachers in their study did not model their own responses enough and rarely took on the role of 'literary curator' – both roles that might have supported students' growing literary awareness. Roser and Martinez (1985) identified three roles that teachers and parents seemed to take as they read and talked about stories with preschoolers: (1) co-responder; (2) informer; and (3) director. As a co-responder, the adult entered the conversation as a participant and modelled literary meaning making and response; as the informer, the adult interpreted aspects of the story and guided children through the process of constructing meaning. The director role was one of assuring procedures and routines typically unrelated to story understanding. In a study of the storybook readaloud styles of six teachers of five-year-olds, Martinez and Teale (1993) documented differences in three facets of their readaloud style: (1) the focus of the teacher talk; (2) the type of information that the teachers and students talked about; and (3) the instructional strategies used by the teachers.

As part of their role during storybook readaloud time, many teachers ask questions to prompt and maintain discussion. McGee (1992), in her study of the 'grand conversations' of five- and six-year-olds, compared the level of interpretive discourse before and after teachers inserted one interpretive question into the literary conversation. After reading each story, the discussion leaders simply asked, 'What do you think?' In each case, children talked freely about one of three picturebooks, with the teacher initially following the children's conversational leads. Teachers asked no questions as the children talked and made comments only to clarify. Then, as the discussion waned, the teacher leaders posed one previously prepared interpretive question intended to focus children on the significance of the story as a whole (but not intended to elicit a single 'right' answer). McGee's analysis revealed that students made more interpretive responses and produced more focused responses after the question than before it. McGee concluded that:

> although it seemed important for students to explore stories on their own terms, switching from topic to topic in an open-ended conversation prompted by their own responses and questions, it also seemed important to focus the conversation around a teacher-posed interpretive question which called for students to reflect on the work as a whole and to use inferential and critical thinking. (1992: 186).

The teacher's role in creating an environment conducive to literary meaning making was explored in a study of Spanish/English bilingual kindergarten children using their knowledge of languages to respond to stories read aloud (Battle, 1993; 1995). The bilingual teacher contributed to children's collaborative meaning making in English and Spanish by encouraging her children's responses in three ways during storytime. First, during story discussion, the teacher made it 'safe to talk' by focusing on what the children had to say rather than the language forms they used. Secondly, *throughout* the readaloud the teacher encouraged questions, observations, and opinions. At times, she repeated, paraphrased, or added to the children's talk, sharing her own enthusiasms. Thirdly, the teacher provided multiple invitations to speak, but did not demand or require response. Battle concluded that this teacher's participation encouraged, supported, and maintained thought and talk in book discussion in both languages:

> The teacher's role seemed to be to highlight either the aspects of text or the children's comments and questions that might hold potential for ... discussion, and then to allow the children to talk. (1993: 166)

Nevertheless, not all storybook readaloud experiences are equally rich opportunities for young children to participate in literary meaning making. Cochran-Smith (1984) observed the storybook readalouds that occurred when her subjects visited the library and found that some adults discouraged interaction during the readaloud. Rather, the librarian in her study expected the children to listen to the story and reserve their talk until after the readaloud. In her study of the literacy opportunities in three communities in the Piedmont area of the Carolinas in the United States, Heath (1982) found that families in two of the three communities read to their children. However, in one community parents typically expected their children to sit quietly during the readaloud and then answer follow-up 'what' questions (as opposed to 'why' questions). By contrast, the families in the community that Heath described as 'school-oriented' engaged their children in interactive readaloud experiences and also helped their children use book meanings to make sense of their world. Similar evidence comes from a series of three case studies of teacher-led readalouds in preschools: McGill-Franzen and Lanford (1994) found that preschoolers in lower socio-economic areas received fewer opportunities for open-ended, higher-level literary discussions than those in higher socio-economic areas.

LEARNING TO CONSTRUCT LITERARY MEANING IS A COMPLEX TASK

Against contemporary pressures to attend to only part of children's literacy learning, Sipe and Bauer have cautioned:

> Too often, the view is that literary understanding is a frill, and that what children really need is more drill and skill approaches. The crisis of literacy ... may not best be solved by these more fragmented methods, but by capitalizing on ... the meaning-making and interpretive richness that children bring to literacy and literature. (2001: 340)

When we understand more about how and why children approach stories and make meanings, we become better positioned to teach. Fortunately, as a learning community, we are becoming ever more understanding (and appreciative) of children's understandings (Duckworth, 1987). We have learned that students' responses to literature vary with development, with experience, with the text, with the tasks, and across readers. As a learning community of researchers and teachers, we value opportunities for children to reveal their literary meanings and to be supported in the process of making meaning.

If literary meaning making is to be both an avenue to and an outcome of children's literacy learning, a number of factors seem implicated. First, it appears important to let children hear, read, and *talk about* stories and texts. As James Britton wrote, 'Perhaps the most important general implication for teaching ... is to note that anyone who succeeded in outlawing talk in the classroom would have outlawed life' (1970: 223). Secondly, children seem to require (beyond rich language learning opportunities) time to revisit favourite stories repeatedly. Rereading both reacquaints and reassures, as well as reopens to new discoveries and understandings. Thirdly, the richest meaning making appears to occur in interactive experiences in which children share with and learn from other listeners and readers. Fourthly, children seem to require multiple opportunities to respond (and demonstrate their meanings) in a variety of formats. Fifthly, some of the best meaning making opportunities seem to occur in the presence of the most inviting texts – stories with powerful language and themes that inspire ideas and feelings, thought and talk (Martinez and Roser, 1995). Sixthly, literary meaning making is rigorous activity. Meanings are not, as Rosenblatt cautions, all of equal value. The most value is assigned to those literary responses that can be supported by returning to the text. Seventhly, teachers can introduce children to a variety of texts using a wide range of media. For example, by providing time for discussion of televised texts, teachers can help to create more informed and critical viewers and consumers (Robinson, 1997). Finally, the role of knowledgeable teacher/leader must be seriously shouldered. By selecting texts, reading evocatively, modelling responses, thinking aloud, prompting students with the well-placed comment or question, drawing children's attention (or noticing their attention) to the authors' and illustrators' craft, teachers scaffold young children's thinking and meaning making abilities.

DIRECTIONS FOR FUTURE RESEARCH

While existing research has revealed a great deal about children as constructors of literary meaning,

questions remain. The earliest strand of response research explored differences in children's meaning construction across age levels. While this work was pioneering in nature, subsequent research has been increasingly grounded in literary theory and has relied on more sophisticated techniques for collecting and analysing data. There would be value in revisiting the question of how children's meaning construction differs across ages, grounding that research in our deepened understanding of the nature of literary response. We are also at a very beginning point in understanding the nature of young children's textual knowledge (e.g. their knowledge of genre features, narrative devices, author and illustrator styles), how they acquire this knowledge, and how this knowledge impacts their construction of meaning. Further, researchers investigating young children's meaning construction have focused primarily on children's responses to picturebooks. Perhaps this comes as no surprise given that picturebooks are the form of printed literature to which most children are first introduced. However, through readalouds many young children at home and school are also introduced to chapter books. There have been no investigations of how young children learn to navigate these lengthier and more complex works of literature. The cultural realm of response is one that especially deserves our attention as researchers. We need to explore differences in the construction of meaning that may exist among cultural and ethnic groups, especially the differences that may exist among groups that come from oral storytelling traditions rather than narrative traditions grounded in printed texts or the media. A portrait of young literary thinkers has begun to take shape from existing research; yet that portrait is one that is likely to take on increasing depth and richness as we continue to pursue investigations of children as meaning makers.

REFERENCES

Applebee, A. (1978) *The Child's Concept of Story.* Chicago: University of Chicago Press.

Bakhtin, M.M. (1986) *Speech Genres and Other Late Essays.* Austin, TX: University of Texas Press.

Battle, J. (1993) 'Mexican-American bilingual kindergartners' collaborations in meaning making', in D.J. Leu and C.K. Kinzer (eds), *Examining Central Issues in Literacy Research, Theory, and Practice.* Forty-Second Yearbook of the National Reading Conference. Chicago: National Reading Conference. pp. 163–9.

Battle, J. (1995) 'Collaborative story talk in a bilingual kindergarten', in N. Roser and M. Martinez (eds), *Book*

Talk and Beyond: Children and Teachers Respond to Literature. Newark, DE: International Reading Association. pp. 157–67.

Bloem, P.L. and Manna, A.L. (1999) 'A chorus of questions: readers respond to Patricia Polacco', *The Reading Teacher*, 52: 802–8.

Britton, J. (1970) *Language and Learning.* Harmondsworth: Penguin.

Cochran-Smith, M (1984). *The Making of a Reader.* Norwood, NJ: Ablex.

Crago, H. and Crago, M. (1976) 'The untrained eye? A preschool child explores Felix Hoffman's "Rapunzel"', *Children's Literature in Education*, 22: 135–51.

Donaldson, M.C. (1978) *Children's Minds.* New York: Norton.

Duckworth, E. (1987) *'The Having of Wonderful Ideas' and Other Essays on Teaching and Learning.* New York: Teachers College Press.

Eeds, M.A. and Wells, D. (1989) 'Grand conversations: an exploration of meaning construction in literature study groups', *Research in the Teaching of English*, 23: 4–29.

Flint, A.S. (2000) 'Know-it-alls, identifiers, defenders, and solidifiers (KIDS): examining interpretive authority within literacy events', *Reading Research and Instruction*, 39: 119–34.

Fox, C. (1993) *At the Very Edge of the Forest: the Influence of Literature on Storytelling by Children.* London: Cassell.

Frank, C.R., Dixon, J.C. and Brandts, L.R. (1998) '"Dear book club": a sociolinguistic and ethnographic analysis of literature discussion groups in second grade', in *National Reading Conference Yearbook*, vol. 47. Chicago: National Reading Conference. pp. 103–15.

Galda, L., Ash, G. and Cullinan, B. (2000) 'Children's literature', in M.L. Kamil, P.B. Mosenthal, P.D. Pearson and R. Barr (eds), *Handbook of Reading Research*, vol. III. Hillsdale, NJ: Erlbaum. pp. 361–80.

Green, G.M. (1982) 'Competence for implicit text analysis: literary style discrimination in five-year-olds', in D. Tanner (ed.), *Analyzing Discourse: Text and Talk.* Washington, DC: Georgetown University Press. pp. 142–63.

Heath, S.B. (1982) 'What no bedtime story means: narrative skills at home and school', *Language in Society*, 11: 49–76.

Hepler, S. and Hickman, J. (1982) '"The book was okay. I love you": social aspects of response to literature', *Theory into Practice*, 21: 278–83.

Hickman, J. (1979) 'Response to literature in a school environment, grades K through 5'. Unpublished doctoral dissertation, Ohio State University.

Hickman, J. (1981). 'A new perspective on response to literature: research in an elementary school setting', *Research in the Teaching of English*, 15: 343–54.

Keenan, J.W. (1993) 'The Jolly Postman comes to call: primary writers' response to literature', in K. Holland, R.A. Hungerford and S.B. Ernst (eds), *Journeying: Children Responding to Literature.* Portsmouth, NH: Heinemann. pp. 72–88.

Kelly, P.R. (1990) 'Guiding young students' response to literature', *The Reading Teacher*, 43: 464–70.

Kiefer, B. (1983) 'The responses of children in a combination first/second grade classroom to picture books in a variety of artistic styles', *Journal of Research and Development in Education*, 16 (3): 14–20.

Kiefer, B. (1986) 'The child and the picture book: creating live circuits', *Children's Literature Association Quarterly*, 11: 63–8.

Kiefer, B. (1988) 'Picture books as contexts for literary, aesthetic, and real world understandings', *Language Arts*, 65: 260–71.

Langer, J.A. (1995) *Envisioning Literature: Literary Understanding and Literature Instruction.* Newark, DE: International Reading Association and Teachers College Press.

Lehr, S. (1988) 'The child's developing sense of theme as a response to literature', *Reading Research Quarterly*, 23: 337–57.

Lehr, S.S. (1991) *The Child's Developing Sense of Theme: Responses to Literature.* New York: Teachers College Press.

Lindfors, J. (1999) *Children's Inquiry: Using Language to Make Sense of the World.* New York: Teachers College Press.

Madura, S. (1995) 'The line and texture of aesthetic response: primary children study authors and illustrators', *The Reading Teacher*, 49: 110–18.

Martinez, M. and Roser, N.L. (1985) 'Read it again: the value of repeated readings during storytime', *The Reading Teacher*, 38: 782–6.

Martinez, M. and Roser, N.L. (1994) 'Children's responses to a chapter book across grade levels: implications for sustained text', in C.K. Kinzer and D.J. Leu, (eds), *Multidimensional Aspects of Literacy Research, Theory, and Practice.* Forty-Third Yearbook of the National Reading Conference. Chicago: National Reading Conference. pp. 317–24.

Martinez, M. and Roser, N.L. (1995) 'The books make a difference in story talk', in N.L. Roser and M. Martinez (eds), *Book Talk and Beyond: Children and Teachers Respond to Literature.* Newark, DE: International Reading Association. pp. 32–41.

Martinez, M. and Roser, N.L. (2002) 'Children's responses to literature', in J. Flood, D. Lapp, J.R. Squire and J.M. Jensen (eds), *Handbook of Research on Teaching the English Language Arts*, 2nd edn. Mahwah, NJ: Erlbaum. pp. 799–813.

Martinez, M. and Teale, W.H. (1993) 'Teachers storybook reading style: a comparison of six teachers', *Research in the Teaching of English*, 27 (2): 175–99.

Martinez, M., Roser, N.L., Hoffman, J.V. and Battle, J. (1992) 'Fostering better book discussions through response logs and a response framework: a case description', in C.K. Kinzer and D.J. Leu (eds), *Literacy Research, Theory, and Practice: Views from Many Perspectives.* Forty-First Yearbook of the National Reading Conference. Chicago: National Reading Conference. pp. 303–11.

McGee, L.M. (1992) 'An exploration of meaning construction in first graders' grand conversations', in C.K. Kinzer and D.J. Leu (eds), *Literacy Research, Theory, and Practice: Views from Many Perspectives.* Forty-First Yearbook of the National Reading Conference. Chicago: National Reading Conference. pp. 177–86.

McGee, L.M., Courtney, L. and Lomax, R.G. (1994) 'Teachers' roles in first graders' grand conversations', in C.K. Kinzer and D.J. Leu (eds), *Multidimensional Aspects of Literacy Research, Theory, and Practice.* Forty-Third Yearbook of the National Reading Conference. Chicago: National Reading Conference. pp. 517–26.

McGill-Franzen, A. and Lanford, C. (1994) 'Exposing the edge of the preschool curriculum: teachers' talk about text and children's literary understandings', *Language Arts*, 71: 264–73.

McGinley, W. and Kamberelis, G. (1996) 'Maniac Magee and Ragtime Tumpie: children negotiating self and world through reading and writing', *Research in the Teaching of English*, 30: 75–113.

Meek, M. (1988) *How Texts Teach What Readers Learn.* Stroud: Thimble.

Morrow, L.M. (1988) 'Young children's responses to one-to-one story readings in school settings', *Reading Research Quarterly*, 23: 89–107.

National Reading Panel (2000) *Teaching Children to Read: an Evidence-Based Assessment of the Scientific Research Literature on Reading and its Implications for Reading Instruction.* Washington, DC: National Institute of Child Health and Human Development.

Oyler, C. and Barry, A. (1996) 'Intertextual connections in read-alouds of information books', *Language Arts*, 73: 324–9.

Paley, V.G. (1997) *The Girl with the Brown Crayon.* Cambridge, MA: Cambridge University Press.

Pellegrini, A. and Galda, L. (1998) *The Development of School-Based Literacy.* New York: Routledge.

Robinson, M. (1997) *Children Reading Print and Television.* London: Falmer.

Rosenblatt, L.M. (1938/1976) *Literature as Exploration.* New York: Noble and Noble.

Rosenblatt, L.M. (1978) *The Reader, the Text, the Poem: the Transactional Theory of the Literary Work.* Carbondale, IL: Southern Illinois University Press.

Roser, N. and Martinez, M. (1985) 'Roles adults play in preschoolers' response to literature', *Language Arts*, 62: 485–90.

Shine, S. and Roser, N. (1999) 'The role of genre in preschoolers' response to picture books', *Research in the Teaching of English*, 34: 197–254.

Short, K.G. (1992) 'Intertextuality: searching for patterns that connect', in C.K. Kinzer and D.J. Leu (eds), *Literacy Research, Theory, and Practice: Views from Many Perspectives.* Forty-First Yearbook of the National Reading Conference. Chicago: National Reading Conference. pp. 187–97.

Sipe, L.R. (1996) 'The construction of literary understanding by first and second graders in response to picture storybook read-alouds'. Unpublished doctoral dissertation, Ohio State University, Columbus.

Sipe, L.R. (1998a) 'How picture books work: a semiotically framed theory of text–picture relationships', *Children's Literature in Education*, 29: 97–108.

Sipe, L.R. (1998b) 'Individual literary response styles of first and second graders', in T. Shanahan and F.V. Rodriguez-Brown (eds), *Forty-Seventh Yearbook of the National Reading Conference.* Chicago: National Reading Conference. pp. 76–89.

Sipe, L.R. (2000a). 'The construction of literary understanding by first and second graders in oral responses to picture storybook read alouds', *Reading Research Quarterly*, 35: 252–75.

Sipe, L.R. (2000b) '"Those two gingerbread boys could be brothers": how children use intertextual connections during storybook readalouds', *Children's Literature in Education*, 31: 73–90.

Sipe, L.R. (2001) 'A palimpsest of stories: young children's construction of intertextual links among fairytale variants', *Reading Research and Instruction*, 40: 333–51.

Sipe, L.R. and Bauer, J. (2001) 'Urban kindergartners' literary understanding of picture books', *The New Advocate*, 14 (4): 329–42.

Snow, C.E., Burns, M.S. and Griffin, P. (eds) (1998) *Preventing Reading Difficulties in Young Children.* National Research Council Committee on the Prevention of Difficulties in Young Children. Washington, DC: National Academy Press.

Styles, M. and Arizpe, E. (2001) 'A gorilla with "Grandpa's eyes": how children interpret visual texts–a case study of Anthony Browne's Zoo', *Children's Literature in Education*, 32: 261–81.

Trousdale, A.M. and Harris, V.J. (1993) 'Missing links in literary response: group interpretation of literature', *Children's Literature in Education*, 24 (3): 195–207.

Vygotsky, L. (1978) *Mind in Society: the Development of Higher Psychological Processes* (1969). Cambridge, MA: MIT Press.

Wolf, S.A. (1991) 'Following the trail of story', *Language Arts*, 68: 388–95.

Wolf, S.A. and Heath, S.B. (1992) *The Braid of Literature: Children's Worlds of Reading.* Cambridge, MA: Harvard University Press.

Wollman-Bonilla, J.E. (1989) 'Reading journals: invitations to participate in literature', *The Reading Teacher*, 43: 112–20.

Wollman-Bonilla, J.E. and Werchadlo, B. (1995) 'Literature response journals in a first-grade classroom', *Language Arts*, 72: 562–70.

Yaden, D. (1988) 'Understanding stories through repeated read-alouds: how many does it take?', *The Reading Teacher*, 41: 556–60.

20

Verbal and Visual Literacy: the Role of Picturebooks in the Reading Experience of Young Children

MARIA NIKOLAJEVA

There seems to be a common understanding among scholars and educators that referring to the reading experience of young children we often speak about texts in which words and pictures are equally represented. Although young children are naturally exposed to other types of texts, narrative as well as non-narrative – for instance, fairytales and stories, nursery rhymes, and songs – these will most likely be presented in oral form. By contrast, the child's first encounter with written texts probably includes images as well as words. Examining a large number of overviews and textbooks in children's literature, we can clearly see that in those arranged by the readers' age, in chapters devoted to ages up to seven, illustrated books prevail (Hearne, 1990; Tucker, 1981). Further, textbooks overtly dealing with literature for young children (Bennett, 1982; McCann and Richard, 1973; Renck, 1988) are likely to consider picturebooks.

While such an attitude is by no means an absolute truth, and while there is no comprehensive empirical research showing that young children's aesthetic appreciation of reading is indeed dependent on visual support, it is a fact that printed reading matter for young children, including fairytales, verse and song collections, consists exclusively of books containing both words and pictures. Thus this chapter will focus on research into picturebooks and their significance for early literacy. As mediators of literature to young children, we should be aware of the complexity of the texts we provide, and before we can seriously examine the young readers' responses to literature, we should investigate the texts themselves in order to see the potentials and problems of what they offer. While young children in the past were mainly referred to primers for their reading practices, today they – or rather their parents and teachers – can choose from a vast and extremely diverse body of printed materials that have different premises and offer different aesthetic, social and educational experiences. The intention of this chapter is to show how our knowledge and assessment of this diversity are relevant for the development of early literacy.

In mapping the research into picturebooks, I will start by looking into the role of picturebooks throughout history and in different countries and cultures. I will then discuss the word/image interaction as the most significant aspect of meaning making, and the various kinds of picturebooks that provide different reading challenges for the child. I will further probe into the ways picturebooks are used for socialization purposes, as well as some research into visual literacy as such. The last aspect I will deal with briefly concerns the dual readership of picturebooks.

In this chapter, I use the terms 'picturebooks' and 'illustrated books' interchangeably, even though many critics, as will be shown, make a clear distinction between the two concepts. I have also decided for the solid spelling of the word 'picturebook', so far more widely adopted by British scholars (for instance, Lewis, 2001).

PICTUREBOOKS THROUGHOUT HISTORY

The first aspect essential for the adult mediator of picturebooks to be familiar with is their historical and social context. Illustrated children's books are a relatively late phenomenon in human history. Although one of the earliest books unquestionably intended for young readers, *Orbis sensualium pictus* (1685), was exactly what we today call a picturebook, with pictures supporting words, the emergence of illustrated books was impossible until the development of printing technology enabled mass production of full-scale colour illustrations. Naturally, illustrated books do not appear in a vacuum, and it is essential to study them in the context of children's literature at large. Any historical survey of children's literature will provide information about the social, economic and educational background for the emergence of illustrated printed matter for young readers (see e.g. Hunt, 1995). It is, however, important to bear in mind that illustrated books, as we know them in our society, are not necessarily included in children's literature in every country and culture. Furthermore, the view of children's literature in different countries may vary, and thus in some countries picturebooks may have purely entertaining purposes, while in others they may be chiefly used for educational and ideological goals. These factors are valuable to take into consideration in order to understand the role of picturebooks in the development and promotion of literacy.

The history of children's book illustrations is presented in a number of studies with a wide variety of purposes, from very broad and general, focusing on thematic and stylistic diversity (Feaver, 1977; Hürlimann, 1968; Marantz and Marantz, 1995; Whalley, 1974; Whalley and Chester, 1988), to devoted to just one country (Bader, 1976; Bergstrand, 1993; Birkeland and Storaas, 1993; Christensen, 2003; Doderer and Muller, 1973; Muir, 1982; Parmegiani, 1989; Steiner, 1999; Stybe, 1983). Historical surveys are also found in catalogues for illustration exhibitions (Alderson, 1973; Barr, 1986; Blake, 2002; Hearn et al., 1996; Thiele, 1997; Ziersch, 1986). In most of these sources, each illustrator is represented by one single

picture. The sequential nature of picturebooks is ignored, as individual pictures are taken out of their context and considered outside their relation to the narrative text. Even though such publications can be useful for general orientation, they hardly address the question of how picturebooks communicate with their readers. Panoramas of contemporary international picturebooks can be found in a number of books and essay collections (Cotton, 2000; Halbey, 1997; Schwarcz, 1982, Schwarcz and Schwarcz, 1991; Styles and Bearne, 2003), and some essays try to capture the specific nature of a particular country or area (Cotton, 2001). National volumes often contain historical surveys, theoretical approaches, and presentations of specific illustrators (Baumgärtner, 1968a; Baumgärtner and Schmidt, 1991; Edström, 1991; Escarpit, 1978; Fridell, 1977; Goga and Mjør, 1999; Hallberg and Westin, 1985; Mørck, 2000; Paetzold and Erler, 1990; Peltsch, 1997; Rättyä and Raussi, 2001; Thiele, 1991). Thus for anyone wishing to become acquainted with a broad variety of international picturebooks, the opportunities are ample, even though, for obvious reasons, Western European and North American publications dominate. Yet, there are substantial gaps in the mapping of international illustration art, owing both to the absence of illustrated books as such in many countries (often because of the dominance of oral culture) and to insufficient research.

If one is interested in a particular illustrator, the sources are more limited; however, the most prominent picturebook creators have become objects for critical study. Maurice Sendak is, not unexpectedly, the artist who has attracted most attention from the scholars, resulting in several book-length studies (Cech, 1995; Lanes, 1980; Sonheim, 1991; Tabbert, 1987). The works of Sendak have also been analysed in articles by North American (Ball, 1997; Roxburgh, 1983; Shaddock, 1997; Sipe, 1996; 1998; Scott, 1997; Stanton, 2000), British (Doonan, 1986a; 1994), French (Nières, 1980), German (Halbey, 1997) and Swedish researchers (Rhedin, 1992), to name just a few. Most of these are devoted either to *Where the Wild Things Are* or *We Are All the Dumps with Jack and Guy*, and take a variety of approaches, from semiotic to socio-ideological.

Another outstanding picturebook creator is Beatrix Potter, with several books and essay collections devoted to her art (MacDonald, 1986; Mackey, 1998; 2002; Taylor, 1986) and a number of chapters and journal articles (Carpenter, 1985: 138–50; Sale, 1978: 127–63; Scott, 1992; 1994). Great Victorian illustrators such as Walter Crane (Spenser, 1975), Kate Greenaway (Taylor, 1991) and Randolph Caldecott (Engen, 1988) have been thoroughly studied. A recent book-length study examines the reception of Crane, Caldecott and Greenaway (Lundin, 2001). We can also find books on Jean de Brunhoff, the author of *Babar* (Hildebrand, 1991; Weber, 1989), Wanda Gág (Hoyle, 1994), and Ezra Jack Keats (Alderson, 1994). Among contemporary illustrators, Anthony Browne (Bradford, 1998; Doonan, 1983; 1986b; 1998; 2000; Perrot, 2000), Chris van Ahlsburg (Neumeyer, 1990; Stanton, 1996), Satoshi Kitamura (Doonan, 1991) and Peter Sís (Latham, 2000) have received much attention. A recent volume on Russell Hoban contains several essays on his picturebooks (Allison, 2000). As clearly seen from these references, apart from de Brunhoff, all the illustrators mentioned are British or American, which is hardly surprising, but far from satisfactory.

Events such as the Illustration Biennale in Bratislava and the Andersen Medal for illustration usually get noticed in the scholarly world; a collection of essays is occasionally published (Perrot, 1998), and journals in children's literature, notably *Bookbird*, carry essays on the winners. A special issue of *Bookbird* (vol. 40 no. 2, 2002) is devoted to picturebooks and features countries such as India, Croatia, and Turkey. A large number of publications in many countries offer short presentations of illustrators and picturebook creators, often brought out by library services. The volume of *Touchstones*, published under the auspices of the Children's Literature Association, contains essays on best-known picturebooks, including Virginia Lee Burton's *The Little House*, Wanda Gág's *Millions of Cats*, Robert Lawson's *The Story of Ferdinand*, and Maurice Sendak's *Where the Wild Things Are* (Nodelman, 1989).

THE SIGNIFICANCE OF WORD/IMAGE INTERACTION

Until recently, studies of picturebooks have been strictly divided into two separate categories: those carried out by art historians and those carried out by children's literature experts. While the first group paid attention to aspects such as line, colour, light and dark, shape, and space, ignoring not only the textual component, but frequently also the sequential nature of the picturebook narrative (Cianciolo, 1970; Klemin, 1966; Lacy, 1986), the second group treated picturebooks as any other children's books, applying either literary or educational approaches, but often without taking into consideration the importance of text/image interaction (Kiefer, 1995; Stewig, 1995; Spitz, 1999). The latter is certainly a legitimate position with its own premises and by no means outdated; yet it is in a way problematic to

discuss picturebooks without paying special attention to how words and pictures cooperate to create a meaning. Picturebooks are in fact different from other literary texts in their conveyance of meaning, and as mediators we should be aware of their specific nature. The German volume *Aspekte der gemalten Welt,* edited by Alfred Clemens Baumgärtner (1968a), was a pioneer work in this respect. The essays discuss mostly visual aspects, such as the influence of contemporary art on picturebooks, as well as psychological and educational issues. Baumgärtner (1968b) raises the question of the relation between words and pictures, but gives the verbal text priority in the creative and interactive process, considering primarily how textual structures are transformed into images. In a later essay Baumgärtner (1990) touches upon the unique nature of picturebooks in their combination of spatial (image) and temporal (word) means of expression, moving from his earlier standpoint toward accentuating the complete parity of word and image. Another early venture into the problem appears in a French study (Durand and Bertrand, 1975: 83–162), where the dialogue between word and image is investigated.

Among the first to bring the text/image interaction into the limelight, as the most essential feature of picturebooks, were Joseph Schwarcz (1982: 9–20; 1991: 1–19), Kristin Hallberg (1982), Stephen Roxburgh (1983), David Topper (1984), Perry Nodelman (1984), Blair Lent (1988), John Stephens (1989), and Peter Neumeyer (1990). Two important landmarks were the special issues of *The Lion and the Unicorn* (vol. 7/8, 1983) and *Children's Literature Association Quarterly* (vol. 9 no. 1, 1984). All these studies emphasize the unique character of picturebooks as an art form based on the combination of two levels of communication, the verbal and the visual. This aspect has been further developed by Clare Bradford (1993), who regards the complex text/image interaction as a part of the general postmodern trend in contemporary literature for young readers; Lawrence Sipe (1998), who also provides an excellent overview of earlier research; and Bettina Kümmerling-Meibauer (1999), who focuses on the ironical tension between the two narrative levels. In *Criticism, Theory and Children's Literature* (1991: 175–88), Peter Hunt draws our attention to the obvious lack of metalanguage for discussing the complexity of modern picturebooks. Such metalanguage has been under expansive development during the past decade. In the introductory chapter to the German essay collection *Neue Erzählformen im Bilderbuch* (1991), Jens Thiele also calls for a syntax of picturebook language, for working tools and concepts necessary to read and understand 'new' picturebooks, that is, picturebooks based on complex interrelations between word and image. Several scholars in the volume (Grünewald, 1991) emphasize this inter-relationship and comment on some specific traits of picturebook narrative, such as movement from left to right, linear development, framing, simultaneous succession, and point of view. The theoretical chapters in Thiele's *Das Bilderbuch* (2000: 36–89) and Hans Adolf Halbey's *Bilderbuch: Literatur* (1997: 149–82) add substantially to the general discussions on picturebook aesthetics. David Lewis (2001: 31–45) and Nina Christensen (2000c) provide a good overview of the field.

Among the terms proposed to describe the tension between words and images we find iconotext (Hallberg, 1982), composite text, duet, poly-systemy, and counterpoint (Schwarcz, 1982), contra-diction (Stephens, 1992), synergy (Sipe, 1998), and congruence (Thiele, 2000), which all emphasize that the true meaning of a picturebook is created only by the joint efforts of the verbal and the visual communication. The variety in the terminology reveals some clear difficulties: while 'iconotext' or 'composite text' refer to the static unity of text and pictures, 'counterpoint' or 'synergy' point at the complex dynamics of interaction in the process of meaning making. Closer to a more subtle reflection of the wide spectrum of visual–verbal narrative is Joanne Golden (1990: 93–119), who distinguishes several types of text/image interaction: (1) the text and pictures are symmetrical; (2) the text depends on picture for clarification; (3) illustration enhances, elaborates text; (4) the text carries primary narrative, while the illustration is selective; and (5) the illus-tration carries primary narrative, while the text is selective. Some of the favourite picturebooks used by scholars to illustrate how words and pictures can tell two separate stories are *Rosie's Walk* by Pat Hutchins, *Come Away from the Water, Shirley* by John Burningham, *Not Now, Bernard* and *I Hate My Teddy Bear* by David McKee, and *Nothing Ever Happens on My Block* by Ellen Raskin. Interestingly enough, an investigation of picturebook translations also reveals the importance of balance between text and pictures (Desmet, 2001; O'Sullivan, 1999; Oittinen, 2000: 100–14; Nikolajeva and Scott, 2001a: 31–41), as does a study of books with the same illustrations, but different texts (McCann and Hiller, 1994).

Although few of these studies focus on the young reader, such approaches lead to a better understand-ing of the role of picturebooks in the development of a child's literacy. In learning to read, we make the arbitrary connections between words – signi-fiers – and the objects or concepts they refer to – signifieds. The relationship between the signifier and the signified in a picturebook can be simple, as in ABC books or picture dictionaries, or substantially more complex; yet picturebooks provide an excellent training in understanding the relationship as such. While the empirical studies of young readers' responses to picturebooks reveal how they make sense of what they see and read or what is read to them (see Martinez, Roser and Dooley, in this volume), theoretical studies of text/image interaction offer mediators guidelines in introducing books to children at appropriate levels.

Nevertheless, some of the most comprehensive studies of picturebooks, such as Joseph Schwarcz's pioneer book *Ways of the Illustrator* (1982) and Jane Doonan's *Looking at Pictures in Picture Books* (1993), while offering excellent tools to decode individual illustrations, do not pay sufficient atten-tion to the dilemma emerging when the story is told in two different media. Yet, these works produce an important counterbalance to many studies of picture-books where pictures are ignored or treated as mere decorations, as pointed out by Kenneth Marantz (1988). Both Doonan and Schwarcz discuss thoroughly the *pictures* in picturebooks, and their specific way of conveying space, movement, and other visual aspects.

Similarly, while Perry Nodelman's *Words about Pictures* (1988) repeatedly states that the meaning in a picturebook is revealed only through the inter-action of words and pictures, the focus is primarily on the visual aspects, mainly the individual com-municative elements of the visual text, such as colour, shape, the mutual position of objects on the page, or the depiction of movement. Thus the book emphasizes extracting information from individual pictures rather than extracting a meaning out of the interaction of picture and words, although it does pinpoint the ways pictures add to the meaning of words. Nodelman's book provides an excellent grammar for reading and understanding pictures in picturebooks which, because of their sequential nature, need a very different approach from that which views pictures as individual works of art. A similar comprehensive grammar is to be found in William Moebius' essay 'Introduction to picture-book codes' (1986).

The most systematic investigation of the nature of text/image relationships is to be found in the studies by Maria Nikolajeva and Carole Scott (2000; 2001a), where five categories are proposed – symmetry, complementarity, enhancement, coun-terpoint, and contradiction – all of which can work independently on the different levels of the picturebook narrative, such as plot, setting, charac-terization, perspective, and so on. Nikolajeva's Swedish-language textbook (2000) is based on the same theoretical ground. Whatever terminology one chooses, it is necessary to bear in mind that text/image interaction can be both relatively simple and extremely complex, and that the readers' understanding of complex interaction is part of the literary competence that can and should be trained.

TYPES OF PICTUREBOOKS

While scholars indeed agree that word/image interaction is the essential element of any illustrated text, there is no agreement on the various types of interaction. In assessing children's understanding of illustrated texts, it is, however, important to realize that words and pictures may carry different loads in meaning making, and that the relationship between words and images can considerably affect the young reader's perception of the book. One of the first attempts at a picturebook typology is found in a short article by the Dane Torben Gregersen (1974), who makes the distinction between (1) a picture dictionary that carries no narrative, (2) a picture narrative, wordless or with very few words, (3) a picturebook, or picture storybook, in which text and picture are equally important, and (4) an illustrated book, in which the text can exist independently. Most (of the few) scholars who have probed into this area distinguish between the illustrated book, where the verbal text can exist on its own, and the picturebook, an inseparable entity of word and image, cooperating to convey a message. Schwarcz does not identify any principal difference between illustrated book and picturebook; however, he does observe the quantitative ratio of text and pictures in different types of illustrated books (1982: 11). Nodelman (1988) does not problematize the concept. His material ranges across many categories from picture dictionaries to illustrated fairytales; he also includes photographic books and non-fiction illustrated books.

The Swedish scholar Ulla Rhedin, in *The Picturebook: Towards a Theory* (1992), partly leaning on Nodelman, suggests three picturebook concepts: (1) the epic, illustrated text; (2) the expanded (or staged) text; (3) the genuine picturebook. While the first category, the illustrated text, also appears in the other scholars' classifications, the two other categories are somewhat artificial, for the difference is very subtle and obviously subjective, and no clear criteria are proposed once Rhedin has exemplified each category by one single picturebook. John Stewig suggests three types: picture books (including alphabet books, counting books, and concept books), picture storybooks, and illustrated books (1995: 3–7). These few examples show that there is no more consensus among scholars about the possible subcategories of picturebooks than about the nature and variety of text/image interaction. Yet, the different approaches clearly demonstrate that the corpus of illustrated books for young children is far from homogeneous, which is necessary to bear in mind when assessing their exposure to literature. A child's understanding of a text is obviously different depending on whether the words or the images are dominant, and on whether the child is better trained in verbal or visual literacy.

The ability to recognize genre conventions is an important aspect of literary competence, and since picturebooks are the first written texts a child usually meets, the diversity of picturebooks sets the reader's genre expectations. In most standard textbooks on children's literature, picturebooks are treated as a separate genre, alongside fairytales, fantasy, adventure, domestic stories, animal stories, and so on (Cullinan, 1981: 150–217; Lukens, 1990: 210–39; Lynch-Brown and Tomlinson, 1993: 54–86; Nodelman, 1996: 215–44; Norton, 1999: 212–75, just to name a few). The same is true of general histories of children's literature (Meigs et al., 1969: 369–76, 633–53; Townsend, 1990: 318–46) or thematic essay collections (Egoff, 1996: 236–75; Powling, 1994: 41–72). However, even a very brief look at the examples discussed in such chapters reveals that picturebooks encompass all of these genres. There are hundreds of picturebooks based on classical and contemporary fairytales; books such as *Where the Wild Things Are* or *Outside Over There* have all the unmistakable features of fantasy; and domestic and animal stories are too many to enumerate. Obviously, genre is not a sufficient category to differentiate picturebooks from other kinds of children's literature, and within the scope of picturebooks we can distinguish a number of separate genres or kinds. While some of these are similar to genres in fiction for older children (fantasy, adventure, school story, family story), picturebooks display a few unique generic categories, for instance picture dictionaries, ABC books, counting books, concept books, and wordless picturebooks. While there are no book-length studies devoted to any of these categories, chapters in general studies of picturebooks often touch upon the specifics of a particular kind. Most often, ABC books and picture dictionaries are treated as educational tools used for language acquisition, without taking the aesthetic aspect into consideration. One of the most illuminating recent studies examines the changing concept of the ABC book from a simple, symmetrical relationship between word and image ('A is for apple') toward a complex and playful interaction, involving the young readers' imagination and developing their sense of language as well as visual perception (Coats, 2000). Studies such as this one emphasize that picturebooks can enhance young readers' understanding of literature not merely as a simple reflection of the external reality (a direct connection between word and object), but as a complex network of referential relationships.

Similarly, while there are no book-length studies of illustrated fairytales, some essays bring forward illustrators' choices that reflect not only individual styles, but quite often the values and ideology of the culture within which they were produced (Bergstrand, 1985; Freudenburg, 1998; Hendrickson, 2000; MacMath, 1994; Mellon, 1987). These are valuable aspects to take into consideration when assessing children's perception of stories. Illustrated poetry books containing at least one poem or verse on each doublespread, accompanied by at least one illustration, seem to be a neglected kind, apparently because the category itself is largely marginal (some classic examples are C.M. Barker's *Flower Fairies* or the Swiss Ernst Kreidolf's floral fairytales; good modern examples are Michael Rosen's illustrated verses).

Finally, a special category of picturebooks is non-fiction or information books. Here, a striking difference from general criticism can be observed, revealing the specific nature of children's literature research. While there are few, if any, critical studies of non-fiction for adults, information picturebooks receive a lot of attention owing to their educational purpose. Most studies of picturebooks include chapters on non-fiction, which, however, seldom take illustrations into consideration beyond simple acknowledgements of their existence.

The vast majority of picturebooks fall into the loosely defined category of picture storybooks, that is, narratives in which words and pictures are used together to convey a meaning. The verbal text can be written in prose or in verse, and the word/image interaction is one of the above-discussed types, that is, symmetrical, complementary, enhancing, and so on. Themes vary from everyday stories to fantasy, and styles from refined to grotesque. The characters can be human beings, animals or animated objects. There are some interesting studies examining the role of animal (Scott, 1992; 1994) and object (Schwarcz, 1982: 150–68) characters in picturebooks. For an overview of themes and styles, Nodelman (1988), Schwarcz (1982) and Schwarcz and Schwarcz (1991) are the best sources.

Most often, a young reader will move from books with very little text (such as picture dictionaries, which sometimes do not have any text at all) toward books with verbal dominance. However, the prevalence of words does not necessarily imply a more complex text; in fact, an illustrated story or fairytale is fairly undemanding in terms of meaning making. It is therefore important for mediators to be aware of the various subcategories of picturebooks and the text/image interaction in them in order to provide young readers with adequate reading experience.

SOCIALIZATION THROUGH PICTUREBOOKS

While some of the above-mentioned sources focus on the aesthetic aspects of picturebooks and the development of visual literacy in young readers, the overwhelming majority of studies are devoted exclusively to the content of picturebooks and their socialization purposes. Often picturebooks are treated as an integral part of children's fiction, with critics employing a literary approach, discussing themes, issues, ideology, or gender structures. However, such literary studies frequently neglect the visual aspect or treat pictures as secondary. Although many of the texts discussed by John Stephens in his well-known study *Language and Ideology in Children's Fiction* (1992: 158–201) are picturebooks, he concentrates on the topics, the depiction of society, ideological values, and adult control, rather than upon the dynamics of the picturebook form. Most studies, in fact, ignore the vast potential of images to convey ideology enhancing or occasionally subverting the messages expressed by words. Since pictures convey ideology implicitly, it is all the more important to train young readers to read visual messages alongside the verbal ones.

Yet this is far from common, as most studies are satisfied with discussing the overt social issues of the books. The chapter titles in Patricia Cianciolo's handbook *Picture Books for Children* (1990) are typical: 'Me and My Family', 'Other People', 'The World I Live In', and 'The Imaginative World'. Such thematic approaches are helpful for teachers looking for particular topics. Ellen Handler Spitz's *Inside Picture Books* (1999) is an example of a study in which picturebooks are examined in connection with developmental psychology, and which focuses upon their therapeutic effect on the child reader. Though Spitz is an art critic, this work concentrates on the messages that picturebooks send, and the chapters are organized by the relevance of the lessons they teach to various childhood experiences: 'It's Time for Bed', 'Please Don't Cry', 'Behave Yourself'. The treatment of texts is rather superficial, and the approach as such feels primitive and outdated. The psychological approach to picturebooks also appears in the study of Tove Jansson's three picturebooks by Lena Kåreland and Barbro Werkmäster (1994); in the various examinations of bedtime stories (Moebius, 1991; Galbraith, 1998); or in articles exploring the tension between children and adults (Bradford, 1994; Christensen, 2000b).

Another approach is investigating the social aspects of picturebooks. Schwarcz and Schwarcz (1991) offer a wide panorama of themes and issues in picturebooks (for instance, the family, the representation of grandparents, the quest for identity, the portrayal of the socially disadvantaged, war and peace), concentrating on educational and social functions of picturebooks, as well as the psychological aspects of visual perception. Learning about the world, in a very broad sense, is something a young child is likely to do through books. It can be questions of international awareness (Christensen, 1999; 2000a), multiculturalism and ethnicity (Cummins, 2000; Iskander, 1997; Kroll, 1999; LaFaye, 2001; Lamme, 2000; Lempke, 1999; McCallum, 1997; Sands-O'Connor, 2001; Smith, 1999; Stephens, 1995; Tabbert, 1995), traumatic war experiences (Galbraith, 2000a; 2000b), violence (Koehnecke, 2001), disability (Christensen, 2001), or other social issues. In these studies, the main focus is on the didactic aspects of the narrative. Holocaust education has become a prominent subject where picturebooks, according to some critics, can be more effective than novels (Kertzer, 2000; Thiele, 2000: 170–6; Williams, 2001). Gender is yet another issue that at least a few articles have touched upon (Chatton, 2001; Pace and Lowery, 2001). The imperialist values of some picturebooks, such as *Babar* (Kohl, 1995: 3–29; Malarté-Feldman and Yeager, 1998) and *Curious George* (Cummins, 1997), have been repeatedly interrogated. The weakness of many studies is that they fail to observe that images can take the narrative in the opposite direction from the words. For instance, the text can be gender-balanced and even convey a strong feminist message, while pictures present characters as clearly stereotypical. The text can appear neutral and fairly innocent in its treatment of power structures, while images can produce an undesirable effect. On the other hand, tokenism, for instance the superficial portrayal of an ethnic group, is more likely to appear in the visual part of the narrative. Before we can teach young children to discern covert ideology in images, it is essential that we are aware of it ourselves. Here, research into picturebooks has vast potentials.

One area where little effort so far has been made is a more general discussion of the connection between the socializing function of picturebooks and their aesthetic function. The Swede Kristin Hallberg (1996) has developed a theory of 'pedagogy as poetics', claiming that the overt didacticism of picturebooks is their specific aesthetic feature, and that there is in fact no contradiction between pedagogical and literary values. Since picturebooks, at least allegedly, address very young children, the incentive to convey practical knowledge, from potty training and table manners to mastering aggressions and coping with death, undoubtedly affects the way picturebook narratives are constructed, on the verbal as well as the visual level. Graeme Harper (2001) offers an interesting sociohistorical perspective, tracing the changes in visual representation as reflecting the changing views on childhood. Some remaining questions are whether complex artistic forms always produce a stronger effect on the young reader and thus underscore the socialization purpose; here, empirical research could illuminate theoretical argument.

VISUAL LITERACY AND AESTHETIC PERCEPTION

The awareness of visual literacy being a significant part of literacy in general is a relatively new insight in pedagogy; until recently, verbal literacy has been given priority. Much general research has been done on visual depiction, and many children's literature scholars find inspiration in the works of Rudolf Arnheim (1954), and more recently W.J.T. Mitchell (1994) and Gunther Kress and Theo van Leeuwen (1996), to name just a few. One of the latest contributions to the understanding of the importance of visual education is the bilingual volume *Siest du das? Die Wahrnehmung von Bildern in Kinderbücher – Visual Literacy* (1997). Its main concern is reader response, and all the chapters, focused on concrete cases, emphasize the importance of images for early literacy. Yet the most profound resource in this area is Molly Bang's *Picture This: How Pictures Work* (2000). In this highly unusual book, the award-winning illustrator explains everything one might need to know about visual perception. Using four colours and some basic shapes, she demonstrates how composition, size, shape, and colour affect our 'reading' of pictures. She starts with some exciting pictorial experiments while creating one single illustration to 'Little Red Riding Hood', offering her own insights in a plain and comprehensible language. She then proceeds to discuss the most essential elements of visual design, generously sharing her discoveries, based on her own work as well as on classroom experience.

Most general studies of picturebooks already mentioned (Doonan, 1993; Nodelman, 1988; Schwarcz, 1982; Stewig, 1995) include chapters or sections on reading and understanding images. They embrace such pictorial elements as shape, line, edge, colour, proportion, detail, and space. Some pay attention to the various techniques employed by illustrators (drawing, watercolour, woodcut, etching) and book design elements. The composition of individual pictures is thoroughly discussed, and some critics notice the essential difference between composition in paintings and in picturebooks, for instance that the centre of gravity in a picturebook picture is normally shifted toward the right edge. Thus, an analysis of a picturebook is somewhat different from traditional art criticism. One of the important observations is that picturebooks contain doublespreads (or openings) rather than pages, and unless a doublespread is one single illustration, the balance between the left-hand page (verso) and the right-hand page (recto) is essential. Essays by Isabelle Nières (1993; 2000) treating space and composition open interesting new vistas. Nodelman (2000) discusses the specific demands that picturebook aesthetic puts on the reader/ viewer. Quite a few contemporary picturebook scholars, notably Doonan and Stephens, have found inspiration in the study by Gunther Kress and Theo van Leeuwen *Reading Images: The Grammar of Visual Design* (1996). The problem with using this source for picturebook analysis is, however, that while it certainly offers excellent (though hardly revolutionary) tools for analysing visual signs, it provides no insights into the text/image collaboration characteristic of picturebooks, or into the sequential nature of the visual narrative. While the book has no intention of addressing these issues, this fact often affects the way picturebook studies influenced by Kress and van Leeuwen approach their material.

Two areas within visual literacy are of special significance: point of view and modality. Nodelman (1991) was among the first to problematize the use of first-person narration in the verbal text of picturebooks. Pictures in picturebooks seldom convey first-person point of view, which creates a confusing contradiction. Picturebooks are supposed to be addressed to a young, inexperienced audience, yet they use within the same story two different points of view. While identification with the 'I' of the verbal text in itself presents a problem for young children, the contradictory perspective of the visual text is rather confusing. In a picturebook, a consistent first-person visual narrator would mean that, while we share his point of view, we never see him appear in any picture (corresponding to the so-called 'subjective camera' in film). For an unsophisticated reader, this would present considerable difficulties. Nikolajeva and Scott (2001a: 117–38) discuss some more or less successful ways in which this dilemma can be circumvented.

Modality is a linguistic category expressing the possibility, impossibility, contingency or necessity of a statement. Modality enables us to decide on the degree of truth in the communication we receive. The term is used by Kress and van Leeuwen (1996) to describe the way images convey the sense of reality, ascribing photography a higher degree of modality ('closer to truth') and abstract or surrealist art a lower degree ('far away from truth'). Stephens (2000) makes use of this concept in his picturebook analysis. Yet, while this use of the term is certainly acceptable and perhaps fruitful for reading visual images, it is less applicable to word/image interaction.

Since modality is a purely linguistic category, a visual image in itself cannot convey modality. Beholding a single picture unaccompanied by words, we cannot as a rule decide whether what we see is real or unreal, a dream, a wish, a prescription, a permission or a doubt. However, even in isolated pictures artists have means, based on conventions, to manipulate the viewers to interpret the image in a certain way, for instance as a fantasy. A sequence of visual images immediately creates a potential for modality. By adding verbal statements, the author can further force the viewer to adopt a particular interpretation. In picturebooks, complex modality can be achieved through the interaction of words and images. While the verbal story is often told from a child's point of view presenting the events as true, the details in pictures may suggest that the story only takes place in the child's imagination. The pictures thus subvert the verbal narrative as an objective story. Nikolajeva and Scott (2001a: 173–210) propose three modalities applicable in picturebook analysis: indicative (expressing objective truth), optative (expressing desire) and dubitative (expressing doubt).

Studies of perspective and modality, as well as analyses of picturebooks representing internal life (Nikolajeva and Scott, 2001b) take the discussion of visual literacy to a higher level, beyond the questions of composition and style. Other aspects worth mentioning in this connection are the growing metafiction (Lewis, 1990; Mackey, 1990; Stephens, 1991; Trites, 1994) and intertextuality (Desmet, 2001; Nières, 1995; Thiele, 2000: 31–5; Beckett, 2001) of contemporary picturebooks. These two aspects are especially prominent in postmodern picturebooks, the subject of David Lewis' (2001) book. Metafiction implies that a text consciously draws the reader's attention to itself as an artistic construction; in picturebooks, it is frequently expressed by frame breaking (for instance, a character stepping out of the picture frame and 'entering' the neutral space between the narrative and the reader). Intertextuality (sometimes referred to as 'intervisuality' in picturebook context) encompasses the various connections to other texts: pictorial quotations and allusions, imitations and parodies. Among contemporary picturebook authors, Anthony Browne has especially elaborated various intertextual devices.

While metafiction and intertextuality certainly can be appreciated by young readers, much of their appeal may just as well be addressed to the adult co-reader. This brings me to the final aspect of research into picturebooks that I would like to point out, namely their dual audience, which falls within the recent critical concept of cross-writing. Picturebooks, more than any other kind of children's literature, are read and appreciated by children and adults together, most often with the adult reading the book to a child or a group of children. Contemporary picturebook creators seem to be very much aware of this reading situation, addressing the adult co-reader parallel to the child, for instance, through specific intertextual and interpictorial references. This does not, however, imply that the adult is addressed at the expense of the child (the infamous 'double address'); on the contrary, an intelligent picturebook takes into consideration the dual audience, offering both parts something to appreciate and enjoy. An illustrator's experience confirms this statement (Ormerod, 1992). Crosswriting child and adult in picturebooks has so far been investigated on a very modest scale (Rhedin, 1991; 1999; Scott, 1999; Beckett, 2001); yet it appears to be one of the most promising directions of further inquiry.

CONCLUSION

I started this chapter by maintaining that illustrated books are the most essential source of reading experience for young children. The reading experience is here understood in a very broad sense, as enjoyment, knowledge of the world, self-knowledge, moral and social lessons, and so on. Contemporary research provides some insights into these aspects. Picturebooks are one of the many contemporary multimedia in which the receiver is challenged to assemble the meaning from different means of communication. Therefore picturebooks provide excellent training for many other later reading experiences. Further, picturebooks are by no means a homogeneous body of texts, but offer a wide variety of challenges in extracting meanings. Contemporary research shows that, contrary to common belief, picturebooks are far from simple and can offer profound aesthetic and psychological experience. Yet not all picturebooks do so, and not all of them intend to do so. Knowing this, and knowing exactly how different types of picturebooks are supposed to affect the

readers, we would be able to supply young readers with books that satisfy their needs according to their cognitive level and individual interests, while also meeting educational and socializing demands.

REFERENCES

Alderson, B. (1973) *Looking at Picture Books.* London: National Book League.

Alderson, B. (1994) *Ezra Jack Keats: Artist and Picturebook Maker.* Gretna, LA: Pelican.

Allison, A. (ed.) (2000) *Russell Hoban: Forty Years. Essays on His Writing for Children.* New York: Garland.

Arnheim, R. (1954) *Art and Visual Perception: a Psychology of the Creative Eye.* Berkeley, CA: University of California Press.

Bader, B. (1976) *American Picturebooks: from Noah's Ark to the Beast Within.* New York: Macmillan.

Ball, J.C. (1997) 'Max's colonial fantasy: rereading Sendak's "Where the Wild Things Are"', *Ariel*, 28 (1): 167–79.

Bang, M. (2000) *Picture This: How Pictures Work* (1st edn. 1991). New York: SeaStar.

Barr, J. (1986) *Illustrated Children's Books.* London: British Library.

Baumgärtner, A.C. (ed.) (1968a) *Aspekte der gemalten Welt: 12 Kapitel über das Bilderbuch von heute.* Weinheim: Beltz.

Baumgärtner, A.C. (1968b) 'Erzählung und Abbild: zur bildnerischen Umsetzung literarischer Vorlagen', in Alfred Clemens Baumgärtner (ed.), *Aspekte der gemalten Welt: 12 Kapitel über das Bilderbuch von heute.* Weinheim: Beltz. pp. 65–81.

Baumgärtner, A.C. (1990) 'Das Bilderbuch: Geschichte–Formen–Rezeption', in Bettina Paetzold and Luis Erler (eds), *Bilderbücher im Blickpunkt verschiedener Wissenschaften unter Fächer.* Bamberg: Nostheide. pp. 4–22.

Baumgärtner, A.C. and Schmidt, M. (1991) *Text und Illustration im Kinder- und Jugendbuch.* Würzburg: Königshausen and Neumann.

Beckett, S. (2001) 'Parodic play with painting in picture books', *Children's Literature*, 29: 175–95.

Bennett, J. (1982) *Learning to Read with Picture Books.* Stroud: Thimble.

Bergstrand, U. (1985) 'Det var en gång: om mötet mellan sagan och bilderboken', in Kristin Hallberg and Boel Westin (eds), *I bilderbokens värld.* Stockholm: Liber. pp. 143–63.

Bergstrand, U. (1993) *En bilderbokshistoria: Svenska bilderböcker 1900–1930.* Stockholm: BonniersJunior. Summary in English: 'The history of Swedish picture-books 1900–1930'.

Birkeland, T. and Storaas, F. (1993) *Den norske biletboka.* Oslo: Cappelen.

Blake, Q. (ed.) (2002) *Magic Pencil: Children's Book Illustration Today.* London: British Council/British Library.

Bradford, C. (1993) 'The picture book: some postmodern tensions', *Papers: Explorations in Children's Literature,* 4 (3): 10–14.

Bradford, C. (1994) 'Along the road to learn: children and adults in the picture books of John Burningham', *Children's Literature in Education,* 25 (4): 203–11.

Bradford, C. (1998) 'Playing with father: Anthony Browne's picture books and the masculine', *Children's Literature in Education,* 29 (2): 79–96.

Carpenter, H. (1985) *Secret Gardens: the Golden Age of Children's Literature.* London: Unwin Hyman.

Cech, J. (1995) *Angels and Wild Things: the Archetypal Poetics of Maurice Sendak.* Philadelphia: Pennsylvania State University Press.

Chatton, B. (2001) 'Picture books for preschool children: exploring gender issues with three- and four-year-olds', in Susan Lehr (ed.), *Beauty, Brains and Brawn: the Construction of Gender in Children's Literature.* Portsmouth, NH: Heinemann. pp. 57–66.

Christensen, N. (1999) 'Teaching tolerance: a comparative reading of two Danish picture books', *Bookbird,* 37 (4): 11–16.

Christensen, N. (2000a) 'An attempt to create an international identity: the picture book in a literary, didactic and historical perspective', in Jean Webb (ed.), *Text, Culture and National Identity in Children's Literature.* Helsinki: Nordinfo. pp. 109–23.

Christensen, N. (2000b) 'Magtens sødme: en tekst- och billedanalytisk undersøgelse af billedbøgers fremstilling af barne- og forældreroller', in Anne Mørck Hansen (ed.), *Børns billedbøger og bilder.* Copenhagen: Høst. pp. 113–34.

Christensen, N. (2000c) 'Billedbogen som genre og analysobjekt: teoretiske positioner', in Nina Christensen, Torben Weinreich and Ea Kock Hansen (eds), *Nedslag i børnelitteraturforskningen.* Frederiksberg: Roskilde Universitetsforlag. pp. 8–38.

Christensen, N. (2001) 'What's the difference? The depiction of Down syndrome in picture books', *Bookbird,* 39 (1): 11–16.

Christensen, N. (2003) *Den danske billedbog 1950–1999.* Roskilde: Roskilde Universitetsforlag.

Cianciolo, P. (1970) *Illustrations in Children's Books.* Dubuque, IA: Browne.

Cianciolo, P. (1990) *Picture Books for Children,* 3rd edn. Chicago: American Library Association.

Coats, K. (2000) 'P is for patriarchy: re-imagining the alphabet', *Children's Literature Association Quarterly,* 25 (2): 88–97.

Cotton, P. (ed.) (2000) *Picture Books sans Frontières.* London: Trentham.

Cotton, P. (2001) 'The Europeanness of picture books', in Margaret Meek (ed.), *Children's Literature and National Identity.* London: Trentham. pp. 111–20.

Cullinan, B.E. (1981) *Literature and the Child.* San Diego, CA: Harcourt Brace Jovanovich.

Cummins, J. (1997) 'The resisting monkey: "Curious George", slave captivity, and the postcolonial condition', *Ariel,* 28 (1): 69–83.

Cummins, J. (2000) 'The Jewish child in picture books?', *The Five Owls,* 15 (2): 38–40.

Desmet, M.K.T. (2001) 'Intertextuality/intervisuality in translation: the Jolly Postman's intercultural journey from Britain to the Netherlands', *Children's Literature in Education,* 32 (1): 31–43.

Doderer, K. and Müller, H. (eds) (1973) *Das Bilderbuch: Geschichte und Entwicklung des Bilderbuchs in Deutschland von den Anfängen bis zur Gegenwart.* Weinheim: Belz.

Doonan, J. (1983) 'Talking pictures: a new look at Hansel and Gretel', *Signal,* 42: 123–31.

Doonan, J. (1986a) 'Outside over there: a journey in style', *Signal,* 50: 92–103, 51: 172–87.

Doonan, J. (1986b) 'The object lesson: picture books of Anthony Browne', *Word and Image,* 2: 159–72.

Doonan, J. (1991) 'Satoshi Kitamura: aesthetic dimensions', *Children's Literature,* 19: 107–37.

Doonan, J. (1993) *Looking at Pictures in Picture Books.* Stroud: Thimble.

Doonan, J. (1994) 'Into the dangerous world: we are all in the dumps with Jack and Guy', *Signal,* 75: 155–71.

Doonan, J. (1998) 'Drawing out ideas: a second decade of the work of Anthony Browne', *The Lion and the Unicorn,* 23 (1): 30–56.

Doonan, J. (2000) 'Stimmen im Park und Stimmen im Schulzimmer: Rezeptionsbezogene Analyse von Anthony Brownes "Stimmen im Park"', in Jens Thiele (ed.), *Das Bilderbuch: Ästhetic, Theorie, Analyse, Didaktik, Rezeption,* Oldenburg: Isensee. pp. 142–56.

Durand, M. and Bertrand, G. (1975) *L'Image dans le livre pour enfants.* Paris: l'Ecole des Loisirs.

Edström, V. (ed.) (1991) *Vår moderna bilderbok.* Stockholm: Rabén and Sjögren. Summary in English: 'the modern Swedish picture-book'.

Egoff, S. et al. (eds) (1996) *Only Connect: Readings on Children's Literature,* 3rd edn. Toronto: Oxford University Press.

Engen, R.K. (1988) *Randolph Caldecott: 'Lord of the Nursery'.* London: Bloomsbury.

Escarpit, D. (ed.) (1978) *L'Enfant, l'image et le récit.* Paris: Mouton.

Feaver, W. (1977) *When We Were Young: Two Centuries of Children's Book Illustrations.* London: Thames and Hudson.

Freudenburg, R. (1998) 'Illustrating childhood: "Hansel and Gretel" ', *Marvels and Tales,* 12 (2): 263–318.

Fridell, L. (ed.) (1977) *Bilden i barnboken.* Gothenburg: Stegeland. Summary in English: 'On pictures in children's books'.

Galbraith, M. (1998) '"Goodnight Nobody" revisited: using an attachment perspective to study picture books about bedtime', *Children's Literature Association Quarterly*, 23 (4): 172–80.

Galbraith, M. (2000a) 'Agony in the kindergarten: indelible German images in American picture books', in Jean Webb (ed.), *Text, Culture and National Identity in Children's Literature.* Helsinki: Nordinfo. pp. 124–43.

Galbraith, M. (2000b) 'What must i give up in order to grow up? The Great War and childhood survival in transatlantic children's books', *The Lion and the Unicorn*, 24 (3): 337–59.

Goga, N. and Mjør, I. (eds) (1999) *Møte mellom ord og bilde: ein antologi om bilderbøker.* Oslo: Cappelen.

Golden, J.M. (1990) *The Narrative Symbol in Childhood Literature: Exploration in the Construction of Text.* Berlin: Mouton.

Gregersen, T. (1974) 'Småbørnsbogen', in Sven Møller Kristensen and Preben Ramløv (eds), *Børne- og ungdomsbøger: problemer og analyser.* Copenhagen: Gyldendal. pp. 243–71.

Grünewald, D. (1991) 'Kongruenz von Wort und Bild: Rafik Schami und Peter Knorr: der Wunderkasten', in Jens Thiele (ed.), *Neue Erzählformen im Bilderbuch.* Oldenburg: Isensee. pp. 17–49.

Halbey, H.A. (1997) *Bilderbuch: Literatur. Neun Kapitel über eine unterschätzte Literaturgattung.* Belz: Athenäum.

Hallberg, K. (1982) 'Litteraturvetenskap och bilderboksforskningen', *Tidskrift för litteraturvetenskap*, 3–4: 163–8.

Hallberg, K. (1996) 'Pedagogik som poetik: den moderna småbarnslitteraturens berättelse', in Anne Banér (ed.), *Konsten att berätta för barn.* Stockholm: Centre for the Study of Childhood Culture. pp. 83–104.

Hallberg, K. and Westin, B. (eds) (1985) *I bilderbokens värld.* Stockholm: Liber.

Harper, G. (2001) 'Enfranchising the child: picture books, primacy, and discourse', *Style*, 35 (3): 393–409.

Hearn, M.P., Clark, T., Clark, H. and Nichols, B. (1996) *Myth, Magic, and Mystery: One Hundred Years of American Children's Book Illustration.* Boulder, CO: Roberts Rinehart.

Hearne, B. (1990) *Choosing Books for Children: a Commonsense Guide*, 2nd rev. edn. New York: Delacorte.

Hendrickson, L. (2000) 'The view from Rapunzel's tower', *Children's Literature in Education*, 31 (4): 209–23.

Hildebrand, A.M. (1991) *Jean and Laurent de Brunhoff: the Legacy of Babar.* New York: Twayne.

Hoyle, K.N. (1994) *Wanda Gág.* New York: Twayne.

Hunt, P. (1991) *Criticism, Theory and Children's Literature.* London: Blackwell.

Hunt, P. (ed.) (1995) *Children's Literature: an Illustrated History.* Oxford: Oxford University Press.

Hürlimann, B. (1968) *Picture-Book World,* trans. and ed. Brian W. Alderson. London: Oxford University Press.

Iskander, S. (1997) 'Portrayal of Arabs in contemporary American picture books', *Bookbird*, 35 (3): 11–16.

Kåreland, L. and Werkmäster, B. (1994) *En livsvandring i tre akter.* Uppsala: Hjelm. Summary in English: 'Life's journey in three acts: an analysis of Tove Jansson's picture-books'.

Kertzer, A. (2000) 'Saving the picture: Holocaust photographs in children's books', *The Lion and the Unicorn*, 24 (3): 402–31.

Kiefer, B. (1995) *The Potential of Picturebooks: from Visual Literacy to Aesthetic Understanding.* Englewood Cliffs, NJ: Prentice Hall.

Klemin, D. (1966) *The Art of Art for Children's Books.* New York: Potter.

Koehnecke, D. (2001) '*Smoky Night* and *Crack*: controversial subjects in current children's stories', *Children's Literature in Education*, 32 (1): 17–30.

Kohl, H. (1995) *Should We Burn Babar? Essays on Children's Literature and the Power of Stories.* New York: New Press.

Kress, G. and van Leeuwen, T. (1996) *Reading Images: the Grammar of Visual Design.* London: Routledge.

Kroll, J. (1999) 'The New Fringe Dwellers: the Problem of Ethnicity in Recent Australian Children's Picture Books', *Papers: Explorations in Children's Literature*, 9 (2): 31–9.

Kümmerling-Meibauer, B. (1999) 'Metalinguistic awareness and the child's developing concept of irony: the relationship between pictures and texts in ironic picture books', *The Lion and the Unicorn*, 23 (2): 157–83.

Lacy, L.E. (1986) *Art and Design in Children's Picture Books: an Analysis of Caldecott's Award-Winning Illustrations.* Chicago: American Library Association.

LaFaye, A. (2001) 'You've come a long way, daddy: affirmations of fatherhood in recent African American picture books', *Bookbird*, 39 (2): 28–33.

Lamme, L.L. (2000) 'Images of poverty in picturebooks with international settings', *The New Advocate*, 13 (4): 347–64.

Lanes, S. (1980) *The Art of Maurice Sendak.* New York: Abrams.

Latham, D. (2000) 'Radical visions: five picture books by Peter Sís', *Children's Literature in Education*, 31 (3): 179–93.

Lempke, S.D. (1999) 'The faces in the picture books', *The Horn Book Magazine*, 75 (2): 141–7.

Lent, B. (1988) 'There's much more to the picture than meets the eye', in Robert Bator (ed.), *Signposts to Criticism of Children's Literature.* Chicago: American Library Association. pp. 156–61.

Lewis, D. (1990) 'The constructedness of texts: picture books and the metafictive', *Signal,* 62: 131–46. Reprinted in Sheila Egoff et al. (eds), *Only Connect: Readings on Children's Literature.* 3rd edn. Toronto: Oxford University Press. pp. 259–75.

Lewis, D. (2001) *Reading Contemporary Picturebooks: Picturing Text.* London: Routledge.

Lukens, R.J. (1990) *A Critical Handbook of Children's Literature,* 4th edn. New York: HarperCollins.

Lundin, A. (2001) *Victorian Horizons: the Reception of the Picture Books of Walter Crane, Randolph Caldecott, and Kate Greenaway.* Lanham, MD: Scarecrow.

Lynch-Brown, C. and Tomlinson, C.M. (1993) *Essentials of Children's Literature.* Boston: Allyn and Bacon.

MacDonald, R.K. (1986) *Beatrix Potter.* Boston: Twayne.

Mackey, M. (1990) 'Metafiction for beginners: Allan Ahlberg's *Ten in a Bed*', *Children's Literature in Education,* 21 (3): 179–87.

Mackey, M. (1998) *The Case of Peter Rabbit: Changing Conditions of Literature for Children.* New York: Garland.

Mackey, M. (ed.) (2002) *Beatrix Potter's Peter Rabbit: a Children's Classic at 100.* Lanham, MD: Scarecrow.

MacMath, R. (1994) 'Recasting Cinderella: how pictures tell the tale', *Bookbird,* 32 (4): 29–34.

Malarté-Feldman, C.L. and Yeager, J. (1998) 'Babar and the French connection: teaching the politics of superiority and exclusion', in Meena Khorana (ed.), *Critical Perspectives on Postcolonial African Children's and Young Adult Literature.* Westport, CT: Greenwood. pp. 69–77.

Marantz, K. (1988) 'The picture book as art object: a call for balanced reviewing', in Robert Bator (ed.), *Signposts to Criticism of Children's Literature.* Chicago: American Library Association. pp. 152–6.

Marantz, S. and Marantz, K. (1995) *The Art of Children's Picture Books: a Selective Reference Guide,* 2nd edn. New York: Garland.

McCallum, R. (1997) 'Cultural solipsism, national identities and the discourse of multiculturalism in Australian picture books', *Ariel,* 28 (1): 101–16.

McCann, D. and Richard, O. (1973) *The Child's First Books: a Critical Study of Pictures and Texts.* New York: Wilson.

McCann, H. and Hiller, C. (1994) 'Narrative and editing choices in the picture book: a comparison of two versions of Roberto Innocenti's *Rose Blanche*', *Papers: Explorations in Children's Literature,* 5 (2–3): 53–7.

Meigs, C., Thaxter Eaton, A., Nesbitt, E. and Hill Viguers, R. (1969) *A Critical History of Children's Literature.* New York: Macmillan.

Mellon, C. (1987) 'Folk tales as picture books: visual literacy or oral tradition?', *School Library Journal,* 33 (10): 46–7.

Mitchell, W.J.T. (1994) *Picture Theory: Essays on Verbal and Visual Representation.* Chicago: University of Chicago Press.

Moebius, W. (1986) 'Introduction to picturebook codes', *Word and Image,* 2 (2): 141–58.

Moebius, W. (1991) 'Room with a view: bedroom scenes in picture books', *Children's Literature,* 19: 53–74.

Mørck Hansen, A. (ed.) (2000) *Børns billedbøger og bilder.* Copenhagen: Høst.

Muir, M. (1982) *A History of Australian Children's Book Illustration.* Melbourne: Oxford University Press.

Neumeyer, P. (1990) 'How picture books mean: the case of Chris Van Allsburg', *Children's Literature Association Quarterly,* 15 (1): 2–8.

Nières, I. (1980) 'Des illustrations exemplaires: "Max et les Maximonsters" de Maurice Sendak', *Le Francais aujourd'hui,* 50: 17–29.

Nières, I. (1993) 'Et l'image me fait signe que le livre est fini', in J. Perrot (ed.), *Culture, texte et jeune lecteur.* Nancy: Presses Universitaires de Nancy. pp. 209–17.

Nières, I. (1995) 'Writers writing a short history of children's literature within their texts', in M. Nikolajeva (ed.), *Aspects and Issues in the History of Children's Literature.* Westport, CT: Greenwood. pp. 49–56.

Nières-Chevrel, I. (2000) 'Jean de Brunhoff, inventer Babar, inventer l'espace', *La Revue des livres pour enfants,* 191: 109–20.

Nikolajeva, M. (2000) *Bilderbokens pusselbitar.* Lund: Studentlitteratur.

Nikolajeva, M. and Scott, C. (2000) 'Dynamics of picturebook communication', *Children's Literature in Education,* 31 (4): 225–39.

Nikolajeva, M. and Scott, C. (2001a). *How Picturebooks Work.* New York: Garland.

Nikolajeva, M. and Scott, C. (2001b) 'Images of the mind: the depiction of consciousness in picturebooks', *CREArTA,* 2 (1): 12–36.

Nodelman, P. (1984) 'How picture books work', in Harold Darling and Peter Neumeyer (eds), *Image and Maker: an Annual Dedicated to the Consideration of Book Illustration.* La Jolla, CA: Green Tiger. pp. 1–12. Reprinted in S. Egoff et al. (eds), *Only Connect: Readings on Children's Literature.* 3rd edn. Toronto: Oxford University Press. pp. 242–53.

Nodelman, P. (1988) *Words about pictures: the Narrative Art of Children's Picture Books.* Athens, GA: University of Georgia Press.

Nodelman, P. (ed.) (1989) *Touchstones: Reflections on the Best in Children's Literature.* Vol. 3: *Picture Books.* West Lafayette, IN: Children's Literature Association.

Nodelman, P. (1991) 'The eye and the I: identification and first-person narratives in picture books', *Children's Literature,* 19: 1–30.

Nodelman, P. (1996) *The Pleasures of Children's Literature,* 2nd edn. New York: Longman.

Nodelman, P. (2000) 'The implied viewer: some speculations about what children's picture books invite readers to do and be', *CREArTA,* 1 (1): 23–43.

Norton, D.E. (1999) *Through the Eyes of a Child: an Introduction to Children's Literature,* 5th edn. Upper Saddle River, NJ: Merrill.

Oittinen, R. (2000) *Translating for Children.* New York: Garland.

Ormerod, J. (1992) 'The inevitability of transformation: designing picture books for children and adults', in M. Styles, E. Bearne and V. Watson (eds), *After Alice: Exploring Children's Literature.* London: Cassell. pp. 42–55.

O'Sullivan, E. (1999) 'Translating Pictures', *Signal,* 90: 167–75.

Pace, B.G. and Lowery, R.M. (2001) 'Power, gender scripts, and boy codes: possibilities and limitations in picture books', *The New Advocate,* 14 (1): 33–41.

Paetzold, B. and Erler, L. (eds) (1990) *Bilderbücher im Blickpunkt verschiedener Wissenschaften under Fächer.* Bamberg: Nostheide.

Parmegiani, C.A. (1989) *Les Petits français illustrés 1860–1940.* Paris: Éditions du cercle de la libraire.

Peltsch, S. (ed.) (1997) *Auch Bilder erzählen Geschichten,* special issue of *Beiträge Jugendliteratur und Medien 8.*

Perrot, J. (ed.) (1998) *Tomi Ungerer.* Paris: In press editions.

Perrot, J. (2000) 'An English promenade', *Bookbird,* 38 (3): 11–16.

Powling, C. (ed.) (1994) *The Best of Book for Keeps: Highlights from the Leading Children's Book Magazine.* London: Bodley Head.

Rättyä, K. and Raussi, R. (eds) (2001) *Jutkiva katse kuvakirjaan/Critical Perspectives on Picture Books.* Tampere: SNI.

Renck Jalongo, M. (1988) *Young Children and Picture Books: Literature from Infancy to Six.* Washington, DC: National Association for the Education of Young Children.

Rhedin, U. (1991) 'Resan i barndomen: Om bilderböcker för barn och vuxna', in V. Edström (ed.), *Vår moderna bilderbok.* Stockholm: Rabén and Sjögren. pp. 155–88.

Rhedin, U. (1992) *Bilderboken: på väg mot en teori.* Stockholm: Alfabeta. Summary in English: 'The picture book: towards a theory'.

Rhedin, U. (1999) 'Det konsekventa barnperspektivet i barnlitteraturen', in U. Palmenfelt (ed.), *Barndomens kulturalisering.* Åbo: Nordiskt närverk för folkloristik. pp. 93–108.

Roxburgh, S. (1983) 'A picture equals how many words? Narrative theory and picture books for children', *The Lion and the Unicorn,* 7/8: 20–33.

Sale, R. (1978) *Fairy Tales and After.* Cambridge: Cambridge University Press.

Sands-O'Connor, K. (2001) 'Why are people different? multiracial families in picture books and the dialogue of difference', *The Lion and the Unicorn,* 25 (3): 412–26.

Schwarcz, J.H. (1982) *Ways of the Illustrator: Visual Communication in Children's Literature.* Chicago: American Library Association.

Schwarcz, J.H. and Schwarcz, C. (1991) *The Picture Book Comes of Age.* Chicago: American Library Association.

Scott, C. (1992) 'Between me and the world: clothes as mediator between self and society in the works of Beatrix Potter', *The Lion and the Unicorn,* 16 (2): 192–8.

Scott, C. (1994) 'Clothed in nature or nature clothed: dress as metaphor in the illustrations of Beatrix Potter and C.M. Barker', *Children's Literature,* 22: 70–89.

Scott, C. (1997) 'The subversion of childhood: Maurice Sendak and the American tradition', in A.L. Lucas (ed.), *Gunpowder and Sealing-Wax: Nationhood in Children's Literature.* Hull: Troubador. pp. 39–47.

Scott, C. (1999) 'Dual audience in picture books', in S. Beckett (ed.), *Transcending Boundaries: Writing for a Dual Audience of Children and Adults.* New York: Garland. pp. 99–110.

Shaddock, J. (1997) 'Where the wild things are: Sendak's journey into the heart of Darkness', *Children's Literature Association Quarterly,* 22 (4): 155–9.

Siest du das? Die Wahrnehmung von Bildern in Kinderbücher – Visual Literacy (1997) Zürich: Chronos.

Sipe, L.R (1996). 'The private and public worlds of *We Are All in the Dumps with Jack and Guy*', *Children's Literature in Education,* 27 (2). 87–108.

Sipe, L.R (1998) 'How picture books work: a semiotically framed theory of text–picture relationships', *Children's Literature in Education,* 29 (2): 97–108.

Smith, K.P. (1999) 'Landscapes of the heart, sharings of the soul: illustrated universes in Australian Aboriginal picture books of the 1990s', *Bookbird,* 37 (1): 19–24.

Sonheim, A. (1991) *Maurice Sendak.* New York: Twayne.

Spenser, I. (1975) *Walter Crane.* London: Studio Vista.

Spitz, E.H. (1999) *Inside Picture Books.* New Haven, CT: Yale University Press.

Stanton, J. (1996) 'The dreaming picture books of Chris Van Allsburg', *Children's Literature,* 24: 161–79.

Stanton, J. (2000) 'Maurice Sendak's urban landscapes', *Children's Literature,* 28: 132–46.

Steiner, E. (1999) *Stories for Little Comrades: Revolutionary Artists and the Making of Early Soviet Children's Books.* Seattle: University of Washington Press.

Stephens, J. (1989) 'Language, discourse and picture books', *Children's Literature Association Quarterly,* 14 (3): 106–10.

Stephens, J. (1991) '"Didn't I tell you about the time I pushed the Brothers Grimm off Humpty Dumpty's wall?" Metafictional strategies for constituting the audience as agent on the narratives of Janet and Allan Ahlberg', in M. Stone (ed.), *Children's Literature and Contemporary Theory.* Wollongong: University of Wollongong. pp. 63–75.

Stephens, J. (1992) *Language and Ideology in Children's Fiction.* London: Longman.

Stephens, J. (1995) 'Representation of place in Australian children's picture books', in M. Nikolajeva (ed.), *Voices from Far Away: Current Trends in International*

Children's Literature Research. Stockholm: Centre for the Study of Childhood Culture. pp. 97–118.

Stephens, J. (2000) 'Modality and space in picture book art: Allen Say's *Emma's Rug*', *CREArTA,* 1 (1): 44–59.

Stewig, J.W. (1995). *Looking at Picture Books.* Fort Atkinson, WI: Highsmith.

Stybe, V. (1983) *Fra billedark til billedbog. den illustrerede boernebog i Danmark indtil 1950.* Copenhagen: Nyt nordisk.

Styles, M. (ed.) (2002) *Reading Pictures.* London: Trentham.

Styles, M. and Bearne, E. (eds.) (2003) *Art, Narrative and Childhood.* Stoke-on-Trent: Trentham.

Tabbert, R. (ed.) (1987) *Maurice Sendak: Bilderbuchskünstler.* Bonn: Bouvier Grundmann.

Tabbert, R. (1995) 'National myth in three classical picture books', in Maria Nikolajeva (ed.), *Aspects and Issues in the History of Children's Literature.* Westport, CT: Greenwood. pp. 151–63.

Taylor, I. (1991) *The Art of Kate Greenaway: a Nostalgic Portrait of Childhood.* Exeter: Web and Bower.

Taylor, J. (1986) *Beatrix Potter: Artist, Storyteller and Countrywoman.* London: Warne.

Thiele, J. (ed.) (1991) *Neue Erzählformen im Bilderbuch.* Oldenburg: Isensee.

Thiele, J. (ed.) (1997) *Experiment Bilderbuch. Impulse zur künstlerischen Neubestimmung der Kinderbuchillustration.* Oldenburg: Bublioteks- und Informationssystem det Universität Oldenburg.

Thiele, J. (2000) *Das Bilderbuch: Ästhetic, Theorie, Analyse, Didaktik, Rezeption,* mit Beiträgen von Jane Doonan, Elisabeth Hohmeister, Doris Reske und Reinbert Tabbert. Oldenburh: Isensee.

Topper, D. (1984) 'On some burdens carried by pictures', *Children's Literature Association Quarterly,* 9 (1): 23–5.

Townsend, J.R. (1990) *Written for Children: an Outline of English-Language Children's Literature,* 6th edn. London: Bodley Head.

Trites, R.S. (1994) 'Manifold narratives: metafiction and ideology in picture books', *Children's Literature in Education,* 25 (4): 225–42.

Tucker, N. (1981) *The Child and the Book: a Psychological and Literary Exploration.* Cambridge: Cambridge University Press.

Weber, N.F. (1989) *The Art of Babar: the Works of Jean and Laurent de Brunhoff.* New York: Abrams.

Whalley, J.I. (1974) *Cobwebs to Catch Flies: Illustrated Books for the Nursery and Schoolroom 1700–1900.* London: Elek.

Whalley, J.I. and Chester, T.R. (1988) *A History of Children's Book Illustration.* London: Murray.

Williams, L. (2001) 'Då orden inte räcker: förintelsen i bilderboken', *Horisont,* 48 (2): 9–15.

Ziersch, Amélie (1986) *Bilderbuch: Begleiter der Kindheit.* München: Museum Villa Stuck.

21

Textbooks and Early Childhood Literacy

ALLAN LUKE, VICTORIA CARRINGTON
AND CUSHLA KAPITZKE

TEXTS AS ARTIFACTS OF CHILDHOOD

If childhood is a social construction, then its social practices are contingent on historically evolving cultural technologies and artifacts. These technologies include the domestic implements of infant care and childrearing, those utilitarian objects of women's work. They also include the core technologies of modern childhood: toys and books. In the contemporary political economy of childhood, toys and books have a special place. They have become linked and co-marketed pedagogic commodities. They are the aesthetic and didactic objects of children's work and desire. But they are also the cultural artifacts that parents, families and caregivers purchase with income that is surplus to basic requirements for food, shelter, and health care.

The centrality of the book and the textbook in childhood is a recent phenomenon. Walter Ong (1958: 150) observes that the coming of the book created a 'pedagogical juggernaut' which 'made knowledge something a corporation could traffic in, impersonal and abstract'. Since the Protestant Reformation and the emergence of state-sponsored schooling in the fifteenth and sixteenth centuries, Anglo-European childhood has involved institutional training with print, in schools and churches (cf. Elson, 1964). Indeed, the orientation towards common core text study was a characteristic of Confucian educational traditions, predating these developments in the West and spreading throughout China, Korea, Thailand and other Asian countries (Nozaki et al., in press). Nonetheless, and despite long-standing Muslim, Hebraic and alterior Judaeo-Christian traditions of hermeneutic training and exegetic study by youth (Kapitzke, 1995), what counts as the textbook and its centrality in formal schooling continues to be strongly defined by modernist Western/Northern postwar educational theory and practice. Over the past decade, this pattern has typically been reinforced by the extension of neoliberal educational practices and policies by governments, aid and non-government organizations under the auspices of economic globalization into developing and newly industrialized countries (Burbules and Torres, 2000).

Throughout the history of schooling, formal education of children has come to entail a formal pedagogical interaction with an official school text: the textbook. The textbook is a print or digital artifact comprising written text designed for pedagogical purposes. That is, textbooks are didactic in form and content, authored and authorized for the selection, construction and transmission of valued knowledges and practices to apprentice readers. As such 'the forms and contents, ideologies and discourses of textbooks constitute an official and authorised version of cultural knowledge and literate practice' (Luke, 2000: 186).

In the current 'political economy of textbook publishing' (Apple and Christian-Smith, 1991), school-based early childhood literacy involves primers, basal readers, and, more generally, reading instructional series including graded or levelled storybooks for children in the initial years of schooling. This current situation has been linked to varying forms and kinds of political control of early reading instruction via policy imperatives around systems 'accountability' (Willis and Harris, 2000). Fifty years ago, the development of print materials reached its zenith in the large scale deployment, adoption and sales of reading series and adjunct materials by publishers like Scott Foresman, Ginn, Harcourt Brace, Macmillan and others. These textbooks have evolved to include home study and readings for an expanded educational marketplace. Changes in current cultures and economies of childhood are marked by two major developments. First, there is an increased targeting by multinational publishers of middle and upper socio-economic classes concerned about their children's early literacy and numeracy. Secondly, there is an accelerated uptake of digital technology, mass media, and linked children's toys and consumables among these same classes of child/parent consumers. So while current analyses have focused on the role of standardized texts and tests in the remaking of school literacy, our concern here is what has been a major move in the economy and production of textbooks that has gone relatively unremarked amongst educational researchers: the articulation of new technologies, popular culture and textbooks in home and out-of-school pedagogy.

What follows is a historical introduction to issues of ideology and political economy of the school textbook, describing its design principles and current policy uses. We then propose to expand the definition of textbooks on two axes. First, an overview is developed of 'graded' children's and infants' literature and reading materials that are commercially marketed for home, preschool and childcare reading events. We then examine consumer and popular texts as new key genres of home and public pedagogies.

TEXTBOOKS AND THE PRODUCTION OF THE MODERN READING CHILD

Childhood and the 'reading child' have been objects of pedagogical discourses and practices for over five centuries (Aries, 1962). The development of a formalized, transportable and replicable technology for the production of the child through literature was realized in the earliest Reformation textbooks. One of the earliest and most successful reading textbooks for children was written by the German churchman, Johann Comenius. His Latin primer, *Orbis Sensualium Pictus (The Visible World in Pictures)*, was printed in 1658 and subsequently used across England, Europe and America for 200 years (Venezky, 1992). Comenius' text was different from other incunabular paediatric and pedagogical literature because of its illustrations, which

were included to assist reading comprehension. Typical of Protestant Reformation primers, readership and identity were tied to the exigencies of religious belief and the German state. The technology of the printing press coupled with religious zeal in Protestant Germany generated new discourses and practices for and about children. In stated purpose, reading and writing linked the lives and identities of children – which were often brutally short – to issues of eternity. Pragmatically, however, textual practice related to the pressing issues of social and cultural control. Work with these textbooks prescribed for children how and what one could read, in what lingua franca, for what cultural and religious, social and economic purposes. As Carmen Luke's (1989) analysis of Reformation pedagogy points out, compulsory state schooling, the mandating of basic early childhood literacy teaching, the development of secular reading textbooks, and the invention of a school inspectorate to monitor and control classroom practices with the book were parallel institutional strategies used by Martin Luther and colleagues.

Residual traces of Comenius' influence on the design and format of textbooks remained until the second half of the twentieth century. Textbook production and use in this premodern era was *ad hoc* and particularistic. Written and published by individuals, textbooks were also brought to school by individual students. Some teachers kept small, eclectic collections in their classrooms, but these were used with individuals and small groups, rather than with whole classes. In the US, spelling was taught from a range of texts, which might include Noah Webster's *Spelling Book* (c. 1783), or Dilworth's (c. 1740) and Perry's (c. 1777) common spellers. Other significant textbooks in the development of literacy acquisition and public schooling during this era included McGuffey's Eclectic Readers (c. 1836), and Latin primers such as Kennedy's *The Public School Latin Primer* (c. 1866) and Arnold's *Latin Prose Composition* (c. 1839). Whilst these texts each had their own curriculum and instructional method, in large part, they had continuing influences on reading and writing instruction for more than 100 years until the collapse of Latin grammar as a curricular field in the 1950s (Westbury, 1990).

The historical development of the early literacy textbook, then, was strongly tied to religious and moral training, affiliated with Protestant state ideology, and featured overt attacks on other belief systems: Webster's *Spelling Book*'s depiction of the Pope is a case in point.

With the eighteenth and nineteenth century spread of empire, textbooks and early literacy training became ideal vehicles for the inculcation of colonial values and allegiance to the crown (Pennycook, 1998). Hence, books like the Irish Readers (*c.* 1830), the Royal Readers (*c.* 1890), the Ontario Readers (*c.* 1880) all presented strong colonial themes of empire and race, national and linguistic hegemony. Prior to the emergence of cheap, accessible and widely distributed books in the early twentieth century, for many rural and urban communities in the US, Canada, Australia and New Zealand, early school textbooks and affiliated religious texts (e.g. the Bible, hymnals, prayer books, *Paradise Lost*) were the only available print materials in many homes, and were the staples of family and communal readings. In this regard, before the advent of mass commercial print culture, the influence of the textbook on moral and ideological formation was profound, by virtue of its near-universal availability and relative exclusivity. Further, home-based early childhood literacy events and those of the schools often shared religious and colonial literary contents (Luke and Kapitzke, 1994; Kapitzke, 1999).

Development of the basal reading series by American educational psychologists in the early twentieth century has, to this day, profoundly affected the shaping of what counts as literacy, literacy instruction and reading in early childhood. Historical studies by Shannon (1989) and Luke (1988) document the emergence of the commercially structured, 'scientifically' designed and mass marketed reading textbooks in the US in the early and mid twentieth century. The prototype of the contemporary reading series was William S. Gray and May Hill Arbuthnot's Dick and Jane (*c.* 1925) series, which dominated early literacy instruction in the US, Canada and other parts of the English-speaking world for over half a century.

A continuing focal point of public and scholarly debate is the matter of overt moral and cultural content of early childhood reading materials. It is not surprising that since the Dick and Jane prototypes, questions about textbook ideological representation have been recurrent. These include critiques of the representation of gender relations in early readers, the exclusion of minority identities and cultures in children's literature, and, indeed, the construction of a particular middle class version of childhood itself (Baker and Freebody, 1987). In this way, content analyses have called attention to the degree and extent to which textbooks construct, rather than represent, worlds of childhood, prescribing national, regional and local forms of cultural identity and social action (e.g. see articles in Apple and Christian-Smith, 1991; Chen, 2002; Nozaki et al., in press).

In contrast with the Protestant and colonialist traditions, the designers of modern textbooks consistently have focused on literacy instruction *qua* scientific method rather than ideological and moral training. It is this view of the textbook as codification of pedagogic method that is the dominant paradigm of American educational science, more specifically, of reading psychology.

But what is distinctive is not only the particular 'scientific' approach to reading of any given textbook *per se*. In the case of Dick and Jane, the books were premised on then contemporary models of word recognition, while current officially sanctioned approaches in the US have moved towards direct instruction in 'alphabetics' and phonics. More profound was the very premise of the modern textbook: that the actual narrative reading text could be designed on the basis of psychological theories of instruction and skill, whether behaviourist, cognitive or psycholinguistic, and *not* on literary content or religious values *per se*; that a whole suite of 'teacher-proofed' curricular commodities including guidebooks, student workbooks, adjunct visual and instructional materials, and tests could be delivered; and that standardized tests could be developed on comparable design principles to assess teacher and system efficacy at delivery of the whole package. This, as Larson (2002) explains, sets the ground not only for a redefinition of literacy pedagogy as the object of science and pseudoscience, a move formalized in the current US and UK policy environments, but also for multinational corporate production and marketing and, indeed, 'snake oil sales'.

To this day, then, the early reading textbook is an archetype of modernist design. But it is also a powerful economic phenomenon in its own right: a multinational product that can be adapted, translated, and niche marketed in a range of national and regional markets; a comprehensive suite of educational commodities with a pedagogic reach that extends far beyond children's narrative reading text; a scientifically 'tested' and 'proven' product. The typical US or UK reading series is modified by local experts and marketed in several English-speaking markets. The educational effects of this model speak to ongoing policy questions about literacy instruction in the UK and US. There, the textbook is a central policy tool for a regulatory system that aims at standardization and quality assurance of classroom literacy events. While the Reformation textbook was a response to the demands of mass schooling in the newly invented secular nation-state, the modern reading series was the response of educational sciences and large publishing houses to the demands of modernist, urban society *par excellence*. As an embodiment of pedagogic method (e.g. phonics, word recognition), it promises discipline, standardization and accountability in the mass delivery of literacy skills. As an educational commodity, large scale adoption across state systems guarantees efficient economies of scale, interstate and transnational export potential, and, increasingly, viable economies of scope for the development of further editions, adjunct and affiliated products in other areas of educational demand and consumption.

There is some recent evidence of the enlistment of many of these approaches to textbook development, with their attendant epistemological and curricular assumptions, in the educational systems of rapidly industrializing and globalizing states in Asia, the Pacific and Africa (e.g. Suaysuwan and Kapitzke, in press). In some instances, as in Korea, this has entailed a direct and explicit textual translation of the values, ideologies and semiotic codes of American reading series (Lee, in press). The role of the state in the political economy of the textbook, of course, depends upon nation or region specific regulation and policy. In the case of many developing countries, the state has retained responsibility not only for the adoption and monitoring of textbook form and content, but often for their production and distribution (Suaysuwan and Kapitzke, in press). In the North and West, the political economy of textbook production, adoption and implementation tends to be more complex, linking government policy, assessment and accountability systems, and the establishment of regional and state 'marketplaces' for multinational educational commodities. The current debates over literacy and reading in the US and UK are cases in point.

In the last three years, the implementation of the UK National Literacy Strategy and the findings of the US National Reading Panel have again focused policy and academic debate on methods, reviving simmering debates over the place of phonics, direct instruction, literature study and, of course, over the use of standardized achievement tests as principal systemic measures for assessing school and programme efficacy. In many ways, these debates begin from the baseline assumptions of the technocratic model. The first assumption concerns the advent of 'evidence-based policy', that the best methods for teaching literacy and the best textbook packages can be determined by reference to an evidence base wholly reliant on classical psychological experimental design and achievement tests.

The second assumption is that the optimal instructional method can be coded, broadcast and implemented across large educational jurisdictions through the mandating of preferred textbooks and affiliated instructional sequences – with current controversies over the US federal government's moves to only provide support for those reading programmes (e.g. Open Court) based on 'scientific evidence' (Cunningham, 2001; Garan, 2001).

THE CROSSOVER OF TEXTBOOKS INTO HOME READING

Goodman et al. (1988) used the term 'basalization' to refer to the textbook development practices described above. Typically, this involves: (1) the attachment of a teachers' guide to direct the pragmatic use of texts, the 'running metatextual commentary' (Luke et al., 1989) on the children's narrative; and (2) a control of the 'level' of the text, usually through the application of a conventional readability scheme that places limits on vocabulary, lexical density and syntactic complexity. Texts are levelled and 'graded' for the incremental introduction of digraph and dipthong combinations and core word recognition patterns for sequenced skill outcomes.

These and other linguistic, semiotic and physical characteristics of the textbook have evolved in relation to the sociolinguistic and cultural context where they are most likely to be read and used, the classroom. There are ongoing debates among early childhood educators about how, when, and with which techniques children should receive formal and informal instruction in literacy, whether this should occur in schools or homes, under whose professional jurisdiction and so forth. There has been an international push to extend and formalize aspects of early literacy experience into earlier years of schooling, and home and childcare settings. In part, this reflects the policy focus on early intervention, widespread concern about home–school transitions for children from lower socio-economic, cultural and linguistic minority groups, and an affiliated movement for 'family literacy', home reading activities preparatory to formal schooling (Carrington and Luke, 2003). At the same time, the market in both print materials and educational toys amongst middle class parents who seek to accelerate their children's skill and intellectual development has expanded.

The early twentieth century architects of the literacy textbook worked in an era in which the sales of Dick and Jane readers to schools for consumption by teachers and small children would have been the largest market available. In the early to mid twentieth century, working families still relied greatly upon public and school libraries for access to books. To this day funding cutbacks in public libraries have their most direct effects on those communities without the surplus income to purchase books (Luke and Kapitzke, 1999). Yet few publishers could have imagined the market possibilities of the extension of the market for early reading instructional materials into homes. The use of books in home and community settings for formal and informal introductions to literacy practices now constitutes a significant and growing proportion of the trade publishing industry.

By recent accounts, the children's literature market is now a multibillion dollar transnational enterprise. According to Cummins (2001), the average American book price of all children's and young adult titles is $US8.41 for paperbacks and $17.57 for hardbounds, rising on average 5.7% per year in cost. The Achuka Children's Book Resources website (www.achuka.co.uk) describes UK children's books as a £225 million industry. This industry includes, of course, bestselling children's books, with over 10 million copies of Beatrix Potter books in print, and bestseller lists that include such early childhood classics as Mercer Mayer's *Just Me and My Dad*, with almost 5 million copies in print, of Dr Seuss, 'Sesame Street' reading materials and other books, and the current bestselling *America: A Patriotic Primer* by Lynne Cheney.

In recent years there has been an extension of textbooks into the home reading environment, beginning with the movement of 'graded' texts into trade markets. Trade journals like the *School Library Journal* have long categorized 'children's and young adult titles' sales by age/grade, for example, 'preschool to grade 4', 'grade 5 and up'. But more recently, marketing has involved increased 'basalization' and branding by level. Series like the bestselling *I Can Read* series and many Golden Books have long branded reading ages through readability formulae. But in the UK and many other countries, popular bookstore chains like W.H. Smith have begun to list, shelve and market books by official National Literacy Strategy levels. Textbook-style design features are crossing over into the general trade children's literature field, and home reading is being brought into alignment with the official categories and practices of official school literacy events.

In its most overt form, this involves crossover product development and marketing by multinationals like McGraw-Hill. McGraw-Hill's Open Court reading series has received official sanction from the US federal government's recent moves to legislate 'scientific' approaches to reading (there are hotlinks to the relevant legislation for teachers and educators on the McGraw-Hill publishing website www.sra-4kids.com). Beginning from an enhanced market share position in early childhood textbooks, McGraw-Hill has expanded its range of affiliated products into the home market. Graded readers similar to those used in Open Court are sold on the McGraw-Hill Children's Publishing website, an Amazon-style operation, for parents:

> Your first grader has been introduced to math, phonics and language art skills at school. This is the perfect opportunity to initiate your child's study habits and help build their confidence level at the same time. With workbooks, software and flashcards from McGraw-Hill Children's Publishing, your child can practice these tough new subjects. Practicing with McGraw-Hill … materials will help eliminate confusion. (www.mhkis.com/cgi-bin/gradeprod.cgi?grade=1).

In this marketing text, the push is on for parents to better align their home reading practices to those of the reading series, through the purchase of textbook-like commodities. But this doesn't stop with reading and literature *per se*. In the same catalogue, grades 1 and 2 test preparation materials are marketed to parents: 'Test preparation material from the nations #1 school testing company!' is said to 'offer … children the preparation they need to achieve success on standardized tests'. All of this occurs under the umbrella of official endorsement of a co-marketed product by the federal government and various scientific 'experts'.

Textbooks for the teaching of reading – and their affiliated worksheets, flashcards and standardized tests – are no longer the focus of formal instruction solely in schools. Textbook design and marketing principles have been extended into the non-school market, making for a *de facto* institutionalization and domestication of home reading – among those social classes with sufficient surplus income – by state literacy policy. This involves both the levelling and the scientific grading of texts, their marketing in relation to official school levels, badged products which are based on product recognition and loyalty (e.g. SRA), print and multimedia that are derived from school series, and activities and texts officially adopted for school use. The modern textbook thus is extending into the home, into 'family literacy', 'early intervention' and new constructions of early childhood, abetted by a multinational political economy of text production. These developments mark the confluence of state intervention in the shaping of what counts as literacy, the standardization of school reading practices, and the expansion of consumer markets by multinational publishers.

NEW TEXTS, NEW IDENTITIES, NEW LITERACIES

Children, parents, and carers alike have become key participants in global industries and economies founded on the advertising and marketing of images and identities of 'child' and 'childhood' (Carrington, 2002). Homes and communities are locations for the flows of consumer culture – magazines, advertising, television guides, and their co-branded digital and media texts (Marsh, 2000). The impacts of popular culture and digital toys and media, and the study of how these are leading to hybridized and blended social practices, are key areas of current ethnographic and sociological research (e.g. Marsh and Millard, 2000; Pahl, 2002).

Basal readers and canonical children's literature alike have tended to present a ready-made possible world, replete with characters, scenery and story-lines. Many of the texts of popular culture, however, are firmly and unapologetically rooted in the practices of everyday life in consumer societies. These texts rely heavily on a direct connection to the consumer and media world outside the text. In this sense, the texts of consumer culture engage children with the flows of multinational culture rather than insulating them in a distinct, child-appropriate world of play, development, fantasy and so forth. With their emphasis on a perpetual present, consumer culture texts are constructed to create a kind of semiotic isomorphism between portrayed world and that of the reader. While they principally are marketed to particular social class and cultural demographic 'niches', like Dick and Jane they act almost inversely to establish an ostensive equality of a universal, white, Anglo-American middle class childhood and neighbourhood. This is done in different ways. *Barbie Magazine*, for instance, makes use of pronouns, particularly 'you', throughout its text to create instant familiarity: 'And you think you're clumsy' (August 2002: 10); 'Start with a scarf like us' (76); 'You'll love these fun cool summer outfits'; 'Subscribing to *Barbie Magazine* is totally cool.'

In order to establish product loyalty and flexible economies of scope, consumer texts are characteristically intertextual: *Barbie Magazine* makes explicit and repeated reference to Barbie dolls, fashion, jewellery, videos and computer games and to other magazines. Its relationship with the reader is to instruct her/him in the world around and outside the text; to equip the reader with relevant and up-to-date knowledge so as to construct appropriate identities in a consumer culture. The multimodal nature of these texts, that is, where one message or meaning is presented in multiple formats (e.g. narrative text in multiple colour and fonts, accompanied by photographs, set next to graphic images and witty one-liners) reinforces key messages about the value and desirability of particular products, and their affiliated lifestyles and identities. This is enhanced by the complex visual layout of these texts, with different fonts and many small text boxes.

The genre here is a form of infotainment. In represented fashion spreads ('Look like a princess!'), ostensible ideological content and advertising for affiliated products are identical. The pedagogic nature of identity construction extends beyond each single text. In a surf-themed text, for example, as well as fashion spreads, surfing tips and personalized recounts of surfing lifestyle, there are descriptions of particular musical genres and movies to watch. Like the pieces of an identikit, readers are taught what pieces go together to create particular identities and, by their absence, what pieces do not fit this particular identity puzzle.

Consumer texts thus are didactic and pedagogic texts of a particular force and power, bridging and transgressing traditional text genres. Readers learn that the text's message is multilevelled, contained in the multiply layered juxtapositions and overlays of pictures, text and font styles. As on the Internet, s/he learns to track visual/semiotic pathways, following the font, colour and picture cueing systems as much, if not more, than the print itself. Where traditionally the message was text-based with pictorial references, the childhood texts of consumer culture do not follow this format. They are aggressively non-linear and, rather than the left to right, top to bottom pathway of print-focused text, they require new directionalities across and through.

At the same time, 'adult' texts and knowledge are increasingly available to children via a number of channels – television, satellite and cable TV, the Internet. Adults are unable to control the type and amount of information available to children. This shift presents a challenge to existing boundaried notions of childhood and, just as surely, to classroom-based pedagogies. Our point is that a deluge of texts now claim the authority to instruct children in how to participate in childhood and consumer culture. These constitute a blend of 'public pedagogy' (Luke, 1996) and what we term 'household pedagogy'. In his analysis of 'unschooled learning', Mahiri (2001) argues that the official curriculum and the institutionalized school are at risk of being superseded. Where earlier generations of children were socialized primarily within the boundaries of family, school, religious organization and community, consumer and popular culture is now *the* principal mode of early childhood socialization (Kline, 1993). The case we have chosen (Barbie) is illustrative only – and we could alternatively have studied a range of other popular figures, from Teletubbies and Garfield to now traditional multimodal representations of Richard Scarry characters. We have discussed two elements of the extension of 'texts' and, indeed, textbooks beyond their traditional domains of schooling and curriculum into home and community contexts: the extension of school-like reading scheme materials into commodity ranges targeting the middle class, and the ubiquitous texts of popular culture that are found in most lounge rooms and bedrooms in late capitalist societies.

FROM TEXTBOOKS TO PEDAGOGIC TEXTS

Ong's (1958) print-based 'pedagogical juggernaut' rolls on. Aided by current policy settings that emphasize accountability via standardized testing, the modern textbook continues to assert a dominant influence on early childhood literacy. More than a corpus of valued knowledges, official ideologies and beliefs, the reading series acts as a codification of instructional approach, of educational 'science', and as a way of steering from a distance teachers' and children's interactions with literacy. As we have shown here, textbooks, primers, basal readers, and the common 'graded' or 'levelled' texts designed for pedagogical and literary uses in the home remain a central part of childhood in print-based economies and cultures.

The political economy of text publishing is actively seeking out new products, new markets and new niches for children, parents and teachers as text consumers. If there is an axiom that arises from the commodification of school knowledge and literacy, it is that publishers and their affiliated knowledge and entertainment corporations necessarily establish, constitute and build new consumer needs, new communities and new target groups of youth and parents. Emergent information technologies have helped to shape and accelerate these developments.

At the same time, the traditionally print-based industry has expanded, consisting of an interesting blend of smaller 'start-up' publishers and large multinational affiliates of larger media/entertainment corporations. The crossover effects we have described are not just from textbooks to children's literature, but also involve the co-development and co-marketing of toys and parenting products, movies and websites, video games and other mass media products (Cope and Kalantzis, 2001). On bestseller lists we find children's literature and reading series with spinoff connections to movies and cartoons. In this way, narrative literature acts to directly market products, from Arthur stuffed figures to Bob the Builder toolkits. Band-Aids, cereals and household products also are spun off of these characters and themes. Movie and video

games producers routinely purchase the rights of bestselling children's books to produce other textual products based on these characters and stories. While its hegemony in the school-based production of the literate subject remains unrivalled, the textbook has lost any monopoly on children's moral, intellectual and psychological development that it might have had. In information societies and economies of signs, the textbook has become one of an array of textual products which are changing the face of early childhood literacy practices.

In ways that early analysts and critics from Ong (1958) to Elson (1964) couldn't have foreseen, the textbook is morphing into new shapes, both as a textual genre and as a commodity, an object of media crossover and textual/semiotic convergence (Kalmbach, 1997). Exploded diagrams and 'callouts' in textbooks illustrate this process of intertextual transference and hybridity. Callouts, copied from technical illustrations of the 'model kit' and 'repair manual' genre, are the captions of visual/verbal display in exploded diagrams. Each callout assembles an arrangement of descriptive and contextual details that complement and extend the visual image. This shift to visual display in school textbooks is to be expected as designers, authors and illustrators – who themselves were reared on 'Sesame Street', MTV, video and computer games – enter the publishing industry.

The advent and spread of a postmodern consumer culture based on the commodification and consumption of texts and discourse have already had a visible impact on the reshaping of the experiences and discourses of childhood (Lee, 2001) and of children's early literacy texts and literate practices. In the 'semiotic economies' (Luke, 2003) of 'developed' and advanced capitalist societies, the production and consumption of text and discourse have become key economic and cultural foci. Early childhood in home and school, mass media and shopping mall is being reframed as a training ground for early literacy. At the same time, these sites have become focal points for the commodification of childhood. At once, the literacy textbook is reasserting its traditional authority over the shaping of what counts as literacy in the school, while it inexorably seeks out new niches, new crossovers, new forms and new markets.

NOTE

The authors wish to thank Peter Freebody for calling our attention to Ong (1958) and to Arlette Willis for critical commentary on an earlier draft.

REFERENCES

Apple, M.W. and Christian-Smith, L.C. (eds) (1991) *The Politics of the Textbook*. New York: Routledge.

Aries, P. (1962) *Centuries of Childhood: a Social History of Family Life*, trans. R. Baldick. New York: Knopf.

Baker, C.D. and Freebody, P. (1987) *Children's First Schoolbooks*. Oxford: Blackwell.

Barbie Magazine (August 2002) No. 61. Haymarket, NSW: EMAP Australia.

Burbules, N. and Torres, C. (eds) (2000) *Globalization and Education: Critical Perspectives*. New York: Routledge.

Carrington, V. (2002) *New Times: New Families*. Amsterdam: Kluwer.

Carrington, V. and Luke, A. (2003) 'Reading, homes, and families: from postmodern to modern?', in A. van Kleeck, S. Stahl and E. Bauer (eds), *On Reading to Children: Parents and Teachers*. Mahwah, NJ: Erlbaum. pp. 231–52.

Chen, J. (2002) 'Reforming textbooks, reshaping school knowledge: Taiwan's textbook deregulation in the 1990s', *Pedagogy, Culture and Society*, 10 (1): 39–72.

Cope, B. and Kalantzis, D. (eds) (2001) *Print and Electronic Text Convergence*. Altona: Common Ground.

Cummins, J. (2001) 'Average book prices '01: dead trees and wooden nickels', *School Library Journal*, 3 January, accessed at slj.reviewsnews.com.

Cunningham, J. (2001) 'The National Reading Panel Report', *Reading Research Quarterly*, 36 (3): 326–35.

Elson, R.M. (1964) *Guardians of Tradition: American Schoolbooks of the Nineteenth Century*. Lincoln, NB: University of Nebraska Press.

Garan, E. (2001) 'Beyond the smoke and mirrors: a critique of the National Reading Panel report on phonics', *Phi Delta Kappan*, 82 (7): 500–6.

Goodman, K., Shannon, P., Freeman, Y. and Murphy, S. (1988) *Report Card on Basal Readers*. Katonah, NY: Owen.

Kalmbach, J.R. (1997) *The Computer and the Page: Publishing, Technology, and the Classroom*. Norwood, NJ: Ablex.

Kapitzke, C. (1995) *Literacy and Religion*. Amsterdam: Benjamins.

Kapitzke, C. (1999) 'Literacy and religion: the word, the holy word and the world', in D.A. Wagner, R.L. Venezky and B.V. Street (eds), *Literacy: An International Handbook*. Boulder, CO: Westview. pp. 113–18.

Kline, S. (1993) *Out of the Garden: Toys, TV and Children's Culture in the Age of Marketing*. London: Verso.

Larson, J. (ed.) (2002) *Literacy as Snake Oil: Beyond the Quick Fix*. New York: Lang.

Lee, I. (in press) 'The representation of new times in Korean language textbooks', in Y. Nozaki, R. Openshaw and A. Luke (eds), *Struggles over Difference: Curriculum, Texts and Pedagogy in the Asia–Pacific*. Albany, NY: State University of New York Press.

Lee, N. (2001) *Childhood and Society: Growing Up in an Age of Uncertainty*. Philadelphia: Open University Press.

Luke, A. (1988) *Literacy, Textbooks, and Ideology: Postwar Literacy Instruction and the Mythology of Dick and Jane*. London: Falmer.

Luke, C. (ed.) (1989) *Pedagogy, Printing, and Protestantism: the Discourse on Childhood*, Albany, NY: State University of New York Press.

Luke, C. (1996) *Feminisms and Pedagogies of Everyday Life*. Albany, NY: State University of New York Press.

Luke, A. (2000) 'Social perspectives on textbooks and primers', in D. Wagner, R.L. Venezky and B.V. Street (eds), *Literacy: an International Handbook*. Boulder, CO: Westview. pp. 186–92.

Luke, A. (2003) 'Literacy and the other: a sociological approach to research and policy in multilingual societies', *Reading Research Quarterly*, 34 (1).

Luke, A. and Kapitzke, C. (1994) 'Pedagogy and paradox: teaching interpretation in a religious community', in H. Parret (ed.), *Pretending to Communicate*. Berlin: de Gruyter. pp. 124–40.

Luke, A. and Kapitzke, C. (1999) 'Literacies and libraries: archives and cybraries', *Pedagogy, Culture and Society*, 7 (3): 467–91.

Luke, C., de Castell, S. and Luke, A. (1989) 'Beyond criticism: the authority of the school textbook', in S. de Castell, A. Luke and C. Luke (eds), *Language, Authority and Criticism*. London: Falmer. pp. 245–60.

Mahiri, J. (2001) 'Pop culture pedagogy and the end(s) of school', *Journal of Adolescent and Adult Literacy*, 44 (4): 382–5.

Marsh, J. (2000) 'Teletubby tales: popular culture in the early years language and literacy curriculum', *Contemporary Issues in Early Childhood*, 1 (2): 119–33.

Marsh, J. and Millard, E. (2000) *Literacy and Popular Culture: Using Children's Culture in the Classroom*. London: Chapman/Sage.

Nozaki, Y., Openshaw, R. and Luke, A. (eds) (in press) *Struggles over Difference: Curriculum, Texts and Pedagogies in the Asia–Pacific*. Albany, NY: State University of New York Press.

Ong, W. (1958) *Ramus: Method and the Decay of Discourse*. Cambridge: Harvard University Press.

Pahl, K. (2002) 'Ephemera, mess and miscellaneous piles: texts and practices in families', *Journal of Early Childhood Literacy*, 2 (2): 145–66.

Pennycook, A. (1998) *English and the Discourses of Colonialism*. London: Routledge.

Shannon, P. (1989) *Broken Promises: Reading Instruction in Twentieth Century America*. South Hadley, MA: Bergin and Garvey.

Suaysuwan, N. and Kapitzke, C. (in press) 'Thai English language textbooks, 1960–2000: postwar, industrial, and global changes', in Y. Nozaki, R. Openshaw and

A. Luke (eds), *Struggles over Difference: Curriculum, Texts and Pedagogy in the Asia–Pacific*. Albany, NY: State University of New York Press.

Venezky, R.L. (1992) 'Textbooks in school and society', in P.W. Jackson (ed.), *Handbook of Research on Curriculum*. New York: Macmillan. pp. 436–59.

Westbury, I. (1990) 'Textbooks, textbook publishers, and the quality of schooling', in D.L. Elliott and A. Woodward (eds), *Textbooks and Schooling in the United States*. Chicago, IL: University of Chicago Press. pp. 1–22.

Willis, A.I. and Harris, V. (2000) 'Political acts: literacy learning and teaching', *Reading Research Quarterly*, 35 (1): 72–88.

22

The Nature of Young Children's Authoring

DEBORAH WELLS ROWE

What is authoring? How does one recognize it? At what age do children begin to exhibit activities that we might call authoring? Is authoring confined to written language or does it include children's ways of weaving together talk, print, play, art, and music to express their meanings?

Imagine for a moment that you are new to the field of early literacy research and in search of answers to these questions. You pick two monographs from a list of recommended readings. You first tackle Ferreiro and Teberosky's *Literacy before Schooling* (1982). You easily conjure up the research scenario. Researchers dictate words and ask young children to write them. Children wrinkle their brows as they consider how to map oral language to print. Ferreiro and Teberosky's analyses convince you that authoring occurs in the mind of the child. To understand it, researchers must track children's hypotheses about the nature of the writing system. Next you pick up Dyson's *Writing Superheroes* (1997) and begin to read. Here the tale unfolds in a different direction. Dyson allows you to peep over the shoulders of Tina and Sammy as they negotiate writing activities in their classroom. Here young authors are making choices about what to write, who to write with, and how their texts will eventually be received by their teacher and classmates. Dyson's children are almost certainly making decisions about spelling and other encoding issues – you can see this in the unconventional texts reproduced in the monograph's illustrations – but this is not what seems most important. Instead, Dyson's analyses highlight how these children negotiate access to meanings and social roles that are available (or not) to persons of their gender, age,

ethnicity, and class. Authoring seems to occur not so much in the mind of the child but between children. You come away convinced that borrowing from popular culture texts like *X Men* positions young authors as certain kinds of writers in the official world of the classroom and certain kinds of kids in peer culture.

The divide between Ferriero and Teberosky and Dyson seems a large one, not because their work is irreconcilable, but because they look at children's authoring from such different vantage points. Even cursory reading leaves the strong impression that there is more than one 'story' of young children's authoring. The theoretical perspectives adopted by these researchers serve to differentially frame the authoring act – as to who or what is observed, under what conditions, and what aspects of the authoring event are subjected to intensive analysis, interpretation, and theorizing.

SCOPE OF THE REVIEW

My goal in this chapter is to explore the theoretical vantage points researchers use to draw boundaries around authoring and child authors. This review began with a search of international research literature published between 1990 and 2002 and focused on authoring of children from birth to age seven. Authoring was broadly defined to include children's construction and expression of meanings in a variety of communications systems. However, in order to limit the scope of the review, I included only studies that in some way explored children's writing (i.e. their attempts at recording linguistic messages on paper), though some studies also included authoring in other symbol systems such as talk, drawing, gesture, and dramatic play.

While there are many possible frames one might apply, in this review, studies were categorized according to major two properties of authoring: location and semiotic system. With regard to location, investigations of childhood authoring have taken two broad approaches. Researchers working from cognitive, psycholinguistic, sociocognitive, and sociopsycholinguistic perspectives have located authoring *in the mind of the child* and designed studies focusing on children's hypotheses about print and their formation in interaction with others. Researchers working from sociocultural, situated cognition, and New Literacy Studies perspectives have located authoring as occurring collectively *between children and others* in their communities. This research has focused on describing socially situated authoring practices, and on analysing the ideological underpinnings of authoring. While scholarship on early literacy learning has given most attention to cognitive and cultural dimensions of authoring, researchers' decisions about a second property of authoring – its semiotic boundaries – have also been influential. Therefore, this review concludes with a discussion of studies adopting multimodal views of young children's authoring.

LOCATING AUTHORING: COGNITIVE AND SOCIOCOGNITIVE PERSPECTIVES

Authoring as a cognitive process

In the last three decades, much of the research on young children's authoring has focused on describing the cognitive processes involved in text production. In general, this work has taken a constructivist view of young children's authoring. That is, children are seen as building their own understandings about the nature of the writing system (Ferreiro, 1990). They do so by constructing and testing hypotheses about print (Ferreiro and Teberosky, 1982; Clay, 1991; Harste et al., 1984; Rowe, 1994; Teale and Sulzby, 1986) rather than learning through direct imitation of print in the environment. It is because young children's hypotheses are 'true constructions' (Ferreiro, 1990; Ferreiro et al., 1996; Besse, 1996; Goodman, 1990; Kamii et al., 2001; Schickedanz, 1990) and do not entirely mirror adult views of writing that their products often look so unconventional to adult eyes. These writing behaviours that precede and develop into conventional literacy have been

termed 'emergent literacy' (Sulzby, 1989; Teale and Sulzby, 1986).

Researchers working from an emergent literacy perspective, then, have defined young children's writing in terms of children's mental processes rather than textual products (Harste et al., 1984). Intentionality – the intention to create a text for a particular context (Hall, 1989; Harste et al., 1984) – rather than conventionality of the resulting product is viewed as the defining characteristic of authoring. Children become authors when they indicate that they have created a message with the intention to communicate, or at least that they understand that their marks might be meaningful to others if their audience knows how to interpret them. Thus, children who ask an adult 'What did I write?' are authors (Clay, 1975; Harste et al., 1984).

Further, analysis of child authors' unconventional texts and talk reveal pragmatic, semantic, syntactic, and graphophonemic organization (Goodman, 1980; 1986; Hall, 1989; Harste et al., 1984) suggesting that young children's authoring *processes* are not qualitatively different from those used by older writers (Harste et al., 1984; Teale and Sulzby, 1986). Young children have been shown to metacognitively monitor the adequacy of their written texts for particular audiences (Rowe, 1994; Sipe, 1998; Wollman-Bonilla, 2001a) and to use strategies to revise texts at the word and meaning levels (Calkins, 1994; Graves, 1994; Sipe, 1998). From this perspective, almost as soon as children pick up a pencil they become authors. Even in the years between birth and age five, many young children are already developing understandings of the functions and forms of writing, and accepting the social role of writer (Goodman, 1986; 1990: Teale and Sulzby, 1986).

Given the constructivist frame outlined above, it is not surprising that a considerable amount of attention has been devoted to describing children's hypotheses about authoring including understandings about differences between drawing and writing, speech–print links, spelling, grammar, concept of word, written language functions, and genre features. (See Sulzby, 1991; Sulzby and Teale, 1991; Teale and Sulzby, 1986; Yaden et al., 2000 for previous reviews.) Research in the last decade has tended to confirm earlier findings and to extend them to different populations by designing studies with younger or slightly older children, speakers of other languages, and children with special needs.

Findings of a number of recent studies support claims of intentionality and organization in young children's unconventional texts. Research has confirmed earlier findings that very young children have different physical action plans for drawing and writing (Brenneman et al., 1996), and distinguish writing from numerals (Landsmann, 1996) even though their products look unconventional to the adult eye. Though children's texts often demonstrate unconventional spatial organization and serial order (i.e. random placement of words, right to left sequencing, and lack of spaces between words), like other aspects of writing, children's hypotheses become more conventional over time (Clay, 1975; Sipe, 1998).

Considerable research attention has been devoted to confirming earlier descriptions of children's hypotheses about orthography, both before and after children develop the alphabetic principle and begin to create 'invented spellings' (Bear and Templeton, 1998; Henderson and Beers, 1980; Gentry, 2000). A number of Piagetian researchers, working with different language groups, have provided support for Ferreiro and Teberosky's (1982) description of a sequenced progression of hypotheses leading to the construction of the alphabetic hypothesis. These studies include work with children learning Italian and Spanish (Ferreiro and Teberosky, 1982), French (Besse, 1996), Portuguese (Grossi, 1990) and English (Kamii et al., 2001; Branscombe and Taylor, 1996). Other researchers (e.g. Sulzby, 1989) have described the progression of children's emergent writing forms from scribbling to random and patterned letter strings (Bloodgood, 1999; Olson and Sulzby, 1991).

With regard to spelling, there is considerable consensus that spelling, too, develops in a fairly predictable way with children developing a series of qualitatively different hypotheses about how speech is represented in print (Fresch, 2001; Hughes and Searle, 1991; Korkeamaki and Dreher, 2000; Mayer and Moskos, 1998) – though there is some debate about the best scheme for dividing and labelling spelling stages (Bear and Templeton, 1998; Gentry, 2000; Read, 1971). (See Zutell and Scharer, in this volume, for a detailed review of this work.) Despite many differences in method (data collection techniques, instructional contexts, and different oral and signed languages), many studies support a developmental progression of learning to spell. Interestingly, Mayer and Moskos (1998) found that deaf children (ages five to nine) followed a similar trajectory.

While much of the last decade's cognitively oriented research on young children's writing has focused on children's understanding of graphophonemic aspects of writing, studies of children's understanding of written genre have given more equal attention to semantic and syntactic organization. Kress (1994) has argued that learning to write is not a generic process, but is instead a process of learning the demands and potentials of different genres. By age four or five many children are able to code-switch between oral and literate registers when they dictate a text (Cox et al., 1997). There is a growing body of work substantiating children's understanding of genre features including spatial organization and syntactic and semantic structures (Donovan, 2001; Kamberelis and Bovino, 1999; Wollman-Bonilla, 2000; Zecker, 1999). Even six- and seven-year-olds have been shown to have considerable knowledge of micro-level features of story and information genre (Kamberelis and Bovino, 1999) including cohesion, tense, vocabulary, and word order (Donovan, 2001). Overall, children's ability to produce genre-appropriate meanings outstripped their ability to record them in writing (Donovan, 2001; Zecker, 1999). In general, children's stories were more conventional than information pieces such as science reports (Kamberelis and Bovino, 1999). Overall, their command of genre features appeared to be closely tied to experience and instruction (Wollman-Bonilla, 2000). Genre knowledge, like other aspects of children's authoring, appears to develop early and become more complex with age (Chapman, 1995; Donovan, 2001; Kamberelis and Bovino, 1999). To summarize, while children's hypotheses, forms, and meanings are not always conventional, they are clearly sensitive to the demands and potentials of different genres.

Trajectory

There is considerable research tracking the trajectory of children's authoring hypotheses and textual forms, and there is little debate that, in general, children's writing becomes more conventional over time. Nevertheless, there is disagreement among researchers about how stage-like and invariant such a progression may be. Research using Piagetian interviews has most often found strict adherence to stage progressions. For example, using clinical interview techniques, Kamii and her colleagues (2001) found an invariant progression in the sequence of children's literacy hypotheses. Gentry (2000), whose spelling research is, in part, based in this tradition, agrees that spelling strategies will become more sophisticated with age, but contends that a range of spelling abilities may be displayed at any one time especially as children transition between stages – a finding supported by Korkeamaki and Dreher (2000).

Sulzby (1996) agrees with the notion that children's trajectory toward conventional forms involves adding more sophisticated forms and hypotheses, but disagrees that there is a strict progression through stages. She and her colleagues

(Olson and Sulzby, 1991) found that children retain older, less sophisticated hypotheses and forms in their repertoire, thereby producing texts that show evidence of more and less sophisticated forms. This pattern of creating texts with 'mixed' forms was particularly prominent when children were writing in the new environment of the computer. Other researchers (Clay, 1975; Harste et al., 1984) also challenge the notion of a fixed sequence of hypotheses or stages through which all children must pass. They suggest that differences in children's hypotheses and the sequence in which they are formed may be related to differences in their experiences and because they attend to different aspects of their environment.

Thus, views of an early literacy learning trajectory range from those that hold a strictly sequenced stage theory, to those who emphasize individual variation related to differences in children's experiences and personal inclinations. One likely reason for these differences is the effect of different research tasks. Only those researchers using standardized clinical interviews find invariant sequences of development. Once researchers begin to draw their data from a broader array of tasks, including observations of children's writing in natural contexts, more variation appears. Secondly, researchers are not always discussing the same aspects of literacy development, making it possible that certain kinds of literacy knowledge may develop in more predictable patterns while others are more dependent on social experiences.

Individual authoring in a social world

Social interaction lurks just off-stage in most of the studies just reviewed. Following Piaget (1976), several emergent literacy researchers (Ferreiro, 1990; Goodman, 1986; 1990; Teale and Sulzby, 1986) argue that children construct literacy knowledge through a process of accommodation and assimilation as they interact with the environment. Sociopsycholinguistic perspectives (Harste et al., 1984) build on these views to highlight the inherently social nature of children's cognitive processes. Both authoring processes and children's texts bear the stamp of the social and cultural contexts in which they are formed. From this perspective, young children's authoring is still seen as occurring in the mind of the child, but this learning is now seen as socially mediated and context specific (Vygotsky, 1978). Therefore, it is crucial to describe children's individual authoring processes as they are formed and shaped in interaction with a social world (Rowe, 1994).

The importance of social interaction is demonstrated by research describing global links between social contexts and children's authoring outcomes. Working in settings where children had entered the first years of formal schooling in the United States (Diffily, 1995; Freppon et al., 1995) and Italy (Formisano, 1996), researchers have documented variation in children's writing in different instructional contexts (e.g. traditional skills-based instruction, emergent literacy instruction, whole language instruction). Differences include children's definitions of writing (Diffily, 1995), amount and complexity of text generated (Freppon et al., 1995), genre of writing (Freppon et al., 1995), understanding of the functions of writing (Formisano, 1996) and development of hypotheses about speech–print relationships (Formisano, 1996).

Other research has taken a fine-grained look at specific features of young authors' interactions with others, including parents, siblings, classmates, and teachers. With regard to adult interaction styles, research shows that when adults exert less control during a writing event, children express more interest in writing (Fang, 1999) and initiate more verbal interaction (Burns and Casbergue, 1992; Zucchermaglio and Scheuer, 1996) but also produce less conventional texts than when adults use a controlling style. However, it may be that once some children enter school they are already focused on conventions, and differences in adult style have less impact on conventionality of children's texts (DeBaryshe et al., 1996). Adults appear to scaffold children's writing by tracking the child's progress and meanings and matching their contributions to the child's current needs and independent writing level (DeBaryshe et al., 1996; Lancaster, 2001; Lysaker, 2000). Following Vygotsky (1978) researchers describe such interactions as developing shared consciousness with an adult and suggest that social interaction of this type supports children in crossing the zone of proximal development. Adult scaffolding allows children to do things collaboratively that they could not yet accomplish on their own (DeBaryshe et al., 1996; Lancaster, 2001; Lysaker, 2000).

When children interact with parents and other familiar adults during writing, there clearly is a relational component to their authoring processes. Adult–child interactions include physical closeness, shared rituals and celebrations of writing progress (Lysaker, 2000). Children engage in writing events to initiate and maintain friendships with peers and to communicate with present and absent audiences (Dyson, 1989; Rowe, 1994; Wollman-Bonilla, 2001a; 2001b). Dyson (1989) has argued that there is a dialectical relationship between cognitive and social aspects of authoring. Children's literacy strategies are developed to accomplish social purposes and those social purposes in turn shape the strategies children develop and explore (Heath, 1991).

Several studies conducted in classroom settings with hearing (Condon and Clyde, 1996; Dyson, 1989; Labbo, 1996; Rowe, 1994; Rowe et al., 2001) and deaf children (Troyer, 1991; Williams, 1999) have described young children's interactions with peers in writing events. When children were free to talk and write with others they took a variety of interactive roles including observing other authors; assisting another author by scribing, providing spellings, or sharing ideas; mirroring other authors' texts and processes; sharing different parts of a writing task to complete a single text; and working collaboratively to co-author texts. Children used talk to negotiate and define their roles (Troyer, 1991), to request and provide help and information (Rowe, 1994; Sipe, 1998; Williams, 1999) and to challenge and question peers' authoring practices (Rowe, 1994; Williams, 1999). When parents responded to children's school writing through family message journals, they played many of the same roles including providing feedback and modelling appropriate genres (Wollman-Bonilla, 2001b).

One way social interaction has been shown to impact children's authoring processes is by providing demonstrations of culturally appropriate authoring forms, processes, and meanings. A number of studies have recorded the ways that young children use 'live' authoring demonstrations and the resulting texts as a means of learning about genre-appropriate content, authoring processes, and purposes for authoring (Chapman, 1996; Rowe, 1994; Harste et al., 1984; Wollman-Bonilla, 2001b). One of the most frequent findings of these studies is that children linked their texts to those of other authors with whom they interacted. In some cases children used other authors' demonstrations conservatively – sticking close to the form and content of another author's text (Rowe, 1994). Kress (1997) and others (Dyson, 1989; Newkirk, 1989; Rowe, 1994) have argued that even in cases where children's authoring processes appear to be imitative, they involve constructive work. There is no such thing as mere copying (Kress, 1997). Instead, children analyse other texts through the frames provided by their current hypotheses and reconstruct the forms, meanings, and functions in their own way. Children also use demonstrations as starting points or for authoring as they combine and recast elements of other authors' texts to accomplish new purposes (Dyson, 1998; Rowe, 1994). What young authors choose to appropriate from a demonstration is motivated by their current hypotheses (Harste et al., 1984), individual purposes (Dyson, 1989) and social interest (Kress, 1997).

Social interaction also appears to play an important role in children's construction and testing of literacy hypotheses. Constructivist theories of learning suggest that literacy learning occurs through a cycle of hypothesis testing in which children attempt to use their existing hypotheses to account for their experiences (Piaget, 1976; Harste et al., 1984; Ferreiro and Teberosky, 1982; Goodman, 1990; Short et al., 1996). When children cannot assimilate the new information in their existing schemes, the anomalies motivate a re-examination of the situation, and the construction and testing of new hypotheses. Social interaction becomes an integral part of children's authoring in several ways. Sometimes children use interaction as a means of confirming their existing literacy hypotheses (Rowe, 1994). However, peer questions and comments also frequently challenge their understandings, pushing young authors to clarify, expand, and refine their intended meanings and the forms used to represent them (Condon and Clyde, 1996; Rowe, 1994). In the process, children shift stances to consider the audience's perspective and monitor the effectiveness and appropriateness of their texts (Rowe, 1994; Wollman-Bonilla, 2001a).

Gregory's (2001) study of siblings' writing interactions in home settings provides an interesting complement and extension to classroom-based work. She found a kind of learning 'synergy' that went beyond Vygotskian notions of scaffolding where learning opportunities are thought to occur only for the less advanced partner. As in the classroom-based studies, social interactions around writing provided opportunities for the younger child to observe demonstrations and to ask for and receive help. However, the younger child also served as a kind of 'trigger' for the older child's learning by asking them to think, explain, and assist. Social interaction around authoring, then, was a learning opportunity for both siblings.

Overall, these studies make a strong case for the social nature of literacy processes and knowledge. While general cognitive processes such as assimilation and accommodation or hypotheses testing are proposed as key elements of authoring, this line of research argues for the need to study authoring in relation to the social context in which it is embedded.

AUTHORING AS SOCIAL PRACTICE: SOCIOCULTURAL PERSPECTIVES ON WRITING

The research reviewed thus far has viewed authoring as an 'in-head' phenomenon, albeit one that is shaped by people and social situations. Recently researchers interested in social and cultural aspects of authoring have challenged the notion of authoring as an individual mental act, suggesting, instead, that authoring occurs *between* people as they negotiate authoring processes, meanings, and textual forms as part of their everyday activities. As Barton and Hamilton argue: 'Literacy becomes a community resource, realised in social relationships rather than a property of individuals' (2000: 13). They note that at a micro level, literacy events are often accomplished jointly by a number of participants with the resulting literacy practices moving beyond the individuals' understandings and meanings. At a macro level, communities create social rules and hold taken-for-granted assumptions about who can use and produce particular literacies under what circumstances (Barton and Hamilton, 2000; Santa Barbara Discourse Group, 1992).

From this perspective, authoring is seen as social practice – the accepted and valued ways of 'doing' writing (or art or talk) in a particular community (Barton and Hamilton, 2000; Lave and Wenger, 1991; Lemke, 1995; Solsken, 1993). While literacy practices are, in part, defined by observable behaviours involving print, they also involve values, attitudes, feelings and social relationships (Barton and Hamilton, 2000; Street, 1995). Authoring practices include definitions of text and authoring, the ways community members talk about authoring, ideological views of literacy, and participants' socially constructed identities. Embedded in literacy practices are power relations that determine the use and distribution of texts and who has access to various positions in authoring events. Social practices are ideological in that they support the power of one social group to dominate another (Lemke, 1995).

Two major strands of research framed by the notion of young children's authoring as social practice are discussed below. The first concerns itself with the ways that children and others co-construct situated literacies, and the second analyses the ideological nature of literacy practices.

The social construction of situated literacies

When authoring is seen as a socially situated act, it is no longer possible to discuss 'the' authoring process as if it were a generic characteristic of mind. Instead, young children's authoring must be investigated as it occurs within the social practices of particular communities (Gee, 2001). Researchers working from this theoretical perspective have focused on culturally based variation in beginning literacy learning and the ways that different community practices lead to different patterns of

literacy knowledge and processing. Heath's (1983) classic study of variation in the literate practices of three communities in the Piedmont Carolinas is a precursor to more recent studies investigating the nature of young children's participation in classroom communities. Kantor et al. (1992), for example, tracked the way that preschoolers and their teachers co-constructed meanings about literacy through everyday interactions. They concluded that each classroom activity's materials, purposes, and participant structures framed literacy in distinctive ways. A number of other studies (Manyak, 2001; Larson, 1995; 1999; 2000; Power, 1991) have carefully described children's participation in communities of practice formed around authoring events in American first-grade classrooms. Power (1991), for example, tracked the development of 'pop-ups' (i.e. portions of illustrations affixed so they stood out from the page) as a text convention in a first-grade classroom. By documenting the development of this text feature across time and across the texts of different children, she demonstrated how the classroom community co-constructed its own local definition of text. Unlike cognitively oriented studies of children's genre knowledge that typically begin with researcher assumptions about conventional genre features, studies framed by a social practice perspective focus on the ways local literacy knowledge is shaped in face-to-face interactions and reflect the group's values and experiences.

In addition to documenting the situated nature of classroom literacies, researchers have explored the consequences of classroom literacy practices for children's participation and literacy learning. Following Lave and Wenger (1991), some early literacy researchers (Larson, 1999; Manyak, 2001) argue that children learn culturally situated literacies through legitimate peripheral participation in communities of practice. That is, children participate in literacy events by adopting authoring roles that approximate those of more experienced authors while providing additional support that opens up the practices to newcomers (Wenger, 1998). Through participation in the social life of families, schools, churches and other groups, children adopt community definitions of authoring, including ideas about acceptable meanings, and ways of constructing text.

The notion that literacy learning occurs through joint participation in literacy events has spurred investigators to document *how* children participate in authoring events. It appears that some classroom literacy events are accomplished through participation structures that allow children and teachers to flexibly shift between roles as experts and novices (Manyak, 2001), and as teacher, author, co-author, overhearer, and so on (Larson, 1995; 1999; 2000).

Findings suggest that these shifts in participation allow children to take on new responsibilities for writing and learning. Though these studies do not directly analyse linkages between student positions and learning outcomes, the authors suggest that the nature of participation in authoring practices has consequences for literacy learning.

Authoring as an ideological practice

In the studies just described, literacy researchers were interested in describing the situated and distributed nature of authoring practices. Others working from a social practice perspective have studied the ideological nature of literacy practices; that is, they have focused on the ways that a group's common-sense views of literacy create and maintain power over others, and are framed by relations of status and dominance within a larger political context (Lemke, 1995; Sheridan et al., 2000; Solsken, 1993). Not only are children's authoring roles embedded within hierarchies of social relationships, but the 'stuff' of authoring is also ideologically loaded. When children construct written texts, they are doing more than selecting words. They are manipulating ideological symbols of power (or weakness) (Dyson, 2000a) and displaying an (often implicit) interdependence between meanings and the social and political positions they occupy (Lemke, 1995). When young children write, they appropriate cultural materials as a means of cultural production (Dyson, 2001).

From this perspective, authoring is co-constructed in local interactions and as part of larger social and political relations (Dyson, 1998; Solsken, 1993). As Solsken argues: 'There is no politically neutral ground for literacy learning, either in families or schools' (1993: 219). When they pick up the pen, children, their teachers, classmates, and families reproduce, resist, and transform hierarchies of social relations and their positions within them. For researchers working within this frame, authoring is seen as a process of negotiating social relationships and ideological views of the world. Children's participation in authoring practices must be read against the structuring processes of race, gender, and class in the larger society (Dyson, 2000a). Authoring is also seen as an act of self-definition. Learning to write involves much more than adding new skills to the child's cognitive repertoire. It requires them to take on new cultural identities and affects their sense of self in profound ways (Dyson, 2001; Rowe et al., 2001; Sheridan et al., 2000; Solsken, 1993). Key questions for these researchers are: what texts and positions are available for use by children of different genders, ethnicities, and social classes? What

forms of agency do children exercise? How do they accept, resist, and transform textual practices and social positions?

Dyson's (1989; 1993; 1997) research in culturally diverse American classrooms has been particularly influential in opening young children's authoring practices to ideological analysis. Her work demonstrates how young authors use texts to construct social affiliations with their peers, as well as to accept and resist the ways they are positioned by others (Dyson, 1995; 2000b). Overall, Dyson found that children not only flexibly reframed culturally available signs, but also recast existing social relationships and social practices. Dyson's (2001) analyses demonstrate that authoring involved assuming a 'social voice' that positioned children in particular ways in relation to the ongoing dialogue in their classroom community and in relation to the texts and practices of the larger society. She identified social and symbolic flexibility and recontextualization processes as key authoring processes used by child authors as they moved across symbolic, social, and ideological boundaries (Dyson, 1998; 2000b; 2001).

Ideological analyses have highlighted the intercultural nature of classroom authoring events (Lemke, 1995). Because children are simultaneously positioned in the overlapping communities of official and peer culture, the same authoring activities often have very different meanings for the children's positions as students in the official world and as friends in the peer world (Dyson, 1993; Rowe et al., 2001).

Several researchers have also conducted ideological analyses of the gendered nature of authoring practices and the ways that writing may reify or transform the social positions occupied and available to young authors. Both Gallas (1998) and Henkin (1998) report that gender and ethnicity strongly influenced the ways children were positioned in authoring events by their peers, with girls and ethnic outsiders sometimes having limited access to powerful roles. Taking a different methodological approach, MacGillivray and Martinez (1998) analysed gender roles displayed in six- to nine-year-olds' texts. They found that while many of the children's story characters displayed traditional gender roles, some of the female students created texts where gender roles were not so rigidly categorized. For this latter group of girls, authoring became an opportunity to create worlds, explore multiple positions, and explore alternative definitions of power. Solsken (1993) also explored the ways middle class five- and six-year-olds' orientations toward literacy were framed by gender and class relations in their families and the larger society. She found that boys' and girls' literacy biographies were impacted by societal ideologies about gender, especially the division of labour in the middle class homes where mothers took major responsibility for supporting children's literacy learning.

Overall, defining authoring as social practice challenges the autonomous model of literacy, as outlined by Street (1995), that is implicit in cognitive and sociocognitive research on young children's writing. Authoring is neither generic nor politically neutral. Children learn situated ways of making meaning with print that vary according to the literacy practices of their communities. When children write, they take up, adapt, or resist positions in existing systems of power relations. Negotiating their places in these cultural systems is a key part of authoring.

EXPANDING THE BOUNDARIES OF AUTHORING: SEMIOTIC PERSPECTIVES

Though discussion of cognitive and cultural aspects has dominated early literacy research, many researchers have commented on children's tendencies to combine writing with other semiotic systems such as talk, drawing, gesture, and dramatic play. As Kress states: 'Multimodality is an absolute fact of children's semiotic practices' (1997: 137). Authoring for young children involves language, vocalization, gesture, gaze, bodily action, and graphic production (Lancaster, 2001). While adults and older children are more likely to have adopted dominant views of writing as separate from other forms of communication, very young children have less cultural experience and so are less constrained by boundaries between sign systems (Kress, 1997). For young children, written language is intimately connected to other sign systems (Dyson, 2001).

The question for researchers is whether young children's multimodal authoring practices should be viewed as immature processes that will one day be replaced by writing-only practices or whether children are, instead, at the beginning of a lifelong process of learning how their communities weave together writing, talk, art, drama, and other sign systems. Both theoretical positions are evident in recent research. As discussed earlier in this chapter, emergent literacy research continues to explore children's abilities to distinguish writing from drawing, and to describe the development of writing along a path where multimodal texts are considered less sophisticated than those that rely only on print. Like other ideological positions, the definition of 'good' authoring as confined to written language is often unexamined even by researchers

who systematically analyse other facets of young children's authoring.

Though many school literacy events privilege authoring practices that isolate print from other sign systems, there are at least two important forces pressing early literacy researchers to broaden the semiotic boundaries for authoring. First, despite school and societal pressures to learn print-only practices, young children's texts and authoring continue to be multimodal (Dyson, 1986; 2001; Harste et al., 1984; Kress, 1997; Newkirk, 1989; Rowe, 1994; Williams, 1999). To limit the focus of research to children's writing is to ignore a large part of young children's meaning making. Secondly, literacy research is being influenced by new technologies that produce adult texts that are increasingly multimodal. Internet websites link print, graphics, video clips, music, animation and more. Even traditional print media such as newspapers and magazines devote an increasing amount of space to photos and graphics, with a resulting decrease in print. In such an environment, young children's penchant for 'symbol weaving' (Dyson, 1986) is increasingly being normalized and valued as part of dominant literacy practices (Harste, 2000; Kress, 1997).

Both classic and more recent studies document children's flexible interweaving of semiotic systems (e.g. Berghoff and Hamilton, 2000; Clyde, 1994; Dyson, 1986; Gallas, 1994; Harste et al., 1984; Hubbard, 1989; Lancaster, 2001; Kress, 1997; Rowe, 1994; Newkirk, 1989; Upitis, 1992). Most often described have been authoring practices that combine writing, art, and oral language (Hubbard, 1989; Newkirk, 1989; Olson, 1992), but researchers have also noted children's connections between writing, music, dance, dramatic play, and drama (Dyson, 1989; Gallas, 1994; Rowe, 1994; Rowe et al., 2001; 2003; Upitis, 1992). They argue that multimodal authoring practices allow children to draw on meanings formed in a variety of sign systems and to gain access to authoring events using non-linguistic forms of communication (Clyde, 1994; Harste, 2000). This appears to be particularly important for beginning writers and those whose strength is not language (Harste, 2000; Rowe et al., 2001).

Several researchers have described transmediation (Siegel, 1995) or transduction (Kress, 1997) as an important part of multimodal authoring activities. Harste (2000) argues that this movement of meanings across sign systems is part of all authoring events. Because there is often no one-to-one match between sign systems, children are encouraged to reflect on both meanings and forms (Siegel, 1995; Dyson, 2000b; Kress, 1997; Rowe et al., 2003).

When researchers broaden the semiotic boundaries of authoring, another outcome is increased attention to the embodied and material nature of authoring practices. For both hearing (Lancaster, 2001) and deaf or hard of hearing (Williams, 1999) preschoolers, authoring involves bodily action. As Williams observes, young children *perform* their early writings with gesture, facial expression, and pantomime. Embodied practices such as gaze and body posture carry important meanings, and are closely monitored by adults who interact with young authors (Lancaster, 2001). Multimodal authoring practices are also strongly influenced by the physical materials that are available in the environment (Dyson, 2000b). As Kress (1997) points out, the materiality of the objects is important in that children are adopting and adapting culturally significant elements of complex signs when they combine paper, writing tools, and objects from their environment, with gesture, talk, and drama.

Overall, it is clear that though young children initially see the boundaries between writing and other sign systems as more permeable than do adults, they quickly begin to explore print-centred views about meaning making. Nevertheless, throughout the early years, children's authoring continues to be multimodal – a characteristic that some researchers consider a strength rather than a weakness. They view authoring as a material and embodied process through which children adapt and transform cultural resources, and which necessarily involves weaving together and moving across a variety of sign systems.

PROVOCATIVE QUESTIONS AND FUTURE DIRECTIONS

Cognitive, cultural and semiotic perspectives provide different answers to questions about the nature of childhood authoring posed at the beginning of the chapter. While these perspectives represent a rough map of new directions surfacing in the field over the last three decades, it should not be assumed that the initial frames have been abandoned. Instead, active research agendas are being pursued in each of these areas.

In general, research on childhood authoring began with attention to young children's unconventional hypotheses about writing. This was followed by interest in the ways children constructed literacy as they interacted with researchers, parents, teachers, and peers. More recently, some researchers have used sociocultural theories to reframe descriptions of authoring in everyday settings as a collective

rather than an individual act. This work has emphasized the situated and ideological nature of children's authoring as they negotiate local definitions of literacy. The semiotic boundaries of childhood authoring are also increasingly of interest, with researchers broadening the definition of authoring to explore children's strategies for creating multimodal texts. Overall, researchers are more frequently adopting multiple foci to look for the mutual shaping of cognitive, social, ideological, and semiotic aspects of authoring (Dyson, 2001) or at least acknowledging the impact of all aspects, even if not all are studied directly.

New theories provoke new kinds of thinking. They also suggest interesting directions for future research. It is clear that both individual and cultural theories make important contributions to our understanding of childhood authoring. Future research would profit from analysing research data from multiple theoretical perspectives. At the same time, researchers should work toward developing multidimensional theoretical frameworks that more powerfully account for both cognitive and cultural aspects of authoring.

Secondly, researchers may want to reconsider intentionality as a necessary condition for defining childhood authoring. If learning to write is co-constructed with others through participation in the social life of the community (Lave and Wenger, 1991), then the beginnings of authoring are likely to precede the young child's individual intention to communicate through print. It is quite possible to imagine a situation in which very young children participate in writing events even before they recognize their social significance. In such a scenario, intention, like other literacy knowledge, should result from participation rather than preceding it, suggesting that we need to study even younger children and their families in order to witness the beginning of authoring.

Thirdly, theoretical perspectives that advance the notion of socially situated literacies expose the tendency of early literacy research to privilege the textual practices of mainstream children and families as 'normal' and marginalize the practices of non-mainstream families by considering these children 'at risk' (Dyson, 2000b). Research describing the diversity of community authoring practices and the relation of those practices to dominant literacies has the potential for opening new dialogues about the richness of non-mainstream practices and the ways that children who adopt them may be differentially positioned in school literacy events.

Finally, if authoring is more broadly defined as making meaning using all available semiotic resources, young children's 'symbol weaving' (Dyson, 1986) becomes a viable focus for investigation and theorizing. Despite the interest of some researchers in multimodal authoring practices, literacy research remains largely print-centred with connections to other sign systems relatively under-developed. Given the changing face of communication technologies, it seems important to describe and nurture children's capacity for multimodal authoring. We may find that, in this area, young authors are leading the way toward twenty-first century literacies.

REFERENCES

Barton, D. and Hamilton, M. (2000) 'Literacy practices', in D. Barton, M. Hamilton and R. Ivanic (eds), *Situated Literacies: Reading and Writing in Context*. London: Routledge. pp. 7–15.

Bear, D. and Templeton, S. (1998) 'Explorations in spelling: foundations for learning and teaching phonics, spelling, and vocabulary', *The Reading Teacher*, 52: 222–42.

Berghoff, B. and Hamilton, S. (2000) 'Inquiry and multiple ways of knowing in a first grade', in B. Berghoff, K. Egawa, J. Harste and B. Hoonan (eds), *Beyond Reading and Writing. Inquiry Curriculum, and Multiple Ways of Knowing*. Urbana, IL: National Council of Teachers of English. pp. 17–38.

Besse, J. (1996) 'An approach to writing in kindergarten', in C. Pontecorvo, M. Orsolini, B. Burge and L. Resnick (eds), *Children's Early Text Construction*. Mahwah, NJ: Erlbaum. pp. 127–44.

Bloodgood, J. (1999) 'What's in a name? Children's name writing and name acquisition', *Reading Research Quarterly*, 34: 342–67.

Branscombe, N.A. and Taylor, J. (1996) 'The development of Scrap's understanding of written language', *Childhood Education*, 72: 278.

Brenneman, K., Massey, C., Machado, S. and Gelman, R. (1996) 'Young children's plans for writing and drawing', *Cognitive Development*, 11: 397–419.

Burns, M.S. and Casbergue, R. (1992) 'Parent–child interaction in a letter-writing context', *Journal of Reading Behavior*, 24: 289–312.

Calkins, L.M. (1994) '*The Art of Teaching Writing*. Portsmouth, NH: Heinemann.

Chapman, M. (1995) 'The sociocognitive construction of written genres in first grade', *Research in the Teaching of English*, 29: 164–92.

Chapman, M. (1996) 'More than spelling: widening the lens on emergent writing', *Reading Horizons*, 36: 317–39.

Clay, M.M. (1975) *What Did I Write?* Auckland: Heinemann.

Clay, M.M. (1991) *Becoming Literate: the Construction of Inner Control*. Portsmouth, NH: Heinemann.

Clyde, J.A. (1994) 'Lessons from Douglas: expanding our visions of what it means to "know"', *Language Arts*, 71: 22–33.

Condon, M. and Clyde, J.A. (1996) 'Co-authoring: composing through conversation', *Language Arts*, 73: 587–96.

Cox, B., Fang, Z. and Otto, B. (1997) 'Preschoolers' developing ownership of the literate register', *Reading Research Quarterly*, 32: 34–53.

DeBaryshe, B., Buell, M. and Binder, J. (1996) 'What a parent brings to the table: young children writing with and without parental assistance', *Journal of Literacy Research*, 28: 71–90.

Diffily, D. (1995) 'Are you a reader? Are you a writer? Answers from kindergarten students', *Reading Horizons*, 36: 23–37.

Donovan, C.A. (2001) 'Children's development and control of written story and informational genres: insights from one elementary school', *Research in the Teaching of English*, 35: 394–447.

Dyson, A.H. (1986) 'Transitions and tensions: interrelationships between drawing, talking, and dictating of young children', *Research in the Teaching of English*, 20: 279–409.

Dyson, A.H. (1989) *Multiple Worlds of Child Writers: Friends Learning to Write*. New York: Teachers College Press.

Dyson, A.H. (1993) *Social Worlds of Children Learning to Write in an Urban Primary School*. New York: Teachers College Press.

Dyson, A.H. (1995) 'The courage to write: child meaning making in a contested world', *Language Arts*, 72: 324–33.

Dyson, A.H. (1997) *Writing Superheroes: Contemporary Childhood, Popular Culture, and Classroom Literacy*. New York: Teachers College Press.

Dyson, A.H. (1998) 'Making sense in children's worlds: the meaning of Tina and the weeping superheroes', in M.E. Graue and D.J. Walsh (eds), *Studying Children in Context: Theories, Methods, and Ethics*. Thousand Oaks, CA: Sage. pp. 192–206.

Dyson, A.H. (2000a) 'Linking writing and community development through the children's forum', In C. Lee and P. Smagorinsky (eds), *Vygotskian Perspectives on Literacy Research*. Cambridge: Cambridge University Press. pp. 127–49.

Dyson, A.H. (2000b) 'On reframing children's worlds: the perils, promises, and pleasures of writing children', *Research in the Teaching of English*, 34: 352–67.

Dyson, A.H. (2001) 'Where are the childhoods in childhood literacy? An exploration of outer (school) space', *Journal of Early Childhood Literacy*, 1: 9–39.

Fang, Z. (1999) 'Expanding the vista of emergent writing research: implications for early childhood educators', *Early Childhood Education Journal*, 26: 179–82.

Ferreiro, E. (1990) 'Literacy development: psychogenesis', in Y. Goodman (ed.), *How Children Construct*

Literacy: Piagetian Perspectives. Newark, DE: International Reading Association. pp. 12–25.

Ferreiro, E. and Teberosky, A. (1982) *Literacy before Schooling.* Portsmouth, NH: Heinemann.

Ferreiro, E., Pontecorvo, C. and Zucchermaglio, C. (1996) 'PIZZA or PIZA? How children interpret the doubling of letters in writing', in C. Pontecorvo, M. Orsolini, B. Burge and L. Resnick (eds), *Children's Early Text Construction.* Mahwah, NJ: Erlbaum. pp. 146–64.

Formisano, M. (1996) 'Literacy in first grade: traditional and experimental situations', in C. Pontecorvo, M. Orsolini, B. Burge and L. Resnick (eds), *Children's Early Text Construction.* Mahwah, NJ: Erlbaum. pp. 287–302.

Freppon, P., McIntyre, E. and Dahl, K. (1995) 'A comparison of young children's writing products in skills-based and whole language classrooms', *Reading Horizons*, 36: 150–65.

Fresch, M.J. (2001) 'Journal entries as a window on spelling knowledge', *The Reading Teacher*, 54: 500–13.

Gallas, K. (1994) *The Languages of Learning: How Children Talk, Write, Dance, Draw, and Sing their Understanding of the World.* New York: Teachers College Press.

Gallas, K. (1998) *'Sometimes I Can Be Anything': Power, Gender, and Identity in a Primary Classroom.* New York: Teachers College Press.

Gee, J. (2001) 'Foreword', in C. Lewis, *Literacy Practices as Social Acts.* Mahwah, NJ: Erlbaum. pp. xv–xix.

Gentry, J.R. (2000) 'A retrospective on invented spelling and a look forward', *The Reading Teacher*, 54: 318–32.

Goodman, Y. (1980) 'The roots of literacy', in M.P. Douglas (ed.), *Claremont Reading Conference, 44th Yearbook.* Claremont, CA: Claremont Colleges. pp. 1–32.

Goodman, Y. (1986) 'Children coming to know literacy', in W. Teale and E. Sulzby (eds), *Emergent Literacy.* Norwood, NJ: Ablex. pp. 1–14.

Goodman, Y. (1990) 'Discovering children's inventions of written language', in Y. Goodman (ed.), *How Children Construct Literacy: Piagetian Perspectives* Newark, DE: International Reading Association. pp. 1–11.

Graves, D. (1994) *A Fresh Look at Writing.* Portsmouth, NH: Heinemann.

Gregory, E. (2001) 'Sisters and brothers as language and literacy teachers: synergy between siblings playing and working together', *Journal of Early Childhood Literacy*, 1: 301–22.

Grossi, E. (1990) 'Applying psychogenesis principles to the literacy instruction of lower-class children in Brazil', in Y. Goodman (ed.), *How Children Construct Literacy: Piagetian Perspectives.* Newark, DE: International Reading Association. pp. 99–114.

Hall, N. (1989) 'Introduction', in N. Hall (ed.), *Writing with Reason: the Emergence of Authorship in Young Children.* Portsmouth, NH: Heinemann. pp. viii–xvi.

Harste, J. (2000) 'Six points of departure', in B. Berghoff, K. Egawa, J. Harste and B. Hoonan (eds), *Beyond Reading and Writing: Inquiry Curriculum, and Multiple Ways of Knowing.* Urbana, IL: National Council of Teachers of English. pp. 1–16.

Harste, J., Woodward, V. and Burke, C. (1984) *Language Stories and Literacy Lessons.* Portsmouth, NH: Heinemann.

Heath, S.B. (1983) *Ways with Words: Language, Life, and Work in Communities and Classrooms.* Cambridge: Cambridge University Press.

Heath, S.B. (1991) 'The sense of being literate: historical and cross-cultural features', in R. Barr, M. Kamil, P. Mosenthal and P. D. Pearson (eds), *Handbook of Reading Research*, vol II. New York: Longman. pp. 3–25.

Henderson, E. and Beers, J. (eds) (1980) *Developmental and Cognitive Aspects of Learning to Spell: a reflection of Word Knowledge.* Newark, DE: International Reading Association.

Henkin, R. (1998) *Who's Invited to Share? Using Literacy to Teach for Equity and Social Justice.* Portsmouth, NH: Heinemann.

Hubbard, R. (1989) *Authors of Pictures, Draughtsmen of Words.* Portsmouth, NH: Heinemann.

Hughes, M. and Searle, D. (1991) 'A longitudinal study of the growth of spelling abilities within the context of the development of literacy', in J. Zutell, S. McCormick, L. Caton and P. O'Keefe (eds), *Learner Factors/ Teacher Factors: Issues in Literacy Research and Instruction.* Fortieth Yearbook of the National Reading Conference. Chicago: National Reading Conference. pp. 159–68.

Kamberelis, G. and Bovino, T. (1999) 'Cultural artifacts as scaffolds for genre development', *Reading Research Quarterly*, 34: 138–70.

Kamii, C., Long, R. and Manning, M. (2001) 'Kindergartners' development toward "invented" spelling and a glottographic theory', *Linguistics and Education*, 12: 195–210.

Kantor, R., Miller, S. and Fernie, D. (1992) 'Diverse paths to literacy in a preschool classroom: a sociocultural perspective', *Reading Research Quarterly*, 27: 185–201.

Korkeamaki, R. and Dreher, M.J. (2000) 'Finnish kindergartners' literacy development in contextualized literacy episodes: a focus on spelling', *Journal of Literacy Research*, 32: 349–94.

Kress, G. (1994) *Learning to Write*, 2nd edn. London: Routledge.

Kress, G. (1997) *Before Writing: Rethinking Paths to Literacy.* London: Routledge.

Labbo, L. (1996) 'Beyond storytime: a sociopsychological perspective on young children's opportunities for literacy development during story extension time', *Journal of Literacy Research*, 28: 405–28.

Lancaster, L. (2001) 'Staring at the page: the functions of gaze in a young child's interpretation of symbolic forms', *Journal of Early Childhood Literacy*, 1: 131–52.

Landsmann, L. (1996) 'Three accounts of literacy and the role of the environment', in C. Pontecorvo, M. Orsolini, B. Burge and L. Resnick (eds), *Children's Early Text Construction*. Mahwah, NJ: Erlbaum. pp. 101–26.

Larson, J. (1995) 'Talk matters: the role of pivot in the distribution of literacy knowledge among novice writers', *Linguistics and Education*, 7: 277–302.

Larson, J. (1999) 'Analyzing participation frameworks in a kindergarten writing activity: the role of overhearer in learning to write', *Written Communication*, 16: 225–57.

Larson, J. (2000) 'Co-authoring classroom texts: shifting participant roles in writing activity', *Research in the Teaching of English*, 34: 468–97.

Lave, J. and Wenger, E. (1991) *Situated Learning: Legitimate Peripheral Participation*. Cambridge: Cambridge University Press.

Lemke, J. (1995) *Textual Politics: Discourse and Social Dynamics*. London: Taylor and Francis.

Lysaker, J. (2000) 'Beyond words: the relational dimensions of learning to read and write', *Language Arts*, 77: 479–84.

MacGillivray, L. and Martinez, A.M. (1998) 'Princesses who commit suicide: primary children writing within and against gender stereotypes', *Journal of Literacy Research*, 30: 53–84.

Manyak, P. (2001) 'Participation, hybridity, and carnival: a situated analysis of a dynamic literacy practice in a primary-grade English immersion class', *Journal of Literacy Research*, 33: 423–65.

Mayer, C. and Moskos, E. (1998) 'Deaf children learning to spell', *Research in the Teaching of English*, 33: 158–80.

Newkirk, T. (1989) *More than Stories: the range of Children's Writing*. Portsmouth, NH: Heinemann.

Olson, J.L. (1992) *Envisioning Writing: Toward an Integration of Drawing and Writing*. Portsmouth, NH: Heinemann.

Olson, K. and Sulzby, E. (1991) 'The computer as a social/physical environment in emergent literacy', in J. Zutell, S. McCormick, L. Caton and P. O'Keefe (eds), *Learner Factors/Teacher Factors: Issues in Literacy Research and Instruction*. Fortieth Yearbook of the National Reading Conference. Chicago: National Reading Conference. pp. 111–18.

Piaget, J. (1976) *The Grasp of Consciousness: Action and Concept in the Young Child*. Cambridge, MA: Harvard University Press.

Power, B.M. (1991) 'Pop-ups: the rise and fall of one convention in a first grade writing workshop', *Journal of Research in Childhood Education*, 6: 54–65.

Read, C. (1971) 'Preschool children's knowledge of English phonology', *Harvard Educational Review*, 41: 1–34.

Rowe, D.W. (1994) *Preschoolers as Authors: Literacy Learning in the Social World of the Classroom*. Cresskill, NJ: Hampton Press.

Rowe, D.W., Fitch, J.F. and Bass, A. (2001) 'Power, identity, and instructional stance in the writers' workshop', *Language Arts*, 78: 426–34.

Rowe, D.W. Fitch, J.F. and Bass, A. (2003) 'Toy stories as opportunities for reflection in writers' workshop', *Language Arts*, 80: 363–74.

Santa Barbara Discourse Group (1992) 'Do you see what we see? The referential and intertextual nature of classroom life', *Journal of Classroom Interaction*, 27: 29–36.

Schickedanz, J. (1990) *Adam's Righting Revolutions: One Child's Literacy Development from Infancy through Grade One*. Portsmouth, NH: Heinemann.

Sheridan, D., Street, B. and Bloome, D. (2000) *Writing Ourselves: Mass Observations and Literacy Practices*. Cresskill, NJ: Hampton.

Short, K., Harste, J. and Burke, C. (1996) *Creating Classrooms for Authors and Inquirers*, 2nd edn. Portsmouth, NH: Heinemann.

Siegel, M. (1995) 'More than words: the generative power of transmediation for learning', *Canadian Journal of Education*, 20: 455–75.

Sipe, L. (1998) 'Transitions to the conventional: an examination of a first grader's composing process', *Journal of Literacy Research*, 30: 357–88.

Solsken, J. (1993) *Literacy, Gender, and Work in Families and in School*. Norwood, NJ: Ablex.

Street, B. (1995) *Social Literacies: Critical Approaches to Literacy in Development, Ethnography, and Education*. London: Longman.

Sulzby, E. (1989) 'Assessment of writing and of children's language while writing', in L. Morrow and J. Smith (eds), *The Role of Assessment and Measurement in Early Literacy Instruction*. Englewood Cliffs, NJ: Prentice-Hall. pp. 83–109.

Sulzby, E. (1991) 'The development of the young child and the emergence of literacy', in J. Flood, J. Jensen, D. Lapp and J. Squire (eds), *Handbook of Research on Teaching the English Language Arts*. New York: Macmillan. pp. 273–85.

Sulzby, E. (1996) 'Roles of oral and written language as children approach conventional literacy', in C. Pontecorvo, M. Orsolini, B. Burge and L. Resnick (eds), *Children's Early Text Construction*. Mahwah, NJ: Erlbaum. pp. 25–46.

Sulzby, E. and Teale, W. (1991) 'Emergent literacy', in R. Barr, M. Kamil, P. Mosenthal and P.D. Pearson (eds), *Handbook of Reading Research*, vol II. New York: Longman. pp. 727–58.

Teale, W. and Sulzby, E. (1986) 'Introduction: emergent literacy as a perspective for examining how young children become writers and readers', in W. Teale and E. Sulzby (eds), *Emergent Literacy*. Norwood, NJ: Ablex. pp. vii–xxv.

Troyer, C. (1991) 'From emergent literacy to emergent pedagogy: learning from children learning together', in J. Zutell, S. McCormick, L. Caton and P. O'Keefe (eds), *Learner Factors/Teacher Factors: Issues in Literacy Research and Instruction*. Fortieth Yearbook of the National Reading Conference. Chicago: National Reading Conference. pp. 119–26.

Upitis, R. (1992) *Can I Play You My Song? The Compositions and Invented Notations of Children*. Portsmouth, NH: Heinemann.

Vygotsky, L. (1978) *Mind in Society*. Cambridge, MA: Harvard University Press.

Wenger, E. (1998) *Communities of Practice: Learning, Meaning, and Identity*. Cambridge: Cambridge University Press.

Williams, C.L. (1999) 'Preschool deaf children's use of signed language during writing events', *Journal of Literacy Research*, 31: 183–212.

Wollman-Bonilla, J.E. (2000) 'Teaching science writing to first graders: genre learning and recontextualization', *Research in the Teaching of English*, 35: 35–65.

Wollman-Bonilla, J.E. (2001a) 'Can first-grade writers demonstrate audience awareness?', *Reading Research Quarterly*, 36: 184–201.

Wollman-Bonilla, J.E. (2001b) 'Family involvement in early writing instruction', *Journal of Early Childhood Literacy*, 1: 167–92.

Yaden, D., Rowe, D. and MacGillivray, L. (2000) 'Emergent literacy: a matter (polyphony) of perspectives', in M. Kamil, P. Mosenthal, P.D. Pearson and R. Barr (eds), *Handbook of Reading Research*, vol. III. Mahwah, NJ: Erlbaum. pp. 245–54.

Zecker, L.B. (1999) 'Different texts, different emergent writing forms', *Language Arts*, 76: 483–90.

Zucchermaglio, C. and Scheuer, N. (1996) 'Children dictating a story: is together better?', in C. Pontecorvo, M. Orsolini, B. Burge and L. Resnick (eds), *Children's Early Text Construction*. Mahwah, NJ: Erlbaum. pp. 83–98.

23

The Development of Spelling

PATRICIA L. SCHARER AND JERRY ZUTELL

In *The Barnhart Dictionary of Etymology* (Barnhart, 1988), the verb *to spell* is defined first as to 'name the letters of'. Along with the related noun form *spell*, meaning 'words supposed to have magical powers, incantation, charm', *to spell* is related to an older root, 'in part probably developed from Old English *spellian* to tell, declare, relate, speak' (1988: 1044) and occurs in compound form in *Gospel*, the 'good story' of Christ's life on earth. Spelling is clearly an important aspect of effective written communication, of our ability to tell our stories well. (Ironically, given the definition of the noun form, English spelling often also has the reputation of being mysterious and/or mystifying. Good spellers may be considered *charmed* in their ability to master the system, though the system itself is rarely thought of as *charming*!)

The perspective guiding this chapter is that spelling represents the development of the child's gradual understanding and control over a complex system, universal in its general structure but also very specific to the child's spoken and written language environment. Understanding how children go about figuring out the specific characteristics of their language system as readers and writers can provide insights into their sociocognitive processes, their literacy development, and the ways they learn over time in response to their instructional contexts. Exploring the relationships between reading, writing, and spelling is a significant part of literacy scholarship. Further, spelling can have a permanence that contrasts with the transience of the reading event. The speller reveals his understanding and mastery of the language's writing system through both correct and approximate attempts. Thus, spelling has been perceived as an important indicator of literacy competence and a record of school performance that is available for both examination and criticism by parents and the general public as well as by educators.

This chapter will review research and scholarship about how young children up to the age of eight unravel some of the mysteries of how their language is represented in print. Specifically, we will deal with how words are represented through spelling systems and how students understand this relationship as manifested in their writing and spelling attempts and the change in those attempts over time. The chapter will be organized into five sections. The first section will provide an introductory discussion of how writing systems map spoken language to written forms. The second section will deal with how young children acquire basic and broad concepts about the relationship between written and spoken language. Then we will review research on learning to spell as a developmental process as well as discuss differing perspectives and critiques of stage theories. The fourth section will address significant issues including the debate surrounding invented (temporary) spellings and recent approaches to assessment and instruction. A concluding section offers future directions.

HISTORY AND THE NATURE OF WRITING SYSTEMS

Before exploring how children gain control of their spelling system, it is important to review some basic principles about the nature of writing systems and how orthographies represent linguistic units in print. Coulmas asserts that 'a conventional relation between graphical sign and linguistic unit is crucial for writing' (1989: 27). He defines the process by which graphical signs with concrete references came to be associated with linguistic signs for those objects as 'phonetization' (1989: 26). Once the primary value of the written sign became a sound it was transformed from icon to symbol. Young children must come to understand this essential characteristic.

Each language uses a particular system for mapping pronunciations of significant units to a system of written symbols. *In theory*, writing systems can be divided into two general classes: (1) those whose symbols represent units of sound, which combine to form pronunciations of linguistic units, and (2) those whose symbols cue meanings, which are then mapped to particular pronunciations. The first class can be further divided into alphabetic systems, which map symbols to sounds at the phonemic level, and syllabic systems in which each symbol represents a spoken syllable. Examples of alphabetic systems include most Western European systems, e.g. English, French, Spanish. Korean Han'gul is an often-cited example of a syllabic system, and Chinese of a meaning-based system. Alphabetic systems have the advantage of using a small number of symbols to represent a very large number of pronunciations, but at the cost of a high level of abstractness. The Chinese system is said to be less abstract, but requires the learning of a large number of distinct characters. Syllabic systems fall between these extremes.

In reality, well-developed systems tend to be multilayered in representing relationships, with trade-offs between the demands of sound, visual pattern, meaning, and historical influences. Letter combinations represent meanings as well as sounds, and spellings sometimes preserve meanings when variations in pronunciations are predictable from the phonological context. For example, the English morpheme **s**, meaning plural, is spelled the same in **cats** and **ribs** though the pronunciation is /s/ in the first word and /z/ in the second. A further consideration is that the development of most writing systems has been greatly affected by historical, social, and political factors along with linguistic ones. Once writing systems were initially established for a language, both the oral language and the written language evolved over time somewhat independently but also in connection with each other. These developmental changes have had a direct impact on the relationship between spellings and pronunciations. In some cases, a relatively slow rate of orthographic change (once print had been relatively standardized) has interacted with a greater change in pronunciation over time and place to add considerable complexity to the relationship between spelling and sound.

English is a particularly noteworthy example in this respect. (See Henderson, 1990, and Venezky, 1999, for fuller historical treatments.) While English began as a Germanic language, and is typically categorized as such, the Norman Conquest led to the eventual blending of Anglo-Saxon and Norman French into a new language. Many new spelling conventions were adopted from French as well; other changes are believed to have been made by scribes in order to make handwriting clearer, sometimes at the expense of phonological accuracy. For example, the replacement of **u** by **o** in **ton** and **woman** was supposedly motivated by the desire to break the confusion of a succession of a large number of vertical strokes (Venezky, 1999). As the need to represent new ideas increased, Latin and Greek elements (prefixes, roots, and suffixes) were used to build new word forms. The sound–letter relationships in such multisyllabic words are further complicated by the English pattern of distributing stress unequally across syllables depending on the number of syllables per word, as in the following set of words from the same root: **oppose**, **opposite**, and **opposition**. In such cases, spelling tends to preserve and make visible connections that may not be as apparent in pronunciation.

During the Age of Discovery, contact with new peoples and other European languages in new environments led to a large number of adoptions and adaptations of foreign words that did not always correspond to typical English letter–sound relationships. Contrast, for example, the borrowings of **vanilla** and **tortilla** from Spanish. Note, too, the various pronunciations of **ch** in **child** (Anglo-Saxon), **chef** (French) and **chorus** (Greek) but the /ch/ sound in **cello** (Italian). The spread of English-speaking peoples to new parts of the word and the military, political, and commercial prominence of British and later American institutions and culture have led to the development of varieties of English across the globe.

The result is a set of orthographies in which contentions between phonetic, visual, semantic, and etymological demands are resolved at the expense of simple, straightforward, sound–letter relationships (Cummings, 1988). It would seem that the demands of such a system on a beginning learner would be higher than on those learning one with simpler, more phonetically transparent and regular relationships.

Similarly, though the Chinese system has often been simplistically described as logographic, the vast majority of Chinese characters are compounds with both meaning and phonetic elements that combine to specify a distinct morphemic-syllabic unit. A compound Chinese character consists of two elements: a classifier that conveys something about the meaning of the overall character, and a phonetic element that provides information about its pronunciation. Coulmas gives the example of the phonetic element, pronounced *tang*, which, when combined with the classifier for water, yields the compound character meaning 'pond' (1989: 101).

However, an important difference between Chinese and alphabetic systems is that in Chinese the phonetic and meaning elements occur in *separate parts* of the character. In alphabetic and syllabic systems the meaning and pronunciation are conveyed simultaneously by the combination of symbols. The English spelling **m-a-n** cannot be broken into distinct parts representing the pronunciation on the one hand, and the meaning (adult masculine human) on the other. Further, the phonetic element in the Chinese character cannot be parsed into subunits that map to individual phonemes in the character's pronunciation, which is the basis of alphabetic systems. Thus, while both kinds of systems provide information about sound and sense, they do so in very different ways. Some scholars hypothesize that such differences in how information is presented may lead to differences in how it is processed. For example, preliminary findings suggest that Chinese readers attend to phonetic information later during word reading processes than do readers of alphabetic scripts (Ju and Jackson, 1995).

HOW CHILDREN ACQUIRE EARLY WRITTEN LANGUAGE UNDERSTANDINGS

The brief analysis above points to the complexity of the task children face as they learn about their writing system and its unique characteristics. Researchers studying preschool children for the past 30 years have sought to document, describe, and analyse the processes through which children become conventional spellers. The distinction made by Coulmas (1989) between three tiers (writing system, script, and orthography) is a useful way to consider the levels of understanding required for children to become conventional spellers. At one level, learners must grasp the general principles underlying a writing system as it relates to oral language (e.g. consistency in directionality). At another, they must become familiar with the features of the specific kind of script (e.g. letters or characters) that accompanies the language they speak. In addition, they must master the specific rules and patterns of that orthography, in terms both of internal visual rules and of how pronunciations and meanings of oral linguistic units are mapped to

particular written forms. To illustrate, though English has 26 letters in its alphabet, not all letters are used in the same way orthographically; for example, English words never start with **ck** or end with a **q**. Furthermore, English in the US and English in the UK have varying spelling patterns (such as **theater/theatre** or **honor/honour**).

Given these layers of understandings, it is no small task for children to learn the complexities of their writing system and its accompanying script and orthography. This includes learning many aspects of how print 'works' in their language. Children must learn that written symbols are different from objects or pictures, that there are specific features of their script, that the writing system has a consistency, and also that there are complex characteristics of the writing system such as directionality and concept of word.

In this section we argue that although these aspects are often individually described in developmental ways based upon studies of children of various ages, there is also reciprocity between these understandings such that what children learn about one may support the development of a more complex understanding of another. Sulzby writes that 'each child acquires the abilities to read and to write within a culture in which both oral and written language are being acquired simultaneously, and that the two together comprise "language" ' (1996: 28). Goswami (1992) argues that children's emerging knowledges of phonological and orthographic concepts interact, each refining the other as the child's understanding becomes more complete. Because of the literate nature of our society, children experience both print and oral language simultaneously as they begin to understand how language carries messages and also the specific characteristics and organization of the script that they see around them.

Thus, learning to spell must be discussed within the context of learning not merely the relationship between symbols and sounds but also how symbols map on to language in a manner that begins with approximations and moves to conventions. Goswami's (1992; 1994; 2001) work on children's phonological awareness focuses on the relationships between learning about print and the oral aspects of language including children's abilities to recognize, categorize, and manipulate spoken language in the absence of print. This work emphasizes that children's phonological awareness, as well as their understandings of the match between written and spoken forms, is in the process of development. Students' abilities to represent spoken language will be affected by their current phonological understandings. For example, in a recent review of the research on early phonological development, Goswami (2001) suggests that there is a developmental progression from phonological awareness of larger to smaller units. Her findings suggest that (1) syllables are natural units of analysis for English speakers; (2) onsets and rimes are particularly salient for young learners as their phonology becomes more segmented; (3) children are able to use onset and rime as the basis for analogy at a young age; (4) phonological awareness of onset and rime predicts later success in reading and spelling; and (5) phonemic awareness develops through instruction in alphabetic orthography. At the beginning stages of language development, phonological processing is, for the most part, holistic. As vocabularies expand

> there is considerable developmental pressure to represent these words in the brain in a way that will distinguish them from other words and allow the child to recognize them accurately and quickly during speech comprehension ... To distinguish between these similarly sounding words both quickly and accurately, child linguists argue that children must begin to represent the sequences of sounds that constitute each known word in their brains. They must represent the 'segmental phonology' of the words they know. (2001: 113)

From another perspective, children must understand the concepts relative to wordness in both oral and written contexts. The concept of word operates primarily in literate societies and, in some ways, is defined by the writing system (Coulmas, 1989). For adults, the definition of a spoken word may seem simple; but, for children, it is an understanding that takes many years of experiences with oral and written language to refine. Papandropoulou and Sinclair (1974) approached their study of young children (ages four to 10) with a Piagetian lens and found that the youngest children did not differentiate between words and things; they typically described words as either objects or actions (**strawberry** is a word because it grows in the garden or **pencil** is a word because it writes). For these children, the length of the word was relative to the size or location of the object (**train** is a long word because it goes and goes). Later, between the ages of five and seven, children described words as 'what you use to say about something' (1974: 244) but limited this definition to comments (proposing full sentences as words) or labels of objects, explaining that **the** is not a word because you need something else like **the truck** to be a word. By the ages of six to eight, however, words are seen as part of a larger more meaningful expression (bits of a story). This development of a concept of word is both gradual and complex: 'Gradually words become detached from the objects and events they refer to, and it is only fairly late in cognitive development that they are regarded as meaningful

elements inside a systematic frame of linguistic representation' (1974: 249).

Clay also describes children's simultaneous learning across various aspects of written language, arguing that 'The individual child's progress in mastering the complexity of the writing system seems to involve letters, words, and word groups all at the one time, at first in approximate, specific and what seem to be primitive ways and later with considerable skill' (1975: 19). Children begin to learn the general characteristics of the script accompanying their writing system as they begin to draw, scribble, or write mock letters loosely reflecting conventional print. For Portecorvo and Orsolini, the distinction between drawing and writing is the first phase of writing development followed by a time when 'children explore the graphic and syntactical regularities of the notation system' (1996: 15). In a manner that parallels the drawings of the cave dwellers, pictures carry the meanings of young children who, when asked to look at the story, may attend only to the picture (Clay, 1975). Pictures are broad and interpretive; but the symbols children must learn representing spoken language units are narrow and specific.

Harste et al. (1982) asked four-year-old children from a variety of international backgrounds to write everything they could write. Children's writing samples were clearly influenced by their environments, as the English-speaking child wrote in cursive-like scribbles; the Israeli child's sample looked much like the Hebrew alphabet; and the Arab child pointed out that the researchers wouldn't be able to read her sample since Arabic has more dots than English. None of these children wrote a recognizable word or could read their message, yet their samples reflected an initial understanding of the nature of three different orthographies. Harste and his colleagues argued that these children were creating hypotheses about how written language works that were constantly being challenged and revised as they learned more and more about 'how the grapho-phonemic, syntactic, and semantic systems of language operate in relation to one another and in relation to those things known about the world' (1982: 65).

As children learn the specific visual qualities of the system, their attempts reveal an element of experimentation as they explore the various ways to make letter forms. They often repeat pictures, letter-like shapes, or individual words to make longer messages, a phenomenon that Clay (1975) calls the 'recurring principle'. Children often learn the letters of their names first; these letters are a key feature of later writings. According to Ferreiro and Teberosky, a child's name is tremendously important and 'in many cases, the child's own name functions as the first stable form endowed with meaning' (1982: 213). It is this meaning that anchors the child's understanding that a specific written form consistently represents a particular meaning, a concept critical to further development. As children gain control over their name, they may repeat one or more letters of their name reorganized into a new pattern, employing what Clay calls the 'generating principle' to create messages with more complex letter arrangements. A longitudinal case study by Martens (1999) documented the importance of learning to write her name in one child's literacy development from ages two to five. Similarly, extensive use of letters found in children's names was documented in Bloodgood's (1999) research, as data analysis revealed that the letters in children's names accounted for nearly half of the random letter writing done by four- and five-year-old children as they used the same letters over and over to write their messages.

As children become more familiar with letter forms and their names, they also begin to develop hypotheses about how these forms are linked to sounds in the stream of speech, to oral words. Kamii and Manning (1999) reviewed findings in this area, beginning with Ferreiro and her colleagues' delineation of four levels of writing revealed when analysing children's spellings in Spanish: (1) letter strings, made up of similar letters, but of different lengths (see discussion of Clay's work, above); (2) letter strings with a fairly fixed range of length, with more letter-like forms included and some differentiation of letters used and/or their order to indicate word differences; (3) use of one character per syllable, but usually no phonetic connection between the letter and the sounds in the syllable (though, within this level, some children begin to use a vowel for each syllable); and (4) evidence of considerable knowledge of grapho–phono correspondences. Kamii et al. (1990) found that English-speaking children generally followed the same levels as the Spanish-speaking children in the Ferreiro studies, with some important differences. At the third level, Spanish-speaking children focus on syllables, using a vowel for each; English-speaking children at this level focus on consonants. They suggest that these differences are likely due to differences in the phonologies of the two languages. In a follow-up study, Kamii and Manning (1999) asked students to write related word pairs in which one word had more syllables than the other (e.g. **ham/hamster**). They found that some students at the second level began to differentiate between the two words by using longer strings for the words with more syllables, though the letters might be totally different. Other students within this level used the same letters for similar parts in the

words, though still using letter strings without grapho–phono correspondences. So, while children's writings may appear somewhat random to adults, closer analysis reveals a developing system of organization and relationships even at this early stage.

While children are developing a conceptual understanding about spoken words as abstract or arbitrary labels distinct from the objects themselves, basic regularities inherent in print, and general features particular to their own scripts, they are also beginning to make links between oral and written words in more systematic ways. Morris (1993) considers the ability to match spoken words in reading with written words in text as a crucial event in learning to read and write. In his year-long study of emergent readers in three kindergarten classrooms, he documented the pivotal nature of this critical element and concluded that beginning consonant knowledge facilitates children's matching of oral and written words, which then further facilitates phonemic segmentation, a skill supporting word recognition. Uhry's (1999) results were consistent with these findings. Hughes and Searle (1991; 1997) also found that to 'develop as fully phonemic spellers, the children had to establish a stable voice-print match, demonstrated by pointing accurately to words as they read memorized text' (1991: 167).

Such connections between reading and spelling reflect fairly recent lines of research. For most of the twentieth century, scholars and educators focused on the differences in spelling and reading rather than the connections between them. This focus was reflected in the clear separation between reading/phonics instruction and spelling practice, often done at very different parts of day with separate, unconnected instructional materials used for each (Read and Hodges, 1982). More recently, research and scholarship have focused on the important similarities and connections between the word processing required for reading and spelling. Frith (1985) proposed a model in which 'phonemic awareness in reading develops as a consequence of spelling experience' (Goswami, 1994: 292). In fact, Morris and Perney (1984) found that a developmental spelling measure administered at the beginning and middle of first grade (ages six to seven years) was a strong predictor of sight word acquisition by the end of the year. This finding is not surprising in light of the fact that a considerable body of research has now demonstrated strong positive relationships between phonemic awareness, spelling, and success in learning to read (e.g. Ehri, 1987; Griffith, 1991; Tangel and Blachman, 1992).

Developmentally sensitive measures, like the one Morris used, capture changes in phoneme awareness as children move from *pre-phonetic* to *semi-phonetic* to *letter name* spellings and beyond

(Richgels, 2001). Based on findings from a later study, Morris has proposed an interactive, sequential process of early literacy learning in which knowledge of beginning consonants (as demonstrated by the child's early spelling attempts) provides a textual anchor for examining word form in greater detail. As the ability to match spoken and oral work accurately stabilizes, supportive text provides the opportunity for matching word pronunciations to letter sequences. Phonemic awareness is thus extended and is reflected in more sophisticated invented spellings. Words are initially learned and successfully identified mostly in supportive contexts with partial letter cues (in the pattern of first; first and last; first, last, and middle). As the specifics of the alphabetic principles are internalized, words are more fully processed, and a stable and expanding sight vocabulary gradually emerges (Morris, 1993).

Several other studies suggest that connections between reading and spelling remain strong beyond beginning stages. In a study of children's ability to notice and report letters in reading specially taught words, Invernizzi (1992) found that the ability to recall the presence or absence of specific letters was clearly related to stage of spelling development and dependent on the complexity of the feature to which the letter belonged. For example, spellers at *within-word pattern* and beyond were very good at recalling the presence of e-markers, while letter name spellers only performed at chance on this feature. Bear (1992) compared first-graders' developmental spellings to the fluency of their oral readings and found that spelling measures could account for three-fifths of the variance in reading rate. *Letter name* spellings were significantly and negatively correlated with fluency, while performance on selected *within-word pattern* features was strongly associated with fluency measures. In both cross-sectional and longitudinal studies, Zutell (Zutell, 1992; Zutell and Fresch, 1991; Zutell and Rasinski, 1989) found that reading and developmental spelling measures were highly correlated for third- and fifth-grade students, with factor analysis strongly supporting a single factor solution which Zutell labelled underlying word knowledge.

A significant finding of these lines of research is that children's written productions that may appear random in nature actually reveal complex thinking on several dimensions, indicating that children's initial, inchoate understandings are moving toward increasingly refined hypotheses about orthography even before they make clear letter–sound connections. Such studies begin to describe the complex and inventive nature of the development of print concepts that happen simultaneously, sequentially, and

reciprocally as young children become increasingly proficient with reading and writing tasks.

HOW CHILDREN ACQUIRE PROFICIENCY AS SPELLERS: SPELLING STAGE THEORIES

Current understandings of spelling development, once children grasp the alphabetic principle, are highly indebted to the seminal work of Charles Read (1971; 1975; 1986) and are heavily grounded in his findings and insights. Read's initial study focused on the spelling attempts of preschool children. He discovered that children from different settings and without formal instruction often produced similar misspellings. Most remarkably, his analysis demonstrated that such errors were neither random nor the result of auditory/phonological immaturity or deficit. Many were, in fact, quite logical, given the knowledge base the children were operating with (knowledge of the names of the letters, but little sight word knowledge) and the complex way English spelling maps phonological relationships to print. For example, Read pointed out that the spelling of /dr/ blends with initial **J** or **G** and the spelling of /tr/ blends with initial **H** or **CH** was due not to 'mishearing' or 'mispronunciation' but to the ambiguity created by the fact that the pronunciation of the first element in each is affricated in the environment of the /r/; that is, it shares a feature of articulation with the related sound and the letters associated with it. The first phoneme in **drag** *does* sound like and is articulated like the first phoneme in **jet**. In similar fashion, Read found that children often misspell short vowel sounds in particular ways (for example, **E** for 'short i', as in **SET** for sit, **A** for 'short e' as in **BAG** for **beg**, **I** for 'short o' as in **MIP** for **mop**). Due to vowel shift, a major historical change in the pronunciation of English long vowels, short vowels and long vowels are not paired in spelling as they are in sound. Read argued that children were using a letter name strategy; that is, they were matching the phonemes heard in words with letters whose names also include those phonemes. Since short vowels are not used as the names of letters in English, children classified those sounds as similar to the closest long vowel letter name. The vowel sound in **beg** *is* more similar to the name of the letter **A** than it is to the name of the letter **E**. Thus Read argued that children were not memorizing spellings but constructing or *inventing* their own plausible system based on abstract phonological relationships. They were recognizing relationships that adults had learned to ignore in the course of becoming literate (Read, 1971; 1975).

While Read's initial study was conducted with a limited number of children, the importance of Read's observations and analyses cannot be over-estimated. His later work and that of other spelling scholars confirmed and extended those early findings. As a result of his work, the study of children's spellings gained in respect and attention. Researchers applied his techniques and insights in case studies of young children (e.g. Bissex, 1980; Gentry, 1982) and in studies of children in the early grades of formal instruction, generally confirming, often refining and elaborating on our understandings of children's strategies (Beers and Henderson, 1977; Treiman, 1993).

The late Edmund Henderson had been collecting and categorizing young children's spellings over several years before Read's work was published. He recognized Read's work as the 'Rosetta Stone' of spelling research in that it provided the key to deciphering and understanding the mental processes underlying children's attempts (Henderson and Beers, 1980). Over the last 30 years Henderson, his students and colleagues, and their students and colleagues have pursued a line of research focusing on the developmental and conceptual nature of children's understandings and learning, extending their investigations on the one hand to younger and/or less knowledgeable children, not yet fully using the *letter name* strategies that Read described, and on the other to mature students grappling with the complexities of the derivational and etymological aspects of English orthographies (Henderson and Beers, 1980; Morris, 1989a; 1989b; Templeton and Bear, 1992). They proposed a stage-like quality to spelling development in which attempts change over time, both in terms of how words are misspelled and in terms of which features (e.g. consonant blends, long vowel markers) and word types are spelled correctly. Patterns of development are affected by the child's knowledge base, strategies, and the complexity and familiarity of the features and words under examination (Gentry, 1978; Henderson, 1990; Schlagal, 1992).

Henderson (1990) suggested the following early levels of development. The first is *pre-phonetic*, characterized by letter strings that represent concepts and ideas, but without a discernible match between letters and sounds (see above for a closer analysis of patterns of attempts at this stage). The second is *semi-phonetic*, characterized in the early part by the use of single consonants to represent beginning or particularly salient sounds in the word. Over time children include letters for both beginning and ending sounds, with long vowels generally represented before short ones. The third is *letter name* (now often labelled *phonetic* or *alpha-betic*), characterized by the ability to consistently match first-to-last in spoken words with left-to-right in the written forms, generally representing each phoneme in a word regularly with the logic Read described. It is at this stage that students begin to develop a working sight vocabulary for reading that also supports developing knowledge of and hypotheses about visual and meaning-based features (Ehri, 1992; Morris, 1992). The fourth is *within-word pattern* (also called *transitional*), characterized by correct spelling of well-known words and single consonants and many blend and consonant digraph patterns, and by good control of short vowel patterns. At this stage children begin to include visual features like vowel markers and other silent letter patterns into their spellings, though they may only gradually do so with accuracy on a regular basis. They are also more likely to use analogy strategies as they are able to process letters in 'chunks' rather than individually. Because of the particular complexity of English visual patterns and their relationships to sound and meaning, full control of these elements may require several years of experience and study (see also Goswami, 1994; 1999).

Henderson also suggested two higher-level stages: *syllable juncture*, in which students grapple with patterns for combining syllables, including consonant doubling and e-drop patterns; and *derivational constancy*, in which students deal with the morphological patterns in English multisyllabic words whose pronunciations often obscure the links in meaning and spelling among words in the same root-word families (e.g. **cave**, **cavity**, **excavation**). Recently the distinct and sequential nature of these stages has been called into question (Ehri, 1992: Gentry, 2000), and current descriptions view these as aspects or phases of later development that may parallel and/or overlap with each other and the later part of the within-word pattern stage (Bear et al., 2000). Other scholars have made significant contributions paralleling and complementing this line of research. One area that has received considerable recent attention is children's understanding of morphological markers and their complex representation in oral and written form. As noted above, English orthography tends to preserve the same spelling in such markers when pronunciation changes predictably in different phonological environments. For example, the spellings of **-s, -es** for plural and third-person singular remain stable when the phonological environment requires /s/,/z/ or /^z/ in pronunciation (e.g. **desks**, **swims**, **dresses**). Studies have generally found that young spellers (six to eight years old) become aware of and gain control over this feature relatively early (Beers and Beers, 1992; Read, 1975). In a similar vein, Treiman (e.g. Treiman and Cassar, 1996) has found that in highly focused conditions young children show sensitivity to morphology in their spellings of identical sounds depending on their relationships to morphemic units. For example, nasal omission, a misspelling Read had initially noted, was more likely to occur in **brand** (one morpheme) than in **tuned** (two morphemes with the second phoneme in the final blend functioning as a morpheme).

Bryant et al. (1999) report a detailed three-year study of the acquisition of the past tense morpheme with children who began the study at ages six, seven, and eight. In English, the -**ed** spelling is maintained in regular verbs whether the pronunciation is /t/, /d/, or /^d/ (e.g. **skipp*ed***, **trimm*ed***, **want*ed***). On the other hand, 'strong' or irregular English verbs tend to vary the vowel while maintaining the direct phoneme–grapheme match for the past tense morpheme (e.g. **sleep**, **sl*ept***; **find**, **f*ound***). The situation is further complicated by the fact that the same final consonant blend pronunciations exist in words unrelated to past tense (**soft**, **blind**). Bryant et al.'s findings support a stage model that includes; (1) a *pre-phonetic* stage in which endings are not represented in a consistent way; (2) a *phonetic* stage in which all endings are spelled phonetically, including those for regular past tense verbs; (3) a stage of *generalizations and overgeneralizations* in which the -**ed** ending is applied to both strong verbs (**SLEPED** for **slept)** and single morpheme words (**SOFED** for **soft**); (4) a *generalizations only* stage in which strong verbs may be spelled with -**ed**, but single morpheme words are spelled conventionally; and (5) a *correct* stage in which strong verb endings are again spelled phonetically. They also found that children's movement through the stages is strongly related to their specific sensitivity to grammatical distinctions, as measured by analogy tasks like those developed by Berko-Gleason (1958). As with other studies, these results support a model of learning to spell that goes beyond memorization to include constructive processes in which children use their growing linguistic knowledge to generate hypotheses and refine them over time as their base of knowledge and experience expands.

Criticisms of spelling stage theory, particularly as proposed by Henderson and his colleagues, tend to focus on details of features of a particular stage, labels for the stages, and/or boundaries between stages (e.g. Ehri, 1992; Treiman, 1993). Consequently, researchers continue to explore and refine these concepts. Others have raised questions about the inviolability of the sequential nature of stages and their ability to account for the full range of individual behaviours. On the one hand, the sequence of stages for young children (through

within word pattern**)** have been fairly well established. On the other, Henderson's stage model and that of his colleagues does not assume to explain every spelling that a student might generate. Individual spellings in a given stage will naturally be affected by reading experiences, word familiarity, the spelling situation (for example, writing a story or making a list), instruction, human factors (e.g. weariness, anxiety, inattention) or other situational or individual differences. Rather, the theory suggests broad steps in development justified by the overall character of children's performance.

The knowledge base, concepts, and techniques developed in the spirit of Read's work and developmental perspectives have been extended in two other noteworthy ways. First, differences between normal functioning and low-ability readers/spellers have been re-examined in light of these understandings. Boder (1973) had suggested three categories: *dysphonetic*, *dyseidetic*, and *mixed* spellers. But reanalysis of her findings in light of Read's descriptions of logical spellings called into question the true number of dysphonetic spellings in her data (Henderson, 1992). Further, with the growing recognition of the importance of instructional level in spelling assessment and instruction (Morris et al., 1986; 1995; Schlagal, 1992), recent studies have compared low-functioning spellers at their instructional level with younger spellers at the same level of ability rather than with average spellers in the same grade. Under these conditions, differences between groups are greatly reduced in comparison to earlier studies (Invernizzi and Worthy, 1989). This finding suggests that *delay in learning* and a need for more processing time (Abouzeid, 1992), rather than *differences in processing*, is a more viable explanation of disabled spellers' difficulties. (However, Alegria and Mousty, 1997, contend that there is some evidence to support subtle visual deficits in disabled readers for which the crucial variables have not yet been fully identified.)

Secondly, there is a small but growing body of research on spelling development in languages and scripts other than English. (Though, admittedly, this literature is likely more extensive, as we are limited to reports published in English.) Results of investigations of children's spelling patterns for Spanish (Temple, 1978; Valle-Arroyo, 1990), French (Gill, 1980), Portuguese (Pinheiro, 1995) and Greek (Porpodas, 1989) suggest a movement away from strictly phonetic strategies to increasing use of strategies based on orthographic and morphographemic knowledge. Investigations of children's spellings in Portuguese (Nunes-Carraher, 1985, as reported by Bryant et al., 1999) and in French (Fayol et al., 1999) have found patterns for the development of morphological markers parallel to those found by Bryant et al. (1999) discussed above.

Shen and Bear (2000) examined spelling errors of Chinese students in grades one through six, both in spontaneous writing and on a specially constructed list. They found a gradual increase in graphemically and semantically based errors and a decrease in phonologically based errors as grade level increased, with young children using mostly phonological strategies. However, this finding is somewhat confounded by the fact that in the early grades students are taught Pinyin, a phonetically based system for representing Chinese pronunciations. The overwhelming phonological strategy used in the early grades was to substitute Pinyin symbols for characters. This speaks to the complex relationships between social factors and writing systems and their impact on children's behaviours. Interestingly enough, Shen and Bear note the presence of partial phonetic spellings in the use of Pinyin in the early grades, a phenomenon they believe warrants further investigation.

On the other hand, some studies do suggest clear contrasts with English. As noted above, Ferreiro and Teberosky (1982) found Spanish-speaking children represented vowel elements in their spellings while Kamii et al. (1990) found English-speaking children at about the same stage represent consonants. They attributed this to differences in the phonologies of the language. Yet Wimmer and Landerl (1997) found that first-grade German-speaking children and dyslexic children with two years of instruction did not have the same difficulty with consonant clusters that has often been reported for English-speaking children, although the languages seem to be comparable in this respect. They conclude that the overall consistency of an orthography (German being more consistent than English), combined with an instructional regime focusing on segmentation, may have a profound impact on spelling development, and they caution that teachers and researchers working in more consistent orthographies should not base their theories and choices solely on English findings. It seems, then, that studies of developmental spelling in multiple languages have identified some similar patterns across languages but also unique qualities shaped by the characteristics of each language and, possibly, the circumstances under which they are taught and learned.

To summarize, the contributions of developmental spelling studies and related research are considerable. Such studies have focused attention on the quality of children's spellings, provided teachers and researchers with tools for making sense of student behaviours, and increased our understanding of the conceptual nature of learning to spell in the face of the traditional focus on memorization. In addition, such research has generated approaches to assessment and instruction that respect and build on student knowledge and strategies.

SPELLING INSTRUCTION: FROM MEMORIZATION TO CONCEPTUALIZATION

Early instructional methods for alphabetic systems, dating back to Greco-Roman times, emphasized memorization of letters that were then applied to the spelling and pronunciation of words. This technique was commonly called the ABCDery method (Otto, 1973). Early American spelling instruction emphasized lengthy recitations and memorization; spelling research focused on the identification of practice and study techniques for learning letter combinations and words. This perspective was motivated by a characterization of English spelling as highly irregular and by a behaviourist, stimulus–response view of the learning process (Templeton and Morris, 2000).

At the beginning of the twentieth century, however, research shifted to analysing the characteristics of words relative to their spelling difficulty, resulting in 'demon' lists of challenging words. Teachers were encouraged to help students learn these words by visualizing (Lee and Lee, 1941) and taking tests leading to mastery. Research focused on developing frequency counts of words in reading and writing (high-frequency words as deserving the most attention), tracking student errors in terms of control of letter–sound matches, and discovering effective practice techniques and time plans to enhance memorization. High-frequency words were taught by having children copy sentences with words commonly used in children's writing and complete dictation exercises in hopes that children would become accustomed to spelling correctly (Scharer, 1992).

By the middle of the twentieth century, grade-level consumable spelling books were a common mode of formal spelling instruction requiring that young children cycle through a different set of words each week by completing various workbook exercises culminating in a final test on Friday. These materials, however, were criticized because students were often required to study words they already knew or were too difficult for them to learn developmentally, and the activities did not help children to learn orthographic patterns or to transfer spelling lessons to their writing (Gill and Scharer, 1996; Zutell, 1994).

More recently, two lines of research have significantly influenced early spelling instruction. First, research has begun to document a positive correlation between a young child's ability to perform tasks of phonological awareness (an awareness of aspects of spoken language such as syllables, rhymes, and individual phonemes), phonemic awareness (a conscious awareness that words are made up of phonemes that can be both isolated and manipulated), and later achievement in both reading and spelling (Adams, 1990; Ball and Blachman, 1991; Ehri, 1980; Goswami, 1999; Griffith, 1991; National Reading Panel, 2000; Richgels, 2001). For example, as reported in Goswami (1999), Bradley and Bryant (1983) studied the impact of phonological training on children (ages four to five) with poor phonological awareness. Two years of training for the experimental group focused on onset and rime through picture sorts of rhyming words and manipulation of plastic alphabet letters to create new rhyming words. One control group was taught semantic classification; the other was unseen. After training, children in the experimental group were eight months ahead of the semantic classification group in reading and a full year ahead in spelling; experimental scores were one year ahead of the unseen control group in reading and two years ahead in spelling.

Further, based upon their meta-analysis, the US National Reading Panel (2000) concluded that phonemic awareness training interventions of 20 hours or less supported kindergarten children as spellers. But, while promising, this analysis was unable to determine specific teaching techniques that were most effective and engaging for both teachers and students or to document positive effects for disabled spellers. Recommendations regarding instruction are further complicated by studies documenting the reciprocity between the development of phonological and phonemic awareness and learning to read and write (Adams, 1990; Goswami, 2001; Silva and Alves-Martins, 2002). Silva and Alves-Martins (2002) found that *either* two weeks of phonological awareness training *or* guided discussions of children's invented spellings enabled young children to move from presyllabic writing to syllabic writing.

While specific training interventions appear successful, McGee and Richgels write with concern that recommendations for phonological or phonemic awareness training in classroom contexts may result in scripted programmes 'so divorced from actually reading and writing of authentic texts for real purposes as to be counterproductive for those students who already have phonemic awareness, or are on their way to acquiring it in other, more functional and contextualized ways' (2000: 212). Consequently, educators are challenged to determine an appropriate curricular sequence, emphasis,

and instructional balance between attention to phonological awareness, phonemic awareness, reading instruction, and writing instruction to support children's literacy development.

A second influential line of research is the three decades of developmental spelling studies, which have also led to innovative ideas about instruction. The issue of correctness in writing, for example, takes on a new perspective as invented spellings are viewed as windows into a child's thought processes, and assessment targets children's developmental stages in ways that can effectively influence instruction (Richgels, 2001). Looking at each child developmentally calls into question practices of having the same grade-level curriculum for every child in the class in favour of providing instruction based upon the needs of groups and individuals. In a year-long study using spelling materials matching students' developmental levels, Morris and his colleagues (1995) found that low-achieving students using materials at the appropriate level scored higher then low spellers taught with more difficult materials. Thus, developmental research calls for teachers to identify students' appropriate levels and plan instruction to meet those needs. This instruction places new demands upon teachers' expertise when compared to whole class instruction using published spelling programmes (basals). Both of these issues – invented spelling and meeting the needs of individuals as spellers – are addressed below.

Invented spelling

Although issues relative to invented spelling often focus on the early years of school, spellers of all ages use invented spelling any time they approximate an unknown word. For young children 50 years ago, writing meant copying sentences and independent writing was not encouraged until children's conventional spellings matched the messages they wrote to ensure accuracy. More recently, however, instructional recommendations have focused on encouraging young children to create and write messages using the knowledge they have of the system, no matter how incomplete. Consequently, preschool and kindergarten children find writing materials in play centres (Morrow, 1990), opportunities for journal writing, and teachers who encourage and celebrate their early writing attempts.

Concerns that children will not learn conventional spellings if allowed to write words unconventionally have been countered with arguments describing the advantages of encouraging young children to see themselves as writers and write stories and messages each day (Clarke, 1988; Morris, 1981; Read, 1986). Adams' review of research, for example, concluded that:

> the process of inventing spellings is essentially a process of phonics … The evidence that invented spelling activity simultaneously develops phonemic awareness and promotes understanding of the alphabetic principle is extremely promising. (1990: 387)

Additional studies indicate that students encouraged to invent spellings seem to write longer, higher-quality texts and are more successful in spelling unfamiliar words correctly (Gettinger, 1993; Griffith et al., 1992).

A key component of the arguments surrounding invented spelling focus on the role of instruction, reflecting concerns that children will not learn the conventions of print without a daily spelling programme. Although whole language supporters such as Wilde (1990) have documented the spelling gains of students who read widely and write daily without formal spelling instruction, Richgels (1995) argues that children need both: (1) the opportunity to learn about grapho-phonemic relationships through both wide reading and many opportunities to write their own messages; and (2) planned instruction modelling conventional spellings and teaching orthographic features based upon student needs.

Such instruction, however, need not focus on worksheets or isolated drills. During interactive writing lessons, for example, the teacher models conventional spellings and teaches specific orthographic features as the teacher and children craft their message together; work together to write the message word by word, by saying the word slowly and writing the sounds that are heard; share the pen such that children write the letters they know; and reread the message to ensure accurate representation of the text (McCarrier et al., 2000). 'What can you show us?' is another instructional context for kindergarten children to develop both phonemic awareness and early concepts about letters, sounds, and words (Richgels et al., 1996) by asking children to examine a text with enlarged print (such as a poem, a big book, or a language experience chart) and demonstrate what they know about the text. Such instruction teaches concepts such as letter or word identification, letter–sound correspondences, rhyming words, or other text features. Spelling instruction in these contexts is placed securely within the contexts of reading and writing meaningful texts.

An important point, however, is that attention to early concepts must be addressed instructionally as it is not sufficient to assume that all children will learn them incidentally. Morris (1993) compared two different approaches to kindergarten instruction – one with a language experience approach and one emphasizing oral language and play. By May, 84% of the children in the kindergarten classroom using a language experience approach were successful with the concept of word task; only 50% of the children in the classroom emphasizing oral language and play understood the concept of word. Similarly, 71% of the students in the language experience classrooms could segment words into phonemes, but only 18% of the students in the language/play classroom could successfully perform the same task. This study highlights the importance of teaching young children concepts about words, which will then facilitate phonemic segmentation, letter–sound relationships, and word recognition through activities such as shared writing, language experience stories, shared reading, and helping children to write their own texts.

Matching instruction with assessment

Planning instruction based upon each student's needs first requires that teachers have appropriate tools for determining developmental levels. The line of developmental spelling research has yielded spelling assessments such as Schlagal's (1989) Qualitative Inventory of Word Knowledge (QIWK), spelling inventories for primary and intermediate learners by Bear et al. (2000), and Ganske's (2000) Developmental Spelling Analysis (DSA). Each of these assessments provides lists of carefully selected words that gradually increase in both familiarity and feature difficulty. Analysis of children's spelling attempts on these assessments enables teachers to determine each child's developmental level and gain preliminary information about the orthographic features the child controls.

Bear et al. (2000) encourage teachers to find out what children are 'using but confusing', demonstrating as yet incomplete knowledge of spelling concepts, and to target their instruction accordingly. For example, children who represent each word with letter-like shapes demonstrating few graphophonemic relationships are not yet ready for formal spelling instruction but can benefit from rhyming games, shared readings of poems, songs, and stories, sorting activities with pictures, and attention to learning the letters of their names. Based on his series of studies on concept of word, Morris (1993) concluded that formal spelling instruction should be delayed until the child has a firm concept of word to avoid both confusion and frustration.

Spellers who begin to demonstrate the accurate use of initial and final consonants and some evidence of short vowel understandings can benefit from studying CVC word patterns through word sorts, word hunts, word families and rhyming words (Ganske, 2000). Johnston encourages teachers to carefully consider when to teach word families, arguing that 'well-timed instruction with word families can help children solidify tentative understandings, sort out current confusions, and move along to new understandings in the most efficient manner' (1999: 67). As children develop a concept of word and begin to move beyond the sounds of letter names that they hear, they may begin to demonstrate some knowledge of silent letters which signals a need for instruction featuring more complex word sorts with VCe or CVVC patterns. The teacher's role, then, is to build the instructional programme by organizing instruction to teach spelling features and concepts based upon students' developmental levels.

Such instruction, however, contrasts sharply with the widespread use of basal spellers, typically one book for each grade level with a specific sequence of word lists and features. Such materials have been criticized for a one-size-fits-all approach that does not meet the needs of many children in a particular grade. Schlagal (2002) recognizes both the limitations of singular, grade-level spelling materials and the challenges faced by teachers attempting to respond to the individual needs of each student. He proposes that teachers use the resources found in a range of spelling basals, with their organized, progressively more difficult lists, to plan instruction for small groups of children with similar abilities, thereby matching instruction with ability to scaffold learning.

FUTURE DIRECTIONS

Recent research has provided significant information about how young children learn to spell. However, further studies are needed to clarify questions related to process, development, and instruction. There is relatively little information on developmental differences or similarities within and across different language systems. Future studies should help distinguish those aspects of learning about printed language that are more or less universal and those particular to specific types of orthographies. Not only are studies needed within and across different language systems, but studies are also needed about how children's learning is affected by their exposure to one or more systems simultaneously. With the increased globalization of society, many students are learning to speak and write in two languages at the same time – in their native language and a second language in which they will be expected to function in a literate manner. It is also important to distinguish between situations in which the second language is learned as a foreign language (i.e. situations in which the primary mode of oral and written communication at home, school, and community is the native language) and contexts in which the second language is the principal means of communication in school and the larger community (e.g. for immigrant populations). These would be rich, though complex, contexts in which to more carefully explore developmental issues.

Other important questions relate to differences between normally developing and disabled readers/spellers. Preliminary studies suggest that differences may be more related to time for learning than to differences in perceptual/cognitive processing and/or abilities. Further research may help to resolve this discussion. Increasingly advanced technology available for the study of brain activity during language and literacy processing may yield significant insights about brain function with important instructional implications for students experiencing learning difficulties.

A large proportion of spelling studies done thus far have focused on children as they begin formal schooling, but relatively few have been done with younger students. This emerging line of research has documented that important concepts about spelling are formed early and are developing during preschool and the early years of formal education. Studies are needed to examine the implications of instruction for three- to five-year-old children by identifying appropriate assessment tools, sensitive to young children's needs; by exploring instructional practices in preschool settings that foster accelerated development; and by examining appropriate practices to provide early intervention for children at risk. Such studies could contribute to current questions about the relationship between development and instruction; that is, how does instruction foster or impede spelling development?

A theme throughout this review has been that learning to spell is a complex task as children learn to understand oral language and its functions, develop concepts about the visual aspects of print, and learn the specific relationships between oral and written language unique to their orthographic system. The line of research followed by Morris (1981; 1989a; 1989b; 1992; 1993) exploring the relationship between a learner's concept of word and spelling has begun to provide insights into the relationships between complex factors. More research is needed to identify how learning about the orthographic system through reading and writing relate to one another over time.

Correlational and experimental studies on phonological and phonemic awareness and their relationship to spelling development have been gaining interest in the research community. But many of these studies have been criticized for limitations in their design. In a review of experimental methodology on interventions to develop phonological awareness, Troia (1999) reviewed 39 studies and found that most had serious methodological flaws. In fact, only seven of the studies met two-thirds or more of the evaluative criteria; all had at least one fatal flaw. Such reviews point to the challenges of designing valid and reliable research to inform the field about early spelling teaching and learning. Experimental studies often focus on single aspects of oral or written language in fragmented, isolated ways, leaving important questions about the application of findings to complex classroom contexts. New and creative methodologies are required, building on the experimental research of the past, to inform future classroom instruction.

Lines of early spelling research have typically focused on children and their learning processes. However, given the critical role of teachers in helping children to become conventional spellers, research must also focus on teachers and what they need to know and do in classrooms of diverse learners. At one time, instructional materials and professional development activities provided teachers with rather scripted, dogmatic (and sometimes erroneous) information about the nature of the orthographic system. Later, attention to spelling was limited, in preference to a focus on more holistic methods of literacy instruction. Currently there is renewed interest in providing teachers with accurate and useful information about the nature of the writing system and developmental processes. Models of spelling instruction based on developmental research recognize the range of abilities found in classrooms and reject one-size-fits-all, grade-level programmes. Such models require that teachers have a new level of knowledge about: how spelling systems work, how children learn, how to assess students' knowledge, and how to organize classrooms to facilitate learning for diverse learners. Teacher education programmes might increase their efforts to develop, implement, and document innovative pre-service and in-service programmes that provide teachers with the knowledge, skills and dispositions they need to make such effective instruction a reality in their classrooms.

REFERENCES

Abouzeid, M.P. (1992) 'Stages of word knowledge in reading disabled children', in S. Templeton and D.R. Bear (eds), *Development of Orthographic Knowledge and the Foundations of Literacy: a Memorial Festschrift for Edmund H. Henderson.* Hillsdale, NJ: Erlbaum. pp. 279–306.

Adams, M.J. (1990) *Beginning to Read: Thinking and Learning about Print.* Cambridge, MA: MIT Press.

Alegria, J. and Mousty, P. (1997) 'Lexical spelling processes in reading disabled French-speaking children', in C.A. Perfetti, L. Reiben and M. Fayol (eds), *Learning to Spell: Research, Theory, and Practice across Languages.* Mahwah, NJ: Erlbaum. pp. 115–28.

Ball, E.W. and Blachman, B.A. (1991) 'Does phoneme awareness training in kindergarten make a difference in early word recognition and developmental spelling?', *Reading Research Quarterly,* 24 (1): 49–66.

Barnhart, R.K. (ed.) (1988) *The Barnhart Dictionary of Etymology: the Core Vocabulary of Standard English. Produced by American Scholarship.* New York: Wilson.

Bear, D.R. (1992) 'The prosody of oral reading and stages of word knowledge', in S. Templeton and D.R. Bear (eds), *Development of Orthographic Knowledge and the Foundations of Literacy: a Memorial Festschrift for Edmund H. Henderson.* Hillsdale, NJ: Erlbaum. pp. 137–90.

Bear, D.R., Invernizzi, M., Templeton, S. and Johnston, F. (2000) *Words Their Way: Word Study for Phonics, Vocabulary, and Spelling Instruction.* Englewood Cliffs, NJ: Prentice Hall.

Beers, C.S. and Beers, J.W. (1992) 'Children's spelling of English inflectional morphology', in S. Templeton and D.R. Bear (eds), *Development of Orthographic Knowledge and the Foundations of Literacy: a Memorial Festschrift for Edmund H. Henderson.* Hillsdale, NJ: Erlbaum. pp. 231–52.

Beers, J.W. and Henderson, E.H. (1977) 'A study of developing orthographic concepts among first graders', *Research in the Teaching of English,* 2: 133–48.

Berko-Gleason, J. (1958) 'Children's learning of English morphology', *Word,* 14: 150–77.

Bissex, G. (1980) *GYNS AT WRK: A Child Learns to Write and Read.* Cambridge, MA: Harvard University Press.

Bloodgood, J.W. (1999) 'What's in a name? Children's name writing and literacy acquisition', *Reading Research Quarterly,* 34 (3): 342–67.

Boder, E. (1973) 'Developmental dyslexia: a developmental approach based on three atypical reading–spelling patterns', *Developmental Medicine and Child Neurology,* 15: 663–87.

Bradley, L., and Bryant, P.E. (1983) 'Categorising sounds and learning to read: a causal connection', *Nature,* 3 (10): 419–21.

Bryant, P., Nunes, T. and Bindman, M. (1999) 'Morphemes and spelling', in T. Nunes (ed.), *Learning to Read: an Integrated View from Research and Practice.* Dordrecht: Kluwer. pp. 15–41.

Clarke, L.K. (1988) 'Invented versus tradition spelling in first graders' writings: effects on learning to spell and read', *Research in the Teaching of English*, 22: 281–309.

Clay, M. (1975) *What Did I Write?* Portsmouth, NH: Heinemann.

Coulmas, F. (1989) *The Writing Systems of the World*. New York: Blackwell.

Cummings, D.W. (1988) *American English Spelling: an Informal Description*. Baltimore: Johns Hopkins University Press.

Ehri, L.C. (1980) 'The development of orthographic images', in U. Frith (ed.), *Cognitive Processes in Spelling*. New York: Academic. pp. 311–38.

Ehri, L.C. (1987) 'Learning to spell and read words', *Journal of Reading Behavior*, 19: 5–31.

Ehri, L.C. (1992) 'Review and commentary: stages of spelling development', in S. Templeton and D.R. Bear (eds), *Development of Orthographic Knowledge and the Foundations of Literacy: a Memorial Festschrift for Edmund H. Henderson*. Hillsdale, NJ: Erlbaum. pp. 307–32.

Fayol, M., Thevenin, M.G., Jarousse, J.P. and Totereau, C. (1999) 'From learning to teaching French written morphology', in T. Nunes (ed.), *Learning to Read: an Integrated View from Research and Practice*. Dordrecht: Kluwer. pp. 43–64.

Ferreiro, E. and Teberosky, A. (1982) *Literacy before Schooling*. Portsmouth, NH: Heinemann.

Frith, U. (1985) 'Beneath the surface of developmental dyslexia', in K. Patterson, M. Coltheart and J. Marshall (eds), *Surface Dyslexia*. Cambridge: Academic. pp. 301–30.

Ganske, K. (2000) *Word Journeys: Assessment-Guided Phonics, Spelling, and Vocabulary Instruction*. New York: Guilford.

Gentry, J.R. (1978) 'Early spelling strategies', *Elementary School Journal*, 79: 88–92.

Gentry, J.R. (1982) 'An analysis of developmental spelling in *Gnys at Wrk*', *The Reading Teacher*, 36: 192–200.

Gentry, J.R. (2000) 'A retrospective on invented spelling and a look forward', *The Reading Teacher*, 54 (3): 318–32.

Gettinger, M. (1993) 'Effects of invented spelling and direct instruction on spelling performance of second-grade boys', *Journal of Applied Behavior Analysis*, 3: 281–91.

Gill, C.E. (1980) 'An analysis of spelling errors in French'. PhD dissertation, University of Virginia.

Gill, C.H. and Scharer, P.L. (1996) '"Why do they get it on Friday and misspell it on Monday"? Teachers inquiring about their students as spellers', *Language Arts*, 73: 89–96.

Goswami, U. (1992) 'Annotation: phonological factors in spelling development', *The Journal of Child Psychology and Psychiatry*, 33 (6): 967–75.

Goswami, U. (1994) 'Development of reading and spelling skills', in M. Rutter and D.F. Hay (eds), *Development through Life: a Handbook for Clinicians*. London: Blackwell Scientific. pp. 284–302.

Goswami, U. (1999) 'Integrating orthographic and phonological knowledge as reading develops: onsets, rimes, and analogies in children's reading', in R. Klein and P. McMullen (eds), *Converging Methods for Understanding Reading and Dyslexia*. Cambridge, MA: MIT Press. pp. 57–75.

Goswami, U. (2001) 'Early phonological development', in S.B. Neuman and D.K. Dickinson (eds), *Handbook of Early Literacy Research*. New York: Guilford. pp. 111–25.

Griffith, P.L. (1991) 'Phonemic awareness helps first graders invent spellings and third graders remember correct spellings', *Journal of Reading Behavior*, 23 (2): 215–33.

Griffith, P.L., Klesius, J.P. and Kromrey, J.D. (1992) 'The effect of phonemic awareness on the literacy development of first grade children in a traditional or a whole language classroom', *Journal of Research in Childhood Education*, 6 (2): 85–92.

Harste, J.C., Burke, C.L. and Woodward, V.A. (1982) 'Children's language and world: initial encounters with print', in J.A. Langer and M.T. Smith-Burke (eds), *Reader Meets Author/Bridging the Gap: a Psycholinguistic and Sociolinguistic Perspective*. Newark, DE: International Reading Association. pp. 105–31.

Henderson, E.H. (1990) *Teaching Spelling, 2nd edn.* Boston: Houghton Mifflin.

Henderson, E.H. (1992) 'The interface of lexical competence and knowledge of written words', in S. Templeton and D.R. Bear (eds), *Development of Orthographic Knowledge and the Foundations of Literacy: a Memorial Festschrift for Edmund H. Henderson*. Hillsdale, NJ: Erlbaum. pp. 1–30.

Henderson, E.H. and Beers, J.W. (eds) (1980) *Developmental and Cognitive Aspects of Learning to Spell: a Reflection of Word Knowledge*. Newark, DE: International Reading Association.

Hughes, M. and Searle, D. (1991) 'A longitudinal study of the growth of spelling abilities within the context of the development of literacy', in J. Zutell and S. McCormick (eds), *Learner Factors/Teacher Factors: Issues in Literacy Research and Instruction*. Chicago: National Reading Conference. pp. 159–68.

Hughes, M. and Searle, D. (1997) *The Violent E and other Tricky Sounds: Learning to Spell from Kindergarten through Grade 6*. York, ME: Stenhouse.

Invernizzi, M. (1992) 'The vowel and what follows: a phonological frame of orthographic analysis', in S. Templeton and D.R. Bear (eds), *Development of Orthographic Knowledge and the Foundations of Literacy: a Memorial Festschrift for Edmund H. Henderson*. Hillsdale, NJ: Erlbaum. pp. 105–36.

Invernizzi, M.A. and Worthy, M.J. (1989) 'An orthographic comparison of the spelling errors of learning disabled and normal children across four grade levels of spelling achievement', *Reading Psychology*, 10 (2): 173–88.

Johnston, F.R. (1999) 'The timing and teaching of word families', *The Reading Teacher*, 53 (1): 64–75.

Ju, D. and Jackson, N.E. (1995) 'Graphic and phonological processing in Chinese character identification', *Journal of Reading Behavior*, 27 (3): 299–313.

Kamii, C. and Manning, M. (1999) 'Before "invented" spelling: kindergartners' awareness that writing is related to the sounds of speech', *Journal of Research in Childhood Education*, 14 (1): 16–25.

Kamii, C., Long, R., Manning, M. and Manning, G. (1990) 'Spelling in kindergarten: a constructivist analysis comparing Spanish-speaking and English-speaking children', *Journal of Research in Childhood Education*, 4 (2): 91–7.

Lee, D.M. and Lee, J.M. (1941) 'The spelling load is too heavy', in J.S. Hudson, N.V. Lind and W. Jacob Jr (eds), *Language Arts in the Elementary School*. pp. 484–7.

Martens, P.A. (1999) '"Mommy, how do you write 'Sarah'?" The role of name writing in one child's literacy', *Journal of Research in Childhood Education*, 14 (1): 5–15.

McCarrier, A., Pinnell, G.S. and Fountas, I.C. (2000) *Interactive Writing: How Language and Literacy Come Together, K-2*. Portsmouth, NH: Heinemann.

McGee, L.M. and Richgels, D.J. (2000) *Literacy's Beginnings: Supporting Young Readers and Writers*, 3rd edn. Needham Heights, MA: Allyn and Bacon.

Morris, D. (1981) 'Concept of word: a developmental phenomenon in the beginning reading and writing processes', *Language Arts*, 58 (6): 659–68.

Morris, D. (ed.) (1989a) *Reading Psychology: an International Quarterly*, 10 (2) (whole issue).

Morris, D. (ed.) (1989b) 'A developmental perspective on spelling', *Reading Psychology: An International Quarterly*, 10 (3): iii–vi.

Morris, D. (1992) 'Concept of word: a pivotal understanding in the learning-to-read process', in S. Templeton and D.R. Bear (eds), *Development of Orthographic Knowledge and the Foundations of Literacy: a Memorial Festschrift for Edmund H. Henderson*. Hillsdale, NJ: Erlbaum. pp. 53–78.

Morris, D. (1993) 'The relationship between children's concept of word in text and phoneme awareness in learning to read: a longitudinal study', *Research in the Teaching of English*, 27 (2): 133–54.

Morris, D. and Perney, J. (1984) 'Developmental spelling as a predictor of first-grade reading achievement', *Elementary School Journal*, 84 (4): 440–57.

Morris, D., Nelson, L. and Perney, J. (1986) 'Exploring the concept of "spelling instructional level" through the analysis of error-types', *Elementary School Journal*, 66 (2): 28–41.

Morris, D., Blanton, L., Blanton, W.E., Nowacek, J. and Perney, J. (1995) 'Teaching low-achieving spellers at their "instructional level"', *Elementary School Journal*, 96 (3): 163–78.

Morrow, L.M. (1990) 'Preparing the classroom environment to promote literacy during play', *Early Childhood Research Quarterly*, 5: 537–54.

National Reading Panel (2000) *Report of the National Reading Panel. Teaching Children to Read: an Evidence-Based Assessment of the Scientific Research Literature on Reading and its Implications for Reading Instruction. Report of the Subgroups*. Washington, DC: US Department of Health and Human Services.

Nunes-Carraher, T. (1985) 'Exploracoes sobre o desenvolvimento da competencia em orlographia em portugueus', (Exploring the development of spelling in Portuguese), *Psicologia, Theoriae Pesquisa*, 1: 269–85.

Otto, H.J. (1973) 'Historical roots of contemporary elementary education', in J.I. Goodlad and H.G. Shane (eds), *The Elementary School in the United States*. Chicago: University of Chicago Press. pp. 36–58.

Papandropoulou, I. and Sinclair, H. (1974) 'What is a word? Experimental study of children's ideas on grammar', *Human Development*, 17: 241–58.

Pinheiro, A.M.V. (1995) 'Reading and spelling development in Brazilian Portuguese', *Reading and Writing: An Interdisciplinary Journal*, 7: 111–38.

Porpodas, C.D. (1989) 'The phonological factor in reading and spelling of Greek', in P.G. Aaron and R.M. Joshi (eds), *Reading and Writing Disorders in Different Orthographic Systems*. Dordrecht: Kluwer. pp. 177–88.

Portecorvo, C. and Orsolini, M. (1996) 'Writing and written language in children's development', in C. Pontecorvo, M. Orsolini, B. Burge and L.B. Resnick (eds), *Children's Early Text Construction*. Mahwah, NJ: Erlbaum. pp. 3–23.

Read, C. (1971) 'Pre-school children's knowledge of English phonology', *Harvard Educational Review*, 41 (1): 1–34.

Read, C. (1975) *Children's Categorization of Speech Sounds in English. Monographs of the National Council of Teachers of English*, no. 17.

Read, C. (1986) *Children's Creative Spelling*. London: Routledge and Kegan Paul.

Read, C. and Hodges, R. (1982) 'Spelling', in H. Mitzel (ed.), *Encyclopedia of Educational Research*, 5th edn. New York: Macmillan. pp. 1758–67.

Richgels, D.J. (1995) 'Invented spelling ability and printed word learning in kindergarten', *Reading Research Quarterly*, 30 (1): 96–109.

Richgels, D.J. (2001) 'Invented spelling, phonemic awareness, and reading and writing instruction', in S.B. Neuman and D.K. Dickinson (eds), *Handbook of Early Literacy Research*. New York: Guilford pp. 142–55.

Richgels, D.J., Poremba, K.J. and McGee, L.M. (1996) 'Kindergartners talk about print: phonemic awareness in meaningful contexts', *The Reading Teacher*, 49 (8): 632–42.

Scharer, P.L. (1992) 'From memorization to conceptualization: history informing the teaching and learning of spelling', *Journal of Language Experience*, 11 (1): 43–58.

Schlagal, R. (1989) 'Constancy and change in spelling development', *Reading Psychology*, 10 (3): 207–29.

Schlagal, R.C. (1992) 'Patterns of orthographic development into the intermediate grades', in S. Templeton and D.R. Bear (eds), *Development of Orthographic Knowledge and the Foundations of Literacy: a Memorial Festschrift for Edmund H. Henderson*. Hillsdale, NJ: Erlbaum. pp. 31–52.

Schlagal, R. (2002) 'Classroom spelling instruction: history, research, and practice', *Reading Research and Instruction*, 42 (1): 44–57.

Shen, H.H. and Bear, D.R. (2000) 'Development of orthographic skills in Chinese children', *Reading and Writing: an Interdisciplinary Journal*, 13: 197–236.

Silva, C. and Alves-Martins, M. (2002) 'Phonological skills and writing of presyllabic children', *Reading Research Quarterly*, 37 (4): 466–83.

Sulzby, E. (1996) 'Roles of oral and written language as children approach conventional literacy', in C. Pontecorvo, M. Orsolini, B. Burge and L.B. Resnick (eds), *Children's Early Text Construction*. Mahwah, NJ: Erlbaum. pp. 25–46.

Tangel, D.M. and Blachman, B.A. (1992) 'Effects of phoneme awareness instruction on kindergarten children's invented spelling', *Journal of Reading Behavior*, 24: 233–61.

Temple, C. (1978) 'An analysis of spelling errors in Spanish'. PhD dissertation, University of Virginia.

Templeton, C. and Morris, D. (2000) 'Spelling', in M.L. Kamil, P.B. Mosenthal, P.D. Pearson and R. Barr (eds), *Handbook of Reading Research*, vol. III. Mahwah, NJ: Erlbaum. pp. 525–43.

Templeton, S. and Bear, D. (eds) (1992) *Development of Orthographic Knowledge and the Foundations of Literacy: a Memorial Festschrift for Edmund H. Henderson*. Hillsdale, NJ: Erlbaum.

Treiman, R. (1993) *Beginning to Spell: a Study of First-Grade Children*. New York: Oxford University Press.

Treiman, R. and Cassar, M. (1996) 'Effects of morphology on children's spelling of final consonant clusters', *Journal of Experimental Child Psychology*, 63: 141–70.

Troia, G.A. (1999) 'Phonological awareness intervention research: a critical review of the experimental methodology', *Reading Research Quarterly*, 34 (1): 28–52.

Uhry, J.K. (1999) 'Invented spelling in kindergarten: the relationship with finger-point reading', *Reading and Writing: an Interdisciplinary Journal*, 11: 441–64.

Valle-Arroyo, F. (1990) 'Spelling errors in Spanish', *Reading and Writing: an Interdisciplinary Journal*, 2: 83–98.

Venezky, R.L. (1999) *The American Way of Spelling: the Structure and Origin of American English Orthography*. New York: Guilford.

Wilde, S. (1990) 'A proposal for a new spelling curriculum', *The Elementary School Journal*, 90 (3): 275–89.

Wimmer, H. and Landerl, K. (1997) 'How learning to spell German differs from learning to spell English', in C.A. Perfetti, L. Reiben and M. Fayol (eds), *Learning to Spell: Research, Theory, and Practice across Languages*. Mahwah, NJ: Erlbaum. pp. 81–96.

Zutell, J. (1992) 'An integrated view of word knowledge: correlational studies of the relationships between spelling, reading, and conceptual development', in S. Templeton and D.R. Bear (eds), *Development of Orthographic Knowledge and the Foundations of Literacy: a Memorial Festschrift for Edmund H. Henderson*. Hillsdale, NJ: Erlbaum. pp. 213–30.

Zutell, J. (1994) 'Spelling instruction', in A.C. Purves, L. Papa and S. Jordan (eds), *Encyclopedia of English Studies and Language Arts*. New York: Scholastic. pp. 1098–100.

Zutell, J. and Fresch, M.J. (1991) 'A longitudinal study of reading and spelling connections for third and fifth grade students'. Paper presented at the 36th Annual Convention of the International Reading Association, Las Vegas, Nevada.

Zutell, J. and Rasinski, T. (1989) 'Reading and spelling connections in third and fifth grade students', *Reading Psychology*, 10 (2): 137–55.

24

Writing the World

FRANCES CHRISTIE

Research into writing development is a particularly satisfying aspect of literacy research because writing represents the productive mode in literacy development. Thus, in early childhood, as one traces what it is young children can *do* in writing, one also traces a great deal of their emergent control of aspects of experience, and of ways to represent it. In other words, one traces much more than, for example, their growing control of such things as handwriting, spelling or punctuation, though these are often thought of as the 'basic' elements of literacy and of writing. Of much greater importance, one traces emergent control of different meanings and how to shape these, at least as they are represented in the written mode. There is at least some parallel with development in the oral language: in learning the mother tongue, one learns a fundamental resource with which one shapes, organizes and represents experience. There is a sense in which, in learning to write, young children also learn to represent experience, and they thereby add to their repertoire of semiotic or symbolic resources with which to represent the world. However, the parallel should not be pushed too far, for the oral and written modes are actually very different; the two are learned differently and they serve fundamentally different goals. In fact, talking and writing are quite different behaviours, which evolved in the human species at very different points in its overall history, and which thus emerged to serve very different social needs. While growth in the individual is not to be confused with evolution in the species, it is no accident that the oral language develops first in young children, while a degree of proficiency in speech needs usually to be established before they can embark on the rather different enterprise of learning to write and to read.

The term 'literacy' is open to many interpretations in the contemporary world, and often to considerable debate. I share some of the concerns expressed by Kress (2001: 22) about what he has termed the rather 'profligate' manner in which the term 'literacy' is sometimes used. Happily, it is not part of my brief in this chapter to define 'literacy'. However, it is important that I indicate what I mean by 'writing behaviour', as a basis for suggesting something of the way such behaviour emerges in young children. Writing behaviour, then, involves expression and shaping of meaning through manipulation of a writing code, where this includes mastery of the grammatical, spelling, writing and punctuation systems of that code. Two matters are of importance for me in such a seemingly unremarkable definition of writing behaviour. First, the concern for meaning in written language is primary: learning to write is one aspect of learning 'how to mean' (a term first used by Halliday, 1975, when discussing early language development in talk). Secondly, in indicating the range of resources to be mastered in order to learn how to mean in writing, I have placed the grammatical system first: contrary to much mythology, it is this which one learns, while also learning the graphemes (the alphabet or its equivalent) and their various combinations (the spelling system) that make possible the representation of the written language on the page. It is perhaps worth adding that the notion of 'grammar' as discussed here has nothing to do with school grammar, with its connotations of the traditional prescriptive rules for the writing of sentences. Instead, the sense in which 'grammar' is used owes most to various functional approaches, of the kind adopted some years ago for example by Perera (1984), when she analysed children's writing development, and also found in the systemic functional (SF) linguistic tradition associated with Halliday (1994) and various SF genres theorists who draw on his theory (e.g. Christie et al., 1990a; 1990b; 1992; Derewianka, 1990; Martin, 1992; Coffin, 1997; Veel, 1997; Macken-Horarik, 2002; Feez, 2002). In the functional sense referred to, a language – and hence its grammar – is a resource for organizing, constructing and communicating meaning. The interest here, then, is in aspects of how that resource is mastered in early writing development.

WRITING DEVELOPMENT AND SCHOOL LEARNING

This discussion of aspects of early writing will be based on two broad assumptions, the first to do with the nature of overall writing development across the years of childhood and adolescence, and the other to do with writing and its role in school learning.

To take the first of these assumptions, early writing is but one step in the wider developmental process of becoming a writer, and this process lasts many years. In fact, in one sense, like development in the oral mode, writing development never finishes, since life brings constant new challenges in shaping (and reading) new forms of literate language. No doubt some of us meet more frequent challenges than others in forming literate language, depending upon the course our lives and careers take; potentially, however, the challenge is there for all. A significant body of research (e.g. Perera, 1984; Derewianka, in press; Christie, 2002; in preparation; Foley and Thompson, 2003; Coffin, 1997; Veel, 1997; Martin, 2002) suggests that very considerable changes occur in the grammatical organization of written language as children pass from early childhood to late childhood, to adolescence and hence to adult life. As we shall see later, the initial steps in control of written language reflect the relatively stronger grasp that young children have over the grammar of speech than that of writing, though as we shall also see, the first steps in writing often reveal much simpler expressions than children are capable of in talk. That is because the challenge of mastering the physical activities of handling pen and paper and forming letters on the page is sufficiently demanding to absorb a great deal of young children's energies for a time.[1]

A number of linguistic measures have been identified by which the initial patterns of written language of early childhood change with growing maturity, not all of which can be discussed here because of space. (The interested reader might consult Perera, 1984, for an account of development in the primary years, while Christie, 2002, discusses development from early childhood to late adolescence.) Some general observations can be made, some of which will be referred to later. Thus, patterns of reference and textual coherence change as students develop an enhanced sense of the grammatical differences between speech and writing, increasingly building written language whose linguistic organization is reasonably context independent. Patterns of clauses and clause relations change as children move away from creating series of clauses overtly linked by simple additive and/or temporal conjunctions, creating greater variety in clause types, and often making use of various dependent non-finite clauses. A third matter worthy of comment is the growing density of written language as children learn to control written language, learning to create the relatively dense patterns found in much adult life, marked as these are by nominalization, among other grammatical resources, and leading to capacity to build abstraction, generalization and argument. Emergence of dense, abstract language (of the kind found in this volume, as a case in point!) is a developmental feature of late childhood to adolescence, though it is clear in the research I have done in Melbourne secondary schools that some adolescents do not grasp it particularly well, creating significant problems in their learning.

This brings me to the second of my assumptions in this chapter. It is that writing is a critically important resource for all young people in coming to terms with school learning. While this might seem obvious, I nonetheless state it by way of indicating that this discussion will concern writing in schools. An interest in writing development beyond the school would be a legitimate matter to address, though it is not one I have chosen to take up. Some years ago, Bernstein (1971: 214–15) made a useful distinction between 'commonsense' and 'uncommonsense' knowledge. The former refers to 'everyday community knowledge, of the pupil, his family and his peer group'. 'Uncommonsense' knowledge on the other hand is 'knowledge freed from the particular, the local through the various explicit languages of the sciences, or implicit languages of the arts which make possible either the creation or the discovery of new realities'. Both forms of knowledge are important, and indeed without the capacity to handle 'commonsense' knowledge, entry to the 'uncommonsense' would be impossible. It is clear that a function of school learning is that students steadily move into control of many forms of 'uncommonsense' knowledge and, in this process, they must learn to write and read a considerable range of text types or genres, many of them of an increasingly specialized kind as the areas of knowledge become more esoteric and abstract. For the purposes of this chapter, my interest is in writing development as an aspect of coming to terms with the demands of school learning. This is itself a fundamentally important aspect of 'learning to write the world'.

WHOSE WORLD?

I have suggested that in learning to write young children learn to represent aspects of their world. Yet the world is a very variable place and young children's opportunities are extremely variable, so that what they learn to do in writing is very much constrained by what social and educational practices make possible. The point is important. I live in Australia, an affluent nation, though numbers within it – including many of our indigenous people – live in conditions of great poverty. In such conditions, young children often have limited opportunity to learn to write. Furthermore, travelling as I often do into Asia and South East Asia, I am aware that in many instances, especially in large cities, young children have considerable educational opportunity, though elsewhere, often in rural parts, the young children receive no schooling. In such conditions, it is not uncommon that children as young as five or six are required to work and contribute to the domestic economy. How early childhood is conceived is also very much a matter of local sociocultural values and practices; the extent to which young children learn to write, and what they learn to write, are not matters about which it is always easy to generalize. Bearing these matters in mind, I shall develop this discussion by reference to data collected in Australia. In developing the discussion, I shall, where it is relevant, draw on the SF grammar (e.g. Halliday and Matthiessen, 1999) since, for reasons alluded to above, such a functional model of grammar provides a tool for analysis and interpretation of written texts. It allows one to analyse both the grammatical choices and the meanings realized in them.

DRAWING AND WRITING

The first encounter many young children have with some of the physical tools needed to learn to write is with a set of coloured pencils or crayons, and their first expressions on paper are typically drawings. The early preschool experiences of drawing involve some experimentation with a range of semiotic resources that very young children use to order

Figure 24.1   The jugglers

experience and hence construct aspects of their world (see Kress, 1997, for some discussion). Indeed, many parents encourage their children to draw, and it is not uncommon for parents as well as many early childhood teachers to advise their children to 'draw a picture and then write about it', even when, strictly speaking, the children are unable or unwilling to construct a coherent written message. Figure 24.1 reproduces a picture and its primitive accompanying writing. This was produced by a boy called David in the first few months of his schooling. The picture involved two jugglers who had visited the school, bringing an old tricycle. One juggler had performed while also riding on the tricycle. The picture depicts the two jugglers and the tricycle. Because he had learned to spell his name, David wrote it at the top of the page, while the piece of writing read *I saw a juggler*. The handwriting is uncertain, suggesting he still has trouble controlling the pencil. Accepting the rudimentary nature of the grasp of the letters, we can say that the spelling is a reasonable estimate of the sounds David wants to reproduce. What are we to make of the meanings and the grammar here? The child selects a personal pronoun (*I*) to write of himself, a process of perception (expressed in the verb choice *saw*) to represent what he did, and a simple nominal group (*a juggler*) to represent what he saw.

The written language is very simple, and the grammatical choices are close to those of speech; one would expect that in a child so young, for he knows far more about the grammar of speech than of writing at this stage of his development. But there are at least two other matters to which we can draw attention. First of all, the child was already capable of talking animatedly and at some length about such an event as a school visit by a juggler, but he was not at this stage able to produce much more than he did in writing, and it was effortful to produce what he did. This is because a young child's language development regresses for a time after the initial entry to literacy, so considerable is the effort of mastering the written code. While the teacher would probably have not put the matter in these terms, she seems intuitively to have understood this: hence, in talk with David, she wrote the text that can be seen displayed, thereby modelling other possibilities for meaning making in writing.

The second matter to be mentioned is that the juxtaposition of the drawing and David's writing is of interest for what it tells us of his learning at this stage about the semiotic resources available to him. Two semiotic systems – those of drawing and of writing – are in operation here. It would seem that David has understood the significance of both, though it is doubtful that he could articulate the matter. The two deal with related information, though the representations involved are different, and the aspect of the information chosen for representation in each case is certainly different. The picture represents the actual event of the jugglers performing, one of them sitting on the tricycle. The writing represents the language involved in reporting, after the event, that David saw the juggler. More than this, however, the writing represents language on the page, while the drawing represents an event that is reasonably concrete and observed.

According to Halliday (1985: 12–15) there was a significant 'leap' in the development of the human species when it was realized that language could be thus represented, by using, for example, marks on a stone, a tablet or a parchment. The activity of representing language in such a manner probably grew out of early drawing activity, though there is some debate about the origins of writing systems in different parts of writing. (See discussions in Halliday, 1985; DeFrancis, 1989 ; Coulmas, 1989; Schmandt-Besserat, 1996.) In any event, the shift into writing represented a mental shift of a quite different order in the human species – a movement from the representation of the relatively concrete to the relatively abstract. In a related fashion, Halliday has suggested, the child goes through a considerable 'leap' in understanding when it is grasped that language itself can be represented with marks on the page. I would add that the potential shift in cognition is enormous, opening the way to later developments in control of the more abstract patterns of written language to which I alluded earlier, and which become critically important in the creation of 'uncommonsense' knowledge. A very good and detailed discussion is provided by Painter (1999) tracing the early oral language growth of her own child as he developed the resources in language in the preschool years that

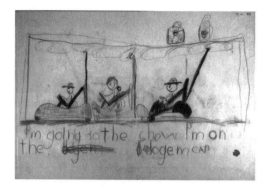

Figure 24.2 The show

would make possible his 'leap' into literacy and, eventually, 'uncommonsense' knowledge.

Figure 24.2, produced when David was a little older, was written in school but about an out-of-school experience. A great deal of the earliest writing activity found in the schools in which I have done research has involved inviting the children to write about pleasurable experiences with family and wider community. In this sense, it draws on the 'commonsense' experience of the young learner, though the choice of the text reflects something of the school's interest in developing in children some capacity in representing experience. Initially, opportunities to represent commonsense experience will typically have been provided in preschool and out-of-school activities. That schooling values them is apparent both in the tendency of teachers to encourage rehearsal of such representation of experience in talk in activities like 'morning news' (sometimes called 'show and tell' or 'sharing time'), and in the associated tendency to encourage it in early writing. More than one researcher (e.g. Michaels, 1980; 1986; Cazden and Michaels, discussed in Cazden, 1988, 7–28; Christie, 1989) has remarked on the relationship between the patterns of language rehearsed in such oral language activities and the patterns of writing they produce. I shall refer to this matter again below.

In Figure 24.2 David demonstrates a more confident control of both and the handwriting and the spelling systems than was true of the first piece. Here he wrote, quite clearly and intelligibly, *I'm going to the show I'm on the dogem car*. The word 'dodgem' is misspelt, though David's attempt at it is a good approximation. The picture and associated writing were inspired by the fact that the annual show had come to the city where he lived, and among the many activities available for children like himself was the exhibition where he could ride on the dodgem cars. Like Figure 24.1, then, this picture involved representing an aspect of David's world by producing both a picture and a written accompaniment. In the case of the second image David writes two clauses, not one as in the first, and the matter is worthy of some comment. In the adult world, as a general principle, length is no reliable measure of the writer's capacities. However, given the effortful nature of the enterprise of learning to handle the pen and the handwriting and spelling systems, as well to control aspects of language sufficiently to shape a written meaning, the child's writing of two clauses here is significant. A review of his earliest attempts at writing, developed over several weeks of schooling, revealed that his original efforts constituted one clause, and sometimes not even that. The move to writing two clauses revealed some developmental progress. The personal pronoun *I* is used again in both clauses, making it clear that it is personal experience that is represented. The first process realized is a material or action process (*I'm going to the show*) and the second creates an attribute of David (*I'm on a dogem car*).

The tense choices in Figure 24.2 are different from in Figure 24.1 Here David uses the present continuous tense in the first clause and the simple present in the second clause. The relationship of the information in the writing and image is thus different from what was the case in the first image. That image is to do with the experience of a visit of a juggler and David's viewing of that: hence he reports what we might term essentially 'received experience'. Figure 24.2 is to do with reporting an aspect of his own experience of riding on a dodgem car, and this we might term 'lived experience'.

Just as was true of the first piece, the second piece is very simple grammatically, and I have suggested this reflects the child's greater knowledge of speech than of writing. While that observation certainly holds, I can say rather more of why the child chose the grammatical selections he did. This was very much dependent upon the model of the simple reading materials he was given in his first 18 months of schooling, which in turn sought to exploit the children's knowledge of oral language. The materials, developed in the school, though based on other reading programmes, including some commercial ones, involved the children in learning to read such items as the following, all of which were accompanied by a simple drawing:

I'm on a swing
I'm going to the show.
I've got a dog.

That's a ball.
Look at the tadpole.

While the children were learning to read these, they were also regularly read to by their teacher, using very much richer models of written language in the books she chose.

The models of the early written pieces for reading just cited certainly are instances of simple texts, though they do not really constitute instance of genres as such, because they are so simple and minimal in nature.[2] Together with the models of other materials read with and by the teacher, they provided a resource on which David and his classmates could build. What can we say of the earliest genres that often appear in young children's writing, and of the models on which they seem to draw in constructing them?

EARLY GENRES FOR WRITING

Two genres appear very early in the texts of young Australian children, and they are apparently elemental in an English-speaking culture. They are recounts and procedures. They are elemental both because they are learned in the earliest years of life in the oral mode, and because they continue to find expression throughout life both in speech and in writing. They represent two quite fundamental ways of making meaning, the one reconstructing events for the benefit of others, the other telling others what to do in participating in such events. Both genres are used in a great deal of early literacy learning. Recounts constitute one of the several ways of *narrating about experience* rehearsed in such activities as sharing time and morning news, and referred to in discussions by Cazden and Michaels, alluded to above. Michaels (1986) points to the difficulties of identifying types of narratives for the purposes of her study. I should note that in using the term 'narrating about experience' I intend no particular association with any narrative structure: instead I refer to the activity of recreating in a relatively sustained way some aspect(s) of experience, often assisted by the intervention of the teacher. In my own research (Christie, 1989), several possible structures emerged, though I shall not detail these here.

The two texts displayed below were written in the same classroom about the same class activity, which involved making a 'hairy monster'. For anyone unfamiliar with the practice of making these monsters in early childhood classrooms, a word of explanation will be in order. The teacher will provide an old sock, put in some wheat seeds and fill it with soil, and then place this in a shallow tray with a little water. Left in a suitably warm place in the classroom, the seeds will soon sprout through the old sock, thus producing what is termed a 'hairy monster'. The activity is seen as a simple way to introduce some scientific information about germination.

Text 1 A recount	*Text 2 A procedure*
1 We got a sock.	1 Get an old sock.
2 We put on the eyes.	2 Stitch on two eyes.
3 We put on the mouth.	3 Stitch on a mouth.
4 We put the seeds in the hairy monster.	4 Put some wheat seeds in the sock.
5 We put the dirt in.	5 Put some dirt in the sock.
6 We watered it.	6 Water the dirt in the sock.
7 We put the hairy monster down the back.	7 Place the sock in a tray in the sunlight at the back of the room.
8 We watered the next day.	8 Water the sock each day.

The class activity had been concluded and the teacher asked the children to 'write about the hairy monster', encouraging them to recall the steps undertaken in their correct sequence, and to number them. No more overt advice in terms of any genre was offered. It is of interest, then, that within the same group of children, some opted for a recount, others for a procedure. The two genres involved offer two perspectives on the same phenomenon: the one telling what 'we' did, the other telling 'you' what to do. Each, in other words, has a different function and social purpose. The recount, then, uses the past tense to reconstruct events, and it uses a series of material or action processes (*we got*, *we put*, *we watered*) to build the actions, while the sense of personal experience is expressed in the regular repetition of the personal pronoun *we*, and in the consistent use of the declarative mood, as of one giving information. The procedure, on the other hand, while it uses the same series of material processes, removes human agency and adopts the imperative mood to direct the behaviours of others: *get an old sock*, *stitch on two eyes*. The practices of telling others what we did, and of guiding or directing the behaviours of others, as I have noted, are encountered first in the patterns of oral language before young children come to school. Recounting personal experience is then often practised in early schooling. But beyond this, these two genres are later endlessly recycled,

so that they reappear not only in later school life but in life beyond school. Think, for example, of the various recounts used in personal letters and diaries but also in works of history (including historical accounts of the lives of individuals in scientific textbooks), and of the many ways in which procedures appear and reappear in things as various as recipes, manuals, and accounts of scientific experiments. These genres, then, while learned in reconstruction of 'commonsense' experience, often have subsequent significance in later construction of the 'uncommonsense'.

The children in the classroom where they made a hairy monster selected from the repertoire of genres available to them, and while aspects of these had been encountered in talk, as I have suggested, they had succeeded in using them to control some written language. They drew on the grammatical resources of English rather differently to construct two rather different kinds of meanings. They had selected from their world two possible ways of making meaning in language, and they had both used them successfully to represent aspects of their world. Both created coherent genres that had unity, order and purpose. Neither text needed the support of any picture and in that sense, unlike the very early pieces produced by David, the two managed to 'stand alone', and this marks important progress in achieving control of the grammar of writing. Speech normally accompanies action – is in fact a form of action – and for that reason it often makes use of exophoric references to matters outside the text, as in the following made-up examples: *Pass me that please*; *Look at this*; *Where is it*? A necessary aspect of learning to control the grammar of writing, as distinct from that of speech, is learning to control the referential items in such a way that a text that is relatively 'content independent' is created. Another way to state the point is to suggest that the language of a written text *constitutes* the meanings involved, while speech is more typically ancillary to it.

With the exception of a couple of lapses, the meanings in the two hairy monster texts were constituted in the written language. One lapse occurs in the recount where the writer assumes that the reader knows the identity of *we*, a defensible feature of early writing; the other occurs in the same text with the reference to *down the back*, which would more completely be expressed as 'down the back of the room'. Overall, these young writers had grasped a great deal of the values and purposes of writing for much school learning and they could create coherent written texts that were largely context independent. In so doing, they had taken some steps towards learning how to handle the grammar of written language.

All this points to an important observation: it is that the selections of experiences and of grammar that children make to create their first written pieces will necessarily draw on such models as they have available to them. The point may seem obvious, though it is an important one to make. Children do not 'invent' the nature of the language selections they write, as some ideologies to do with self-expression in children's writing development of the past have tended to suggest (Gilbert, 1990, discusses the problems of such ideologies). On the contrary, they draw on the linguistic resources made available to them as part of participating in their world. Once those linguistic resources have been learned and internalized, then children are to that extent released to fashion and shape meanings in what will become increasingly independent ways. It is through this means that they develop the tools and knowledge with which to express self.

An important consequence of all this is the pedagogical significance that attaches to selecting appropriate materials with which students can take their first steps in learning to read and write. It also points to the importance of the role of the mentor – be that parent or teacher – in supporting the young in learning to handle written language. The more deprived the children in terms of exposure to reading and writing experiences, then the more critical becomes the role of the teacher. This brings me to say something of the values of joint construction of written texts, and the values of considerable rehearsal of the language patterns needed in order to create coherent written texts.

JOINT CONSTRUCTION OF EARLY WRITTEN TEXTS

These days, it has become almost a commonplace to talk of the values of scaffolding children's learning generally, as well as their language learning in particular. (Cazden, 1992: 99–113; Painter, 1999; and Hammond, 2001, offer useful and rather varied accounts of aspects of scaffolding language learning.) Good teachers have of course always understood the values of joint construction and modelling of written language, and this was true long before the term 'scaffolding' had achieved the currency it now has. I want to illustrate the values of joint construction in early writing development by examining some aspects of the experience of a group of young Australian Aboriginal children and their teacher. Aboriginal children in many parts of Australia live in poverty, their access to print materials being severely limited. The Aboriginal children I allude to here lived in bush camps around

their town and their parents were keen to see them break the poverty trap by achieving an education. The educational programme they followed was one developed by several people, though Gray (1998) had a particular role in its shaping and development, and it is from his work that I shall develop this discussion. The programme was designed to build with very young children their language resources, both for handling school learning generally and for handling written discourse. Significant fields of knowledge were selected for class discussion including, for example, the life cycle of chickens, and these became the focus of attention for some weeks of work. The children were read stories about hens and chickens and factual materials about chickens; these they sometimes had reread so that the children could follow aspects of the written language and learn how to spell numbers of the words involved, which were also displayed in the classroom. They even cooked eggs in the classroom, while an incubator was also installed so that the children could follow the development of some chickens till they eventually hatched. While the period of incubation was in progress, the teacher and children regularly revisited the book she had selected which gave an account of the process of growth in the egg.

After a quite sustained period of time, the teacher was ready to involve the children in joint construction of a factual text about chickens. She actually advised them they would write a 'story', a general term she seemed to use for most written texts. It is impossible here to reproduce all the talk developed in the course of several lessons. I shall reproduce the finished text the teacher and children produced over three lessons, making some comments beneath about the manner in which it was rehearsed and written. This is what I would term a 'transitional' text, in that it is not a totally coherent and independent text, of the kind that more mature writing requires. Its transitional nature is apparent in several ways, but most notably in its uses of exophoric references to matters, an understanding of which is shared by participants in the context, but which ideally would be given overt or endophoric reference in a more mature piece.

Text 3

Completed in the first lesson

We didn't have a mother hen so we used an incubator to keep the eggs warm. The incubator has a thermometer that tells how hot the eggs are. The orange light comes on every time the eggs start to get cold. When the arm [of the incubator] turns over it moves the eggs around to give the little chicks exercise.

Completed in the second lesson

First, we switched on the electricity and put the eggs in. The little chick looked like a dot. It stays in the egg for twenty one days. His food is the yolk. The little chick grows a little bit bigger. He grows a tiny head, a tiny heart, tiny eyes and tiny blood vessels. Then he grows tiny ears, tiny wings and tiny legs. Next he grows a tiny tail and a tiny beak. Then he grows tiny feathers and an egg tooth.

Completed in the third lesson

While the little chick is in the egg it is floating in a water sac. When it is twenty one days the little chick cracks open the egg with his egg tooth. It's hard work. At last the chick is out. He is all wet and weak and wobbly. When he dries out he is soft and fluffy.

The fact that the text was jointly constructed from shared reading and class activity was evident for example in such expressions as: *We didn't have a mother hen so we used an incubator to keep the eggs warm.* It was also apparent in such expressions as: *First, we switched on the electricity and put the eggs in.* In both cases, the use of the personal pronoun *we* indicates that personal experience, in part at least, is at issue. In other words, this was not an entirely context independent piece of scientific written language, and the teacher drew on the children's shared experience to shape the text. Elsewhere and in a much earlier lesson, considerable discussion had ensued about the role of the 'arm' of the incubator in turning it to ensure adequate movement of the developing chicken, as well as the function of the electric light on the incubator which came on and off at certain times, signalling that an appropriately warm environment for the developing chicken was being maintained. Talk of these matters led to such exchanges as the following:

Teacher:	What turns it (the incubator) Jenny? What turns the incubator?
Several children:	That arm. The arm. (They point excitedly)
Teacher:	Yeah. That little arm.
Jenny:	And the arm ... the arm ... the arm goes over the screen.
Another child:	You don't have to turn it with your finger.
Teacher:	No.
Same child:	You just leave it and (unclear).
Naomi:	The arm goes over to the screen.
Teacher:	The arm goes over to the screen and the little egg just turns around slowly.

Jenny:	And then it comes back.
Teacher:	And then it comes back and the little egg turns like that.

Here it will be noted that there is a great deal of exophoric reference out of the text to aspects of the context, most notably to features of the incubator, e.g. *that arm; the arm goes over to the screen; and the little egg turns like that.* All this contributed to the eventual writing of the sentence that reads: *When the arm turns over it moves the eggs around to give the little chicks exercise.* Here the reference to *the arm* remains exophoric, and its status as an aspect of the incubator is not made clear in the written text.

As the text proceeds, especially in those parts written in the second and third sessions, the written language moves away from uses of the first person towards using the third person to create a series of clauses in which the chick, or some aspect of its anatomy, is the subject. The process types selected to construct what happens in development are sometimes material or those of action, as in: *he grows tiny feathers and an egg tooth*, or *the little chick cracks open the egg with his egg tooth*. Others still build attributes of the chick, as in: *At last the chick is out*, or *He is all wet and weak and wobbly.* These expressions and other like them derive in part from the model of the books the children had had read them by their teacher, though that in no way diminishes the achievement of the children in working with their teacher to create them. We can also note that a strong sense of the temporal sequence of the steps in chicken development is constructed through a series of conjunctive relationships:

He grows a tiny head, a tiny heart, tiny eyes and tiny blood vessels.
Then he grows tiny ears, tiny wings and tiny legs.
Next he grows a tiny tail and a tiny beak.
Then he grows tiny feathers and an egg tooth.

and

While the little chick is in the egg it is floating in a water sac.
When it is twenty one days the little chick cracks open the egg with his egg tooth.
At last the chick is out.
When he dries out he is soft and fluffy.

The effect of creating such a sequence of clauses, in which it was the chicken that was emphasized by being placed in subject position, was to build knowledge and experience that were not personal, but researched. I have suggested the text was transitional in that it displayed some language features that are more properly associated with the grammar of speech, and whose effect was to create a text which was not entirely context independent and coherent. It was, however, a very appropriate piece of jointly constructed writing, in which the children had been assisted to create some 'uncommonsense' knowledge about an interesting and important aspect of their world.

Overall, the activity of joint construction was of critical importance. It meant that the children enjoyed the benefits of shared participation in the creation of the written text, working together under teacher guidance to create a text they could not have produced independently at that stage of their development. It also meant that they participated in the building of significant knowledge – knowledge, that is, that required some research and effort in its mastery, so that it constituted an intellectual challenge for the young learners involved. And because it meant these things, the activity necessarily involved the children in learning patterns of language use for shaping written knowledge.

Joint construction in the manner outlined is particularly relevant for young literacy learners. The principles developed by Gray and others have actually been applied in provision of early literacy programmes in Thailand (Rattanavich and Christie, 1993; Rattanavich and Walker, 1996) among children of ethnic minorities learning the Thai national language, while related principles have also been used in similar programmes for the children of ethnic minorities in Vietnam (Woolley et al., 1995; 1996; 1998).

The processes of moving into capacity independently to create coherent written genres are variable, for individuals differ. However, by the age of seven years, few children will have effected the transition into full control of the grammar of coherent written language, though many will have made good progress. I shall turn in my last section to some consideration of the writing of one child who had made good progress by age six years.

ONE CHILD WRITES HER WORLD

Among the first genres young children attempt is a narrative with the classic orientation, followed by some kind of complication, followed by some evaluation, which is followed by a resolution, as originally described by Labov and Waletzky (1967). The pattern, with many variations and adaptations, endures into adult life, and is constantly revisited in the many films, videos and books encountered by adults. That the pattern – or at least attempts at it – finds its way into young children's writing is not surprising, since so many children encounter it in the books that are read in the school room, as well,

in many cases, as in the family context. Narratives are highly valued in English-speaking cultures. Apart from their value as sources of entertainment, they seem to serve an important function in affirming many values. On occasion the values are to do with facing and overcoming adversity, and sometimes they are to do with giving support and help to others, though other values may be involved. Consider the following little narrative, written by Anna aged six years (taken from Aidman, 1999). The model from which she borrowed will be familiar. I have set it out to show the elements of structure, though Anna did not write it this way. I should perhaps note that the story was written in some free time in school, and the class teacher had not devoted any time to discussing narrative structures.

Text 4   The Bee
Orientation

Once upon a time there was a Bee.

Complication

He lost his parents. So he said to the Possum, 'I am a Bee, please will you help me find my parents?' 'No,' said the Possum, 'I can't.' So the Bee said to the Spider, 'I am a Bee, please will you help me find my parents?'

Resolution/evaluation

'Yes,' said the Spider, 'Come on.' So they went to find the parents. *When they found them the Bee was happy.* 'Come on, let's go home.' When they were home they had some lunch. The Spider went home. 'Goodbye Spider,' said the Bee.

(The *italic* sentence indicates the point in the text at which evaluation is introduced in the story, signalling the significance of the events to an important protagonist in the tale.)

The narrative depends for its structure on many other similar stories of its kind, the tale of the 'Little Red Hen' being just one, involving considerable repetition of certain passages of dialogue. Young children take particular pleasure in such repetition, both because they appear to enjoy the repetition of the sounds, and because it assists them to predict what is to come in their reading. Anyone who has sat in an early childhood classroom will know the manner in which young children like such stories to be reread, so that they can anticipate and hence read along with their teacher, even when they are not yet sufficiently competent to read the text independently.

Anna's motives in selecting such a model for writing are not difficult to see: it gave her a structure around which she then constructed a text of her own. It was knowledge of the schematic structure and of the necessary language choices to create it that enabled her to compose a written narrative of her own.

By several standards this is a successful piece of writing. Anna had mastered the particular schematic model well, giving the text a sense of completion. Such a sense of completion included the introduction of the important evaluation element. Many young children neglect to include such an element, though it is quite crucial for an understanding of the significance of the events, and ultimately for an understanding of the social purpose of such a genre. It is because the bee lost his parents and then found them that he was happy, and the reader can empathize with that emotion: without it, the narrative would be less significant. But apart from that, there are other ways in which we can tell the young writer had successfully created a coherent text constituting its own meanings. Note, for example, how the first sentence, employing a time-honoured opening, introduces the central character, using an indefinite article to do so, and then the text goes on to build internal or endophoric references back to that character (through the definite article or the pronoun), so that the text binds together:

Once upon a time there was a Bee.

He lost his parents.

So he said to the Possum, 'I am a Bee. ...'

Subsequent sentences use instances of the definite article to refer to *the Possum* and *the Spider* when they are brought into the tale, though it seems to me that this is a common manner of introducing such characters in this kind of tale, once the story has been instituted and the sequence of events unfolds. Such at any rate is the case in at least one copy of the 'Little Red Hen' I consulted in writing this chapter.

I shall turn to reference in the latter elements, demonstrating how successfully this works to build the meanings – and hence the world – of this text:

So the Bee said to the Spider,

'I am a Bee, please will you help me find my parents?'

'Yes,' said the Spider, 'Come on.'

So they went to find the parents,

When they found them

the Bee was happy.

'Come on, let's go home.'

When they were home

they had some lunch.

The Spider went home.

'Goodbye Spider,'

said the Bee.

Anna, the writer of Text 4, was a bilingual child, fluent in both Russian and English. She had had many stories read to her, in both languages, from a very early age, and she early developed an interest in writing. She knew a great deal about how to construct her world in writing, and she actively drew on the models of written language available to her. She had, in other words, internalized a great deal of the grammar of written language, as well as knowledge of the social purposes of at least some familiar genres.

Like the Aboriginal children in the case of Text 3 earlier, Anna had been scaffolded into control of written genres, though in her case, the processes of scaffolding were somewhat different. She had enjoyed considerable familial support in mastering ways of writing and reading in English (as well as Russian), of a kind that less advantaged children do not typically enjoy.

CONCLUSION

What then can we say of the processes by which the young learn 'to write their world'? Development of writing ability very often grows out of young children's early experiments in drawing and in playing with ways to organize ideas and experiences with pencils, crayons and, these days, with computers and computer games. The recognition that the ephemeral thing that is language is capable of being represented in some way on the page or computer screen is a significant step forward in young children's awareness of the semiotic resources available to them. It leads initially to experimentation with ways to construct and organize simple messages, normally of one clause but sometimes even less than that. Such early experimentation, undertaken while also learning the skills of controlling the handwriting and spelling systems, leads in time to rather longer but still rudimentary written texts. In the latter, young children seek to come to terms with controlling aspects of the grammar of writing, while also seeking to master features of the first genres they will construct. As they learn these things, so too do young children learn a great deal of ways of representing experience in a manner valued in their culture. Such ways, once internalized, are then used increasingly by the young as they grow into independence in their uses of written language. Critical along the way will be the role of the teacher and of the models of written language made available, if children are to recognize and internalize both the patterns of written language and the social purposes fulfilled in adopting particular genres. In an important sense, learning the written language patterns of one's culture is an essential aspect of being successfully apprenticed into that culture. The role of the teacher in selecting written patterns to read, practise, discuss, jointly construct, play with and rehearse is essential, not least for its relevance in assisting children to enter into the 'uncommonsense' knowledge of schooling.

NOTES

1 It was partly in an effort to assist children over the hurdle of dealing with such matters that some years ago those who developed the 'Breakthrough to Literacy' programme (Mackay et al., 1970) invented the sentence maker, which gave children correctly spelled words they could take and shape into written passages of their own.

2 All kinds of passages of language can be judged instances of texts, in that they have the linguistic properties that give texture and coherence. A genre is recognized on related but essentially different grounds. It will have an overall schematic structure giving it some kind of staging that indicates a particular social purpose. The presence of the stages is tested by examining all aspects of the grammar. An introductory discussion of the approach has been provided by Derewianka (1990).

REFERENCES

Aidman, M. (1999) 'Biliteracy development through early and mid-primary years: a longitudinal case study of bilingual writing'. PhD thesis, University of Melbourne, Australia.

Bernstein, B. (1971) *Class, Codes and Control. Vol. I: Theoretical Studies towards a Sociology of Language.* London: Routledge and Kegan Paul.

Cazden, C. (1988) *Classroom Discourse: the Language of Teaching and Learning.* Portsmouth, NH: Heinemann.

Cazden, C. (1992) *Whole Language Plus: Essays on Literacy in the United States and New Zealand.* New York: Teachers College Press.

Christie, F. (1989) 'Curriculum genres in early childhood education: a case study in writing development'. PhD thesis, University of Sydney, Australia.

Christie, F. (2002) 'The development of abstraction in adolescence in subject English', in M. Schleppegrell and C. Colombi (eds), *Developing Advanced Literacy in First and Second Languages: Meaning with Power.* Mahwah, NJ: Erlbaum. pp. 45–66.

Christic, F. (in preparation) *Learning to Write, Writing to Learn.*

Christie, F., Gray, P., Gray, B., Macken, M., Martin, J.R. and Rothery, J. (1990a, 1990b, 1992) *Language: a Resource for Meaning. Procedures: Books 1–4 and Teacher Manual. Reports: Books 1–4 and Teacher Manual. Explanations: Books 1–4 and Teacher Manual.* Sydney: Harcourt Brace Jovanovich.

Coffin, C. (1997) 'Constructing and giving value to the past: an investigation into secondary history', in F. Christie and J.R. Martin (eds), *Genre and Institutions: Social Processes in the Workplace and School.* London: Continuum. pp. 196–230.

Coulmas, F. (1989) *The Writing Systems of the World.* Oxford: Blackwell.

DeFrancis, J. (1989) *Visible Speech: the Diverse Oneness of Writing Systems.* Honolulu: University of Hawaii Press.

Derewianka, B. (1990) *Exploring How Texts Work.* Sydney: Primary English Teachers' Association.

Derewianka, B. (in press) 'Grammatical metaphor in the transition to adolescence', in A.M. Simon Vandenbergen, M. Taverniers and L. Ravelli (eds), *Lexicogrammatical Metaphor: Systemic and Functional Perspectives.* Amsterdam: Benjamins.

Feez, S. (2002) 'Heritage and innovation in second language education', in A.M. Johns (ed.), *Genre in the Classroom: Multiple Perspectives.* Mahwah, NJ: Erlbaum. pp. 43–69.

Foley, J. and Thompson, L. (2003) *Language Learning: a Lifelong Process.* London: Arnold.

Gilbert, P. (1990) 'Authorising disadvantage: authorship and creativity in the language classroom', in F. Christie (ed.), *Literacy for a Changing World.* Melbourne: Australian Council for Educational Research. pp. 54–78.

Gray, B. (1998) 'Accessing the discourses of schooling: English language and literacy development with Aboriginal children in mainstream schools'. PhD thesis, University of Melbourne, Australia.

Halliday, M.A.K. (1975) *Learning How To Mean: Explorations in the Development of Language.* London: Arnold.

Halliday, M.A.K. (1985) *Spoken and Written Language.* Geelong, Australia: Deakin University Press.

Hallidays M.A.K. (1994) *An Introduction to Functional Grammar.* London: Arnold.

Halliday, M.A.K. and Matthiessen, C. (1999) *Construing Experience through Meaning: a Language-Based Approach to Cognition.* London: Cassell.

Hammond, J. (2001) *Scaffolding*: *Teaching and Learning in Language and Literacy Education*. Sydney: Primary English Teaching Association.

Kress, G. (1997) *Before Writing*: *Rethinking the Paths to Literacy*. London: Routledge.

Kress, G. (2001) '"You've just got to learn how to see": curriculum subjects, young people and schooled engagement with the world', in J. Cumming and C. Wyatt-Smith (eds), *Literacy and the Curriculum*: *Success in Senior Secondary Schooling*. Melbourne: Australian Council for Educational Research. pp. 21–31.

Labov, W. and Waletzky, J. (1967) 'Narrative analysis: oral versions of personal experience', in J. Helm (ed.), *Essays in the Verbal and Visual Arts. American Ethological Society, Proceedings of Spring Meeting 1966*. Washington: University of Washington Press. pp. 12–44.

Mackay, D., Thompson, B. and Schaub, P. (1970) *Breakthrough to Literacy. Teachers Manual: the Theory and Practice of Teaching Initial Reading and Writing*. London: Longmans, for the School Council.

Macken-Horarik, M. (2002) '"Something to shoot for": a systemic functional approach to teaching genre in secondary school', in A.M. Johns (ed.), *Genre in the Classroom*: *Multiple Perspectives*. Mahwah, NJ: Erlbaum. pp. 17–42.

Martin, J.R. (1992) *English Text*: *System and Structure*. Philadelphia: Benjamins.

Martin, J.R. (2002) 'Writing history: construing time and value in discourses of the past', in M. Schleppegrell and C. Colombi (eds), *Developing Advanced Literacy in First and Second Languages*: *Meaning with Power*. Mahwah, NJ: Erlbaum. pp. 87–118.

Michaels, S. (1980) 'Sharing time: an oral preparation for literacy'. Paper presented at the Ethnography in Education Research Forum, University of Pennsylvania, Philadelphia.

Michaels, S. (1986) 'Narrative presentations: an oral preparation for literacy with first graders', in J. Cook-Gumperz (ed.), *The Social Construction of Literacy*. Cambridge: Cambridge University Press. pp. 94–116.

Painter, C. (1999) *Learning through Language in Early Childhood*. London: Cassell.

Perera, K. (1984) *Children's Writing and Reading*: *Analysing Classroom Language*. Oxford: Blackwell.

Rattanavich, S. and Christie, F. (1993) 'Developing text-based approaches to the teaching of literacy in Thailand', in G. Gagné and A.C. Purves (eds), *Papers in Mother Tongue Education 1*. New York: Waxmann Münster. pp. 97–110.

Rattanavich, S. and Walker, R.F. (1996) 'Literacy for the developing world', in F. Christie and J. Foley (eds), *Some Contemporary Themes in Literacy Research*. New York: Waxmann Münster. pp. 17–45.

Schmandt-Besserat, D. (1996) *How Writing Came About*. Austin, TX: University of Texas Press.

Veel, R. (1997) 'Learning how to mean – scientifically speaking: apprenticeship into scientific discourse in the secondary school', in F. Christie and J.R. Martin (eds), *Genre and Institutions*: *Social Processes in the Workplace and School*. London: Continuum. pp. 161–95.

Woolley, M., Pigdon, K. and Molyneux, P. (1995) *Report on Development of Modules 4, 5 and 6 for Multigrade Teacher Training Program, Hoa Binh, Vietnam*. UNESCO Office, Hanoi.

Woolley, M., Pigdon, K. and Molyneux, P. (1996) *Report on Development of Modules 7 and 10 for Multigrade Teacher Training Program, Nha Trang, Vietnam*. UNESCO Office, Hanoi.

Woolley, M., Pigdon, K. and Hartman, D. (1998) *Report on a Writing Camp Held at Lao Cai*. World Bank Primary Education Project, Multigrade and Bilingual Education Sub-component. UNESCO Office, Hanoi.

Part IV

LITERACY IN PRESCHOOL SETTINGS AND SCHOOLS

25

Talk and Discourse in Formal Learning Settings

JOANNE LARSON AND SHIRA MAY PETERSON

Recent studies on talk and discourse in early childhood literacy events have dealt with a wide variety of productive research issues that promise to significantly impact early childhood education. While there is a great deal of overlap and consensus in the research topics, underlying these research programmes are a number of diverse and often incompatible ideological positions that shape the researchers' choice of method, conclusions, and recommendations for educational practice. In particular, two theoretical issues currently fragment the field of early childhood literacy research. The first concerns the nature of literacy. Street's (1995) distinction between ideological and autonomous conceptions of literacy is well known and has been broadly incorporated into literacy research and theory. Street posits a continuum between research that frames literacy as a neutral set of skills and research that understands literacy as a social practice. A second issue concerns the purpose or function of literacy. We argue that researchers fall along a continuum between viewing successful literacy outcomes as fixed, marked by the achievement of traditional notions of literacy success, and viewing literacy outcomes as fluid, characterized by emergent and multiple forms of collaboratively constructed meaning. Competing ideologies have made it increasingly difficult for readers of the research to understand how to interpret research findings. The current diversity of positions has also discouraged researchers from reading across ideological positions.

This chapter presents a theoretical framework for situating research on talk and discourse in formal learning contexts that combines the two continua of ideological versus autonomous and fixed versus fluid outcomes, resulting in a four-quadrant grid with which we analyse the literature. This theoretical heuristic provides a framework for our review of research that focuses on the social, cultural, historical, and political context of literacy learning in formal learning settings, which we identified as schools, preschools, churches, and both formal and family day care centres. The goal of locating research studies within their respective ideological positions is to illuminate the underlying historical contexts that have shaped current research on language and literacy in early childhood.

We define talk as social action in which interlocutors co-construct meaning in interaction in everyday activity (Duranti, 1997; Goodwin, 1990). Ochs defines discourse as a 'set of norms, preferences, and expectations relating linguistic structures to context, which speaker-hearers draw on and modify in producing and interpreting language in context' (1988: 8). This distinction between talk and discourse is echoed in Gee's (1999) notion of 'little d' and 'big D' D/discourse. 'Discourse' with a 'big D' represents the various culturally organized ways of acting and being in the world, or 'forms of life', that are enacted, reproduced, or transformed through language in use, or what Gee calls discourse with a 'little d'. We use discourse here to describe what Bakhtin (1981; 1986) terms a social language that has a particular speech genre. Bakhtin's unit of analysis focuses on the utterance as an active representative of the voice or voices that are reflected in and produced from an organized social context, such as schools and classrooms.

Additionally, we draw on definitions of discourse in critical discourse analysis to explore how discourse in local sites and in larger social structures constructs and positions human subjects (Foucault, 1972; Luke, 1995). Critical discourse analysts acknowledge the dialectical relationship between discourse in use and the larger social structures, each constituting and transforming the other through social interactions (Fairclough, 1992). A critical discourse analysis perspective investigates the constitutive and constructive links between discourse in everyday interactions and the differential distribution of power and subjectivity in macrolevel social structures (Luke, 1995).

Given contemporary debates about the definition of research in the US, we feel it necessary to explain the definition of research we used in this review. The Bush administration has recently passed the No Child Left Behind Act of 2001 and national reading legislation in which a federally sanctioned definition of research effectively eliminates all forms of qualitative research from recognition as valid science. This move should not be surprising when one considers that the traditional psychological model is still the dominant paradigm in the majority of educational research, and that politicians seeking a 'quick fix' to educational problems will typically rely on traditional methods of inquiry (Larson, 2001), rather than risking controversy by considering what are often termed 'alternative' forms of research. We know a good deal about talk, discourse, and literacy learning in early childhood due in large part to the variety of research available. To eliminate whole fields of literacy research seems remarkably shortsighted and potentially damaging. In an effort to combat the reductionist view of research currently mandated in the US, we include both quantitative (experimental designs) and qualitative (ethnographic designs) in our review.

ANALYTIC HEURISTIC

We use the four-part grid described earlier to organize and understand the various research perspectives that have been applied to the study of talk and discourse in early childhood literacy events (Heath, 1983). We want to emphasize that this framework is meant to be used as a fluid analytic heuristic and not as a rigid structure within which to hierarchically determine research orientations.

The first continuum represents varying ideological perspectives on the definition and nature of literacy. *Ideological models* define literacy as a social practice grounded in social, historical, cultural and political contexts of use. In this view, the nature and

meaning of literacy are created in the specific social practices of participants in particular cultural settings. In contrast, *autonomous models* define literacy as a unified set of neutral skills that can be applied across contexts (Street, 1995). Literacy is isolated as an independent variable or set of variables that imply standard cognitive and economic consequences. The autonomous definition of literacy is typically based on the essay text genre and generalized to apply to all contexts in which literacy is used. Until recently, nearly all of the research on talk in early childhood literacy events has been dominated by an autonomous view of literacy. Based in a traditional psychological paradigm, these studies treat talk as 'input' into the child's language acquisition system. Simple causal models are used to trace the effects of talk on child outcomes, typically measured by standardized tests of language and literacy skills, administered in a laboratory setting.

An ideological view of literacy assumes that literacy is a set of social practices that are historically situated, highly dependent on shared cultural understandings, and inextricably linked to power relations in any setting (Irvine and Larson, 2001; Street, 1995). From this anthropological perspective, social and linguistic practices are mutually constituted within past and present power relations among people who write and read to accomplish social goals. In this model, the context is constituted by local, culturally specific practices that outline who has access to learning to read and write which kinds of texts for which purposes.

While the ideological/autonomous distinction has been widely discussed in the literacy research community, our second continuum has not received the same level of attention. This continuum represents differing views on the purpose or functions of literacy. We distinguish those approaches that view literacy outcomes as fixed (meaning is defined from an etic point of view) from those that view literacy outcomes as fluid (meaning is defined from an emic point of view). The fixed view of literacy outcomes is one that posits prespecified goals in the process of learning literacy. Whether defined as 'skills', 'competencies', or 'repertoires', these outcomes are determined *a priori*, deriving from the theoretical assumptions of the researchers. Typically, these outcomes are based on traditional notions of school-based literacy. In contrast to the fixed approach, in which 'schooled' types of literacy and meaning are privileged, the 'fluidly defined outcomes' approach takes a more relativistic stance towards meaning making, viewing both school- and home/community-based forms of meaning as collaborative 'forms of life' (Wittgenstein, 1958). In addition, the fluidly defined outcome approach emphasizes emergent meaning, rather than classifying meaning according

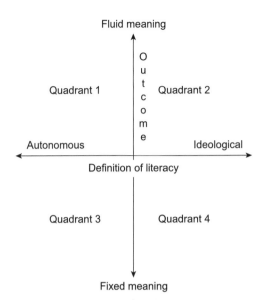

Fluid meaning

Quadrant 1   Outcome   Quadrant 2

Autonomous   Ideological

Definition of literacy

Quadrant 3   Quadrant 4

Fixed meaning

Figure 25.1   Framework for research perspectives on early talk and discourse

to fixed categories. An emergent view sees meaning as continuously changing with context and inter-action, rather than fitting into prespecified definitions. This perspective values the creative and non-standard forms of literacy that children produce in the process of meaning making. Figure 25.1 graphically illustrates the quadrant structure of this heuristic.

In reviewing and analysing the literature, we used the following set of questions to guide the analysis: what is the definition of literacy? What is the implied or articulated learning outcome? What is the position of the learner in relation to text? What is the role of language in literacy learning? What is the research methodology? How are talk and discourse defined? Given this handbook's defi-nition of early years, we limited our review to studies of talk and discourse in formal learning settings with children eight years old and younger. While we focus our review on current research studies, these studies are contextualized through their place-ment in one of the four quadrants in our grid, link-ing them historically to previous foundational research perspectives from which they arose.

QUADRANT 1: AUTONOMOUS, FLUID MEANING

The studies reviewed in quadrant 1 focus on teach-ing children the explicit process of becoming literate subjects and encouraging children to produce creative expressions within conventional, school-based texts. Researchers, both qualitative and quantitative, focus on the fluid construction of meaning as the academic outcome of schooled lit-eracy. Researchers view children's language and social interactions during writing activities as a window into children's understanding of reading and writing processes. In this quadrant, discourse is conceptualized as what Cazden (1988) has called a catalyst or scaffold for student learning. This per-spective views discourse as a tool through which adults can effectively impart objectified knowledge to children. Because research in this quadrant draws on an autonomous model of literacy, reproduction logic or connections to macro social, cultural, and political processes are not examined.

The process model of literacy learning is a repre-sentative area of research in this quadrant. We cat-egorized writing process work as using an autonomous definition of literacy because the explicit and implicit goal is to teach students school-based literacy competencies or academic literacy that is rooted in essayist text (Street, 1995). However, learning to write is understood to be a social process embedded in meaning making. Writing process researchers have made an invalu-able contribution to our understanding of writing in the early years by making internal writing processes available to students through modelling and sup-porting children's multiple literacies. While the process approach to writing focuses on constructing personal meaning, it has been critiqued for its romanticized view of writing and writer's work as art (Willinsky, 1990). Lensmire (1994) has pointed out the potential risks of reproducing race, class, and gender inequities through unproblematized sharing of student writing in writers' workshops.

The work of Donald Graves (1983; 1991; 1994) serves as our case example of research on writing processes. Graves' (1983) research in *Writing: Teachers and Children at Work*, in which he exam-ined the composing processes of seven-year-olds, and subsequent research examining writing devel-opment in early childhood helped to establish the process model of writing instruction in schools. The book itself is a descriptive, hands-on guide for teachers that clearly delineates how to create a studio-craft atmosphere in the classroom. Graves focuses on writing as a craft in which the goal is to build on children's natural desire to write. Children are seen as writers who need to be instructed to find their own processes for expression. Access to understanding these learning processes is gained through analysis of talk and interaction in class-rooms and through examination of children's texts.

Lucy Calkins (1994) built on Graves' work in her research in early childhood classrooms while participating in the Teachers' College Writing Project. Like Graves, Calkins produced a practitioner's handbook outlining the hows of teaching writing to elementary school children that has become one of the guiding works for writing process teachers. She presents a detailed outline of children's writing development and offers explicit strategies for teaching preschool, kindergarten, and first- and second-grade children. Children are viewed as authors who learn to write when they see writing done for real purposes. The focus on audience, purpose, and conventions (defined as school-based notions of correctness) comes into play when making writing public. While the goal is to produce creative expression, the means is through conventional, school-based text, thereby meriting placement in quadrant 1.

Arguing that the primary concern of education is 'with enabling individual students both to contribute to society and to achieve their human potential … just as important as the acquisition of productive skills for the marketplace' (2001: 173), Wells' recent edited volume presents an analysis of talk in process-oriented literacy events in which knowledge is understood to be constructed through discourse. In Chapter 2 of the same volume, Donoahue (2001) examines the development of classroom community in her second-grade classroom. Through weekly class meetings designed to teach children speaking and listening skills that would facilitate community development, she found that children indeed felt a strong sense of community, enhancing their ability to work together during literacy activities. These researchers make the argument that the community skills revealed in this research are needed in the contemporary workplace.

A clear emphasis found among these studies was a focus on using children's spontaneous utterances as a valuable source of information about children's thinking as it is embedded in literate action (Dahl, 1993). In a study of Finnish kindergarten children's literacy development, Korkeamaki and Dreher (2000) examined how classroom discussions contributed to the development of children's spelling ability over time, finding that classroom discussions about letters and sounds allowed children to infer more specific understandings of the alphabetic principle. Analysis of student utterances revealed the students' metacognitive awareness of sound–symbol relationships, self-appraisal and self-management strategies, developmental patterns, text patterns, and the relationship of reading and writing (Dahl, 1993). The research illustrates that young children have a clear sense that text is meaningful and predictable and that they monitor their own understanding of written text. Thus, as other researchers have found, interaction around writing activity can provide information about children's internal processes (Daiute et al., 1993).

Researchers in this quadrant argue that the writing and reading processes of 'real' authors and readers need to be made explicit for young children in classroom instruction through modelling and mini-lessons. The goal is for students to understand the craft of writing as a means for meaningful personal expression. However, the definition of literacy remains grounded in autonomous, school-based literacy practices.

QUADRANT 2: IDEOLOGICAL, FLUID MEANING

Quadrant 2 is characterized by research focusing on how teachers and children can negotiate meaning in literacy events through incorporating children's literacy practices into the official curriculum. Researchers in this area stress the need for teachers to acknowledge the intertextuality of children's literacy understandings, and to validate the social worlds that they bring to the official school world (Dyson, 1993). Teachers must not only learn to appreciate their students' multiple ways of knowing about literacy, but also expand their own views of appropriate participation and ways of interacting with text, in order to allow for more meaningful types of learning (Larson, 2002) and to acknowledge the ways in which children negotiate social membership (Danby, 1996). Classrooms that capitalize on children's propensity towards participating in a community enable the creation of co-constructed forms of literacy knowledge (Gallas, 1994). Research in quadrant 2 also illustrates the ways that the dominant definition of literacy contributes to inscribing children's bodies with ways of talking and acting that serve to maintain power relations and result in curriculum as 'training to be trained' (Luke, 1992).

While approaches to literacy based on an autonomous model assume that literacy skills are context-independent, an ideological definition seeks to understand how literacy forms and practices have evolved to serve culturally specific purposes. In Street's conception of literacy as ideological, the cognitive processing of linguistic parts is wholly dependent on context because it takes place 'within cultural wholes and within structures of power' (1995: 161).

In an ideological model of literacy education, students would have opportunities to use reading and writing to access the world, not as objects of instruction, but as the subjects of meaning making

(Coles, 1998; Edelsky, 1996; Freire and Macedo, 1987). Moreover, language is understood to mediate literacy learning as children actively participate in and are socialized into culturally organized activities (Cole, 1996; Duranti, 1997; Heath, 1983; Ochs, 1988; Rogoff, 1994). Some quadrant 2 researchers tend to define discourse in ways that align with Ochs' definition described earlier, or as what Cazden (1988) describes as reconceptualization/recontextualization. In this view, discourse enables learners to revise their conceptions based on previous experience and interactions with others. Other researchers draw from critical discourse analysis (Gee, 1999; Fairclough, 1992; Luke, 1995) to connect micro language and literacy practices to macro social, cultural, historical, and political processes. Grounded in anthropological theories of culture and language, most of the research in this quadrant uses ethnography, or other forms of ethnographic and qualitative methods, to study language and literacy practices in contexts of use.

Anne Dyson's ethnographic research in early childhood classrooms is our representative case example for this quadrant (Dyson, 1992; 1993; 1996; 1997a; 1997b; 1999; 2000). Dyson's research has provided the field with in-depth analyses of children's literacy practices. Starting from a socio-cultural perspective on language learning, Dyson focuses on the social practices of children as they participate in meaningful literacy activities. Across her research, Dyson defines literacy as a social practice grounded in the social, cultural, historical, and political practices of children's communities. She focuses on the personal and social meanings children collaboratively and interactively construct in academic learning contexts. One of her major contributions to our understanding of children's literacy learning was the finding that school contexts typically separate the social and the academic in ways that inhibit the interactive potential of socially mediated learning.

In *Social Worlds of Children Learning to Write in an Urban Primary School* (1993), Dyson challenges the rigidity of school boundaries by examining the ways in which young children interactively negotiate their social and academic worlds. In the classrooms she studied, children negotiated the official classroom culture by mixing diverse genres and traditions on 'the classroom stage' (1993: 215). We learn about Jameel's boundary crossing as he made a home in school by bringing in cartoons as a legitimated writing genre. Lamar and Eugenie took 'curricular side roads' through peer talk during officially sanctioned activities. All the students and teachers Dyson worked with operated in what she calls a 'permeable curriculum' (1993: 38) that

dialogically engages children's interest in the meaning, context, and complexity of social worlds.

Dyson expanded her analysis to include the ways in which children's culture was incorporated into both oral and written classroom stories (Dyson, 1996; 1997a; 1997b; 1999). Children's identities were textually constructed as they took control of stories, placing themselves in superhero roles as they interpreted, analysed, compared and contrasted texts (Dyson, 1997a). Children's social goals were enacted through affiliating, resisting, and negotiating classroom social life as it shaped text. This negotiation of classroom texts in turn shaped classroom life. In sum, Dyson's point of interest is in the intertextual links between popular culture and academic culture seen in the talk and discourse of classroom interaction. She argues that pedagogy should help children extend the textual knowledge they bring to school into the official school world (Dyson, 2000).

Deborah Hicks and colleagues carry the argument Dyson makes to actively build on young children's language and literacy practices further. Hicks and Kanevsky (1992) use a sociocultural theoretical frame to analyse one first-grade African-American student's use of language within and across activity settings. They found that through his use of multiple modalities of language use – verbalization, writing, and drawing – the student came to assume an authorial voice, to use classic narrative themes, and to develop complex, fictional characters. In another study of an urban first-grade classroom, Hicks (1996) studied how two children reconstructed their understandings of popular superhero texts through talk and writing during journal activities. Children socially enacted meaning in their peer collaborations, creatively transforming the discourses of the classroom and the larger community. All of the research described in this quadrant thus far provides evidence of the utility of children's language and literacy practices and makes compelling arguments for actively using, not simple 'valuing', these resources in the early childhood curriculum.

Several studies we assigned to this quadrant examined competing ideologies of literacy between teachers and students and the resultant conflicts in literacy practices and meaning making that occurred. Like Dyson and Hicks, Rymes and Pash (2001) explore how the social lives of children mediate their participation in school literacy events. In their study of one second-language learner in a mainstream second-grade classroom, Rymes and Pash argue that the student's concern for maintaining his social identity as an 'ordinary' student sometimes conflicted with the teacher's academic goals for classroom literacy activities. The authors argue that teachers must be aware of how conflict between the various language games enacted in the classroom may limit students' academic learning.

Children bring multiple intertextual, multimodal understandings of language and literacy to school, even at the young ages examined in this volume; however, these practices are often not valued in school settings (Ballenger, 1996; Harris and Trezise, 1997; Sipe, 2000). When students' practices are not valued or are actively dismissed, they become increasingly marginalized in the lessons and in classroom social life (Harris and Trezise, 1997; Larson and Irvine, 1999). Furthermore, young children's multiple literacy understandings tend to be acknowledged by the teacher only when they are consistent with the teacher's expectations. When this is not the case, children's responses are often misconstrued as 'misconceptions' (Harris and Trezise, 1997). Teachers who engage children's multiple literacies can enhance student participation and overall classroom experience. For example, Ballenger found that Haitian children's 'shadow curriculum' (1996: 318) provided them with nurturance and comfort in literacy activities, making them more motivated to learn.

Constructing meaning across home and school provides another area of research that builds on the argument for understanding and using children's cultural, linguistic and literacy practices in the classroom. Drawing from anthropology, these studies seek to understand the fluid construction of meaning situated in local communities. For example, Goodman (2000) argues that analysis of classroom discourse reveals students' and teachers' implicit understandings of text and particular beliefs and values that all classroom participants bring from home and other discourse communities. Understanding the multiple discourse communities that are at work in classrooms, then, becomes a key factor in the construction of the early childhood literacy curriculum.

Duranti et al. (1995) reconsider the relationship between home and school and between home and community in their comparison of literacy instruction in pastors' schools in Western Samoa and in a Samoan-American Sunday school in Los Angeles. In both communities, teachers instructed the children in the Samoan alphabet using an educational tool called the Pi Tautau. However, because of the differences in linguistic repertoires and identities of the students and teachers in the two settings, the two instructional activities had different meanings. The authors note the changing meaning of the Pi Tautau, originally used as an instrument of Westernization of Samoan culture by Protestant missionaries, but held up today as a powerful symbol of Samoan culture in the Samoan-American community.

Furthering the argument that children's socially and contextually situated understandings of literacy are necessary contributions to curriculum, Gallas (1992; 1994; 1997; 2001) contends that children should have the opportunity to acquire multiple discourses (literacies) in school and that discourse acquisition is the point at which educational equity occurs. Children acquire discourse through the bridging of the child's imaginative life with the world of school in authorship processes (Gallas, 2001). She argues strongly that a classroom should be a 'sharing community that privileges all kinds of talk and values every child's cultural membership' (1992: 173).

Gallas' (1994) contribution has been a careful examination of narrative as a source of knowledge for young children and as a vehicle for learning that makes children's thinking visible. In a study of her own first- and second-grade classrooms, Gallas analysed sharing time as a speech event to understand her role as a central figure in classroom talk. She implemented what she called a 'noninterventionist' (1994: 17) style during sharing time to explore what would happen if children became the primary audience or ratifiers of classroom discourse. She found that multiple language genres were constructed by the students and were used as an interactive social force that produced an ethic of social inclusion in the classroom community.

Examining how language is used in everyday classroom interactions as a starting point for examining equity of access to participation in literacy events, Larson's body of work (1995; 1997; 1999; 2002) focuses on language and literacy practices in early childhood classrooms and how those practices mediate literacy learning. Through microanalysis of talk and interaction using classroom participation frameworks (Goffman, 1981) as a unit of analysis, Larson articulates a range of ways in which young children participate in literacy events that includes traditional understandings of speaker–hearer dyads to more complex frameworks. In particular, Larson problematizes the conception of overhearer as a passive role in the participation framework and argues that overhearer participation is active and meaningful (Larson, 1995; 1997; Larson and Maier, 2000).

Not only can early childhood classrooms be places where students' language and literacy practices are excluded, they can also be places where reductionist literacy practices and unequal power relations are reproduced. Luke (1992) analysed classroom discourse in an Australian grade 1 classroom and offers a model of ideological transmission in which the body becomes a political object of literacy instruction. He argues that there is no monolithic dominant ideology of literacy that directly mediates ideological reproduction; rather school practices are a form of moral and political discipline. Teachers inscribe the body during routinized literacy events and lessons through the use of strict IRE (initiation, response, evaluation: Mehan, 1979) discourse patterns and directed group recitation, or what Luke calls 'training the mouth' (1992: 120). He claims that while so-called natural learning approaches acknowledge classroom events as being grounded in social context and are opposed to skill and drill instruction, they are still lacking in political theorization of classroom discourse and literacy learning in early childhood as a means of correct training. He concludes that the forms of cultural capital taught in school are not important for today's linguistic market; rather, they are solely for the purpose of discipline and promotion within the school institution. In other words, young children are 'training to be trained' (1992: 126).

Using critical discourse analysis, Luke (1995) and Luke et al. (1994) studied the reading and writing practices in four mixed Aboriginal/Islander and Anglo-Australian students in four first-grade classrooms. They found that basal reader texts and accompanying pictures constructed a subject position of monocultural, middle class family life and gender roles that excluded the realities of the working class Aboriginal and Islander children. Group reading events following a round robin structure positioned students as characters in the text in ways that made their own sociocultural realities invisible. In writing events, the subjectivity of the child as gendered literate writer/author was constructed in classroom talk. The child 'is positioned to reproduce and naturalize particular forms of cultural logic and social identity under the guise of the transmission of particular cultural techniques of authorship' (Luke, 1995: 29).

In sum, the researchers in this quadrant argue strongly that, rather than continuing to devalue students' linguistic, cultural, and discursive practices and simply train them to be trained (Luke, 1992), schools need to understand more deeply how intentions, multiple approaches to text meaning, children's social worlds, and multiple discourses can be used as resources for curriculum. Specifically, understanding children's multiple interpretations of text (Sipe, 2000) and the multiple literacies children use to interpret and use text (MacGillivray, 1997) may begin to address issues of educational equity (Gallas, 1997). Finally, a critical discourse analysis perspective argues that examining the various subject positions established within and across texts reveals how power relations constitute and are constituted by texts (Luke, 1995).

QUADRANT 3: AUTONOMOUS, FIXED MEANING

Research in quadrant 3 is characterized by an autonomous model of literacy and an emphasis on the acquisition of a prespecified set of school-specific literacy skills. Literacy is understood as a set of skills that children need to learn in order to succeed in school, in college, and in the world. The research in this quadrant is influenced to a large extent by traditional psychological theories of literacy development, which posit a developmental continuum in the cognitive and linguistic achievements necessary for literacy acquisition. Most studies in this quadrant are characterized by quantitative methods, including scores on standardized tests of language and literacy and quantitative coding and analysis of naturalistic language.

Studies in this tradition often focus on giving children from 'disadvantaged' backgrounds (those from minority or impoverished families, and native speakers of a language other than English) opportunities to develop the type of language and literacy skills that their home environment is thought to lack, in order to help them 'catch up' with their middle class peers (Bereiter and Engelmann, 1966; Hart and Risley, 1995). This perspective highlights the differences between oral language and literacy, presuming that only certain types of oral language, which replicate some of the demands of literacy, are related to literacy development (Dickinson and Tabors, 2001). While many researchers in this quadrant focus on the social contexts in which children acquire such language and literacy skills, the skills themselves are not treated as contextualized or historical. Rather, traditionally defined literacy skills are accepted as important to children's success in school. This conception views literacy knowledge as an objective commodity that is transmitted from the teacher to the student, whether it is through direct transmission (Bereiter and Engelmann, 1966) or scaffolding (Bruner, 1975).

Collectively, the research studies located in quadrant 3 point to the importance of particular oral language practices as precursors for children's later literacy abilities. Researchers recommend that early childhood environments provide children with ample opportunities to engage in complex conversations with adults and peers, including such 'extended discourse' forms as narratives, explanations, pretend play, and other forms of complex conversation (Dickinson and Tabors, 2001). The finding that not all children participate in these types of language practices at home leads to the recommendation that teachers engage 'disadvantaged' children more often in such practices.

The Home School Study of Language and Literacy, led by David Dickinson and Catherine Snow, is a representative case in this quadrant. The purpose of this large-scale study was to identify the linguistic features of children's home and classroom environments that predict their later literacy abilities, as measured by standardized tests of oral language and emergent literacy. Data were collected from home and school experiences of 64 children from low-income families over a period of two years, beginning when the children were three years old. The same children completed a battery of language and literacy measures in kindergarten called the SHELL–K (the School–Home Early Language and Literacy Battery–Kindergarten: Snow et al., 1995). These tasks were intended to measure the skills that support or relate to literacy acquisition. They included narrative production, picture description, formal definitions, superordinates, story comprehension, emergent literacy (including writing concepts, letter recognition, story and print concepts, sounds in words, and environmental print), and receptive vocabulary as measured by the Peabody Picture Vocabulary Test (PPVT).

Of primary interest in this study is the use of 'extended discourse' in adult–child conversations. Extended discourse is characterized as talk that replicates some of the demands of literacy. It is defined in this study as 'talk that requires participants to develop understandings beyond the here and now and that requires the use of several utterances or turns to build a linguistic structure' (Dickinson and Tabors, 2001: 2). Examples given in the study are narratives, explanations, pretend talk, and other non-immediate talk. The concept of extended discourse has its roots in Bernstein's (1962) distinction between restricted and elaborated codes. Elaborated or extended language has also been variously characterized as cognitively challenging (Smith and Dickinson, 1994), disembedded (Wells, 1981), representational talk that is used to communicate information rather than control behaviour (Dickinson and Tabors, 2001), decontextualized (in which the audience is at a distance from the speaker, whether physically or socially: Snow, 1991), and explicit (talk that depends on linguistic, rather than contextual, cues to represent meaning). Previous research has suggested that experience with this type of language is related to children's later literacy abilities (Hart and Risley, 1995; Snow, 1983; 1987; Sulzby, 1985; Wells, 1981).

The results of the Home School Study demonstrated that several aspects of preschool teachers' language predicted children's scores on the kindergarten measures. These include low rates of teacher talk to child talk, using rare words in conversation with children, using a 'performance-oriented' book reading style rather than a 'didactic' style, using strategies to direct children's attention during large group time, extending children's comments in conversation, and engaging children in cognitively challenging, analytic, interactive conversations.

Furthermore, the analysis reveals that children's participation in extended discourse with teachers in preschool is a strong predictor of their language and literacy skills in kindergarten. A number of previous studies point to the fact that teachers' language in formal early childhood settings is rarely used for complex thinking purposes such as reasoning, predicting, and problem solving (Makin, 1994; Tizard and Hughes, 1984; Tough, 1977). Dickinson and Snow conclude from the Home Study findings that young children should be given opportunities in preschool to participate in the types of extended discourse forms identified in this study.

Other researchers in this quadrant have investigated teacher talk in early childhood formal learning environments as a predictor of children's acquisition of the oral language skills that are thought to precede literacy. While many studies have shown that expressive language ability is an important predictor of literacy, receptive language (the ability to take information from incoming language) is an often overlooked but equally important component of literacy. In a study of early childhood classrooms in Korea, French and Song (1998) found that Korean teachers support children's receptive language skills through extensive use of extended adult talk during large-group activities. Listening to long stretches of teacher talk about interesting, child-appropriate subjects gives children a basis to practise several pre-literacy skills such as drawing inferences, making predictions, and interpreting new information (French and Song, 1998). Other researchers have identified contextual factors that affect teacher talk in preschools, including programme type (McGill-Franzen and Lanford, 1994) and activity setting (Kontos, 1999; Mistry and Martini, 1993).

The ability to compose an oral narrative is highlighted by the research in this quadrant as an important component of children's literacy development (Dickinson and McCabe, 1991). The development of personal narratives in European North American children has been well documented (see McCabe and Peterson, 1991). Recent studies with Japanese (Minami, 1995) and Venezuelan (Shiro, 1995) preschool children have reported structural differences in the personal narratives of four- and five-year-olds. By age five, children in these diverse countries typically develop an understanding of their culture's canonical narrative form. In addition to narrative, researchers have also identified explanation as an important oral language skill that predicts literacy success (Dickinson and Tabors, 2001). Peterson (2002) found that through participation in extended conversations with teachers, children in a science-based preschool programme made significant gains in their oral explanations for physical phenomena.

Many researchers in this quadrant emphasize that early childhood educators can give children opportunities to learn school-based forms of oral language through scaffolding (Bruner, 1975). Speidel (1993) found that comprehension reading lessons in a Hawaiian first-grade classroom (part of the Kamehameha Early Education Program, or KEEP) became opportunities for scaffolding children to use standard English forms. Researchers have also identified peer interaction as another way that children can learn to participate in school-based literacy practices. In one multiage (K-2) classroom, Stone and Christie (1996) found that 40% of children's time in the sociodramatic play centre was engaged in school forms of literacy activities and that most of these activities were in collaborative interactions with an older or a younger child. The authors suggest that multiage classrooms have the potential to naturally foster 'communit[ies] of learners' (1996: 133) due to the children's wide range of literacy expertise.

As a whole, researchers in quadrant 3 have argued that experience with school-based oral language practices is related to children's later success in school-based forms of literacy. Students who lack experience with such language and literacy forms are frequently disadvantaged when it comes to participating in school-based literacy practices and performance on standardized measures of literacy. The orientation in this quadrant to an autonomous view of literacy leads to suggestions for educational practices that are focused on the types of language and literacy typically expected of students in school. On the whole, these researchers agree that early childhood educators should give children ample opportunities to participate in extended discourse forms, including narratives, explanations, pretend talk, and other forms of complex conversation, in order to achieve successful school-based outcomes.

QUADRANT 4: IDEOLOGICAL, FIXED MEANING

Researchers in quadrant 4 subscribe to an ideological model of literacy, in which literacy practices are understood in cultural and historical context, yet their ultimate focus is on children's participation in school-based literacy practices. From this perspective, researchers problematize traditional definitions of literacy and school success, acknowledging that they represent only one of many types of literacy understandings based in cultural practices. However, they also recognize that the traditional definition of literacy is the one that carries the most political and ideological weight in mainstream cultures in the US, as well as in most Western nations (Delpit, 1988). An ideological approach views literacy knowledge as constructed through participation in literacy events, during which children appropriate cultural knowledge through language, participating in ways of talking and acting that are preferred by the cultural and social group in which the child lives (Gee, 2001). While all of these types of literacy understandings are valuable to the child, children who are not familiar with school-based literacy practices are at a disadvantage in mainstream school settings and in a global capitalist workforce. Researchers in quadrant 4 advocate that school should provide children with opportunities to learn 'legitimate' forms of literacy, in order for them to become familiar with and appropriate the *cultural capital* (Bourdieu, 1977) of school-based ways of approaching literacy.

Like researchers in quadrant 3, those in quadrant 4 acknowledge that extended discourse forms as characterized by Snow and Dickinson are privileged in school settings, and children's facility with such forms predicts their acquisition of traditional literacy knowledge. However, researchers in quadrant 4 do not assume that this kind of school talk (Genishi and Fassler, 1999) is explicit and decontextualized in absolute terms. As Gee argues, school language is simply 'inexplicit and contextualized in a different way' (1999: 31). 'Schooled literacy' (Street, 1995) represents a particular set of social practices and a particular kind of language use that are considered the 'legitimate' form in schools. Researchers of this view focus on ways that teachers either expose or conceal their expectations for 'legitimate' literacy participation from children. Researchers in quadrant 4 urge teachers to integrate children's home discourse practices into the classroom. This approach acknowledges the diversity of language practices that children bring with them to school, and makes use of this knowledge through discourse that provides for reconceptualization/recontextualization (Cazden, 1988) in teaching children the 'legitimate' literacy practices of mainstream school culture. Both quantitative and qualitative research methods can be found in this quadrant.

For our case study in this quadrant, Shirley Brice Heath defines literacy events as 'occasions in which written language is integral to the nature of participants' interactions and their interpretive processes and strategies' (1982: 74). Heath proposes that ways of taking meaning from the printed word are interdependent with ways children learn to talk in social interactions, a view that challenges the validity of the oral–literate dichotomy. In her study of three communities in the Piedmont Carolinas (1982; 1983), Heath describes the ways in which families from different communities differ in their literacy practices with their children. While children in a white, middle class community (Maintown) participate in ways of talking that are parallel to classroom interactions, children in a white, working class community (Roadville) and in a black, working class community (Trackton) experience language and literacy practices in ways that do not necessarily prepare them for what they find in the classroom.

Trackton children in particular score poorly on reading readiness tests, yet Heath observes that they excel at a variety of language abilities, such as analogy skills, which are not tapped in the school setting. Heath suggests that children who are not socialized to 'school talk' at home are at a considerable disadvantage when they enter school, due to the different expectations that teachers have of children's language. She argues that Roadville children need opportunities to practise new forms of discourse, and to learn distinctions in discourse strategies and structures, especially related to interactions with books. Trackton students need to learn to take meaning from books, to adapt their creative language abilities for use in learning to read, to recount factual events, and to learn the mainstream discourse appropriate to school.

Like Heath's work, the work of Sarah Michaels identifies ways that children's home experiences with literacy are devalued in school settings. Michaels' (1984; 1985) research on talk in early childhood classrooms focuses on the diverse literacy understandings that children bring to the classroom. She proposes that children's school success is hindered by teachers' evaluations, which are often unconsciously based on their discourse expectations of children. When asked to judge transcripts of children's sharing time narratives, white adults responded more positively to linear, 'topic centred' stories produced by most white children, while black adults responded positively to both 'topic centred' stories and 'topic associating' stories, used more often by black children (Michaels, 1984). Michaels argues that, while control over various language forms should be the ultimate goal, the focus of sharing time should be more concerned with allowing children to use the forms and strategies they are most familiar with in order to successfully

express themselves. This attitude is prevalent among teachers participating in the structural equivalent of sharing time in Spanish classrooms, known as *la ronda* (Poveda, 2001). Instead of a lesson in discourse forms, *la ronda* is primarily seen as a means of socializing students into a moral community. Consequently, Spanish teachers have fewer expectations for children's discourse forms, are less intrusive in correcting children's stories, and allow for more individual differences in children's participation, including permitting students not to participate if they do not wish to.

Researchers in this quadrant focus on exposing the consequences of teachers' tacit expectations for children's participation. In a study of an elementary school in the Piedmont Carolinas, Edwards and Davis (1997) found that the middle class white teachers frequently judged their Appalachian and African-American students' answers to be off-topic when they were in fact 'mishearing' the children's language. Furthermore, the researchers found teachers' questions to be ambiguous in that they carried implicit expectations that were not clear in the language and were not made clear to the children. The authors reiterate Au's (1993) suggestion that teachers create 'culturally composite classrooms' where a diversity of languages is acknowledged.

Gregory's (1993) study of nine children in one urban, multilingual early childhood classroom in the UK revealed that the teacher blurred the boundaries between the text and her commentary on it. Successful children in this classroom 'ignore[d] the teacher's explicit instructions [to talk about what they think] … and work[ed] within her implicit expectations of "getting the story" (1993: 218), that is, adhering to the teacher's assumptions about what was relevant in the story. Gregory also found that children who were unsuccessful at participating in the reading activity were given less feedback about their performance than the successful children, hindering their future participation and achievement. Gregory argues that the 'legitimate' (school-based) interpretation of literacy is important for children's later school reading success (1993: 223). Teachers should become aware of their own expectations for children's participation in literacy events and encourage children's awareness of social practices surrounding literacy.

In sum, research in quadrant 4 deals with ways that educators can help children to participate in school-based literacy practices, while at the same time acknowledging and integrating the multiple language and literacy resources that children bring from home. By recognizing the differences in local conceptions of 'doing literacy', educators can more effectively teach children from various backgrounds the forms of cultural capital that are valued in school and in mainstream social institutions. Viewing school-based literacy through an ideological lens, researchers in this quadrant emphasize the importance of making explicit the multiple conceptions of literacy held by students, their families, teachers, schools, and mainstream society, so that children's literacy knowledge may be incorporated in the classroom as an important resource in children's overall literacy development.

CONCLUSIONS/IMPLICATIONS FOR FUTURE RESEARCH

The research reviewed in this chapter represents four approaches to the study of talk and discourse related to children's literacy learning, falling within the two continua of ideological versus autonomous approaches to literacy and fluid versus fixed meaning outcomes. In reviewing the research on talk and discourse in formal early childhood settings, we noticed a number of trends across the studies. First, researchers tend not to read across ideological positions and as a result do not build on each other's work. This practice limits the potential advances we can make in the field. It is our recommendation that researchers take an ideological approach to the research and acknowledge multiple ways of knowing in the different research communities from which we approach the subject of talk and discourse. To do this, researchers must position themselves as critical readers of research and view individual studies as located within a historical, a social, and an ideological framework. This practice to a large extent depends upon researchers acknowledging their own assumptions in their research, which brings us to our second point.

In writing this review, it became clear that some researchers whom we placed on the autonomous side of the continuum are in fact beginning to draw from ideological models. We found that a number of researchers in quadrants 3 and 4 are focusing on the same issues as researchers in quadrants 1 and 2, although their research did not articulate the same ideological position. This phenomenon made placing researchers into a particular quadrant problematic, since it was not always obvious what ideological position the researchers actually held. The lesson that emerges from this analysis, then, is that researchers should ideally be explicit about acknowledging their theoretical assumptions so that their findings can be interpreted in light of their view of literacy and their focus on outcomes for educational practice.

A third finding is that, in spite of the rhetoric of the reading wars, most of the research we examined was located in quadrant 2, indicating a growing appreciation of literacy as a social practice and talk as a means of meaning making. Perhaps this distribution can be attributed to a lack of focus on classroom talk by researchers who are interested in school-based literacy skills.

Fourthly, while we now know a good deal about how teachers and students use talk and discourse in the construction of literacy in the early school years, we know much less about the use of talk in the preschool years. We therefore identify a need for more research conducted in the various formal settings for the education of young children, such as church schools, day care centres, and family day care programmes. With the current political climate in the United States and other countries focusing increasingly on the preparation of young children for school, we expect to see a dramatic increase in the coming years in the number of studies examining the kinds of talk that are occurring in preschool and day care settings.

Finally, we found that studies on talk and discourse in formal early childhood learning settings constitute a robust field of research, characterized by important research questions concerning the role of talk in young children's literacy learning. In the future, we hope that researchers in this area begin to ask, and hopefully answer, some of the following important questions: how does talk mediate the impact of technological advances affecting children's literacy learning in schools? What is the relationship between participation framework, literacy activity, and children's experiences in the construction of literacy knowledge? How do curriculum and pedagogy affect discourse interactions in literacy events? How can future research move the field toward a more critical analysis of how young children are positioned as objects of literacy instruction in traditional literacy events?

REFRENCES

Au, K. (1993) *Literacy Instruction in Multicultural Settings*. New York: Harcourt Brace.

Bakhtin, M. (1981) *The Dialogic Imagination*. Austin, TX: University of Texas Press.

Bakhtin, M.M. (1986) *Speech Genres and Other Late Essays*. Austin, TX: University of Texas Press.

Ballenger, C. (1996) 'Learning the ABCs in a Haitian preschool: a teacher's story', *Language Arts*, 73: 317–23.

Bereiter, C. and Engelmann, S. (1966) *Teaching Disadvantaged Children in the Preschool*. Englewood Cliffs, NJ: Prentice Hall.

Bernstein, B. (1962) 'Social class, linguistic codes and grammatical elements', *Language and Speech*, 5: 31–46.

Bourdieu, P. (1977) *Outline of a Theory of Practice*. Cambridge: Cambridge University Press.

Bruner, J.S. (1975) 'The ontogenesis of speech acts', *Journal of Child Language*, 2 (1): 1–19.

Calkins, L. (1994). *The Art of Teaching Writing*, new edn. Portsmouth, NH: Heinemann.

Cazden, C. (1988) *Classroom Discourse: the Language of Teaching and Learning*. Portsmouth, NH: Heinemann.

Cole, M. (1996) *Cultural Psychology: a Once and Future Discipline*. Cambridge, MA: Harvard University Press.

Coles, G. (1998) *Reading Lessons: the Debate Over Literacy*. New York: Hill and Wang.

Dahl, K.L. (1993) 'Children's spontaneous utterances during early reading and writing instruction in whole-language classrooms', *Journal of Reading Behavior*, 25 (3): 279–94.

Daiute, C., Campbell, C., Griffin, T., Reddy, M. and Tivnan, T. (1993) 'Young authors' interactions with peers and a teacher: toward a developmentally sensitive sociocultural literacy theory', in C. Daiute (ed.), *The Development of Literacy Through Social Interaction*. San Francisco: Jossey Bass. pp. 41–63.

Danby, S. (1996) 'Constituting social membership: two readings of talk in an early childhood classroom', *Language and Education*, 10 (2–3): 151–70.

Delpit, L. (1988) 'The silenced dialogue: power and pedagogy in educating other people's children', *Harvard Educational Review*, 58 (3): 280–98.

Dickinson D.K. and McCabe, A. (1991) 'A social inter-actionist account of language and literacy development', in J. Kavanaugh (ed.), *The Language Continuum*. Parkton, MD: York.

Dickinson, D.K. and Tabors, P.O. (eds) (2001) *Beginning Literacy with Language: Young Children Learning at Home and at School*. Baltimore: Brookes.

Donoahue, Z. (2001) 'An examination of the development of classroom community through class meetings', in G. Wells (ed.), *Action, Talk, and Text: Learning and Teaching Through Inquiry*. New York: Teachers College Press.

Duranti, A. (1997) *Linguistic Anthropology*. Cambridge: Cambridge University Press.

Duranti, A., Ochs, E. and Ta'ase, E.K. (1995) 'Change and tradition in literacy instruction in a Samoan American community', in B. McLaughlin, B. McLeod and S. Dalton (eds), *Teaching for Success: Reforming Schools for Children from Culturally and Linguistically Diverse Backgrounds*.

Dyson, A.H. (1992) ' "Whistle for Willie", lost puppies, and cartoon dogs: the sociocultural dimensions of young children's composing', *Journal of Reading Behavior*, 24 (4): 433–62.

Dyson, A.H. (1993) *Social Worlds of Children Learning to Write in an Urban Primary School*. New York: Teachers College Press.

Dyson, A.H. (1996) 'Cultural constellations and child-hood identities: on Greek gods, cartoon heroes, and the social lives of schoolchildren', *Harvard Educational Review*, 66 (3): 471–95.

Dyson, A.H. (1997a) 'Rewriting for, and by, the children: the social and ideological fate of a media miss in an urban classroom', *Written Communication*, 14 (3): 275–312.

Dyson, A.H. (1997b) *Writing Superheroes: Contemporary Childhood, Popular Culture, and Classroom Literacy*. New York: Teachers College Press.

Dyson, A.H. (1999) 'Coach Bombay's kids learn to write: children's appropriation of media material for school literacy', *Research in the Teaching of English*, 33 (4): 367–402.

Dyson, A.H. (2000) 'On reframing children's words: the perils, promises, and pleasures of writing children', *Research in the Teaching of English*, 34 (3): 352–67.

Edelsky, C. (1996) *With Literacy and Justice for All: Rethinking the Social in Language and Education*, 2nd edn. Bristol, PA: Taylor and Francis.

Edwards, B. and Davis, B. (1997) 'Learning from class-room questions and answers: teachers' uncertainties about children's language', *Journal of Literacy Research*, 29 (4): 471–505.

Fairclough, N. (1992) *Discourse and Social Change*. Cambridge: Polity.

Foucault, M. (1972) *The Archaeology of Knowledge*, trans. A. Sheridan Smith. Oxford: Blackwell.

Freire, P. and Macedo, D. (1987) *Literacy: Reading the Word and the World*. South Hadley, MA: Bergin and Garvey.

French, L. and Song, M. (1998) 'Developmentally appro-priate teacher-directed approaches: Images from Korean kindergartens', *Journal of Curriculum Studies*, 30 (4): 408–30.

Gallas, K. (1992) 'When the children take the chair: a study of sharing time in a primary classroom', *Language Arts*, 69: 172–82.

Gallas, K. (1994) *The Languages of Learning: How Children Talk, Write, Dance, Draw, and Sing their Understanding of the World*. New York: Teachers College Press.

Gallas, K. (1997) 'Story time as a magical act open only to the initiated: what some children don't know about power and may not find out', *Language Arts*, 74 (4): 248–54.

Gallas, K. (2001) ' "Look, Karen, I'm running like Jell-O": imagination as a question, a topic, a tool for literacy research and learning', *Research in the Teaching of English*, 35 (4): 457–92.

Gee, J. (1999) *An Introduction to Discourse Analysis: Theory and Method*. New York: Routledge.

Gee, J. (2001) 'Reading, language abilities, and semiotic resources: beyond limited perspectives on reading', in J. Larson (ed.), *Literacy as Snake Oil: Beyond the Quick Fix*. New York: Lang. pp. 7–26.

Genishi, C. and Fassler, F. (1999) 'Oral language in the early childhood classroom: building on diverse foundations', in C. Seefeldt (ed.), *The Early Childhood Curriculum: Current Findings in Theory and Practice*, 3rd edn. New York: Teachers College Press.

Goffman, E. (1981) *Forms of Talk*. Philadelphia: University of Pennsylvania Press.

Goodman, D.L. (2000) 'Becoming literate in an inner-city, whole language school'. Unpublished doctoral dissertation, Michigan State University.

Goodwin, M.H. (1990) *He-Said-She-Said: Talk as Social Organization among Black Children*, Bloomington, IN: Indiana University Press.

Graves, D. (1983) *Writing: Teachers and Children at Work*. Portsmouth, NH: Heinemann.

Graves, D. (1991) *Building a Literate Classroom*. Portsmouth, NH: Heinemann.

Graves, D. (1994) *A Fresh Look at Writing*. Portsmouth, NH: Heinemann.

Gregory, E. (1993) 'What counts as reading in the early years' classroom?', *British Journal of Educational Psychology*, 63: 214–30.

Harris, P. and Trezise, J. (1997) 'Intertextuality and beginning reading instruction in the initial school years', *Journal of Australian Research in Early Childhood Education*, 1: 32–9.

Hart, B. and Risley, T.R. (1995) *Meaningful Differences in the Everyday Experience of Young American Children*. Baltimore: Brookes.

Heath, S.B. (1982) 'What no bedtime story means: narrative skills at home and school', *Language in Society*, 11: 49–76.

Heath, S.B. (1983) *Ways with Words: Language, Life, and Work in Communities and Classrooms*. Cambridge: Cambridge University Press.

Hicks, D. (1996) 'Contextual inquiries: a discourse-oriented study of classroom learning', in D. Hicks (ed.), *Discourse, Learning, and Schooling*. Cambridge: Cambridge University Press. pp. 104–41.

Hicks, D. and Kanevsky, R. (1992) 'Ninja Turtles and other superheroes: a case study of one literacy learner', *Linguistics and Education*, 4: 59–105.

Irvine, P.D. and Larson, J. (2001) 'Literacy packages in practice: constructing academic disadvantage', in J. Larson (ed.), *Literacy as Snake Oil: Beyond the Quick Fix*. New York: Lang. pp. 45–70.

Kontos, S. (1999) 'Preschool teachers' talk, roles, and activity settings during free play', *Early Childhood Research Quarterly*, 14 (3): 363–82.

Korkeamaki, R. and Dreher, M.J. (2000) 'Finnish kindergartners' literacy development in contextualized literacy episodes: a focus on spelling', *Journal of Literacy Research*, 32 (3): 349–93.

Larson, J. (1995) 'Talk matters: the role of pivot in the distribution of literacy knowledge among novice writers', *Linguistics and Education*, 7: 277–302.

Larson, J. (1997) 'Indexing instruction: the social construction of the participation framework in kindergarten journal writing activity', *Discourse and Society*, 8 (4): 501–21.

Larson, J. (1999) 'Analyzing participation frameworks in kindergarten writing activity: the role of overhearer in learning to write', *Written Communication*, 16 (2): 225–57.

Larson, J. (ed.) (2001) *Literacy as Snake Oil: Beyond the Quick Fix*. New York: Lang.

Larson, J. (2002) 'Packaging process: consequences of commodified pedagogy on students' participation in literacy events', *Journal of Early Childhood Literacy*, 2 (1): 65: 95.

Larson, J. and Irvine, P.D. (1999) ' "We call him Dr. King": reciprocal distancing in urban classrooms', *Language Arts*, 76 (5): 393–400.

Larson, J. and Maier, M. (2000) 'Co-authoring classroom texts: shifting participant roles in writing activity', *Research in the Teaching of English*, 34: 468–98.

Lensmire, T. (1994) *When children write: Critical Re-visions of the Writing Workshop*. New York: Teachers College Press.

Luke, A. (1992) 'The body literate: discourse and inscription in early literacy training', *Linguistics and Education*', 4: 107–29.

Luke, A. (1995) 'Text and discourse in education: an introduction to critical discourse analysis', *Review of Research in Education*, 21: 1–48.

Luke, A., Kale, J., Singh, M.G., Hill, T. and Daliri, F. (1994) 'Talking difference: discourse on Aboriginal identity in grade one classrooms', in D. Corsen (ed.), *Discourse and Power in Educational Organizations*. Creskill, NJ: Hampton. pp. 211–24.

MacGillivray, L. (1997) ' "I've seen you read": reading strategies in a first-grade class', *Journal of Research in Childhood Education*, 11 (2): 135–46.

Makin, L. (1994) 'Quality talk in early childhood programs', *Journal for Australian Research in Early Childhood Education*, 1: 100–8.

McCabe, A. and Peterson, C. (1991) *Developing Narrative Structure*. Hillsdale, NJ: Erlbaum.

McGill-Franzen, A. and Lanford, C. (1994) 'Exposing the edge of the preschool curriculum: teachers' talk about text and children's literacy understandings', *Language Arts*, 71 (4): 264–73.

Mehan, H. (1979) *Learning Lessons*. Cambridge, MA: Harvard University Press.

Michaels, S. (1984) 'Listening and responding: hearing the logic in children's classroom narratives', *Theory into Practice*, 23 (3): 218–24.

Michaels, S. (1985) 'Hearing the connections in children's oral and written discourse', *Journal of Education*, 167 (1): 36–56.

Minami, M. (1995) *Japanese Preschool Children's Personal Narratives: a Sociolinguistic Study*. Research report. US Department of Education.

Mistry, J. and Martini, M. (1993) 'Preschool activities as occasions for literate discourse', in R. Roberts (ed.), *Coming Home to Preschool: the Sociocultural Context of Early Education*. Norwood, NJ: Ablex. pp. 220–46.

Ochs, E. (1988) *Culture and Language Development: Language Socialization and Language Acquisition in a Samoan Village*. Cambridge: Cambridge University Press.

Peterson, S.M. (2002) 'Explanatory discourse in preschool science lessons'. Paper presented at the annual meeting of the American Educational Research Association, New Orleans, LA.

Poveda, D. (2001) '*La ronda* in a Spanish kindergarten classroom with a cross-cultural comparison to sharing time in the U.S.A', *Anthropology and Education Quarterly*, 32 (3): 301–25.

Rogoff, B. (1994) 'Developing understanding of the idea of communities of learners', *Mind, Culture, and Activity*, 1 (4): 209–29.

Rymes, B. and Pash, D. (2001) 'Questioning identity: the case of one second-language learner', *Anthropology and Education Quarterly*, 32 (3): 276–300.

Shiro, Martha (1995) 'Focus on research: Venezuelan preschoolers' oral narrative abilities', *Language Arts*, 72 (7): 528–37.

Sipe, L.R. (2000) 'The construction of literary understanding by first and second graders in oral response to picture storybook read-alouds', *Reading Research Quarterly*, 35 (2): 252–75.

Smith, M.W. and Dickinson, D.K. (1994) 'Describing oral language opportunities and environments in Head Start and other preschool classrooms', *Early Childhood Research Quarterly*, 9: 345–66.

Snow, C.E. (1983) 'Literacy and language: relationships during the preschool years', *Harvard Educational Review*, 53: 165–89.

Snow, C.E. (1987) 'Beyond conversation: second language learners' acquisition of description and explanation', in J. Lantolf and A. Labarca (eds), *Research in Second Language Learning: Focus on the Classroom*. Norwood, NJ: Ablex. pp. 3–16.

Snow, C. E. (1991) 'The theoretical basis for relationships between language and literacy in development', *Journal of Research in Childhood Education*, 6 (1): 5–10.

Snow, C.E., Tabors, P., Nicholson, P. and Kurland, B. (1995) 'SHELL: A method for assessing oral language and early literacy skills in kindergarten and first grade children', *Journal of Research in Childhood Education*, 10 (1): 37–48.

Speidel, G.E. (1993) 'The comprehension reading lesson as a setting for language apprenticeship', in *Coming Home to Preschool: the Sociocultural Context of Early Education*. Norwood, NJ: Ablex pp. 247–74.

Stone, S.J. and Christie, J.F. (1996) 'Collaborative literacy learning during sociodramatic play in a multiage (K-2) primary classroom', *Journal of Research in Childhood Education*, 10 (2): 123–33.

Street, B.V. (1995) *Social Literacies: Critical Approaches to Literacy in Development, Ethnography and Education*. New York: Longman.

Sulzby, E. (1985) 'Children's emergent reading of favorite storybooks: developmental study', *Reading Research Quarterly*, 20 (4): 458–81.

Tizard, B. and Hughes, M. (1984) *Young Children Learning*. Cambridge, MA: Harvard University Press.

Tough, J. (1977) 'Children and programmes: how shall we educate the young child?', in A. Davies (ed.), *Language and Learning in Early Childhood*. London: Heinemann.

Wells, G. (1981) 'Some antecedents of early educational attainment', *British Journal of Sociology of Education*, 2 (2): 181–200.

Wells, G. (2001) *Action, Talk, and Text: Learning and Teaching through Inquiry*. New York: Teachers College Press.

Willinsky, J. (1990) *The New Literacy: Redefining Reading and Writing in the Schools*. New York: Routledge.

Wittgenstein, L. (1958) *Philosophical Investigations, 2nd edn*. Edited by G.E.M. Anscombe and R. Rhees. Translated by G.E.M. Anscombe. Oxford: Blackwell.

26

Effective Literacy Teaching in the Early Years of School: A Review of Evidence

KATHY HALL

Learning to read and write is arguably the most important curricular aspect of early years education. This chapter explores the literature on effective literacy teaching in the early stages of schooling, where early years is defined as ranging from five to eight years. The focus is not so much about the relative effectiveness of various teaching methods, instructional programmes, teaching materials, or the 'natural' development of literacy in young children as it is about what characterizes teacher expertise in the intentional promotion of literacy in the early years classroom.

There is now considerable (Roskos and Christie, 2001; Bissex, 1980; Bussis et al., 1985; Teale and Sulzby, 1986; Geekie et al., 1999; Adams, 1991; Snow et al., 1998), though not total (Gee, 1999), agreement in the research field regarding how young children acquire literacy and develop as readers and writers, but this consensus does not extend to literacy pedagogy which still remains quite controversial (e.g. Raphael and Brock, 1998; Foorman et al., 1998; Taylor et al., 2000a; Hall, 2003). More fundamentally, what constitutes literacy is also a contested issue (e.g. Gee, 1999). Moreover, the specific area of effective literacy teaching or expertise in the promotion of literacy, however 'effective' is defined, has a short history. Although reviews of instructional research exist (e.g. Hiebert and Raphael, 1996; Roehler and Duffy, 1996; Raphael and Brock, 1998), much of the available research up to the 1990s did not involve detailed observations of teachers in practice. Only six years ago Pressley et al. (1996) reported a gap in the literature, and in 1998 Wharton-McDonald et al., with particular reference to the early years, noted that 'There is a lack of systematic study of effective literacy teachers, a lack of understanding of their practices and perspectives' (102). However, since the 1990s several researchers have begun to determine what exemplary literacy teaching looks like and it is primarily this relatively new and recent line of enquiry that is of particular interest here.

While the chapter primarily draws on and foregrounds the smaller body of research on effective literacy teachers and their teaching, it also draws on the more general scholarship on literacy teaching that provides theoretical and empirical insights in order to describe the role of teachers in fostering effective early years literacy education. My goal is to integrate a variety of empirical perspectives on literacy to develop an understanding of literacy teaching in the service of an increasingly pluralistic society. The empirical studies discussed in the review all bear on early years classrooms even though several studies incorporated higher grades or classes in their design, in addition to early years classes. The organization of the chapter reflects the kinds of questions that guided the initial search of the literature:

- What characterizes the practices of effective early years literacy teachers and how is 'effective' defined?
- How are these teachers distinguished from their less expert colleagues?
- What theoretical perspectives appear to underpin their practices?
- What are the critical areas in need of further study?

CHARACTERIZING AND DISTINGUISHING EFFECTIVE EARLY YEARS LITERACY TEACHING

The body of empirical research reviewed here derives mainly from the US, but also from the UK, and to a lesser extent New Zealand. The overarching message is that effective literacy teachers integrate two major aspects of the subject. What seems to be key is the integration and balancing of the learning of the codes of written language with uses and purposes of literacy that are meaningful to the learner (Knapp et al., 1995; Pressley et al., 1996; 2001; Wharton-McDonald et al., 1998; Pressley, 1998; Medwell et al., 1998; Morrow et al., 1999; Taylor et al., 1999; 2000b; Rankin-Erickson and Pressley, 2000; Block, 2000; Block, et al., 2002; Au, 1997; Tharp, 1982; Wilkinson and Townsend, 2000). On the one hand, they provide extensive opportunities for their pupils to read and respond to children's literature and to write for a variety of authentic purposes. On the other hand, they attend to the codes of written language: sound–symbol correspondence, word recognition, spelling patterns, vocabulary, punctuation, grammar, and text structure.

THE RESEARCH OF MICHAEL PRESSLEY AND OTHERS

I will illustrate further with reference to the first significant series of studies in terms of scale and scope about effective early literacy teaching. This US-based work was initiated and led by Michael Pressley in the mid 1990s, beginning with an interview survey of kindergarten, grade 1, and grade 2 teachers (Pressley et al., 1996). It proceeded to a more fine-grained, qualitative analysis of outstanding and more typical grade 1 teachers in New York. This research involved observational literacy assessments of pupils, in-depth teacher interviews, close classroom observations, and cross-case analyses of classrooms where achievement was high, i.e. in which the pupils were reading grade-level books, end-of-year writing was extended and mechanically sound relative to other first-graders, and task involvement during literacy lessons was high (Wharton-McDonald et al., 1997; 1998). So the definition of 'effective' and 'outstanding' teaching here bears on pupils' high literacy achievement as revealed by their ability to read and write at a minimum level expected for their grade. It then tested the findings emerging from this ethnographic study in a national investigation of effective teaching in five different areas of the US using a similar range of methodological data-gathering techniques and cross-case analyses methods, and involving 30 'outstanding' and 'more typical' teachers (Block and Pressley, 2000; Pressley et al., 2001).

These studies included mostly children from middle- to lower-middle-income communities and incorporated pupils from a variety of ethnic backgrounds, but they appear not to have represented well the very lowest-income groups, a point I will return to later. Exemplary teachers were nominated by supervisors according to pre-specified criteria, which prioritized their success in raising pupils' literacy achievement levels. However, a major strength of this work is that such nominations were only the starting point and the research team's final samples were based on a subset of teachers whose pupils demonstrated consistently higher levels of achievement in reading and writing and of task engagement in literacy activities (Wharton-McDonald et al., 1998; Pressley et al., 2001). Researchers themselves assessed pupil achievement and on-task engagement using qualitative measures. For example, in the national study, teachers selected as most effective were ones where more than 90% of their pupils were engaged in productive reading and writing more than 90% of the time; where, by the end of the year during which they participated in the study, their pupils were reading picturebooks with several sentences per page; and where their pupils' written compositions were coherent, quite well structured, and several pages long. The outcomes from this series of studies are highly consistent, with the findings of the second study being confirmed by the more broadly based third one. Moreover, findings from a survey of instructional practices of special education teachers nominated as effective teachers of literacy (Rankin-Erickson and Pressley, 2000: 218) were 'strikingly similar' to the findings in Pressley et al. (1996) which was based on a sample of primary teachers nominated as outstanding. Taken together, all these studies offer a consensus on what exemplary literacy teachers do in their classrooms and how they do it. In addition, the findings from one smaller-scale, qualitative study of the reading practices of four outstanding early years teachers, nominated as effective, in New Zealand are also in line with the US evidence (Wilkinson and Townsend, 2000).

Exemplary teachers offer a variety of literacy experiences to their pupils from partner reading, shared reading, independent reading and book choosing to explicit instruction using familiar and new texts, and from daily writing in journals and workshop settings to mini-lessons about the mechanics of writing based on children's needs. Guided reading lessons typically incorporate mini-lessons on phonics and phonemic awareness, the use of new and familiar text, the introduction and use of new vocabulary. These teachers show their pupils how to use a range of reading cues (graphophonic, picture, syntactic and semantic cues) in the context of ongoing reading and writing activity and explicit methods are used for the development of comprehension. The teaching of the mechanics of writing, such as punctuation, occurs in the context of real writing and teachers increasingly emphasize the process of writing such as planning and revising as pupils move from kindergarten to grade 2.

The most effective teachers consciously integrate the teaching of skills with authentic literacy experiences. Indeed integration, as already noted, would appear to be a salient feature of their practice. This means that pupils are encouraged to apply their literacy skills in a variety of reading and writing situations. Literacy for these teachers permeates the curriculum. Writing, for example, is integrated into content areas or other curriculum areas and also thoroughly integrated into reading. The books pupils read and the topics for writing are connected and there is much emphasis on oracy. The researchers conclude that the 'extremely strong presence of themes taught through cross-curricular connections was one of the most extraordinary characteristics of outstanding first-grade literacy instruction' (Morrow et al., 1999: 469).

The grounded theoretical nature of the research orientation used in this line of enquiry allowed the researchers to describe, in ways that have high 'relatability' for practitioners, how these teachers balanced different aspects:

In addition to – and often as part of – explicit skills instruction, the high-achievement teachers provided many opportunities for students to engage in authentic reading and writing activities. Students in these classes read many books alone, in pairs, and with the teacher. They heard good literature read aloud. They used books to search for information on topics of interest. They wrote letters and notes, recorded plant growth in their gardens, and described the growth and development of the chicks hatching in their classrooms. All of these activities were meaningfully linked to ongoing themes and instruction in specific skills. (Wharton-McDonald et al., 1998: 114)

The classrooms are organized for whole-group, small-group, paired, and one-to-one teaching. But perhaps more significantly, these teachers make extensive use of scaffolding whereby they tune into their learners' thinking; have a grasp, through careful monitoring, of their pupils' conceptions and misconceptions; and then intervene with assistance as necessary. They demonstrate a keen awareness of their pupils' thinking and are able to intercede at

just the right moment to ensure the acquisition of some skill or concept. They are expert in seizing the 'teachable moment' and they are not tightly bound by the planned lesson (Block, 2000). Arguably, for this reason they are also especially adept at pitching pupils' work at what might be described as a level of 'easy difficulty' for individual pupils. The researchers noted, 'we observed time and time again the most effective teachers making sure that students were reading books just a little bit challenging for them' (Pressley et al., 2001: 47). They are experts at differentiating tasks according to pupil need. Similarly, Wilkinson and Townsend (2000) reported that their effective teachers continually sought opportunities to move students along a gradient of difficulty with an appropriate level of interactive support. What enabled the New Zealand teachers to achieve such a close fit between the tasks they set their pupils and their learning needs was a combination of their thorough knowledge about their learners (obtained through close observations and running records) and their extensive knowledge of children's literature and the texts that were generally in use in the classroom.

What distinguishes outstanding teachers from their more average colleagues is their ability to incorporate multiple goals into a single lesson. The researchers termed this 'instructional density', saying this was one of the most striking characteristics of practices in high-achievement classes (Wharton-McDonald et al., 1998). In contrast, these teachers' counterparts spend time on activities that are less cognitively complex and less literacy relevant; their lessons are typically of a single teaching goal; and they do not deviate as much from their intended plan to seize an incidental learning opportunity.

The more effective teachers overtly model what they wish their pupils to do. For instance one teacher was observed writing on a chart how she had helped her mother prepare Thanksgiving dinner before asking pupils to write about a time when they helped someone. Similarly, the effective teachers model comprehension by making predictions about what might be in the text that they read to pupils, and they identify questions and major messages that the text suggests as the reading occurs (Morrow et al., 1999). They also exhibit excellent classroom management, including the coordination of support and special teachers; they are well planned; they carefully monitor their pupils' literacy activities, for example as they write; they have well-established routines that children understand and work within; and pupils are expected to be self-regulated and independent (Pressley et al., 2001).

Recently published research by Block et al. (2002) based in seven English-speaking countries sought to identify the qualities of teaching expertise that distinguished highly effective instruction at different grade levels. Highly effective kindergarten teachers, for instance, are described as 'masterful guardians, catching, cradling, and championing every child's discoveries about print' (2002: 189). Interestingly, when their pupils do not learn in their initial attempt, these teachers repeat those literacy experiences again, and again, reusing the same text and context – unlike their counterparts at preschool and grade 1 levels. Highly effective kindergarten teachers believe that frequent repetition enhances background knowledge and facilitates 'ah ah' connections with print. These teachers are described as having 'exceptional talents in creating classrooms that are inviting, print-rich, and home-like' (2002: 189). Highly effective first-grade teachers are expert 'reteachers': they distinguish themselves in their ability to teach literacy all day, motivating pupils by varying the breadth, depth and speed of literacy lessons, teaching up to 20 different skills in a single hour.

What the literature, so far, shows is the complexity of excellent literacy teaching; that expertise involves the smooth interweaving of a whole host of elements; and that outstanding literacy teachers do not adhere to one particular method of teaching.

UK-BASED RESEARCH

UK-based research on effective literacy teaching converges strongly with the above. Descriptive of the range of primary classrooms, and thus not only confined to early years classrooms, the research commissioned by the government's Teacher Training Agency and carried out by Jane Medwell, David Wray, Louise Poulson and Richard Fox compared the teaching of a sample of teachers whose pupils made effective literacy gains with a more random, comparison (validation) sample of teachers whose pupils made less progress in reading (Medwell et al., 1998; Poulson et al., 2001; Wray et al., 2001). The 'effective' teachers were chosen from a list of teachers recommended as effective by advisory staff. The key criterion used by the research team for their selection from this list was evidence of above-average learning gains in reading for the their pupils. The research design incorporated questionnaires, close observations of and interviews with 26 teachers, and a quiz to test teachers' knowledge. It is worth pointing out that this research was carried out in England at a time when there was unprecedented central governmental interest in literacy pedagogy and a highly prescriptive framework for the promotion of literacy was being developed (see Hall, 2001).

Effective literacy teachers in England generally seek to contextualize their teaching of language conventions to maximize its meaningfulness to pupils. This means that letter–sound correspondence, word recognition, and vocabulary, for example, are taught within the context of interacting with whole texts – often shared texts like 'big books'. Effective teachers are distinguished by their explicitness of the functions of what their pupils are learning in literacy and why what they are learning is necessary and useful for them. Other UK research by Lynda Graham (2001) on how reluctant writers overcome their difficulties confirms the significance of meaningfulness, integration of reading, writing, and oracy, and collaboration and sharing texts. Although not specifically on effective teachers, her ethnographic work offers teacher explanations for their pupils' success as writers. Another aspect that Graham's teachers advanced to explain their children's writing progress was small-group work – a feature identified in several studies as important for literacy achievement (see below).

Like the US work, and also based on observational evidence, Medwell et al. found that their effective teachers use short, regular teaching sessions to promote word recognition which involve them modelling to their pupils how sounds work. They use a wider range of texts than their validation colleagues. They tend to use grammar to describe language whereas their colleagues tend to use grammar to prescribe rules for the use of language.

They also adopt very clear assessment procedures involving focused observation and systematic record keeping. They are adept at differentiating the support they offer pupils during the completion of tasks. While effective teachers in England might set all pupils in the group or class the same task and expect them to achieve the same learning outcome, the more effective teachers offer struggling readers and writers more or different support to achieve this outcome. In the light of this, it is not surprising that more effective teachers are also more 'highly diagnostic' in their interpretations of their pupils' written work; they are better and quicker than their validation colleagues at offering explanations as to why children read or write as they do.

Medwell et al.'s cross-sectional samples could not be considered particularly representative of teachers working with pupils from ethnic minority groups or from areas of poverty: they were not designed to be so. Other research on teacher effectiveness has shown that different pupils benefit from different types of teaching (e.g. Good and Brophy, 1991) and research from the field of literacy confirms this (Au, 1980; Au and Carroll, 1997; Moll et al., 1992).

RESEARCH BASED ON MORE DIVERSE POPULATIONS

In this regard, research conducted at the US-government-funded Center for the Improvement of Early Reading Achievement (CIERA) (Taylor et al., 1999; 2000b; Taylor, 2000; Adler and Fisher, 2001; Hiebert and Pearson, 2000) and research by Knapp et al. (1995) are especially insightful. Although not so focused on what specifically characterizes effective literacy teachers and their teaching, some studies of school effectiveness in urban areas of the US (e.g. Designs for Change, 1998; Puma et al., 1997) also provide insights about distinctive teacher practices that are especially relevant to success with low-income catchments and more ethnically diverse populations. And finally, the ongoing longitudinal work of Kathy Au in Hawaii (Au, 1997; Au and Carroll, 1997), though again not specifically designed to explore effective teachers' practices, provides valuable insights into effective literacy teaching with minority ethnic groups.

A national study of effective schools and accomplished teachers at CIERA sought to understand the practices of accomplished teachers in schools that were *beating the odds*, or more precisely, that were achieving unexpectedly high results (Taylor et al., 1999; 2000b). Based on 14 high-achieving, high-poverty, inner-city schools and 70 teachers of kindergarten to grade 3 (i.e. five- to eight-year-olds), this research used a range of quantitative and qualitative data-gathering methods and cross-case analyses determining similarities and differences across settings, especially across effective and ineffective settings. Two teachers from each class, kindergarten to grade 3, were observed and achievements in reading (word recognition, accuracy, fluency and comprehension) were measured by the researchers at the beginning and end of the school year. Michael Knapp et al. (1995) investigated 140 'high-poverty' grades 1–6 classrooms across three US states also using a combination of qualitative and quantitative approaches including the testing of pupils. The results of both studies are largely consistent and in line with the other US and UK evidence, but some additional and specific insights merit some discussion and integration with the previous literature.

First, reading is a priority for teachers in the most effective schools and the most accomplished teachers devote more time to reading activities (including independent reading and writing in response to reading) than the moderately and least effective schools (Taylor et al., 1999; 2000b). Pupils of effective teachers read more and write extended

texts about topics they care about. Creativity and self-expression are important (Knapp et al., 1995). They spend more time on task and, apparently, enjoy what they do (Taylor et al., 2000b).

Secondly, accomplished teachers are distinguished from their counterparts in spending more time in small-group teaching which includes teacher-directed text activity, literature circles, and explicit teaching in phonics, comprehension and vocabulary. This is not altogether surprising when one considers the likelihood that the small-group context allows for activities to be personalized as well as differentiated or targeted more directly at pupils' needs and for teaching to be repeated as needed so children can internalize and better understand. Previous research on early reading demonstrates that whole-class phonics instruction, for example, is not likely to be effective for the majority of children (Juel, 1994). As Connie Juel (1996) concludes, based on a study of what makes one-to-one tutoring effective, providing verbal interaction and tasks that are differentiated according to need is simply not as easy in the whole-class setting. But it is also important to note that in the CIERA study the greater time allotted to small-group teaching is a collaborative decision that is made at school level – could only be made at school level – by all four of the most effective schools (Adler and Fisher, 2001). This small-group work is characterized by regular, special education, and by resource teachers working together to provide small-group teaching. Much like the effective small-group teaching in the New Zealand study (Wilkinson and Townsend, 2000) groups are similar-ability based, although the accomplished teachers in the study refer to it as 'instructional-level grouping', the composition of which changes frequently in the light of assessments and continuous monitoring. Previous literacy research (e.g. Allington, 1983) shows that similar-ability grouping meant that those consigned to the lower-ability groups were frequently given work that was low in cognitive demand. But in the CIERA study pupils in the lower 'instructional-level group spent as much time on higher-order activities as did average achievers' (Taylor et al., 2000b: 156). The authors point out that the success of this strategy is due not merely to the accomplished teachers but to school culture, i.e. to the school-level decisions that led to flexible deployment of teaching staff together with a common assessment system that ensured flexible movement between groups. Indeed one of the substantive strengths of the CIERA study is its linkage of school and classroom effectiveness measures. What comes across from the evidence is that the classrooms of the most effective teachers are more discursive, conversational and dialogic places to be: one gets a sense of negotiation, tentativeness, and power-sharing, yet there is explicitness, clarity about expectations, and a sense of security for children.

Thirdly, the most effective teachers explicitly build on children's personal and cultural backgrounds (Knapp et al., 1995) and teachers in the most effective schools reach out more to communicate with and involve parents (Taylor et al., 1999; Designs for Change, 1998; Puma et al., 1997). This suggests a view of literacy that involves social and cultural interactions at home and at school, a view that recognizes that some children have home cultures that differ from the culture of the school and that such cultural conflict may impede literacy learning (e.g. Dyson, 1998; Heath, 1983; Hicks, 2001; Schmidt, 1995). The effective teachers' emphasis on the sociocultural aspect is in line with previous, longitudinal research in classrooms (Au, 1992; 1997), and in line with a perspective on literacy learning that does not separate cognitive and affective aspects. Au's work, for example, has demonstrated the benefits of bridging the gap between school and community literacies (Tharp, 1982). She has researched the Kamehameha Elementary Education Program (KEEP) in Hawaii for over two decades, a programme based on Vygotskian theory and, more specifically, on the idea that pupils from diverse and poor neighbourhoods have rich funds of knowledge and community literacy practices. The success of this programme suggests that a culturally responsive curriculum is important for improving literacy among pupils who do not come from middle class backgrounds – pupils whose home and community culture may not align with the traditional school culture of literacy.

The fourth insight is entirely in line with previous studies. While explicit word recognition strategies are taught in all schools, what distinguishes the most accomplished teachers is their additional 'coaching' of pupils (as opposed to telling or recitation which is more evident among the least accomplished teachers) in how to apply their word recognition skills to their everyday texts (Taylor et al., 2000a). This contrasts with most teachers who tend to teach word recognition skills in isolation from their application to real texts (Taylor et al., 1999; 2000b; Knapp et al., 1995; Designs for Change, 1998; Puma et al., 1997). A major distinguishing feature of the most successful first-grade teachers, Knapp et al. claim, is that 'skills are taught as tools to be used immediately (or very soon) in the work of making sense of the printed page, not be mastered for their own sake without applications to the act of reading' (1995: 74). And when skills are taught separately they are integrated into games and there is much emphasis on recognizing learning patterns through rhyme and story.

The limited number of research studies on effective literacy teaching in the early years that could be included in this review means that conclusions have to be viewed as exploratory. However, the consistency across the findings permits their integration under three interrelated headings: curricular, organizational and pedagogical. Table 26.1 highlights the range of practices that distinguish the most effective literacy teachers. The effective literacy teacher is not someone who has a single identifying approach but rather is someone who weaves and interweaves several literacy goals and literacy practices through attending to a variety of curricular, organizational and pedagogical matters. Effective teachers appear to approximate to a 'cognitive apprenticeship' model (Collins et al., 1989). This model focuses on learning through guided experience, it highlights the cognitive and metacognitive processes involved in expert performance, and in this way learners are made sensitive to the details of expert performance. It also embeds knowledge, skills and strategies in their social and functional contexts. It is clear that outstanding literacy teachers in the early years of school build upon the variety of rich language acquisition strategies which children have informally developed outside of school. They appear to act on the Hallidayan theory that meaning is the driving force in literacy growth. In other words it is from an understanding of what language does (semantically and pragmatically) that children learn its form (both syntactically and graphophonemically) (see Harste et al., 1994, for a full account).

A discussion of theories of literacy learning is beyond the scope of this chapter, but it is worth noting that the cognitive apprenticeship model does not preclude an emphasis on decontextualizing knowledge (Collins et al., 1989), albeit applied in context 'soon' or even immediately. However, that effective teachers are adept at seizing the 'teachable moment', and that they closely observe and act on children's literate practices as they occur in a variety of classroom contexts, suggest that they also draw on a kind of situated learning theory that emphasizes the creation of learning contexts for which literacy can be used to meet the demands of a situation. In this view, activities create the context that stimulates learners to construct their own knowledge (Rogoff, 1982; Neuman and Roskos, 1997).

EFFECTIVE LITERACY TEACHERS' THEORETICAL PERSPECTIVES

So far attention has tended to focus largely on the characteristic classroom practices of exemplary early years teachers of literacy. A fuller understanding

Table 26.1 *Distinguishing characteristics of effective literacy teachers' practices*

Curricular
- Their pupils read more and write more extended text
- Their pupils read and write about what matters to them
- Word recognition, vocabulary, spelling, comprehension and writing skills are explicitly taught through application
- They teach their pupils multiple cues for word recognition
- These teachers offer greater variety in literacy experience: partner reading, shared reading, independent reading, book choosing, explicit teaching using new and familiar texts, writing for a variety of purposes, collaborative writing

Organizational
- Excellent class management, incorporating routines that support pupil independence, thorough planning, and strong emphasis on literacy-rich classroom environments, on specific feedback about progress, and on positive reinforcement
- These teachers spend more time on cognitively demanding and literacy-relevant tasks
- They coordinate support staff to maximize curricular integrity and task differentiation according to pupil need
- They provide organizational variety: small-group teaching, pair work, one-to-one and whole-class teaching
- They spend more time on teacher-directed, similar-ability, small-group work, the composition of which changes frequently due to careful monitoring
- They establish close links with parents and community

Pedagogical
- Integration and balance: reading and writing are integrated by these teachers, so pupils write in response to texts read; thematic approach is used to integrate the content areas; balance between reading good quality literature, writing for meaningful purposes and learning the conventions of print; literacy knowledge and skills are applied to real texts as they are learned
- Teacher models literate behaviour to make learning and thinking explicit for pupils
- More extensive scaffolding of pupil learning and providing the right level of support, and monitoring and giving feedback as pupils complete tasks
- More emphasis on self-regulation and pupil independence
- Greater use of opportunistic/incidental teaching; instructional density; and multiple goals for a single lesson
- Explicit building on children's cultural backgrounds

of their expertise is facilitated through an examination of the thinking and perspectives they bring to bear on their decision making in the classroom. Some of the above studies together with other, smaller-scale studies shed light on this.

Research conducted on effective teachers during the 1960s and 1970s focused almost exclusively on the teacher behaviours in the classroom that related to pupil achievement (e.g. Rosenshine and Furst, 1973; Brophy, 1973; see Hoffman, 1991, for a review in relation to literacy). The largely behaviourist perspective underpinning this line of enquiry meant that little or no attention was paid to the teacher as critical decision maker. The constructivist thinking underlying the more recent literature, however, does consider the significance of the teachers' prior beliefs and knowledge and their reasoning behind their practices. The more recent studies seeking to illuminate expert literacy teaching practices incorporate data on teacher thinking about and explanation for their actions. This information is typically elicited through semi-structured interviewing, that is conversations about lessons just observed or about samples of their pupils work, although questionnaires have also been used (e.g. Poulson et al., 2001). In addition, since experts in a

profession tend to have a privileged understanding of what they do and are able to give valid and accurate accounts of the decisions they make (Wharton-McDonald et al., 1998), highly competent literacy teachers are extremely well positioned to provide insights into the nature of effective teaching.

What additional insights then are available about outstanding early years teachers' literacy practices? The first point to be made here is that the most effective teachers exhibit continuity between their pedagogical philosophies and their practices.

A questionnaire survey within the UK study, designed to assess teachers' orientations to different literacy perspectives, found that there are differences in theoretical beliefs between effective teachers and the comparison or validation sample (Poulson et al., 2001). First, the effective teachers of literacy show a higher level of consistency between their theoretical beliefs and choice of teaching activities than the comparison sample. The effective teachers claim to be more committed to principles of whole language in their teaching of reading, that is, they place more emphasis on their pupils making sense of text, on authentic as opposed to decontextualized texts, on literacy processes, and on writing for a range of purposes.

Differences between the two samples in relation to orientation to writing are less clear-cut. There are also differences between the validation teachers and the effective teachers regarding what they think children need to know about reading and writing. While all emphasize the importance of coming to grips with the codes of written language, the more effective teachers accord much more status to children recognizing the purposes and functions of the literacy tasks they are set.

The most accomplished teachers hold consistently high expectations for *all* their pupils. They define all their pupils as capable of becoming successful readers and writers and their practices bear this out (Wharton-McDonald et al., 1998; Block et al., 2002; Taylor et al., 2000b; Wilkinson and Townsend, 2000). The New Zealand teachers, for example, are described as holding a developmental view of ability, a notion of ability as 'learnable' and incremental rather than innate or immutable. Effective teachers also exhibit a keen awareness of purpose. The most effective teachers are strikingly different from their less effective colleagues in their detailed descriptions of why their pupils were allocated specific tasks (Block, 2000; Medwell et al., 1998). They talk about their philosophies with reference to specific children. While typically teachers can 'talk the talk' in that they tend to be familiar with the latest literacy terminology, the most effective teachers go beyond general terms and general descriptions and apply their theoretical understanding to individual children (Block, 2000).

Interestingly, these teachers know they are effective. In one study (Block and Pressley, 2000: 8–9) they allocated themselves the highest possible ranking in meeting the needs of pupils with special literacy needs and they could also explain how their teaching contributed to pupils' literacy growth: they could cite, for example, 'what part of their actions, instructional program, or teaching repertoire had scaffolded the success of individual students'. Similar findings emerged from the UK research (Medwell et al., 1998). In the UK study the most effective teachers are described as being very specific about how literacy activities at the whole-text, word and sentence levels contribute to children's meaning making. They are also found to have more detailed and well-developed knowledge about literacy: they are described by the researchers as having a 'coherent belief system' which appears to be related to their more considerable experience of in-service professional development.

On the basis of the above, the most effective teachers implicitly define their pupils as active, thinking, feeling sense makers, rather than mere rememberers or forgetters. They implicitly define themselves as powerful enablers whose task it is to understand what their learners already know and can do in various literacy contexts, to recognize what motivates and engages them, and to extend their literacy repertoires by building on their strengths. Becoming literate is implicitly defined as becoming increasingly adept at using literacy to do things for purposes that are valued by them and within their communities. We can also conclude that effective teaching involves evidence-informed practices, to use a fashionable phrase, with evidence not only about literacy learning *per se* but, fundamentally, about specific children's literacy practices and dispositions.

CONCLUSION

The research reviewed here demonstrates that effective literacy teaching in the early years of school is about far more than 'method'. Rather it is a complex mix of philosophy, method, teacher development and school culture. Effective teachers are clearly eclectic in their approach to literacy teaching, and dichotomies such as phonics-oriented versus literature-based approaches seem not to be relevant to real-life contexts. The complexity of what effective literacy teachers do, which, to varying degrees, fits with what we know about the complexity of children's early learning about written language (e.g. Adams, 1991; Snow et al., 1998; Roskos and Christie, 2001; Bissex, 1980; Bussis et al., 1985; Teale and Sulzby, 1986; Geekie et al., 1999; Kress, 1997; Dyson and Genishi, 1994) should lead us to question the validity of perspectives that seek to find a single best approach (Foorman et al., 1998; DfEE, 1998). The effective teaching of literacy cannot be packaged in teacher-proof scripts or prescriptive programmes on the assumption that 'one size fits all'.

Children benefit from a combination of teaching approaches to become successful readers and writers and effective teachers know and act on this. This conclusion is not only justified via the research on teacher effectiveness reviewed here; it is also confirmed by research that focuses on different pedagogical approaches to literacy development. To illustrate, Sachs and Mergendoller (1997) showed that the kindergarten pupils in their study who had very little knowledge of literacy benefited more from a whole-language approach than from a phonics-oriented approach at that particular point in their learning. Juel and Minden-Cupp (2001) demonstrated that when teachers use the same approach with all first-grade pupils, its impact differs according to the children's varying entry profile to that class. Those first-graders who already had considerable experience of and success in literacy activities benefited from an emphasis on real texts and good quality children's literature and were disadvantaged by an emphasis on phonics training. The opposite was the case for lower-achieving pupils in the first grade: they benefited from an emphasis on phonics training. Once pupils appreciate that print carries meaning and once they master some initial skills, it seems that more direct attention to specific reading strategies is timely. The point of this illustration is that children in kindergarten (or any year/grade) are not homogeneous and teachers have to base their teaching on a knowledge of their pupils' specific literacy strengths and weaknesses in order to maximize their effectiveness. And this is what effective literacy teachers are adept at doing. They recognize the need for careful differentiation. Moreover, our children are increasingly diverse, not just academically, but linguistically and culturally, making it highly unlikely that a single approach to teaching literacy can be found.

The CIERA research demonstrates that school and classroom factors interact to influence the quality of the child's literacy experience. Further research needs to continue to explore the nature of the relationship between school-level and classroom-level decision making about literacy pedagogy. In addition, while it is clear that effective literacy teachers liaise closely with parents, the nature of this contact merits closer scrutiny, especially in diverse classrooms and in areas of poverty. The evidence shows, for example, that effective teachers explain to pupils the purposes of the literacy activities set for them. But perspectives about the functions of literacy may differ in different social and cultural groups. Metsala et al. (1996), for instance, found that middle-income parents are more inclined to see literacy as a source of entertainment, whereas lower-income parents tend to see it more as skill to be developed with consequent expectations about how they expect it to be fostered in school (see McCarthy, 2000, for a review). Moreover, children learn culturally appropriate ways of using language to construct meaning from texts in their early years at home. The evidence for the significance of shared understanding about community practices is persuasive. Teachers who are more effective with children from diverse cultural and language groups are likely to know more about their pupils and their pupils' communities (McNaughton, 2001; Heath, 1983; Darling-Hammond, 1998). Currently we do not have sufficient evidence about how effective teachers interface with culturally and ethnically diverse families and how they build on young children's home literacies. In the interests of fairness and democracy this kind of inquiry is urgently needed.

Only three years ago, Elizabeth Hatton (1999) argued, with reference to Australia, that there is 'alarmingly little to go on in terms of what day to day life in schools is like', and in particular noted that there is little known about how teachers and schools address issues of social justice – her specific concern. Research on effective teachers, generally, and on effective early years literacy teachers in particular, is still in its infancy and future research needs to explore the extent to which the apparent current consensus in the field applies more globally. I should at this point note that a large-scale, government-funded investigation of what constitutes effective literacy teaching and learning practices in the early years of schooling is currently in progress under the direction of William Louden at Australia's Edith Cowan University.

Research on literacy engagement (Guthrie et al., 1996), which combines the construct of self-regulation with intrinsic motivation, describes engaging classroom contexts as those that: focus on substantive themes rather than reading skills; allow choice of themes and texts and promote autonomy; offer explicit teaching of reading strategies; are collaborative, emphasizing social construction of meaning; create opportunities for self-expression and group interaction; and are coherent in that they integrate classroom activities and tasks. The theoretical perspective offered by Guthrie et al. is that these are the very classroom qualities that accelerate the development of literacy engagement. One can speculate, therefore, that the practices of the most effective early years teachers are those that turn out children who not only *can* read and write, but who *do* read and write inside and outside of school. Future research on effective teaching might usefully incorporate evidence of out-of-school literacy practices of the pupils of those deemed to be outstanding teachers to determine their impact beyond the classroom. Such research might usefully incorporate the learner's voice more directly than the existing research.

Research and development programmes to improve schools in urban areas of poverty where children are not 'beating the odds' are already in progress, following the research conducted by CIERA. This is based on the expectation that the quality of classroom literacy teaching can be enormously enhanced through research-based intervention programmes. This work is certainly important and opportune, given the considerable consensus that exists within the research of literacy teacher effectiveness.

But the existing studies on literacy teacher effectiveness imply a model of literacy that is restricted largely to the interpretation and production of print. This brings me, finally, to the implicit theory of literacy and literacy acquisition underlying the studies of effectiveness reviewed in this chapter. Contemporary literacy practices suggest the need for pedagogic research that incorporates a fuller range of symbolic tools that are available to children to support meaning making, drawing especially on popular culture and information technologies (see Kress, 1994 ; Marsh, and Comber, in this volume). Research on children's ways of using written language (e.g. Dyson, 1994; Kress 1997) which demonstrates the non-linearity of literacy development offers new perspectives for policy and practice. Dyson, for example, views written language development within a broad context of children's development as symbolizers. She demonstrates how children's use of written language is interrelated in complex ways with their use of other media and with the relationships they form through interaction with other people. Viewing written language development as part of the child's developing symbolic repertoire and changing social relationships offers new ways of thinking about its development in the classroom. The talking, drawing, playing, storytelling and experiences with print all provide resources which teachers and children can draw on to build new possibilities. As Dyson notes, we do not yet understand how educators might build from such an array of resources.

It is arguable too that the studies reviewed here tend to set up a false tension between abstracting the codes of language and learning their application for meaningful purposes. The emphasis on the integration of the two in practice leaves intact the underlying assumption that somehow they are discrete entities that have to be integrated. The assumption seems to be that pupils have to be inculcated into the forms of written language through a kind of diligent apprenticeship: they are positioned as users of an existing system. The work of Kress, acknowledging that we are entering a new age of the image, invites a much more 'serious engagement with form' but 'form as meaning' as opposed to 'form as formalism' (1997: xvi). He accepts that there is an intrinsic relationship between the expression of a meaning and the form used to express it. And he sees children (and adults) as not merely users but transformers, makers and remakers of communication systems. How young children in early years classrooms act transformatively on the cultural resources of their environments and the implications of this for forms of teaching are aspects that merit a great deal of further investigation.

NOTE

This chapter is based on research which was supported by a grant from the United Kingdom Reading Association (UKRA). I should also like to acknowledge the assistance of Dr Jon Tan, who conducted electronic literature searches.

REFERENCES

Adams, M.J. (1991) *Beginning to Read: Thinking and Learning about Print.* Cambridge, MA: MIT Press.

Adler, M.A. and Fisher, C.W. (2001) 'Early reading programs in high-poverty schools: a case study of beating the odds', *The Reading Teacher*, 54 (6): 616–29.

Allington, R.L. (1983) 'The reading instruction provided readers of differing abilities', *Elementary School Journal*, 83: 548–59.

Au, K. (1980) 'Participation structures in a reading lesson with Hawaiian children: analysis of a culturally-appropriate instructional event', *Anthropology and Education Quarterly*, 11 (2): 91–115.

Au, K. (1992) 'Constructing the theme of a story', *Language Arts*, 69 (2): 106–11.

Au, K. (1997) 'A sociocultural model of reading instruction: the Kamehameha Elementary Education Program', in S.A. Stahl (ed.), *Instructional Models in Reading.* Mahwah, NJ: Erlbaum. pp. 181–202.

Au, K. and Carroll, J. (1997) 'Improving literacy achievement through a constructivist approach: the KEEP demonstration classroom project', *The Elementary School Journal*, 97: 203–21.

Bissex, G.L. (1980) 'Gnys at Work: a Child Learns to Write and Read'. Cambridge, MA: Harvard University Press.

Block, C.C. and Pressky, M. (2000) 'It's not scripted lessons but challenging and personalized interactions that distinguish effective from less effective primary classrooms'. Paper presented at the National Reading Conference, Phoenix, December.

Block, C.C., Oakar, M. and Hurt, N. (2002) 'The expertise of literacy teachers: a continuum from preschool to grade 5', *Reading Research Quarterly*, 37 (2): 178–206.

Brophy, J. (1973) 'Stability of teacher effectiveness', *American Educational Research Journal*, 10: 245–52.

Bussis, A., Chittenden, F., Amarel, M. and Klausner, E. (1985*) Inquiry into Meaning: an Investigation of Learning to Read.* Hillsdale, NJ: Erlbaum.

Collins, A., Brown, J.S. and Newman, S.E. (1989) 'Cognitive apprenticeships: teaching the crafts of reading, writing and mathematics', in L.R. Resnick (ed.), *Knowing, Learning and Instruction.* Hillsdale, NJ: Erlbaum. pp. 453–91.

Darling-Hammond, L. (1998) 'Teachers and teaching: testing policy hypotheses from a National Commission report', *Educational Researcher*, 27 (1) 5–15.

Designs for Change (1998) 'What makes these schools stand out: Chicago elementary schools with a seven-year trend of improved reading achievement', Chicago Public Schools, http://www.dfc1.org.

DfEE (1998) *The National Literacy Strategy: Framework for Teaching*. London: Department for Education and Employment.

Dyson, A.H. (1994) 'Viewpoints: the word and the world – reconceptualizing written language development, or, do rainbows mean a lot to little girls? in R.B. Ruddell, M.R. Ruddell and H. Singer (eds), *Theoretical Models and Processes of Reading*, 4th edn. Delaware: International Reading Association. pp. 297–322.

Dyson, A.H. (1998) 'Folk processes and media creatures: reflections on popular culture for literacy educators', *The Reading Teacher*, 51 (5): 392–402.

Dyson, A.H. and Genishi, C. (eds) (1994) *The Need for Story: Cultural Diversity in Classroom and Community*. Urbana, IL: National Council of Teachers of English.

Foorman, B.R., Francis, D.J., Fletcher, J.M. and Mehta, P. (1998) 'The role of instruction in learning to read: preventing reading failure in at-risk children', *Journal of Educational Psychology*, 90 (1): 37–55.

Gee, J.P. (1999) 'Critical issues: reading and the new literacy studies: reframing the National Academy of Sciences report on reading', *Journal of Literacy Research*, 31 (3): 355–74.

Geekie, P., Cambourne, B. and Fitzsimmons, P. (1999) *Understanding Literacy Development*. Stoke-on-Trent: Trentham.

Good, T.L. and Brophy, J.E. (1991) *Looking in Classrooms*, 5th edn. New York: Harper Collins.

Graham, L. (2001) 'From tyrannosaurus to Pokémon: autonomy in the teaching of writing', *Reading*, 35 (1): 18–26.

Guthrie, J.T., Van Meter, P., Dacey-McCann, A., Wigfield, A., Bennett, L., Poundstone, C.C., Rice, M.E., Faibisch, F.M., Hunt, B. and Mitchell, A.M. (1996) 'Growth in literacy engagement: changes in motivations and strategies during concept-oriented reading instruction', *Reading Research Quarterly*, 31 (3): 306–32.

Hall, K. (2001) 'An analysis of primary literacy policy in England using Barthes' notion of "readerly" and "writerly" texts', *Journal of Early Childhood Literacy*, 1 (2): 153–65.

Hall, K. (2003) *Listening to Stephen Read: Multiple Perspectives on Literacy*. Buckingham: Open University Press.

Harste, J.C., Burke, C.L. and Woodward, V.A. (1994) 'Children's language and world: initial encounters with print', in R.B. Ruddell, M.R. Ruddell and H. Singer (eds), *Theoretical Models and Processes of Reading*, 4th edn. Delaware: International Reading Association. pp. 48–69.

Hatton, E. (1999) 'Contemporary classroom practice in Australian primary classrooms', *Asian–Pacific Journal of Teacher Education*, 27 (3): 215–37.

Heath, S.B. (1983) *Ways with Words: Language, Life and Work in Communities and Classrooms*. Cambridge: Cambridge University Press.

Hicks, D. (2001) 'Literacies and masculinities in the life of a young working-class boy', *Language Arts*, 78 (3): 217–26.

Hiebert, E. and Pearson, D. (2000) 'Building on the past, bridging to the future: a research agenda for the centre for the improvement of early reading achievement', *Journal of Educational Research*, 93 (3): 133–44.

Hiebert, E.H. and Raphael, T.E. (1996) 'Psychological perspectives on literacy and extensions to educational practice', David C. Berliner and Robert C. Calfree (eds), *Handbook of Educational Psychology*. New York: Macmillan. pp. 550–602.

Hoffman, J.V. (1991) 'Teacher and school effects in learning to read', in R. Barr, M.L. Kamil, P.B. Mosenthal and P.D. Pearson (eds), *Handbook of Reading Research*, vol. 2. New York: Longman. pp. 911–50.

Juel, C. (1994) *Learning to Read and Write in One Elementary School*. New York: Springer.

Juel, C. (1996) 'What makes literacy tutoring effective?', *Reading Research Quarterly*, 31 (3): 268–89.

Juel, C. and Minden-Cupp, C. (2001) 'Learning to read words: linguistic units and instructional strategies', *Reading Research Quarterly*, 35 (4): 458–93.

Knapp, M.S. and Associates (1995) *Teaching for Meaning in High-Poverty Classrooms*. New York: Teachers' College Press.

Kress, G. (1994) *Learning to Write*, 2nd edn. London: Routledge.

Kress, G. (1997) *Before Writing: Rethinking the Paths to Literacy*. London: Routledge.

McCarthy, S.J. (2000) 'Home–school connections: a review of the literature', *Journal of Educational Research*, 93 (3): 145–53.

McNaughton, S. (2001) 'Co-constructing expertise: the development of parents' and teachers' ideas about literacy practices and the transition to school', *Journal of Early Childhood Literacy*, 1 (1): 40–58.

Medwell, J., Wray, D., Poulson, L. and Fox, R. (1998) *The Effective Teachers of Literacy Project*. Exeter: University of Exeter.

Metsala, J., Barker, L., Sonnenschein, S., Serpell, R., Scher, D., Fernandez-Fein, S., Munstermann, K., Hill, S., Goddard-Truitt, V. and Danesco, E. (1996) Early literacy at home: children's experiences and parents' perspectives. *The Reading Teacher*, 50: 70–2.

Moll, L., Amanti, C., Neff, D. and Gonzalez, N. (1992) 'Funds of knowledge for teaching: using a qualitative approach to connect homes and classrooms', *Theory into Practice*, 31: 132–41.

Morrow, L.M., Tracey, D.H., Woo, D.G. and Pressley, M. (1999) 'Characteristics of exemplary first-grade literacy instruction', *The Reading Teacher*, 52 (5): 462–76.

Neuman, S.B. and Roskos, K. (1997) 'Literacy knowledge in practice: contexts of participation for young writers and reader', *Reading Research Quarterly*, 32 (1): 10–32.

Poulson, L., Avramidis, E., Fox, R., Medwell, J. and Wray, D. (2001) 'The theoretical beliefs of effective teachers of literacy: an exploratory study of orientations to literacy', *Research Papers in Education*, 16 (3): 1–22.

Pressley, M. (1998) *Reading Instruction That Works: the Case for Balanced Teaching.* New York: Guilford.

Pressley, M., Rankin, J. and Yokoi, L. (1996) 'A survey of the instructional practices of outstanding primary-level literacy teachers', *Elementary School Journal*, 96: 363–84.

Pressley, M., Wharton-McDonald, R., Allington, R., Block, C.C., Morrow, L., Tracey, D., Baker, K., Brooks, G., Cronin, J., Nelson, E. and Woo, D. (2001) 'A study of effective first-grade literacy instruction', *Scientific Studies of Reading*, 5 (1): 35–58.

Puma, M.J., Karweit, N., Price, C., Ricciuti, A., Thompson, W. and Vaden-Kiernan, M. (1997) *Prospects: Final Report on Student Outcomes (Title 1).* Washington, DC: US Department of Education, Planning and Evaluation Service.

Rankin-Erickson, J.L. and Pressley, M. (2000) 'A survey of instructional practices of special education teachers nominated as effective teachers of literacy', *Learning Disabilities Research and Practice*, 15 (4): 206–25.

Raphael, T.R. and Brock, C.H. (1998) 'Instructional research in literacy: changing paradigms', in C. Kinzer, D. Leu and H. Hinchman (eds), 46th *National Reading Conference Yearbook.* Chicago: National Reading Conference.

Roehler, L.R. and Duffy, G.G. (1996) 'Teachers' instructional actions', in R. Barr, M.L. Kamil, P. Mosenthal and P.D. Pearson (eds), *Handbook of Reading Research*, Vol. 2. Mahwah, NJ: Erlbaum. pp. 861–83.

Rogoff, B. (1982) 'Integrating context and cognitive development', in M.E. Lamb and A.L. Brown (eds), *Advances in Developmental Psychology.* Hillsdale, NJ: Erlbaum. pp. 125–61.

Rosenshine, B. and Furst, N. (1973) 'The use of direct observation to study teaching', in R.M.W. Travers (ed.), *Second Handbook of Research on Teaching.* Chicago: Rand McNally. pp. 122–83

Roskos, K. and Christie, J. (2001) 'Examining the play–literacy interface: a critical review and future directions', *Journal of Early Childhood Literacy*, 1 (1): 59–89.

Sachs, C.H. and Mergendoller, J.R. (1997) 'The relationship between teachers' theoretical orientation toward reading and student outcomes in kindergarten children with different initial reading abilities', *American Educational Research Journal*, 34 (4): 721–39.

Schmidt, P.R. (1995) 'Working and playing with others: cultural conflict in a kindergarten literacy program', *The Reading Teacher*, 48 (5): 404–12.

Snow, C.E., Burns, M.S. and Griffin, P. (1998) *Preventing Reading Difficulties in Young Children.* Washington, DC: National Academy Press.

Taylor, B.M. (2000) 'Highly accomplished primary grade teachers in effective schools'. Paper presented at the National Reading Conference, Phoenix, December.

Taylor, B.M., Pearson, D.P., Clark, K.F. and Walpole, S. (1999) 'Effective schools/accomplished teachers', *The Reading Teacher*, 53 (2): 156–9.

Taylor, B.M., Anderson, R.C., Au, K.H. and Raphael, T. (2000a) 'Discretion in the translation of research to policy: a case from beginning reading', *Educational Researcher*, 29 (6): 16–26.

Taylor, B.M., Pearson, P.D., Clark, K.F. and Walpole, S. (2000b) 'Effective schools and accomplished teachers: lessons about primary-grade reading instruction in low-income schools', *The Elementary School Journal*, 101 (2): 121–65.

Teale, W.H. and Sulzby, E. (eds) (1986) *Emergent Literacy: Writing and Reading.* Norwood, NJ: Ablex.

Tharp, R.G. (1982) 'The effective instruction of comprehension: results and description of the Kamehameha Early Education Program', *Reading Research Quarterly*, 17 (4): 503–27.

Wharton-McDonald, R., Pressley, M., Rankin, J., Mistretta, J., Yokai, L. and Ettenberger, S. (1997) 'Effective primary-grades literacy instruction equals balanced literacy instruction', *The Reading Teacher*, 50: 518–21.

Wharton-McDonald, R., Pressley, M. and Hampston, J.M. (1998) 'Literacy instruction in nine first-grade classrooms: teacher characteristics and student achievement', *Elementary School Journal*, 99 (2): 101–28.

Wilkinson, I.A. and Townsend, M.A. (2000) 'From Rata to Rimu: grouping for instruction in best practice New Zealand classrooms', *The Reading Teacher*, 53 (6): 460–71.

Wray, D., Medwell, J., Fox, R. and Poulson, L. (2001) 'The teaching practices of effective teachers of literacy', *Educational Review*, 52 (1): 75–84.

27

Creating Positive Literacy Learning Environments in Early Childhood

LAURIE MAKIN

This chapter is based on the notion that creating positive literacy learning environments is a different proposition today than it was in previous years, since what we think of as literacy is changing, how we do it is changing, and the skills children need are changing. The print-saturated environment of the world outside of educational settings is seldom replicated within them. Nevertheless, there is a rich research literature relating to how settings can be made more effective by paying attention to the creation of print-rich environments in early childhood education and to the mediation of literacy learning within these environments.

The term 'environment', when applied to early childhood educational settings, is an aggregate of conditions and influences on learning, including both the physical environment (layout, range of resources, access, and use) and the psychosocial environment (interactions between staff and children, among peers, and between the setting and its wider contexts of homes and communities). The educational environment reflects underlying philosophical beliefs about how children learn, how they should be taught, what they should learn and why.

Recent sociocultural perspectives on literacy have led to a recognition that what counts as literacy is inextricably entwined with power, that texts are not neutral, and that failure to achieve success in school literacy may often result from gaps between home and school literacies. Print-rich environments may be rich for some groups and poor for those groups that do not see themselves or their social literacy practices reflected in the environment. Interactions around print may enrich some children's knowledge and develop their predispositions to read and write, but may marginalize and disenfranchize other children.

Positive learning environments support children's learning. The focus in this chapter is on identifying aspects of both the physical and the psychosocial environment that support literacy learning. A review of the research suggests that two aspects of the environment are of particular importance in literacy learning: availability of appropriate resources; and interactions between children and adults who mediate their literacy learning. It also suggests areas for further research.

SOME ENVIRONMENTAL PREDICTORS OF SUCCESSFUL LITERACY

Congruence between home and preschool/school literacies

Literacy begins practically from birth in a literate society. Children's environments have changed dramatically over the last few decades (Moss, 1990; OECD, 2001a), with increasing numbers of children in educare environments, because of social changes and financial pressures. Hence children's early literacy experiences will take place in various contexts: home, community and a range of early childhood settings.

Increasingly, literacy and life opportunities are linked. Reports from different countries (see, for example, Comber and Hill, 2000; Gregory, 1994; Snow et al., 1998; Sylva et al., 2001) confirm that 'at-risk' children usually come from low income, low literacy, and/or bilingual homes. Disadvantage has a cumulative nature, but the first factor, poverty, appears to be a particularly powerful predictor of problematic literacy.

Support for children at risk of low literacy can be present in their homes and communities, their early educational settings, or, ideally, in both. Research supports the belief that the home environment is an important environmental factor affecting children's literacy learning (see, for example, Cairney, in this volume; Purcell-Gates, 1996; Saracho, 2002). A key factor appears to be the degree of congruence between the literacies of home and school (Heath, 1983; Cairney, 2002). Despite the fact that this notion is now widely accepted, acceptance does not appear to have been translated into environmental change, especially in schools. Not only do the same groups persistently experience difficulties and often do poorly on national assessments, but there are growing indications (Alloway and Gilbert, 1997; Millard, in this volume) that gender differences in literacy engagement and success are also affected by school literacy environments that are not aligned with children's literacy interests and experiences.

High quality educare environments

A well-known, widely used scale for measuring the general environment in early childhood settings prior to school entry is ECERS–R, the Early Childhood Environmental Rating Scale–Revised (Harms et al., 1998). In its earlier form (Harms and Clifford, 1980), ECERS has been used by researchers throughout the world (for example, Bryant et al., 1994; Dunn et al., 1994; Scarr et al., 1994) and is considered to have good predictive validity. The newer version, ECERS–R, has the same general rationale as the original and retains the earlier scale's broad definition of 'environment' as including all those features that directly affect children and adults in early childhood settings. There are seven subscales reflecting what the authors consider to be the most important features of high quality early childhood environments: space and furnishings, personal care routines, language-reasoning, activities, interaction, programme structure, and parents and staff. The revised scale includes more emphasis on inclusive practices, cultural diversity and use of technology.

ECERS–R focuses on the environment in general, not on literacy. There have been two recent attempts to extend or revise ECERS–R in order to focus more directly on the literacy environment in early childhood settings. Sylva and Siraj-Blatchford (2001) report on development within the Effective Provision of Pre-School Education (EPPE) Project of ECERS–E (Early Childhood Environmental Rating Scale–English). ECERS–E extends ECERS–R to include desirable learning outcomes that map onto the English National Curriculum. ECERS–E appears to be a useful tool for evaluating the strengths of various types of early childhood settings. Two findings are of particular interest here. One is that high scores on ECERS–E as a whole (i.e. including non-language aspects of the environment as well as aspects relating directly to language) were significantly related to progress between the ages of three and five years in language, the foundation of literacy learning. The other is that high scores on the ECERS–E literacy subscale, which includes a focus on letter recognition and contextualized phonological awareness, were significantly related to children's progress in pre-reading skills. This suggests that high quality learning environments in general support literacy learning in particular, and that a specific focus on key predictors of successful school literacy achieves positive results.

In Australia, Makin et al. (1999) adapted a number of ECERS–R items and added a new subscale on literacy practices to map the literacy environment in 79 early childhood settings. New and modified items were incorporated for the purposes of the project into a shortened form of the ECERS–R, renamed the Early Childhood Language and Literacy Scale (ECLLS). Many areas of the literacy environments studied were rated as in need of improvement, in particular, literacy interactions during dramatic play and in relation to children's literacy learning experiences, encouragement of metalinguistic and phonological awareness, and inclusion of technology. ECLLS has been piloted, but is still in the process of refinement. Reliability and validation statistics are needed.

A play-based approach to literacy in early childhood settings

Roskos and Christie (2001) review 20 recent studies investigating the interface between play and literacy and judge that a strong case has been made to support the importance of play in early literacy learning in the provision of scenarios that promote literacy activities, hence helping children develop skills, strategies, oral language, and an understanding of connections between oral and written expression. An environment in which guided and free play is the primary mode of teaching and learning is one in which children can act positively upon their environment and be in control of their learning. If literacy artefacts are available within their play contexts, children's emergent reading and writing activities increase dramatically, although Roskos and Christie report some mixed findings relating to connections between such activities and various assessment measures used when children begin school.

Many early childhood educators (for example, Galda et al., 1989; Vukelich, 1994) support literacy-enriched dramatic play. Long term evaluations of the High/Scope project (Schweinhart et al., 1993) found that the greatest long term benefits were demonstrated by the children who had experienced a play-based curriculum. With increasing pressures in the UK, the USA, and Australia on more tests at ever earlier ages and more formal teaching methods, it may be time to attempt to regain the high ground for play-based literacy learning.

A play-based approach can be especially important for young children who may not be best served by a more academic approach to literacy (Nielsen and Monson, 1996). Additional support for this view comes from the PISA study, (OECD, 2001b), which found that, in Finland, high quality, play-based educare prior to school entry and delaying formal reading instruction until the age of seven or eight years does not have deleterious results – indeed, quite the contrary. These findings are of particular relevance in the first years of school in countries such as the UK and the USA, where, increasingly, literacy is seen as academic instruction. The work of insightful researchers (see, for example, Paley, 1984; Dyson, 1996; Marsh, 1999) offers situated examples of how play can be used to extend children's literacy interests and repertoires.

From a perspective of literacy as social practice (Makin and Jones Diaz, 2002), sociodramatic play in early childhood classrooms becomes centrally important in literacy learning, as it is through sociodramatic play that children role-play being a literate adult, just as they may role-play being a parent, a shop keeper, a superhero, and so on. On one level the implication of this perspective is that the contexts of sociodramatic play need to be literacy-enriched through the provision of literacy artefacts and resources, not simply to affect children's performance in school-based assessments, but to widen and deepen their understanding of how literacy works in society and what it means to be a literate person. However, there exists a deeper level of justification beyond simply providing a site for literacy tool usage, one which has been explored by Hall (1998) and Hall and Robinson (2003). Within a curriculum world based around decontexualized versions of literacy, sociodramatic play is the one area within which children on their own almost invariably generate a situated context for literacy, for example when the baby is ill, the doctor calls

and writes a prescription. Inevitably, within complex events literacy is only a part of an event and takes its rightful place as one of a series of features (Hall and Robinson, 1998). The play is thus oriented around events in which literacy is a part, not the end in itself, and this is directly analogous to ways in which literate people engage with literacy outside of schooling. Thus in sociodramatic play and life, literacy exists as a means to an end; only in a school curriculum is literacy an end in itself.

Helping children create effective literacy-related social contexts in play can be facilitated by adult aid or intervention. Chang and Yawkey (1998) and Pahl (1999) explore relationships between literacy and sociodramatic play and suggest that the symbolic nature of such play offers children opportunities to engage in the literacy practices of their societies, both with each other and with adult staff members who scaffold their learning. Studies of literacy-enriched sociodramatic play environments (Neuman, 2001; Makin et al., 1999) have found that, even when a print-rich play environment is created, adult involvement and mediation are necessary for children to extend their play to include social practices of literacy with which they may be largely unfamiliar, for example, what one does in a hospital, an office or a garage (see Hall and Robinson, 2003).

Opportunities to develop specific knowledge about literacy

A number of large-scale studies identify predictors of successful literacy learning prior to school entry that are congruent both with each other and with the ECERS-related studies reported above. These predictors are directly related to children's environmental experiences. Burgess (1997) reviews a number of research studies, concluding that most important for children are oral language ability, the ability to recognize environmental print, early knowledge of letters and the sounds they make, and early knowledge of the mechanics of print. Similarly, Snow et al. note that among those children who begin school less prepared to learn to read are those who need more knowledge 'in certain domains, most notably letter knowledge, phonological sensitivity, familiarity with the basic purposes and mechanisms of reading, and language ability' (1998: 137). Other researchers (for example, Jordan et al., 2000; Dickinson and Tabors, 2001) emphasize the importance of extended discourse that goes beyond the here and now.

Sylva and her colleagues (2001) identify certain experiences as key predictors of successful literacy, i.e. being read to frequently, having opportunities to play with letters and sounds, adults' drawing children's attention to print and later letters, learning songs and nursery rhymes, and visiting the library often. Many studies over the last two decades (see, for example, Sulzby, 1985; Wells, 1981; 1985; Snow and Ninio, 1986) confirm the importance of reading aloud to children regularly from an early age. Gambrell (1996) reports that reading aloud in school environments is also important. Shared book reading is conducive to the extended discourses that are central to oral language development.

National emphasis on the importance of literacy teaching and learning

Large-scale research studies relating to literacy have been carried out in the United Kingdom since the late 1940s, following the end of World War II, and in the United States since the early 1970s, following Russian successes in the exploration of outer space. In Australia, basic skills tests were introduced in the last decade, with the impetus being a re-examination of Australia's place in the Asia–Pacific. High stakes testing, as the process is often referred to, is by necessity restricted in what it can measure, especially when assessments are sought that are genuinely equivalent across countries, involving translation of texts and the reading of texts developed within particular cultural frameworks (Shiels and Cosgrove, 2002). Many educators claim that such testing exercises are of little direct benefit. However, they offer opportunities to examine a range of environmental factors impacting on reading achievement – policy support, curriculum documents, remedial support, teaching strategies – and to reflect on related factors such as gender, indigeneity and socioeconomic status.

Three recent large-scale international assessments of children's reading are (1) the International Association for the Evaluation of Educational Achievement (IEA) Reading Literacy Study (RLS) (Elley, 1992; 1994); (2) the Program for International Student Assessment (PISA) (OECD, 1999; 2001b); and (3) the IEA's Progress in International Reading Literacy Study (2001). The first two focused on high school students, the third on nine-year-olds. Although none of the three focused on early childhood, defined internationally as birth to eight years, they demonstrate educational outcomes that build on earlier experiences. Findings confirm the importance of the educational environment, both physical and psychosocial, and of the wider national environment.

The results of the third study will not be available until 2003. Certain similarities have been found in the results of the first two. In both IEA/RLS and PISA, Finland had the highest ranking overall. Elley (1992) suggests that this may relate in part to the country's relatively high socioeconomic status and a social emphasis on the importance of literacy, both aspects of the macro environment affecting literacy in educational settings. Aunola et al. (2002) confirm the high status of literacy in Finland, attributing it in part to the historical value placed on literacy since the seventeeth century, when the church insisted on basic reading ability as a precursor to marriage.

This emphasis on the larger social environment reminds us that education does not function in a vacuum and that pedagogical practices and curriculum documents are influenced by forces within the wider external environment, including the availability of high quality early childhood education. A recent OECD review (2001a) of early childhood education and care found high quality, play-based programmes in Finland, with excellent staff–child ratios, aesthetically pleasing environments, and supported educare for all children under school age, with no formal reading instruction until school entry at the age of seven years.

POSITIVE LITERACY ENVIRONMENTS: SOME RESOURCE ISSUES

Provision of literacy resources

An early learning environment that provides high quality early childhood education in general, and access to literacy resources in particular, appears to be crucial in laying firm foundations for school literacy in the years prior to school entry. Considerations of what sorts of resources are (and should be) offered in early childhood settings and how they should be used raise issues relating to access and use. At the preschool or school level, provision of and access to literacy resources are influenced in part by teacher philosophy. In some studies of early childhood settings prior to school entry, even the most basic features of a print-rich environment have been found to be lacking. Dunn et al. (1994), for example, in a snapshot study of 30 community-based day care classrooms in the US, found the classrooms were lacking even in terms of conventional literacy practices, with only nine even having books. To some extent, this may be the result of earlier maturationist and developmental approaches to literacy, which tended to see literacy as school-related and inappropriate for preschool settings. It is relatively recently, since the 1980s, that educators have become aware of the importance of literacy prior to school entry, and even more recently, that studies such as those referred to earlier (Sylva et al., 2001; Snow et al., 1998; Burgess, 1997) have identified what is most needed in this period.

Dowhower and Beagle (1998) compared 'holistic' teachers, who take a top-down approach to literacy, starting with texts, and 'conventional' teachers, who take a bottom-up approach, starting with individual letters and sounds. They found that holistic teachers placed a strong emphasis upon literature, on learning in context and on reading for meaning. They provided more writing tools, more literacy centres, less commercial print and more child- and teacher-created print. They also had more books in their classroom libraries.

Even when environments are print-rich in terms of the quantity of resources available, they may offer children access that is restricted to a narrow range of books, paper and writing implements. Recent researchers have explored ways in which the educational environment can be adapted to reflect more closely the wider external environment in general, offering relevant ways of engaging children who may not otherwise choose to engage with more traditional school literacy practices. Gender is one area of increasing interest to researchers. Young and Brozo (2001) review American studies indicating that there are societal pressures acting to deter boys from success in literacy and refer to similar findings by Australian researchers. Millard and Marsh (2001) report a preference among boys for comics and magazines in reading. Yet Dowhower and Beagle (1998) found no magazines or newspapers in any of the classroom library collections they studied, and Worthy et al. (1999) found an ever-increasing gap between student reading preferences and school reading resources. There is research suggesting that different text types appeal to different children (see Millard, in this volume) and influence interaction patterns (Neuman, 1996; Reese and Harris, 1997), as well as facilitating children's ability to develop as literate members of society. The same appears to hold for opportunities to write as well as read different text types (see, for example, Zecker, 1999, who questions the overemphasis on narratives in the first years of school).

Access to literacy resources

Access to resources can depend upon socioeconomic, linguistic and geographical factors. Often, these intersect with one another to produce formidable barriers for children. Duke, in a study of 20 first-grade classrooms, suggests that, 'Literacy is

another domain through which schools may contribute to lower levels of achievement among low-SES children' (2000: 441). Duke uses the term 'semiotic capital', to refer to an important currency in many institutions and settings in largely literate societies. Analysis of literacy practices in classrooms with children from very different socioeconomic backgrounds indicated that low-SES children had access in their classrooms to less semiotic capital than children from high-SES backgrounds. They encountered less print, were exposed to less extended forms of text, were less likely to experience print integrated throughout the curriculum, had fewer opportunities for choice, lower degrees of authorship, smaller classroom libraries, and less time to use them. They spent at least as much, and sometimes more, time on print activities, but the nature of the activities was different. The children were read to less often, could choose what they read less often, and spent more time on copying and completing worksheets rather than in more authentic literacy learning activities. Children need experience in reading and writing a wide range of genres from the earliest years: shopping lists, letters, stories, procedures, reports, notices and so on. Dickinson and DeGisi (1998) cite frequency, variety, relevance, and authenticity as the key factors.

There are also factors outside the classroom that impact upon access to resources, for example, the socioeconomic status of the community, whether it is rural or urban, and the extent to which it is culturally diverse. Dowhower and Beagle (1998), in a study of 18 urban, suburban, and rural classrooms, found that suburban children tended to be better resourced. Eleven of the classrooms in their study had no environmental or functional print on show, and 14 had no or very little student-generated print. Rural children had fewest writing tools and (presumably as a consequence) generated least print.

Within urban and suburban environments, there are also differences. Neuman and Celano (2001) suggest that unequal provision of community literacy resources may impact on children's literacy. Examples they give include disfigured, difficult to read public signage, food outlets designed to encourage quick turnover as opposed to encouraging patrons to linger and read newspapers or magazines, and libraries with fewer books in worse condition.

Provision of a print-rich environment in culturally diverse classrooms may need particular attention in settings whose programmes are developmentally based. A focus on individuals can mean that the setting itself, its staff and its programmes may be shielded from observation and reflection. Alloway states that, 'by its very nature, an individualist framework does not invite challenge to curricular and pedagogical practices that enfranchise particular groups of students while disenfranchising others' (1999: 2). This warning is particularly relevant in the current climate of high stakes testing. Both child knowledge and adult scaffolding within the educare environment must be taken into account if all children are to experience a positive literacy environment.

When a print-rich environment is restricted to the dominant language, children whose home language is a language or dialect other than the standard language or dialect of power within a society face many difficulties in literacy learning, especially when, as is the case in the majority of early childhood settings in Australia, Canada (with the exception of immersion classes), the US, and the UK, they share classes with children who are already fluent in the language of power. Research studies confirm that cultural as well as linguistic differences are often overlooked in such cases and that children often learn the new language or dialect at the expense of their community languages or dialects (see, for example, Gregory, 1994; Siraj-Blatchford and Clarke, 2000; Hohepa and McNaughton, 2002). The subtractive nature of a dominant-language-only environment is currently of increasing concern to many researchers (see, for example, Gutiérrez et al., 2002) in the wake of increasing emphasis on English-only teaching and testing in countries whose official language is English.

All children need access to the literacy practices and discourses of society's dominant groups. However, this need not come at the expense of other literacies and should be an additive rather than a subtractive process (Cairney, 2002). Walters writes that, 'The language of a literate classroom is in the identities of the language user' (1998: 8). These identities include socioeconomic status, indigeneity, gender, and language.

Information and communication technology (ICT)

The paradigm of literacy in Western societies has been shifting since the 1970s to one in which literacy is seen as social practices done differently by different people in different contexts (Gee, 1990; Luke, 1993; Makin and Jones Diaz, 2002; Knobel and Lankshear, in this volume). The literate behaviours of people in Western societies have changed enormously within the space of a few years, with the explosion of home computers, mobile telephones, short messaging systems (SMS), multimedia texts, faxes, digital videos, and so on. This shift has broadened our definition of literacy to include areas such as techno-literacy, and increased emphasis on areas such as visual literacy (Anstey and Bull, 2000) and critical literacy (Bradshaw, 1998). However, these areas are not yet commonly reflected in early childhood settings.

Integration of technology into literacy learning environments is still in the process of development in many early childhood settings. Its absence is often particularly evident in sociodramatic play. For example, while many settings have a shop, few extend this to include, for example, a real or make-believe computer-based inventory or cash-out machine. Few home corners contain a real or make-believe computer for e-mail, information searches, or online shopping. Yet, competency in ICT-related negotiations increasingly comprises a centrally important part of what it means to be a literate person, as one uses automatic tellers, the Internet, online banking, and so on. In early childhood settings, computers are often used only for skill and drill games, or digital worksheets. Reports of classroom-based action research which aims to improve practice (see, for example, Walker and Yekovich, 1999; Hill with Broadhurst, 2002) show exceptions to this situation and offer examples of the type of innovative, authentic literacy experiences children can take part in when teachers provide appropriate resources and mediate children's experiences with technology.

Karchmer (2001), in a study of the reaction of 13 teachers to the Internet, reminds readers that the nature of literacy has always been dependent upon, and a product of, communication technology, affecting what is read and written, by whom, and in what media. Digital communication, animation, graphics, hyperlinks and so on affect the current nature of literacy and the skills children need. Goldstone (2002) suggests that opportunities offered by interactive multimedia texts to create substories, fill in gaps, and connect to other texts are changing children's books themselves to become less linear and more self-referential and ironic in tone. Smith's (2001) study of her son's exploration of three types of storybook media, including CD-ROM storybooks, between the ages of 2.5 and 3.5 years, suggests that current reconceptualizations of literacy must include recognition of the unique contributions to literacy development that can be made through ICT resources. Her study demonstrates clearly the literacy learning opportunities offered by a print-rich environment that includes multiple media.

Not only is technology reflective of the literacy which children will encounter in their everyday lives within society. It also has the potential to positively affect the social environment of the classroom, for example, increasing on-task communication when computer use is integral and involves software that is both developmentally appropriate and appropriate to the classroom's learning outcomes (Richards, 2000). Use of the Internet widens this social learning environment beyond individual settings to include international communication (Offman-Gersh, 2001; Hill with Broadhurst, 2002).

POSITIVE LITERACY ENVIRONMENTS: SOME MEDIATION ISSUES

Teacher expectations

Research supports the notion that the psychosocial environment is as important as the physical environment in terms of children's literacy. Literacy environments that work not only provide children with access to resources, but also provide them with motivation to engage with these resources. McMahon et al. (1998) remind us that teachers who believe children learn through social interaction and exploration in meaningful activities will have classrooms that are very different from those in which teachers believe children learn through drill and practice. Bouas et al. (1997) report that if teachers believe that kindergarten children can write, they will write, supported by a print-rich environment, a regular, scheduled time for writing, teacher modelling, short individualized conferences, and opportunities to share writing with their peers.

A literate environment provides children with appropriate physical surroundings and supportive interpersonal relationships (Neuman and Roskos, 1997). Group as well as individual characteristics should be familiar to the teacher and reflected in the environment. This is more easily said than done. Expectations of teacher–child–family interactions, home and community literacy practices, and what is deemed to constitute 'appropriate' physical surroundings are all culturally determined. Many researchers (for example, Heath, 1983; Purcell-Gates, 1996; Freebody et al., 1995) warn of the dangers of adopting a 'one size fits all' approach to literacy learning.

Snow et al. (1998) warn of the dangers of low teacher and school expectations, which can result in an undemanding curriculum. The increasingly formal teaching methods seen in some responses to the perceived need to raise national literacy levels may, paradoxically, reinforce low expectations by teachers of children who do not respond to these methods. Purcell-Gates and Dahl (1991) emphasize the importance of print-rich environments that provide varied, meaningful and functional opportunities for literacy engagement, and teacher expectations that children will be active co-constructors of literacy knowledge, not the passive recipients of teacher-led direct instruction.

Interactions in educare settings

Dickinson and Tabors (2002), in a longitudinal study of 74 children, compared different home and preschool environments and found that kindergarten language ability was highly predictive of literacy and vocabulary at later ages. However, several studies (see, for example, Wells and Nichols, 1985; Dunn, 1993; Rolfe, 1999) support views of restricted teacher–child talk in early childhood settings.

The source of such restricted interactions may arise from an intersection of several factors, including initial teacher preparation, staff qualifications, and staff–child ratios. Rosemary and Roskos (2002) suggest that it may be the first of these that needs particular attention. In their study of three childcare centres, literacy interactions (defined as talk related to reading and writing) represented only 10% of the total, and tended to be instrumental with brief exchanges getting information about print and checking understanding, i.e. transmission teaching – telling about literacy rather than scaffolding children's understanding of literacy. Higher teacher qualifications affected the amount of literacy interaction, but not the overall interaction pattern. Rolfe (1999) reports similar findings in her naturalistic study of infant educare. Most interactions between the children and staff were very brief, often made from a distance, and overwhelmingly functional in nature, although the subjective impression of the staff was that the interactions were both more frequent and longer than they were in fact. She interprets this to reflect the hurried environment of infant/toddler rooms with inadequate staff–child ratios, which do not allow for individual, child-centred responsiveness.

Staff interactions as well as adult–child interactions are an important part of educare environments. Munns' (1995) study of eight preschools in the UK found that, in environments that supported children's literacy and numeracy development, staff treated one another as equals, despite different levels of qualifications, and hence were able to engage in exploratory and reflective discussions of the environment and their own role in supporting children's literacy and numeracy development.

Positive literacy environments as a 'productive pedagogy'

All learning environments teach children – either consciously or unconsciously. Early childhood practitioners support children's literacy when they provide positive, supportive, and respectful literacy learning environments in which young children view themselves as increasingly competent, literate members of society.

Snow et al. (1998) identify provision of a positive language and literacy environment as one of the most important conditions contributing to successful reading, and an important preventive effort for children at risk of low school literacy. A positive environment is defined as one that is rich in oral language, interactive reading, and language play, with opportunities for children to both observe and participate in the functions of literacy. In Australia, provision of a supportive classroom environment has been identified as one of four categories of 'productive pedagogies' (Education Queensland, 1999), i.e. strategies that can focus instruction and improve student outcomes, thus placing the environment firmly in the foreground of factors to be considered in planning for literacy. Within this category of productive pedagogies, relationships are seen to be of crucial importance in developing people who not only are able to engage as literate members of society in a range of ways, but choose to do so.

When literacy environments are boring or disempowering, they are an unproductive pedagogy. Some researchers argue that this is often the case for boys. Barrs (2001), in a study of seven- to nine-year-olds, found that there were more boys than girls in the categories of children who were able to read but chose not to, and children who neither could nor did read. See Millard (in this volume) for further discussion of the intersections between gender and literacy in school literacy learning environments.

There are additional issues for children at risk of low school-based literacy assessments. One of these is the gap that may exist between home and community literacy proficiency and school-assessed literacy proficiency (Heath, 1983; Gregory, 1994; Hanlen, 2002; Rogers, 2002). The ideology associated with different discourse contexts can have negative effects on the less powerful because they may internalize too well, from early literacy learning environments, the constructions by the more powerful of what counts as literacy and what it means to be a literate person.

DIRECTIONS FOR FUTURE RESEARCH

In this chapter, I have reviewed many areas in which various research studies that explore positive literacy learning environments support and confirm each other, for example: the importance of access to and experience with literacy tools and technologies;

frequent reading aloud accompanied by extended discourse; modelling by adults; opportunities to engage in everyday literacy experiences; opportunities to explore environmental print and to play with sounds; and a play-based curriculum for young children.

In some areas, it seems less a matter of needing more research than a matter of translating research into practice. An example of this is the need for schools to widen their view of literacy to be more inclusive of the wide range of home and community literacy practices in which children engage. Since the 1980s, with seminal research such as that of Heath (1983), research has confirmed the need to address this area seriously. However, there has been little far-reaching change in the literacy learning environments in early childhood settings. On the contrary, it can be argued that, over the last decade in particular, school literacy environments are increasingly constrained and restricted, reflecting a set of values and strategies that excludes many children.

In other areas, there is a need for future research into the provision of positive literacy environments, in terms of both their physical and their psychosocial aspects. We need, for example, more studies identifying ways in which technology can be appropriately integrated into early childhood education; studies of the long term impact on children's literacy dispositions of an environment that accepts and works with popular culture; more research into mediation strategies and the effects of changing the discourse in classrooms; a deeper understanding of the environmental predictors of literacy learning in infants and toddlers; thick descriptions of transitions in literacy learning environments between preschool and school settings; and fine-grained linguistic analyses of literacy interactions between children and between adults and children to identify key features of peer and teacher mediation.

This latter area is of particular importance in the current climate of external, decontextualized testing of children's literacy. Learning outcomes are a product of interaction and mediation as well as cognitive ability, and assessment must include an understanding of what children experience. We need to hear the voices and ideas of children as well as adults. Such understanding might assist in identification of ways to provide physical and psychosocial environments that offer educational advantage to children of poverty, support indigenous literacy, and develop true partnerships between teachers and families in promoting children's literacy learning.

Our collective report card seems to indicate a judgement of 'can do better', in terms of providing resource-rich, mediation-rich environments that support the early literacy of all children, so that they not only are able to function as literate people in society, but see themselves as competent, confident, literate members of society, disposed to engage in an ever widening repertoire of literacy practices.

REFERENCES

Alloway, N. (1999) 'Reconceptualising early literacy achievement: moving beyond critique-paralysis', *Australian Journal of Early Childhood*, 24 (4): 1–6.

Alloway, N. and Gilbert, P. (1997) 'Boys and literacy: lessons from Australia', *Gender and Education*, 9 (1): 49–58.

Anstey, M. and Bull, G. (2000) *Reading the Visual: Written and Illustrated Children's Literature*. Sydney: Harcourt.

Aunola, K., Nurmi, J., Niemi, P., Lerkkanen, M. and Rasku-Puttonen, H. (2002) 'Developmental dynamics of achievement strategies, reading performance, and parental beliefs', *Reading Research Quarterly*, 37 (3): 310–27.

Barrs, M. (2001) 'Boys and literacy: building and sustaining a literate culture for both genders', *Practically Primary*, 6 (3): 36–8 (reprinted from *Language Arts*, 77 (4), 2000).

Bouas, M., Thompson, P. and Farlow, N. (1997) 'Self-selected journal writing in the kindergarten classroom: five conditions that foster literacy development', *Reading Horizons*, 38 (1): 3–12.

Bradshaw, D. (ed.) (1998) *Knowledge of Texts: Theory and Practice in Critical Literacy*. Melbourne: Language Australia.

Bryant, D., Burchinal, M., Lau, L. and Sparling, J. (1994) 'Family and classroom correlates of Head Start children's developmental outcomes', *Early Childhood Research Quarterly*, 9: 289–309.

Burgess, S. (1997) 'The role of shared reading in the development of phonological awareness: a longitudinal study of middle to upper class children', *Early Child Development and Care*, 127–8: 191–9.

Cairney, T. (2002) 'Bridging home and school literacy: in search of transformative approaches to curriculum', *Early Child Development and Care*, 172 (2): 153–72.

Chang, P. and Yawkey, T. (1998) 'Symbolic play and literacy learning: classroom materials and teacher's roles', *Reading Improvement*, 35 (4): 172–7.

Comber, B. and Hill, S. (2000) 'Socio-economic disadvantage, literacy and social justice: learning from longitudinal case study research', *Australian Educational Researcher*, 27 (3): 79–97.

Dickinson, D. and DeGisi, L. (1998) 'The many rewards of a literacy-rich classroom', *Educational Leadership*, 55 (6): 23–33.

Dickinson, D. and Tabors, P. (eds) (2001) *Beginning Literacy with Language: Young Children Learning at Home and School*. Baltimore: Brookes.

Dickinson, D. and Tabors, P. (2002) 'Fostering language and literacy in classrooms and homes', *Young Children*, 57 (2): 10–19.

Dowhower, S. and Beagle, K. (1998) 'The print environment in kindergartens: a study of conventional and holistic teachers and their classrooms in three settings', *Reading Research and Instruction*, 37 (3): 161–90.

Duke, N. (2000) 'For the rich it's richer: print experiences and environments offered to children in very low- and very high-socioeconomic first-grade classrooms', *American Research Journal*, 37 (2): 441–78.

Dunn, L. (1993) 'Proximal and distal features of daycare quality and children's development', *Early Childhood Research Quarterly*, 8: 167–92.

Dunn, L., Beach, S. and Kontos, S. (1994) 'Quality of the literacy environment in daycare and children's development', *Journal of Research in Childhood Education*, 9 (1): 24–34.

Dyson, A. (1996) 'Cultural constellations and childhood identities: on Greek gods, cartoon heroes, and the social lives of schoolchildren', *Harvard Educational Review*, 66: 471–95.

Education Queensland (1999) *The Next Decade: a Discussion about the Future of Queensland State Schools*. Brisbane: Education Queensland.

Elley, W. (1992) *How in the World Do Students Read?* Hamburg: IEA.

Elley, W. (1994) *The IEA Study of Reading Literacy: Achievement and Instruction in Thirty-Two School Systems*. Oxford: Pergamon.

Freebody, P., Ludwig, C. and Gunn, S. (1995) 'Everyday literacy practices in and out of schools in low SE urban communities'. Faculty of Education, Griffith University, Nathan, Queensland, Australia.

Galda, L., Pellegrini, A. and Cox, S. (1989) 'A short-term longitudinal study of preschoolers' emergent literacy', *Research in the Teaching of Reading*, 32 (3): 292–309.

Gambrell, L. (1996) 'Creating classroom cultures that foster reading motivation', *The Reading Teacher*, 50 (1): 14–24.

Gee, J. (1990) *Social Linguistics and Literacies: Ideology in Discourse*. London: Taylor and Francis.

Goldstone, B. (2002) 'Whaz up with our books? Changing picture book codes and teaching implications', *The Reading Teacher*, 55 (4): 362–70.

Gregory, E. (1994) 'Cultural assumptions and early years' pedagogy: the effect of the home culture on minority children's interpretation of reading in school', *Language, Culture and Curriculum*, 7 (2): 111–24.

Gutiérrez, K., Asato, J., Pacheco, M., Moll, L., Olson, K., Horng, E., Ruiz, R., García, E. and McCarty, T. (2002) '"Sounding American": the consequences of new reforms on English language learners', *Reading Research Quarterly*, 37 (3): 328–43.

Hall, N. (1998) 'Real literacy in a school setting: five-year-old take on the world', *The Reading Teacher*, 53 (3): 8–17.

Hall, N. and Robinson, A. (1998) 'Developing young children's understanding of work as a social institution', *Children's Social and Economics Education*, 3 (2): 81–93.

Hall, N. and Robinson, A. (2003) *Exploring Writing and Play in the Early Years*, 2nd edn. London: Fulton.

Hanlen, W. (2002) 'Emerging literacy in rural and urban indigenous families'. Unpublished PhD dissertation, University of Newcastle, Australia.

Harms, T. and Clifford, R. (1980) *Early Childhood Environment Rating Scale*. New York: Teachers College Press.

Harms, T., Clifford, R. and Cryer, D. (1998) *Early Childhood Environment Rating Scale–Revised Edition*. New York: Teachers College Press.

Heath, S. (1983) *Ways with Words: Language, Life and Word in Communities and Classrooms*. Cambridge: Cambridge University Press.

Hill, S. with Broadhurst, D. (2002) 'Technoliteracy and the early years', in L. Makin and C. Jones Diaz (eds), *Literacies in Early Childhood: Changing Views, Callenging Practice*. Sydney: MacLennan and Petty. pp. 269–88.

Hohepa, M. and McNaughton, S. (2002) 'Indigenous literacies: the case of Maori literacy', in L. Makin and C. Jones Diaz (eds), *Literacies in Early Childhood: Changing Views, Challenging Practice*. Sydney: MacLennan and Petty. pp. 197–214.

Jordan, G., Snow, C. and Porche, M. (2000) 'Project EASE: the effect of a family literacy project on kindergarten students' early literacy skills', *Reading Research Quarterly*, 35 (4): 524–44.

Karchmer, R. (2001) 'The journey ahead: thirteen teachers report how the Internet influences literacy and literacy instruction in their K–12 classroom', *Reading Research Quarterly*, 36 (4): 442–66.

Luke, A. (1993) 'The social construction of literacy in the primary school', in L. Unsworth (ed.), *Literacy Learning and Teaching*. Melbourne: Macmillan.

McMahon, R., Richmond, M. and Reeves-Kazelskis, C. (1998) 'Relationships between kindergarten teachers' perceptions of literacy acquisition and children's literacy involvement in classroom materials', *The Journal of Educational Research*, 91 (3): 173–92.

Makin, L. and Jones Diaz, C. (eds) (2002) *Literacies in Early Childhood: Changing Views, Challenging Practice*. Sydney: MacLennan and Petty. pp. 197–214.

Makin, L., Hayden, J., Holland, A., Arthur, L., Beecher, B., Jones Diaz, C. and McNaught, M. (1999) *Mapping Literacy Practices in Early Childhood Services*. Research report prepared for NSW DoCS and NSW DET, Sydney.

Marsh, J. (1999) 'Batman and Batwoman go to school: popular culture in the literacy curriculum', *International Journal of Early Years Education*, 7 (2): 117–31.

Millard, E. and Marsh, J. (2001) 'Sending Minnie the Minx home: comics and reading choices', *Cambridge Journal of Education*, 31 (1): 25–38.

Moss, P. (1990) *Childcare in the European Community 1985–1990*. Brussels: European Commission Childcare Network.

Munns, P. (1995) 'The role of organized preschool learning environments in literacy and numeracy development', *Research Papers in Education*, 10 (2): 217–52.

Neuman, S. (1996) 'Children engaging in storybook reading: the influence of access to print resources, opportunity', and parental interaction, *Early Childhood Research Quarterly*, 11: 495–513.

Neuman, S. (2001) 'The role of knowledge in early literacy', *Reading Research Quarterly*, 36 (4): 468–75.

Neuman, S. and Celano, D. (2001) 'Access to print in low-income and middle-income communities: an ecological study of four neighborhoods', *Reading Research Quarterly*, 36 (1): 8–26.

Neuman, S. and Roskos, K. (1997) 'Literacy knowledge in practice; contexts of participation for young writers and readers', *Reading Research Quarterly*, 32 (1): 10–32.

Nielsen, D. and Monson, D. (1996) 'Effects of literacy environment on literacy development of kindergarten children', *The Journal of Educational Research*, 89 (5): 259–75.

OECD (1999) *Measuring Student Knowledge and Skills: a New Framework for Assessment*. Paris: Organization for Economic Co-operation and Development Available at http://www.pisa.oecd.org.

OECD (2001a) *Starting Strong: Early Childhood Education and Care*. Paris. Organization for Economic Co-operation and Development.

OECD (2001b) *Knowledge and Skills for Life: First Results of PISA 2000*. Paris. Organization for Economic Co-operation and Development.

Offman-Gersh, S. (2001) 'Technology's role in creating the shared learning environment', *Multimedia Schools*, 8 (5): 48–52.

Pahl, K. (1999) *Transformations: Children's Meaning Making in a Nursery*. Stoke-on-Trent: Trentham.

Paley, V. (1984) *Boys and Girls: Superheroes in the Dolls' corner*. Chicago: University of Chicago Press.

Purcell-Gates, V. (1996) 'Stories, coupons and the TV guide: relationships between home literacy experiences and emergent reading knowledge', *Reading Research Quarterly*, 31 (4): 406–28.

Purcell-Gates, V. and Dahl, K. (1991) 'Low-SES children's success and failure at early literacy learning in skills–based classroom', *Journal of Reading Behavior*, XXXIII (1): 1–34.

Reese, D. and Harris, V. (1997) '"Look at this nest!" The beauty and power of using informational books with young children', *Early Child Development and Care*, 127–28: 217–31.

Richards, G. (2000) 'Why use computer technology?', *English Journal*, 90 (2): 38–41.

Rogers, R. (2002) 'Between contexts: a critical discourse analysis of family literacy, discursive practices', and literate subjectivities, *Reading Research Quarterly*, 37 (3): 248–77.

Rolfe, S. (1999) 'Training for quality educare in infant childcare: Bowlbian dreams and the tyranny of economic rationalism', keynote paper in *Proceedings of the Seventh Early Childhood Convention*, Whakatu–Nelson, New Zealand.

Rosemary, C. and Roskos, K. (2002) 'Literacy conversations between adults and children at child care: descriptive observations and hypotheses', *Journal of Research in Childhood Education*, 16 (2): 212–31.

Roskos, K. and Christie, J. (2001) 'Examining the play–literacy interface: a critical review and future directions', *Journal of Early Childhood Literacy*, 191: 59–89.

Saracho, O. (2002) 'Family literacy: exploring family practices', *Early Child Development and Care*, 172 (2): 113–22.

Scarr, S., Eisenberg, M. and Deater–Deckard, K. (1994) 'The measurement of quality in child care centers', *Early Childhood Research Quarterly*, 9: 131–51.

Schweinhart, L., Barnes, H. and Weikart, D. (1993) *Significant Benefits: the High/Scope Perry Preschool Study through Age 27*. Monographs of the High/Scope Educational Research Foundation no. 10. Ypsilanti, MI: High/Scope Press.

Shiels, G. and Cosgrove, J. (2002) 'International assessments of reading literacy', *The Reading Teacher*, 55 (7): 690–92.

Siraj-Blatchford, I. and Clarke, P. (2000) *Supporting Identity, Diversity and Language in the Early Years*. Buckingham: Open University Press.

Smith, C. (2001) 'Click and turn the page: an exploration of multiple storybook literacy', *Reading Research Quarterly*, 36 (2): 152–83.

Snow, C. and Ninio, A. (1986) 'The contracts of literacy: what children learn from learning to read books', in W. Teale and E. Sulzby (eds), *Emergent Literacy*. Norwood, NJ: Ablex.

Snow, C., Burns, M. and Griffin, P. (eds) (1998) *Preventing Reading Difficulties in Young Children*. Washington, DC: National Academy Press.

Sulzby, E. (1985) 'Children's emergent reading of favorite storybooks: a developmental study', *Reading Research Quarterly*, 20: 458–81.

Sylva, K. and Siraj-Blatchford, I. (2001) 'The relationship between children's developmental progress in the preschool period and the two rating scales'. Paper presented at the International ECERS Network Workshop, Santiago, Chile.

Sylva, K., Sammons, P., Siraj-Blatchford, I., Melhuish, E. and Quinn, L. (2001) 'The Effective Provision of Pre–School Education (EPPE) Project'. Symposium presented at the BERA Annual Conference, Leeds.

Vukelich, C. (1994) 'Effects of play interventions on young children's reading of environmental print', *Early Childhood Research Quarterly*, 9: 167–69.

Walker, C. and Yekovich, F. (1999) ' TRALEs to literacy', *Educational Leadership*, 57 (2): 57–60.

Walters, T. (1998) 'The language of a literate classroom: rethinking comprehensive directions', Education Digest ED418430, ERIC Clearinghouse.

Wells, G. (1981) 'Some antecedents of early educational attainment', *British Journal of Sociology of Education*, 2: 181–200.

Wells, G. (1985) *Language, Learning and Education*. Windsor: NFER-Nelson.

Wells, G. and Nichols, P. (eds) (1985) *Language and Learning: an Interactional Perspective*. London: Falmer.

Worthy, J., Moorman, M. and Turner, M. (1999) 'What Johnny likes to read is hard to find in school', *Reading Research Quarterly*, 34 (1): 12–27.

Young, J. and Brozo, W. (2001) 'Conversations: boys will be boys, or will they? Literacy and masculinities', *Reading Research Quarterly*, 36 (3): 316–25.

Zecker, L. (1999) 'Different texts, different emergent writing forms', *Language Arts,* 76 (6): 483–90.

28

Computers and Early Literacy Education

LINDA D. LABBO AND DAVID REINKING

Computers are a part of young children's literacy experiences in their homes, communities, and classrooms. By the time many young children begin formal schooling, they are likely to have had countless experiences involving digital forms of communication, for example sitting in the lap of an adult who is corresponding with a relative via e-mail or who is making an online purchase over the Internet. Or, they may participate in engaging interactive multimedia stories and games on a home computer (Lauman, 2000). Children who attend preschool are likely to have had experiences with computers, at least occasionally, involving educational games designed to teach the alphabet (Duffelmeyer, 2002) or programs designed to encourage drawing and creative play (Labbo, 1996; Haugland, 1999). Even children who, for sociocultural or economic reasons, have not had such opportunities, the computer is a part of everyday experiences ranging from seeing people use computerized, interactive devices in stores and banks to using an interactive digital kiosk that provides information at a subway station.

In fact, for at least a decade, educators have noted that for many youngsters literacy activities involving computers prior to and outside of school are typically more frequent, richer, and more meaningful than are such activities they encounter when they enter elementary school (Green and Bigum, 1993; Mackey, 1994; Unsworth, 2001). That discrepancy and the increasing integration of digital forms of reading and writing into everyday life suggest that considering the role of technology in the literacy development of young children is a timely and important topic. That it is timely and important is reflected by the fact that computers are now considered to be essential in outfitting the modern classroom and they are readily available for use in most elementary schools (e.g. Technology Counts, 1999), by the fact that there is a growing body of literature addressing the use of computers in early literacy (e.g. see Blok et al., 2002), and by the fact that there is an extensive array of commercial, educational multimedia software designed for young children and numerous free websites for young children on the World Wide Web (cf. Davis and Shade, 1994; Duffelmeyer, 2002; Haugland, 1999; 2000).

Indeed, national governments and international professional associations for educators are establishing literacy instruction, guidelines and standards for using computers in instruction (Alberta Learning, 2000; Leu, 1997). For example, the International Reading Association and the National Association for the Education of Young Children (1996) issued a joint statement indicating that early childhood educators must be prepared to examine critically and use effectively new technologies for the benefit of children. On a national level, Prime Minister Tony Blair (1999) announced his goal to link every school in the United Kingdom to the Internet. Likewise, the governments of New Zealand, Australia, and Finland have established initiatives to integrate technology into their education systems (Leu, 2000). In the United States, although there is no national policy, a national survey (National Center for Education Statistics, 1999) documented that schools have invested $4 billion to place computers in 90% of K-5 classrooms with more than half of teachers in the survey reporting that they have at least two classroom computers. However, 80% of the teachers surveyed indicated that they do not feel adequately prepared to use computer technology for instruction.

It is clear that various stakeholders in education recognize the importance of computers in the literacy development of young children. Likewise, they are vitally interested in determining how best to take advantage of the presence and power of computer technologies to enhance instruction, to expand or transform teaching approaches, and to support children's literacy development while avoiding long-standing pitfalls and difficulties inherent in integrating new technologies into classroom instruction (Cuban, 2001; Newman, 1990; Sheingold, 1991). In this chapter we consider the role that research has played, is playing, and might play in addressing this timely and important topic.

CAVEATS AND MULTIPLE REALITIES

Several important caveats and multiple realities shape our consideration of research pertaining to computers and the development of young children's literacy. First, the research base is broad and shallow. It is broad because digital technologies have implications for virtually all areas and issues of reading and writing and because they introduce new topics for consideration (Reinking, 1994; 1998). It is shallow as illustrated by the US National Reading Panel's (2002) report indicating that only 21 quantitative studies addressing the use of computers in early reading instruction met its stringent criteria for consideration (see also Kamil and Lane, 1998; Kamil et al., 2000).

Further, as we have argued previously (Labbo and Reinking, 1999), the connection between research and practice can only be considered in relation to the multiple realities represented by those who conceptualize and conduct research and by those who seek guidance from it. The theoretical stances (or lack thereof) of researchers and the pedagogical assumptions of practitioners create multiple realities influencing what research is carried out and what findings are considered important and relevant. For example, early childhood educators and researchers influenced respectively by the perspectives of educators such as Chall, Vygotsky, Brunner, Piaget, Montessori, or Malaguzzi may have much different conceptions of how technology might benefit young children.

A related caveat is that research pertaining to the use of computers with young children has been conceptualized and conducted within a rapidly shifting landscape affecting what topics are considered relevant. During the relatively short history of educational computing and the research pertaining to it, the power and range of computer-based applications for children inside and outside school have expanded exponentially, as have educators' understanding and imaginative exploration of how computer technology might play a role in child development. Likewise, views of early literacy and literacy instruction have changed and have become politicized, particularly in the US and in the UK. Finally, the methods and epistemologies of educational research have broadened to include naturalistic forms of inquiry.

Despite these caveats and multiple realities, we believe that a broad look at the research, which includes not only experimental studies but also methods such as ethnographies, case studies surveys, and formative experiments, may lead to useful insights about the use of computers with young children. Findings are rarely definitive and firm principles are hard to find. Nonetheless, at the very least, the directions and issues pursed by researchers suggest some major themes and tentative conclusions that might focus the attention of both researchers and educators on how digital technologies might be integrated into the literacy development of young children. In this chapter we outline those directions, themes, and conclusions, taking a focused look at the recent relevant literature.

A BRIEF HISTORY

Research on the role of computers in literacy education has had a relatively short, yet peripatetic, and sometimes tumultuous history that reflects not only often grudging acceptance of new and rapidly changing technologies but also broader shifts in perspectives on literacy pedagogy and research methodologies. A brief overview of that history helps contextualize the direction and findings of research. It also clearly illustrates the multiple realities that define what research is considered relevant by whom under what circumstances.

The earliest studies on the use of computers for reading instruction were conducted in the 1960s by Richard Atkinson and his colleagues at Stanford University (Atkinson and Hansen, 1966–7). Their goal was unapologetically ambitious, and in retrospect naive: to use a mainframe computer to deliver beginning reading instruction that would develop competent readers without the need for a teacher. Although their work laid the foundation for subsequent commercial materials, interest in using computers for early literacy development remained dormant through the 1970s due in part to the strong reaction against the Stanford project by the mainstream education community (Spache, 1967), but mainly because of the technological and practical limitations of mainframe computers.

However, with the appearance of the personal microcomputer, the early 1980s witnessed the beginning of research and publications focusing on using computers in the early grades (e.g. Alexander, 1983; Barnes and Hill, 1983; Bradley; 1982; Clements, 1983–4; Cuffaro, 1984; Hungate, 1982; Lavin and Sanders, 1982). Readiness and skill-based perspectives reflected in drill-and-practice applications dominated commercial software developed during the 1980s and into the 1990s and consequently influenced how computers were used in early literacy instruction during that period. Researchers investigated the effects of these new applications and also quickly determined that even preschool children had no difficulty acquiring the skills needed to interact with a computer (Binder and Ledger, 1985; Clements and Nastasi, 1993a; 1983b; Gore et al., 1989; Hess and McGarvey, 1987; Watson et al., 1986). It also became clear that computer-based technologies could uniquely accommodate the needs of young children in ways that went beyond conventional printed materials (e.g. special alphabetically arranged keyboards) and by eliminating the need for independent reading skills for beginning literacy activities (e.g. digitized or synthesized speech to provide directions and feedback).

Resurrecting the goals of the Stanford project (Atkinson and Hansen, 1966–7), several comprehensive computer-based curricular and management programmes referred to as integrated learning systems (ILSs) became prominent in the 1980s. One prominent ILS of this period, *Writing to Read* (Martin, 1986), was heavily promoted by IBM Corporation and was adopted by many schools across the US. Interestingly, it combined skills-based phonics instruction delivered by the computer with writing activities (using IBM typewriters) and children's literature that were more characteristic of whole language perspectives. Nonetheless, it appealed more to those with a skills-based, phonics orientation than those invested in more child-centred approaches. The research conducted on *Writing to Read* is illustrative of an often-repeated pattern for other commercial ventures. Initially, positive results are reported from studies conducted or sponsored by the company or organization developing the programme. Then, independent researchers point out flaws in the research or conduct their own studies that produce less favourable findings (e.g. Krendl and Williams, 1990; Slavin, 1991). Amid debates about whether the research does or does not support the programme, individual teachers adapt the programme to their own needs and perspectives, often in ways that are different from the intent of those who designed the programme (Labbo et al., 1995–6; see also Bruce and Rubin, 1993).

ILSs such as *Writing to Read* became less popular in the early 1990s because of their expense, their lack of clearly demonstrated success (Becker, 1992), and their inconsistencies with popular views of early literacy instruction. However, as Patterson et al. (in press) have argued, ILSs experienced a resurgence of popularity in the late 1990s. This resurgence may be explained in part by the increasing emphasis particularly in the US on skills-based phonics instruction in early reading that is a consequence of politically driven initiatives aimed at promoting that perspective (e.g. the Reading First Act and the No Child Left Behind initiative in the US). However, Patterson et al. (in press) concluded in their study of the Waterford Program (www.waterford.org/), a heavily phonics-based ILS, that it too did not live up to claims of increasing achievement more than control classrooms. More importantly, they found that teacher variables including type of management and interaction patterns explained much more variance in achievement than did the ILS.

Educational trends in the 1990s affected the content and direction of research pertaining to computers and the development of young children's literacy, creating new realities. For example, pervasive use of e-mail and the World Wide Web during the 1990s made it much clearer that new conceptions of literacy and literate behaviours are needed (Leu and Kinzer, 2000). Likewise, software developers exploited the exponential expansion of computing memory and speed to create multimedia activities. For example, many CD-ROMs entered the market as multimedia versions of popular children's stories that engaged children in a variety of interactions with the story that were not possible in printed form. And, as before, these technological developments stimulated research into these new uses and capabilities (e.g. Labbo and Kuhn, 1998). Also during the 1990s definitions of literacy began to include non-print media (e.g. Flood et al., 1997). Reinforcing this broader view was a shift towards sociocultural perspectives that emphasized dimensions of literacy related to contextual factors in school (and notably now outside school), social interactions, and the ideologies that shaped conceptions of literacy and literacy development.

Research too took a turn toward more naturalistic methods. For example, rather than investigating the immediate effects of whether hundreds of children in many classrooms using a computer-based phonics activity for a relatively short time outperformed those who used some other medium, a researcher in the 1990s was as likely to conduct an ethnographic or case study investigating how computers may affect patterns of social interaction and language complexity during writing activities (e.g. Kent and

Rakestraw, 1994). There was also a corresponding interest in the process of how new technologies became integrated into literacy instruction (Bruce and Rubin, 1993; Garner and Gillingham, 1998) and how children learned *with* a computer not *from* a computer (Clements and Nastasi, 1993a). This line of research has been supported by the considerable evidence that new technologies are not readily integrated into instruction, nor do they readily transform traditional patterns of instruction (e.g. Cuban 2001; Windschitl and Sahl, 2002).

Nonetheless, counterbalancing this trend during the 1990s was an increasing politicization of reading instruction, particularly in the US and to some extent in other countries such as the UK (e.g. Beard, 2000), with central governments and governmental agencies and commissions valuing and sanctioning conventional product-oriented achievement through legislative and funding initiatives that privilege experimental over qualitative methods (e.g. the National Reading Panel in the US). In addition, that governmental influence has been relatively narrowly focused on phonemic aspects of beginning reading rather than literacy development broadly considered. Thus, as we write this chapter, we would argue that unfortunate bifurcations exist within the research community, particularly across theoretical, methodological and disciplinary lines, and that this general condition is clearly reflected in the current state of research concerning the use of computers with young children (see Leu, 2000, and Kamil et al., 2000, for additional support for this view). However, some recent studies employing new approaches to research, often using mixed methods (e.g. Karchmer, 2001; Patterson et al., in press; Reinking and Watkins, 2000), offer some promise to cross these boundaries. In addition, some researchers have advocated taking a broader ecological perspective (e.g. Bruce and Hogan, 1998) in considering how new technologies of written communication may affect reading and writing.

So, given the rapid shifts and multiple influences and realities evident during this relatively brief history, what, if anything, do we know about the role of computers in early literacy development? What have we learned from research? What themes emerge as important, beyond those we have already highlighted? What research is needed? What theoretical positions might be useful? We now turn to these and related questions.

ISSUES, FINDINGS, AND THEORIES

In this section we synthesize pedagogical issues, research findings, and theoretical perspectives by presenting five broad themes spanning the divergent historical trends and multiple realities discussed in the previous section. The themes clearly overlap to some extent, and they are certainly not the only themes that might be generated. Nonetheless, this admittedly personal list allows us to provide some structure to a broad and divergent area of research. The five themes are as follows: in relation to young children's literacy development, computers (1) support writing, (2) contribute to the development of phonological abilities, (3) enable more independent reading, (4) foster social interaction and collaboration, and (5) transform instruction and introduce new literacy skills and awareness.

Supporting writing development

A growing body of research indicates that computer technology can support young children's development of writing ability. Research has focused on how computers can support that development from the perspective of emergent literacy and process writing and through the use of word processing and other software aimed at creative expression. An emergent literacy perspective with its emphasis on creative, natural experimentation with writing (Teale and Sulzby, 1986) is well matched to the capabilities of the computer. For example, in our work (Labbo, 1996) kindergarten children who worked independently to produce stories using a software application that allowed students to express themselves with pictures and text achieved cognitive growth, child-initiated collaborative work, and development of literacy insights as they attempted to solve problems they encountered while composing. Activities involving the computer provided multimedia scaffolding not available in conventional printed material, allowing children to explore symbolic representations but also providing them with opportunities to develop conventional literacy skills such as letter recognition, directionality, punctuation, and sound–symbol correspondence (see Bangert-Drowns, 1989; Rosengrant, 1988) and on how they could represent their intended meaning in symbolic form (Borgh and Dickson, 1986; Rosengrant, 1988). Likewise, working from the perspective of emergent literacy (Teale and Sulzby, 1986), Lomangino et al. (1999) documented that many children begin to form mental connections among writing, print, and symbol making as they engage in acts of writing with computers.

Standard word processing applications aimed at more advanced writers have also been made available to young children. Cochran-Smith (1991) suggested that word processing programs have the potential to support children's ability to engage in sophisticated writing processes and production. She stated that word processors overcome 'difficulties of print production that often preoccupy young writers, and facilitate the physical manipulation and revision of text without necessitating rewriting and recopying – tasks which are often laborious and sometimes even counterproductive for elementary school age children' (1991: 108). One long-standing line of research has focused on the influence of word processing programs on young children's written expression, literacy development and benefits when writing with a computer as compared to writing with pens and pencils (e.g. Cochran-Smith, 1991; Edinger, 1994; Olson and Johnston, 1989). However, some scholars have questioned the advisability of conducting research aimed at comparing paper and pencil to computer writing (Kelly and O'Kelly, 1993; Leu, 1997; Reinking, 1994) because word processing has proven by its widespread use that it is clearly superior for most purposes. Nonetheless, this generalization may not hold for young children.

Studies report mixed results on the effects of word processors on children's literacy development and ability to write (Hunter, 1990; Joram et al., 1992); however, the overall conclusion seems to be that they are beneficial. Word processing has been found to increase the amount of children's metacognitive, self-guiding talk, their number of revisions, and the overall lexical density and organizational cohesiveness of written products when compared to writing generated with paper and pencil (Jones and Pellegrini, 1996; Moeller, 1993). Likewise, word processing enhanced students' abilities to maintain a specific topic focus throughout their writing efforts (Cochran-Smith et al., 1991), provided encouragement for non-motivated writers (Cochran-Smith et al., 1988), resulted in more writing (Chang and Osguthorpe, 1990; Clements, 1987; Daiute, 1988; Rosengrant, 1986), and supported children's improvement of writing skills (Moxley and Warash, 1992). Phenix and Hannan (1984) describe how young children utilized printouts to read a legible version of what they had written by hand (the original text was extremely difficult to read).

Studies also indicate that writing with computers facilitates a process approach to writing (Calkins, 1983; 1986; Graves, 1983) by enhancing, for example, brainstorming, drafting, revising, publishing). Children have been found to gain confidence in their writing abilities (Phenix and Hannan, 1984) and to exhibit positive attitudes toward writing and writing process approaches (Bangert-Drowns, 1989; Leher et al., 1987) when using word processors and other computer-based applications that encourage and facilitate writing. Leher et al. (1987) note that

preschoolers, who playfully wrote with word processors, exhibited an ability to brainstorm and collect their thoughts as they generated ideas for a topic before they wrote. Apparently, as children brainstorm, write drafts, revise, edit, and publish with a word processing program, they can focus more on managing and organizing their ideas and less on tedious or mechanical aspects of writing (Jones, 1994).

More recent studies have focused more specifically on aspects of children's writing that may be affected by writing with computers. For example, there is some evidence that children who have access to revising tools on computer screens also have opportunities to conceptually grasp the notion that print is changeable and that composing involves the manipulation and refinement not only of text but also of ideas (Labbo and Kuhn, 1998). Fletcher (2001) reported a case study in which students who used computers made better editing decisions; however, they did not consistently utilize feedback provided by editing tools such as spell or grammar checks. Tancock (2002), on the other hand, noted that young children did not consistently benefit from spell-check options because their attempts to spell were not close enough to conventional spelling to result in a display of options for correctly spelled words. Kahn (1997) found that children writing with a computer were able to shift their perspectives from seeing writing as primarily an activity that involved the production of neatly printed text to seeing writing as centred on audience awareness, sharing information, and focusing on a particular topic.

Developing phonological abilities

From the earliest days of instructional computing, computers have been considered useful for teaching sound–symbol correspondences, inspiring researchers to investigate how the computer might enhance early literacy instruction in this area (e.g. Atkinson and Hansen, 1966–7). Interest in this area was spawned in part because it is relatively easy to conceptualize and program tutorial and drill-and-practice instruction in entertaining game-like formats when content can be specified as a hierarchy of discrete skills, as is typically the case for learning letter names and the sounds. Despite cautions from many literacy educators that drill-and-practice applications may undermine the goals of early literacy instruction (e.g. Clements, 1999), others have pointed out that such applications can play an important role in developing phonological abilities (e.g. Barker and Torgesen, 1995).

The research literature provides considerable support for the contention that computers can contribute to the development of phonological abilities. Much of that literature involves investigating applications in which the computer provides audio support for children who have not yet become fluent decoders. For example, using the computer to generate synthesized or digitized speech and isolated speech sounds has been an ongoing area of software development and research. Several of these research efforts have led to commercial products (e.g. *Hint and Hunt* based on research by Roth and Beck, 1987) or have investigated the effectiveness of commercial products (e.g. Barker and Torgesen's 1995 research on *Daisy Quest* and *Daisy's Dilemma*). The underlying assumption of these efforts is that the computer can enhance individualized instruction and provide independent practice in learning various phonological aspects of written language. Studies that have demonstrated increases in phonological awareness using this capability with a variety of populations include Foster et al. (1994) and Reitsma and Wesseling (1998) with emergent readers; Wise and Olson (1995) and Barker and Torgesen (1995) with developing readers experiencing problems in learning to read; Barron et al. (1998) with neurologically impaired children; Lundberg (1995) with special education students; and Ho and Ma (1999) with Chinese dyslexic children.

A longitudinal study by Reitsma and Wesseling (1998) is noteworthy. They investigated the effects of computer-based activities designed to increase phonological awareness with children who moved from kindergarten to first grade in the Netherlands. This study offers strong evidence that computer-based activities can develop phonological awareness, because it took into account multiple factors: (1) computer application factors (e.g. programs that specifically target phonemic blending activities administered outside of the classroom focus on the computer screen as a learning environment); (2) child factors including not only phonological ability but also literacy factors in the home based on extensive interviews with caregivers; (3) classroom teacher factors (e.g. classroom observations and teacher questionnaires); and (4) impact and durability of the training (e.g. follow-up testing to determine children's decoding and word recognition abilities and transfer of learning to tasks without the computer).

We believe that this comprehensive and rigorous approach (e.g. a comparison group that used the computer for vocabulary instruction) that employs quantitative and qualitative data gathered longitudinally is exemplary, and thus this study provides especially convincing findings. Further, their findings offer three important insights that are consistent with previous research. First, the computer learning environment offered a successful approach to supporting children's development of foundational skills. Children trained in phonological awareness skills using the computer gained significantly more in blending skill abilities than control group children. Secondly, the classroom learning environment influenced children's acquisition of basic skills. Thirdly, the skills gained were durable and transferable outside of the initial learning environment. When post-tests were administered to children at the six-month stage of first grade, children who engaged in the computer-based activities remained significantly better decoders.

Thus, there is considerable evidence that computers offer effective instructional options for helping young children acquire phonological abilities. Some of the studies highlighted in the following sections add support to this conclusion.

Enabling independent reading

Digital texts can provide various supports during independent reading that are not available in printed texts. They may employ diverse media effects including speech, sound, animation, movies, and rapid links to diverse textual and graphic representations. For example, children reading a story in digital form might click on an unfamiliar word to hear it pronounced or to obtain its meaning; they might select an option to hear the entire story read aloud by the computer; or they might click on objects in an illustration to see them animate. Together these capabilities remove some of the barriers to independent reading and comprehension that are inherent in conventional materials. Thus, digital texts may be less difficult to read and understand, and they may be more engaging, and thus more likely to be read independently by young children.

The widespread introduction of CD-ROM technology in the 1990s gave considerable impetus to this area of computer use, particularly in the development of computerized versions of popular children's books. Two series of books on CD-ROM were introduced respectively by Discis Books (1990) and Living Books (1990) during this period. Such stories and capabilities were and are quite popular in schools and homes and widely used, and they have begun to migrate to the Internet. But what does the research have to say about the use of such capabilities and their ability to facilitate independent reading and learning among young children? Can children who interact with digital texts with various supports and media effects develop (or perhaps lose) a sense of story structure, gain foundational concepts about printed and digital reading and writing, increase vocabulary, incidentally acquire sight words, read more independently?

Unlike areas of research involving computers, the research investigating computer-based activities to enhance independent reading and comprehension has been guided by theoretical perspectives (Reinking, 1998). For example, Salomon et al. (1989) saw the computer as a 'reading partner' that helped children read in their 'zone of proximal development' in the Vygotskian (Vygotsky, 1978) sense. They found that children were more often able to read and comprehend texts when the computer provided support during independent reading in the following categories: modelling, activating relevant cognitive processes, and offering guidance.

Using the computer's capability to allow children support during independent reading has led to increases in conventional reading skills. For example, Reitsma (1988) found that Dutch children who used the assistance available in electronic passages learned target words more readily than children in a comparison group (see Olson et al., 1986, for similar results with learning disabled students). More recent work with eight-year-old children in Canada (Miller et al., 1994) indicated that children who engage in multiple readings of electronic text over time access word pronunciations less frequently, a finding which may indicate growth in word recognition rates and abilities. Other research conducted along these lines of inquiry suggests that listening to an electronic story helps young children develop a sense of story, extends vocabulary, increases knowledge of words, enhances story comprehension for children who read below grade level, and enriches concepts about print (Lewin, 1995; McKenna, 1998). These findings indicate the potential of talking books to introduce very young children to foundational concepts about print.

In a recent series of experiments McKenna and his colleagues (McKenna, 1998; McKenna et al., 2001; McKenna and Watkins, 1994; 1995; 1996) investigated young children reading digital versions of children's books. They termed these books 'talking books', because the computer provided audio reading of the text, the pronunciation of unfamiliar words, and phonics analogies (e.g. comparing 'bat' and 'cat') depending on the condition. They viewed these forms of assistance as 'electronic scaffolds'. However, specifically they were interested in determining if and under what forms of assistance kindergarten and first-grade children might acquire phonological and sight word knowledge while reading high quality children's literature. Among the findings that emerged from these studies are that providing pronunciations alone does not enhance phonological awareness, that children who have little knowledge of the alphabetic principle do not benefit from phonics analogies, and that increases in sight word knowledge are related to increases in phonological awareness.

Another major line of theoretically grounded research includes studies using qualitative methods to investigate children's interactions with stories in digital form, delivered via commercial CD-ROMs. In our work (Labbo and Kuhn, 2000) in this area we employed Wittrock's (1986) generative learning model as a qualitative case study frame for understanding a kindergarten child's meaning making processes and story comprehension. Extending to electronic narratives Armbruster and Anderson's (1984) notion of considerate and inconsiderate expository texts, we were interested in determining what features of the electronic texts enhanced children's interaction with the story in relation to their recall of the narrative. Findings indicated that considerate CD-ROM talking books enabled the child to cohesively retell the story and utilize meaning making processes that chained together complex affective, cognitive and metacognitive processes. Inconsiderate CD-ROM talking books interfered with the child's comprehension as evidenced by a fragmented retelling. Furthermore, interactions during reading generated passive viewing and suspended efforts to make meaning. We surmised that when teachers wish to support children's comprehension of story with electronic stories, it is vital to determine if the content and multimedia features are congruent or incongruent with the narrative (see also Scoresby, 1996; Smith, 2001).

Lewin (1996) has also raised concerns about the use of talking books for young children's literacy development. She wondered about the long-term consequences if children become so dependent on the computer to pronounce unknown words that they do not begin to develop adequate word recognition strategies. She raises concerns that talking books might result in fewer thoughtful interactions and more passive viewing behaviours (see Carroll, 1999). On the other hand, researchers continue to report benefits of talking books (Matthew, 1997; McKenna and Watkins, 1994; 1995; 1996; Talley and Lancy, 1995). However, contextual factors may often outweigh the benefits of even the most carefully designed and research-based application. For example, Talley and Lancy's (1995) study of children in a Head Start programme indicated that CD-ROM talking books were useful if they were integrated as an enhancement to an existing developmentally appropriate instructional programme.

Fostering social interaction and collaboration

Social interaction and collaboration are valued among those interested in developing young children's literacy, and that view has been frequently supported by sociocognitive views of literacy development as proposed most notably by Vygotsky (1978). Although some have expressed concerns that computers may reduce first-hand social interactions, that concern has not been supported in research involving the use of computers with young children in schools. In fact, when computers are integrated into classroom instruction in more than perfunctory ways, they have been shown to enhance significantly social interaction and collaboration, often involving reading and writing activities.

For example, early research indicated that word processing activities increased young children's collaboration during writing (Bruce et al., 1985; Hoot and Kimler, 1987; Phenix and Hannan, 1984) and that children who are more capable or knowledgeable may scaffold less able children's literacy development and ability to write (Tharp and Gallimore, 1988). Wild and Braid (1996) noted that collaborative or cooperative computer-related word processing experiences foster children's engagement with meaning making, cognitively oriented discussions, and task-focused talk. Dickinson (1986) found that computer monitors provided a shared viewing platform that made children's writing more public, accessible and readable for peers. Thus, as children shared computer composing spaces, computer composing tools (e.g. keyboards, mice), or writing goals they felt more accountable to discuss their writing plans, to elicit ideas and to respond thoughtfully to the writing of others.

More recently Lomangino et al. (1999) delved more closely into the nature of children's computer-related collaborations by exploring three case studies of child dyads. They reported inconsistencies in children's ability to successfully collaborate. For example, during computer collaborations, many children's interactive conversational patterns consisted in large part of a struggle for control about using technology tools and whose ideas to use in. Children's friendship relationships and status in the class also influenced the tone and benefits of collaborations. Liaw (1997) conducted a related study investigating interactions among third-grade students who had limited language proficiency (LEP) while they were engaged in reading computerized versions of books that made available various types of assistance: corners to show page turn, music and sound effects. The children's comments began by focusing on computer functions. However, after several sessions, talk shifted to story content, leading Liaw to conclude that, 'regardless of their grade levels and English language proficiency levels, the LEP children used English to read, command, suggest, question, respond, explain, express emotion, express opinions, and describe images and actions' (1997: 69).

Computers have also been used to enhance interactions among young children through socio-dramatic play and learning centres. Learning and development through play have long been recognized as an important component of early childhood classrooms (Glickman, 1979). Young children naturally engage in play, and their play with peers in early childhood classrooms may involve complex role playing, decision making, and socially negotiated problem solving that make important contributions to their cognitive, social, and emotional development (Morrow, 1990; Neuman and Roskos, 1992). Some educators have raised concerns that computers may not afford adequate learning environments for children to playfully engage with literacy learning in developmentally appropriate ways (Elkind, 1996; Healy, 1998). However, we believe that research supports the possibility that computers can be integrated into learning environments in productive ways that capitalize on young children's natural eagerness to learn through play (Freeman and Somerindyke, 2001; Gillen, 2002; Labbo et al., 1996; Smith, 2001), and that indeed young children are capable of various forms of play that involves computers (Escobedo, 1992).

An example from our own work (Labbo et al., 1996) illustrates the possibilities for enhancing literacy development of young children through sociodramatic computer play. We used a cardboard model of a computer as a prop in a centre set up as a flower shop. The children first went to an actual flower shop to learn how the computers were used, which included correspondence, printing greeting cards, creating signs, and so forth. In the classroom, students pretended they were running a flower shop at the play centre which included telephones, order forms, and the computer as literacy. Children playfully mimicked the workplace literate activities they had observed in the real flower shop, which we believe reinforced perceptions of a computer as a natural tool for literacy.

Insights about computers and play can be found in a year-long qualitative study conducted by Smith (2001) on her 2.5-year-old son, James. Her analysis revealed that James' playtime with CD-ROM stories developed his conceptual and practical understanding of various links and symbolic modes. She explained that, while the sequence of the story pages and presentation of CD-ROM talking book text is not altered, various multimedia effects and information links offer differing story paths. Smith notes that her son's non-computer playtime was just as likely to involve pretending to be a hypertextual screen object as it was to involve pretending to be Batman. Interestingly, James' computer experiences extended to other life events. For example, he told his mother that he used a 'dream mouse' to click and stop a bad dream.

A promising line of research on the role of culturally responsive, playful computer learning environments is provided in a formative, exploratory study. Pinkard (1999) evaluated two computer games that were intended to build on the out-of-school language play engaged in by many young African-American children. When the seven-through 10-year-old children, who enjoyed rap music, playground chants, jump rope rhymes, and clapping games, participated in the games created by the researcher, they encountered language activity with which they were already familiar, but that focused on more conventional literacy skills such as phonological awareness. Results indicated that students were highly motivated to play with the programs, and they progressed in sight word knowledge as measured by delayed post-tests.

Another natural way to integrate computers into instruction is to use them in less socially oriented classroom centres. However, some educators have cautioned that using computers in classroom learning centres does not constitute an appropriate learning environment for young children because the computer exacerbates the limited opportunities using oral language in interaction with others (Healy, 1998; Henninger, 1994). Those who take this perspective are likely to view children's computer work in centres as an isolated, solitary activity involving low-level skills. Indeed, that may be the case, but we do not believe that it must be.

For example, Kelly and Schorger's (2001) recent six-month study examined the number of utterances made by 25 kindergarten children during free time play in computer and in traditional centres (e.g. blocks, classroom library, art, and sociodramatic play). Findings indicated that there were no significant differences in the majority of the children's mean length of utterance. The researchers posited that when children use computers as a self-selected activity, their language is as rich, expressive, and regulatory as is the language they use in more traditional centres. In a related line of inquiry, Freeman and Somerindyke (2001) used an observational approach aimed at understanding whether four- and five-year-old children could serve as mutually supportive peers in accomplishing computer activities. They found that children assumed mutually supportive roles including offering assistance in using a mouse and in sharing strategies for navigating through computer applications.

Our own qualitative investigations suggest that when children are given ample time, individually and collaboratively, to playfully explore computer applications during their centre work, they have occasions to learn keyboard functions (e.g. making upper-case letters), action schemes (manipulating a string of computer operations to accomplish a goal),

and vocabulary terms (e.g. metalinguistic knowledge that enables shared problem solving: Labbo, 1996). However, we also found that five-year-old children's attempts to collaborate indicated that teachers play a key role in setting up a context that allows for all children to benefit (Labbo et al., 2000).

In sum, these studies indicate the rich possibilities that computers offer for fostering social interaction and collaboration. Computers can be incorporated into playful activities, and there is some evidence that doing so may contribute substantively to language and literacy development. However, successful implementation and tangible benefits are dependent on a variety of contextual factors.

Transforming instruction and introducing new literacy skills

Among those who write about the use of computers in education there is a common view that educators have been slow to integrate technology into instruction and that they have been slow to recognize the desirable and needed transformations that new technologies afford (Cuban, 2001; International Society for Technology in Education, 2002; Leu and Kinzer, 2000). Papert (1993) went so far as to compare the typical school's stance towards computers to white blood cells attacking an invading virus. Yet, in our view, we see the computer making gradual, but steady, inroads into instruction with many teachers integrating technology more fully into their instruction and also recognizing the need to address the new literacy skills that are increasingly evident in everyday life. In this section we highlight what we see to be some of the more promising and needed areas of transformation in light of relevant research.

Communicating via e-mail is now ubiquitous in modern nations, providing many opportunities for personally meaningful reading and writing. Likewise, the World Wide Web puts people easily in contact with diverse information and individuals worldwide. With the increased availability of computers and Internet access in schools, even young children now have opportunities to communicate and to locate information online. For example, e-mail has encouraged exchanges between students around the world (Garner and Gillingham, 1998; Tao and Reinking, 2000; Tao et al., 1997), and Zhao et al. (1999) observed that the Internet offers a high level of connectivity that is an especially appealing avenue for literacy instruction. They stated, 'Connectivity relates to the capacity for communication among peers and between students and experts as students access information beyond the classroom walls, but also enables seamless data sharing across activities' (1999: 5). For example, e-mail and the Internet have the potential to engage students in reading that is inherently meaningful, which is not only motivating but also provides opportunities to practise and reinforce developing reading skills in authentic contexts.

Garner and Gillingham (1998) present a good illustration of this potential, although their research involved mostly students beyond the primary grades. They present six case studies of e-mail use by teachers in diverse settings. They documented how e-mail exchanges between students in one typical American classroom and students in Alaska provided an opportunity to experience writing in a context that promoted sociocultural understandings. They also documented how elementary school children gained new literacy skills. For example, students learned to embed topics in ongoing exchanges to create a meaningful context for their geographically, and often socially, distant correspondents; how to delete irrelevant details; and how to be appropriately responsive to messages.

That e-mail may be a useful activity for the development of literacy in the young can be seen in Yost's (2000) first-person narrative documenting e-mail use by kindergarten. She reported a progression in the way that she employed e-mail. She began by allowing the few children whose parents had e-mail accounts to send notes home (e.g. reminders about overdue library books etc.). Later, when she realized that all of the families had access to e-mail, it became an integral part of her kindergarten literacy curriculum. Children engaged in more writing, but they also needed to be provided with choices about, for example, what type of spelling they would use, when they would send messages, and what they would communicate. Interestingly, she found that after pre-service teacher educators volunteered to type children's dictation, many children withdrew because they felt writing had become an obligation. We believe more research along these lines would provide important insights into how e-mail might be incorporated into activities in the preschool and primary grades and into what factors seem associated with positive outcomes for literacy development.

Internet access supports inquiry projects, and integrated, thematic cross-disciplinary activities, which are an influential way to invite children to learn about and share relevant content while employing all of the language arts. When children's purposes are to assemble and communicate knowledge from various resources (print based and screen based), they are likely to become more strategic and self-directed. Such approaches have great potential for integrating computers into the fabric of classroom life and for leveraging the power of multimedia to enhance children's electronic literacy development.

For example, in our own work (Labbo et al., 1995) we investigated children's opportunities for literacy development when a class of nine-year-old children in Taiwan exchanged e-mail questions with their counterparts in an American classroom. The third-grade students were motivated to frequently exchange electronic messages, which was more affordable, accessible and quicker than placing telephone calls or sending letters. The topics of children's exchanges focused on material culture (e.g. lifestyles, food choices, parents' careers, typical school day).

On the other hand, when Upitis (1990) explored the use of e-mail as a cross-cultural communicative tool, she found that teachers initially thought of the communications in terms of contrived and traditional paper and pencil activities. When Canadian keypals were paired with students in Boston, children wrote introductions in a traditional letter format. Furthermore, the teachers selected topics and projects they thought would be interesting. Children quickly lost interest because it did not allow them to become personally invested in authentic communication for authentic purposes. However, interestingly, after the project was abandoned, children initiated their own e-mail correspondences that entailed a series of exchanges focused on playfully pretending and role playing messages from creatures from outer space. Upitis concludes that educators need to make 'A distinction between really needing a tool and creating a use for a tool, arguing that too many contrived projects rely on the second option' (1990: 92). This finding again illustrates that sometimes subtle contextual factors and variations in implementation may determine the success of any computer-based activity.

Karchmer (2001) reported on 13 K-12 exemplary teachers' perceptions of how the Internet influences their literacy instruction. Insights from semi-structured interviews indicated that the Internet did influence the elementary teachers' decision making and instruction, and they reported devoting a great deal of time to locating appropriate and accurate Internet materials. Appropriate materials were considered to be within a range of reading levels present in their classrooms, include audiovisual aids or digitized speech to support children's comprehension, and connect to class themes. A kindergarten teacher reported, 'The biggest problem are Web sites with too much text. I find sites with graphics. Pictures [and] any kind of animated graphics are very intriguing to my students' (2001: 455). Most teachers reported publishing students' work on the Internet, which they believed was beneficial to literacy development.

We believe more research is needed to investigate not only how teachers of young children use computers in transformative ways, but how they come to understand and accept new roles, responsibilities, and opportunities in light of now common digital forms of written communication. One way that this may occur is by seeing computer-based activities as a logical extension of the long-standing pedagogical perspectives and roles associated with teachers of young children. Two examples are sociodramatic play and classroom learning centres, to which we now turn.

FUTURE DIRECTIONS

As we move into the twenty-first century, diverse viewpoints and many controversies continue to permeate discussions of the computer's role in education and child development. For some, the steadily increasing role of computers in education, the empirical evidence, and the future potential of computers in classrooms represent an epic journey that will profoundly transform literacy and promote new educational paradigms that offer educational benefits for children (Bolter, 1991; Clements and Nastasi, 1993a; 1993b; Gilster, 1997; Leu, 1997; Papert, 1993; Sheingold, 1991; Tapscott, 1998). These advocates extol the capacities of computers to open new vistas of learning for youngsters who may use computers to go on virtual field trips to Mars, to conduct inquiry projects with students in geographically and culturally distant classrooms, and to publish their multimedia work for a worldwide audience on the Web (see, Leu, 1997). Their enthusiasm and confidence are often grounded in a reality that supports a transformation of instruction toward more progressive, child-centred instruction (e.g. International Society for Technology in Education, 2002). Other enthusiasts, with a more teacher-directed and curriculum-based reality, see the benefits of computers in terms of their potential to deliver instruction more reliably and individually, especially for children experiencing problems in developing conventional literacy skills (e.g. Olson et al., 1997).

For others, the same unfolding chronicle of educational computing is a story of unrealized promise and credible dangers (Barnes and Hill, 1983; Bikerts, 1995; Clements, 1987; Elkind, 1987; Healy, 1998). Such views are even held by those outside of the educational arena. For example, medical authorities, albeit with little evidence, caution that computer games may promote violence, dangerous stereotypes, lowered self-esteem, and a passive, sedentary lifestyle (American Academy of Pediatrics, 2000). During the previous two decades, the tensions that exist between outright pessimism and unfailing optimism concerning the use of computers in classrooms have been especially apparent in the realm of early childhood literacy education (Clements, 1987; Clements and Nastasi, 1993a; Cuban, 2001).

In this chapter we have argued that a sufficient body of research currently exists to provide guidance for researchers and practitioners about what constitutes useful, necessary, and appropriate early literacy instruction in relation to digital technologies. However, we also acknowledge that some research in the area of young children's computer-related literacy development is exploratory and continues to emerge. Thus, findings are not definitive and clearly more research is needed, especially given the rapidly changing landscape of digital communication. Taking a historical perspective, we have noted that conceptions of relevant research have persistently changed as computer-based technologies have evolved; as perspectives on early literacy have shifted; as qualitative research methodologies and related theoretical perspectives have gained recognition among researchers; and as educators have begun to realize that digital forms of literacy activities change virtually everything about conventional print-based conceptions of literacy instruction. Furthermore, we have taken the perspective of multiple realities (Labbo and Reinking, 1999) that takes into consideration the contextual complexities involved in addressing the role of computer technologies in early childhood classrooms.

It is clear from our review of relevant research that many forces come into play when considering the effects of computer technologies on young children's literacy development. Computer learning environments are complex and influenced by various factors including children's literacy abilities, features of computer applications, the use of computer applications within larger classroom contexts, and the nature of learning conditions set up by teachers. Thus, it is also clear that context counts when it comes to effective use of computers in early childhood classrooms (see Kamil et al., 2000; Leu, 2000).

Teachers play a key role in orchestrating and determining the overall influence of computer technologies on children's literacy development. When viewed as an integral component of classroom instructional life, computers do not serve as a stand-alone centre where children, connected to individual headphones, work in isolation at the mercy of never-ending worksheets presented on a computer screen. It is imperative for pre-service teacher education programmes and in-service teacher professional development efforts to emphasize the potentially transformative role that computers can play in young children's literacy development; however, such training is likely to have little effect unless relevant factors pertaining to children, to computer applications and aspects of the technology, and learning environment are taken into consideration.

The field would benefit from more research agendas that acknowledge the multiple factors and multiple realities that may affect useful and appropriate uses of computers in the development of literacy among young children. This is no small challenge. New technologies such as hand-held computers, e-books, and other wireless, portable devices that are emerging at the time we are writing this chapter reflect a constantly changing technological landscape. Even more important and unpredictable is the way we incorporate these devices into our social worlds and how in turn we conceptualize reading and writing and our goals for developing literacy. The evolution of newer technologies also requires the thoughtful identification of theoretical constructs and practical principles of instruction that may be applied across various classroom contexts. We look forward to the next chapter in this unfolding story, and we hope that we have contributed in a small way here to addressing the challenges facing researchers and practitioners who are seeking informed guidance in addressing how computers can contribute to the development of literacy in young children.

REFERENCES

Alberta Learning (2000) *Information and Communication Technology, Kindergarten to Grade 12.* Edmonton, AB. Available at ednet.edc.gov.ab.ca.

Alexander, D. (1983) *Children's Computer Drawings.* Medford, MA: Tufts University.

American Academy of Pediatrics (2000) *Understanding the Impact of Media on Children and Teens.* Elk Grove Village, IL. Available at www.aap.org.

Armbruster, B.B. and Anderson, T.H. (1984) *Producing 'Considerate' Expository Text: Or, Easy Reading Is Damned Hard Writing.* Reading Education Report no. 46. Urbana, IL: Center for the Study of Reading.

Atkinson, R. and Hansen, D. (1966–7) 'Computer-assisted instruction in initial reading: the Stanford project', *Reading Research Quarterly,* 2: 5–26.

Bangert-Drowns, R.L. (1989) *Research on Word Processing and Writing Instruction.* Paper presented at the meeting of the American Educational Research Association, San Francisco, March 1989.

Barnes, B.J. and Hill, S. (1983) 'Should young children work with microcomputers Logo before Lego?', *Computing Teacher,* May: 11–14.

Barker, T.A. and Torgesen, J. (1995) 'An evaluation of computer-assisted instruction in phonological awareness with below average readers', *Journal of Educational Computing Research,* 13 (1): 89–103.

Barron, R., Lovett, M. and McCabe, R. (1998) 'Using talking computers to remediate reading and spelling disabilities: the critical role of the print-to-sound unit', *Behavior Research Methods, Instruments and Computers,* 30 (4): 610–16.

Beard, R. (2000) 'Long overdue? Another look at the National Literacy Strategy', *Journal of Research in Reading,* 23: 245–55.

Becker, H.J. (1992) 'Computer-based integrated learning systems in elementary and middle grades: a critical review and synthesis of evaluation reports', *Journal of Educational Computing Research,* 8: 1–41.

Bikerts, S. (1995) *The Gutenberg Elegies: the Fate of Reading in an Electronic Age.* New York: Fawcett.

Binder, S. and Ledger, B. (1985) *Preschool Computer Project Report.* Oakville, ON: Sheridan College.

Blair, T. (1999) 'The knowledge economy and government Internet policy', Speech by Prime Minister Tony Blair, 13 September. Available at www.techlawjournal.com.

Blok, H., Oostdam, R., Otter, M.E. and Overmaat, M. (2002) 'Computer-assisted instruction in support of beginning reading instruction: a review', *Review of Educational Research,* 72: 101–30.

Bolter, J.D. (1991) *Writing Space: the Computer, Hypertext, and the History of Writing.* Hillsdale, NJ: Erlbaum.

Borgh, K. and Dickson, W.P. (1986) 'Two preschoolers sharing one microcomputer: creating prosocial behavior with hardware and software', in P.F. Campbell and G.G. Fein (eds), *Young Children and Microcomputers.* Reston, VA: Reston. pp. 37–44.

Bradley, V.N. (1982) 'Improving students' writing with microcomputers', *Language Arts,* 50 (7): 732–43.

Bruce, B.C. and Hogan, M.P. (1998) 'The disappearance of technology: toward an ecological model of literacy', in D. Reinking, M. McKenna, L.D. Labbo and R.D. Kieffer (eds), *Literacy for the 21st Century: Technological Transformations in a Post-Typographic World.* Mahwah, NJ: Erlbaum. pp. 369–81.

Bruce, B.C. and Rubin, A. (1993) *Electronic Quills: a Situated Evaluation of Using Computers for Writing in Classrooms.* Hillsdale, NJ: Erlbaum.

Bruce, B.C., Michaels, S. and Watson-Gegeo, K. (1985) 'How computers can change the writing process', *Language Arts,* 62: 143–9.

Calkins, L. (1983) *Lessons from a Child.* Portsmouth, NH: Heinemann.

Calkins, L. (1986) *The Art of Teaching Writing.* Portsmouth, NH: Heinemann.

Carroll, M. (1999) 'Dancing on the keyboard: a theoretical basis for the use of computers in the classroom', *Reading Online.* Available at www.readingonline.org.

Chang, L. and Osguthorpe, R. (1990) 'The effects of computerized picture-word processing on kindergartners' language development', *Journal of Research in Childhood Education*, 5: 73–84.

Clements, D. (1983–4) 'Supporting young children's Logo programming', *Computing Teacher*, 11 (5): 24–30.

Clements, D.H. (1987) 'Computers and young children: a review of the research', *Young Children*, 43 (1): 34–44.

Clements, D.H. (1999) 'The uniqueness of the computer as a learning tool: insights from research and practice', in *Dialogue on Early Childhood Science, Mathematics, and Technology Education*. Project 2061. Washington, DC: American Association for the Advancement of Science. Available at www.project2061.org.

Clements, D.H. and Nastasi, B.K. (1993a) 'Electronic media and early childhood education', in B. Spodek (ed.), *Handbook of Research on the Education of Young Children*. New York: Macmillan. pp. 251–71.

Clements, D.H. and Nastasi, B.K. (1993b) 'Computers and early childhood education', in M. Gettinger, S.N. Elliot and T.R. Kratochwill (eds), *Advances in School Psychology: Preschool and Early Childhood Treatment Directions*. Hillsdale, NJ: Erlbaum. pp. 187–246.

Cochran-Smith, M. (1991) 'Word processing and writing in elementary classrooms: a critical review of related literature', *Review of Educational research*, 61: 107–55.

Cochran-Smith, M., Kahn, J. and Paris, C.L. (1988) 'When word processors come into the classroom', in J.L. Hoot and S.B. Silvern (eds), *Writing with Computers in the Early Grades*. New York: Teachers College Press. pp. 43–74.

Cochran-Smith, M., Paris, C.L. and Kahn, J. (1991) *Learning to Write Differently*. Norwood, NJ: Ablex.

Cuban, L. (2001) *Oversold and underused: Computers in the Classroom*. Cambridge, MA: Harvard University Press.

Cuffaro, H.K. (1984) 'Microcomputers in education: why is earlier better?', *Teachers College Record*, 85: 559–68.

Daiute, C. (1988) 'The early development of writing abilities: two theoretical perspectives', in J.L. Hoot and S.B. Silvern (eds), *Writing with Computers in the Early Grades*. New York: Teachers College Press. pp. 10–22.

Davis, B.C. and Shade, D.D. (1994) *Integrate, Don't Isolate? Computers in the Early Childhood Curriculum*. Urbana, IL: ERIC Clearinghouse on Elementary and Early Childhood Education.

Dickinson, D.K. (1986) 'Cooperation, collaboration, and a computer: integrating a computer into a first-second grade writing program', *Research in the Teaching of English*, 20: 357–78.

Discis Books (1990) 'Interactive computer books for children', *TechTrends*, 35 (5): 35–38. Available at www.discis.com.

Duffelmeyer, F.A. (2002) 'Alphabet activities on the internet', *The Reading Teacher*, 55: 631–5.

Edinger, M. (1994) 'Empowering young writers with technology', *Educational Leadership*, 51 (7): 58–60.

Elkind, D. (1987) 'Early childhood education on its own terms', in S. Kagan and E. Zigler (eds), *Early School: the National Debate*. New Haven, CT: Yale University Press. pp. 98–115.

Elkind, D. (1996) 'Young children and technology: a cautionary note', *Young Children*, 51 (6): 22–3.

Escobedo, T.H. (1992) 'Play in a new medium: children's talk and graphics at computers', *Play and Culture*, 5 (2): 120–40.

Fletcher, D.C. (2001) 'Second graders decide when to use electronic editing tools', in *Information Technology in Childhood Education Annual*, pp. 155–74.

Flood, J., Heath, S.B. and Lapp, D. (eds), (1997) *Handbook of Research on Teaching Literacy through the Communicative and Visual Arts*. New York: Macmillan.

Foster, K.C., Erickson, G.C., Foster, D.F., Brinkman, D. and Torgeson, J.K. (1994) 'Computer assisted instruction in phonological awareness: evaluation of the Daisy Quest program', *Journal of Research and Development in Education*, 27: 126–37.

Freeman, N. and Somerindyke, J. (2001) 'Social play at the computer: preschoolers scaffold and support peers' computer competence', in *Information Technology in Childhood Education Annual (*ITCE), 2001 no. 1, pp. 87–103.

Garner, R. and Gillingham, M.G. (1998) 'The Internet in the classroom: is it the end of transmission-oriented pedagogy?', in D. Reinking, L.D. Labbo, M.C. McKenna, and R.D. Kieffer (eds), *Handbook of Literacy and Technology: Transformations in a Post-Typographic World*. Mahwah, NJ: Erlbaum. pp. 221–31.

Gillen, J. (2002) 'Moves in the territory of literacy? The telephone discourse of three- and four-year-olds', *Journal of Early Childhood Literacy*, 2 (1): 21–43.

Gilster, P. (1997) *Digital Literacy*. New York: Wiley.

Glickman, C. (1979) 'Problem: declining achievement scores. Solution: let them play', *Phi Delta Kappan*, 60: 545–55.

Gore, D.A., Morrison, G.N., Maas, M.L. and Anderson, E.A. (1989) 'A study of teaching reading skills to the young children using microcomputer assisted instruction', *Journal of Educational Computing Research*, 5: 179–85.

Graves, D. (1983) *Writing: Teachers and Children at Work*. Portsmouth, NH: Heinemann.

Green, B. and Bigum, C. (1993) 'Aliens in the classroom', *Australian Journal of Education*, 37 (2): 119–41.

Haugland, S.W. (1999) 'What role should technology play in young children's learning?', *Young Children*, 54 (6): 26–31.

Haugland, S.W. (2000) 'Early childhood classrooms in the 21st century: using computers to maximize learning', *Young Children*, 55 (1): 12–18.

Healy, J. (1998) *Failure to Connect: How Computers Affect Our Children's Minds – for Better or Worse.* New York: Simon and Schuster.

Henninger, M.L. (1994) 'Computers and preschool children's play: are they compatible?', *Journal of Computing in Childhood Education*, 5 (3–4): 231–9.

Hess, R. and McGarvey, L. (1987) 'School-relevant effects of educational uses of microcomputers in kindergarten classrooms and homes', *Journal of Educational Computer Research*, 3: 260–87.

Ho, C. and Ma, R. (1999) 'Training phonological strategies improves Chinese dyslexic children's character reading skills', *Journal of Research in Reading*, 22 (2): 131–42.

Hoot, J. and Kimler, M. (1987) *Early Childhood Classrooms and Computers: Programs with Promise.* Urbana, IL: University of Illinois.

Hungate, H. (1982) 'Computers in the kindergarten', *Computing Teachers*, 3: 15–18.

Hunter, W.J. (1990) 'Research of writing technologies in grades K-12', *Writing Notebook: Creative Word Processing in the Classroom*, 8 (2): 36–7.

International Society for Technology in Education (2002) 'The National Educational Technology Standards (NETS) Project'. Available at cnets.iste.org.

Jones, I. (1994) 'The effect of a word processor on the written composition of second grade pupils', *Computers in the Schools*, 11 (2): 43–54.

Jones, I. and Pellegrini, A.D. (1996) 'The effects of social relationships, writing media, and microgenetic development on first-grade students' written narratives', *American Educational Research Journal*, 33 (3): 691–718.

Joram, E., Woodruff, F., Bryson, G. and Lindsay, H. (1992) 'The effects of revising with a word processor on written composition', *Research in the Teaching of English*, 26 (2): 167–93.

Kahn, J. (1997) 'Scaffolding in the classroom: using CD-ROM storybooks at a computer reading center', *Learning and Leading with Technology*, 25: 17–19.

Kamil, M.L. and Lane, D.M. (1998) 'Researching the relation between technology and literacy: an agenda for the 21st century', in D. Reinking, M.C. McKenna, L.D. Labbo and R.D. Kieffer (eds), *Handbook of Literacy and Technology: transformations in a Post-Typographic World.* Mahwah, NJ: Erlbaum. pp. 323–42.

Kamil, M.L., Kim, H. and Intrator, S. (2000) 'Effects of other technologies on literacy and literacy learning', in M.L. Kamil, P.B. Mosenthal, P.D. Pearson, and R. Barr (eds), *Handbook of Reading Research*, vol. 3. Mahwah, NJ: Erlbaum. pp. 773–91.

Karchmer, R.A. (2001) 'The journey ahead: thirteen teachers report how the Internet influences literacy and literacy instruction in their K-12 classrooms', *Reading Research Quarterly*, 36: 442–66.

Kelly, Anthony E. and O'Kelly, James B. (1993) 'Emergent literacy: implications for the design of computer writing applications for children', *Journal of Computing in Childhood Education*, 4 (1): 3–14.

Kelly, K.L. and Schorger, J.R. (2001) '"Let's play "Puters": expressive language use at the computer center', in *Information Technology in Childhood Education Annual*, pp. 125–38.

Kent, J.F. and Rakestraw, J. (1994) 'The role of computers in functional language: a tale of two writers', *Journal of Computing in Childhood Education*, 5: 329–37.

Krendl, K.A. and Williams, R.B. (1990) 'The importance of being rigorous: research on writing to read', *Journal of Computer-Based Instruction*, 17: 81–6.

Labbo, L.D. (1996) 'A semiotic analysis of young children's symbol making in a classroom computer center', *Reading Research Quarterly*, 31: 356–85.

Labbo, L.D. and Kuhn, M.R. (1998) 'Electronic symbol-making: young children's computer related emerging concepts about literacy', in D. Reinking, M.C. McKenna, L.D. Labbo and R.D. Kieffer (eds), *Handbook of Literacy and Technology: Transformations in a Post-Typographic World.* Mahwah, NJ: Erlbaum. pp. 79–92.

Labbo, L.D. and Kuhn, M.R. (2000) 'Weaving chains of affect and cognition: a young child's understanding of CD-ROM talking books', *Journal of Literacy Research*, 32 (2): 187–210.

Labbo, L.D. and Reinking, D. (1999) 'Negotiating the multiple realities of technology in literacy research and instruction', *Reading Research Quarterly*, 34: 478–92.

Labbo, L.D., Field, S.L. and Watkins, J. (1995) 'Narrative as action research: one teacher's story'. Paper presented at the Qualitative Research Interest Group (QUIG) Conference, Athens, GA, January.

Labbo, L.D., Phillips, M. and Murray, B. (1995–6) '"Writing to read": from inheritance to innovation and invitation', *The Reading Teacher*, 49 (4): 314–21.

Labbo, L.D., Reinking, D., McKenna, M., Kuhn, M. and Phillips, M. (1996) *Computers Real and Make Believe: Opportunities for Literacy Development in an Early Childhood Sociodramatic Play Center.* Instructional Resource no. 26. National Reading Research Center, Athens, GA: University of Georgia.

Labbo, L.D. and Sprague, L., with Montero, K. and Font, G. (2000) 'Connecting a computer center to themes, literature, and kindergartners' literacy needs', *Reading Online*. Available at www.readingonline.org.

Lauman, D.J. (2000) 'Student home computer use: a review of the literature', *Journal of Research on Computing in Education*, 33 (2): 196–203.

Lavin, R.J. and Sanders, J.E. (1982) *Longitudinal Evaluation of the Computer Assisted Instruction,* Title I Project, 1979–82.

Leher, R., Levin, B.B., DeHart, P. and Comeaux, M. (1987) 'Voice feedback as a scaffold for writing: a comparative study', *Journal of Educational Computing Research*, 3: 335–53.

Leu, D.J. (1997) 'Caity's question: literacy as deixis on the Internet', *The Reading Teacher*, 41: 62–7.

Leu, D.J. (2000) 'Literacy and technology: deictic consequences for literacy education in an information age', in M.L. Kamil, P.B. Mosenthal, P.D. Pearson and R. Barr (eds), *Handbook of Reading Research*, vol. III. Mahwah, NJ: Erlbaum. pp. 743–70.

Leu, D.J. and Kinzer, C.K. (2000) 'The convergence of literacy instruction with networked technologies for information, communication, and education', *Reading Research Quarterly*, 35: 108–27.

Lewin, C. (1995) *The Evaluation of Talking Book Software: a Pilot Study*. Technical Report no. 220. London: Centre for Information Technology in Education, The Open University.

Lewin, C. (1996) *Improving Talking Book Software Design: Emulating the Supportive Tutor*. Technical Report no. 222. London: Centre for Information Technology in Education, The Open University.

Liaw, M. (1997) 'An analysis of ESL children's verbal interaction during computer book reading', *Computers in Schools*, 13 (3/4): 55–73.

Living Books (1990) *Brøderbund*, Novato CA 94948. http://broderbund.com/

Lomangino, A.G., Nicholson, J. and Sulzby, E. (1999) *The Nature of Children's Interactions While Composing Together on Computers*. CIERA Report no. 2–005, Center for the Improvement of Early Reading Achievement, University of Michigan, Ann Arbor.

Lundberg, I. (1995) 'The computer as a tool of remediation in the education of students with reading disabilities: a theory-based approach', *Learning Disability Quarterly*, 18 (2): 89–99.

Mackey, M. (1994) 'The new basics: learning to read in a multimedia world', *English in Education*, 28 (1): 9–19.

Martin, J. (1986) *Writing to Read: Teacher's Manual* 2nd edn. Boca Raton, FL: IBM.

Matthew, K. (1997) 'A comparison of the influence of interactive CD-ROM storybooks and traditional print storybooks on reading comprehension', *Journal of Research on Computing in Education*, 29 (1): 263–75.

McKenna, M.C. (1998) 'Electronic texts and the transformation of beginning reading', in D. Reinking, M.C. McKenna, L.D. Labbo and R.D. Kieffer (eds), *Handbook of Literacy and Technology: Transformations in a Post-Typographic World*. Mahwah, NJ: Erlbaum. pp. 45–59.

McKenna, M.C. and Watkins, J.H. (1994) 'Computer-mediated books for beginning readers'. Paper presented at the meeting of the National Reading Conference, San Diego, December.

McKenna, M.C. and Watkins, J.H. (1995) 'Effects of computer-mediated books on the development of beginning readers'. Paper presented at the meeting of the National Reading Conference, New Orleans, November.

McKenna, M.C. and Watkins, J.H. (1996) 'The effects of computer-mediated trade books on sight word acquisition and the development of phonics ability'. Paper presented at the meeting of the National Reading Conference, Charleston, SC, December.

McKenna, M.C., Reinking, D. and Bradley, B.A. (2001) 'The effects of electronic trade books on the decoding growth of beginning readers'. Paper presented at NATO Advanced Study Institute on Literacy Acquisition, Assessment, and Intervention: the Role of Phonology, Orthography, and Morphology, Il Cioco, Italy, November.

Miller, L., Blackstock, J. and Miller, R. (1994) An exploratory study into the use of CD-ROM storybooks', *Computers and Education*, 22: 187–204.

Moeller, B. (1993) 'Literacy and technology', *News from the Center for Children and Technology and the Center for Technology in Education*, 2 (4): 1–4.

Morrow, L.M. (1990) 'Preparing the classroom environment to promote literacy during play', *Early Childhood Research Quarterly*, 5: 537–54.

Moxley, R.A. and Warash, B.G. (1992) 'Writing strategies of three prekindergarten children on the computer', *Journal of Computing in Childhood Education*, 3 (2): 137–9.

National Association for the Education of Young Children (1996) *Technology and Young Children Ages 3–8*. Position statement. Washington, DC. Available at www.naeyc.org.

National Center for Educational Statistics (1999) *National Center for Educational Statistics Issue Brief: Internet Access in Public Schools and Classrooms 1994–1998*. Available at nces.ed.gov.

National Reading Panel (2002) *Teaching Children to Read: Summary Report*. Available at www.nationalreadingpanel.org.

Neuman, S.B. and Roskos, K. (1992) 'Literacy objects as cultural tools: effects on children's literacy behaviors in play', *Reading Research Quarterly*, 27: 202–25.

Newman, D. (1990) 'Opportunities for research on the organizational impact of school computers', *Educational Researcher*, 19: 8–13.

Olson, K. and Johnston, J. (1989) *The Use of the Computer as a Writing Tool in a Kindergarten and First Grade Classroom*. CIEL Pilot Year Final Report, Part 2. Ann Arbor, MI: Ann Arbor School of Education.

Olson, R.K., Foltz, G. and Wise, B.W. (1986) 'Reading instruction and remediation with the aid of computer speech', *Behavior Research Methods, Instruments, and Computer*, 18: 93–9.

Olson, R.K., Wise, B., Ring, J. and Johnson, M. (1997) 'Computer-based remedial training in phoneme awareness and phonological decoding: effects on the post training development of word recognition', *Scientific Studies in Reading*, 1: 235–53.

Papert, S. (1993) *The Children's Machine: Rethinking School in the Age of the Computer.* New York: Basic.

Patterson, W.A., Henry, J.J., O'Quin, K.R., Ceprano, M. and Blue, E. (in press). 'Investigating the effectiveness of an integrated learning system on early emergent readers', *Reading Research Quarterly.*

Phenix, J. and Hannan, E. (1984) 'Word processing in the grade one classroom', *Language Arts*, 61: 804–12.

Pinkard, N. (1999) *Learning to Read in Culturally Responsive Computer Environments.* CIERA Report no. 1–004, Center for the Improvement of Early Reading Achievement. Available at www.ciera.org.

Reinking, D. (1994) *Electronic Literacy.* Perspectives in Reading Research no. 4, National Reading Research Center, Athens, GA: University of Georgia.

Reinking, D. (1998) 'Synthesizing technological transformations of literacy in a post typographic world', in D. Reinking, M. McKenna, L.D. Labbo and R. Kieffer (eds), *Handbook of Literacy and Technology.* Mahwah, NJ: Erlbaum. pp. xi–xxx.

Reinking, D. and Watkins, J. (2000) 'A formative experiment investigating the use of multimedia book reviews to increase elementary students' independent reading', *Reading Research Quarterly*, 35: 384–419.

Reitsma, P. (1988) 'Reading practice for beginners: effects of guided reading, reading while listening, and independent reading with computer-based speech feedback', *Reading Research Quarterly*, 23: 219–35.

Reitsma, P. and Wesseling, R. (1998) 'Effects of computer assisted training of blending skills in kindergarten', *Scientific Studies of Reading*, 2 (4): 301–20.

Rosengrant, T.J. (1986) 'Using the microcomputer as a scaffold for assisting beginning readers and writers', in J. Hoot (ed.), *Computers in Early Childhood Education: Issues and Practices.* Englewood Cliffs, NJ: Prentice Hall. pp. 128–43.

Rosengrant, T.J. (1988) 'Talking word processors for the early grades', in J.L. Hoot and S.B. Silvern (eds), *Writing with Computers in the Early Grades* New York: Teachers College Press. pp. 143–59.

Roth, S.F. and Beck, I.L. (1987) 'Theoretical and instructional implications of assessment of two microcomputer word recognition programs', *Reading Research Quarterly*, 22: 197–218.

Salomon, G., Globerson, T. and Guterman, E. (1989) 'The computer as zone of proximal development: internalizing reading-related metacognitions from a reading partner', *Journal of Educational Psychology*, 81: 620–7.

Scoresby, K. (1996) 'The effects of electronic storybook animation on third graders' story recall'. Unpublished doctoral dissertation, Brigham Young University.

Sheingold, K. (1991) 'Restructing for learning with technology: the potential for synergy', *Phi Delta Kappan*, 3 (1): 17–27.

Slavin, R. (1991) 'Reading effects of IBM's "Writing to Read" program: a review of evaluations', *Educational Evaluation and Policy Analysis*, 13: 1–11.

Smith, C. (2001) 'Click and turn the page: an exploration of multiple storybook literacy', *Reading Research Quarterly*, 36 (2): 152–83.

Spache, G.D. (1967) 'A reaction to "Computer-assisted instruction in initial reading: the Stanford project"', *Reading Research Quarterly*, 3: 101–9.

Talley, S.D. and Lancy, D.F. (1995) 'The effects of a CD-ROM storybook program on Head Start children's emergent literacy'. Paper presented at the Biennial Convention of the Society for Research in Child Development, Indianapolis, April.

Tancock, S.M. (2002, April) 'Reading, writing, and technology: a healthy mix in the social studies curriculum', *Reading Online*, 5 (8). Available at www.readingonline.org.

Tao, L. and Reinking, D. (2000) 'E-mail and literacy education', *Reading and Writing Quarterly*, 16: 169–74.

Tao, L., Montgomery, T. and Pickle, M. (1997) 'Content analysis in e-mail research: a methodological review', in C.K. Kinzer, K.A. Hinchman and D.J. Leu (eds) *Inquiries in Literacy Theory and Practice.* Chicago: National Reading Conference. pp. 474–82.

Tapscott, D. (1998) *Growing Up Digital: the Rise of the Net Generation.* New York: McGraw-Hill.

Teale, W.H. and Sulzby, E. (eds) (1986) *Emergent Literacy: Writing and Reading.* Norwood, NJ: Ablex.

Technology Counts (1999) Market Data Retrieval, unpublished tabulations from 1998–1999 School Technology Survey and published tabulations from earlier MDR surveys, *Education Week*, 23 September: 64.

Tharp, R.G. and Gallimore, R. (1988) *Rousing Minds to Life.* New York: Cambridge University Press.

Unsworth, L. (2001) *Teaching Multiliteracies across the Curriculum: Changing Contexts of Text and Image in Classroom Practice.* Buckingham: Open University Press.

Upitis, R. (1990) 'Real and contrived uses of electronic mail in elementary schools', *Computers in Education*, 15: 233–43.

Vygotsky, L.S. (1978) 'Internalization of higher psychological functions', in M. Cole, V. John-Steiner, S. Scribner and E. Souberman (eds), *Mind in Society.* Cambridge, MA: Harvard University Press.

Watson, J.S., Chadwick, S.S. and Brinkley, V.M. (1986) 'Special education technologies for young children: present and future learning scenarios with related research literature', *Journal of the Division for Early Childhood*, 10: 197–208.

Wild, M. and Braid, P. (1996) 'Children's talk in cooperative groups', *Journal of Computer Assisted Learning*, 12: 216–21.

Windschitl, M. and Sahl, K. (2002) 'Tracing teachers' use of technology in a laptop computer school: the interplay of teacher beliefs, social dynamics and institutional culture', *American Educational Research Journal*, 39: 165–205.

Wise, B. and Olson, R. (1995) 'Computer-based phonological awareness and reading instruction', *Annals of Dyslexia*, 45: 99–122.

Wittrock, M.C. (1986) 'Students' thought processes', in M.C. Wittrock (ed.), *Handbook of Research on Teaching*. New York: Macmillan. pp. 297–314.

Yost, N. (2000) 'Electronic expressions: using e-mail to support emergent writers', *Computers in the Schools*, 16: 17–28.

Zhao, Y., Englert, C.S., Chen, J., Jones, S.C. and Ferdig, R. (1999) *TELE-Web: Developing a Web-Based Literacy Learning Environment*. CIERA Report no. 1–006, Center for the Improvement of Early Reading Achievement, University of Michigan, Ann Arbor.

29

Critical Literacy: What Does It Look Like in the Early Years?

BARBARA COMBER

The work of early childhood educators in facilitating children's literacy acquisition has never received more attention than at the turn of the new millennium. Media hype about literacy crises, falling standards, and teacher quality and government promises of minimum standards for all children have simultaneously increased the 'visibility' of literacy and the stakes for school performance. Indeed the last decade could be seen as an age of pronouncements with respect to literacy, with politicians internationally promising to cure supposed low literacy with standardized tests and mandated programmes. At the same time as the rhetoric around literacy intensifies, many late capitalist economies are experiencing shifts which have increased the gaps between rich and poor, changed the very nature of work, and fundamentally altered the cultural mix of their populations. More and more children attending schools where English is the language of instruction speak it as a second or third language. Many children have experienced the effects of war, terrorism, migration and poverty. Many live in fractured, fragmented and changing families. Teacher populations are changing too. In some places ageing teacher workforces mean that there is already a shortage of qualified teachers. Literacy is also changing as the impact of digital technologies on global and local communication, economies and knowledges begins to bite in everyday and working lives. In times such as these it is interesting to think about how spaces for the emergence and sustenance of critical literacy in early childhood education might be created.

Critical literacy is a relative newcomer to early childhood educational discourse. Early childhood literacy education has typically been dominated by developmental theory with its attendant assumptions of the naturally developing child and emergent literacy (Luke and Luke, 2001; Reid and Comber, 2002). Ideologies of child innocence and the 'goodness' of literacy permeate the field and infuse literacy curricula and pedagogy. The child literacy learner is positioned as a maturing individual – a biological subject – who grows and blossoms with the right conditions and support. Indeed this developmental discourse is central to the notion of 'readiness', a key word in early schooling and literacy, a yardstick by which some children are judged as ready to come to school and/or ready for reading and others not (Comber, 1999). Critical literacy, with its focus on power and language, has not been a force in early childhood literacy education. Indeed critical literacy, if discussed at all, is often seen as most appropriate for older or more advanced students. However for the past two decades, there have been studies in early childhood literacy which have taken a critical position and these have alerted early childhood literacy educators to the non-neutrality of literacy, the non-innocence of young children's textual work and play, and their potential for complex analytical textual practice.

In this chapter I first introduce the concept of critical literacy. I consider what can be learnt from studies of mainstream early literacy education that have taken a critical perspective. The next section focuses on research which addresses questions of power, language and representation in early childhood literacy education. Next I discuss studies of early childhood education which take a multicultural or anti-racist perspective. I then move to explore in some detail two classroom-based projects where the early childhood educators explicitly set out to build and investigate critical literacies in their classrooms. Finally I outline a number of questions for further research in critical literacy.

CRITICAL LITERACY: AN EVOLVING CONCEPT

The history of *critical literacy* is located more in adult and community sites (e.g. Freire, 1972; Kamler, 2001; Lankshear and McLaren, 1993; Wallace, 2001) and high schools (e.g. Bigelow, 2001; Janks, 1993; Mellor et al., 1987; Searle, 1993) than in primary schooling. Paolo Freire is typically credited with its genesis and his phrase 'reading the word, reading the world' (Freire and Macedo, 1987) is emblematic of critical literacy internationally. Freire's insistence that literacy could and should position people to argue for their rights underpins much of the work of educators committed to critical literacy (Edelsky, 1999; Giroux, 1993; Lankshear, 1994; Luke, 2000; Powell, 1999). Defining critical literacy goes against the grain of those who promote its repertoires of practices which foreground 'debate, dissonance and difference' (Luke and Freebody, 1997: 16), in that it needs to be locally contingent, dynamic and subject to revisions in terms of its effects (Kamler and Comber, 1996; Luke, 2000). It is also important that researchers specify how critical literacies are constituted in different situations (Comber and Simpson, 2001; Luke 2000).

Critical literacy educators have drawn on perspectives from feminism, anti-racist education, critical discourse analysis, multiculturalism, theories of social justice and more. In the US for instance, critical literacies have developed out of a politicized whole language approach, multiculturalism, cultural and critical theory. In the United Kingdom critical linguistics, cultural, literary and literacy studies influenced critical approaches to teaching English literacy. In South Africa a critical language awareness model based upon the work of Norman Fairclough and others has been a powerful catalyst for change particularly in secondary schools and tertiary institutions. Clearly this developed alongside anti-Apartheid political activism. And there are other histories in other places. There is not one generic critical literacy; rather it is an evolving concept. While it would be worthwhile, a genealogy of critical literacy is beyond the scope of this chapter. As the focus here is on critical literacy in early years literacy education, this chapter is selective in that it attends to work which has had a demonstrable effect on early years policy and practice. Recently

Luke and Freebody, whilst also underscoring the range of approaches, have suggested critical literacy marks out:

> a coalition of educational interests committed to engaging with the possibilities that the technologies of writing and other modes of inscription offer for social change, cultural diversity, economic equity and political enfranchisement. (1997: 1)

Notwithstanding different preferred methods and starting points, what is clear is a common standpoint towards social equity through textual and representational practices. More specifically, Luke et al., explain:

> By 'critical' we mean ways that give students tools for weighing and critiquing, analysing and appraising textual techniques and ideologies, values and positions. The key challenge, then, is how to engage students with the study of how texts work semiotically and linguistically – while at the same time taking up how texts and their affiliated social institutions work politically to construct and position writers and readers in relations of power and knowledge. (1994: 139)

In this context critical literacy is seen as an evolving repertoire of practices of analysis and interrogation which move between the micro features of texts and the macro conditions of institutions, focusing upon how relations of power work through these practices. In practice, critical literacy involves at least three principles for action:

- repositioning students as researchers of language
- respecting student resistance and exploring minority culture constructions of literacy and language use
- problematizing classroom and public texts (Comber, 1994).

By this account teachers start with an analysis of who the students are, and what they can already do with words, and then help them to research and analyse social and textual practices. The aim is to have them assemble repertoires of practices they can use to understand the work texts do and to make texts that work for them. In early childhood classrooms this often involves three key pedagogical moves (Comber, 2001a): recognizing and mobilizing children's analytic resources (Dyson, 1997), examining existing critical texts (Baker and Davies, 1993; Harste and Leland, 2001) and offering children new discursive resources (O'Brien, 1994a; 1994b; Vasquez, 2001a; 2001b).

In Australia, Freebody and Luke's (1990; Luke and Freebody, 1997) model of reading has been highly influential at the level of policy and curriculum. They argue that reading incorporates four roles:

- code breaker (How do I crack this?)
- text participant (What does this mean?)
- text user (What do I do with this, here and now?)
- text analyst (What does this do to me?).

In later iterations of their model they have renamed the roles as resources – coding, pragmatic, semantic and critical (Luke and Freebody, 1997) – to reflect their sociological rather than psychological approach to literacy as assembling repertoires of practices. A social view of reading requires that teachers give attention to the sociopolitical nature of their work and the non-neutrality of textual practices. They suggest that critical literacy practices might include:

- asking in whose interests particular texts work
- examining multiple and conflicting texts
- examining the historical and cultural contexts of discourses in texts
- reading texts against one another
- comparing the vocabularies and grammars of related texts
- investigating how readers are positioned by the ideologies in texts
- making multiple passes through texts.

Along with analysis, they also include transforming and redesigning texts as part of critical literacy (Luke and Freebody, 1999). Similarly a critical orientation is taken as applicable to visual, electronic texts and the hybrid multimedia and multimodal texts of everyday life (Luke and Luke, 2001). Importantly they argue that a sociological approach with its focus on situated practices allows educators to move away from deficit models of learners.

Early childhood teachers have for the most part been held responsible for children learning to 'crack the code' and to 'make meaning' from texts. The four-resources model of literacy acknowledges the importance of dimensions of literacy with which early childhood educators are already familiar (code breaking and understanding the text). Precisely because it is an inclusive approach to literacy in that it does not discount the importance of any aspect of literate practice, 'the four-resources model' has made critical literacy more attractive to teachers and policy makers. That is, it adds to what educators do already. It does not contest that code breaking or meaning making are essential, but it does stress that they are insufficient for proper literacy today. Further they argue that these dimensions of literacy need to be learnt together; that critical literacy is as important in early childhood as adult literacy or secondary school English. As part of the four-resources model, critical literacy has been taken up in many Australian state literacy strategies and curricula,

and indeed resources have been provided for teachers (e.g. Department for Education and Children's Services, 1995; Education Queensland, 2000). In moving to an understanding of literacy as repertoires of practices, unproductive debates about one kind of literacy versus another or one kind of method as more effective than another are bypassed. In this way critical literacy becomes part of a coherent model of literacy as social practice which now informs early childhood literacy education. In explaining the critical dimension of the model they emphasize that learners need to:

> Critically analyse and transform texts by acting on knowledge that texts are not ideologically natural or neutral – that they represent particular points of view while silencing others and influence people's ideas – and that their designs and discourses can be critiqued and redesigned in novel and hybrid ways. (Luke and Freebody, 1999)

Later in this chapter several examples of early childhood teachers attempting to enact and research such practices are described. Along with the reframing of literacy to include a critical component there has also been a strong and growing trend towards feminist and critical readings of both early childhood education and literacy education and this scholarship has paved the way for thinking differently about young children and early literacy. It is to this burgeoning field of inquiry that we now turn.

CRITICAL ANALYSES OF THE EARLY CHILDHOOD LITERACY CURRICULUM

Since the 1980s a number of researchers have taken a critical position with respect to the major tenets of early childhood theorizing (e.g. Burman, 1994; Cannella, 1997; Polakow, 1989; Walkerdine, 1984). The notion of 'childhood' itself had already been put to question (e.g. Aries, 1962). The dominance of an essentialist view of the naturally developing male child and how this positioned mothers and female teachers was contested (e.g. Walkerdine, 1984). The ways in which early childhood theories position working class, poor and minority culture women as deficient (Polakow, 1993; Burman, 1994; Cannella, 1997), in not making available the conditions upon which 'normal development' was supposedly contingent, were made visible. This chapter does not revisit this very productive field of scholarship. Rather it acknowledges that such critiques provided the foundation for much emerging feminist and critical work, thereby accomplishing a 'discursive shift' (Fairclough, 1992) in the field of early childhood education theorizing. Developing an explicit social justice agenda for early childhood education is a continuing project that has its genesis in this earlier scholarship (see Cannella, 2000; 1997; Mac Naughton, 2000). Early literacy education became a site that was worthy of attention and critique for educational theorists and sociologists. The beginning of schooling is particularly fruitful as there its goals (including literacy), what it takes for granted about itself (and its subjects), its informing dominant discourses, and its mundane everyday practices are perhaps more acutely visible. Critical analyses of aspects of early years literacy education have focused on, amongst other things, the texts (read and produced), the positioning of students as literate subjects, gendered relations of power, the quality of content and the positioning of parents.

A central technology in beginning literacy instruction is the basal reader or reading series (see Luke, Carrington and Kapitzke, in this volume). Luke (1988) analysed a historical corpus of basal readers, to interrogate the kinds of messages and ideologies produced therein. He demonstrated how such books constitute versions of typical childhood, induct children into particular kinds of knowledge of the world and position them as instructional subjects/readers. While such books claim neutrality they offer a selected range of ideologies and ethics, whether it is a Protestant work ethic, loyalty to the mother country or families behind white picket fences (Luke, 1991). Similarly, Baker and Freebody (1989) provided a comprehensive analysis of the production of the school literate child through the selection and treatment of beginning school reading materials for young children in Australia. Such books provide repeated information about how one is to be a child in the context of adult–child relations and portray mundane everyday worlds. In this way apparently innocent texts teach children what should be familiar, what their lives should be like, what mothers and fathers and children should do – a normative training (see also Baker and Davies, 1993). Baker and Freebody (1989: 161) also analysed the talk around texts, in lessons incorporating enlarged books. Interactions around text can be seen as 'providing guidelines to the students on how to produce right answers in question–answering sequence in classrooms' (1989: 161). Hence children are introduced to the teachers' preferred interpretations of texts and how and when to produce these. In critiquing the ubiquitous basal reader or beginning reading texts, Luke, Baker and Freebody shifted attention away from best materials or methods of instruction to questions about the ideological work of early literacy lessons.

At a similar time a number of writing researchers recognized that the process approach to writing produced risks for different children in elementary schools. These included the use of 'free writing' for gender harassment (Gilbert, 1989; Kamler, 1994; Lensmire, 1994) and the dominance of personal narrative at the expense of 'genres of power' (Christie, 1989; Martin, 1985), in particular for children who may not access such forms in their out-of-school lives (Walton, 1993) (see Christie, in this volume). In early childhood education writing has received less critical attention; however, insights from these researchers about racial, class-based and gender-based peer aggravation in the writing classroom have alerted educators to revisit children's writing and drawing as practices to watch, rather than simply to be celebrated.

Since the 1980s many researchers have questioned the content, process and texts of early literacy lessons in terms of the restriction of genres, the infantilization of the content, the non-innocence of children's writing, the raced, classed and gendered nature of literate identities. Yet despite the growing field of critical research about literacy education, the normative model of literacy development (Muspratt et al., 1997) has remained hard to shake in early childhood education (Comber, 2001b; Dyson, 1999; Gregory and Williams, 2000; Luke and Luke, 2001), particularly at a time when policy makers and politicians are preoccupied with standards (Comber, 2001b).

Luke and Freebody suggest that key questions are about:

> who gets access to which technologies and practices of writing and representation – and how schools and literacy education are active participants in the construction of the social division of textual and discursive work along ... traditional fractures of gender, culture and class. (1997: 9)

Critical accounts of normative or traditional models of literacy education and their effects are integral to understanding both theories and practices of critical literacy pedagogies which have been developed. How one understands the problem of 'non-critical literacies' impacts the alternative critical literacies which educators have sought to produce and negotiate. While many of the socially critical studies of early literacy document mainstream practices which severely limit children's opportunities for analytical textual work and play, some researchers have continued to focus on young children's sense making in classrooms where teachers make the space for that to occur.

POWER, LANGUAGE AND REPRESENTATION IN EARLY LITERACY LESSONS

Although the term 'critical literacy' has only recently been taken up in early childhood education contexts, it has been clear for some time that addressing questions about power, language and representation was certainly possible in early childhood classrooms (Dyson, 1989; 1993; 1997). In an extensive series of ethnographic case studies over two decades in the US, Anne Haas Dyson has shown that young, poor, urban children of colour can and do deal with the complexity of power relations and bring to bear multiple sophisticated representational resources in their classroom writing. Drawing theoretically on Bakhtin's notion of the dialogic nature of texts – 'in a world riddled with voices talking to, past, and over each other' – Dyson (1993: 6) demonstrates that children operate strategically and logically to create texts which work for them in their classroom social worlds. Children employ 'sociocultural intelligence' (Dyson, 1993) in constructing texts that position them powerfully and productively in their classroom contexts.

Dyson's work shows that young children are not simply media dupes or TV sponges but that they selectively appropriate material from popular culture which they assemble anew with home language traditions and school genres. As young children compose texts they simultaneously compose spaces for themselves in the world. Dyson shows too that such composing may be marked by irreverent play, jokes, songs and parodies, not always the serious display of scholarship, but nevertheless an effective method of contesting dominant discourses of the official realms of schooling and beyond. Dyson's extensive corpus of work, whilst not overtly locating itself within a tradition of 'critical literacy', provides more than ample evidence of young children's and their teachers' capacities to engage with complex analyses of language as they produce their stories filled with characters grappling for power, influence and social effects. Along with other researchers of children's writing (Gilbert, 1991; Kamler, 1994; Lensmire, 1994) Dyson illustrates persuasively that gender, class and race impact strongly on children's writing and their responses to each other's writing.

While Dyson eschews the sometimes 'oppressive academic jargon' of 'critical language awareness' (1993: 226) her work is a testimony to young children's demonstrable understandings and interest in how language works in their real and imaginary worlds. Moreover Dyson's work indicates what particular children can do with their peer, popular, home, literary and school discourses and genres within a 'permeable curriculum' (1993: 224) that allows them to make use of all the meaning making resources they have whilst appropriating those they do not. Her research also strongly suggests that, when it comes to an analysis of language

and power, young children have greatest investments in situations and texts that arise in their immediate social classroom worlds. She confirms too the importance of pleasure and play in investigating language and power. The 'critical literacies' invented in the sites Dyson reports arise from the productive interplay of young children's social goals with the teachers' academic agenda. When children work and play on classroom narratives and dramatic performances in which they have palpable investments, their identity work and their literacy work fuse in fruitful ways. Their struggles over who can speak, who can play which roles, which characters are good, evil, strong, weak, powerful, passive, provide fertile ground for the teacher to raise questions about how these texts work.

Dyson steadfastly refuses categories which consign children to deficit positions and categories about her own work. She has worked against the negative effects of bandwagons and the exclusivity of academic discourse which alienates many teachers. While she doesn't name her work as part of a critical literacy tradition, the questions she explores are at the heart of a social justice project in early literacy education. Along with her cooperating teacher colleagues she provides the evidence that young children are more than capable of practising critical literacies. Indeed they assemble such analytic practices as they learn to interact through language and play with symbolic and actual representational resources and engage with systematic interactions which require them to attend to specific features of texts in contexts, notice patterns across texts and anticipate the effects on participants, readers and viewers.

Dyson's research raises many questions for early childhood educators about keeping professional and personal knowledges, school and home practices separated in different boxes. She demonstrates repeatedly how seriously we underestimate what children do intellectually and socially within the micro-politics of their everyday lives in classrooms:

'Innocent' children, adults may feel, should be free from such complexities, free to play on playground and paper. But children's imaginative play is all about freedom from their status as powerless children. Tales about good guys and bad ones, rescuers and victims, boyfriends and girlfriends allow children to fashion worlds in which *they* make the decisions about characters and plots, actors and actions. Thus for children, as for adults, freedom is a verb, a becoming; it is experienced as an expanded sense of agency, of possibility for choice and action. (1997: 166, emphasis in original)

Dyson works at the interfaces between recognized genres and vernacular resources, between work and play, between oral and written, between the popular and the literary, the critical and the pleasurable. In particular, her respect for young children's social agency and their appropriation and reworkings of popular cultural texts has informed international curriculum design and classroom-based research in a range of very different early childhood settings (Kavanagh, 1997; O'Brien and Comber, 2000; Marsh, 2000, and in this volume; Sahni, 2001; Vasquez, 2003). For example Sahni explains how she negotiated a responsive literacy curriculum within 'circles of mutuality' (2001: 22), whereby young children in rural India developed powerful performative social literacies through poetry, songs and drama as well as drawing and writing stories. For these young children empowerment through literacy was associated with identity formation and social relations in everyday life. Her message is that teachers find ways of incorporating children's social and imaginary worlds, and include dramatic, performative and pleasurable aspects of everyday life into their design for critical literacy. Dyson explains:

> At any age, critical literacy is always a personal as well as political (power-related) matter because it entails reconsidering one's own experience ... And critical literacy is always a local as well as a societal matter because it is something we do in response to others' words and actions, including their voiced views on the social world. (2001: 5)

CRITICAL LITERACIES IN EARLY CHILDHOOD EDUCATION: MAKING DISCURSIVE SPACE

As critical literacy is a relative newcomer to the discourses of early childhood education it is not surprising that little classroom research has been done so far. For this reason I briefly review a selection of studies which are more broadly concerned with social justice in early childhood education and then feature the work of two early childhood teacher-researchers who have explicitly set out to design, implement, and systematically research a critical literacy curriculum with young children in their own classrooms.

Research which explicitly addresses social justice, multiculturalism and/or anti-racism can be seen as related to critical literacy (or at least a parallel movement) in the sense that it contributes to the production of a discursive space, allowing educators to rethink their work in overtly political ways. Some researchers question the effects of English as the dominant language of education for children who speak English as a second language or

as dialect; others argue that socially critical literacy should be primarily concerned with inducting children into the language of power (Cope and Kalantzis, 1993). As Pennycook puts it, what constitutes a transformative pedagogy concerns:

> whether teachers see their pedagogical goal primarily as giving marginalized students access to the mainstream through overt pedagogical strategies or as trying to transform the mainstream by placing greater emphasis on inclusivity. (1999: 337)

Similarly, in a recent international collection dealing with critical multiculturalism May writes:

> a critical multiculturalism needs both to recognize and incorporate the differing cultural knowledges that children bring with them to school, *while at the same time* address and contest the different cultural capital attributed to them as a result of wider hegemonic power relations. (1999: 32, emphasis in original)

May argues that the goal of critical multiculturalism is to foster 'students who can engage critically with all ethnic and cultural backgrounds, including their own' (1999: 33). What counts as critical literacy and/or critical multiculturalism in multiracial and multilingual schools remains an unresolved question for researchers and early childhood educators. In Giroux's (1993) terms the real crisis about literacy education is a crisis about the politics of difference. He argues that:

> Educating for difference, democracy and ethical responsibility is not about creating passive citizens. It is about providing students with the knowledge, capacities and opportunities to be noisy, irreverent and vibrant. Central to this concern is the need for students to understand how cultural, ethnic, racial, and ideological differences enhance the possibility for dialogue, trust and solidarity. (1993: 374–5)

The relationship between literacy and a politics of difference underlies critical literacy in theory and in practice. In the United States there has been a strong tradition of arguing for bilingual education as a key move in respecting minority children's identities and cultures (e.g. de la Luz Reyes, 2001; Moll, 2001). Internationally, sociocultural literacy research has contested normative educational discourse by promoting respect for poor and culturally diverse communities by highlighting neighbourhood 'funds of knowledge' (Moll et al., 1992), the 'resourcefulness' of families (McNaughton, 1995) and the children's use of syncretized (or blended) literacies (Gregory and Williams, 2000). Whilst these studies do not name their objectives as critical literacy they are directly concerned with the relationships between language, power and identity. Moll refers to several US projects to explain:

these projects by virtue of defining diversity as an asset in theory and practice, are 'counterhegemonic' in nature. Although neither project necessarily features explicit discussions of ideologies and power *per se*, they do provide alternative ways of defining cultural resources, and of forming new social relations for promoting change. They also provide, through their agency, strategies for developing new 'subjectivities' with the participants, either collectively in terms of how groups of people may be defined or in terms of individual children and their potentials for learning. (2001: 24)

Such research which debunks deficit discourses about the poor is still needed to make inroads on the pervasiveness of blame and derision (Comber, 1997, Freebody, 1992). Research which contests the mainstream normative model of early literacy, with its insistence on mothers reading to children as the single and preferable readiness route to literacy (Carrington and Luke, 2002: Dyson, 1999; Panofsky, 2000), can be seen as making space for different and culturally inclusive literacies that are part of a critical literacy agenda which operates beyond the individual teacher and classroom to change the discourses that pervade and delimit early literacy instruction.

Several UK-based studies concerned with anti-racism and anti-sexism also have relevance here. Epstein (1993) argues that the place to start is the site of children's everyday experiences of oppression. Epstein invited the five- and six-year-old children in her class to consider topics such as 'what mothers were like', to write freely at first, then to discuss what mothers actually did and then to write again. They were then asked to compare their pieces of writing. This led a group of children to survey what mothers were shown doing in the reading books in their classroom and report their results on the limited options available to storybook mothers. Epstein reports that re-examining their own texts and classroom texts led to a raised consciousness amongst the children about gender bias. They returned to this concept to examine different forms of play pursued by boys and girls. They also applied their practice of critically reviewing texts to questions of racial representations. Epstein describes in some detail how she 'went with' the issues which arose from children's lives in and out of school. She states that it is important to work on issues which already matter to the children, in which they already have affective as well as cognitive engagement.

Babette Brown's *Unlearning Discrimination in the Early Years* (1998) draws on her work as a nursery educator in the United Kingdom. She argues strongly that the early years is the time to begin working forcefully against any form of discrimination based on stereotypical thinking about race,

colour, ethnicity, language, sexuality, gender, or ability. Brown draws on her own practice and a substantial review of research to show that very young children quickly learn to behave and think in dangerous and discriminatory ways and that teachers and early childhood workers can begin to contest this 'misinformation'.

Other chapters in this volume (see Baquedano-López, Gregory and Kenner, and Razfar and Gutiérrez) more fully address research about cultural and linguistic diversity. Traditions such as multicultural education, anti-racism and anti-sexism have contributed (and still do) to the emergence of critical literacy. This will be evident as we consider closely the work of two early childhood teacher-researchers who designed and investigated critical literacy practices with young children. Equally importantly these educators manage this without fostering relentless political correctness or cynicism. A great deal of what they do in developing a text analytic approach is based on reading and rereading popular texts. This work starts from sites of children's pleasures and investments in cultural and media phenomena and mobilizes their knowledge and analytic capacities (Comber, 2001a).

CRITICAL READING IN EARLY CHILDHOOD CLASSROOMS: STARTING WITH TEXTS

Jennifer O'Brien developed her approach to critical literacy in early childhood classrooms working with five- to eight-year-old children in culturally diverse low to middle socio-economic communities in South Australia. She was profoundly influenced by poststructuralist feminist theory, gender and literacy (e.g. Gilbert and Rowe, 1989), critical discourse analysis and critiques of early childhood and progressive pedagogies. Such theories suggested that children's capacities were being underestimated in literacy classrooms. In a series of studies O'Brien developed a language and a pedagogy of critical literacy that would make sense to and engage young children. Working with feminist poststructuralist theory and critical literacy approaches developed for high school students (Mellor et al., 1987; Janks, 1993) as her guide, plus the critiques of early childhood literacy and progressive pedagogies (Baker and Freebody, 1989; Luke, 1988) on her mind, O'Brien adapted, reshaped and invented ways of examining texts with young children and assignments which positioned them as text analysts and researchers.

O'Brien believed that children learning to decode could take up analytical stances in relation to texts. Influenced by Dyson's ethnographic accounts of young children's grasp of power relations in their writing and also by Au and Mason's (1981) work indicating that the patterns of talk around text could be altered, she was confident that children had the capacities for critical literacy. O'Brien's main goal was that children question the social worlds constructed in texts. This meant children understanding that texts are constructed by authors and illustrators who make particular decisions about who and what to show and how, who and what not to show, about the scripts and actions different characters are given and so on. O'Brien's tasks drew attention to the craftedness of texts. For example, referring to contrasting versions of the Hansel and Gretel story she asked the children to consider both the stepmother and the father:

> Draw the woman as you think Anthony Browne will draw her. Show her face and her clothes. Use a speech bubble to show what she says.
>   Draw the man as you think Anthony Browne will draw him. Show his face and his clothes. Use a speech bubble to show what he says. (O'Brien and Comber, 2000: 159)

In this way she mobilized children's existing cultural knowledge about representations of women and men in texts. The commonalities and differences between children's predictions became the object of study. O'Brien attempted to increase children's awareness of the ways in which their reading practices were constructed. She took a similar approach with picturebooks, school reading series (both fact and fiction) and everyday texts (O'Brien, 2001a; 2001b) and she invited children to consider how texts position their readers. Referring to *My First Book of Knowledge* (Petty, 1990), O'Brien invited children to consider the content that adults include in such books:

> I wonder what Kate Petty and the other people who produced this book decided to put in this book for you to read about.

O'Brien positioned children as readers who could and should question the texts that were produced for them. As the children began to critically examine the text and to point out mistakes in the pictures, O'Brien broadened their inquiry and invited them to look at other factual texts in the school reading series to see if there were similar problems there: 'Let's look out for other examples of authors not taking the trouble to get things right for young readers.' In particular, they examined how 'science texts' designed for young readers construct knowledge. The children discovered that such texts contained many inaccuracies, a mixture of fact and fiction, and underestimated what they already knew.
    O'Brien positioned young students as critical from the start. She invited them to interrogate, to

examine, and to compare other texts and their own knowledge, to dare to question the authority of the text. She frequently focused on the representation of the family or family members in children's literature, basal readers and everyday texts. She is perhaps best known for working with young children to deconstruct everyday texts, such as junk mail, using questions such as the following:

- Who are the important people (powerful, good etc.) in the family created in this text?
- How do they behave?
- What kinds of words does the writer/illustrator think you should know about family members?
- Who are the unimportant people in this family?
- How can you tell they are less/more important for the writer/illustrator?
- How does this compare with your experience? (O'Brien and Comber, 2000: 164)

O'Brien's feminist stance meant that she focused a great deal on the ways in which men and women were depicted in textual families – as kings, queens, princesses, aunts, mothers and fathers and so on. Her work over several years with different groups of children, examining Mothers' Day catalogues and the wider cultural event of Mothers' Day (O'Brien, 1994a; Luke et al., 1994), provided an accessible approach to introducing critical literacy to young children.
    Luke, in analysing this work with O'Brien and Comber, points out four key moves in critical text analysis, which are evident here (Luke et al., 1994):

1 talk about the institutional conditions of production and interpretation
2 talk about the textual ideologies and discourses, silences and absences
3 discourse analysis of textual and linguistic techniques in relation to 1 and 2
4 strategic and tactical action with and/or against the text.

While O'Brien employed a planned approach to critical literacy such as the Mothers' Day unit, like most early childhood teachers she worked with everyday events and incidental texts in the context in which they appeared (O'Brien, 1998). O'Brien was a trailblazer in building, designing and documenting her innovations with critical reading practices. References to her work appear in many state department materials for teachers. In this chapter considerable space has been devoted to describing her actual framing of tasks and questions around specific texts and events because a major contribution of O'Brien's work is its customization of discourses of critical literacy for pedagogical work with young children. Few educators or researchers had grappled with such issues and indeed, this review suggests that only a limited amount of research focusing on the pedagogy of critical literacy in the early years has been done at this time.

O'Brien also conducted research in her classroom which addressed different children's responses to her critical literacy curriculum. She reported (O'Brien, 1994b) that there was a differential response to the disruptive feminist discourse she had made available, mainly along gender lines, with some girls taking up socially critical positions and transferring this approach into new texts and tasks. Indeed one young student even appropriated the discourse to the point where she explained that, 'It's written in our head.' This seven-year-old had understood O'Brien's point that texts follow culturally familiar storylines. Yet several boys in the class were less enthusiastic about her disruptive readings and did not take up these positions themselves. O'Brien's research raises important questions about what young children do with discursive practices and ideological positions which are different to their own. This relates to what might be seen as the 'limits of English' (Patterson, 1997) or literacy teaching. Patterson suggests that advocates of critical literacy need to think about 'training' children in particular kinds of critical reading techniques and strategies – sets of capacities which they can bring to bear in particular situations, rather than ethical positions which we ask them to take up. O'Brien's research certainly demonstrated that young children could read critically. Sometimes some children resisted her invitations to do so. Questions about differential response, take-up and transfer require further research.

CHILDREN'S CULTURAL AND SOCIAL QUESTIONS ABOUT EVERYDAY LIFE AS CURRICULUM

Vivian Vasquez was a kindergarten teacher working in a highly multicultural Catholic school in Toronto when she first encountered O'Brien's classroom research, along with the theoretical resources of scholars such as Allan Luke, Carole Edelsky and other literacy educators. Vasquez decided to make her whole language pedagogy more overtly political, by taking up children's questions about justice in representational and schooling practices. Part of her strong justice standpoint grew from painful memories of her own school experiences in Canada as an immigrant child from the Philippines (Vasquez, 2001a; 2003).

Vasquez (2001a) designed her critical literacy curriculum around children's issues, interests, questions and observations. Often these focused around school and family life. For instance children raised

questions about why as the youngest children in the school they were sometimes excluded from events and places (e.g. a school café), why they had to wait for certain privileges (e.g. receiving a sacrament), differences between men and women in various media representations (e.g. Canadian Mounted Police), people's rights to different cultural preferences and practices (e.g. vegetarianism, McDonald's), languages taught at school (e.g. why French rather than Spanish or Chinese?).

Vasquez believed in making the curriculum and her research visible. She and the children collected and posted key artifacts and products of their work – transcripts of their conversations, covers of texts discussed, photographs, drawings, written responses and so on – on a wall (40 feet × 6 feet) of the classroom she had covered in paper. Children got to see what was recorded as significant and worth exploring. This Vasquez described (following Harste, 1998) as the 'audit trail':

> Retracing thinking invites theorizing. As I constructed the audit trail, I began to think about using it as a tool for critical conversation with young children … By the end of the school year, the audit trail had become a joint construction between teacher and children and a means of generating and reflecting on the classroom curriculum … Each of the artifacts became a way for us to make visible the incidents that caused us to want to learn, the issues we had critical conversations about, and the action we took to resist being dominated and to reposition ourselves within our community. They became our demonstration of and our site for constructing critical curriculum for ourselves. (2001b: 57–8)

Vasquez reports that over the school year children frequently referred to objects on the wall and revisited earlier conversations. Topics raised and explored included fairness, gender, the media, the environment and, as Vasquez puts it, a range of questions about 'power and control'. Because the wall was visible to all, parents and guardians became involved. Children regularly polled their own class and others about school matters; they wrote a petition; they organized a speaker's corner; they conducted their own conference to which parents and other children and teachers were invited. In short the children were inducted into the social use of literate practices in specific situations. Over time Vasquez reports that the children became questioners. While many parents were delighted by the children's engagement, some teachers saw them as 'radical, rude and disrespectful' (Vasquez, 2001b: 59) because they questioned how things were. These children were clearly not performing normal kindergartner subjectivities. Vasquez's work makes it clear that when young children begin to interrogate and research things that matter to them it is a continuously generative process – 'an incidental unfolding of social justice issues' (Vasquez, 2001a).

Reluctant to 'frontload' social justice topics selected by the teacher, Vasquez's approach is to work with the everyday issues that are often put to one side in classrooms or seen as disruptive. The repertoires of language and literacy practices she assists young children to assemble – public speaking, letter writing, surveys, petitions – are goal-directed and situation-specific, teaching children how to make a difference through talk and writing (or attempt to!).

Whereas O'Brien tended to focus on questions of representation in texts, Vasquez emphasized writing, conversation and action within the classroom and school community, 'grounding the curriculum in the lives of students' (2001a: 211). Yet both these early childhood teachers start with the everyday – either everyday texts or everyday life. Both examine school practices and texts. Both are committed to a political standpoint of social justice informed by feminism and critical multiculturalism. Both invite young children to become co-researchers and explore the secrets of institutional life and what's hidden in texts.

CRITICAL LITERACY IN EARLY CHILDHOOD EDUCATION: A RESEARCH AGENDA

Research about critical literacy in the early years is still in its infancy. Yet we know from what has been done that young children can appreciate how relations of power are produced through textual practices. We know they can deal with questions of fairness and justice. However there is a great deal more that needs to be explored. We need to know more about what constitutes critical literacies in different early years classrooms and the extent to which the critical can or should be given priority (Hall, 1998). The timing is right for some systematic studies of what critical literacy looks like in different communities and what different groups of children do with the critical discourses which are made available to them. We need to conduct micro analyses of the ways different children participate in critical literacy curricula and what they take from that into their everyday literate practices. We need to look closely at the connections and overlap between critical media literacy, multimodal literacies and new e-literacies (Alvermann and Hagood, 2000; Kress, 2000; C. Luke, 1997; Myers et al., 2000; Nixon, 2003) and critical literacy (see Kress,

and Robinson and Mackey, in this volume). We need to explore the relationship between the critical, the popular and the everyday. Recent studies continue to confirm the value of incorporating drama and media studies in early years critical literacy pedagogy. The relationship between critical literacy and children's appreciation and pleasure in popular culture also needs closer grounded investigations (Dyson, 1997; Marsh, 2000). Productive connections may be made with critical scientific literacy (Roth and Desautels, 2002) and place studies (Smith, 2002) where local action on and within the environment is stressed (Healy, 1998; Powell, 2001; Comber et al., 2001). We need to look systematically at what constitutes critical literacy in different nation-states in relation to literacy policy and accountability frameworks.

Recent publications suggest that teachers and researchers have begun to build on the ground-breaking work of theorists and of classroom-based early years teacher-researchers (Arthur, 2001; de la Luz Reyes, 2001; Jones Diaz et al., 2002; Martello, 2001). The International Reading Association and the National Council of Teachers of English have cosponsored a task force focusing on a critical perspective on literacy. Recent issues of the *Australian Journal of Language and Literacy* and *Language Arts* have had themed issues on critical literacy. However the extent to which critical literacy is being taken up is questionable. Recent large-scale school-based studies of literacy (Comber and Hill, 2000; Lankshear et al., 1997) indicate that critical or analytical literacy practices are not yet common in Australian classrooms generally. Given this it may be that critical literacy remains rare in early childhood sites and may be even less visible in nations where it is not yet part of the authorized curriculum. It may be, as Luke (2000: 459) recently suggested, that it's not whether governments bring critical literacy into state curriculum policy but rather a 'matter of government getting out of the way so that "critical literacies" can be invented in classrooms'. Added to this must be a reciprocal alliance between theorists, researchers and teachers to document and analyse these critical literacies as they are produced and to gauge the effects on students in different communities (Comber, 2001c). While there has been a discursive shift in early childhood education at the levels of theory and policy, it seems that on the ground there is still work to be done in terms of imagining, inventing and adapting the discourses of critical literacy for productive learning in early childhood settings. Given the neo-conservative push towards minimal measurable standards in literacy, advancing a critical literacy agenda is both urgent and difficult.

NOTES

I am grateful to Helen Nixon, Jackie Marsh, Valerie Munt and Vivian Vasquez for helpful feedback on earlier versions of this chapter.

REFERENCES

Alvermann, D. and Hagood, M. (2000) 'Critical media literacy: research, theory, and practice in "New Times"', *Journal of Educational Research,* 93 (3): 193–205.

Aries, P. (1962) *Centuries of Childhood: a Social History of Family Life,* trans R. Baldick. New York: Vintage.

Arthur, L. (2001) 'Young children as critical consumers', *Australian Journal of Language and Literacy,* 24 (3): 182–94.

Au, K. and Mason, J. (1981) 'Social organisational factors in learning to read: the balance of rights hypothesis', *Reading Research Quarterly,* xvii (1): 115–52.

Baker, C. and Davies, B. (1993) 'Literacy and gender in early childhood', in A. Luke and P. Gilbert (eds), *Literacy in Contexts: Australian Perspectives and Issues.* London: Allen and Unwin. pp. 55–67.

Baker, C. and Freebody, P. (1989) *Children's First School Books: Introductions to the Culture of Literacy.* Oxford: Blackwell.

Bigelow, B. (2001) 'On the road to cultural bias: a critique of the Oregon Trail CD-ROM', in B. Comber and A. Simpson (eds), *Negotiating Critical Literacies in Classrooms.* Mahwah, NJ: Erlbaum.

Brown, B. (1998) *Unlearning Discrimination in the Early Years.* Stoke-on-Trent: Trentham.

Burman, E. (1994) *Deconstructing Developmental Psychology.* New York: Routledge.

Cannella, G.S. (1997) *Deconstructing Early Childhood Education: Social Justice and Revolution.* New York: Lang.

Cannella, G.S. (2000) 'Critical and feminist reconstructions of early childhood education: continuing the conversations', *Contemporary Issues in Early Childhood,* 1 (2): 215–21.

Carrington, V. and Luke, A. (2002) 'Reading, homes and families: from postmodern to modern?', in A. van Kleeck, S. Stahl and E. Bauer (eds), *On Reading Books to Children: Parents and Teachers.* Mahwah, NJ: Erlbaum.

Christie, F. (1989) 'Curriculum genres in early childhood education: a case study in writing development'. Unpublished PhD thesis, University of Sydney.

Comber, B. (1994) 'Critical literacy: an introduction to Australian debates and perspectives', *Journal of Curriculum Studies,* 26 (6): 655–68.

Comber, B. (1997) 'Literacy, poverty and schooling: working against deficit equations', *English in Australia,* 119–20: 22–34.

Comber, B. (1999) 'Coming ready or not: what counts as early literacy!', *Language and Literacy Journal,* 1 (1). Available at educ.queensu.ca/~landl.

Comber, B. (2001a) 'Critical literacy: power and pleasure with language in the early years', *The Australian Journal of Language and Literacy,* 24 (3): 168–81.

Comber, B. (2001b) 'Literacy development and normative fantasies: what can be learnt from watching students over time?'. Paper presented at the Australian Association for Research in Education Annual Conference, Fremantle, 2–7 December. Paper index, available at com01438.htm, www.aare.edu.au/index. htm.

Comber, B. (2001c) 'Critical literacy and local action: teacher knowledge and a "new" research agenda', in B. Comber and A. Simpson (eds), *Negotiating Critical Literacies in Classrooms.* Mahwah, NJ: Erlbaum. pp. 271–82.

Comber, B. and Hill, S. (2000) 'Socio-economic disadvantage, literacy, and social justice: learning from longitudinal case study research, *The Australian Educational Researcher,* 27 (9): 1–19.

Comber, B. and Simpson, A. (eds) (2001) *Negotiating Critical Literacies in Classrooms.* Mahwah, NJ: Erlbaum.

Comber, B., Thomson, P. with Wells, M. (2001) 'Critical literacy finds a "place": writing and social action in a neighborhood school', *Elementary School Journal,* 101 (4): 451–64.

Cope, B. and Kalantzis, M. (1993) *The Powers of Literacy: a Genre Approach to the Teaching of Writing.* London: Falmer.

de la Luz Reyes, M. (2001) 'Unleashing possibilities: biliteracy in the primary grades', in M. de la Luz Reyes and J. Halcon (eds), *The Best for Our Children: Critical Perspectives on Literacy for Latino Students.* New York: Teachers College Press.

Department for Education and Children's Services (1995) *Texts: the Heart of the English Curriculum.* Adelaide: DECS.

Dyson, A.H. (1989) '*Multiple Worlds of Child Writers*: *Friends Learning to Write.* New York: Teachers College Press.

Dyson, A.H. (1993) *Social Worlds of Children Learning to Write in an Urban Primary School.* New York: Teachers College Press.

Dyson, A.H. (1997) *Writing Superheroes: Contemporary Childhood, Popular Culture, and Classroom Literacy.* New York: Teachers College Press.

Dyson, A.H. (1999) 'Transforming transfer: unruly children, contrary texts, and the persistence of the pedagogical order', *Review of Research in Education,* 24: 141–71.

Dyson, A.H. (2001) 'Relational sense and textual sense in a U.S. urban classroom: the contested case of Emily, girl friend of a Ninja', in B. Comber and A. Simpson (eds), *Negotiating Critical Literacies in Classrooms*, Mahwah, NJ: Erlbaum. pp. 3–18.

Edelsky, C. (ed.) (1999) *Making Justice Our Project: Teachers Working Towards Critical Whole Language Practice*. Urbana IL: National Council of Teachers of English.

Education Queensland (2000) *Why Wait? A Way into Teaching Critical Literacies in the Early Years*. Brisbane: State of Queensland, Department of Education.

Epstein, D. (1993) *Changing Classroom Cultures: Anti-Racism, Politics and Schools*. Stoke-on-Trent: Trentham.

Fairclough, N. (1992) *Discourse and Social Change*. Cambridge: Polity.

Freebody, P. (1992) 'Social class and reading', *Discourse*, 12 (2): 68–84.

Freebody, P. and Luke, A. (1990) '"Literacies" programs: debates and demands in cultural context', *Prospect: the Journal of Adult Migrant Education Programs*, 5 (3): 7–16.

Freire, P. (1972) *Pedagogy of the Oppressed*. New York: Seabury.

Freire, P. and Macedo, D. (1987) *Literacy: Reading the Word and the World*. Westport, CT: Bergin and Garvey.

Gilbert, P. (1989) 'Student text as pedagogical text', in S. De Castell, A. Luke and C. Luke (eds), *Language Authority and Criticism: Readings on the School Textbook*. London: Falmer.

Gilbert, P. (1991) 'Writing pedagogy: personal voices, truth telling and "real" texts', in C. Baker and A. Luke (eds) *Towards a Critical Sociology of Reading Pedagogy*. Amsterdam: John Benjamins.

Gilbert, P. and Rowe, K. (1989) *Gender, Literacy and the Classroom*. Carlton North, VA: Australian Reading Association.

Giroux, H. (1993) 'Literacy and the politics of difference', in C. Lankshear and P. McLaren (eds), *Critical Literacy: Politics, Praxis and the Postmodern*. Albany, NY: State University of New York Press.

Gregory, E. and Williams, A. (2000) *City Literacies: Learning to Read across Generations and Cultures*. London: Routledge.

Hall, K. (1998) 'Critical literacy and the case for it in the early years of school', *Language, Culture and Curriculum*, 11 (2): 183–94.

Harste, J. (1998) 'The work we do: journal as audit trail', *Language Arts*, 75 (4): 266.

Harste, J. and Leland, C. (2001) 'That's not fair! Critical literacy as unlimited semiosis', *Australian Journal of Language and Literacy*, 24 (3): 208–19.

Healy, A. (1998) 'The Woody Kids', in M. Knobel and A. Healy (eds), *Critical Literacies in the Primary Classroom*. Newtown, NSW: Primary English Teachers Association.

Janks, H. (ed.) (1993) *Critical Language Awareness*, series. Johannesburg: Witwatersrand University Press and Hodder and Stoughton.

Jones Diaz, C., Beecher, B. and Arthur, L. (2002) 'Children's worlds and critical literacy', in L. Makin and C. Jones Diaz (eds), *Literacies in Early Childhood: Challenging Views, Challenging Practice*. Sydney: Maclennan and Petty.

Kamler, B. (1994) 'Lessons about language and gender', *The Australian Journal of Language and Literacy*, 17 (2): 129–38.

Kamler, B. (2001) *Relocating the Personal: a Critical Writing Pedagogy*. Albany, NY: State University of New York Press.

Kamler, B. and Comber, B. (1996) 'Critical literacy: not generic – not developmental – not another orthodoxy', *Changing Education*, 3 (1): 1–9.

Kavanagh, K. (1997) *Texts on Television: School Literacies through Viewing in the First Years of School*. Adelaide: Department of Education and Children Services.

Kress, G. (2000) 'Multimodality', in B. Cope and M. Kalantzis (eds), *Multiliteracies: Literacy Learning and the Design of Social Futures*. South Yarra, VA: Macmillan.

Lankshear, C. (1994) 'Critical literacy'. Occasional paper no. 3. Australian Curriculum Studies Association, Canberra.

Lankshear, C. and McLaren, P. (1993) *Critical Literacy: Politics, Praxis and the Postmodern*. Albany, NY: State University of New York Press.

Lankshear, C. Bigum, C., Green, B., Wild, M., Morgan, W., Snyder, I., Durrant, C., Honan, E. and Murray, J. (1997) *Digital Rhetorics: Literacies and Technologies in Education – Current Practices and Future Directions*. Canberra: Department of Employment, Education and Youth Affairs.

Lensmire, T. (1994) *When Children Write: Critical Revisions of the Writing Workshop*. New York: Teachers College Press.

Luke, A. (1988) *Literacy, Textbooks and Ideology: Postwar Literacy Instruction and the Mythology of Dick and Jane*. London: Falmer.

Luke, A. (1991) 'The political economy of reading instruction', in *Towards a Critical Sociology of Reading Pedagogy: Papers of the XII World Congress on Reading*. Amsterdam: Benjamins. pp. 3–26.

Luke, A. (2000) 'Critical literacy in Australia: a matter of context and standpoint', *Journal of Adolescent and Adult Literacy*, 43 (5): 448–61.

Luke, A. and Freebody, P. (1997) 'Critical literacy and the question of normativity: an introduction', in S. Muspratt, A. Luke and P. Freebody (eds), *Constructing Critical Literacies: Teaching and Learning Textual Practice*. Sydney: Allen and Unwin.

Luke, A. and Freebody, P. (1999) 'Further notes on the four resources model', *Reading online*. Available at www.readingonline.org.

Luke, A. and Luke, C. (2001) 'Adolescence lost/childhood regained: on early intervention and the emergence of the techno-subject', *Journal of Early Childhood Literacy*, 1 (1): 91–120.

Luke, A., O'Brien, J. and Comber, B. (1994) 'Making community texts objects of study', *The Australian Journal of Language and Literacy*, 17 (2): 139–49.

Luke, C. (1997) 'Media literacy and cultural studies', in S. Muspratt, A. Luke and P. Freebody (eds), *Constructing Critical Literacies: Teaching and Learning Textual Practice*. Sydney: Allen and Unwin. pp. 19–50.

Mac Naughton, G. (2000) *Rethinking Gender in Early Childhood Education*. St Leonards, NSW: Allen and Unwin.

Marsh, J. (2000) '"But I want to fly too!": girls and superhero play in the infant classroom', *Gender and Education*, 12 (2): 209–20.

Martello, J. (2001) 'Drama: ways into critical literacy in the early childhood years', *Australian Journal of Language and Literacy*, 24 (3): 195–207.

Martin, J. (1985) *Factual Writing: Exploring and Challenging Social Reality*. Geelong: Deakin University Press.

May, S. (1999) *Critical multiculturalism: Rethinking Multicultural and Antiracist Education*. London: Falmer.

McNaughton, S. (1995) *Patterns of Emergent Literacy*. Oxford: Oxford University Press.

Mellor, B., Patterson, A. and O'Neill, M. (1987) *Reading Stories*. Perth: Chalkface.

Moll, L. (2001) 'The diversity of schooling: a cultural-historical approach', in M. de la Luz Reyes and J. Halcon (eds), *The Best for Our Children: Critical Perspectives on Literacy for Latino Students*. New York: Teachers College Press.

Moll, L., Amanti, C., Neff, D. and Gonzalez, N. (1992) 'Funds of knowledge for teaching: using a qualitative approach to connect homes and classrooms', *Theory into Practice*, 31 (2): 132–41.

Muspratt, S., Luke, A. and Freebody, P. (1997) *Constructing Critical Literacies: Teaching and Learning Textual Practices*. Sydney: Allen and Unwin.

Myers, J., Hammett, R. and McKillop, M. (2000) 'Connecting, exploring, and exposing the self in hypermedia projects', in M. Gallego and S. Hollingsworth (eds), *What Counts as Literacy: Challenging the School Standard*. New York: Teachers College Press.

Nixon, H. (2003) 'Exploring the communicational webs of popular media culture in English language arts curriculum', in R.F. Hammett and B.R.C. Barrell (eds), *Digital Media, Cultural Studies and Technology*. Calgary: Detselig of University of Calgary.

O'Brien, J. (1994a) 'Show mum you love her: taking a new look at junk mail', *Reading*, 28 (1): 43–6.

O'Brien, J. (1994b) 'It's written in our head: the possibilities and contradictions of a feminist poststructuralist discourse in a junior primary classroom', Unpublished masters of education thesis, University of South Australia.

O'Brien, J. (1998) 'Experts in Smurfland', in M. Knobel and A. Healy (eds), *Critical Literacies in the Primary Classroom*. Newtown, NSW: Primary English Teaching Association.

O'Brien, J. (2001a) 'Children reading critically: a local history', in B. Comber and A. Simpson (eds), *Negotiating Critical Literacies in Classrooms*. Mahwah, NJ: Erlbaum.

O'Brien, J. (2001b) '"I knew that already": how children's books limit inquiry', in S. Boran and B. Comber (eds), *Critiquing Whole Language and Classroom Inquiry*. Urbana, IL: Whole Language Umbrella and National Council of Teachers of English.

O'Brien, J. and Comber, B. (2000) 'Negotiating critical literacies with young children', in C. Barratt-Pugh and M. Rohl (eds), *Literacy Learning in the Early Years*. Crows Nest, NSW: Allen and Unwin.

Panofsky, C. (2000) 'Examining the research narrative in early literacy: the case of parent–child book-reading activity', in M. Gallego and S. Hollingsworth (eds), *What Counts as Literacy: Challenging the School Standard*. New York: Teachers College Press.

Patterson, A. (1997) 'Setting limits to English', in S. Muspratt, A. Luke and P. Freebody (eds), *Constructing Critical Literacies: Teaching and Learning Textual Practice*. Sydney: Allen and Unwin.

Pennycook, A. (1999) 'Introduction: critical approaches to TESOL', *TESOL Quarterly*, 33 (3): 329–47.

Petty, K. (1990) *My First Book of Knowledge*. London: Conran Octopus.

Polakow, V. (1989) 'Deconstructing development', *Journal of Education*, 171 (2): 75–87.

Polakow, V. (1993) *Lives on the Edge: Single Mothers and their Children in the Other America*. Chicago: The University of Chicago Press.

Powell, R. (1999) *Literacy as a Moral Imperative: Facing the Challenges of a Pluralistic Society*. Lanham, MD: Rowman and Littlefield.

Powell, R. (2001) 'Saving black mountain: the promise of critical literacy in a multicultural democracy', *The Reading Teacher*, 54 (8): 772–81.

Reid, J. and Comber, B. (2002) 'Theoretical perspectives in early literacy education: implications for practice', in L. Makin and C. Jones Diaz (eds), *Literacies in Early Childhood: Challenging Views, Challenging Practice*. Sydney: Maclennan and Petty.

Roth, W.M. and Desautels, J. (eds) (2002) *Science Education as/for Sociopolitical Action*. New York: Lang.

Sahni, U. (2001) 'Children appropriating literacy: empowerment pedagogy from young children's perspective', in B. Comber and A. Simpson (eds), *Negotiating Critical Literacies in Classrooms*. Mahwah, NJ: Erlbaum. pp. 19–35.

Searle, C. (1993) 'Words to a life-land: literacy, the imagination, and Palestine', in C. Lankshear and P. McLaren (eds), *Critical Literacy: Politics, Praxis and the Postmodern*. Albany, NJ: State University of New York Press. pp. 167–91.

Smith, G.A. (2002) 'Place-based education: learning to be where we are', *Phi Delta Kappan*, April: 584–94.

Vasquez, V. (2001a) 'Classroom inquiry into the incidental unfolding of social justice issues: seeking out possibilities in the lives of learners', in S. Boran, and B. Comber (eds), *Critiquing Whole Language and Classroom Inquiry*. Urbana, IL: Whole Language Umbrella and National Council of Teachers of English. pp. 200–15.

Vasquez, V. (2001b) 'Constructing a critical curriculum with young children', in B. Comber and A. Simpson (eds), *Negotiating Critical Literacies in Classrooms*. Mahwah, NJ: Erlbaum. pp. 55–66.

Vasquez, V.M. (2003) *Negotiating Critical Literacies with Young Children*. Mahwah, NJ: Erlbaum.

Walkerdine, V. (1984) 'Developmental psychology and the child-centred pedagogy: the insertion of Piaget into early education', in J. Henriques, W. Hollway, C. Urwin, C. Venn and V. Walkerdine (eds), *Changing the Subject: Psychology, Social Regulation and Subjectivity*. London: Methuen.

Wallace, C. (2001) 'Critical literacy in a second language classroom: power and control', in B. Comber and A. Simpson (eds), *Negotiating Critical Literacies in Classrooms*. Mahwah, NJ: Erlbaum.

Walton, C. (1993) 'Literacy in Aboriginal contexts: re-examining pedagogy', in A. Luke and P. Gilbert (eds), *Literacy in Contexts: Australian Issues and Perspectives*. St Leonards, NSW: Allen and Unwin.

30

Finding Literacy: a Review of Research on Literacy Assessment in Early Childhood

SHARON MURPHY

The vitality of language lies in its ability to limn the actual, imagined and possible lives of its speakers, readers, and writers ... It arcs toward the place where meaning may lie. (Toni Morrison, as cited in Himley, 2000: 131)

Any review of research on literacy assessment creates a double 'language moment'. This doubling is created because texts about literacy assessment are themselves being read and interpreted to investigate how reading and writing are assessed, and the manner in which the reading and writing are assessed in any one instance in these texts tells something about what the author-researchers thought about literacy. Each element – each move and assertion made within the literacy assessment texts themselves, and each inference a reader makes about what these literacy assessment texts represent – 'arcs towards where meaning [about literacy and assessment] may lie' and, in doing so, reveals as much about the meaning makers as it does about literacy.

In this review, I intend to try and work with (or limn) the double language moment to make more apparent how the field of literacy assessment in early childhood education works. Specifically, I will situate my analysis in the idea that assessment, like language, is value laden and that values, in large part, determine what one sees as either literacy or assessment. Drawing upon this theoretical framework I will go on to discuss, in similar terms, research relating to three literacy assessment archetypes in early childhood education and then will suggest future directions for research.

VALUES, LANGUAGE, AND ASSESSMENT

Varied sources highlight the fact that language is undergirded by values. Child developmentalists who study language recognize that a system of shared meaning permeates language. For instance, Katherine Nelson, in exploring the meaning of meaning in language, posits that 'the greater the degree to which an individual's semantic, conceptual, and script systems correspond to the conventional representations of the cultural (or subcultural) group to which the speakers belong, the greater the likelihood of establishing a high degree of shared meaning on any given occasion' (1985: 10). In essence, she is saying that if you share discourse strategies and values with someone, then your likelihood of successfully communicating with them is heightened because the way you interpret the world is similar.

Bakhtin's (1981) argument that the meaning of discourse is an artefact of social history sets the idea of a shared system of meaning and values within a time period lengthier than Nelson's single interchange and highlights the importance of the social practices that become part of language. Linguists such as Simpson explore 'point of view' in texts by considering 'the value systems and sets of beliefs which reside in texts ... in other words, *ideology* in language' (1993: 5). Critical theorists like Fairclough (1989) argue that shared values run so deep that they appear naturalized, that is, people are no longer aware of the ways in which shared values affect what they say, how they say it, and in what circumstances they say it. In essence, all of these perspectives illustrate that language is an interpretive value framework for encountering the world.

The language of assessment, as a subset of language itself, is open to the same varied influences as language is. The recognition of this element foregrounds what is sometimes an unspoken assumption in discourse on assessment: the language of assessment is a language of values and, as such, it is an interpretive framework for viewing not only what is assessed but the nature of the assessment itself. One simple way in which to illustrate this point is to consider word choices in describing assessment options. For example, the words 'formal' and 'informal' are used within the field of literacy assessment to describe particular kinds of assessments (see, for example, Farr and Beck, 1991; Goodman, 1991). These descriptors, whether intended to or not, immediately communicate issues of worth or importance to the assessment. Formal assessments, like formal dress affairs, are considered by many to be performative rather than substantive and, some would argue, mask one's true self. Informal assessments, like casual clothes, may be instruments of day-to-day activity but may be considered by some to be not quite refined enough. Of course, there are other interpretations possible and other elements of comparison between formal and informal assessment; my point is not to perform a comparative analysis but to illustrate that assumptions underlie the language of assessment and these assumptions are value laden.

In addition to values being a part of assessment simply because the language of assessment is a subset of language, it is important to recognize that within the field of assessment, there is considerable explicit theorization about values. At the heart of assessment is validity, a term which shares the same root meaning as value (Kaplan, 1964). If psychometric theorizing about validity is drawn upon, evidence for test interpretation and use is linked with the appropriateness of the consequences of that interpretation and use (Messick, 1985) and the latter is explicitly about values. For example, even though a test (which is the typical focus of psychometric writing) can be demonstrated to assess well a domain of knowledge, if the consequences of the test use are more than the test should bear, then the test should be considered invalid for that use. However, Messick (1985) readily acknowledges that there is considerable slippage between theoretical discourse about assessment and the practice of assessment. If values are an indicator for the 'worthwhileness of implementation', then this slippage suggests that validity theorization is itself an arena for values display.

Assuming then that assessment is and inevitably will continue to be value laden, what are the consequences of this assumption for the field of assessment itself and for literacy assessment in early childhood education in particular? Operationally, I believe that values in large part determine how we 'find' (or see and evaluate) literacy. If our values predispose us to conceptualize literacy in particular ways, then we will tend to look for evidence of our conceptualizations while missing evidence for other types of conceptualizations. I will set the framework for a consideration of how values work in three literacy assessment archetypes by briefly considering the historical path that literacy assessment has taken in early childhood education.

SETTING ARCHETYPES AGAINST A HISTORICAL PERSPECTIVE

The typical point of departure for most reviews of research on literacy assessment in early childhood education is a focus on the readiness movement (see, for example, reviews by Johnston and Rogers, 2001; Stallman and Pearson, 1990). Two strands interlace to form the substance of literacy assessment under this rubric:

1   the testing movement, which arose out of the desire to create a more 'scientific' approach to assessment (Willis, 1991)
2   the developmentalist perspective, with its underlying biological deterministic perspective (Stallman and Pearson, 1990).

The explanations for the move towards a more 'scientific' approach to assessment typically include the desire of what is now the discipline of psychology to become just that, a discipline, with its own associated scientific methods (Gardner, 1984), and the desire to stem criticisms of biases (in the forms of poorly constructed examinations or the influence peddling of high status society members) that plagued the evaluation of performance in schools (Brooks, 1920; 1921). One study commonly associated with the onset of readiness testing was conducted in 1931 by Morphett and Washburne (1983). This report, which correlated reading ability and intelligence, recommended that, so as to reduce the possibility of failure, the onset of reading instruction should begin when children are ready, which in this research was at the mental age of six and a half. The readiness construct remained a relatively intransigent one for three-fourths of the twentieth century, embedded as it was not only in most reading tests (Stallman and Pearson, 1990) but also in the general textbooks developed for pre-service early childhood educators (e.g. Seefeldt, 1980).

Even though accounts reveal that there was debate over whether readiness was biologically or environmentally determined, these accounts also indicate that the concept itself held sway (e.g. Banton-Smith, 1951–2). Indeed, typically little is posited to have changed in literacy assessment until the mid 1960s when theories of literacy learning began to be influenced by fields such as cognitive psychology, linguistics, and anthropology. As these newer theories of literacy became refined and articulated, so too did a critique of the substance of literacy assessment. Alternative frameworks and assessment methodologies for literacy assessment were proposed as part of this 'new literacy' (Willinsky, 1990) movement. A literacy theorization *Zeitgeist* appeared to be at work during this period, with similar theoretical moves afoot globally in Argentina (e.g. Ferreiro and Teberosky, 1982), the United States (e.g. Calkins, 1983; Gentry, 1987; Goodman and Burke, 1972; Goodman and Goodman, 1980; Teale and Sulzby, 1986), Australia (e.g. Holdaway, 1979), New Zealand (e.g. Clay, 1972), Israel (e.g. Tolchinsky Landsman, 1990), Italy (e.g. Pontecorvo and Zucchermaglio, 1990), Brazil (e.g. Grossi, 1990), and Britain (e.g. Meek, 1982; 1988; Rosen and Rosen, 1973). Underlying these different bodies of work were the following premises:

1   The child is constantly hypothesizing about the world.
2   The tasks one uses to describe/assess literacy can conceal as much as they can reveal.
3   Tasks that are situated in activities of the everyday are more likely to yield fuller demonstrations of children's early literacy.
4   The relationship between teaching and learning is not always a causal one; children may learn much that they weren't taught.

Out of these assumptions grew assessment initiatives that related more to the literacy activities of the everyday in both format and substance. These initiatives began to be developed in the 1970s, proliferated in the 1980s and early 1990s, and have reached a relative stability of sorts since that time.

This thumbnail sketch of the history of literacy assessment in early childhood is itself a bit misleading. Indeed, the thumbnail sketch is an example of what occurs when values and assumptions are left unexamined. For instance, absent from most commentaries on the history of early childhood literacy assessment is any reference to the child study movement which began in the nineteenth century and ebbed and flowed in popularity across the twentieth century (Cohen and Stern, 1978). In Britain, in the 1930s, people like Susan Isaacs (1966) advocated the value of qualitative record keeping based on

observation. Isaacs' sample observational notes include lengthy descriptions and summarizations of the literacy activities of children.

Many interpretations can be brought to bear to explain the absence of the child study movement in reviews of research on early childhood literacy assessment:

1   The child study movement did not focus specifically on the theorization of literacy but was more interested in the whole child (although this argument is not persuasive since many standardized assessments of reading used across the twentieth century had weak to non-existent grounding in literacy theories, yet they are referenced).
2   Psychically, the readiness concept and its testing were so dominant in the field of early childhood assessment, that other assessment activities were but footnotes to the field.
3   Disciplinary boundaries were such that early childhood and literacy educators did not interact.

Each of these interpretations is not only a statement about values, but an illustration of how the literacy that is 'found' as a result would lead out of the interpretations. So, for example, if literacy theory was not valued in the child study movement, what was valued instead, and what would literacy look like as a result of such a perspective? Similarly, what view of literacy is found if reading readiness tests are the lens? Rather than answer such questions in relation to the history of literacy assessment, I will explore similar questions by drawing upon research relating to three early childhood education literacy assessment archetypes.

LITERACY ASSESSMENT ARCHETYPES IN EARLY CHILDHOOD EDUCATION

Three archetypical methods for data collection exist in the discourse on literacy assessment in early childhood education: standardized or large-scale group tests, observation and documentary methods, and responsive listening methods. Standardized or large-scale group methods include both commercially available tests and state run tests. Observation and documentation methods include a variety of observational techniques accompanied by some form of record keeping, and the collection of documents generated by children that can illustrate literacy knowledge. Responsive listening involves observation and documentation, but it is dynamic in relation to the child's learning and involves a legitimization of the child's point of view (Gandini, as cited in Rinaldi, 1998). I have deliberately avoided categorizations such as formal and informal, or external (to the classroom – a reference to account-ability) and internal (to the classroom) (Paris et al., 2001), because of the significant ideological weight these terms have for how one finds literacy and in what circumstances.

How standardized large-scale group methods 'find' literacy

Critique abounds with respect to the use of stan-dardized large-scale group methods of assessment (e.g. Murphy, 1997; Murphy et al., 1998: Sacks, 1999). Professional associations such as the American Educational Research Association (2000) and the International Reading Association (1999) have been so concerned that they have issued papers on this topic. Yet, there appear to be national (Hoffman et al., 2001) and global moves afoot (e.g. in Japan: Johnston and Rogers, 2001; in Canada: Murphy, 2001; in England: DfES, 2002) to increase the use of standardized testing. These moves, in part, are being fed by societal reform occurring as consequence of economic and media globalization (Barlow and Robertson, 1994). Countries that at one time were bemused by the newspaper publica-tion of school-by-school standardized test results in the United States now find their own newspapers vying for the eye-catching headlines and politi-cians trying to trump each other with test scores (Murphy, 2001). Given such a context, one would imagine that the way in which standardized large-scale group methods assess literacy must be compelling.

The rhetorical moves (and the values underlying them) associated with standardized testing account for some of the longevity and popularity of this method. Standardized tests are usually referred to as measures (e.g. Farr and Carey, 1986), a term sug-gesting *accuracy* and *precision*. The reporting method is usually numerical, which is further sug-gestive of exactness. Systematic analyses of stan-dardized tests designed for younger readers reveal an emphasis on micro-text elements such as words and word parts (Murphy et al., 1998; Stallman and Pearson, 1990), inherently turning literacy into sets of smaller and smaller components. Indeed, Stallman and Pearson report that for most of the readiness tests they reviewed, 'the clear emphasis (almost half of the subtests) is on sound–symbol knowledge' (1990: 36).

The content of tests, another index of values, determines what is named as literate behaviour. Test content is manifested by the architecture of the test (its format) and the substance of the test (the

material covered). Stallman and Pearson (1990) report that the overarching architectural motif for readiness tests is that of multiple-choice fill-in-the-bubble format, with an emphasis on the recognition rather than the production of elements. Others have found similar patterns (see Murphy et al., 1998). This architectural structuring of standardized tests has many consequences, two of which are parti-cularly significant for the present discussion:

1   The tests have embedded in them such relatively narrow *a priori* definitive assumptions about what and how evidence of literacy is demon-strated, that the literacy knowledge of some is lost to the architecture (e.g. by design, partial knowledge is not given credit on these tests).
2   The tests so constrain the ways in which literacy is manifested that they make it relatively easy to create literacy programmes which mimic the tests and, unsurprisingly, the children engaged in such programmes make significant gains on the tests.

The substance of standardized literacy tests can be addressed at many levels. I have analysed such tests to determine whether they hold up to good psycho-metric design principles and found many problems with the tests (Murphy et al., 1998). However, analyses such as mine are often counteracted with a comment that the analysis offered is that of an adult reader and that, somehow, the traps I or another adult might see would not be fallen prey to by a child who has different values. Until recently, it was difficult to counteract this argument with evidence. Only a small sampling of work (e.g. Fillmore, 1982) exists in which children were used as infor-mants in the critical analysis of standardized test items. However, more recently Hill and Larsen (2000) have included extensive item-by-item responses from children in relation to a comprehen-sive analysis of a pilot-test edition of the Gates–MacGinitie test for eight-year-olds. Using linguistic, genre, and discourse approaches to the analysis of test items (which could be published in full because the items were pilot items), Hill and Larsen's work illustrates how the texts within tests operate as unusual text forms that are systematically biased against certain groups. Hill and Larsen take multiple routes to uncovering what children know and what they might believe a text says and, in doing so, reveal the questionable validity of the texts in the Gates–MacGinitie: right answers are achieved for the wrong reasons, wrong answers (when explained) have inherent justifiable logic, and some of the answers that the test makers indi-cate are the correct answers make no sense at all.

What then, is the literacy found by this assess-ment method? In short, the literacy found is a facsimile of sorts. Superficially it may appear to be not only literacy, but a precise estimate of literacy knowledge; however, when this literacy is probed, as in the case of the Hill and Larsen (2000) research, it disintegrates, and one is left with fragments of possibility but not much else.

How observation and documentary methods 'find' literacy

While standardized tests 'make up people' (Hacking, 1990) by using language and numbers that imply a precision inconsistent with the nature of the phenomenon under study, observation and documentary methods make up people by interpreting their surface actions and the residue they leave behind in the form of literacy artefacts. Observation and documentation methods include selected individualized standardized instruments, portfolio assessments, and observation-based schemes. I include selected individualized standardized instruments here because, although these instruments have made some attempt at standardization in the data–collection tasks that are the focus of the interaction between an adult and a child around a literacy activity, typically the tasks are similar to regular classroom activities.

As the field of emergent literacy (Teale and Sulzby, 1986) came into being, so too did a wealth of assessment tools drawing from that theory. Typically, these tools involve: (1) anecdotal records made by the teacher based on interactions with the child, (2) the collection of literacy artefacts that stand as tokens of literacy development, and (3) observations based on interventions that take the form of tasks typical of classroom activity, such as requesting that a child read aloud. Examples of popular tools include *The Primary Language Record* (Barrs et al., 1988; Barrs, 1993), *An Observation Survey of Early Literacy Achievement* (Clay, 1993) or its earlier variants (e.g. Clay, 1972), and *Reading Miscue Inventory: Alternative Procedures* (Goodman et al., 1987) or its earlier variants (e.g. Goodman and Burke, 1972). Examples of research, the results of which became the material of checklists (e.g. Rhodes, 1993), included Sulzby's (1985) work on storytelling, Doake's (1985) work on reading-like behaviour, Goodman and Altwerger's (1981) work on print awareness, Gentry's (1987) work on spelling, and the work of people like Harste et al. (1984) or Ferreiro and Teberosky (1982) on early literacy development. The nature of the activities undertaken in most of the activities associated with the tools or checklists derived from studies is very much in keeping with the types of activities that occurred in the child study movement;

however, the interpretation of these 'kidwatching' (Goodman, 1978) assessments is informed by theories about literacy learning for young children.

The rhetoric that accompanies these assessment activities is of two sorts: (1) a *justification* rhetoric, and (2) a *descriptive* rhetoric based in theories of emergent literacy. The justification rhetoric essentially amounts to an argument for the validity of the activities; it is implicitly an argument *against* the vacuousness of standardized large-scale group tests. Typical language associated with this argument includes terms such as 'authentic' (e.g. Hiebert, 1994) and 'performance-based' (e.g. Kapinus et al., 1994). The descriptive rhetoric usually draws upon observational research or ethnographic research as a further justification argument.

The format or architecture of observation and documentation methods is wide-ranging – from, for standardized instruments/protocols, *a priori* structuring of the tasks/activities/knowledge deemed to be literate behaviour, to an absence of all *a priori* structuring (in such instance, the structuring of what counts is left up to the observer). It can range from a temporal ordering of indicators of literate behaviour to a description derived out of one or more theories of literacy. In short, much can vary within and among assessment methods of this type.

But the architecture of observation and documentation methods has an additional element that must be considered. That element, the significance of the demonstration of behaviour, is related to two key assumptions built into observation and documentation methods: (1) the knowledge children have about literacy will be demonstrated in observable ways, and (2) the environment is conducive to allowing such demonstrations to happen. When behaviours are not demonstrated in observable ways, the question facing those interpreting observation and documentation methods is whether or not this absence of demonstration should be regarded as indicative of some type of 'lack' on the part of the child. When observations are interpreted or when standardized observation and documentation methods are used, these methods become as much an assessment of the environment as they are the child. So, for example, if there is no opportunity for the child to demonstrate knowledge of an element of literacy knowledge such as quotation marks, because the instructional environment provided no opportunity for their use, then the problem resides with the setting and not with the child. Indeed, using such a rationale, some have advocated theoretically based observation and documentation methods as a means of changing teacher practices (e.g. Searle and Stevenson, 1987).

Like standardized tests, the substance of observation and documentation methods can be addressed at many levels. An in-depth analysis of a large set of observation and documentation methods was conducted by Meisels and Piker (2001). Of the 89 teacher-identified early literacy assessments (for children ages five to nine) that they studied, only 7% were designed to be administered to a group. Therefore, while there is some 'noise' in their findings as a result of the inclusion of these group assessments, many of the patterns described by Meisels and Piker (2001) are useful in considering how literacy is thought about in these assessments. They are at once similar to and distinct from their standardized group assessment peers. Similarities include a high incidence of phonics assessment (61% included some aspect of this element), comprehension (58% included this element) and reading (57% included this element). Unlike the standardized tests, print awareness was assessed in 47% of the instruments and reading strategies in 42%. Also of note is the fact that writing makes a significant appearance in these assessments: writing conventions are examined in 57% and writing process in 48%. The emergent literacy theoretical values appear to have had some impact, in methods such as these, upon what is defined as literate behaviours.

So what kind of literacy is found by observation and documentation methods? A simple answer might be, 'What you see, is what you get.' That is, observation and documentation methods are as much about the behaviour being displayed as they are about the ability of the viewer/interpreters to understand what the display is about.

How responsive listening methods 'find' literacy

Responsive listening methods are not named as such in the literature on early childhood literacy assessment. Indeed, responsive listening methods, like the methods associated with the child study movement, are methods that are the product of childhood education and study, rather than literacy study. Responsive listening methods emerge out of the Reggio Emilia approach to early childhood education originating in Italy. In this approach, children are viewed as:

> hav[ing] their own questions and theories, and ... they negotiate their theories with others. Our duty ... is to listen to the children, just as we ask them to listen to one another. Listening means giving value to others, being open to them and what they have to say. Listening legitimizes the other person's point of view, thereby enriching both listener and speaker. (Rinaldi, 1998: 120)

The effect of a listening stance and the expectation that the child is working from a base of knowledge are dynamic in relation to the child's learning. As the teachers in Reggio Emilia schools accessibly place, throughout the environment, documentation in the form of charts, diaries, tapes and slides, their children 'become even more curious, interested, and confident as they contemplate the meaning of what they have achieved' (Malaguzzi, 1998: 70).

Even though literacy learning *per se* has not been a focus of the published reports on the Reggio Emilia approach, many of the observation and documentation approaches within literacy assessment in early childhood education can be, or have been, extended so that they adhere to the principles of this approach. For instance, the retelling component of the Reading Miscue Inventory (Goodman et al., 1987) is quite open to being treated in a responsive listening fashion, whereas the coding of miscues, which is technical and theoretically driven (Murphy, 1999), would be less open to such techniques with young children. Similarly, Hill and Larsen's (2000) investigations with children as to what formed the basis for their answers to the questions on a multiple-choice standardized test involved a type of listening in which the adults were open to learning what the children thought about standardized testing.

If there is any type of rhetorical move embedded in the responsive listening assessment approach, it is the tendency to focus on *uncovering* children's knowledge (Giudici et al., 2001). The assumption is that much knowledge lies waiting to be revealed. In literacy assessment, one example that incorporates some aspects of responsive listening is the research of Ferreiro and Teberosky (1982) in which they demonstrate the great range of literacy knowledge children have at relatively young ages. These researchers, whose method is adapted from Piagetian-based clinical interviews, describe children's knowledge, not so much as fixed facts, but as sets of hypotheses from which they are working: hypotheses about genre, the role of graphic elements, and what elements of language can be represented in print. However, it should be noted that responsive listening typically does not occur in the format of a clinical interview setting, especially given the literature that indicates the care that must be taken in interviewing young children (e.g. Ginsburg, 1997); rather, for the Reggio Emilia classrooms it occurs in the day-to-day activity of classrooms.

The architecture of the responsive listening approach lies embedded in the structuring of conversation and the response of the adult. The skills of the adult in conversation with or responding to the child result in glimpses into children's thinking that, depending on those skills, can result in the rarely seen or the mundane and the predictable. The responsive listening approach isn't standardized because it is about response to children, but it can be routinized in so far as there is attentiveness and care given to what are assumed to be knowledgeable children. An example of the extent to which this perspective is taken can be found in a discussion of the application of the work of Vygotsky (1978) to teaching and learning. Malaguzzi, in reflecting on Vygotsky's concept of the zone of proximal development (the space between the independent ability of the child and what the child can do with the support of others), comments that:

> The matter [of the zone of proximal development] is ambiguous. Can one give competence to someone who does not have it? … In such a situation [in which the child is about to see what the adult already sees] the adult can and must loan to the children his judgement and knowledge. But it is a loan with a condition, namely, that the child will repay. (1998: 83–4)

The substance of the responsive listening very much depends on the adult's finding the places in conversation where the child's hypotheses can be let loose and where a lending of judgement might be made. Even then, the responsive listening approach is not about getting the child to demonstrate proficiencies (although it surely does that), but it is more about trying to understand how children think about the world and why they might think that way. The approach works away at eroding common assumptions about literacy learning to reveal what was previously unthought-of in terms of children's knowledge of print conventions in relation to both reading and writing.

So, what kind of literacy is found by the responsive listening method? Again, a simple answer: an uncommon kind, one that resists being defined by adults' predisposed biases towards conventional literacy representations and interpretations and that allows for different insight to be made.

WITHIN AND BEYOND ARCHETYPES

For the three archetypes presented, fundamental differences flow from who defines (and values) literacy at the outset. With traditional, standardized approaches, the definitions are established *a priori* and a narrow interpretation of what counts as literate behaviour defines the experience and the result of the assessment. With the observation and documentation methods, *a priori* assumptions exist, but they allow for some interaction with the environment; ultimately, however, these methods rest upon base description and, maybe, the interpretive lenses of literacy theories. The responsive listening method relies less on *a priori* conventional understandings of literacy but asks what the child's understanding of literacy is.

For each of the archetypes, values also feed into what any literacy assessment might mean. On the one hand, we are all witness to the considerable rhetoric that suggests that assessments ought to be related to the purposes to which they are to be used (we get the formal and informal assessment language out of that argument). But, fundamentally, if a literacy assessment is just that – a literacy assessment – then the first criterion to which it must be held, above any other, is that of the quality of its assessment of literacy. All of the archetypes presented suffer in this regard. None provides a complete picture of the literacy knowledge of children, and perhaps no single assessment type can. But some clearly provide better information than others.

As for the standardized test archetype, one point raised by Crossland (1994) bears remembering: the pace at which children's literacy knowledge changes in early childhood is so rapid as to create an educational Doppler effect. That is, by the time we have gathered information about a child's literacy and interpreted what it might mean, the child has moved on to new understandings. The annual or semi-annual standardized literacy test seems especially likely to suffer from such Doppler effects.

As for the other archetypes, to some extent the observation/documentation and the responsive listening methods complement each other in together providing the broadest picture. But the picture is only as large as our minds allow it to be. Two examples of how the literacy picture, and the complementary assessments, might be enlarged come to mind.

The first has to do with the theoretical models that inform the interpretation of any observation/documentation. By and large, the models that are used are those with psycholinguistic or sociopsycholinguistic rootings. Newer interpretive frameworks such as the conceptualization of literacy as social practice might bring different interpretations to bear on the same observations and documentation. For instance, Watrous and Willett considered the matter of reading identity of a student and, in their words, their method:

> looked at the process of group formation and maintenance and at the individual as an aspiring member of the classroom community. It did not highlight John as a failure, as a non-member with little chance of gaining group acceptance. It did not measure his progress against predetermined criteria indicating success or failure as a reader. Instead, it looked at the strategies John employed to establish membership and the degree to which he was successful in his efforts. It also examined

the ways the community both hindered and facilitated those efforts. (1994: 85–6)

Such perspectives locate literacy learning, and ultimately the assessment of literacy learning, not simply in the head of the learner but in the community in which it is practised.

Even when the values of literacy are located more strictly in the learner, perspectives are missing from the current interpretive frameworks. For a second example, consider, for a moment, what an assessment method might look like if it emphasized affect. I am not talking here about superficial concepts of 'fun' or behaviouristic conceptions of 'motivation', in which external referents are the driving force, but about psychoanalytically driven assessments such as are found in the work by Jones (1996). Such work teases out the complex relations between attachments to texts and the roles such attachments have for readers. Consider, for instance, that for Jones' (1996) children, books became transitional objects, objects which could be loved and hated but which were treasured in the same way that a favourite toy might be. What a different relationship her children have with books than others who have not had such experiences.

Both the 'literacy as social practice' and the psychoanalytic perspective reflect a switch from the underlying question of most assessments, which is 'Who do we want you to become as a literate person?', toward a more interesting question, 'Who *are* you as a literate person?' Maybe this is the question that ought to be guiding research and thinking about literacy assessment in early childhood education.

REFERENCES

American Educational Research Association (2000) 'Position statement of the American Educational Research Association concerning high-stakes testing in pre-K-12 education', *Educational Researcher*, 29 (8): 24–5.

Bakhtin, M.M. (1981) 'Discourse in the novel', in M. Holquist (ed.), *Bakhtin*, trans. M. Holquist and C. Emerson. Austin, TX: University of Texas Press. pp. 259–422.

Barlow, M. and Robertson, H. (1994) *Class Warfare: the Assault on Canada's Schools*. Toronto: Key Porter.

Banton-Smith, N. (1951–2) 'Recognizing reading readiness at all levels', *Reading Teacher*, 5: 7–10.

Barrs, M. (1993) 'The primary language record: what we are learning in the U.K.', in C. Bouffler (ed.), *Literacy Evaluation: Issues and Practicalities*. Portsmouth, NH: Heinemann. pp. 52–62.

Barrs, M., Ellis, S., Hester, H. and Thomas, A. (1988) *The Primary Language Record: Handbook for Teachers*. Portsmouth, NH: Heinemann.

Brooks, S.S. (1920) 'Getting teachers to feel the need for standardized tests', *Journal of Educational Research*, 2 (1): 425–35.

Brooks, S.S. (1921) 'Measuring the progress of pupils by means of standardized tests', *Journal of Educational Research*, 4 (3): 161–71.

Calkins, L. (1983) *Lessons from a Child on the Teaching and Learning of Writing*. Portsmouth, NH: Heinemann.

Clay, M. (1972) *The Early Detection of Reading Difficulties*. Portsmouth, NH: Heinemann.

Clay, M. (1993) *An Observation Survey of Early Literacy Achievement*. Portsmouth, NH: Heinemann.

Cohen, D.H. and Stern, V. (1978) *Observing and Recording the Behavior of Young Children*, 2nd edn. New York: Teachers College Press.

Crossland, H. (1994) 'Screening early literacy: ideology, illusion, and intervention', *Educational Review*, 46: 47–62.

DfES (2002) 'Key Stage 1 National Curriculum assessment'. Department for Education and Skills, United Kingdom. Available at www.dfes.gov.uk, accessed 31 March.

Doake, D. (1985) 'Reading-like behavior: Its role in learning to read', in A. Jaggar and M. Trika Smith-Burke (eds), *Observing the Language Learner*. Newark, DE: International Reading Association. pp. 82–98.

Fairclough, N. (1989) *Language and Power*. London: Longman.

Farr, R. and Beck, M.D. (1991) 'Evaluating language development: formal methods of evaluation', in J. Flood, J.M., Jensen, D. Lapp and J.R. Squire (eds), *Handbook of Research on Teaching the English Language Arts*. New York: Macmillan. pp. 489–501.

Farr, R. and Carey, R.F. (1986). *Reading: What Can Be Measured?*, 2nd edn. Newark, DE: International Reading Association.

Ferreiro, E. and Teberosky, A. (1982) *Literacy Before Schooling*. Portsmouth, NH: Heinemann.

Fillmore, C.J. (1982) 'Ideal readers and real readers', in D. Tannen (ed.), *Analyzing Discourse: Text and Talk. Georgetown University Round Table on Languages and Linguistics 1981*. Washington, DC: Georgetown University Press.

Gardner, H. (1984) *The Mind's New Science*. New York: Basic.

Gentry, R. (1987). *Spel---- Is a Four-Letter Word*. Portsmouth, NH: Heinemann.

Ginsburg, H. (1997) *Entering the Child's Mind: the Clinical Interview in Psychological Research and Practice*. Cambridge: Cambridge University Press.

Giudici, C., Rinaldi, C. and Krechevsky, M. (eds) (2001) *Making Learning Visible: Children as Individual and Group Learners*. Cambridge, MA: Project Zero, Harvard Graduate School of Education.

Goodman, K.S. and Goodman, Y.M. (eds) (1980) *Linguistics, Psycholinguistics, and the Teaching of Reading: an Annotated Bibliography*. Newark, DE: International Reading Association.

Goodman, Y.M. (1978) 'Kidwatching: an alternative to testing', *National Elementary School Principal*, 57: 41–5.

Goodman, Y.M. (1991) 'Evaluating language development: informal methods of evaluation', in J. Flood, J.M. Jensen, D. Lapp and J.R. Squire (eds), *Handbook of Research on Teaching the English Language Arts*, New York: Macmillan. pp. 502–9.

Goodman, Y.M. and Altwerger, B. (1981) 'Print awareness in pre-school children. A working paper. A study of the development of literacy in preschool children'. Occasional Paper no. 4, Program in Language and Literacy, University of Arizona, Tucson.

Goodman, Y.M. and Burke, C. (1972) *Reading Miscue inventory Manual: Procedure for Diagnosis and Evaluation*. New York: Macmillan.

Goodman, Y.M., Watson, D. and Burke, C. (1987) *Reading Miscue Inventory: Alternative Procedures*. Katoneh, NY: Owen.

Grossi, E.P. (1990) 'Applying psychogenesis principles to the literacy instruction of lower-class children in Brazil', in Y.M. Goodman (ed.), *How Children Construct Literacy: Piagetian Perspectives*. Newark, DE: International Reading Association. pp. 99–114.

Hacking, I. (1990) *The Taming of Chance*. Cambridge: Cambridge University Press.

Harste, J., Woodward, V.A. and Burke, C.L. (1984) *Language Stories and Literacy Lessons*. Portsmouth, NH: Heinemann.

Hiebert, E.H. (1994) 'Authentic assessment in the classroom and beyond', in S. Valencia, E.H. Hiebert and P.P. Afflerbach (eds), *Authentic Reading Assessment: Practices and Possibilities*. Newark, DE: International Reading Association. pp. 99–102.

Hill, C. and Larsen, E. (2000) *Children and Reading Tests*. Stamford, CT: Ablex.

Himley, M. (2000) 'Descriptive inquiry: "Language as a made thing"', in M. Himley with P.F. Carini (eds), *From Another Angle: Children's Strengths and School Standards. The Prospect Center's Descriptive Review of the Child*. New York: Teachers College Press. pp. 126–34.

Hoffman, J.V., Assaf, L.C. and Paris, S.G. (2001) 'High-stakes testing in reading: today in Texas, tomorrow?', *Reading Teacher*, 54 (5): 482–92.

Holdaway, D. (1979) *The Foundations of Literacy*. Toronto: Scholastic.

International Reading Association (1999) 'High-stakes assessments in reading', *Reading Teacher*, 53 (3): 257–64.

Isaacs, S. (1966) *Intellectual Growth in Young Children*. New York: Schocken.

Johnston, P.H. and Rogers, R. (2001) 'Early literacy development: the case for "informed assessment"', in S.B. Neuman and D.K. Dickinson (eds) *Handbook of Early Literacy Development*. New York: The Guilford Press. pp. 377–89.

Jones, R. (1996) *Emerging Patterns of Literacy: a Multidisciplinary Perspective*. London: Routledge.

Kapinus, B., Collier, G.V. and Kruglanski, H. (1994) 'The Maryland school performance assessment program: a new view of the assessment', in S.W. Valencia, E.H. Hiebert and P. Afflerbach (eds), *Authentic Reading Assessment: Practices and Possibilities*. Newark, DE: International Reading Association. pp. 255–76.

Kaplan, A. (1964) *The Conduct of Inquiry: Methodology for Behavioral Sciences*. San Francisco: Chandler.

Malaguzzi, L. (1998) 'History, ideas, and basic philosophy: an interview with Lella Gandini', in C. Edwards, L. Gandini and G. Forman (eds), *The Hundred Languages of Children: the Reggio Emilia Approach. Advanced Reflections*, 2nd edn. London: Ablex. pp. 49–97.

Meek, M. (1982) *Learning To Read*. Toronto: Bodley Head.

Meek, M. (1988) *How Texts Teach What Readers Learn*. Stroud: Thimble.

Messick, S. (1985) 'The once and future issues of validity: assessing the meaning and consequences of measurement', in H. Wainer and H.I. Braun (eds), *Test Validity*. Hillsdale, NJ: Erlbaum. pp. 33–45.

Miesels, S.J. and Piker, R.A. (2001) 'An analysis of early literacy assessments used for instruction'. University of Michigan School of Education, Center for the Improvement of Early Reading Achievement, Ann Arbor. Available at www.ciera.org.

Morphett, M.V. and Washburne, C. (1983) 'When should children begin to read?', in L.M. Gentile, M.L. Kamil and J.S. Blanchard (eds), *Reading Research Revisited*. Colombus, OH: Merrill. pp. 163–9. (Reprinted from *The Elementary School Journal*, 1931, pp. 496–503).

Murphy, S. (1997) 'Literacy assessment and the politics of identities', *Reading and Writing Quarterly*, 13: 261–78.

Murphy, S. (1999) 'The validity and reliability of miscue analysis', in A. Marek and C. Edelsky (eds), *Reflections and Connections: Essays on the Influence of Kenneth S. Goodman*. New York: Hampden. pp. 95–122.

Murphy, S. (2001) ' "No one has ever grown taller as a result of being measured" revisited: more educational measurement lessons for Canadians', in J.P. Portelli and P. Solomon (eds), *The Erosion of the Democracy in Education: Critique to Possibilities*. Calgary, AB: Detselig/Temeron. pp. 145–67.

Murphy, S. with Shannon, P., Johnston, P. and Hansen, J. (1998) *Fragile Evidence: a Critique of Reading Assessment*. Mahwah, NJ: Erlbaum.

Nelson, K. (1985) *Making Sense: the Acquisition of Shared Meaning*. New York: Academic.

Paris, S.G., Paris, A.H. and Carpenter, R.D. (2001) 'Effective practices for assessing young readers'. Report 3-013, University of Michigan School of Education, Center for the Improvement of Early Reading Achievement. Ann Arbor. Available at www.ciera.org.

Pontecorvo, C. and Zucchermaglio, C. (1990) 'A passage to literacy: learning in a social context', in Y.M. Goodman (ed.), *How Children Construct Literacy: Piagetian Perspectives*. Newark, DE: International Reading Association. pp. 59–98.

Rhodes, L.K. (ed.) (1993) *Literacy Assessment: a Handbook of Instruments*. Portsmouth, NH: Heinemann.

Rinaldi, C. (1998) 'Projected curriculum constructed through documentation. *Progettazione*: an interview with Letta Gandini', in C. Edwards, L. Gandini and G. Forman (eds), *The Hundred Languages of Children: the Reggio Emilia Approach. Advanced Reflections*. London: Ablex. 2nd edn. pp. 113–35.

Rosen, C. and Rosen, H. (1973) *The Language of Primary School Children*. Harmondsworth: Penguin.

Sacks, P. (1999) *Standardized Minds: the High Price of America's Testing Culture and What We Can Do To Change It*. Cambridge, MA: Perseus.

Searle, D. and Stevenson, M. (1987) 'An alternative assessment program in language arts', *Language Arts*, 64 (3): 278–84.

Seefeldt, C. (1980) *Teaching Young Children*. Englewood Cliffs, NJ: Prentice Hall.

Simpson, P. (1993) *Language, Ideology and Point of View*. London: Routledge.

Stallman, A.C. and Pearson, P.D. (1990) 'Formal measures of early literacy', in L.M. Morrow and J.K. Smith (eds), *Assessment for Instruction in Early Literacy*. Englewood Cliffs, NJ: Prentice Hall. pp. 7–44.

Sulzby, E. (1985) 'Children's emergent reading of favorite storybooks: a developmental study', *Reading Research Quarterly*, 20: 458–81.

Teale, W.H. and Sulzby, E. (eds) (1986) *Emergent Literacy: Writing and Reading*. Norwood, NJ: Ablex.

Tolchinsky Landsman, L. (1990) 'Literacy development and pedagogical implications: evidence from the Hebrew system of writing', in Y.M. Goodman (ed.), *How Children Construct Literacy: Piagetian Perspectives*. Newark, DE: International Reading Association. pp. 26–44.

Vygotsky, L. (1978) *Mind in Society*, eds M. Cole, V. John-Steiner, S. Scribner and E. Souberman. Cambridge, MA: Harvard University Press.

Watrous, B.G. and Willett, J. (1994) 'Assessing students as members of a literate community', in K. Holland, D. Bloome and J. Solsken (eds), *Alternative Perspectives in Assessing Children's Language and Literacy*. Norwood, NJ: Ablex. pp. 73–88.

Willinsky, J. (1990) *The New Literacy: Redefining Reading and Writing in the Schools*. New York: Routledge.

Willis, A.I. (1991) 'Panorama: a narrative history of standardized elementary reading comprehension test development and reading test authors in the United States, 1914–1919. Volumes I and II', *Dissertation Abstracts International*, 51 (10): 3374–A.

Part V

RESEARCHING EARLY CHILDHOOD LITERACY

31

Methodologies in Research on Young Children and Literacy

DAVID BLOOME AND LAURIE KATZ

Typically, discussions of research methodologies begin either with a philosophical distinction between empirical and phenomenological approaches or with a distinction among quantitative, qualitative, and other approaches. Useful methodological discussions of literacy research employing these typical categories can be found in Kamil et al. (2000) and Flood et al. (2003), among others. More recently, there have been a small number of discussions of research methodologies that have focused on what Gee and Green (1998) have called 'logic-of-inquiry' that eschews the binary distinctions typically used to categorize research methodologies. In brief, they call for attention to what methodological warrants are provided by the theoretical constructs that frame the study and how the methodology articulates theoretical constructs.

In this chapter, we take a different approach to exploring research methodologies. We are interested in the underlying chronotopes of research studies of young children and literacy. By 'chronotope', we are referring to an implied ideology about how people move through time and space. Every research study has an implied chronotope expressed through its methodology.

We have borrowed the term 'chronotope' from literary theory, and specifically from Bakhtin (1981). Bahktin describes a chronotope as follows:

We will give the name *chronotope* (literally, 'time space') to the intrinsic connectedness of temporal and spatial relationships that are artistically expressed in literature ... [chronotope] expresses the inseparability of space and time ... In the literary artistic chronotope, spatial and temporal indicators are fused into one carefully

thought-out, concrete whole. Time, as it were, thickens, takes on flesh, becomes artistically visible; likewise, space becomes charged and responsive to the movements of time, plot, and history ... it is precisely the chronotope that defines genre and generic distinctions ... The chronotope as a formally constitutive category determines to a significant degree the image of man [*sic*] in literature as well. The image of man [*sic*] is always intrinsically chronotopic. (1981: 84–5)

Bakhtin analyses chronotopes in various literary periods, showing how time and space are differently conceptualized and how the chronotope frames character development, plot, and meaning. For example, Bakhtin analyses the chronotope of Greek romances. In brief, the hero and heroine meet, fall in love, but are separated by events and have to go through a series of adventures and overcome obstacles to rejoin each other and marry. In this 'adventure-time', although the hero and heroine may spend time in the adventure and travel different places,

it is simply days, nights, hours, moments clocked in a technical sense within the limits of each separate adventure. This time – adventure-time, highly intensified but undifferentiated – is not registered in the slightest way in the age of the heroes. In this kind of time, nothing changes: the world remains as it was, the biographical life of the heroes does not change, their feelings do not change, people do not even age. (1981: 90–1)

Bakhtin's analysis of the chronotope of the Greek romance highlights the power of a chronotope to frame human agency and the relationship of the individual to the world in which she or he lives:

All moments of this infinite adventure-time are controlled by one force – chance ... In this time, persons are forever having things happen to them (they might even 'happen' to win a kingdom) ... But the initiative in this time does not belong to human beings.... In [adventure-time] there is no potential for evolution, for growth, for change. As a result of the action described in the novel, nothing in its world is destroyed, remade, changed or created anew. What we get is a mere affirmation of the identity between what had been at the beginning and what is at the end. Adventure-time leaves no trace. (Bahktin, 1981: 95–110).

Every methodology expresses a chronotope (although not necessarily 'adventure-time'). Regardless of whether the researcher is aware of the chronotope or not, the chronotope is a powerful rhetoric influencing how researchers and consumers of research conceptualize young children and literacy. The chronotope becomes all the more powerful when it is taken for granted, invisible, and unexamined.

In order to reveal underlying chronotopes, it is necessary to first examine the methodological grammars of research studies. By methodological grammar we are referring to the components of a research study and their structural relationship (syntax) to each other. What we call methodological grammar might also be called research models.

It is important to make a distinction between methodological grammar and the theory–method connection given and described in a research study. Although a researcher may explain the theoretical and ideological grounding of their research methods, such an explanation by itself does not describe the components of a research study or their syntax or the underlying chronotope. No more so than an author's explanation of his/her intent constitutes a satisfactory explanation of the components and structure of the artistic work, its implicit chronotope, or its rhetorical effect. One must examine the methodology *in use*.

Given the above framing of the analysis of research methodologies, we ask what are the methodological grammars and chronotopes implicit in research methodologies with regard to children and literacy. More specifically, we hold that research methodologies in the human sciences are necessarily arguments, explicitly or implicitly, about what can be known about the nature of human beings in the world. Research methodologies are arguments about what counts as knowledge about people, language (including literacy), and about where people are located in space and time. The methodologies used in research on young children and literacy constitute arguments about the nature of children: what can be known about children, the language (spoken and written) they use, where they

are, where they have been and where they are going (their histories). We use these three dimensions (the nature of children, the nature of language/literacy, and locations) as heuristics to organize this chapter. We note that it is often difficult to separate out these dimensions from each other. For example, it is difficult to discuss the nature of children without also discussing their locations. Nonetheless, we view the three dimensions as useful heuristics because they provide a means for discussing underlying methodological chronotopes.

It may be helpful to note some distinctions we make in the terminology we use in this chapter. We make a distinction between methodology and method. A method is a strategy or technique used within a research study; for example, one might use several different methods for collecting data. Methodological grammar refers to the design components of a research study and the relationship of the components to each other and to the goal of the study. It also refers to the set of manifest theoretical assumptions that warrant the components and their syntax. Manifest assumptions may be articulated by the researchers or the manifest assumptions may be implied or tacit. As noted earlier, we use the term 'methodological grammar' similarly to the way that some use the term 'research model'. For us, methodology refers to methodological grammar and methods taken together. We should also note that we take it as given that attention to the underlying chronotopes of research methodologies is only a partial examination of the ideological foundations of research. Attention is also needed to epistemological assumptions and to the historical evolution of research methodologies, and we earlier noted useful citations for such efforts.

THE NATURE OF CHILDREN

Methodologies for research on children and literacy vary in their assumptions about children. What can be known about children depends on how 'child' is conceptualized, the personhood assigned to the category 'child'. Personhood refers to the notion of the 'person' as an ideological field within a society (Kirkpatrick, 1983; Geertz, 1966; 1973), including the attributes that are viewed as defining the 'person', either explicitly or implicitly (cf. Gergen and Davis, 1985; Shweder and Miller, 1985). Researchers construct the personhood of children through their tacit assignment of attributes to the children in their research studies.

For example, consider the methodology shown in Figure 31.1 which we label the 'child attribute improvement methodology'. The child is conceived

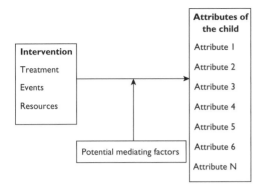

Figure 31.1 Child attribute improvement methodology

as having a series of attributes which are potentially affected by a particular treatment or set of events. The attributes may be age, gender, language competency, intelligence, socio-economic status, family membership, literacy skills (e.g. vocabulary, phonemic awareness, fluency, comprehension etc.). The purpose of the intervention is to examine the effect on one or more of the attributes that define the child. The attributes may be measured by tests or predetermined criteria, the intervention may be simple or complex, and the relationship between the child attributes and the intervention may be viewed as mediated by other factors or not. Regardless, the unit of analysis is the child and particular attributes assigned to the personhood of child.

A study by Lonigan and Whitehurst (1998) of the effects of reading to children provides an illustration of 'child attribute improvement methodology'. They define the child as having the following attributes: age, socio-economic status, home language, gender, race, and language/literacy skills. The children were exposed to a series of events (various formulations of reading to the children) to examine the effect on the child's language/literacy skills. The chronotope underlying the methodology of the study is that as the child moves through time and space, the events change the person/child by increasing (or failing to increase) the person's/child's language/literacy skills. At issue here is not the specific findings or the relationship between methods and findings, but the underlying chronotope. For example, alternative findings are provided in a study by Sénéchal et al. (1998). They found that storybook reading at home was related to the child's oral language skills but not written language skills (which were influenced by parent teaching). Nonetheless, the methodological grammar and underlying chronotope are the same.

In brief, although one could examine and debate the adequacy of the measures of the specified child attributes and the nature and accuracy of the descriptions of the events they experienced, regardless of the measurements used, part of the meaningfulness of a study or a set of studies conducted in the field is in their underlying chronotope, in how it promulgates a conception of children moving through time and space and in how the chronotope defines change. In those studies involving a 'child attribute improvement methodology' each child is conceived of as an individual unit (the children may have collective experiences but the underlying chronotope conceptualizes each child as experiencing the journey as if in isolation from others). The child experiences events (that is, things happen to the child, he/she does not create the events or fundamentally change the events),[1] and each child either increases or fails to increase the attribute of language/literacy skills considered in isolation of potential changes in other attributes, people, events, social relationships etc. It is a type of 'adventure-time' in which the protagonist (the child) goes on a journey (at school and at home) and experiences a series of adventures (reading to child events) which, depending on the nature of the adventure, may increase his/her wealth (language/literacy skills).

Such a chronotope can be found in numerous other studies. They may vary in the attributes assigned to the child, in the change in attributes (increase/decrease), in the events the child experiences, and in the factors that mediate the relationship between the child and the events experienced. Regardless, the underlying grammar of the chronotope is one in which children are conceptualized as individual units, events are experienced, and change in attribute involves an increase or decrease. Analysis of studies employing methodological chronotopes such as the 'child attribute improvement methodology' needs to be concerned with (1) the attributes defining personhood, (2) the dimensionalization of one or more of those attributes along a quantitative scale (e.g. increase/decrease), (3) the nature of the events experienced, but also (4) the assumption of the directionality and relative isolation of event effects on attributes.

A variation of the 'child attribute improvement methodology' is shown in Figure 31.2 which we label the 'complex event–attribute improvement methodology'. Studies that employ this methodology view attributes as influenced by multiple types of events rather than by a single type of event, and view changes in one attribute or set of attributes as influencing the child's behaviour in key events which then influences other attributes of the child. In brief, there is a complex and interactive view of the influence of events on attributes. For example,

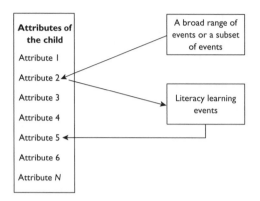

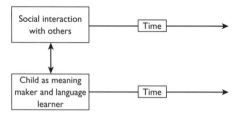

Figure 31.3   Child as meaning maker
and language learner methodologies

Figure 31.2   Complex event-attribute
improvement methodology

in a study by Bus et al. (1997), young children's
literacy skills were viewed as influenced indirectly
by their affective relationships with their parents. In
brief, a broad range of interactions with their
parents were viewed as influencing children's
attachment security which was viewed as influencing children's literacy behaviours (their eagerness
to explore books) which was viewed as influencing
their literacy skills. Unlike the 'child attribute
improvement methodology', the conception of the
child in 'complex event–attribute improvement
methodology' is one in which the child acts on
events in a way that defines the nature of events, at
least in part. Both children and events are malleable. Thus, the 'complex event–attribute improvement methodology' promulgates a substantially
different chronotope than the 'child attribute
improvement methodology' in which the events
were given and experienced.

A different chronotope underlies what we call
'child as meaning maker and language learner
methodologies'. Studies by Wells (1981), Goodman
and Wilde (1992), and Dyson (1989; 1997), for
example, begin with a definition of the child as a
meaning maker and language learner and then ask
what processes influence that meaning making
and language learning. By defining the child as a
meaning maker and language learner such studies
warrant a different methodological grammar and
establish a different chronotope than the methodologies discussed earlier. The child is seen as
actively engaging in a journey through many different events (typically defined as social interaction)
which are influenced by the child's efforts and
which reciprocally influence the child. At issue in
such studies is better understanding of the nature of
the child as a meaning maker and language learner
(by closely examining what the child does with

language over time) and how the events in which
the child participates affects the child's language
learning (by closely examining how the child
responds to what is happening) (see Figure 31.3).

For example, consider Dyson's (1989; 1997)
studies of young children. She begins by defining
children as meaning makers who use a broad range
of semiotic tools. Then, through careful observation
of children in interaction with each other, their
teachers, and others, over time and across a broad
range of classroom situations (including journal
writing, dramatic play, instructional conversations,
free play etc.) and non-classroom situations, she
asks what must constitute language learning and
what must constitute the nature of social events
given her observations and analysis of the events,
texts and other artifacts created by the child in
social interaction with others.

The underlying chronotope in 'child as meaning
maker and language learner methodology' studies
eschews defining the child in terms of a series of
attributes, but rather defines the child organically
(as a language learner) who changes as he/she journeys through numerous events which she/he helps
create. As the child evolves (through social interaction) the journey evolves.

Part of the rhetorical aspect of this chronotope
lies in contrasting the conceptions of children, their
personhood with conceptions of children promulgated by some other chronotope. For example, in
some research studies some children may be viewed
as inherently deficit with regard to literacy because
of their cultural background (their cultural background may be described as impoverished, as having
primarily an oral tradition, lacking formal education,
or otherwise alliterate or illiterate). Such a conception of children redefines language learning and
meaning making as attributes rather than as a definition of a child. Thus, at issue is not just a conception of the child as a facile and proficient meaning
maker and language learner versus a conception
of the child as a deficient meaning maker and
language learner, but a conflict between underlying
methodological grammars and chronotopes. One

cannot simultaneously hold a view of children (all children) as inherent language learners and meaning makers and a view of children as having varying degrees of those attributes. At issue then in studies employing a 'child as meaning maker and language learner methodology' is the validity of the conception of the child as meaning maker and language learner. Goodman and Wilde (1992) provide an illustration. In their study, they document how children from the Tohono O'odham community manifest the same underlying meaning making and language learning processes as children from middle-class Anglo communities. Thus, the rhetorical aspect of their research is not only to illuminate the nature of literacy learning in classrooms over time but to validate the conception of all children as meaning makers and language learners with regard to literacy learning. In brief, to the extent that methodological grammars are warranted by particular conceptions of personhood, studies such as Goodman and Wilde's, Dyson's, and Wells' call into question the validity of particular methodological grammars because the definitions of personhood that warrant them are not valid.

LANGUAGE/LITERACY
USED BY CHILDREN

The methodologies discussed above begin with a definition of the child, its personhood; and the grammar of the research methodologies follows from that definition. The studies discussed in this section, in terms of methodological grammar, begin with a definition of literacy. Definitions of literacy can be categorized as autonomous models or ideological models (cf. Street, 1984; 1995). An autonomous model assumes that literacy consists of a distinct set of skills or cognitive processes that are relatively stable across situations, and social and cultural contexts. An ideological model assumes that literacy is inherently multiple (literacies) and consists of social, cultural, political, economic, and psychological processes that vary across situations. How literacy is manifested in any particular situation depends largely on shared cultural norms (the cultural ideology) for the use of written language for such situations.

Autonomous models of literacy
and methodology

The underlying methodological grammar of research grounded in autonomous models of literacy begins with a definition of reading or writing, and then asks what factors facilitate the reader's enactment of that definition. There are two sets of related studies. The first is concerned with what processes constitute reading or writing. The second set of studies concerns what classroom and environmental factors facilitate the enactment of the definition of reading or writing.

With regard to the first set of studies – what cognitive and linguistic processes constitute reading and writing – the methodological grammar involves the parsing of reading or writing (see Figure 31.4). For example, Cunningham et al. (1999) parse silent reading comprehension into a series of underlying skills in order to develop an assessment of reading. They sought to validate the set of underlying cognitive and linguistic skills through their association with various reading tasks.

Another approach to researching the cognitive and linguistic processes defining reading has been the manipulation of text factors (see Figure 31.5). By manipulating a text and carefully examining the responses of a reader, inferences can be made about the cognitive and linguistic processes that are assumed to have been present. For example, Calhoun and Leslie (2002) investigated the influence of word frequency and rime neighbourhood size on young children's ability to read target words embedded in a story the children read aloud. They studied the effect on children over time (over three years) as a way to explore the effect of texts on the process of learning to read defined as the acquisition of the reading skills that comprise reading.

As shown in Figure 31.5, the relationship between the text and the cognitive processes involved in reading and writing may be mediated by a series of factors including individual differences in children, their background experiences, among others. For example, Cox et al. (1997) examined the effect of producing a text under two conditions (one associated with writing, the other associated with reading) on four- and five-year-old children who varied in their development as readers and writers in order to assess their ability to code-switch into a literate register. They defined a literate register as one involving particular types of textual cohesion associated with conventional reading and writing. Their interest was in the mediating effect of income level and level of each child's development as an emergent reader/writer on the cognitive and linguistic processes employed. They claimed that the effects of the various mediating factors were evidence of particular kinds of cognitive and linguistic processing.

For the purposes of this chapter, debates among researchers over which cognitive and linguistic processes constitute reading or writing are not pertinent. Rather, we are concerned with the underlying chronotope of the methodology regardless of the researcher's advocacy for one set of cognitive

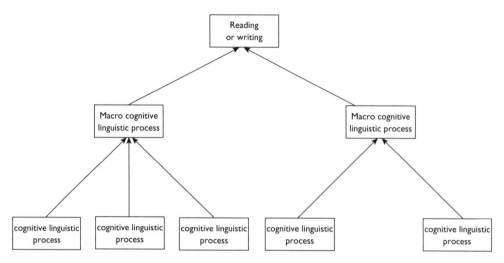

Figure 31.4 Literacy as a set of autonomous cognitive and linguistic processes methodologies

and linguistic processes over another. For those researchers who equate the identification of the cognitive and linguistic processes that constitute reading or writing with the process of learning to read or write,[2] the underlying chronotope of 'literacy as a set of autonomous cognitive and linguistic processes methodologies' is a journey of acquisition of those skills and processes.

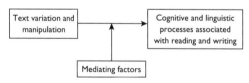

Figure 31.5 Text manipulation methodologies

The second set of studies related to an autonomous model of literacy has primarily been concerned with what classroom and environmental factors facilitate enactment of a given model of reading (with such enactments counting as learning to read). From a methodological perspective, there are three types of studies: input–output studies, process–product studies, and process–process studies. The labelling of these three types of studies derives from Dunkin and Biddle's (1974) classic review of research on the study of teaching. After noting the lack of systematicity and rigour in studies of teaching, they identified three sets of factors considered in classroom research: presage (or input) factors, process (or classroom) factors, and product (or output) factors. They then characterized studies based

on whether they examined the relationship between input and output factors (presage–product studies), process and product factors (what influence did what happened in the classroom have on outcomes), or process and other process factors (what influence did one aspect of the classroom have on other aspects of the classroom) (see Figure 31.6).

Input–output studies examine the consequences of factors such as child background, family income, child age, teacher education, gender, amount of money spent by a district per child, instructional programme, among other givens, on outcome measures such as reading test scores, number of words read during recreational reading, teacher evaluation of student reading, reading strategy assessment. Input–output studies are often described as 'horse race' studies as they explicitly or implicitly pit two or more literacy programmes against each other as a means to determine which is better for children. They are also referred to as 'black box' studies because attention is not paid to how the input factors are manifested in the classroom: only the outcomes are of concern. The underlying chronotope, not surprisingly, is that of a competition between literacy programmes racing through an opaque space (see Figure 31.7).

An example of an input–output study is Santa and Høien's (1999) study of the effects of an early intervention programme called Early Steps. Santa and Høien compared the achievement of first-grade children who participated in the programme with children who did not (who participated in no programme). The children who participated in the programme did better, especially those children who were at risk for reading failure.

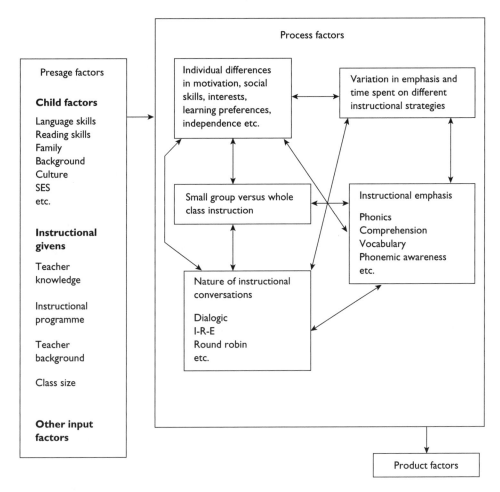

Figure 31.6   Process–process studies

One of the weaknesses associated with input–output studies is that they lack explanatory power. One may know which instructional programme (or other input variable) was associated with improved reading or writing achievement, but how it 'won the race' remains speculation. For example, Santa and Høien describe the theory behind the early intervention programme and its given components. Although they suggest that the achievement gains are the result of enactment of the theoretical constructs that guided the programme and the design of the components, there are no direct data about the enactment of the programme, nor did the methodological grammar allow for identification and examination of complexities and confounding factors.

Perhaps the most famous of the input–output studies of young children and reading instruction

were the 'first-grade studies' (see Bond and Dykstra, 1964). The first–grade studies were conducted in the early 1960s and involved 17 research studies across the United States. Although each study

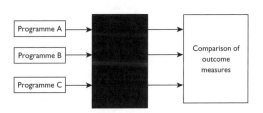

Figure 31.7   Input–output horse race studies

collected some similar data to allow comparison across sites, the studies also varied depending on their goals. For example, some studies compared the use of a basal reading series with the use of a basal reading series supplemented by additional phonics instruction. Another compared the effects of a language experience instructional method with a basal reading instructional method. Another examined the consequences of amount and nature of teacher education on reading achievement. Although almost all of the studies found that their favoured instructional method produced better results, analysis conducted by Bond and Dykstra (1964) across the studies noted that instructional method *per se* was not related to outcome measures; rather, the quality of the teacher was. The findings reported by Bond and Dykstra have led to the decline (and derision[3]) of 'horse race' studies of instructional programmes and methods. In brief, the methodological grammar of input–output studies is viewed as not providing sufficient explanatory power, not having a concern for effects (often any change results in improved achievement), researcher and not educator bias, and the complexity of mediating factors, and not defining instructional programmes and methods in terms of how they are implemented rather than in terms of how they are given. Nonetheless, the methodological grammar of input–output studies is a powerful rhetoric and thus input–output studies continue to be conducted.

Process–product studies examine the relationship of various classroom processes to outcome measures such as reading achievement test scores. Classroom processes include such variables as academic engaged time, instructional strategies, teacher–student interaction, classroom organization, and classroom management, among others. Such factors, either alone or in combination, are correlated with outcome measures. For example, Dahl et al. (1999) examined phonics instruction in whole language classrooms, identifying what occurred and where it occurred (in which instructional activities), and correlated the reading achievement gains for three groups of students differentiated by their knowledge of phonics during pre-testing.

One aspect that differentiates the Dahl et al. study from many process–product studies is that the Dahl et al. study did not assume the existence of the process variable it sought to relate to product outcomes. That is, typically process–product studies begin with an assumption of a process variable and measure its occurrence which is then related to an outcome. Such studies avoid asking whether the classroom process variable identified is more than a speculation or a construction of the researcher, whether it has grounding in actual classroom

dynamics. Without grounding it is difficult to assess the construct validity of process variables.

Studies can be designed to include both an input–output component and a process–product component. For example, Leslie and Allen (1999) examined the difference in achievement for inner city children between those who attended an early literacy intervention project and those who did not; and, they also examined the relationship between classroom factors such as type of instruction received, number of times taught, number of core words taught, and reading achievement. Another example of a combined input–output and process–product study is Neuman's (1999) study of the impact of 'flooding books' into childcare centres. The input variables were the books provided (as a quantity), teacher training in the use of storybooks, and the children's initial literacy level. Process variables included the physical environment of the classroom, teacher–child interactions, amount of storybook reading activity, access to books, and time spent in reading. Outcome measures of reading and literacy development were linked to classroom processes (access to books, storybook reading aloud activities) as well as to input variables (the provision of books and teacher training)

The complexity of classrooms, the large number of potential factors that mediate reading and writing achievement, and the interaction of variables with each other, argue for methodological grammars that are more complex than input–output and process–product 'horse race' studies. Process–process methodologies focus attention on how various classroom processes influence each other.

For example, Juel and Minden-Cupp (2000) studied four classrooms to examine which of the complexities of the classroom influenced which instructional strategies with regard to their success for which students. Among the factors they examined were reading ability level of the child, instructional practices and the distribution of instructional strategies within the classroom (e.g. how much emphasis on vocabulary instruction versus phonemic awareness versus comprehension instruction), teacher modification and use of the instructional practices, and types of texts. At issue were how these variables influenced each other with regard to providing increased reading achievement for children.

Although input–output, process–product, and process–process studies typically refer to studies of classrooms and achievement, the methodological grammar can be applied outside the classroom. For example, Bergin (2001) studied the relationship of quality of parent–child reading (which they quantified) to reading outcome measures (including affective and behavioural dimensions, which were also quantified). The chronotope underlying studies such as Bergin's is similar to that of the input–output, process–product, and process–process studies of classroom reading and writing instruction: that of a race toward a goal – which programme, condition, treatment, or set of variables provides the greatest gain. The race is not between children but among input and process variables.

At issue in input–output, process–product, and process–process studies, whether conducted in classrooms or in families, is how the chronotope defines those factors and events that influence the enactment of a given reading model. First, there is the issue of quantification. The quantification itself is a definition of the variable, as is the isolation of the variable required in order to quantify it. That is, in order to count a phenomenon, it has to have borders to make it countable. Assigning borders makes a phenomenon a discrete entity (even if only for heuristic purposes) and involves the linguistic process of nominalization. Nominalization refers to the process of transforming verbs (actions and states of being) into nouns (cf. Fairclough, 1992). For example, in the Bergin study, for heuristic purposes the quality of parent–child reading is quantified by separating out nine affective variables and quantifying them. Reading, emotion, and learning are transformed from verbs (actions people take with and toward each other) into discrete and isolatable nouns. A second issue concerns the complexity of how classroom (or non-classroom) reading and writing events evolve over time. The methodological grammar of input–output, process–product, and process–process studies requires reducing complexity and codifying change in events. Similarly, the evolution of a reading practice over time, the importance of a single event, and the particularities of a specific event are *non sequiturs* given the methodological grammar. For example, in the Bergin study, parent–child reading is defined in terms of the 'race' toward fluency in reading and a good attitude toward reading. The value and meaning of the activity of parent–child reading in and of themselves are *non sequiturs* in such studies; so too are the goals that the parent and child themselves may have had for engaging in parent–child reading events (e.g. to share a cultural history, to relax before bedtime, to snuggle).[4] Similarly so, in the studies by Dahl et al., Juel and Minden-Cupp, Neuman, Leslie and Allen, the first-grade studies, among other input–output, process–product, and process–process classroom studies, the underlying chronotope defines the purpose of classroom reading (or writing) instruction as reading achievement (winning the race). Such a monolithic definition of classroom events obviates purposes of classroom education associated with

the hidden curriculum, enculturation, stability and change in societal structures, language socialization, the development of social competence, social and cultural identity, as well as the meaning of classroom events within themselves (for example, the importance of a literary experience within a classroom event as meaningful in its own right and not just for development of some future academic literacy skill).

Ideological models of literacy and methodology

With regard to reading, Luke explains an ideological model:

> there are no universal 'skills' of reading. Reading is a social practice, comprised of interpretive rules and events constructed and learned in institutions like schools and churches, families and work places. Implicit in ways of teaching reading are social theories – models of the social order, social power, and social change; models of the institutional everyday life; models of worker/employee relations; and ultimately models of how the literate worker and citizen should look and be. Simply put, reading instruction has always described and prescribed forms of life: of how Dick, Jane, and Spot should be and act as citizens and readers, and indeed of how migrants and workers, women and men, should be and act as citizens and readers. (1995: 97)

Luke's quotation emphasizes the diversity of literacy practices, their connection to social institutions, and their use as an agent of social, cultural, and political socialization. As such, the methodological grammar of one set of studies of literacy practices has been to identify and describe a set of literacy practices, their connections to the social institutions from which they emanate, and the ways in which they foster particular configurations of culture, social relations, social identity, and power relations (see Figure 31.8).

Luke's (1988) study of reading textbooks in Canadian primary schools is one illustration. Through analysis of the texts and through analysis of historical and political documents, Luke is able to identify the reading practices promulgated by the textbooks and the political, social, and cultural processes that produced this particular set of literacy practices. Duranti and Ochs (1986) examined the instructional practices and classroom events in a Samoan village school in order to investigate the potential impact of literacy instruction on Samoan culture. They describe how the ways in which reading was taught promulgated certain Western values, ways of thinking, and social relationships, which contrasted with those of traditional Samoan village

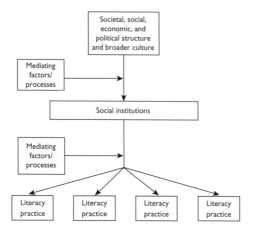

Figure 31.8 Literacy practices as social practices of social institutions and community cultures methodological grammar

Figure 31.9 Adopting and adapting literacy practices methodologies

culture. Duranti and Ochs emphasize that there is no separation between a reading practice and how it is used. The methodological implication is that literacy practices need to be studied in their use. Fishman (1988) provides another illustration. She was able to identify and describe a set of literacy practices across various social institutions (e.g. family, school) within an Amish community, showing how those literacy practices reflected cultural themes in Amish life. Although the methodological grammar of Luke's, Duranti and Ochs', and Fishman's study are similar,[5] there are key differences. Luke describes how literacy practices are employed to enhance state control; Duranti and Ochs describe how literacy practices carry values, culturally specific ways of thinking, and social relationships, while Fishman describes how literacy practices are employed to express a culture.

It is important to note that the relationship between the social, economic, and political structure of a society, its social institutions, and its literacy practices, may be mediated by a series of factors. For example, people may resist the imposition of a particular set of literacy practices because they are associated with the imposition of a dominant culture or social hierarchy (cf. Ogbu and Simons, 1998). For example, Manyak (2001) researched a first- and second-grade immersion English classroom in the United States in a state that had enacted laws that mandated language and literacy instruction and development only in English. Over time, the students and teacher resisted the limitation to English only and engaged in the daily classroom literacy practice of the 'daily news' in both English and Spanish.

The underlying chronotope of 'literacy practices as social practices of social institutions and community cultures methodological grammar' posits the child as moving through various adventures that define the child and define the child's relationship with others and with the world in which he/she lives. The adventures do not change (although they may be resisted). As the child moves through formal and informal instruction in the literacy practices of the social institutions of her/his society, the child is defined and positioned within society.

Street (1993) provides a series of case studies of literacy practices in a broad range of cultures across the world that suggest a different methodological grammar than that discussed above. The case studies describe literacy practices in situations where there is contact between two cultures or social institutions and there are differential power relations between them (one may be attempting to impose its culture and social structure on the other either directly or tacitly). Rather than starting with the dominating culture and its social institutions and examining the production of literacy practices, the case studies in Street (1993) begin with the literacy practices of people's everyday lives and examine how these literacy practices reflect a relationship with dominant social institutions, how people adapt the literacy

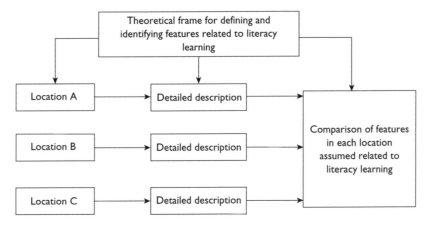

Figure 31.10   Comparative location methodologies

practices of the dominant social institutions to their own needs and way of life, and how people produce literacy practices that eschew dominant social institutions (see Figure 31.9).

With regard to studies of young children and literacy, Heath (1983) documents literacy practices in three communities and describes how differences in those literacy practices create boundaries and obstacles for some of the children and families in classrooms. Taylor (1983) and Taylor and Dorsey-Gaines (1988) provide a series of case studies of literacy practices in families that document family literacy practices and their use to establish social relationships among family members and between the family and other social institutions, such as the school. Similarly, although primarily focusing on the child as a meaning maker and language learner, Dyson (1997; 1999) provides an illustration of the adaptation of literacy practices. The children she studied adapted aspects of popular culture into their writing; they used available cultural tools for their own purposes. At issue in the studies by Heath, Taylor, Taylor and Dorsey-Gaines and Dyson is not just documentation of a range of literacy practices, but rather the social, cultural, economic, and political relationships among social institutions (such as family, school, pop culture, and mass media) grounded in assumptions about what literacy practices mean about who people are (see also Gee, 1996, for a discussion of literacy practices and identity).

The chronotope underlying 'adopting and adapting literacy practices methodologies' involves a protagonist (as an individual or a collective) creatively acting on the adventures in which she/he finds herself/himself, the way forward being based on the consequences of his/her creativity and on how others respond to that creativity.

LOCATIONS OF CHILDREN

In a sense, even if unacknowledged, every methodology locates the child and the use of written language somewhere: in a classroom, a family, a research laboratory etc. However, at issue here are research methodologies whose grammar explicitly foregrounds the location of children and their use of written language as a definition of children and literacy.

One set of location studies has a methodological grammar and underlying chronotope similar to that of the 'horse race' studies discussed earlier. Two or more locations are described in detail and then compared in order to suggest that one will facilitate literacy learning better than the other. For convenience, we label studies that employ such a methodological grammar 'comparative location methodologies' (see Figure 31.10).

For example, Pickett (1998) investigated what occurred in the block area of a first-grade classroom with a special focus on literacy related activities. During one week the block area was 'unenriched', during the second week the block area was 'enriched' with literacy related materials, and during the third week an adult interacted with the students in the enriched block area. Pickett's observations were that the enriched block area produced more behaviours viewed as consistent with literacy learning than the unenriched and that the condition with the adult produced an even greater amount. The methodological grammar, as illustrated by Pickett's study, identifies literacy features in each location based on a given theoretical frame and then compares the locations based on the identified features, again using the given theoretical frame. The methodological grammar positions the

Child and use of written language as part
of a situation of
social relations and structures,
cultural dynamics,
material conditions,
social interaction,
institutional dynamics,
discourse processes,
particularities,
political and economic dynamics and
structures etc.

Figure 31.11   Freeze frame situated
methodologies

theoretical frame as setting the 'standard' for what
counts as a better location for literacy learning, but
it also sets the standard for defining the locations
and what counts as occurring within those locations.

Although literacy activity is placed in a location,
studies employing a 'comparative location
methodology' differ paradigmatically from 'situated
methodologies'. 'Situated methodologies' define
people and their use of written language as part of
a *situation* (cf. Gee, 1996; 2001, for a detailed
discussion of literacy and young children as situated
social practices).[6] The situation can be a
material/physical/geographical one (such as a house
or a playground), an institutional one (such as a
classroom or a family), an event (such as a reading
instruction lesson), or some combination (see
Figure 31.11).

Unlike the chronotope of adventure-time in
which the protagonists experience a series of situations, in 'situated methodologies' there is no separation between the people and the situations within
which they act. The chronotope of 'situated
methodologies' might be compared to the examination of a painting such as Claude Monet's *La Gare
St Lazare* (1877). The painting portrays the train
station not through the presenting of endless and
undifferentiated detail, but by creating impressions
of the whole scene.[7] Although the painting simu-
lates a specific moment in the train station, it represents not a specific moment but a potential of the
situation. Further, although the situation is frozen in
time and place, the painting nonetheless suggests an
ongoing activity. That is, situated methodologies do
not necessarily document movement through space
and time, although they may acknowledge it. The

child and the use of written language can be
described as part of a situation or an event without
consideration of how that situation is related to
other previous or future situations or other locations. It is the freezing of the situation that allows
the depth of analysis and allows an examination of
the complexity and particularities of the situations
and events in which people find themselves. In
brief, the chronotope can be described as a 'freeze
frame'.

An example of a 'situated methodology' is Sipe's
(2000) study of a class of first- and second-grade
students. Although Sipe spent eight months in the
classroom and collected data over time, his analysis
created a detailed freeze frame view of the
responses and interactions the children made to the
books and stories they read. In so doing, Sipe was
able to identify three types of literary impulses and
differentiate five different types of responses and
five different types of literary understanding as a
means to reconceptualize and theorize literary
understanding as a situated process in classrooms.
That is, unlike the input–output, process–product,
and process–process methodologies described
earlier, which focused on antecedents to 'better'
reading, the grammar of the methodology employed
by Sipe focused on theorizing and defining a
phenomenon grounded in the lived experience of
young children reading literature in a classroom.
Although the grammar of the methodology does not
allow for a generalized statement about what factors
lead to increased literary understanding, the grammar
of the methodology does allow for statements about
what literary understanding may be.

Cairney and Ashton (2002) illustrate a situated
methodology that involves multiple locations.
Although superficially similar to 'comparative location methodologies' (described earlier), Cairney
and Ashton's methodology illustrates the use of
comparison to generate theoretical constructs about
the nature of literacy within and across settings; this
is conceptually the opposite of 'comparative location
methodologies', which use theoretical framing to
define and order the relative value of multiple
locations. We label the methodological grammar
underlying situated studies such as Cairney and
Ashton's 'comparative situations theory-building'
(see Figure 31.12).

The nature of the comparison involved in 'comparative situations theory-building' methodologies
involves the situation as the unit of analysis (as
opposed to distinct literacy behaviours). The comparison involves a dialectical process that results in
a theoretical description of the nature and diversity
of literacy practices as situated social phenomena.
Like the 'freeze frame situated methodologies'
described earlier, although the data collection may

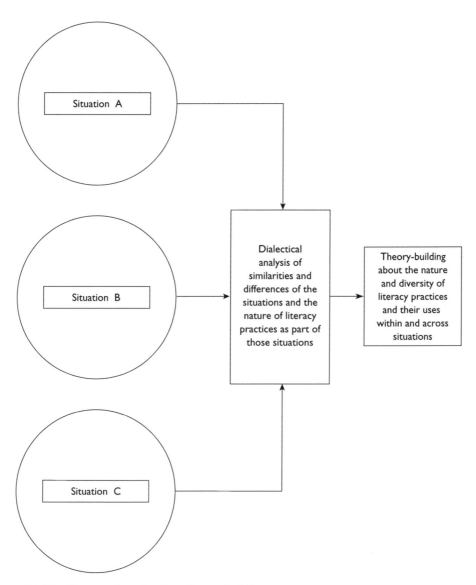

Figure 31.12   Comparative situations theory-building

have occurred over time, 'comparative situations theory-building' presents 'freeze frames' of multiple situations.

The underlying chronotope depends, in part, on each particular 'freeze frame'. That is, part of the goal of 'situated methodologies', including 'comparative situations theory-building', is to provide an emic description of the underlying chronotope of the situation(s) being studied. However, in part, the underlying chronotope of 'situated methodologies' depends on how the study is located. For example,

Cairney and Ashton locate their study of literacy practices in families and schools within a broader discussion of the relationship of schools and families. As children move back and forth across these two social institutions their participation in one may affect their participation in another and, in some cases, with negative consequences. This, then, is the underlying chronotope: the movement of children across locations where they variously experience events based in part on their participation in other social and institutional locations.

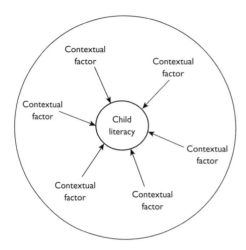

Figure 31.13 Contextualization methodologies

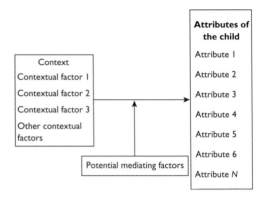

Figure 31.14 Alternative representation of contextualization methodologies

It is important to note that a situated methodology is not the same as a methodology whose grammar highlights the contextualization of people engaged in using written language. Such a methodology defines context as a series of factors that influence the process of a child's use of written language (see Figure 31.13).

'Contextualization methodologies' have a chronotope that is similar to 'child attribute improvement methodologies' discussed earlier, in which the child experiences an event or series of events (the intervention) which increases or decreases an attribute assigned to the child. In 'contextualization methodologies', the child experiences the context (taken either as a set of discrete though naturally occurring factors, or as a complex and inseparable set of factors) which influences (increases or decreases) an attribute of the child (such as the child's ability to read or the child's literacy skills). Thus, it may be more accurate to represent 'contextualization methodologies' as shown in Figure 31.14 as opposed to Figure 31.13.

Earlier, we discussed situated methodologies that did not foreground movement through time and space ('freeze frame' chronotopes). However, situated methodologies are often oriented to movement through time and space. The child (or children) and their uses of written language can be described as part of a set of related or evolving/changing situations. We label such methodologies 'situated over time and space methodologies'[8] (see Figure 31.15).

An example of such a methodology would be the series of studies conducted under the rubric of language socialization (cf. Ochs, 1988). The child is described as part of a set of situations over time in which the nature of the situation and the nature of the child's participation change over time. Although the study may be organized around the case of a child, doing so is only a trope to enable the researcher to select the set of situations to describe. What is foregrounded is not the child and the child's attributes *per se*, but the ways in which a group, a family, a culture, an institution, a community socialize a member to their ways of using written language. For example, Larson and Maier (2000) documented how a first-grade teacher socialized her students into the role of 'author' by engaging them in a series of activities in which she modelled what being an author involved and then which required the children's collaboration with her as co-authors. Although attention is paid to the teacher and children, in studies like Larson and Maier's the unit of analysis is not the child but the social locations/situations that make up the process of language socialization. Personhood is a component of the situation or set of situations examined; it does not exist separate from the situations and events. In our view, this is a major difference with methodologies we described earlier in the chapter ('child attribute improvement methodologies', 'complex event–attribute improvement methodologies', and 'contextualization methodologies'), perhaps a paradigmatic difference, which at best would make combining such methodologies or synthesizing them a complex and difficult theoretical challenge.

For example, Miller et al.'s (1986) study of early reading at home in South Baltimore employs a methodology that foregrounds the family as a unit of analysis. The children, their parents, siblings etc., and their uses of written language are described as

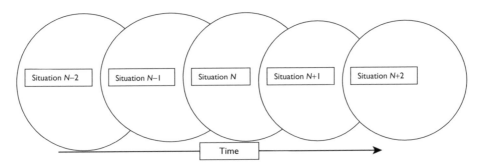

Figure 31.15   Situated over time and space methodologies

part of the family's everyday life, including the family's efforts at preparing their children for school. The families studied shared a neighbourhood and a socio-economic class. The methodology allows Miller et al. to describe literacy as an attribute of enculturation (as a family and class process) rather than an attribute of the child *per se*. The underlying chronotope focuses on the family as it creates and responds to a series of events at home, in the community, and in schools.

Anderson-Levitt et al. (Reed-Danahay and Anderson-Levitt, 1991; Anderson-Levit et al., 1991) provide another example of focusing on location over time but, in contrast to Miller et al. (1986), focus on the school at a national level. Their research on elementary education in France describes, over time, what the elementary school classroom is like and how it embodies a variety of cultural and philosophical/ideological themes that can be compared at a national level (e.g. France versus the United States). Methodologically, Anderson-Levitt et al. take schooling at a national level as a unit of analysis and examine changes in schooling over time and across nations. Literacy education is a function of schooling and reflects the broader themes that might only be identified by taking a broad look at schooling at a national level or by comparing across nations. That is, an assumption is made that cultural, political, philosophical, and ideological themes that pervade schooling might be hidden from educators, students, and researchers because they appear to be 'natural' parts of the schooling experience and might only be revealed through comparison on a national level.

Whether research is conducted at the level of the family, the classroom, or schooling at a national level etc., a key aspect of situated methodologies is a comparative perspective (see Hymes, 1980, for additional discussion of the need for a comparative perspective). Unlike the 'horse race' studies described earlier which compare two instructional

programmes to determine a 'winner', the purpose of comparison in situated methodologies is to reveal otherwise hidden issues and processes that can then be used either theory development or more insightful future research (see Figure 31.16).

One issue in such comparative studies is the selection of the phenomena for comparison. Why compare these two as opposed to those two? Why compare working-class families to middle-class families, or elementary education in France to elementary education in the United States? Anderson-Levitt et al. (1991) describe their rationale for the comparison by noting that elementary education in France presents a case of a centralized, national system while the United States presents a case of a localized system, and thus implicitly there is a comparison of the two approaches. But comparisons may also be oriented to the relationship of the research to a particular audience or to power relations that exist both within and beyond the research study itself. For example, one can assume that the audience of a research study will bring their knowledge and their personal experience to the reading. The comparison in the research study can be viewed, therefore, as a rhetorical tool for challenging and expanding the understandings that the reader has of the foreign situation and of the situation with which he/she is familiar. Alternatively, there may be an unequal power relation between groups and the comparison embedded in the research may provide a way to challenge the rationale that underlies that power relationship. Thus, Miller et al.'s research implicitly challenges the assumption held by some people in the middle class (including middle-class educators) that working-class families are deficit with regard to their concern and activity around their young children's learning to read.

Beyond the selection of a comparative case or situation, there is another key selection issue in the grammar of situated methodologies. Whether

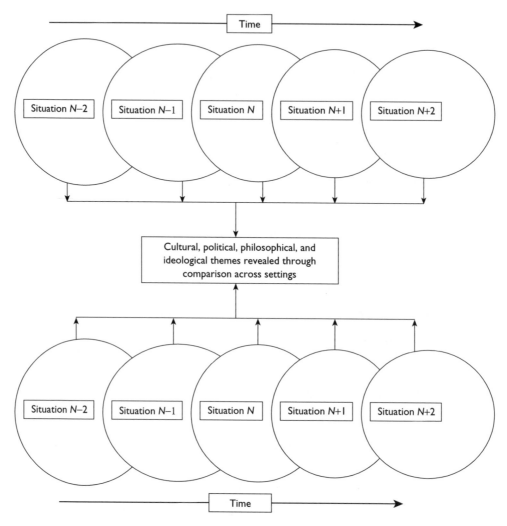

Figure 31.16   Comparative situated methodologies

explicitly stated or not, a 'situated methodology' assumes a relationship between the situation or event analysed (situation *N* in Figure 31.15) and other situations and events (situations *N*–1, *N*–2, *N*+1, *N*+2 in Figure 31.15) or some end goal. The relationship of situations and events to each other needs to be carefully considered and warranted. For example, in the study by Miller et al. there is an assumed relationship among the events of enculturation in the family, school, community, etc. In the Miller et al. study, situations were sampled as part of a whole, the whole being the child rearing culture of the neighbourhood and class. Another approach has been to examine a particular type of situation over time. For example, Borko and

Eisenhart (1987) studied the discourse used in instructional reading groups, focusing on differences among high, middle, and low ability reading groups over time. They examined (1) differences in norms for using spoken and written language across reading groups, and (2) how young children's ways of using spoken and written language within a reading group matched or did not match the norms for language use within the reading groups. Findings aside, their methodology illustrates one principle for selecting the series of situations to be examined: namely, the nature of a particular set of reading practices over time and their consequences for defining children by positioning them within a social organization.

An alternative principle for selecting a set of situations to examine is illustrated by Kantor and colleagues (1992a; 1992b; 1993). Rather than follow a particular type of situation, they examined the different types of situations over time within a classroom, eventually focusing on four types of situations including two small instructional group situations and two situations during daily free play (block area and activity table area). The principle of selection had two dimensions: (1) capturing the range of uses of written language that counted as literacy in the classroom, and (2) a view of literacy learning as part of the process of becoming a member of the classroom culture. Thus, the studies by Kantor et al. share a methodological grammar with the language socialization studies and the study by Borko and Eisenhart (discussed earlier), all of which build on the methodological grammar of 'situated over time and space methodologies'.

FINAL COMMENTS

In this chapter, we have focused attention on the methodological grammars and underlying chronotopes of methodologies used in research on young children and literacy. We have not attempted to be comprehensive in coverage of studies, methodological grammars, or chronotopes. Nor do we claim that our analysis of methodological grammars or underlying chronotopes is the only analysis and interpretation possible. Rather, we only claim that it is one analysis and one interpretation. Our effort was not aimed at presenting a definitive analysis but rather at foregrounding the rhetorical import of the methodological grammars of research on young children.

Methodological grammars and their underlying chronotopes have been discussed within three dimensions for understanding research on young children and literacy: (1) the nature of children, (2) definitions of literacy, and (3) locations of children. Underlying conceptions of how people move through time and space drive both research methodologies and what counts as knowledge derived from research methodologies. At issue, then, in the study of research methodologies, is not simply the rigour or validity of a research methodology, nor is it simply a matter of the trustworthiness of the findings. The meaning of a research study is not just in the bits of knowledge produced, the question asked, or the topic studied, but in the methodological grammar employed and the underlying chronotope. Such recognition makes it possible to unpack hidden assumptions and to generate new insights about the nature of inquiry and the nature of the accumulation of knowledge on young children and literacy.

NOTES

1 We are not suggesting that the children are passive. In the reading to children events designed by Lonigan and Whitehurst the children were active participants in the reading events. Rather, the 'journey' that the children take is one in which they experience a series of prescribed events. They may have to be active participants in these events, even though they do not choose whether or not to participate and they do not create the grammar of the events they experience.

2 Some researchers make a distinction between the parsing of reading and writing into their constituent processes and skills and the process of learning to read or write.

3 One form of derision is the labelling of input–output studies as black box studies, referring to the opaqueness of the classroom (the ignorance of process factors).

4 Care must be taken to separate out the rhetorical consequences of methodological grammar from suggestions about the intent or meaningfulness to the researcher. A researcher may indeed care about and value parent–child reading in its own right without reference to academic goals. Our concern here is with the rhetorical consequences of underlying methodological grammar and chronotopes.

5 Although we argue that the methodological grammar is similar, the methods used by Luke (1988), Duranti and Ochs (1986), and Fishman (1988) are different.

6 The term 'situation' is used differently across research studies and scholarly articles. Here, we use the term 'situation' broadly equivalent to the way the term 'context' is used in some studies and 'event' in others. In this chapter, we distinguish between situation and context as a way to distinguish between situated methodologies and contextualization methodologies (which are explained later).

7 See Van Maanen (1988) for an argument on the legitimacy and usefulness of impressionistic description in ethnographic research.

8 Figure 31.15 derives, in part, from a similar discussion in Weade (1992).

REFERENCES

Anderson-Levitt, K., Sirota, R. and Mazurier, M. (1991) 'Elementary education in France', *The Elementary School Journal*, 92 (1): 79–95.

Bakhtin, M. (1981) *The Dialogic Imagination.* (1935), trans. 1981. Austin, TX: University of Texas Press.

Bergin, C. (2001) 'The parent–child relationship during beginning reading', *Journal of Literacy Research*, 33 (4) 681–706.

Bond, G. and Dykstra, R. (1964) *Report of a Developmental Program; Conference on Coordination of Accepted Proposals for the Cooperative Research Program in First Grade Reading Instruction*. Minneapolis: University of Minnesota.

Borko, H. and Eisenhart, M. (1987) 'Reading ability groups as literacy communities', In D. Bloome (ed.), *Classrooms and Literacy*. Norwood, NJ: Ablex. pp. 107–34.

Bus, A.G., Belsky, J., Ijzendoorn, M.H. and Crnic, K. (1997) 'Attachment and book reading patterns: a study of mothers, fathers, and their toddlers', *Early Childhood Research Quarterly*, 12: 81–98.

Cairney, T. and Ashton, J. (2002) 'Three families, multiple discourses: parental roles, constructions of literacy and diversity of pedagogic practice', *Linguistics and Education*, 13 (3): 303–45.

Calhoun, J.A. and Leslie, L. (2002) 'A longitudinal study of the effects of word frequency and rime-neighborhood size on beginning readers' rime reading accuracy in words and nonwords', *Journal of Literacy Research*, 34 (1): 39–58.

Cox, B., Fang, Z. and Otto, B.W. (1997) 'Preschoolers' developing ownership of the literate register', *Reading Research Quarterly*, 32 (1): 34–55.

Cunningham, J., Erickson, K., Spadorica, S., Koppenhaver, D., Cunningham, P., Yoder, D. and McKenna, M. (1999) 'Assessing decoding from an onset–rime perspective', *Journal of Literacy Research*, 31 (4): 391–414.

Dahl, K., Scharer, P., Lawson, L. and Grogam, P. (1999) 'Phonics instruction and student achievement in whole language first grade classrooms', *Reading Research Quarterly*, 34 (3): 312–41.

Dunkin, M. and Biddle, B. (1974) *The Study of Teaching*. Washington, DC: University Press of America.

Duranti, A. and Ochs, E. (1986) 'Literacy instruction in a Samoan village', in B. Schieffelin and P. Gilmore (eds), *The Acquisition of Literacy: Ethnographic Perspectives*. Norwood, NJ: Ablex. pp. 213–32.

Dyson, A. (1989) *Multiple Words of Child Writers: Friends Learning to Write*. New York: Teachers College Press.

Dyson, A. (1997) *Writing Superheroes: Contemporary Childhood, Popular Culture, and Classroom Literacy*. New York: Teachers College Press.

Dyson, A. (1999) 'Coach Bombay's kids learn to write: children's appropriation of media material for school literacy', *Research in the Teaching of English*, 33 (4): 367–402.

Fairclough, N. (1992) *Discourse and Social Change*, Cambridge: Polity.

Fishman, A. (1988) *Amish Literacy: What and How It Means*. Portsmouth, NH: Heinemann.

Flood, J., Lapp, P., Squire, J. and Jensen, J. (eds) (2003) *Handbook of Research on Teaching the English Language Arts*, 2nd edn. Mahwah, NJ: Erlbaum.

Gee, J.P. (1996) *Social Linguistics and Literacies: Ideology in Discourses*, 2nd edn. London: Taylor and Francis.

Gee, J.P. (2001) 'A sociocultural perspective on early literacy development', in S. Neuman and D. Dickinson (eds), *Handbook of Early Literacy Research*. New York: Guilford. pp. 30–42.

Gee, J.P. and Green, J. (1998) 'Discourse, literacy and social practice', in P.D. Pearson (ed.), *Review of Research in Education*. Washington, DC: American Educational Research Association.

Geertz, C. (1966) *Person, Time, and Conduct in Bali: an Essay in Cultural Analysis*. New Haven, CT: Yale University Press.

Geertz, C. (1973) *The Interpretation of Cultures: Selected Essays*. New York: Basic.

Gergen, Kenneth J. and Davis, Keith E. (eds) (1985) *The Social Construction of the Person*. New York: Springer.

Goodman, Y. and Wilde, S. (1992) *Literacy Events in a Community of Young Writers*. New York: Teachers College Press.

Heath, S. (1983) *Ways with Words*. Cambridge: Cambridge University Press.

Hymes, D. (1980) *Language in Education: Ethnolinguistic Essays*. Washington, DC: Center for Applied Linguistics.

Juel, C. and Minden-Cupp, C. (2000) 'Learning to read words: linguistic units and instructional strategies', *Reading Research Quarterly*, 35 (4): 458–92.

Kamil, M., Mosenthal, P., Pearson, P.D. and Barr, R. (eds) (2000) *Handbook of Reading Research*, vol. III. Mahwah, NJ: Erlbaum.

Kantor, R., Green, J., Bradley, M. and Lin, L. (1992a) 'The construction of schooled discourse repertoires: an interaction sociolinguistic perspective on learning to talk in preschool', *Linguistics and Education*, 4: 131–72.

Kantor, R., Miller, S. and Fernie, D. (1992b) 'Diverse paths to literacy in a preschool classroom: a sociocultural perspective', *Reading Research Quarterly*, 27 (3): 185–201.

Kantor, R., Elgas, P. and Fernie, D. (1993) 'Cultural knowledge and social competence within a preschool peer culture group', *Early Childhood Research Quarterly*, 8: 125–47.

Kirkpatrick, John (1983) *The Marquesan Notion of the Person*. Ann Arbor, MI: UMI Research Press.

Larson, J. and Maier, M. (2000) 'Co-authoring classroom texts: shifting participant roles in writing activity', *Research in the Teaching of English*, 34 (4): 468–98.

Leslie, L. and Allen, L. (1999) 'Factors that predict success in an early literacy intervention project', *Reading Research Quarterly*, 34 (4): 404–25.

Lonigan, C.J. and Whitehurst, G. (1998) 'Relative efficiency of parent and teacher involvement in a shared-reading intervention for preschool children from low-income backgrounds', *Early Childhood Research Quarterly*, 13 (2): 263–90.

Luke, A. (1988) *Literacy, Textbooks and Ideology*. New York: Falmer.

Luke, A. (1995) 'When basic skills and information processing just aren't enough: rethinking reading in new times', *Teachers College Record*, 97 (1): 95–115.

Manyak, P. (2001) 'Participation, hybridity, and carnival: a situated analysis of a dynamic literacy practice in a primary-grade English immersion class', *Journal of Literacy Research*, 33 (3): 423–65.

Miller, P., Nemoiani, A. and DeJong, J. (1986) 'Early reading at home: its practice and meanings in a working class community', in B. Schieffelin and P. Gilmore (eds), *The Acquisition of Literacy: Ethnographic Perspectives*. Norwood, NJ: Ablex. pp. 3–15.

Neuman, S. (1999) 'Books make a difference: a study of access to literacy', *Reading Research Quarterly*, 34 (3): 286–310.

Ochs, E. (1988) *Culture and Language Development: Language Socialization and Language Acquisition in a Samoan Village*. New York: Cambridge University Press.

Ogbu, J. and Simons, H. (1998) 'Voluntary and involuntary minorities: a cultural-ecological theory of school performance and some implications for education', *Anthropology and Education Quarterly*, 29 (2): 155–88.

Pickett, L. (1998) 'Literacy learning during block play', *Journal of Research in Childhood Education*, 12 (2): 225–32.

Reed-Danahay, D. and Anderson-Levitt, K. (1991) 'Backward countryside, troubled city: French teachers' images of rural and working-class families', *American Ethnologist*, 18 (3): 546–64.

Santa, C. and Høien, T. (1999) 'An assessment of Early Steps: a program for early intervention of reading problems', *Reading Research Quarterly*, 34 (1): 54–79.

Sénéchal, M., LeFevre, J., Thomas, E. and Dailey, K. (1998) 'Differential effects of home literacy experiences on the development of oral and written language', *Reading Research Quarterly*, 35 (1): 96–116.

Shweder, Richard A. and Miller, Joan G. (1985) 'The social construction of the person: how is it possible?', in Kenneth J. Gergen and Keith E. Davis (eds), *The Social Construction of the Person*. New York: Springer.

Sipe, L. (2000) 'The construction of literary understanding by first and second graders in oral response to picture storybook read-alouds', *Reading Research Quarterly*, 35 (2): 252–75.

Street, B. (1984) *Literacy in Theory and Practice*. New York: Cambridge University Press.

Street, B. (ed.) (1993) *Cross-Cultural Approaches to Literacy*. Cambridge: Cambridge University Press.

Street, B. (1995) *Social Literacies*. London: Longman.

Taylor, D. (1983) *Family Literacy*. Portsmouth, NH: Heinemann.

Taylor, D. and Dorsey-Gaines, C. (1988) *Growing Up Literate*. Portsmouth, NH: Heinemann.

Van Maanen, J. (1988) *Tales of the Field: on Writing Ethnography*. Chicago: University of Chicago Press.

Weade, G. (1992) 'Locating learning in the times and spaces of teaching', in H. Marshall (ed.) *Redefining Student Learning: Roots of Educational Change*. Norwood, NJ: Ablex. pp. 87–118.

Wells, G. (1981) *Learning through Interaction: the Study of Language Development*. Cambridge: Cambridge University Press.

32

Feminist Methodologies and Research for Early Childhood Literacies

JEANETTE RHEDDING-JONES

Today's newer research methodologies are the effects and the constructs of postmodernism, critical theory, feminisms, postcolonial theory, queer theory and cultural studies. Although these may contain vestiges of earlier research practices, certainties, fixed categories of analysis and statistical information, they are now challenging what counts as knowledge and who the knowers are. Applied to literacy practices and competencies, newer research methodologies are alternative perspectives and practices that shift research fields towards ethics rather than mere information, towards theories rather than mere findings, and towards reconceptualizing practices rather than merely analysing results or reporting.

In all of this the would-be feminist researcher is in a different positioning from the don't-want-to-be feminist researcher, and also from the men well read in feminist theory and/or wanting to work for gender equity. This is because feminism, and any other contemporary 'ism' such as multiculturalism, anti-racism, anti-ageism or postcolonialism, contains a set of unfixed political values, validities and desires for social justice. So for critically and thus politically oriented researchers, taking out your political and cultural standpoints is an impossibility. So is being able to say how much your feminist (or other) affinity is influencing your research practice and the ways that you decide to write it up.

Given word limits for this chapter, I will not write about who is currently publishing what regarding literacies in early childhood. There is not the space here to discuss the work of overtly feminist, sometimes feminist, pro-feminist and non-feminist research about literacy; and how these might intersect with research about gender. Nor is

there space to say what sorts of feminisms and feminist complexities around cultures, sexualities and languages such researchers might be making use of, developing or reconstructing. However, I would point to other chapters in this volume (especially those by Radhika Viruru and by Elaine Millard), and suggest that these are read with an eye to how various feminisms inform their positionings regarding gender; and which feminisms (socialist, conservative right, radical or newer such as global, postmodern, poststructural) appear to be resisted, ignored or acted out agentically through these writers' choices of research methodologies, academic references, writing genres and discourses.

My aim is thus larger than feminism, in that I would like to reconceptualize research and its relationships to practices and theories. I see these as emerging epistemological and ontological issues for early childhood education and the larger discourses contextualizing it. Deconstructing the meta-narrative of how research is done thus represents new scholarship that challenges theories of knowledge, philosophy and childhood studies. Can there be an ethical research with or for young children? What matters as reconstructed research practice? How can higher educations for early schooling and preschool day care effectively develop more appropriate and useful methodologies? Where are the voices of children in all this (Cannella, 1998; Christiansen and James, 2000; Yelland, 1998)? What sense do children make of themselves and of each other as gendered beings? What methodologies can deal with these questions?

In asking such critical questions, feminism must be acknowledged as a beginning point for many women's critical scholarship. It was feminism that got us to see marginalization, and got us into theory in the first place, and got some of us into 'the posts' beyond that (Lather, 1995; Rhedding-Jones, 1995; 1997a; Richardson, 1997). Also, it is feminism that has enabled many women scholars to see the positioning of children and other dominated groups amongst adults as once we saw the positioning of ourselves amongst men (Firestone, 1970). When I gave a draft of this chapter at a recent Nordic conference about education research, the women there insisted that feminism still has much work ahead of it, and that we must never not see how patriarchy continues. This applies not only to the everyday lives of the children we work with and for, but to the gendered injustices of research practices, higher education, prestigious publishing, academic promotion, bureaucratic power and money (Begum, 1994; Huq, 1997; Weiler and Middleton, 1998). Further, a major task of feminist researchers is to make such gendered power dynamics visible.

Regarding literacy, feminists uncover the politics of power giving boys and men educational advantages in a patriarchal agenda. For example, in many Anglo cultures girls have been the clever ones in literacy, yet this has still not given them educational advantages resulting in their later equal financial and employment positioning with men. So following feminist logic: pushing the case of boys and literacy is thus diverting funds away from girls' schooling, and driven by the fear of boys not retaining their natural and rightful dominance in the feminized hothouses of early childhood classrooms. Here the quantitative measures used to demonstrate boys' relative failure in literacy are quite suspect. They request examination by feminists skilled in quantitative arguments, who may then expose such research as functioning politically for patriarchy, rather than scientifically (Gilbert and Gilbert, 1998).

Writing about gender, however, is not the same as writing about feminism, as researchers and theorists of masculinity, sexuality and anti-racist critiques of white women have shown (hooks, 1994; Mac an Ghaill, 1994; Quinlivan, 2002). So this chapter is not about what girls and boys are doing differently from each other, as readers and writers, non-readers and non-writers and various grey shades between these dichotomies. Nor is it about what men and women teachers and parents are doing that is supposedly because of their gender, and gender's effects on literacy 'outcomes' and related semiotics. Instead, this chapter points to how you might do research and what sorts of data you might decide to get. Nevertheless, the topics and the themes of research to some extent decide its methodology, as do the audiences for whom it will be written. I would argue that who you do the

research with and what you decide to (not) research are also your methodological choices. And that your choices are made because of your politics, feminist and otherwise.

IN NORWAY AND NAIROBI

I'll start with Norway because that is where I live. Even when they begin to go to school, at the age of six, children here will be given no assigned tasks (*oppgaver*) and will be controlled by no assessment in terms of marks (*vurdering med karakter*) until they reach the age of 11 or 12. In line with this there is no word in Norwegian for literacy, as children are not forcibly encouraged to take up reading and writing until they themselves show an interest in it and begin to want it. Hence teachers are not overtly into reading and writing activities, and preschool teacher-carers are not noticeably demonstrating them. As teenagers and adults, Norwegians appear no less able to read and write than people anywhere else in capitalist society; although as an Australian I am very conscious of the number of times I hear the word dyslexic (*dyslektisk*) said in everyday conversation, on the radio and in the lecture and tutorial rooms with undergraduates. In school, apart from discourses of special education where dyslexia is the province of special pedagogies rather than literacy experts (at least from my Australian point of view), the children are free to concentrate on social competence activities. In other words this is quite an oral culture, and the culture determines the social competence definition (see also Viruru, in this volume).

So what would you as a feminist or as a researcher informed by feminist theory do in this situation? I think I might start with the patriarchal quality of the psychology that constructs the discourse of dyslexia. Questioning further, I might ask who are the literacy experts that Norway may be denying? Or how do the working conditions and the pay of denied literacy experts and acknowledged dyslexic experts differ on gender lines? Who is selling books for children and students and who is not? Who wants school literacy and why? Who becomes an information technology expert requiring those literacies not taken up by schooling? Who will become the gendered readers of written music, of art and dance, of novels, poetry and private letters?

In contrast, and with contrasting research possibilities and problematics, is the following, which I have taken from Woodhead (2000: 16). Here, four-year-old Henry is in Nairobi. His home is a one-room hut that he shares with his mother and sisters. He attends a preschool classroom with 50–60 other children and one teacher. There are no play materials and no learning materials to speak of except wall charts of the English alphabet. The teacher leads the group and the children recite the letters in unison. Here my feminist perspective cannot be articulated alone. As a literacy researcher I would want to know how close Henry's culture is to shared recitation. How important are formality and respect for adults? Is this regarded locally as a high quality preschool? As a feminist I might ask what Henry's mother is doing with her time, whilst he is in preschool. And is this more important than my Anglo-Australian judgment of colonial literacy practices? Also, what of the gendered professionalism of Henry's teacher? What kinds of masculinity is Henry constructing for himself in his everyday life with his sisters? To what gendered and non-gendered uses might his literacy eventually be put? As you can see, these critical questions are beyond those normalized by literacy researchers wanting to measure and quantify what Henry now does. But I have to work to keep my feminist focus because feminism here is not, apparently, what matters most (Rhedding-Jones, 2001b; 2002).

FEMINISMS

Having now made feminism problematic, I'll try to deal with it. As I see it, feminism as critical theory relates to other critical theories. And feminism as poststructural theory relates to other poststructural theories uncovering power and deconstructing categories, hierarchies and fixedness. Feminism as phenomenology is about interpretations of gendered meanings and hermeneutics. And feminism as positivism attracts social scientists wanting hard sciences, who try to explain and predict in terms of cause-and-effect relations, believing that such findings are not politically motivated, and that method is able to produce reliable findings. In this chapter I spell out some of the implications of this for research about literacy in early childhood.

Whilst not feminist unless its critique or its deconstructions or its interpretations or its statistics and graphs regard gender, or the positioning of women and girls (Glenn, 2000; Hammersley, 1992; Hauser and Jipson, 1998; Rhedding-Jones, 1997b), any doing away with an 'ages and stages' notion in early childhood discourses relates to liberation and resistance. So for today's feminist researchers, learning to resist normalized research practices, normalized evaluations of literacy and normalized notions of 'childhood' matters very much. From such resistance comes awareness of other marginalizations, such as gender together with financial differentiation, gender together with an ethnic

minority positioning, or gender in the ageism shown to children by adults. Hence it is not surprising that many feminists are now taking up the fight against multiple marginalizations including gender. Having been positioned themselves as resisting patriarchy they are now able to work for other people's agencies in a range of discourses of institutionalized power. Literacy is one such institution.

So feminisms vary depending on where and when they are or were located (Rhedding-Jones, 1997b; 2001a), and on who decides that this is feminist. Combining positionings (feminism and anti-ageism, or anti-racism, gay and lesbian rights, social justice for marginalized religions and languages) is likely to be called 'postmodern', especially if the writing style of the researcher also takes up a range of different juxtaposed genres or textual complexities for audiences. A modernist positioning usually takes a singular stance or standpoint, regarding both research focus and authorial voice.

You cannot do work that is feminist without focusing on gender (although as I have said, not all gender research is feminist). Further, feminist research is not about the biological differences between women and men, girls and boys. Rather it is about the social and cultural constructions of what we do about our identities, as the gendered selves we have temporarily or over longer time (Marsh, 2000). So the words 'male' and 'female', as biological terms, are not likely to be there in feminist research, where people are seen as subjects rather than as objects. With research which is about girls or boys but which does not name gender or feminism, it is probable that feminist agendas are at work, but the local situation may be such that they cannot be stated (for example, Rhedding-Jones et al., 2002).

In a country like Norway (Rhedding-Jones, 2001a), where feminism seems assumed (by the general public) to have happened some 30 years ago and not to be overly concerning now, it does not help to point to the average incomes of adult women and men and then to try and link these to the literacy practices of the young. Nor does it help much to accuse pedagogical discourses of preschooling as replicating the desirability of the middle-class home, with the traditionally attending mother always putting 'her' children first. Watching the little boys of Pakistani and Vietnamese backgrounds grow up to become tomorrow's technological wizards (Castleton, 2000; Gliddon, 2001) instead of today's special education's problem schoolboys is similarly unrecognized as a gendered effect. But as three problems for early childhood literacy education and its related research, I suggest that these have high relevance for today's feminists, and not only in Norway.

Yet feminists in general appear not keen to take up the research fields of education: perhaps a sign of their own professional lack of experience here, but maybe also some form of hierarchical ordering of what counts as important in the social sciences. So for whatever reason, feminist research in education is usually the prerogative of feminist educators or feminist ex-teachers, rather than feminist sociologists, anthropologists or literary theorists. When the topic is literacy, the researcher needs to know how people become gradually literate, how they become differently literate, occasionally literate, generically literate, technologically literate, graphically literate and musically literate. This may then be linked to the positionings of the very young, and in particular to how their/our different genderings impact upon their/our literacies and vice versa. As implied, a newer feminist research practice will focus not only on children but also on the adults who are with them: on the borders between multiple realities and fantasies, complex sites and events, diverse texts and contexts.

RESEARCH METHODOLOGIES AND FEMINIST APPROACHES TO SOCIAL SCIENCE

Any piece of research is open to some level of feminist practice, which may involve simply being sensitive to gender matters. A more complex feminist practice is selecting and constructing other forms of analysis, interpretation, critique or deconstruction of the research data (Haug, 1987), so that the gendered aspects of these are made clear, resisted or challenged. A further step is a critical awareness of the gendered processes and discourses by which the research itself is valued. In other words, in feminist research that is not within positivist empiricist approaches, the subjective and political positioning of the researcher may be apparent and accepted (Ellis and Flaherty, 1992). For researchers claiming and wanting objectivity, this is problematic.

This section considers methodologies from positivist, interpretive, critical and poststructural approaches to social science research (Connole, 1998; Deakin University, 1998; Hughes, 2001; Rhedding-Jones, 2000). These may include or reconstruct survey and statistical analysis, historical and current case studies, action research, ethnography and multiple methods. They might involve interviews, so-called observations and recordings, document constructings, discourse analysis and academic writing as the postmodern. Within methodologies are strategies (sometimes called methods) for doing the research: designing questionnaires, writing a research journal, photocopying documents, selecting texts for analysis, audio

recording and photographing (Rhedding-Jones and Atkinson, 1991; Rhedding-Jones, 1993). These are then put together intellectually and analysed, interpreted, critiqued or deconstructed. From this process come findings, statements, suppositions, critiques, undoings, theories and knowledge. You can see that as I have been naming and locating these I have loosely been making left to right orderings, following Western literacy patterns, to structure an understanding of today's methodologies. So this could, with some exceptions and overlaps, be diagrammed and put in a box.

However, feminist research is especially concerned with being (ontology). This is why so many feminists have wanted to take up subjectivity and the problem of language as meaning. And because all knowledge is in some way grounded, and all research methods are linked to theories (epistemology), then it is these that feminists hold suspect (Burt and Code, 1995). Hence the feminist movement into poststructuralism is a way to make explicit complex positionings, including those of the researcher. And to resist the neat little boxes that look so nice as research findings. For literacy researchers, who should be especially knowledgable about language and the crafting of writing, this means that doing research is not going to be easy. Here the challenge in feminist poststructural research is to cause political, pedagogical and agentic change because of the research, and through the academic literacy of the researcher. In the case of early childhood education, this research is for the present and the future of young people.

With this in mind, today's feminist postpositivist research methodologies for literacies may be described as follows. *Interpretive research projects* use case studies or ethnography or their audiovisual or textual strategies of documenting practice. Interviews or observations are interpreted by a researcher who focuses on meaning, hermeneutics or phenomena. The research can be empirical in that theories come from the practices researched (but this is not empiricist or positivist). *Critical research projects* are often action research projects that aim at intervention and change. Or they may follow case study or ethnography and their strategies of interviews and document analysis. Research data may be analysed, critiqued, unpacked, undone or deconstructed. The approach is empirical in that theories and practices both matter. *Poststructural research projects* operate within the postmodern, with deconstructive practices. Research data are thus undone, read differently, de-scribed and reinscribed otherwise. In particular the voice of the researcher is heard, as are the voices of minorities, such as children in situations of adult domination like schooling. As empirical research this may be highly theoretical, in multiple ways. Yet as feminist research it always has a cutting political edge.

What happens if our methodology takes up an *interpretive approach*? If our focus is on masculinity and literacy we might interview men teachers and women teachers, or mothers and fathers, and talk with them in appropriate language about how they see boys relating to early writing and reading experience in various places. Observations here could help us decide how to interpret our interview transcripts in the light of what appears to have happened. This could be further supported by the texts the boys actually produce, perhaps in comparison to the texts produced by some girls. With this approach a researcher's own feminism (or pro-feminism) makes her (or him) the authority as regards the semantics of the situation, as all interpretations are filtered by the professionalism of the researcher. Here a feminist standpoint theory (Harding, 1993) may be made clear. Interpretive approaches may link to modernity or to postmodernity, and may be combined with other approaches. For a feminist, taking up the interpretive is not a particularly radical step, and it need not be personally exposing. But narratives go well here, and suit a general audience. Hence interpretive research usually presents reports, exposés and theoretical explanations as easy to read.

A *critical approach* takes into account the uses of literacy and the people and actions positioned as important. It might be combined with the interpretive or the poststructural. In early childhood education, a critical approach might request a sharp look at psychology as an informing discipline (Cannella, 1998) and at the roles played by adults in the normalized practices of institutionalized child play. Action research (Mac Naughton, 2001) is closely in line with critical theories, following the earlier Frankfurt school, the influential neo-Marxist work in 1980s teacher education, and the new critical theories in early childhood (Bailey, 1997; Grieshaber, 1998; Rhedding-Jones, 2002). Here innovations to practice are documented, critically reflected upon and evaluated before new spirals of introductions recommence. For literacy, this allows for a politics of change, and the questioning of the status quo of pedagogy. Teachers find this an inclusive teaching/researching practice. For some parents also it works well. And feminists get the chance to reconstruct both pedagogy and literacy as more appropriate for the gendering of today's young people. Making a difference is thus one of the successes of action research (Berge and Ve, 1999; Møller, 1996); though critical approaches go far beyond an endpoint of satisfaction. For example, feminists find that what is more problematic than pedagogies and literacies are the people occupying the positions of power: the publishers of bestselling books, the examiners who operate at the other end of schooling and university, the politicians controlling the purse-strings, the school principals and policy makers, the children's fathers and what they (do not) read and write. Researching the gendering of these, with a critical approach, involves also what happens outside the school and preschool.

With a *poststructural approach*, research shifts into multiplicity and uncertainty, by making problematic both meaning and language. Here Australian feminist poststructural theory in education has gained much space internationally (for example, Davies, 1993; 2000; McWilliam, 1994). More than just a clever play with words, this approach to research is beginning internationally to construct a new ethics (Rhedding-Jones, 2000), to challenge knowledge and philosophy, to resist boundaries and to open itself to all forms of difference and complexity. Here the process of research produces a feminist cooperative knowledge, where the researchers must have particular accountabilities to the children and the adults participating in the research, and also to various reading audiences of differing positionings. Women are central here as theoretical resources, and in the development of innovative research methodologies. For literacy, such an approach might engage the girls and the boys as gendered subjects not necessarily so different from each other. And because poststructural theory is about the breakdown of dichotomized thinking, gender itself is deconstructed and reconstructed. As are literacy and early childhood. And research.

I would argue that people experienced in working and playing with the very young can reconstruct research methodology, because of their/our particular positionings (Creaser and Dau, 1995; Grau and Walsh, 1998; Hatch, 1995) in relation to practices, autobiographies, memories, and communications by everyday language(s) and bodies. Working with the very young in fact sharpens these positioning-related skills and arts. Far from looking down on them, an innovative researcher puts such skills/arts to advantage. Yet as with all confrontations between institutions and individuals, the effects of power can be devastating. Hence postgraduate students fail, research grant applications get rejected, articles and books remain unpublished. Challenging research practices (especially those of people wanting not to reject their own values regarding literacy, learning, play, work, age, space, time, and 'isms' like feminism, multiculturalism and postcolonialism) are thus at risk.

As an endnote here: feminist methodologies cannot be fully described or prescribed (Fonow and Cook, 1991; Malterud, 1996; Reinharz, 1992).

Within the various approaches to social science inquiry there are places for a range of feminisms and a range of feminist ways of conducting research. What matters regarding feminisms here are feminist epistemologies and ontologies. For feminist theorists have not just critiqued and reconstructed methodology (Alcoff and Potter, 1993). Their/our critique and reconstruction are resistance to the normalizations that pervade which knowledge counts. We work to show that theories of difference must affect every aspect of the research process and its products.

EARLY CHILDHOOD EDUCATION AND FEMINISTS

Differences in 'Northern' normalized practices of institutionalized childcare and education have led to the dichotomy of early schooling and preschool day care (Penn, 2000). Here if preschooling may be said to represent and construct the private and feminized discourses of the home, then schooling perhaps represents the public space of a normalized masculinity, such as the army, the church or a men's sporting club. For feminist researchers there is much here not yet researched, with little critique as yet having been done by women about our own dominant positioning in early childhood education and its discourses (Jørgensen and Phillips, 1999). That said, we must also ask who are the professors and who writes the books.

Early childhood is usually seen as from birth to age eight. Literacies and their emergent practices (Rhedding-Jones, 1997c) involve children's listening, looking, drawing, speaking, touching, feeling and thinking. What is crucial is what adults do, what other children do and what happens with technology, as well as what children do for themselves. So people, practices, desires, texts, technologies, media and graphics construct the various literacies. In some locations, a written culture is not important. In others it is there, but its measurement and its early manifestation are of little consequence. Researching literacies must then be culturally appropriate to the participants in the literacy events and non-events. Thus sites for literacies, or locating them contextually and culturally, are not only different locally. They must also be seen globally. And the literacy of a child, like orality, might involve more than one culture and more than one language. For feminist (and pro-feminist) researchers, who themselves will have first-hand (or vicarious) experience of marginalization or difference because of their gender, a positioning of otherness because of language and culture should be able to be understood. Unfortunately, this does not always follow.

So young children marginalized linguistically are quite often expected to be integrated into the dominant culture (that is, via standard language in public places, and by not being invited into the homes of the dominant). In practice much integration is in fact assimilation, as in the case of the almost total non-use of community languages in the institutions of early schooling, preschooling and care. Relatedly, and because white feminism has a history of ignoring black people, Asians and people of colour, it cannot be expected that many white feminists will work sympathetically with linguistic (and hence literacy) difference. With newer research though this is beginning to happen (Jones Diaz, 2001). Paying lip service to what used to be called 'the mother tongue', but in practice making sure that literacy develops only through one standard national language, is beginning to be seen as inappropriate literacy pedagogy. Moreover, having one language only to read and write is out of step with today's transnational and hybridized identities (Rhedding-Jones, 2001b). Refusing multiplicities by insisting on a monolingual and a monocultural positioning (Andersen, 2002) is thus an essentially modernist stance. So feminists engaged in global and postcolonial debates (Harding, 1996) will resist such early childhood educations of singular linguistic positioning. Research following this involves awareness not only of the functions of language(s) but of the effects of a postmodern world. Early childhood literacy needs then to be seen as operating not only locally but within global space. Quite often here, the misnamed 'minority' children are far ahead of adults, researching theorists included.

A multilingual or translingual education thus requests research that takes into account the diversity and multiplicity of the cultural positionings of the gendered subjects of literacies. For feminist researchers this means being open to the practices of women and men in other countries, in subcultures within cities, and in minority religions (Levine et al., 2001). We need more than token gestures to representative tourism. Researching such literacy events and sites requires a knowledge of the home cultures and the street cultures of children, of the cultures of their race, of the desires their parents have for their learning. Being sensitive to the gendered difference within cultures is thus the work of the feminist researcher, who aims not to downplay the culture of women or to disregard the culture of men. And when these are not so separate from each other, then perhaps it is the gendered culture of the researcher that must be taken more into account. Furthermore, the roles of research assistants, postgraduate students and children themselves as informing subjects must be critically acknowledged and acted upon.

LITERACIES AND FEMINIST PRACTICES

Measuring or even describing literacy because child development has been the basis of pedagogy has resulted in a literacy of ages and stages. Thus 'the "developing child" is researched within an evaluative frame that is mainly interested in their position on the stage-like journey to mature competence' (Woodhead, 2000: 29). Similarly, literacy is seen as a linear naming of competency in reading and writing, with experts saying what beginning writers and readers can and cannot do. Feminists critical of such namings, fixings and expertise will challenge this positioning, especially as it regards how boys and girls are differently rated, ranked and described (Love and Hamstom, 2001). But feminists without a critical theory of anything except gender will not focus on the more far-reaching problems of who counts as expert and how children are positioned in relation to adults in power.

If reading is about the makings of meanings, as traditionally supposed, how can anyone possibly know what meanings another can make? And if you are a poststructuralist deconstructing meaning as itself always lacking, then what (Gallop, 2000; Tobin, 1995)? Further, not expressing all that we know is a feature not only of writing but also of talking, of acting and of living. So seeing literacy as an engineered thing of reception and expression is thus only a tiny part of a much bigger picture, of which there are many. Examining or measuring ability to read and write thus positions readers and writers as observed and thus as betrayed subjects. Feminist researchers in particular are expected not to be wanting to exploit other people, especially those rendered relatively powerless by age, size and a literacy presumably less developed than their own. But the irony is that adult researchers and teachers assume 'the child' is incompetent, when in fact 'the child' may soon be highly literate in the multimedia and technologies rapidly overtaking traditional texts.

In the case of literacy research about (on, for, with) the very young, the history of its practice is, I think (following Connole, 1998), as follows. *Positivist empiricist* inquiry has research interests that regard prediction, control, explanation and technically exploitable knowledge. Here children are tested to find out what they can do. The researcher is the one who knows and the research product is quoted as absolute, essential to future strategies, financial expenditures and the promotion or sacking of teachers. A far right political agenda is seen to be in line with this: politicians and a general public who want simple answers get them. Economic rationalism is done on the basis of the research results. This is research performed on objectified children who are unable to protest, whose futures as readers and writers are not taken into account in terms of their interests, and whose complex semantic and sociocultural relations to literacy are denied. The ethics here are that the research must be defended as an accurate naming of categories of literacy achievement, and that the results are kept under lock and key until publication. A further ethics here regards the accuracy of the counting of the quantities inherent in the measurement instruments. In other words, there must be no cheating in the compilation of charts, graphs and statistics.

In an *interpretive* approach to literacy research, the researcher's interests regard understanding at the level of everyday language and action, and discovering the meanings and beliefs of teachers, parents, assistants and the children themselves. Here the literacy practices in current use are studied as particular phenomena with hermeneutic value. Classroom research rules, with the words and doings of children and adults coming into the research focus. The ethics are about the accurate or reasonable describing and interpreting of what is seen and heard to happen. Analysing (from videos, for example) and categorizing actions and interactions must be done as faithfully as possible to present the most likely account of what happened. Quite often large numbers of items, institutions or interactions are studied, as if their number validates the research. To generalize excruciatingly about gender here: (1) women seem to like this research practice, usually with no critique of its time-consuming accountability, and of the impossibility of language ever saying everything; (2) men (and women with less time to spare) appear to resist the problems by preferring the discourse of expertise offered by positivism, or by taking up the technical problematics of how to interpret the found phenomena.

Critical theory's research methodology practices may include the interpretive, but always there are layers of critique and sharp questions regarding power. What counts is the critical analysis, which may be of discourses and not only of practices. The interests of critical research are to radically transform human existence, by practical and public involvement in knowledge formation and use. Here many of the new critical theorists in early childhood education have to date been relatively silent regarding literacy. This may be because literacy itself is seen as an undesirable site for research, given radical agendas of child advocacy and social justice. Here the argument is that institutional literacy is usually imposed: a case of adult dominance over the very young, a matter of teacher power. Alternatively, not researching literacy may simply reflect a lack of experience or knowledge amongst researchers, about how texts work and how readers and writers act. But maybe I have been in literacy-less Norway too long: for the last five years I have taught, examined and researched without the concept. This may, of course, simply reflect my own lack of knowledge about the multiplicity of terms Norwegians use for the notion of literacy.

With *poststructural* approaches, the research interests are to question totalizing or unified interpretation and understanding (Scheurich, 1997). This includes self-critique of the positioning of the researcher (as at the end of the last paragraph). What matters regards locating dominant interests and saying or showing how these are produced and maintained. Hence marginal positions matter. For literacy this means literacies, with many acceptable practices, resistances and agencies. Minorities would here include whichever gender is non-dominant; whichever languages are spoken, written and read at home but not in schools and preschools; whoever has their marginalized sexuality or their religion not represented appropriately in the texts used and produced in educational institutions; which social classes in terms of higher education or money are disadvantaged regarding literacy practices; whose literacy at home does not include computer literacy; whose ethnicity and race are not represented by the teachers and the tests of literacy in the schools. Here the ethics regards other people, and attempts to maintain multiplicity: to work for lack of fixedness, including fixedness in research approaches and in understandings of what literacy is or might be.

It can be seen then that the ethics of researching the literacy of young children is not a simple matter. This is not just about getting or constructing data, analysing, interpreting, critiquing or deconstructing them, and writing them up (Blaxter et al., 1996). Ethical research involves for many researchers today (feminist poststructuralists, critical multiculturalists, postcolonial theorists) a reconstruction of what it is to do research. This necessitates thinking critically about particular sites, local events and differing subjectivities. It seems to me (as a feminist) that feminism has helped us see these things by showing us how women and girls (and their literacies and their research) must be considered differently and allowed to be different from men and boys. But if feminism is not itself plural, if it continues to refuse to acknowledge other marginalized groups, or it remains blind to its own locations of power, then there are problems to be dealt with. For these reasons a 'feminist methodology' is suspect.

Despite all this, the newer feminist (and queer theory and anti-racist and postcolonial) practices regarding literacies may arguably be researched as

dividing and blurring between gendered and other ways of being: (1) a teacher (of literacy); (2) a parent (for literacy learning); (3) a researcher (for and of literacies); (4) a policy maker (for literacies); (5) a writer (of texts and computer programs for the becoming literate); (6) a measurement expert (of literacies); (7) a child (who is expected to become literate).

ENDINGS

I have been drawing from classic Anglographic feminist texts on methodologies (Alcoff and Potter, 1993; Burt and Code, 1995; Fonow and Cook, 1991; Harding, 1993; 1996; Reinharz, 1992) to try to answer the question about what feminist research might be. This is a modernist question, because it seeks to categorize researchers as within or without. In postmodernity we can be both. Further, as I have tried to explain, there are many ways of doing feminist research and many related and theoretically driven approaches to inquiry in the social sciences. Not all of these are feminist, whatever that may be and however it shifts in time and space.

But over time, and given changing ideologies and the changing make-ups of workforces and given clientele, the spaces occupied by thematic, methodological and theoretical positionings begin to be taken up by others. In early childhood education the clientele comprises the students and participants of early schooling, preschooling and higher education. Here the employee statistics show the slow shift of ethnic minorities and senior women into the teaching, leading, lecturing and examining forces. Resultantly, changing ideologies and values begin to deal more seriously with locations of difference, multiplicities of meanings and openings for otherness. As effects of these, the themes, the theories and the ways of going about doing research are also changing. Time itself is a causal factor of change, as populations alter their social and scientific priorities, together with their desires for new fields, new modes, new actors and new writers. These shift as history reconstructs practices and values.

Much feminist research has come from a close relationship between the researcher and the researched. In one way, this places it in a similar position to the research of teachers. Teachers' research is produced because of and for the students past and present and future, with whom the researching teacher works. For teachers, teaching and researching go together. As with feminism, there is an ethics here which is not the same as the ethics in the research of an outsider who comes into the field. What then are the ethics and the competence of literacy experts without the professional experience of teachers, and without complex and highly developed literacies of their own?

I hope that this chapter raises many questions. Should men research women's issues? Should adults research the so-called literacy of children? Are the people conducting literacy research themselves lacking all but a basic understanding of what literacy is and how it differs in different situations, cultural contexts and genres? What has been the history of children's exclusion from research conducted about them, and what are the effects of this on today's research practices? Are young people in a position to conduct their own research? What would they do about us? What do we want research for?

Following this, anyone who still decides to research literacy will: (1) attempt to create new subject positions for people to occupy regarding literacies; (2) be prepared to reject existing methodologies and usual audiences for research; (3) constantly critique their own research practices and their own positionings regarding ever widening literacies; (4) not be afraid to theorize, to produce theory from the research, and to read expansively; (5) acknowledge that all knowledge is limited, contestable and must eventually change, because of who people are, where they are, when they produce their knowledge and for whom.

REFERENCES

Alcoff, L. and Potter, E. (eds) (1993) *Feminist Epistemologies*. New York: Routledge, Chapman and Hall.

Andersen, C.E. (2002) 'Verden i barnehagen. Dekonstruksjoner i lys av postkolonial teori: en etnografisk undersøkelse fra en barnehageavdeling' ('The world in the day care centre. Deconstructions in the light of postcolonial theory: an ethnographic investigation from a day care group') (my translation). Hovedfag i barnehagepedagogikk (Masters degree in early childhood education), Oslo University College, Norway.

Bailey, C. (1997) 'A place from which to speak: stories of memory, crisis and struggle from the preschool classroom', in J. Jipson and N. Paley (eds), *Daredevil Research: Re-creating Analytic Practice*. New York: Lang.

Begum, S. (1994) 'The issue of literacy and women's role in the development process', *Empowerment*, Dhaka University, Bangladesh, 1: 13–22.

Berge, B.-M. and Ve, H. (1999) *Action Research for Gender Equity*. Buckingham: Open University Press.

Blaxter, L., Hughes, C. and Tight, M. (1996) *How to Research*. Buckingham: Open University Press.

Burt, S. and Code, L. (eds) (1995) *Changing Methods: Feminists Transforming Practice*. Peterborough: Broadview.

Cannella, G. (1998) 'Early childhood education: a call for the construction of revolutionary images', in W. Pinar (ed.), *Curriculum: Toward New Identities*. New York: Garland. pp. 157–84.

Castleton, G. (2000) 'Workplace literacy: examining the virtual and virtuous realities in (e)merging discourses on work', *Discourse: Studies in the Cultural Politics of Education*, 21 (1): 91–104.

Christiansen, P. and James, A. (eds) (2000) *Research with Children: Perspectives and Practices*. London: Falmer.

Connole, H. (1998) 'Approaches to social science inquiry', in *Research Methodologies in Education*, Deakin University, Geelong, Australia, pp. 7–27.

Creaser, B. and Dau, E. (eds) (1995) *The Anti-Bias Approach in Early Childhood*. Pymble, NSW: Harper.

Davies, B. (1993) *Shards of Glass: Children Reading and Writing beyond Gendered Identities*. St Leonards, NSW: Allen and Unwin.

Davies, B. (2000) *A Body of Writing: 1990–1999*. California: AltaMira.

Deakin University (1998) *Research Methodologies in Education. vol. 1: Reader. vol. 2: Study Guide. vol. 3: Horizons, Images and Experiences: the Rsearch Story Collection*. Faculty of Education, Geelong, Australia.

Ellis, C. and Flaherty, M. (eds) (1992) *Investigating Subjectivity: Research on Lived Experience*. Newbury Park CA: Sage.

Firestone, S. (1970) *The Dialectic of Sex: the Case for Feminist Revolution*. New York: Morrow.

Fonow, M. and Cook, J. (eds) (1991) *Beyond Methodology: Feminist Scholarship as Lived Research*. Bloomington, IN: Indiana University Press.

Gallop, J. (2000) 'The ethics of reading: close encounters', *Journal of Curriculum Theorizing*, Fall: 7–17.

Gilbert, R. and Gilbert, P. (1998) *Masculinity Goes to School*. Sydney: Allen and Unwin.

Glenn, C. (2000) 'Comment: truth, lies and method: revisiting feminist historiography', *College English*, 62 (3): 387–9.

Gliddon, J. (2001) 'Nerds from the underground', *The Bulletin*, Sydney, Australia, 8 May, 119: 60–1.

Grau, E. and Walsh, D. (1998) *Studying Children in Context: Theories, Methods and Ethics*. London: Sage.

Grieshaber, S. (1998) 'Constructing the gendered infant', in N. Yelland (ed.), *Gender in Early Childhood*. London: Routledge.

Hammersley, M. (1992) 'On feminist methodology', *Sociology*, 26 (2): 187–206.

Harding, S. (1993) 'Rethinking standpoint epistemology: what is "strong objectivity"?', in L. Alcoff and E. Potter (eds), *Feminist Epistemologies*, New York: Routledge, Chapman and Hall.

Harding, S. (1996) 'Multicultural and global feminist philosophies of science: resources and challenges', in

L. Nelson and J. Nelson (eds), *Feminism, Science and the Philosophy of Science*. Dordrecht: Kluwer.

Hatch, A. (ed.) (1995) *Qualitative Research in Early Childhood Settings*. Westport, CT: Praeger.

Haug, F. (ed.) (1987) *Female Sexualisation: a Collective Work of Memory*, trans. E. Carter. London: Verso.

Hauser, M. and Jipson, J. (1998) *Intersections: Feminisms/Early Childhoods*. New York: Lang.

hooks, b. (1994) *Teaching to Transgress: Education as the Practice of Freedom*. New York: Routledge.

Hughes, P. (2001) 'Paradigms, methods and knowledge', in G. Mac Naughton, S. Rolfe and I. Siraj-Blatchford (eds), *Doing Early Childhood Research: International Perspectives on Theory and Practice*. Buckingham: Open University Press.

Huq, J. (1997) 'History of literacy efforts for women in Bangladesh: various issues and dimensions', *Empowerment*, 4: 79–104.

Jones Diaz, C. (2001) 'Latino American voices in Australia: negotiating bilingual identity in early childhood education'. Paper presented at Reconceptualizing Early Childhood Education Conference, Teachers College, Columbia University, New York, 3–6 October.

Jørgensen, M.W. and Phillips, L. (1999) *Diskursanalyse som teori og metode* (*Discourse Analysis as Theory and Method*) (my translation). Roskilde: Roskilde Universitetsforlag.

Lather, P. (1995) 'The validity of angels: interpretative and textual strategies in researching the lives of women with HIV/AIDS', *Qualitative Inquiry*, 1 (1): 41–67.

Levine, R., Levine, S. and Schnell, B. (2001) ' "Improve the women": mass schooling, female literacy and worldwide social change', *Harvard Educational Review*, 71 (1): 1–50.

Love, K. and Hamstom, J. (2001) 'Out of the mouths of boys: a profile of boys committed to reading', *The Australian Journal of Language and Literacy*, 24 (1): 31–48.

Mac an Ghaill, M. (1994) *The Making of Men: Masculinities, Sexualities and Schooling*. Buckingham: Open University Press.

Mac Naughton, G. (2001) 'Action research', in G. Mac Naughton, S. Rolfe and I. Siraj-Blatchford (eds), *Doing Early Childhood Research: International Perspectives on Theory and Practice*. Buckingham: Open University Press. pp. 208–24.

Malterud, K. (1996) *Kvalitative metoder i medisinsk forskning: en innføring* (*Qualitative Methods in Medical Research: an Introduction*) (my translation). Oslo: Tano Aschehoug.

Marsh, J. (2000) ' "But I want to fly too!": girls and super-hero play in the infant classroom', *Gender and Education*, 12 (2): 209–20.

McWilliam, E. (1994) *In Broken Images: Tales for a Different Teacher Education*. New York: Teachers College Press.

Møller, J. (1996) 'Aksjonsforskning i spenningsfeltet mellom politikk og vitenskap' ('Action research in the tense/exciting field between politics and epistemology') (my translation), *Nordisk Pedagogik*, Nordic Association for Educational Research, 16 (2): 66–77.

Penn, H. (ed.) (2000) *Early Childhood Services: Theory, Policy and Practice*. Buckingham: Open University Press.

Quinlivan, K. (2002) 'So far so queer? Some ins and outs of working with high school students on issues of sexual diversity'. Paper presented in Network on Schooling Sexualities, at Nordic Educational Research Association Congress, Tallinn, Estonia, 7–9 March.

Reinharz, S. (1992) *Feminist Methods in Social Research*. New York: Oxford University Press.

Rhedding-Jones, J. (1993) 'Gender and readings of literature', in *Fantasy and Feminism in Children's Books. Literary Literacy: Study Guide*. Faculty of Education, Open Campus Program, Geelong, Deakin University. pp. 43–78.

Rhedding-Jones, J. (1995) 'What do you do after you've met poststructuralism? Research possibilities regarding feminism, ethnography and literacy', *Journal of Curriculum Studies*, 27 (5): 479–500.

Rhedding-Jones, J. (1997a) 'The writing on the wall: doing a feminist poststructural doctorate', *Gender and Education*, 9 (2): 193–206.

Rhedding-Jones, J. (1997b) 'Across continents: gender and education'. Review essay of Bjerén, G. and Elgquist–Saltzmann, I. (eds) (1994), *Gender and Education in a Life Perspective: Lessons from Scandinavia*. Avebury: Aldershot. Gaskell, J. and Willinsky, J. (eds) (1995), *Gender In/forms Curriculum: from Enrichment to Transformation*. New York: Teachers College Press. *Australian Research in Education*, 24 (3): 115–23.

Rhedding-Jones, J. (1997c) 'Changing the subject of literacy', *Literacy Learning: Secondary Thoughts*, 5 (1): 58–63.

Rhedding-Jones, J. (2000) 'Fakultetsopponenten sammanfattar' ('Report and academic discussion by the examiner of a doctoral thesis'). For Lenz Taguchi, H. (2000), Emancipation och motstånd: dokumentation och kooperativa läroprocesser i förskolan' ('Emancipation and resistance: documentation and co-operative learning processes in preschooling') (my translation). Studies in Educational Sciences 33, Lärarhögskolan i Stockholm: HLS Förlag. *Pedagogisk Forskning i Sverge* (Educational Research in Sweden), 5 (4): 320–7.

Rhedding-Jones, J. (2001a) 'Gender and education: guest editorial', *Nora: Nordic Journal of Women's Studies*, 3 (2): 11–15.

Rhedding-Jones, J. (2001b) 'Shifting ethnicities: "native informants" and other theories from/for early childhood education', *Contemporary Issues in Early Childhood*, 2 (2): 135–56.

Rhedding-Jones, J. (2002) 'An undoing of documents and other texts: towards a critical multicultural early childhood education', *Contemporary Issues in Early Childhood*, 3 (1): 90–116.

Rhedding-Jones, J. and Atkinson, N. (1991) 'Gender and literacy learning: powerful literacies for boys and girls', in E. Furniss and P. Green (eds), *The Literacy Agenda*. Portsmouth, NH: Heinemann. pp. 58–79.

Rhedding-Jones, J., Halim, S., Chowdhury, O. and Vandsemb, B. (2002) *Girls at School: a Qualitative Review in Bangladesh*, HiO-report 2002, no. 2, Oslo University College. Female Secondary Education Stipend Project (FESP) Phase 2 (NORAD).

Richardson, L. (1997) *Fields of Play: Constructing an Academic Life*. New Brunswick, NJ: Rutgers University Press.

Scheurich, J. (1997) *Research Method in the Postmodern*. London: Falmer.

Tobin, J. (1995) 'Poststructural research in early childhood education', in A. Hatch (ed.), *Qualitative Research in Early Childhood Settings*. Westport, CT: Praeger.

Weiler, K. and Middleton, S. (1998) *Narrative Inquiries in the History of Women's Education*. Buckingham: Open University Press.

Woodhead, M. (2000) 'Towards a global paradigm for research into early childhood', in H. Penn (ed.), *Early Childhood Services: Theory, Policy and practice*. Buckingham: Open University Press. pp. 15–35.

Yelland, N. (ed.) (1998) *Gender in Early Childhood*. London: Routledge.

33

Taking a Naturalistic Viewpoint in Early Childhood Literacy Research

BRIAN CAMBOURNE

This chapter begins with two assumptions. One is that naturalistic research serves unique scientific purposes in education. The other is that literacy education, especially as it relates to early childhood learners, falls within the general ambit of 'education'. Accordingly the first part of the chapter will use examples of naturalistic research conducted in the early childhood literacy field to address the general question, 'What distinguishes a "naturalistic viewpoint" from other viewpoints in educational research?' The chapter will conclude by addressing the issue, 'Naturalistic research in early childhood literacy: why and when?'

WHAT DISTINGUISHES A 'NATURALISTIC VIEWPOINT' FROM OTHER VIEWPOINTS IN EDUCATIONAL RESEARCH?

This question (or a version of it) is frequently discussed in educational research circles. Too often such discussions focus on the relative merits and/or usefulness of naturalistic research methods *vis-à-vis* explicitly controlled, manipulated, laboratory methods. Unfortunately they also frequently deteriorate into polemics and petulant, empty argumentation which spills over into the published literature. This is especially true with respect to the literature of early childhood literacy. In the last decade for example it has been a common occurrence to see such oppositions as 'scientifically based reading research versus anecdotal evidence', ' rigour versus

sloppiness', 'control of variance versus meaningfulness', 'sterile versus real-world and true-to-life', ' thin data versus rich data', and so on appearing in the literature, especially since the re-emergence in the 1980s and 1990s of the adversarial 'code-breaking versus meaning-based' debates which Chall initiated in the 1960s (Chall, 1967; Coles, 2000; 2003).

While the actual words used in these oppositions point to some of the reasons for the adversarial postures adopted by those who engage in such polemics, there are other issues associated with the status of naturalistic research in educational research. One of particular relevance for this chapter is the ambiguity and confusion inherent in distinguishing a naturalistic viewpoint from others. In what follows I intend to explore some of the confusions associated with this ambiguity. In particular I will focus on three overlapping, yet distinct perspectives for addressing the issues inherent in distinguishing naturalistic inquiry from other modes of research. These are:

1 naturalistic research means using a particular set of research behaviours
2 naturalistic research means 'doing what comes naturally'
3 naturalistic research means adopting certain philosophical beliefs.

Naturalistic research means using a particular set of research behaviours

Can a research project be identified as 'naturalistic' on the basis of what researchers actually *do* as they engage in the research process? Is it the overt research behaviours which researchers employ that sets naturalistic research apart from other research traditions?

Let us explore this issue with a concrete example. Between 1981 and 1987 I *spent hundreds of hours observing* children in Australian kindergarten classrooms (Cambourne and Turbill, 1987). I was trying to understand how kindergartners learned to solve what I then called 'the written language puzzle'. In order to achieve this end I engaged in a range of distinctive, more or less 'overt' research behaviours. I *took detailed field notes* of individual children as they created the written texts that their kindergarten teacher expected them to write. I *used video and audio technology to capture and 'freeze' the processes they employed, which I could revisit again and again*. I *asked students lots of questions* about both their learning and their writing; I *had many conversations with their teachers* about what I was seeing and hearing; I *mapped the classroom environment*; I *collected and studied the written products each child, and their teachers, constructed*. The overt research behaviours in which I engaged are italicized. Let's pull them together into a single list:

- spent hundreds of hours observing
- took detailed field notes
- used video and audio technology to capture and 'freeze' the processes they employed, which I could revisit again and again
- asked students lots of questions
- had many conversations with their teachers
- mapped the classroom environment
- collected and studied the written products each child, and their teachers, constructed.

I also spent a lot of time trying to make sense of, or *to understand*, what all these data 'meant'. So perhaps another, less overt (but still relatively obvious) research behaviour associated with a naturalistic viewpoint is the overall purpose of the research. In the 1981–7 studies this was:

- to understand how kindergartners learned to solve 'the written language puzzle'.

Naturalistic researchers are also expected to report on what they learn from engaging in this kind of research. Therefore I *wrote a multiplicity of papers using the data I collected between 1981 and 1987*. These papers in turn were similar in that they *were written in the quasi-narrative genre* that I believed to be characteristic of naturalistic research papers. For example, here's how I wrote the first few pages of one such paper (Cambourne, 1982a). Notice the 'story-like' tenor of the narrative I constructed.

It is the first week of December and the second last week of the school year. Reagan, who is five years eight months old, sits in her kindergarten class, bent over her desk, engrossed in a task which she calls 'Writing a story'. She's been engaged in this task for the last 37 minutes. I've been sitting just behind her right shoulder, observing her, and taking field notes. I wait for a pause in her activity and ask her to share what she's written. She shows me her 'story'.

As I've been observing her every week now since July she knows what I'm going to ask her to do. She anticipates my request and reads her piece to me, pointing to each word as she reads it.

Reagan's reading

'I are staying at my aunties. My cousins are Terry and Cory. My uncle and auntie are Sue and Garry. Mum and dad went to Adelaide to get a new tennis court. It is a hard tennis court. The cement is black and white. Cory asked me if I would like to skate behind his tractor, and my stopper came off. I asked Garry if he would fix it but he was ...'

Nicole, who is in the same class and is the same age (5:8), is also writing at her desk. Like Reagan she's been engaged in the task for the last thirty-seven minutes. Although today's date is December 2, the date on the first page of Nicole's piece is November 3. She's been working on the same piece now for approximately one month. She numbers her last completed page, '27'. When she began this piece a month ago her teacher and I referred to it as 'Nicole's Piece'. Now, four weeks and twenty-seven pages later we facetiously talk about 'Nicole's Thesis'. The first few pages of her 'thesis' look like this:

If we add the last three criteria to the previous list of 'research behaviours' that characterize what

> Nicole 3-11-81
> On The weyKend
> I went to nahhy
> and PoPPy Poppy
> got us an oyscret
> and a Pacit of
> bubollgum and That
> th day aw cuzenz
> came uP to see
> us. We went uP to
> The Pack We had
> a swing. Wen
> we went back
>
> We Went to see
> aw anty Mell
> at The covent
> aw cusenz t
> fownd a Pond.
> then Was a fis
> Ill the Watta
> aw cuzens faw
> a Plastic bag.
>
> Mathyou
> trod to cach him
> and scot tod his
> thongs off. and
> hoPt in the Pond.

naturalistic researchers actually 'do', our final summary list might read something like this.

Naturalistic researchers:

- spend prolonged periods of time observing
- take detailed field notes
- sometimes use video and audio technology to capture and 'freeze' the ongoing behaviours in which humans engage
- repeatedly revisit these frozen records
- ask those whom they're observing lots of questions
- map the physical environment where behaviour occurs
- collect and study the artefacts which those being observed produce
- seek to understand how some phenomena 'work'
- write papers using the data they collect
- write papers in a quasi-narrative genre.

Given this list, can we conclude that what sets naturalistic research apart is the decision to adopt a certain set of overt research behaviours?

I don't believe we can. Certainly the intention in 1981 was to conduct a naturalistic inquiry, but there was much more behind this intention than merely the decision to use a particular set of research behaviours. While they could be potential indicators of naturalistic research, they are merely superficial accoutrements of naturalistic inquiry. As such they *cannot* be accorded the status of defining criteria. To consider them thus would only serve to trivialize naturalistic inquiry. There are factors additional to the overt researcher behaviours which need to be considered in any attempts to clarify and sharpen what distinguishes naturalistic inquiry from other modes of research. Some of these have emerged from attempts to sharpen the meaning of the terms 'natural' and 'naturalistic' and their cognates.

Naturalistic research means 'doing what comes naturally'

When researchers attempt to discuss naturalistic research, one of the first problems they encounter is the meaning of the adjective 'naturalistic'. Willems

(1968) was one of the first to draw attention to this issue in the social sciences when he wrote:

> Too often we hear the word 'natural' used in the sense of 'real' and 'true' as against 'unreal' and 'untrue', or even 'unnatural'. Is the finding from a naturalistic study more 'real' or more 'true' than the finding from a laboratory experiment?

One common response to this issue is to define naturalistic research as research on *natural phenomena*. Unfortunately, such attempts inevitably founder on the issue of circularity. Is the learning which occurs in a classroom 'natural'? Is it more 'natural' than the learning that occurs in the family setting? Is a classroom a 'naturally occurring' phenomenon, or is it an artificially contrived, culturally derived setting? Is it more 'natural' than the family meal setting? At the time of writing I'm not aware of any unambiguous criteria for the concepts 'naturalness' and naturalistic' having been developed.

So where does this leave us? Are we trapped forever in circular argument? Or is there a framework which allows us to hone the meaning of the adjective 'naturalistic', so that it is relevant for empirical investigation?

One interesting attempt to develop such a framework emerged in the mid 1950s and was refined during the 1960s and 1970s by a group which called themselves 'ecological psychologists' (Barker and Wright, 1955; Barker, 1964; 1968; Barker and associates, 1978). In 1968 one of this group, Edwin Willems, published a seminal paper on this issue. Among other things he wrote:

> the set of activities an investigator actually engages in while conducting his [*sic*] research falls somewhere in a two dimensional space. The first dimension, which is most frequently thought of in differentiating research activities, describes *the degree of the investigator's influence upon, or manipulation of, the antecedent conditions of the behaviour studied*, on the assumption that the degree of such influence or manipulation may vary from high to low or from much to none. The second dimension, which is less commonly considered than the first, describes *the degree to which the units are imposed by the investigator upon the behaviour studied*. (1968: 46, emphasis in original)

Figure 33.1 shows these dimensions in orthogonal relation. The texts inside the 'space' relate to different positions which researchers can adopt on each of the two dimensions. Willems explained the figure thus:

> The figure represents a descriptive view of research activities in the following way. Assuming that the target of investigation is some behavioural phenomenon, it is

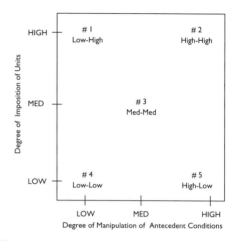

Figure 33.1 Research activities in a two-dimensional space (Willems, 1968)

possible to describe two separate, though often interdependent, ways in which the investigator may function in the process of obtaining behavioural data (a) by influencing or arranging the antecedent conditions of the behaviour, and (b) by imposing restrictions or limitations on the range and spectrum of response, that is the behaviour itself. Furthermore, as described by Figure [33.1] each of these functions can vary on a continuum'. (1968: 47)

How this two-dimensional space describes research activities can be illustrated with a personal example. Many years ago I conducted a study of the language development of Australian children at school entry (Cambourne, 1982b). The specific research question which framed the study was, 'When children first enter the school system, what language abilities do they bring with them?'

I decided to approach this question from two very different directions by actually doing two studies. In the first I decided to conduct a study which could be placed in region 2 of Willems' two-dimensional space, namely 'high–high'. I chose to administer a reputable standardized test to my sample of beginning school children. The standardized test I used was the Illinois Test of Psycholinguistic Abilities (ITPA) (Kirk et al., 1968) which purported to measure the psycholinguistic processes associated with the receptive, expressive and organizational dimensions of language use. My intention was to use the scores which each of my subjects attained on this instrument to answer the question which motivated the study.

In the second study, I decided to do a study which could be placed in region 4 of Willems' space, namely 'low–low'. Rather than give a standardized test, I decided to devise a way of 'spying' on these children as they used their language in situations which were not specifically set up for research purposes. I did this by placing a small radio microphone in my subjects' clothing (which transmitted to a receiver which was in turn hooked up to a recorder), and recording a minimum of four hours continual language use by each of them as they interacted with others at home and/or at school in the everyday ebb and flow of a typical day. I devised a method of quantifying units of language which could be used as indicators of language ability (mean length of T-unit[1] in words and mean number of sentence combining transformations per T-unit: see Cambourne, 1982b, for details).

The first study would be located in the 'high–high' region because I exerted high degrees of influence both on the antecedent conditions of the behaviour I was studying (language use), and on the nature of the responses (units of behaviour) that the subjects could make. The significant antecedent behaviours in this study were the specific input questions in each of the subtests that made up the ITPA battery. At any point in the progress of the research I could predict with high degrees of accuracy what linguistic behaviour would occur, in what order, and so on. This is probably the highest degree of control which can be exerted by a researcher over the 'input end' of a research project. The linguistic responses that resulted from these predetermined questions are also highly predictable. Some require a 'yes' or 'no' or 'true/false' response, some require the subject to point to one of four pictures, some require the subject to repeat a list of digits after hearing them spoken by the tester (me). No other behaviours are allowed or planned. The range of linguistic behaviours imposed by me (the researcher) are limited to 'yes', 'no', 'don't know' and 'no response'.

In the second study this situation was reversed. I had no control over or prior knowledge of what would be said, by whom, to whom, for what purposes. The range of possible meanings that might be expressed in language could range from single words to much longer complex texts, perhaps comprising a multiplicity of sentences. Thus the degree of manipulation of antecedent conditions I imposed, especially any language that might be used, was virtually zero. Similarly the degree to which I imposed units of linguistic behaviour on how subjects would respond to any linguistic event or question that occurred while they were being 'bugged' was also virtually zero. Even though the same subjects were involved, the differences in the empirical findings from these two modes of research suggested there are some important scientific issues which need to be untangled.

Given these examples, does the descriptive space in Figure 33.1 help clarify the meaning of the adjective 'naturalistic'? I think it does, but with important limitations.

While it provides a tenable framework for characterizing research activities which might fall into the extreme ends of each axis, or even those which would fall somewhere on the main diagonal from low–low through med–med to high–high, the further we move from this diagonal, the more the differences are blurred. Although it's a useful framework for classifying research which clusters around this diagonal, it tends to exclude a great number of other research possibilities. Studies which can be located along this diagonal represent only a small proportion of the possible set of educational research activities. Thus Willems' two-dimensional space, while helpful in clarifying some of the ambiguity which inheres in the term 'naturalistic', is not a consistently reliable framework for unambiguously identifying all possible degrees of naturalistic inquiry. While a combination of the methodological tools a researcher employs, and the degree to which a researcher manipulates the axes which make up Willems' two dimensions, might be *necessary* indicators of a naturalistic viewpoint, they are not *sufficient*. What a researcher *believes* about some rather abstract philosophical issues also needs to be included in the search for defining criteria.

Naturalistic research means adopting certain philosophical beliefs

Naturalistic inquiry hasn't always been a strongly preferred research option in education. While it's always had its advocates, it wasn't till Kuhn's (1962) seminal work on the nature of scientific revolutions that it started to generate increased interest from educational researchers. In 1977 a Qualitative Research Special Interest Group was formed from the membership of the American Educational Research Association (AERA). In 1981 Guba and Lincoln observed that the naturalistic paradigm was 'an emergent paradigm that has begun seriously to challenge that orthodoxy'. In the intervening two decades there have been scores of articles and books on the central arguments about the philosophical underpinnings of educational research. While Paul and Marfo (2001) cite the 'publications by Teachers College Press and by Sage Publications in particular' as two of the most prolific providers of 'an intellectually compelling body of work on the philosophy and practice of a whole range of philosophical bases of inquiry', they single out Howe's 'Two dogmas of educational research' (1995) and Guba's *Paradigm Dialog*

(1990) as two of the 'more useful works in clarifying the philosophical issues which impacted on naturalistic inquiry'.

Just what are these 'philosophical issues'? How are they reflected in the discourse of researchers? Let's imagine two hypothetical educational researchers who are committed to conducting research into early childhood literacy. One prefers to work in the rationalistic ('quantitative', 'scientific') mode, and the other in the naturalistic mode. If each were asked to explain these research preferences, the *rationalistic researcher* would answer along these lines:

> Of course I prefer to work in the scientific paradigm. Is there any other valid way to do research? I know it is also referred to by other names such as 'experimental', 'rationalistic', 'logical-positivist', 'empirical', 'measurement-based', 'quantitative', but I prefer to call it 'scientific'. I prefer to locate my research projects within this paradigm of inquiry because I hold certain philosophical beliefs about the nature of reality, the nature of truth and the methods for discovering what these truths are.
>
> For example I believe that the universe is completely and correctly structured in terms of entities, properties, and relations, and that these exist independently of the human mind and human experience. The correct forms of these things, and what they 'mean', also exist independently of the experiences we have 'of' and/or 'with' them. The universe only grudgingly and reluctantly reveals these meanings, never willingly. We have to force it to do so. This is what research is for, namely to discover the correct forms of these entities, properties, and relations and use them to build theoretic models that represent the one true reality that I believe exists 'out there'. The best way to find out these truths is to use the scientific modes of inquiry developed and synthesized over the last 400 years by philosophers and physical scientists in their attempts to understand and explain the complex physical world.
>
> This means l do most of my research in a laboratory or specially contrived setting of some kind, and the fundamental purpose of my research is to prove or disprove cause–effect relationships. Like Newton and Descartes I'm really trying to force nature to reveal the truths on which it's based so that I can move yet another few steps toward revealing what the one true reality actually is. Ultimately I intend to develop predictive theories which describe how this reality 'works'. The method I use to do this will involve controlled experimentation, including testing hypotheses, eliminating and controlling threats to objectivity, measuring effects, and ultimately developing a predictive theory.

On the other hand, if one asked the same question of an *educational researcher* who expressed a preference for working within naturalistic inquiry, he/she would probably respond thus:

I prefer to locate my research within the paradigm of naturalistic inquiry, which is also referred to by other names such as 'qualitative research', 'ethnography', 'anthropological research', 'ecological research', 'case study', 'responsive evaluation', 'grounded-theory research', and so on. You'll also find sociologists, investigative journalists, anthropologists, and responsive evaluators working within this paradigm.

Why do I prefer to conduct this kind of research? While I believe that there is a real world 'out there' that we all experience, unlike my colleague above, I do not believe that meanings which can describe this reality are imposed on us. Rather I believe that that it is us (i.e. the human mind) which imposes meanings on these experiences. Again, unlike my colleague above, this means I do not believe that there is *one correct* set of meanings of or perspective on the entities, properties, and relations associated with any event or concept. While I can see how the canons, principles, and tools of the classical 'scientific method' can be applied to the inanimate physical world of forces, mass, the motion of celestial bodies, test-tubes and billiard balls, I do *not* believe that they can be adapted to the so-called 'social and educational sciences' with the same degree of success. Social scientists, especially those like me with an interest in early childhood literacy, confront problems that the 'pure' physicists, chemists etc. need not consider. Like test-tube contents, mass, force, motion, position in space can be controlled, whereas human behaviours, especially those associated with the meanings which humans construct, frequently refuse to be isolated or compartmentalized for purposes of experimentation

I also prefer to work in the naturalistic mode because the fundamental research questions that intrigue and motivate me are of this ilk: 'How do complex systems (such as early childhood literacy classrooms, the reading and writing processes that students must learn to control etc.) "work"?' Given this research focus, I believe that the most appropriate paradigm to help me understand how the multiplicity of variables which make up the complex phenomenon known as an 'early childhood literacy classroom' etc. actually 'work' in our educational culture is based on the epistemological and ontological principles which underpin the naturalistic paradigm. Obviously I also believe that the kind of learning that is necessary for the development of highly productive, critically literate graduates has its origins in the early years of schooling, *and* is far too complex to be understood by applying simplistic, cause–effect, measurement- based logic.

I also believe that a valid form of 'truth' about such complex systems as Australian early childhood literacy classrooms will ultimately emerge if I am given the opportunity to spend prolonged periods of time being immersed in and experiencing settings where these complex systems can be found. Given this kind of immersion I will be able to identify what is important, pervasive and salient. Furthermore if I conduct my field work and subsequent analysis of data in ways that enhance the credibility and trustworthiness of my findings, the 'truths' which emerge will be ultimately be confirmable.

Given these caveats I'll do field work in natural settings. The major 'instrument' I'll rely on in order to understand what I'm observing will be the human mind. Rather than try to 'prove' or 'disprove' cause–effect relationships, I'll set out to understand how complex phenomena 'work', how all the variables that are operating in such complex phenomena relate to each other, and how these interactions ultimately shape the phenomenon I'm interested in. While I do not take steps to impose control over any of the variables involved in the phenomenon I'm trying to understand, I deliberately take certain steps to increase the credibility and trustworthiness of my findings, as well as minimizing my subjectivity and increasing the neutrality of my analysis.

It has been my experience that the beliefs embedded in these hypothetical discourses are not so explicit in the day-to-day discourse of most literacy researchers. Typically they are implicit, operating at a tacit level of assumption, only becoming explicit when educational researchers are forced to consider these three deeply philosophical issues and address the questions they beg.

1   the *ontological* issue ('What do I assume about the nature of reality?')
2   the *epistemological* issue ('What do I assume about the nature of truth?')
3   the *methodological* issue ('What do I assume about the best way to go about discovering the truths I want to know?').

If we could (metaphorically) 'get inside the heads' of our two hypothetical researchers and help them turn these tacit assumptions into propositional form, what would emerge? Table 33.1 addresses this question.

It seems that what a researcher believes about the nature of 'reality' and 'truth', and about how and why one would go about *coming to know* them, is crucial in determining if a researcher has a naturalistic intent. In other words it is a researcher's philosophical belief system which 'drives' the research process and determines how it will unfold. What sets naturalistic research apart from other modes of research are certain key beliefs about reality, truth, and methods of finding out. These in turn will affect where a research project might be located in Willems' two-dimensional space, as well as the methodological tools and other overt researcher behaviours employed.

Figure 33.2 is a schematic summary of these relationships.

NATURALISTIC RESEARCH IN EARLY CHILDHOOD LITERACY: WHY AND WHEN?

With the information embedded in Table 33.1 and Figure 33.2 in mind, the remainder of this chapter addresses the issue of the role and rationale of naturalistic inquiry in the early childhood literacy domain. In particular it will explore the assumption that 'naturalistic research uniquely serves scientific purposes in early childhood literacy education'. While this assumption is specifically about early childhood literacy education, it is really a special case of the larger domain of education *per se*. Accordingly I intend to explore the assumption first from the perspective of the general case ('naturalistic research serves unique scientific purposes in education *per se*') and then apply what emerges to the specific area of 'early childhood literacy education'.

Researchers in most domains of scientific inquiry have at some time faced the issue of justifying the decision to adopt a naturalistic research viewpoint *vis-à-vis* other paradigms of inquiry. Typically they identify four broad, overlapping categories of 'scientific purpose' which naturalistic inquiry uniquely serves. These are:

1   coercing and enabling unique and important conceptual advances
2   documenting the distribution of phenomena in the world
3   supporting and/or challenging the ecological validity of research findings created by other modes of research
4   informing the design of worthwhile, manipulative, rationalistic studies.

In what follows I intend to explore the relevance of each of these categories for early childhood literacy research.

Naturalistic inquiry serves the scientific purpose of coercing and enabling unique and important conceptual advances

During the last two decades early childhood literacy researchers have engaged in a great deal of what Hull and Schultz (2001) refer to as 'out-of-school research'. An example is Gilmore and Glatthorn's (1982) collection of educational ethnographies, *Children In and Out of School*. In this volume, a common theme running through the different

Table 33.1 *From tacit assumptions to propositions*

Domain of philosophical concern	Our rationalistic researcher's tacit assumptions in propositional form	Our naturalistic researcher's tacit assumptions in propositional form
Ontological Assumptions: 'What do I assume about the nature of reality?'	• A single reality, which is independent of the human mind, exists	• Any realities we come to know are contingent upon the way our nervous systems construct meanings from the stimuli which impinge on our sense organs
	• This reality operates according to immutable laws of cause and effect	• This means that there are a multiplicity of plausible realities which are contingent upon interpretation by a human mind
'And how does it relate to the truth?'	• Truth is a set of propositions that are isomorphic to this single reality	• Truth comprises the inevitable conclusions about what is important, pervasive, salient, and dynamic in a particular human context
Epistemological assumptions: 'What do I assume about the nature of truth?'	• Truth is absolute, immutable, eternal, and fixed (when I use the word 'truth' I *don't* need to put quotation marks around it)	• Truth is problematic (when I use the word 'truth' I *do* need to put quotation marks around it)
	• Truth is an experimentally confirmable hypothesis	• Truth is confirmable through proper conduct of field study and subsequent analysis of data generated by such field work
	• Objectivity is both possible and desirable.	• Objectivity is neither possible nor necessary to the discovery of truths
	• Facts and theory are value- and context-free	• All facts and theories are value-laden
Methodological assumptions: 'What do I assume about the best way to go about discovering the truths I want to know?'	• Controlled experimentation is the fundamental technique	• Field study is the fundamental technique
	• Experimenter bias must be zero; this is made possible by interposing a non-human measuring and/or observational instrument between the experimenter and the data	• Involves use of 'human instrument' in natural settings
	• Potential contaminating variables *can* and *must* be controlled	• Potential contaminating variables *cannot* and *should not* be controlled; rather researcher subjectivity can be explicated and neutrality maximized
	• Predictive, context-independent, immutable, theory is the end-product	• A credible, trustworthy explanation of how and why the multiplicity of variables under observation 'work together' to produce the phenomenon being studied is the end product

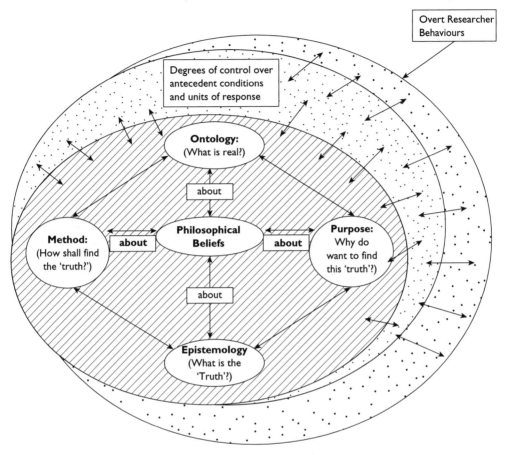

Figure 33.2 Schematic summary of relationships in alternative research approaches

chapters is the concept of schools as cultures with a set of values and beliefs that are not continuous with the cultures from which they draw their clientele. That Jacobs and Jordan (1993) ultimately elevated this discrepancy to the status of the 'continuity–discontinuity theory' is evidence of the kinds of 'conceptual advances' that such naturalistic research can promote. Furthermore it was in the Gilmore and Glatthorn volume that Heath (1982) first alerted the profession to the possibility of viewing education as a process of cultural transmission, and formal schooling as only one part of the process. She thus made an early argument for the need to study schools and classrooms in relation to the broader community or culture.

Heath (1983) continued this thrust in her classic long-term study of three contiguous communities over a decade in the 1960s and 1970s. She illustrated how each community – a black working-class community, a white working-class community, and a racially mixed middle-class community – socialized their children into very different language practices. Heath documented each community's 'ways with words' and explored how these impacted on their school learning. She concluded that 'the place of language in the life of each social group [in these communities and throughout the world] is interdependent with the habits and values of behaving shared among members of that group' (1983: 11). She thus demonstrated how children from different communities were differentially prepared for schooling that promoted and privileged only middle-class ways of using language.

These early out-of-school studies have engendered other research projects, which document both the functions and the uses of literacy practices in various communities and the differential preparation that children from various communities brought to school. These projects included Cochrane-Smith's (1986) description of story reading in a private nursery school, Fishman's (1988) study of an Amish community, Taylor and Dorsey-Gaines' (1988) study of the literacy practices in urban homes, Taylor's volume *From the Child's Point of View* (1993) and my own work on developing an 'educationally relevant theory of literacy learning' (Cambourne, 1995). The conceptual and theoretical advances which this research has made possible have been far reaching. Hull and Schultz (2001) go so far to suggest that such research has 'played pivotal roles in the history and development of literacy research and literacy theory'. Without such research, significant theoretical advances in the ways researchers thought about early childhood literacy would at best have been delayed, and at worst not even have occurred.

Naturalistic research serves the scientific purpose of documenting the distribution of phenomena in the world

Scientists from established domains of inquiry such as zoology, botany, geology, chemistry, and so on have long recognized the need to map the forms, abundance, and distribution of the phenomena which make up their science. This has not been so evident in the social sciences. Psychology is a case in point:

> Every beginning [psychology] textbook tells the student that failure and frustration are important behavior phenomena, and that rewards and punishments are important attributes of man's environment. But where is the information on the forms, abundance, and distribution of these important phenomena outside the very limited, specially contrived situation of psychological laboratories and clinics? As a psychologist, what answer should I give a layman seeking information from me, as a scientific expert, on the occurrence among men of frustration, for example? To what handbook of data should I refer him? (Barker, 1964)

The same could be said of early childhood literacy. The naturalistic studies of the 1970s, 1980s and 1990s enabled us to map 'the forms, abundance, and distribution' of the phenomena in the literacy events associated with paper-based, print based alphabetic literacy. Researchers like Harste et al. (1979) helped us document how young learners encountered and dealt with the literacy phenomena in the print-rich environments in which they moved before formal schooling. Others like Clay (1972) helped us identify and document specific 'concepts of print' which young learners needed to control in order to read and write print-based, paper-based texts. While these kinds of studies were an auspicious beginning for the process of mapping the forms, abundance, and distribution of the phenomena or early childhood literacy in Western democracies, they are already dated.

The rapid growth of screen-based hypertext as media for both the construction and the dissemination of information has heightened our awareness that literacy means more than reading and writing using a paper-based, print-based alphabetic script. So too has naturalistic research into the literacy events and behaviours of non-Western cultures (Street, 1995; Barton, 1994).

Research which sets out to map the forms, abundance, and distribution of the phenomena in the literacy events associated with screen-based texts has been fruitful in adding to the theory and practice of literacy teaching and learning in early childhood. For example, Clay's (1972) famous 'concepts of print' have been extended by Turbill (2003) to include 'concepts of screen' such as 'mouse control' and 'use of navigation tools'. Such print-based metalinguistic awarenesses as 'letter', 'sound', 'left-to-right text flow' have been extended to include screen-based forms such as 'icons', 'hypertext links', 'save', 'boot', 'click', 'double-click', 'exit', 'quit', 'menu' etc. Even the concept of text as a paper-based, print based phenomenon has been challenged. Whereas as a parent in the 1970s I would complain when *my* preschool children pestered me to read 'memorable texts' (Holdaway, 1979) such as *The Gingerbread Man* over and over, now *their* preschool children ask me to sit through multiple viewings of their favourite video shows with them, or to play the same video games *ad nauseam*.

The world of early childhood literacy is in a continual state of change. As a consequence, literacy researchers have continued to employ naturalistic research methods to document the function, form and purpose of the screen-based texts that young children encounter and use outside of school. Already such research has widened the concept of 'literacy' to one of *multiliteracies* (Cope and Kalantzis, 2000). Already the learning theory underpinning certain kinds of computer games is being explored and documented (Gee, 2001). I predict that the growth of information technology will demand continued use of naturalistic methods, if only to keep early child literacy educators abreast of how the phenomena of their science are developing.

Naturalistic research serves the scientific purpose of supporting and/or challenging the ecological validity of research findings created by other modes of research

Determining ecological validity is perhaps the most important purpose that naturalistic inquiry can serve. Ecological validity is at the core of the issue of generalizing findings and laws from research to everyday circumstances. When two different approaches are used to study the same phenomenon and discrepant findings are the outcome, it points to an important scientific function for naturalistic methods, as some well known examples from early childhood literacy research will suggest.

In 1967 Jean Chall published her most famous book, *Learning to Read: The Great Debate*. Chall's work was highly acclaimed and has been one of the most influential studies ever published. It was hailed as a fine example of an objective, carefully controlled scientific enterprise, in the best traditions of research.

In the 1970s Chall's assertions that a code-breaking-based pedagogy had been 'scientifically' proven to be superior for beginning readers came under intense scrutiny. Goodman's (1973; 1978) miscue research was instrumental in focusing this scrutiny because it raised serious doubts about the research on which Chall based her conclusions about the superiority of a code-based pedagogy. It also raised doubts about the ecological validity of the overwhelming majority of research being used at the time to inform curriculum, pedagogy, and assessment practices.

On the one hand Goodman's miscue research questioned the narrow 'prove cause–effect relationships' focus of the traditional research paradigm Chall employed. Rather than using miscue analysis to engage in hypothesis testing for the purpose of establishing cause–effect relationships, Goodman used miscue analysis as a tool to *understand* how reading 'worked'. On the other hand Goodman and his research associates continuously employed the rhetoric of '*real* reading with *real* kids reading *real* books' which highlighted the artificial texts, and the contrived, artificial settings, that characterized the paradigm in which Chall had put so much faith.

The end result of Goodman's miscue work was to challenge and subsequently change the theory that effective reading was merely a matter of automatic word recognition, which in turn was best developed by a drill and practice pedagogy. In the 1980s Graves' (1978) and his co-workers' research into young children learning to write had an almost similar effect on the teaching of writing for young learners.

Willems' (1968: 66) argument for the continued employment of naturalistic methods in behavioural research is valid for the early childhood domain:

1 Appropriate generalization to everyday events is a problem of ecological validity.
2 Achievement of ecological validity requires, at least in part, an ecological or contextual perspective.
3 An ecological/contextual perspective requires naturalistic methods.
4 Therefore naturalistic methods are important in any domain of scientific endeavour.

Naturalistic inquiry serves the scientific purpose of informing the design of worthwhile manipulative, rationalistic studies

From Chall's, (1967) 'great debate' to the current era of the No Child Left Behind Act of 2001, early childhood literacy research seems to have been dominated by the same competing and adversarial points of view surrounding two questions:

1 What kinds of literacy should our schools be teaching?
2 How should it be taught and measured?

The typical response has been to conduct countless numbers of tightly controlled, hypothesis-testing, 'horse-race' studies which compare one instructional method against another, for the purpose of creating 'scientifically based research evidence' which can inform policy and classroom practice. For a host of complex reasons, groundwork naturalistic research, which other scientific endeavours considered to be an essential prerequisite of producing such evidence, has not been considered important.

The history of scientific inquiry indicates that many of the established domains of scientific knowledge such as astronomy, physics, and earth sciences began in similar ways, often motivated by similar kinds of groundwork questions. For example, what we currently know and understand about astronomy began with the study of the solar system. The basic research questions asked by those who pioneered this science were of this order:

1 What happens in this system?
2 How are the phenomena which make up this system distributed?
3 How do these phenomena relate to each other in this system?
4 How do all the phenomena which have been identified in this system 'work'?
5 Why does this system work the way it does; or, what's a possible grounded theory which will explain how these systems work?
6 How can we use this theory to inform what we do?

The same questions are just as relevant for understanding complex systems such as early childhood literacy classrooms. Before we conduct research which attempts to prove that one instructional method is superior to another, perhaps we should first have a very clear picture of what actually does happen in classrooms in the name of teaching and learning literacy. Describing and understanding *what actually does happen* in settings like classrooms is quite different and distinct from describing *what one thinks should be happening* in them.

Michael Pressley (2002), a recognized international leader in literacy research at the time of writing, agrees. At the 47th International Reading Association's annual conference, he expounded at length on this issue. In this address Pressley questioned the narrow nature of the research paradigm being mandated by the current literacy education policy makers in the USA. He argued that:

> valid experimental, hypothesis testing research into teaching and learning literacy should only be conducted by well-informed scientists who have immersed themselves in the ecology of the site where the experimental research is to be carried out, before launching into experiments in them.

Pressley went on to condemn the current spate of intervention studies which are determining literacy education policy in the USA as being the work of uninformed 'scientific extremists' who attempt to design 'comparative intervention studies' before they 'truly understand the intervention they want to study'. The requisite levels of understanding they must first acquire, he argued, can only be achieved after years of naturalistic research in these settings. Only this, he suggests, would enable them to understand the ecology of the system in which they want to conduct their comparative studies. Only then, he asserts, could they hope to achieve results which have even minimal degrees of ecological validity.

CONCLUDING REMARKS

In this chapter I have argued that a naturalistic viewpoint in early childhood literacy research is distinguishable from other research modes by a complex mix of philosophical beliefs, degrees of control over input and output variables exerted by the researcher, and the methodological tools which are chosen to conduct the research. I have also argued that a naturalistic inquiry will continue to serve four important overlapping scientific purposes in early childhood literacy research, and that such research is essential for helping us think anew about literacy and learning across a range of contexts, both in and out of school settings.

Given the gulfs that separate and continue to widen between children and youth who acquire the skills and knowledge of highly productive critical multiliteracies and those who do not, between the privileged and the disenfranchised, and given the attempts of policy makers and politicians to impose mandated instructional strategies and materials on school systems, there is increased pressure on literacy theorists and researchers to ensure that naturalistic viewpoints are accorded equal status in the field, and continue to be used.

NOTE

1 A unit of linguistic analysis first devised by Kellog Hunt in 1965. For Hunt, a 'T-Unit' or 'Minimal Syntactic Unit' is essentially a main clause defined as including all subordinate clauses and other constructions that go with it.

REFERENCES

Barker, R.G. (1964) 'Psychology's third estate'. Kansas City Psychological Association (unpublished mimeo), Kansas City, MO.

Barker, R.G. (1968) *Ecological Psychology*. Stanford, CA: Stanford University Press.

Barker, R.G. and Wright, H.F. (1955) *Midwest and its Children*. New York: Harper and Row.

Barker, R.G. and associates (1978) *Habitats, Environments, and Human Behaviour*. San Francisco: Jossey Bass.

Barton, D. (1994) *Literacy: an Introduction to the Ecology of Written Language*. Oxford: Blackwell.

Cambourne, B.L. (1982a) 'Learning about learning by watching kids write'. University of Wollongong, Wollongong.

Cambourne, B.L. (1982b) 'Test results and the real world: a study of incompatibility', *Australian Journal of Reading*, 5 (3): 129–41.

Cambourne, B.L. (1995) 'Toward an educationally relevant theory of literacy learning: twenty years of inquiry', *The Reading Teacher*, 49 (3): 182–90.

Cambourne, B.L. and Turbill, J. (1987) *Coping with Chaos*. Sydney: Primary English Teachers Association.

Chall, J. (1967) *Learning to Read: the Great Debate*. New York: McGraw-Hill.

Clay, M.M. (1972) *Sand: the Concepts about Print Test*. Auckland: Heinemann.

Cochrane-Smith, M. (1986) 'Reading to children: a model for understanding texts', in B.B. Schieffelin and P. Gilmore (eds), *The Acquisition of Literacy: Ethnographic Perspectives*. Norwood, NJ: Ablex.

Coles, G. (2000) *Misreading Reading: the Bad Science that Hurts Children*. Portsmouth, NH: Heinemann.

Coles, G. (2003) *Reading the Naked Truth*. Portsmouth, NH: Heinemann.

Cope, B. and Kalantzis, M. (eds) (2000) *Multiliteracies: Literacy Learning and the Design of Social Futures*. London: Routledge.

Fishman, A. (1988) *Amish Literacy: What and How It Means*. Portsmouth, NH: Heinemann.

Gee, J.P. (2001) Seminar presented at Center for Expansion of Language and Thinking (CELT) Rejuvenation Conference, Chicago, Illinois.

Gilmore, P. and Glatthorn, A.A. (eds) (1982) *Children In and Out of School: Ethnography and Education*. Washington, DC: Center for Applied Linguistics.

Goodman, K.S. (1973) Theoretical Studies of Patterns of Miscues in Oral Reading Performance. Washington, DC: US Department of Health, Education, and Welfare, Office of Education, Bureau of Research.

Goodman, K.S. (1978) *Reading of American Children Whose Reading Is a Stable Dialect of English or a Language Other than English.* Washington, DC: US Department of Health, Education and Welfare, National Institute of Education.

Graves, D.H. (1978) *Balance in the Basics: Let Them Write.* New York: Ford Foundation.

Guba, E. (ed.) (1990) *The Paradigm Dialog.* Newbury Park, CA: Sage.

Guba, E. and Lincoln, Y. (1981) *Effective Evaluation: Improving the Usefulness of Evaluation through Responsive and Naturalistic Approaches.* San Francisco: Jossey Bass.

Harste, J.C., Burke, C.L. and Woodward, V. (1979) 'Children's initial encounters with print'. National Institute of Education grant proposal.

Heath, S.B. (1983) *Ways with Words.* New York: Cambridge University Press.

Holdaway, D. (1979) *The Foundations of Literacy.* Auckland: Ashton Scholastic.

Howe, K. (1995) 'Two dogmas of educational research', *Educational Researcher*, 14: 10–18.

Hull, G. and Schultz, K. (2001) 'Literacy and learning out of school: a review of theory and research', *Review of Educational Research*, 71 (4): 575–612.

Hunt, K. (1965) 'Grammatical structures written at three grade levels', Research Report No. 3, Urbana, IL: NCTE.

Jacobs, E. and Jordan, C. (eds) (1993) *Minority Education: Anthropological Perspectives.* Norwood, NJ: Ablex.

Kirk, S.A., McArthy, J.J. and Kirk W.D. (1968) *Illinois Test of Psycholinguistic Abilities. Examiner's Manual.* Urbana, IL: University of Illinois Press.

Kuhn, T. (1962) *The Structure of Scientific Revolutions.* Chicago: University of Chicago Press.

Paul, J.L. and Marfo, K. (2001) 'Preparation of educational researchers in philosophical foundations of inquiry', *Review of Educational Research*, 71 (4): 521–47.

Pressley, M. (2002) 'What constitutes evidence in research?'. Address at the 47th Annual Convention of the International Reading Association, San Francisco.

Street, B.V. (1995) *Social Literacies: Critical Approaches to Literacy in Development, Ethnography, and Education.* London: Longman.

Taylor, D. (1993) *From the Child's Point of View.* Portsmouth, NH: Heinemann.

Taylor, D. and Dorsey-Gaines, C. (1988) *Growing Up Literate: Learning from Inner-City Families.* Portsmouth, NH: Heinemann.

Turbill, J. (2003) 'Exploring the potential of the digital language experience approach in Australian classrooms', *Reading Online*, 6 (7).

Willems, E.P. (1968) 'Planning a rationale for naturalistic research', in E.P. Willems and H.P. Raush (eds), *Naturalistic Viewpoints in Psychological Research.* New York: Holt, Rinehart and Winston.

Index

This Handbook provides an overview of up-to-date research into early childhood literacy. It deals with subjects relating to the nature, function and use of literacy and the development, learning and teaching of literacy in early childhood. In addition it covers issues relating to research and will be a guide to those carrying out research in the field.

The handbook particularly emphasises literacy as a socially situated and global experience, one that is evolving in relation to changes in contemporary culture and technological innovation.

The arrangement of chapters reflects a contemporary perspective on research into early childhood literacy. Major sections include:

- perspectives on early childhood literacy
- childhood literacy and families, communities and cultures
- early moves in literacy
- literacy in preschool settings and schools
- researching early childhood literacy.

Nigel Hall is Professor of Literacy Education in the Institute of Education at Manchester Metropolitan University.

Joanne Larson is Associate Professor and Chair of Teaching, Curriculum, and Change at the University of Rochester's Warner Graduate School of Education and Human Development.

Jackie Marsh is Senior Lecturer in the School of Education at the University of Sheffield.